AF716833

THE ARTHUR PAPERS

VOLUME ONE

THE ARTHUR PAPERS

BEING THE CANADIAN PAPERS
MAINLY CONFIDENTIAL, PRIVATE, AND DEMI-OFFICIAL

OF

SIR GEORGE ARTHUR, K.C.H.
Last Lieutenant-Governor of Upper Canada

IN THE MANUSCRIPT COLLECTION OF
THE TORONTO PUBLIC LIBRARIES

EDITED BY
CHARLES R. SANDERSON

VOLUME I

1822-1838

TORONTO PUBLIC LIBRARIES
AND
UNIVERSITY OF TORONTO PRESS
1957

Printed in Canada

Reprinted in 2018
ISBN 978-1-4875-8138-1 (paper)

Pages i–xvi have been issued in 1957 in order to be bound with Parts I and II, published in 1943 and 1947 respectively.

PREFACE

THE Trustees of the Toronto Public Library have hoped for many years to be able to arrange the publication of the Canadian papers of Sir George Arthur which are in the manuscript collection of the Library. Dr. Charles R. Sanderson, Chief Librarian of the Toronto Public Library from 1937 to 1956, had devoted much of his time and energy to this task. Parts of the Arthur Papers which Dr. Sanderson had prepared were printed in 1943, 1947 and 1949.

Dr. Sanderson had planned to complete the work on his retirement, when his sudden illness and death in July, 1956, made this impossible. The Board of Trustees of the Toronto Public Library feel that as a memorial to Dr. Sanderson they would like to recognize his outstanding achievements by continuing the publication of *The Arthur Papers*, in which he was so vitally interested. Dr. Sanderson had done a great deal of work on the remaining unpublished papers, and page proofs of Part IV were being corrected at the time of his death.

The cooperation of the following persons and organizations has made it possible to see the remaining parts through the press. The Carnegie Corporation of New York has given a generous grant to assist the financing of the project. Mr. Marsh Jeanneret, the Director of the University of Toronto Press, and his staff have made the task of completing publication after Dr. Sanderson's death much easier by their ready understanding and support. Dr. D. G. Creighton of the History Department of the University of Toronto has advised on the completion of the work. Miss Edith G. Firth of the Reference Division of the Toronto Public Library has checked the manuscript left by Dr. Sanderson and supervised the arrangements for publishing the final volumes. Miss Laura E. Loeber, head of the Reference Division of the Toronto Public Library prior to her retirement in 1956, undertook to prepare the Index to the papers and has thus ensured that this Index, which is contained in the final volume, matches the standards established by Dr. Sanderson in the transcription of the papers themselves.

In preparing the Introduction, Miss Firth has made use of part of the commentary concerning Sir George Arthur which was written by Dr. Sanderson prior to his death.

It is the hope of the Trustees of the Toronto Public Library and of all who have cooperated in securing the publication of the papers, that by achieving their completion some measure of appreciation has been shown towards the work of Toronto's Chief Librarian who initiated and almost single handed carried out this important project.

Toronto H.C.C.
March 24, 1957

CONTENTS

VOLUME I

ABBREVIATIONS

A.D.	autograph document not signed by sender
A.D.S.	autograph document signed by sender
A.L.	autograph letter not signed by sender
A.L. initialled	autograph letter initialled by sender
A.L.S.	autograph letter signed by sender
A.M.	autograph memorandum not signed by sender
A.M.S.	autograph memorandum signed by sender
D.S.	document not in the handwriting of sender but signed by sender
Df.	draft. This designation is used in conjunction with other designations, when the original is marked or endorsed a draft, or when it is obviously a draft and includes emendations. L. and A.L. are doubtless drafts in some cases.
L.	letter, not in the handwriting of, and not signed by, the sender.
LB.	letter-book, *i.e.* a letter appearing in one of the letter-books; v. (volume) is omitted, and the entry reads LB.1, p. 1–6.
L. initialled	letter not in handwriting of sender, but initialled by sender
L.S.	letter not in handwriting of sender, but signed by sender
M.	memorandum. Not a letter, but an item which can be termed a memorandum in place of the more general designation of "document".
p.	page, pages

INTRODUCTION

SIR GEORGE ARTHUR was born in Plymouth, England, on June 21, 1784. At the age of twenty he entered the army, and served in Italy, Egypt, and Sicily. He was twice wounded, and on the Walcheren expedition of 1809 was thanked in General Orders for his action at the siege of Flushing. On his return to England he received the freedom of both London and Plymouth. He served as Aide and military secretary to the Governor of Jersey, and in 1812 joined the 7th West India Regiment in Jamaica. He received his first administrative appointment in 1814, when he was named Superintendent of British Honduras, a position he held until 1822. Like all his appointments this was not easy, and was complicated by a serious revolt of the slave population. In 1824 he became Lieutenant Governor of Van Diemen's Land, then a convict settlement. It is believed that while there he made the first suggestion for the confederation of the Australian colonies. In March, 1837, he returned to England, accused by his enemies in the colony of official oppression and personal dishonesty. He cleared himself triumphantly, and in November of the same year was appointed Lieutenant Governor of Upper Canada.

Arthur arrived in Toronto on March 23, 1838. Three months later he was informed of the appointment of Lord Durham as Governor in Chief of all five British North American colonies. Durham's stay in Canada was short, and on November 1, 1838, he sailed for England. Arthur's second period of sole responsibility for the government of Upper Canada lasted almost a year. On October 19, 1839, Charles Poulett Thomson, later Lord Sydenham, arrived in Canada as Governor General and Governor in Chief. His main objective, the settlement of the constitutional problem, necessitated much interference in Upper Canadian politics and government. After the passage of the Act of Union in 1841 abolished the office of Lieutenant Governor of Upper Canada, Arthur returned to England.

He was appointed Governor of the Presidency of Bombay in June, 1842. Here again his position was an awkward one, and his relationships with those above and those below him were undefined and full of potential difficulty. He was in India during the occupation of Sind, and was involved in the Napier-Outram controversy. In 1846 he was elected provisional Governor General of India, but was compelled by ill-health to return to England in the same year.

His knighthood was conferred on him for his services in Van Diemen's

Land, and his baronetcy for his work in Upper Canada. After his return from India he was made a privy councillor, and received an honorary D.C.L. from the University of Oxford. He died on September 19, 1854, in London.

Because Arthur served in such widely separated parts of the Empire, his papers are important to historical research in several countries. For this reason they have been divided. Those covering the period of his administration in British Honduras are in the library of the Royal Empire Society in London; his Van Diemen's Land papers are in the Mitchell Library, Sydney, Australia; and his Canadian and Indian papers are in the Toronto Public Libraries, Toronto, Canada. The Canadian papers were considered of such importance that the Toronto Public Library Board of Trustees, assisted by the generosity of the Carnegie Corporation of New York and the University of Toronto Press, has undertaken their publication, under the editorship of the late Chief Librarian, Charles Rupert Sanderson, LL.D., M.A., B.Sc. They were first published in six paper-bound parts, and then in the present three volumes.

Sir George Arthur's papers of the Canadian period consist of six letter-books of ledger size, and about thirteen hundred pieces. They are as a whole confidential, private and demi-official, rather than official, although a few despatches and official papers are copied, apparently because of their particular significance. Generally, the papers are supplementary to the purely official interchange of correspondence and despatches, and there is relatively little duplication of the official material preserved in the Public Archives of Canada, and the Public Records Office, London. The unbound pieces are almost entirely letters received by Arthur, but they also include a few drafts or copies, some in Arthur's handwriting, of outgoing letters and despatches. The letter-books, which have been numbered by the editors, record copies of about eight hundred outgoing letters. Some of the letters are in Arthur's handwriting, many in that of his daughter "Kate", who frequently assisted her father, and others were apparently entered by his secretaries. The volumes are not chronological, and although there is some attempt at classification, it is not consistently carried out. One part of volume [6] contains mainly family and purely personal correspondence during the Canadian period; the other contains official letters written in Van Diemen's Land, which have not been published.

Every attempt has been made in the transcription to present the papers themselves without undue editorial interference. Footnote comment has been deliberately kept to a minimum, the principle being not to attempt to supply information which was as readily available to the reader as it was to the editors. A few entries have been calendared, because of their lack of importance or interest. Great care has been taken in all other entries to reproduce exactly the text of the original documents. The spelling, punctuation, and division of the paragraphs of the letters themselves have been strictly followed.

The items have been arranged chronologically, and have been numbered. Accurate dating of undated items has been carried out as far as this could be done from internal and external evidence, and writers and recipients have similarly been identified as far as possible. No attempt has been made to gather together "enclosures" with their covering documents unless they were found placed together when the papers came into our possession. Every attempt, however, has been made to link up covering documents and enclosures by notes to the separate items. "Markings" have been distinguished from "endorsements". The former are part of the original document, and are transcribed at the beginning of the entry; the latter have been subsequently added by the recipient or other person concerned, and are transcribed at the end of the entry. Full Christian names are used where there is only one Christian name, initials where there are more than one. Names or initials are given except in outstanding cases, e.g. Arthur, Colborne, Durham. The index in Volume Three is as complete as possible. Following these general rules, the editors have sought to present as clearly as possible the exact content of Arthur's papers.

Arthur was in Canada during an exciting, disturbed, and restless time, when old ideas were meeting new ones, and the old guard of professional colonial administrators was being superseded by idealists and opportunists. It was an age of transition both in England and the colonies—an age in which Arthur perhaps represents the best of the older tradition. Nowhere is the turmoil of the period shown more clearly than in Arthur's Canadian papers.

There were certain issues that were present throughout Arthur's term of office in Canada, and which therefore are reflected in all three volumes of his papers. These were the bitterness that was the aftermath of rebellion, the appalling inefficiency of the machinery of government, the clergy reserves and the university question, the awkwardness of militia organization—and the unsatisfactory progress of Arthur's sons at school in England. Each volume, however, has its own special emphasis.

The emphasis in Volume One is on the restoration of order after the Rebellion of 1837, and the defence of the province against invasion and brigandry. The trials of the political prisoners and the prevention of a Tory reign of terror were two problems complicated by differences of opinion with Lord Durham. Defending the border and stamping out lawlessness were complicated by the attitude of the Commander of the Forces, Sir John Colborne, who vacillated between blind optimism and equally blind panic. Volume One closes with the attacks at Prescott and Windsor.

The mood of Volume Two is noticeably calmer. As the imminent danger of attack from without and within receded, the question of the future form of government of the colony became predominant. In the spring of 1839 Lord Durham's Report reached Upper Canada, and its recommendations aroused heated controversy. Sydenham's appointment confirmed the belief that the report was going to be implemented, and Volume Two ends with the passing of the measure for union in both houses of the Upper Canadian legislature.

Volume Three continues the story of the constitutional development of the province. The inner workings of Lord Sydenham's form of practical politics are shown clearly in the manipulating of the elections for the united House of Assembly, and in the choosing of the Executive Council. Robert Baldwin's place in that Council brought the whole question of responsible government into prominence, as Lord Durham's Report had done two years earlier. When Arthur left the province in March, 1841, Sydenham was confident that constitutional stability had at last been achieved. A disturbing feature of Arthur's last days in Canada was the repercussions of the McLeod case, and this too is discussed at length in Volume Three of the papers.

In 1953, M. C. I. Levy wrote *Governor George Arthur, a colonial benevolent despot*. This book is a justification of Arthur's administration in Van Diemen's Land. Dr. Sanderson had hoped to write a similar defence of Arthur's policies in Upper Canada, but death intervened. In 1940, however, he wrote a thesis, *Sir George Arthur, last lieutenant governor of Upper Canada, 1838-1841, a vindication*. This was his introduction:

> Sir George Arthur has not yet been caught up in the limelight of history. By way of individual monographs on him, there was a tiny one said to have been privately published some sixty years ago. It has vanished; perhaps because "the family did not much care for it." At any rate none of them has a copy, and no copy has been traced elsewhere. And there is the 32 page pamphlet by Walter Sage, published as a Queen's University bulletin over twenty years ago.[1]
>
> For the rest, most historical publications tend to ignore Arthur's administration of Upper Canada, or to treat it as unimportant. As an alternative

[1]Sage, Walter. *Sir George Arthur and his administration of Upper Canada.* (Bulletin of the Department of history and political and economic science in Queen's University, Kingston, Ontario, Canada. No. 28, July, 1918.)

he is simply pilloried as the executioner of Lount and Mathews, a man with a tendency for capital punishment, and checked only by the more humanitarian Durham.[2]

Actually, however, as further material becomes available, Arthur's administration is seen to have been neither unimportant nor lacking in interest, and, moreover, the judgments passed on him may have been somewhat hasty. If Sir Francis Bond Head had not been replaced by Arthur, it is far from improbable that Upper Canada might have joined the majority of the components of the first empire. There was certainly more than a chance that the general situation might "send the two tribes after the ten."[3] And so far from Arthur's administration having been merely the last rampart of opposition to reform, it is probable that, constitutionalist though he inevitably was, it was nevertheless due to his work that the province outlived a critical period when anything might have happened to it. To this extent, unknowingly, he conditioned the union, the preliminary to the subsequent establishment of self-government.

Arthur also will be seen to have been a much misused man. At the very outset there was a serious misunderstanding (to give it the most generous interpretation) as to his powers so far as Durham was concerned, and in his attempts to do something for Upper Canada he was hampered by the muddle which Sir Francis Head had left, frustrated by Sir John Colborne's views and obstinacy, and impeded by the incompetency and inefficiency of government officials and methods. In short, he was confronted with an almost impossible task in a country which was carrying the burden of already crippled finances through the continentally-wide depression of 1837.

Ultimately he was completely subordinated to Sydenham, and left with a discarded policy on his hands, a policy which, although by no means unsuccessful, and despite its approbation by the home government, had been completely reversed without his even having been officially informed of just what was to happen. He was made to eat his pride. Acting as a lackey boy for Sydenham, he was placed in a position where he had to help in supplanting the very things which, in response to his repeated instructions, he had loyally struggled to maintain.

It is easy, therefore, standing on the vantage ground of responsible government, to look back at Arthur through the wrong end of the telescope. He can then be made to appear simply as one of the defenders of the old school of colonial government, holding hands with a self-seeking family compact, and amounting merely to one more of the hindrances to progressive reform. This is most unjust. Irrespective of our views to-day, Arthur has to be seen in his own environment as he really was. It is true that he was the product of his background: a soldier, a tory, a churchman, past middle

[2]Even Mr. Sage, in the only extant monograph, introduces him as the lieutenant governor who "lives in Canadian history as the man who refused to reprieve Lount and Matthews [*sic*], and who made common cause with the Family Compact against the Reformers."

[3]Mackenzie to Hume: 1830: Mar. C.O. 42/392: Hume to Murray: Apl. 20.

age and somewhat set in his ideas. But his honesty and integrity stand out clearly. He had a kind heart and a generous nature. His finger was on a pulse that was beating rapidly under the general excitement of the period, and he had at least a partial vision of the course which the unchecked disease would be likely to follow. He planned and introduced improvements which, given a little more time, would have substantially changed the unhappy state of affairs which he had found in the province. He struggled to be loyal to a ministerial policy which seemed to him to change with a bewildering rapidity. Shabbily treated by a home government which used him as a pawn in the game dictated by its own instability, he nevertheless succeeded in making himself respected and liked by a vast portion of the population of Upper Canada.

With the publication of Arthur's Canadian papers in their entirety, a further source of information is made available to those who may wish to learn more of this period in Canada's history.

EDITH G. FIRTH
Reference Division

THE ARTHUR PAPERS

VOLUME ONE

Arthur Papers

[1] [WRITER AND RECIPIENT NOT STATED]: 16p.

[*1822* ?] [*Place not stated.*]

Remarks on the existing State of things in Canada 1822.

The present difficulties in which these Provinces are found, arise from various causes, a leading one of which appears to be the impracticability of Upper Canada enjoying a just participation of the duties levied on imports, at the Port of Quebec, a very large proportion of which are consumed within that Province.—The only constitutional mode of remedying this great evil, would be the *reunion* of the two Provinces under one Government. Unfortunately The wish and object of the House of Assembly of Lower Canada, however they may pretend to disguise it, is to prevent the Lower Province from being settled by any but French Canadians, or as they stile themselves the "*Nation Canadienne,*" and they would willingly keep it a Desert, until their own Population be sufficient to fill it. They are unwilling to afford facilities for improvement, or to remove the obstacles to settlements, or remedy defects in the Laws which are obvious to all, lest a more favorable state of things should people the Country with Emigrants from Great Britain; and they willingly submit to inconveniences, not because they are insensible to them, but because they hope that Strangers may in consequence be deterred from establishing themselves here.

Their expectations hitherto have not been disappointed, for of the many thousand Emigrants which of late Years have come to this country, I do not suppose that 500 have settled in Lower Canada.—The "*Nation Canadienne,*" as they call themselves, assert that their preservation as a separate people, in Religion, Laws, Language & Character, is essential to secure the country as a Colony to Great Britain. The House of Assembly, who are the Representatives of the "*Nation Canadienne*" (for the English Inhabitants are not virtually represented) have even made attempts to extend the *feudal* tenure to Lands yet ungranted. (See pamphlet of Andrew Stuart on that subject). Their real object, *that of rearing up a French Nation* in America, is not to be thought surprising, because it is *natural* that they should desire it—at the same time every Englishman is bound to prevent it: and it is absurd to be deceived by their Hypocritical Cant, in pretending that it is for the sake of being a Colony of Great Britain, & out of affection for the English, that they wish to continue so unlike them, in Laws, & language, as well as everything else, & to exclude, as far as they can, all who speak English from the Country. They well know that there is an age of majority for Colonies, as well as for Individuals, and the question, with regard to Canada, cannot be, whether it is always to remain an appendage to what they are willing for the present, to call the Parent Country,—but whether, when it shall take its separate station among the nations of the Earth, it is still to be an English, or a French Country.

That the reunion of the two Provinces, and the settlement of the country by English Emigrants would hasten the period of separation, is an assertion which might justly be denied—but were it even admitted to be true, how could the interests of a few years more or less, of the temporary existence of this Country as a Colony, be weighed in the Balance against the sort of eternity during which it must have a separate existence, & during which it ought to be an English Country— All North America ought for ever to be English, altho' no part of it may be for ever a Colony of Great Britain. One great object of a Nation founding Colonies must surely be to extend & perpetuate their own language & institutions;— What have the French done for us, that Great Britain should rear up for them, at enormous sacrifice of blood & treasure, a French Nation in North America? And yet this is likely to happen, if there be no reunion; but it would effectually be prevented by such a happy junction, as it would ultimately give to the English Colonists a majority in the Assembly, disposed to favor improvements & emigration to Lower Canada. This measure must be for the interest of the Inhabitants of the Upper Province, as well as all the Lower Canadians who are not *French*, (or Nation Canadienne) & *they* would be found powerless to prevent it, if it be not too long delayed. Even they, when they found it inevitable would speedily reconcile themselves to the change; and the Upper Canadians, and English Inhabitants of Lower Canada, together with the Emigrants from England Scotland & Ireland, who have all one common language, & must have one Common interest, to cause the country to resemble that of their common Ancestors, would soon form a population sufficient to absorb the others, & without injuring anyone, effect a peaceful and bloodless conquest over the foreign language and Gallican Laws which still prevail here, somewhat to the disgrace of old England.

We must not deceive ourselves,—from the inevitable course of things the natural & & [*sic*] permanent feelings of persons descended from hostile Nations will necessarily be hostile, so long as the descendants of each shall retain the language of their ancestors; for so long their respective education and information will be derived from totally opposite and innimical [*sic*] sources; & so long the sympathies, attachments, habits & associations from the earliest dawn of intellect to the latest period of existence, will be at variance in the respective portions of the Population. Their pride & love of Glory can have no unity of object, their vanity & their national affections no similarity of gratification. It is only the use of the same tongue that can permanently destroy animosities and prejudices, by removing opportunities of misrepresenting each other, & that can unite & attach all as one people, by enabling all to draw their knowledge from the sources of a common Country.

The causes of distrust & enmity being natural & permanent among people of hostile origin & different language, no trust or reliance can with safety be placed upon the continuance of their friendship, however flattering, may be the transient & casual indications of Harmony.

The leaven of hate, which however inactive at the moment, is contained in the composition, will always be ready to rise into fermentation upon the slightest warmth of political discussion (See Note A)[.]

Supposing the reunion of Upper & Lower Canada not to take place, the Imperial Parliament is bound in duty & Patriotism to afford at least some speedy relief to to [*sic*] the English part of Lower Canada.— Lower Canada may be divided into two parts vizt Seigniorial, or French Canada. which lies on the banks of the St Lawrence—extending in a narrow Strip of varying breadth of from—15—to 40—miles on each side of the River,—and English Canada, where the Country has been laid out into new Townships & granted in the English tenure of free & common Socage. This latter division or English Lower Canada includes indefinitely the rest of the Province, from the rear of the French Seigniories & is of much greater extent, & capable of containing a much greater population than Seigniorial Canada. At present the New Townships contain about (Note B) 40,000 Inhabitants, who are chiefly Emigrants from the United States, & most of them descendants of the old British Loyalists. They speak nothing but English. In Seigniorial or French Lower Canada there is an English Population of about 40,000 interspersed among the French Canadians (C) But in the Free & Common Socage lands, or English Lower Canada, there are no French Canadians. Nevertheless these latter are not satisfied with seeing the English in Seigniorial Canada subjected to French Laws administered in the French language, which for the present may be tolerated on the ground of the numerical inferiority of the English in Seigniorial Canada, but they labor in direct contradiction to the views contained in the Proclamations & Promises of his late Majesty, as well as in British Statutes (D) to perpetuate the Yoke of the French Laws & Language over the free & common Socage Portion of Lower Canada, where scarce one inhabitant knows a tittle of the Laws, or one word of the Language in which they are contained.

If a feeling, however mistaken, of benevolence & kindness, & there could be no other Motive, induced the British Govt. in 1774 to indulge the French Canadians in Seigniorial Canada with the French laws, (& those Laws were never meant to extend beyond the limits of the Seigniories) surely not merely the same motive of benevolence & kindness, but also Justice, national dignity, patriotism & the sacred pledges of faith & honor wd. require that the Bsh. Govt. shd. grant to the English in the rest of Lower Canada, the benefit of the Laws of their English Ancestors, which have been so often promised to them & to their Fathers.

The Inhabitants of the New Townships do not ask, however reasonable the demand might be, that English Laws should be given to Seigniorial Canada; they only ask that French Laws may not be imposed upon them, An English People, living under English Tenures, in what is at least in name, an English Colony. They do not request, however politic the measure might be, that French Lower Canada should be rendered English, they only beg that English Lower Canada may not be compelled to become French. They do not seek to encroach upon the Territorial limits of the Seigniories,—they only pray that the Seigniorial part of Lower Canada may not be permitted to make any new acquisitions upon English Territory. The French Canadians are certainly sufficiently, if not too much indulged in continuing (to this day, distant half a century from the conquest of the country, & its consequently becoming an English Colony) a separate people, in Language, & Laws, on their own Seigniories, out of which they as yet have no settlements; and it surely cannot be the object of England to allow in addition, (however it may suit the Treacherous system of a french House of Assembly) that the French Language & french Laws, should extend themselves, & make *conquests* beyond the Limits of the Seigniorial part of Lower Canada.

The relief therefore which will be necessary for English Lower Canada, (if the reunion of the Two Provinces does not take place) will be a Statute of the Imperial Parliament, to fulfill the promises express as well as implied, not only of a British King, but of the whole British Legislature, enacting that English Laws & English Courts shall be established in & for the whole of Lower Canada, except the Seigniories; and either that the english Tenures shall have a competent number of Representatives in the House of Assembly of Lower Canada, which may now be called entirely French, or, that that House of Assembly shall not legislate for them.

(Note A) It cannot therefore be impolitic, when the assembly of the "*Nation Canadienne*" attempt to provide Governt support for the rising Generation in the French Language, that the other branches of the Legislature should withhold their assent; for it would be the heig[h]th of absurdity to suppose that an English Govt, in an English Colony ought to contribute to an education having a natural tendency to excite prejudices against the Mother Country, or indeed ought to contribute to ȧny but an English Education. If a different education is required by parental fondness or Parental prejudice, it can surely be no hardship to say that Parents must procure it from their own means & not expect it from Govt.

(Note B) It is now only about 30 years since the new Townships began to be settled, in consequence of the Proclamations of the Executive of Lower Canada, promising grants of land to the old American Loyalists. These Settlements would have advanced infinitely faster than they have done, but they are viewed with much jealousy by the French House of Assembly, who, as far as possible throw impediments in their way, instead of aiding their advancement, like the Legislatures of other British Colonies. Among other Evils such is the state of the Laws, that the Inhabitants have no means of ascertaining, when they purchase land, whether their title is good or not, or whether the Land be not incumbered for ten times its amount. The establishment of Register offices would afford a remedy in this particular, and such offices are established universally in all the other English Colonies. But is it to be expected that a French House of Assembly shall pass Laws that would assist English Emigrants, when several of their Members have declared that Lower Canada ought to be settled by none but French Canadians, & should be kept waste until the French Canadians can settle it.—

(Note C) The English in Quebec & Montreal will probably soon equal the French in numbers if they do not already. Upper Canada probably contains 230,000 Inhabitants, all speaking English, seven eight[h]s of whom have settled here within the last 30 years. The New Townships in Lower Canada, about 40,000 all likewise speaking English: Seigniorial Canada may contain about 40,000 English, in all say 310,000 English. The French Canadians in Lower Canada estimate their numbers at 400,000,—hence there wd at present be an excess of 90,000 in the French Population of Lower Canada over the English in both Provinces; but there will probably be no excess in 5 or 6 years, as the Emigrants from England Scotland and Ireland may be estimated at about 15,000 yearly, almost all of whom however *now* go to Upper Canada (in consequence of the insecurity of acquiring property in the Lower Province, for the want of Register Offices) & therefore do not serve to destroy the preponderance of French influence in Lower Canada.

(Note D) See the Proclamation of the 7th. Octr 1763 after the cession of the Canadas in which His late Majesty promises "that *all persons* inhabiting in, or resorting to, our said Colonies may confide in our Royal Protection for the enjoyment of the benefit of the Laws of our Realm of England &a." See also the British Statutes of 1774 vizt Geo. III cap. 83. By this Statute passed eleven years after the before mentioned

Proclamation, the French Canadians are allowed the French Laws in the Words vizt "in all matters of controversy relative to property & civil rights resort shall be had to the Laws of Canada as the rule for decision of the same &a, ["] but even in this Statute regard is paid to His Majestys Promises in his Proclamations, for in the very next clause of the same Statute, we find those promises confirmed & sanctioned in the following words vizt, "Provided always that nothing in this Act contained shall extend or be construed to extend to any Lands that have been granted by His Majesty, or that shall hereafter be granted *by His Majesty his heirs and Successors* to be holden in free *& common Socage*". Notwithstanding this, by a Legal subtlety# the French Laws are, in practice, actually extended to the new Townships— No English Courts have been Established for them.

#The British Statute of 1774 was passed obviously under the impression & assumption that the English Laws were then *legally* in force throughout the whole Province of *Quebec*, Had this been really the case the restriction of the French Laws to the Seigniories only, under that Statute, would have of necessity applied. But it is held by the Courts, that the English Laws, (altho' they might have been acted upon from 1763 to 1774) had never been *legally* introduced, & therefore that the restrictive clause could have no operation. However correct this doctrine may be, the intent & meaning of His Majesty & of the Legislature, was most plain & obvious, & if the Courts saw from the technical rules of Interpretation to which they were obliged to adhere, that actual effect could not be given to the intent & meaning of the Legislature, would it not have been judicious to have made the Govt. at Home acquainted with the inefficiency of the Law upon that point, to the end that by a positive enacting clause, the difficulty might be removed, & the patriotic intentions of the Imperial Parliament no longer defeated in their operation?—

[2] [WRITER AND RECIPIENT NOT STATED]:

[*1822?*] [*Place not stated.*]

[A tabulation of the dates of five "Capitulations & Treaties relative to Canada", 1759-1783, on a slip of paper watermarked 1820 and endorsed "On the Reunion of U. & L. Canada".]

[3] ROBERT BAYLY: [RECIPIENT NOT STATED]: A.D.S. 7p.

Oct. 18 *Plymouth.*

[A memorandum on the legality of Indian slavery in Honduras. "Col. Arthur's appointment of Commissioner to investigate the claims of the Indians . . . has been the means of obtaining considerable information upon the subject, which may be highly useful in the further consideration of the business. . . . He seems to have acted throughout most meritoriously and humanely".]

[The document is incomplete; a portion of it is apparently prior to the date here given.]

[4] [ARTHUR TO GOULBURN]: Df.A.L. 2p.

1828 [*Van Diemen's Land.*]

July 2 The last arrivals from England conveyed the information of your return to office, and although in a Department of the Government which throws me out of the probability of any official intercourse, with you yet, as I have always entertained a very grateful recollection of your uniform kindness & support whilst I administered the affairs of Honduras I cannot deny the pleasure of expressing the sincere satisfaction wh. I have felt on this occasion.

Such have been the vicissitudes of the political world during the last twelve or 18 months that ere this reaches you some further change may render my congratulations a little too late but I hope better things and at all events it cannot alter the sincere esteem which induces me to offer them.

As this rising Country once engaged much of your attention it will not be unacceptable to you to hear that it is making rapid strides in prosperity, and although the troubles & anxiety of a Convict Colony are scarcely to be described, yet there is a satisfaction mingled with one's cares in marking the visible amelioration which in short interval is produced in such a state of society[;] in fact the elasticity of a young Colony in a fine Climate will carry it forward even though it be populated from Newgate. [A cancelled passage reads: "in fact, Englishmen are Englishmen in every Climate even although they pass through Newgate to reach it—"]

[5] GOULBURN TO ARTHUR: A.L.S. 3p.

Nov. 30 *Downing Street*, [*London*.] [Marked: "Private".]

I have just received your letter of the 2nd of July & beg to return you my sincere thanks for your congratulations on my return to office. It is peculiarly gratifying to me to think that I am indebted for them to your approval of my conduct in the office which I previously held & that the course which I pursued in that office was as agreeable to your feelings as it was consistent with what appeared to me to be just.

Although removed to another department I still take the strongest interest in the advancement of the Colony over which you preside—I am not surprised at the rapid progress which it has made in mitigation & improvement and I shall be rather disappointed if under your superintendance it does not make still further advances—

[6] [ARTHUR] TO MAJOR GENERAL [SIR JOHN] MACDONALD: Df.A.L. 4p.

1831
Apr. 22 *Van Diemen's Land, Government House*. [Marked: "Duplicate".]

By the last opportunity for England I was prevented from writing one single private letter or I should not have failed to have offered my congratulations to you on the step you have gained[1] . . . [Macdonald's brother has succeeded Arthur in command at Honduras, and has supported] all those measures which were so sadly abused by my immediate worthy successors Generals Pye and Codd . . . although there are many worthless characters at Honduras, there are some very worthy persons in whose happiness and prosperity I take great interest . . . [Recounts a domestic scandal involving Captain Robertson, a protégé of Macdonald] with Mrs. Shadforth, the daughter of Judge Stephen of New South Wales., Pray consider this, as it strictly is, a private communication for although nothing can perhaps justify the moral criminality of Captn. Robertson's conduct, there may be some redeeming circumstances when his side of

[1]Probably his appointment as deputy adjutant general.

the question is fully brought forward . . . [Asks for an opinion as to an official application for confirmation of the rank of colonel now held for many years;] a *refusal* would be dreadful. . . .

[On the final sheet appears part of a draft in Arthur's handwriting of another document referring to the indiscriminate retaliation by natives upon other inhabitants for outrages committed by convicts. "But, still, knowing that we are the aggressors it is painful to adopt those measures which are absolutely essential to the security of the Settlers— In all other respects the Colony is most prosperous & Emigrants of the lower class have great cause to be thankful that they are exempted from those severe deprivations which have been so much felt at Home."]

[7] ARTHUR: [RECIPIENT NOT STATED]: Df.A.L. initialled.

July 15 *Hobart.*

Since my return from the Interior I have never been able to devote one single day to my Private affairs until this morning & I lament that the account wh. I am indebted to Mr. Pitcairn & Young[?] stands prominent amongst my neglects.

You will, I trust, excuse what is really very rare with me, the omission of immedly purging a debt. You spoke to Mr. Parramour I find upon the subject, but most unfortunately He quite forgot it until it occurred to myself on opening my Private Drawer this morning . . . [Mentions other personal business matters.]

[8] M [?] FORSTER TO ARTHUR: A.L.S.

1834 *Hobart.*

Apr. 15 [Apologises for neglectfulness.]

[9] [ROBERT BALDWIN TO PETER PERRY]: L.

[*1836*] [*Place not stated.*]

[*Mar. 16*] Extract from a letter addressed by Mr Baldwin, 16th. March 1836, to Mr P. Perry MP.P.

"These desirable [*sic*] would thus be accomplished without in the least intrenching upon the just and necessary prerogatives of the Crown which I consider, ***when administered by the Lieut Governor through the medium of a Provincial Ministry responsible to the Provincial Parliament*** to be an essential part of the Constitution of the Province."

[As in item 15, the watermark of 1839 indicates the above to be a copy made some years later than the original.]

[10] HEAD TO GLENELG: L.

May 14 *Toronto.* [Marked "No. 36".]

I have this morning received your Lordship's despatch No. 43 dated 30 March in which Your Lordship has been pleased (in confirming the appointment of Messrs. Dunn, Baldwin, and Rolph as Executive Councillors) to express your approbation of the course with reference to the conditions attempted to be attached by Mr. Baldwin to his acceptance of the post of Executive Councillor.

I cannot express to your Lordship the satisfaction I have derived from this communication, as it indicates a determination to support me in the arduous duties I have had to perform.

I have no fear whatever of crushing the Republicans in this Province and of reanimating the constitutionists, if I receive from your Lordship a continuance of this support.

[The above appears to have been torn from an official letter book. On the reverse side begins item 11.]

[11] HEAD TO GLENELG: L. 3p.

May 16 *Toronto, Upper Canada.* [Marked: "No. 37." "Private and Confidential".]

In case Your Lordship should deem it advisable to remove me from the Government of this Province in consequence of the request contained in my despatch of the 5th. February and respectfully repeated in No. 33, dated the 8th. Inst. I am desirous calmly to bring before your Lordship's most serious consideration, the importance and urgent necessity of sending out my successor immediately, as I can practically assure you that nothing can be a greater disadvantage to the Lieut Governor as well as to the Province, than his arriving, as I did, ignorant of all the various branches and departments in which the affairs of this Province are conducted.

I beg leave moreover to observe that not only would my successor reap advantage by having a little leisure for observation and reflection before he be actually called upon to determine upon the important subjects which require his decision, but that I myself am becoming every day seriously embarrassed by the uncertainty in which I exist.

During the three months of suspense which elapsed between the first expression of my requests dated 5th. Feby. and your Lordship's reply, I managed with considerable difficulty to advance against the Republicans, hampered by preparations to retreat at a moment's warning, but I foresee that the measures I shall shortly have to take, must unavoidably assume every day a more decisive character and I therefore hope your Lordship will see the propriety of coming at once to a final decision on my case.

With your Lordship's decision I am perfectly prepared to rest satisfied, but as I feel I did not sufficiently explain the grounds of my request I beg leave to do so by the following short statement.

At the time I was requested to assume the Government of Upper Canada, I was in the receipt of the following emoluments.

	£	s
Salary of An Assistant Poor Law Comr.	700	0
Allowance of £1.1s. per day	383	5
Allowance of 9s per day in lieu of travelling	164	5
Pay and allowance to my son as Clerk	180	0
Total annual income which I gave up at the request of H.M. Govt.	1427	10

The following is a list of fines, fees and expenses which were subsequently imposed upon me

	£	s
For my Commission	212	0
For travelling expenses for myself and suite with outfit	800	0

Paid Sir John Colborne for a part of his furniture &c.	1050 .. 0
Extra expenses in England for furniture &c. &c. &c. to be brought out	1000 .. 0
	£ s
	[1]2962 .. 0
Deduct allowance granted to me by H.M. Govt. to defray the above expences	£ s 300 .. 0
	£
Total amount of fees & expences	2762 .. 0

Having given up a permanent income of £1427, and having incurred expences of £2762, I requested in my despatch to your Lordship of the 5th. Feby. that my allowance might be made equal to that of my predecessors, but as that request did not meet with your Lordship's approbation, I abandoned it, adhering to the request of an accession of civil rank free of fees.

If this request be deemed also inexpedient I have begged, and still earnestly desire to be permitted to retire on two grounds.

1st. That I have not sufficient means to enable me to maintain my station, encumbered as I am by a military rank inferior to that of various officers under my command.

2ndly. That in justice to my family I cannot consent to transport them to this country, from which after my services are worn out, I shall return deeply in debt, besides having lost my income and prospects in England.

As far as the public service is engaged, I will pledge myself to tranquillize Upper Canada but I frankly declare to your Lordship that I cannot afford to injure my family, and that the least remuneration I respectfully require, is civil rank free of fees— If this be deemed more than my services are worth, I shall retire from the Colonial service with at least the consciousness of having served it faithfully.

I conclude by again asking your Lordship to do me the favour to inform my family whether they may come to me on the terms I have mentioned, or I to them.

[The above appears to have been torn from an official letter book and begins on the reverse side of item 10.]

[12] J. B. Robinson to [Head]: A.L.S. 2p.

July 9 [*Place not stated.*]

I must beg that you will have the kindness to peruse the inclosed statement[.] I could not rest satisfied till I had made it—and my brother had no objection, though I trust it will turn out that for any other purpose it might have been spared.

I shall take the liberty of calling at an early hour on Monday, if Your Excellency will allow me; to speak on this subject, and on one or two matters unconnected with it.

[Pin marks in the above, corresponding with others in items 13 (which is obviously the enclosure referred to) 14, 107, and 112, indicate that these letters concerning Peter Robinson's defalcations had been kept together for some particular purpose.]

[1]Error in addition not in the final total.

[13] J. B. ROBINSON TO THE LIEUTENANT GOVERNOR [HEAD]: A.L.S. 10p.

July 9 *Toronto.*

I have my brother's[1] permission to make to Your Excellency the following statement.

It would be more agreeable to me, if it can be regarded as confidential, unless a necessity should arise for treating it otherwise. That necessity I know will not arise, so far as the security of the Government is concerned. It is in Your Excellency's discretion, however, to rely on this assurance or not; and (as I should at any rate make this communication,) I withdraw all objection to an official use being made of it, if Your Excellency should desire it; and I shall be ready further to give to Your Excellency in any shape such additional information as I may happen to possess, or may be able to procure upon the subject of this letter.

About 12 or 14 days ago my brother was seized with partial paralysis of his left side, the attack being occasioned, as his physician thinks from an unfortunate accident which occurred in the preceding day—He was not only disabled by it from attending to his official duties, but being naturally apprehensive of a more fatal attack following, he was anxious to make such arrangements of all his affairs as the circumstances called for—

Unfortunately my younger brother was detained in the Country by circumstances which it is not necessary to advert to, but which Your Excellency is aware unavoidably kept him there, for some days. Of course I repaired immediately to my brother, and spent with him all the time I could spare from my public duty. It was his anxious desire to put me fully in possession of the state of his affairs, particularly so far as his public offices were concerned. The current half year was just closing, and the accounts had been for some time in preparation—He told me that there would be found no difficulty in closing his accounts as Commissioner for Crown Lands, and as Commissioner for Clergy Reserves, in which latter department the greatest amount of monies had been received—: that the accounts in those departments had been made up at the end of the last half year, and all the monies received up to that time paid in— But with respect to his accounts as Commissioner for woods and Forrests [*sic*], he said that they would require a careful and thorough examination from the beginning—that an error had been lately discovered of an accidental double charge against himself, of more than £1000, and he thought others would be found—that at present he believed there stood a balance against him of about £6000. He then explained to me upon what grounds he was convinced that he could not be actually chargeable with such arrears, if the truth could be exactly ascertained; but that of course he must be answerable for the apparent balance, whatever it might turn out to be.

He referred me to Mr. Hawk[e] for further particulars, gave me a list of his real property, and suggested that it might if the Government desired it, be at once made over to any person they might appoint, as a security for whatever balance might be found due—

Knowing no more of my brother's accounts, nor of the affairs of his offices, than if I had passed the last ten years in another quarter of the world, knowing on the other hand that my brother's income was large, (for he has always had considerable private means in addition to his salary,) I was equally astonished and distressed at this communication

[1]*i.e.* Hon. Peter Robinson.

which he made to me— My first anxiety has been to arrive as nearly, and as speedily as I could at the truth, in order that I might know the worst, and take measures accordingly, and that I might have at least the satisfaction, if possible, of having no unpleasant doubts remaining which might affect the characters, or involve the feelings of others, when my brother might be no longer able to assist in clearing them up—

I have been urgent therefore with Mr. Hawke to ascertain as early as he could the utmost possible balance for which my brother can be accountable, for I apprehended as it usually turns out on such occasions, that it might much exceed what my brother supposed, though I was convinced it could not be so much more as to involve any risque of an ultimate loss—

Mr. Hawke, and the book keeper in the office have made a hasty minute, from the books & accounts, of the apparent balance which rather exceeds £11,000 Provincial Currency.

They say it will take some weeks to ascertain the balances precisely, and that the further investigation is likely to reduce, but not to increase it, because the receipts are all regularly carried to account at the time, but the disbursements not so certainly and regularly, as many of them require detailed statements and vouchers, before they can be taken into account.—

My brother will not believe that there can turn out to be such a balance against him— In his infirm state of health he has had to depend upon the punctuality of many persons employed by him.— His accounts have been of large amount, and under many heads, and several branches of public service have been at times thrown upon him by the Government, which were not properly part of his duty, and which all increased his responsibility, and chances of loss, and these have been hitherto discharged without any additional remuneration.

His manner of living has been by no means expensive, not nearly so much so I am convinced as his income would have warranted,—and though I can account for some considerable sums disbursed by him beyond his current expences, I am utterly at a loss to conceive how he should turn out to be in arrear in any such large sum— The sums to which I allude are fortunately still available being invested in the purchase of real property in the town— It is satisfactory to me to be able to state that as my brother has not been a wilful defaulter, and has dissipated nothing by extravagance, so there is also the fullest certainty that no loss will be sustained by the Government— He owes no body, and has a large property in lands and houses wholly unincumbered, and generally of a saleable description. He can pay £2000 immediately, and I believe his real estate to be moderately valued at £20,000— It was almost all acquired long before he held any of these offices, and however painful it may be to him, after a long and very arduous service in difficult duties, to be under the necessity of parting with it on such an occasion as I have stated, there will of course be no hesitation— The only question can be as to the best means of avoiding a wasteful sacrifice in turning it to account— There are some claims which my brother says he has always intended to urge upon the Government, under certain heads of service, but these must abide the decision of the Governor & Council, or of His Majesty's Government. I must not omit mentioning one other circumstance which I so little thought I should ever have occasion to remember, that until lately I had dismissed it from my mind. I have been under the impression that I became one of my brother's securities when he entered upon his offices, though I had forgotten the amount, and the names of the persons who were joined with me. When I first learnt the probability of this difficulty I was anxious to know who the sureties were, that I might relieve them by apprising them that they would certainly incur no loss.— I was surprised to find that the bonds which my brother had prepared remained unexecuted—

It was intended I believe that there should be four sureties in £5000 each, and I know that I consented to be one— I am ready now to execute the bond if the government desires it—

[The above is obviously the enclosure referred to in item 12.]

[14] HEAD TO THE CHIEF JUSTICE [J. B. ROBINSON]: A.L.S. 2p.

July 9 [*Place not stated.*] [Marked: "Copy".]

I have this moment read your letter of this day's date, which I shall consider as confidential, and shall not even mention its contents t my council, or t any one.

I write t you immediately, as I think it may relieve your brother and yourself from anxiety.

The affair you mention (as regards your brothers accounts as Comr. of Woods and forests) appears t me t be very simple.

You privately tell me that there is a balance against him of about £11.000 provincial currency, but that his real estate at a moderate estimate amounts t about £20,000.

Under these circumstances, it appears t me, that all that is necessary is, that he should be allowed sufficient time to revise settle and balance his accts. and t this, his long services I think entitle him.

Every consideration which is due t him as a public servant he may depend upon receiving from me, and as I feel confident that he has every proper feeling and honorable desire that his affairs should be creditably wound up, I have no suggestion of any kind t offer[.]

It will give me pleasure to see you on Monday mrng[.]

[15] ROB[ER]T BALDWIN TO GLENELG: L. 54p.

July 13 *4 Trinity Court, Charing Cross,* [*London.*]

[A manuscript copy of the well known letter setting out Baldwin's views on Canadian affairs. A copy of this letter was enclosed in Glenelg to Head, Aug. 20, 1836, and is reprinted in the *Dominion of Canada, report of the Public archives for the year 1923* (*The Durham papers*), p. 329; in the corresponding *report . . . for the year 1936*, p. 431; and in *Statutes, treaties and documents of the Canadian constitution 1713-1929, ed. by W. P. M. Kennedy, 2nd ed., 1930*, p. 335.]

[As in item 9, the watermark of 1839 indicates the above to be a copy made some years later than the original.]

[16] [VAN DIEMEN'S LAND BILL]: 2p.

[*1837*] [A manuscript draft of "An Act to enable the Government for a limited period to remedy Deficiencies in the Circulation by making Treasury Bills a Legal Tender." The act is to continue in force for two years only. It authorises the provision by Proclamation that "all Bills drawn within this Colony by the Assistant Commissary General upon the

Lords Commissioners of His Majesty's Treasury" shall for a specified period not exceeding six months be accepted as legal tender. Arthur is mentioned as lieutenant governor. The Act does not appear in the printed statutes for 1837.]

[Endorsed: "The Clerk of the Councils Copy."]

[17] [WRITER AND RECIPIENT NOT STATED]: 2p.

[*1837?*] [*Place not stated.*]

Statement of Clergy Reserves of Upper Canada—

There have been sold to the end of the year 1836, 368,428 acres of land for Currency £250,655 at an average of 13s/7d per acre.

Received in part payment.......	89 597		
Leaving due and bearing Interest	£161,058		
Of the sum received in part payment for Lands sold vizt.......	£89,597		
There is invested in English 3 per cent Stock, in Sterling £62,278			
Add for difference of Exchange 6 675	68 953	producing Sterling	—£1880
Leaving this amount to be accounted for..........................	£20,644	add 1/9 difference of Exchange	— 209
			2089

The actual Income for the present is, Interest of £62,278 Sterling equal to £68,953 Currency	£ 2089
Ditto of unpaid Instalments of purchase money	2162
Rent of 361,000 acres on Lease	2141
	£ 6392

The following Income it is assumed may be produced	
By Loan of the Sum now in the English Stocks, Currency £68,953 in the Province at 6 pr Cent	£ 4137
By Receipt of Purchase Money due for Land sold £161058—ditto—ditto—	9663
By sale of Land now Leased 361,000 Acres at 12s/ —£189,600—ditto—ditto	11376
	25176
Suppose the Sum lent at 5 per cent only, then deduct 1/6th.	4196
	£20,980

Total Clergy Expenditure for the year 1836		£12,317
		£ 8663
In aid of the Wesleyan Mission	£ 900	
Salary to the Bishop	£1000	£ 1900
(exclusive of House Rent & Travelling Exps.)		
Leaving an unappropriated annual surplus of Curry		£ 6763

Remain for the disposal of the Crown in aid of the Erection of Churches, support of Clergy and general Education 1,525245 Acres at 12/- per acre £915,147.

Sold	368,423
Leased	361,000
	729,423

Clergy Expenditure for the year 1836

Missionaries of the Church of England	£ 2565.12. 6
Ministers of the Church of Scotland	1541.10. 0
Ministers of the United Presby. & Synod of Upper Canada	699.19.11
Priests of the Roman Catholic Clergy	1500. 0. 0
House Rent of Lord Bishop of Quebec	180. 0. 0
Clergy Expenditure	£ 6487. 2. 5
Erection of Parsonage Houses	367. 2. 5
*Missionaries of the Church of England	4500. 7. 0
Archdeacon of York and Kingston	600. 0. 0
Secretary to the Clergy Corporation	270. 0. 0
Contingent Expences of the Office of the Clergy Corporation	92.13.11
	12,317. 5. 9
Independent of the Claim of the Wesleyan Missy Society	900. 0. 0
	£13217. 5. 9

*In aid of this Sum the Society for the Propagation of the Gospel pay the Sum of £3800.

	Acres	
Total quantity of Land reserved	2,254,668	
Sold and Rented	729 423	
Remain to be disposed of for the erection of Churches, in aid of Ministry or for general Education	1 525,245 Acres	
Value of 1,525,245 Acres at 12s/ per acre		£915,147

		Acres
Clergy Reserves granted as Endowments to the Church of England Clergy Patents for which are completed		22931
Ditto—Ditto—Patents for which are not completed		4118
	acres	
Ditto set apart as Glebes	21057	
of these are included in the Return of Endowments	8332	12725

[The above is possibly the enclosure referred to in item 60.]

[18] [Arthur] to [Glenelg?]: Df.A.L. 2p.

[*1837*] [*Place not stated.*]
[*c. Mar.*] [As commanded, submits nominations for assistant protectors of Aborigines.]

[19] F. W. Jerningham to Arthur: A.L.S. 2p.

[*1837*] [*Place not stated.*]
[*c. Mar.*] [Refers to conversation the previous day; enquires concerning a protectorship of Aborigines; encloses copy of letter sent to Wakefield.]

[*Enclosure:*]

[20] [*1837*]
[*c. Mar.*]

F. W. Jerningham to [E. G.?] Wakefield: L. 3p.

[*Place not stated.*] [Marked: "Copy of a letter written to Mr. Wakefield".]

[Refers to conversation "the other day" on emigration to South Australia. Understands it is intended to establish a military force in the Colony; states his qualifications for forming the corps; asks that the commissioners recommend his immediate promotion to a lieutenancy; discusses the duties and prospects.]

[21] Mrs. Marianne Serjeantson to [Arthur?]: A.L.S. 2p.

Apr. 12 *Wanstead, Van Diemen's Land.* [Marked: "Copy—"]
[A widow appeals for intercession in obtaining a grant of land apparently recommended by Arthur but negatived by the secretary of state.]

[22] Arthur to [Captain] T. Fremlin: Df.L. with emendations in Arthur's handwriting.

May 6 *69, Cadogan Place,* [*London.*]

I regret much that I had not the pleasure to see you when you called this morning— I wished, particularly, to thank you for your care of my Baggage, and for the trouble you gave yourself respecting my Servants—

It is a great disappointment to me that you have not included in your account what I am indebted to you for the Claret, and small articles with which you supplied us— I cannot consent that it should be left unadjusted, & have therefore made a small addition [the following words are here deleted: "added twenty Pounds"] to your account which I hope will be satisfactory— I have heard that the "Elphinstone" is again taken up for Convicts, so that I conclude you will erelong be on your own element again, and sincerely hope, if it be the case, that you may have a prosperous voyage.—

[23] J[AMES]S BUCHANAN TO JOHN JOSEPH: A.L.S. 3p.

May 10 *On board the Boat on my way to Quebec.* [Marked: "highly Confidential & private".]

I venture to submit this letter to your discretion, as to communicating the Contents to His Excellency or not. I feel confidant [*sic*] my Motive will not be Mistaken as the information *might* when I am in London be necessary to me.— I am on my way to Quebec to see Lord Gosford as to my son, who in Consequence of my Brothers absence from ill health has for two years performed the duties of his Majestys Agent for Emigrants— I have obtained Leave of Absence to visit England, and I purpose taking my Wife and Daughter with me, after her late bereav[e]ment, and had in View to sail, (if no circumstance should interpose), about the end of this month.— His Majestys Government some years ago had fixed on placing me as his Majesty['s] Commissioner, to reside in the Provinces to rep[ort] on all Measures relating to trade, and I was so Selected by the late Marquess of Londonder[r]y, and Lord Wallace then Vice President of the Board of Trade; without any Application on my part, as my being acquainted with the Trade of the United States, and not being in any way Concerned in Trade, were deemed essential qualities. Lord Bathurst— afterward, as the appointment was View'd by Colonial agents, as likely to supersede their offices, had the Matter suspended, & the Marquess of Londonder[r]y died, and Lord Wallace retired from the Board of Trade— The subject it is understood, is again looked to, but under more Extended operation, a copy of which I beg leave to enclose. If it should be acted on (but from the unset[t]led State of the Ministry I have great fear of their holding their ground—) I no doubt I should be Appointed by his Majesty to preside at the Board, and watch over these interests: And I need not tell you, that I am most anxious to get out of this Democratic Atmosphere, the Emolument would not be better— Indeed such is the desire of my Wife to get to Canada, and leave New York; that half my present Emolu[me]nt would induce us Cheerfully to go— There has been much talk about the Appointment of a Post-Master General for Upper Canada, tho' that Appointment is distinct from the Colonial Department, I should for the reasons mentioned willingly exchange for it, provided it did not interfer[e] with any Views Sir Francis may have respecting it, and I Venture to say, under his Excellencys Auspicees[?], a Change of that Department, both as to Emolument and Efficiency, would be truly apparent. I am decidedly for all Responsibility as to appointments being Vested in the Supreme Head, two Heads to one body is not according to Nature, and undoubtedly Politically wrong. it does not answer in a house,—a ship, an Army, the Cabinet, nor in fact any where productive of that well founded Efficiency Servicibl [*sic*] to the State or Poeple [*sic*]— The object I have Chiefly; (and if you will do me the favor to believe) Chiefly in View, that in case any such Exchange should be Effected, would it in any way interfer[e] with his Excellencys View, as I beg to assure you, *most distinctly and unequi[v]ocally* that Notwith[st]anding our Anxious Wish to remove to Canada, I would on no account accept the office if in my power, without the fullest Approbation of Sir Francis, and I would Venture to add, no Man will fill it, who would yeild [*sic*] more Efficient Service *in accordance with his Excellency.* than I should do.—

I intreat you my dear Sir, to View this laying open to you my Mind, as a Mark of my Sincere respect, and *fullest Confidence*: however I may Mistake the Manner, and that if in error you will not suffer it go further . . .

[P.S.] your reply shall be religiously regarded Confidential[.]

[Enclosure lacking.]

[24] J[AME]S BUCHANAN TO C. A. HAGERMAN: L. 3p.

June 10 *New York.* [Marked: "Copy of letter addressed to me by Mr. Buchanan, British Consul at New York.— C. A. Hagerman".]

I sail this day wind permitting with my wife and daughter for England in the Packet Quebec for Portsmouth and I am happy to tell you I am likely to be consulted on some matters of importance. I need not say to you that tho' we differ about the Church, yet we are firmly united in promoting British Connection, obedience to the laws and hatred of Democracy— The regulation of the Trade of the Provinces will occupy much of my time. I have your Views fully—the prostration here is without any parallel and depend on it next Decr. will be dark and gloomy. The people are against the manufacture of Money out of raggs & Lampblack—or the Community against the Banks—and universal suffrage will prevail—pray command me—letters sent here will be forwarded to me at the Foreign Office— I purpose returning on the 1st. Octr. My Sons have to complain of the Sheriff of Niagara—his deputy Abr. McLeod levied £60. some time ago and offers him £40 provided he gives a discharge—this differs from withholding to pay over Money— I advised my Son to write to Mr. Hamilton about it—he did so but no reply— I do not wish to bring forward a charge, but any Sheriff who would make such a proposition is unworthy of the office and my View of Sir Francis is, that he will not suffer any Officer [*sic*] to hold an Office—Would you, my dear friend, cause a letter to be written to Mr. Hamilton from your Office as my Son finds it very difficult to get at this deputy Sheriff— I shall *confidentially* drop you a Note from Downing Street when I stand on good ground . . .

[25] J. C. WORTHINGTON TO ARTHUR: A.L.S.

[*1837*] [*Place not stated.*]

[*Sep. 20*] [Refers to the prospective sale by Arthur of apples from an orchard. An accompanying printed sheet advertises the Flower Pot Inn, Sunbury, Middlesex, as having been taken over by John Curtis Worthington, and is marked: "Sep 20 ½ Dozen Old Port £1 4s 0d."]

Sep. 22 HEAD TO GLENELG:

[See item 51.]

[26] ARTHUR TO MAJOR [F.] CARPENTER: Df.A.L. 3p.

Oct. 7 [*Place not stated.*] [Marked: "Private".]

Your letter dated the 14th ultimo has followed me in a variety of ways & at length found me Here— I have been travelling in quest of Health having suffered during the last six weeks from a severe relapse of that terrific disorder influenza.

It would afford me sincere pleasure to be of use to you in a pecuniary way if it were in my power—but, at this time, it really is not[.]

Every pound I can command I have urgent occasion for, from circumstances of a most unexpected nature, so that I am obliged again to look for harrassing employment which, by all means, it was my wish to avoid. If I do get an appointment you shall hear from me immediately—not in the way of a *loan*,—but in one that would be far more agreeable to my own feelings.

A man who is on great terms as he says with Mr Bradley has brought an action against me for "Trespass" during my Govornt. of V. D. Land & laid his Damages, I hear, at £15,000—rather a pleasant addition to the plague these worthies have already given me—but I expect to get some credit out of the affair though I would readily be spared the annoyance and anxiety of it.

Oct. 7 HEAD TO GLENELG:

[See item 52.]

[27] F. CARPENTER TO ARTHUR: A.L.S. 3p.

Oct. 12 *24 Dorset Place, [London.]*

I concluded from the lapse of time which had occurred since the writing of my last letter that you were, somewhere on the wing in the search of pleasure.—and lamented to learn that health was the goddess, whose smiles you were courting . . . [Replies in somewhat florid terms to Arthur's letter of October 7.]

Your letter is full of kindness and friendship—were it otherwise it could not, from the pen of my former friend, have originated . . .

[28] ARTHUR TO [JOHN] MEASURE: Df.L.

Oct. 18 *Oak House, [Feltham.]*

I regret very much that circumstances have prevented our attending the happy ceremony this morning; but I beg you will believe me sincere in assuring you, and Dear Charlotte,[1] of our earnest desire that your Union may be productive of much happiness,—and that it may please God to confer upon you every temporal comfort, and, indeed, as much prosperity as may not prove a hindrance to your Christian course . . . [Invites them to visit Oak Hill on returning from Brighton.]

[Endorsed: "dft. of letter to Mr. Measure written and sent 16th. October dated 18th. October 1837."]

[29] F. CARPENTER TO ARTHUR: A.L.S. 2p.

Nov. 6 *24, Dorset Place, Dorset Square, [London.]*

[Again requests financial loan.]

---

[1]*i.e.* Charlotte de Ferrers Smith, Lady Arthur's sister.

[30] COLBORNE TO HEAD: A.L.S. 6p.

Nov. 6 *Sorel.* [Marked: "No. 35".]

As to the intentions of Mr Papineau, it is not of much importance, what they may have been; the effect of his agitation however the Province now feels acutely; and disaffection, which has penetrated deeper than you may imagine, brings the agitator nearer his avowed object.

The sooner you put the good men and true of the Upper Province on their metal, the better. Your determination of liberating the 24th Regt will produce the best effect; Sir Colin Campbell will act on a similar principle. I believe he will call on the Militia to do the military duties, till reinforcements may arrive from the Mother Country; and send every company he can spare to Quebec, from Halifax.

The alarm in this District is great, and rapidly encreasing. In fact the counties between Longue[u]il and the upper part of the Richelieu are in a state of revolt. Many persons who have distinguished themselves for their loyalty, and as friends of order are menaced, and compelled to join the disaffected, or permit their property to be injured. I have received several applications for protection.

The grand point, and pivot, is Montreal. I am endeavouring to collect there such a force as will permit the apprehensive to sleep quietly, and enable us to act with vigour when called upon by the Executive Government[.]

I have ordered the 24th Regt to proceed without delay to the Carillon and Montreal. One company however must be left at Fort Henry. Fifty Soldiers composing the garrison of that Fort will not, in any respect, take away from the effect of your plans and policy.

You incur not the least risk, or responsibility in trusting to the good feeling of the Province of Upper Canada. You are fully warranted in making the arrangements which you have notified to me.

The diversion or demonstration which Mr Mackenzie may make in Yonge Street, or *Alway* in the London District will do no good.

If the company of the 24th Regt which had quitted Toronto for Kingston had been recalled, the effect of a timid measure of that description would have been much felt in the Province. . .

[P.S.] I have received two offers from the Upper Province to bear down with Volunteer Corps on the *Rebels*[.]

[31] [SIR] J[OHN] GARDINER TO ARTHUR: L.S. 4p.

Nov. 7 *Horse Guards,* [*London.*]

The General Commanding in Chief has received a Communication from The Secretary of State for the Colonial Department, accompanied by an Extract of a Letter which you addressed to Lord Glenelg, as also other Documents, respecting the expediency of measures being adopted for the promulgation, throughout the Service, of the System of Restraint and Coercion to which Convicts are subjected in Van Dieman's Land.

Lord Hill concurs fully in the Opinion offered by Lord Glenelg, that the real condition of a Convict should be thoroughly understood in the Army at large, so long as Transportation is resorted to, as the means of upholding its Discipline.

It has been stated, at the same time, by Lord Glenelg, that, certain alterations in the System hitherto pursued, with respect to transported Convicts, are now in contemplation. It is considered, that, the alterations proposed are likely to have the effect of rendering the Punishments more uniform, and more effective, with a view to the prevention of Crime, and the Reformation of the Offenders. . . [Is instructed to request that Arthur, from his intimate knowledge of the existing convict system] will duly consider, and state the System and Penalties to which a Sentence of Transportation subjects a Prisoner, & the Regulations generally, so far at least as You may deem them, important, to promulgate to the Army, in the manner and with a view to the objects, you have recommended. . .

[32] HEAD TO COLBORNE: L. 3p.

Nov. 11 *Toronto.*

I am much obliged to you for the information you have been so good as to give me respecting your "wars and rumours of wars," and it is satisfactory to me that you approve of the peaceful course of policy I am adopting here.

In proportion as you may be driven to adopt forceable measures, Upper Canada should I consider refrain from doing so, as the moral contrast will no doubt have its effect on those who like to live in peace and quietness.—

You will see in print my answer to an address from Kingston to raise a corps of volunteers—it is in fact to tell them I have no authority to sanction their request— You must not think from this that I am lukewarm in your cause, for though I intend to be slow to anger, yet I think I can assure you that in case you should really want help the Militia of Upper Canada shall be once again round their old Master[.]

[33] COLBORNE TO GOSFORD: L. 2p.

Nov. 13 *Montreal.* [Marked: "Copy".]

The affairs of the Province have in a few days taken a turn so decidedly serious and alarming, that not a moment ought, I think, to be lost in preparing for the worst and for an extensively combined revolt. The Revolutionists are running over a large section of the Country armed, & menacing every individual who hesitates to join them— Dr. Cote in Acadie, Mongeau in Rouville are generally accompanied by five or six hundred persons many of which are armed—At La Prairie St. Francis and St Charles armed parties are actively employed in forcing the Habitans to enrol— If we neglect to profit by the offers from the Upper Province, and those from The Inhabitants of Montreal to assist by raising Corps; while we permit the declared Revolutionists to arm quietly we shall lose the Province.— I propose with Your Lordships sanction to form a Company of Pensioners and to station them at Isle aux Noix.

This Fort must be occupied, for it would have the worst effect to let The Borderers under Dr. Cote, to get hold of it, even for a day: and we cannot spare Detachments from our small Force to lock them up in a Garrison— A Few Corps from Upper Canada might occupy Montreal Chambly and St. Johns during the Winter, and liberate a more valuable description of Force— St. Hyacinthe is I understand to be the Head Quarters of the Revolutionists and it is said that Papineau yesterday was invited to go there and declare himself and that Wd. Nelson is to take the lead in case of his refusal[.]

I have had some conversation with a Methodist Preacher who was brought before Dr Cote when on his route to St. Johns— Cote recommended him not to proceed as he intended to enter the village with four or five hundred persons, while a party from St. Athanan would pass the Bridge and meet him—

Two Officers of Militia called on Major Trydell of the 83rd Regt. at St. Helens late on Sunday night and requested him to permit them to lodge their Commissions in his hands, as they expected a visit from a party on the La Prairie side to force them to resign[.]

[34] C. J. FORBES TO COLBORNE: L. 3p.

Nov. 13 *Carillon.* [Marked: "Copy".]

In accordance with my intention to make Your Excellency acquainted with any circumstances that may transpire touching the state of affairs in this District of Country, I have now the honor to submit certain information that I have received from a person in my employ who has just returned from performing the last offices to a deceased near relative at the Grand Brulé, and as it corresponds in all particulars with information I have received from various other quarters I feel assured that it may be fully relied upon—

1st. That the system of enrolment is general throughout the whole of this neighbourhood—

2dly. That great exertions are making to procure Fire Arms, and in repairing such as are found unserviceable among the Habitans—

3dly. That Quantities of Powder is [*sic*] providing for the use of Armed Bodies of Men, and Musquet Balls are casting very extensively—

4thly. That a system of intimidation is generally pursued towards all who dispose of Cattle or Produce to the English, and examples have already been made of some, by injuring, and even destroying their Horses who have had dealings in this neighbourhood.

These are truly alarming symptoms the extension of which to the Counties on the South side of the St Lawrence would lead one to apprehend that one of the principal objects of the Agitators is to cut off the supplies from Montreal during the Winter— This consequence is threatened by our Radicals without the least reserve, as well as the harassing the Troops in this neighbourhood by nightly demonstrations—

How far in the present depressed state of the Mercantile Community at Montreal it will be possible to count upon a sufficiency of flour and grain being laid up in that City for its supply I am not exactly capable of determining; but of this I think we may be fairly assured, that the arrangements of the Merchants will not be found equal to assuring a supply of Forage, Salt Meat, and Cattle for its Inhabitants, and those who may seek refuge there, should the present alarming symptoms not be speedily dissipated— Therefore it may be of the utmost importance that the Communication between The Ottawa and Montreal should be kept open in order to ensure the safe conduct of these indispensible Articles—

That there are many of the Habitans throughout this section of The Country that are well affected to Her Majesty's Government I have strong assurances of, who would gladly assist the efforts of the Executive to put an end to the Insubordination that prevails—but the total want of Magistrates possessing energy to guide the efforts of the well thinking, aided by The Military is a draw back that cannot be conquered— Magistrates much better qualified than those in the neighbourhood invested with the mere power the existing Law gives them would be totally inadequate to the exigencies of The Times— Special Magistrates acting under special Instructions which should be stretched to the utmost Limit would be alone suited to the present Emergencies— And the sooner such appointments were created the better, in order that the proper investigations may be gone [into], by which the Sedition that now reigns paramount may be laid bare and checked; and before the authority of the Government be entirely lost sight of[.]

I may perhaps be excused for anticipating the intentions of Lord Gosford to create such opportunity & I may perhaps wander still wider from the Mark in concluding that His Lordship may meet with difficulty in finding persons possessing the requisite qualifications for the office, but it can do no injury that I should confide to Your Excellency the name of a Gentleman who for firmness of purpose and intelligence is scarcely to be matched, if he could be prevailed with in case of need to accept the appointment— It is the Revd. Joseph Abbott The Episcopal Clergyman of Grenville, with whose character I am intimately acquainted. And I shall at any time be happy to attempt a negotiation with him upon Your Excellency's suggestion[.]

[35] THO[MA]S PETERS TO MRS. URLING SENR. A.L.S.

Nov. 13 *13 Serles Place, Lincoln's Inn,* [*London.*]

[Dison wrote a request to Phillipps, under-secretary of state, to hand over "the Quadruplicate Memorial" to Peters; Everest, a clerk at the Horse Guards, said that all papers sent were undeviatingly retained, but it might be perused and copied; Peters encloses a transcript with answers to the queries proposed by Mason. Refers to "T, N's" last letter.]

[The above is re-addressed to Arthur.]

[Enclosure lacking.]

[36] COLBORNE TO HEAD: A.L.S. 4p.

Nov. 14 *Montreal.*

The whole French population of this Province are now united against the Government; and in many sections of the country are not only organized; but have already taken the lead in active operation by sending out armed parties of three or four hundred persons, that run over the districts and force every individual to join them. If we do not immediately take active measures to arm and organize our friends, the Province will be lost[.]

From the enclosures you will find that if we hesitate in making arrangements for shewing our strength, in the Upper Province, the Revolutionists will carry on their system of intimidation to such an extent as will give them an advantage over us which cannot be recovered.

I think you could, in this hour of danger, constitutionally select a certain number of companies from the Militia for five months service, and send them down to us, if Lord Gosford will accept their aid.

They might be stationed at La Prairie St John's and Chambly. Their occupying these points, would allow the regular force to act with effect immediately.

The habitans in all parts of the Province refuse to pay their rents; as they have been informed by the leaders of the Revolutionists that they are to have their deeds; and that the Seigniorial rights and tithes are to be abolished. Thus they are all interested in the success of the menaced revolt.

I thank you for your communication of the 11th inst., which Mr Lysons has just delivered to me[.]

[Enclosures lacking.]

[37] [SIR] W[ILLIA]M MOLESWORTH TO [ARTHUR?]: A.L.S. 3p.

[*1837*] *[Place not stated.]*
[*Dec.*] I feel exceedingly obliged to you for the books which you have been so kind as to send me & I will carefully peruse them. It is the intention of the Committee to recommend that another committee shall be appointed next session & then I think it would be most admirable to reexamine you upon many subjects to which I abstained from referring merely because the wish of the committee was to finish their business as quickly as possible[.]

[38] JOHN STRACHAN: A.D.S. 4p.

Dec. 2 *Toronto.*

A Report On the Religious state of the Indians in Upper Canada. . .

[For a later copy of this report with slight variations, see item 166. The present copy may have been an enclosure with item 236.]

[39] [ARTHUR TO GLENELG]: Df.L. 4p.

[*1837*] *[Place not stated.]*
[*Dec. 6*] Observing in the Newspapers of this Morning that a Petition was last evg presented to the House of Commons on behalf of Mr Bryan referring to my intended departure for Upper Canada I take the earliest opportunity of making the following statement for your Lordships information.

The action which has been brought against me by Mr. B. is founded upon my having ordered the removal from his charge of several convict-servants who had been indented to him "on loan". Their removal took place in consequence of my conviction that he was not a proper person to retain that trust[.] In taking this step I acted in accordance with an interpretation of the Law which Sr. G Murray had conveyed to me for my guidance, & which interpretation was founded on the Report of the present Ld Abinger & of Sr. E. Sugden the then Atty & Solr. Genl.

I am not aware that my presence in England or my absence can in any manner affect the [the following words are here deleted: "trial of this action"] or the interest, of Mr. B except indeed in the Event of his recovering[?] a final judgt. against me, he wd. not in my absence be able to execute it against my person. But I do not leave England witht. knowing that the most ample provision has been made to satisfy any damages which can possibly be recovered against me. If I could contemplate as possible the contingency that any such damages would not be immediately paid [the following words are here deleted: "after the plaintiff had obtained a final judgement"] I should hold myself bound instantly to return to meet the demand in person—

[40] M. S. BIDWELL TO HEAD: L. 2p.

Dec. 8 *Toronto.* [Marked : "Copy of letter from M. S. Bidwell Esq to Sir Francis Head, in my possession. C. A. Hagerman".]

In consequence of the kind conversation of your Excellency this morning, I have determined to leave this Province for ever[.]

I am aware that the circumstances to which your Excellency alluded, are calculated to give rise to suspicions against me, in relation to this insurrection, and while they would be likely to render my further residence in the Province unpleasant, they make your Excellencys kindness the more worthy of my deep and lasting gratitude.—

I am confident at the same time, that the investigation which will now of course be made, will fully remove those suspicions from your Excellencys mind, and will prove that any (qu: *no*) such attempt was in contemplation.[1]

[41] [ARTHUR] TO GLENELG: Df.L. with emendations in Arthur's handwriting. 6p.

Dec. 9 *U[nited] S[ervices] C[lub,] [London.]*

I have the honor to inform your Lordship that I shall have completed all my arrangements on Wednesday the 20th Inst and shall be prepared to proceed to New York by the first opportunity that may offer after that day.

I venture to submit to Yr Lordship it is of much importance that the two following subjects should be disposed of before my embarkation[.]

First— As respects the Rectories endowed by Sir John Colborne.— If, on further consideration, the Law Officers of the Crown should be of opinion that the measure cannot be disturbed on the ground of its illegality, the advocates for the [the following words are here deleted: "rights of the"] Established Church ought to be, and I think would be, under such circumstances disposed to come into some reasonable adjustment of the general question of Church Reserves.— If, on the other hand, If the Law Officers shall adhere to the opinion that the titles have been illegally issued,—then the position in wh. the advocates of the Estad. Church will be placed affords some reason to hope that they will on other considerations be still disposed to accede to an equitable arrangement [the phrase here originally read: "disposed to listen to reasonable terms"].

The feeling in the Province is so strong upon this subject, that I am persuaded the foundation for an amicable adjustment of the existing differences should be at once laid in this Country, and I presume to hope, that, with yr. Lordships concurrence, much may be done towards it.

Second. As respects the precise terms in wh. the offer should be made to surrender to the Provincial Legislature Her Mys. territorial and casual revenue.

---

[1]This is a copy of the letter which Ryerson said had been essentially mutilated when it appeared in *The Patriot* for April 20, 1838. In the completed version which he subsequently printed in *The Upper Canada Herald* for May 8, 1838, the last clause read: "and will prove that I had no knowledge or expectation that any such attempt was in contemplation." John Joseph, Head's private secretary, apparently sent to Vice-Chancellor Jameson an account of Bidwell's final interview with Head, and attached a "true copy" of Bidwell's letter. In two transcripts of this correspondence in the *Robert Baldwin Papers* and in Baldwin's handwriting, the same omission occurs. In one transcript an interpolation (probably by Baldwin) suggests that "'my ignorance' or some such words appear to be omitted" after the words "will prove." Beyond Ryerson's assertion, there is no evidence of mutilation. A more probable explanation of the discrepancy is that Bidwell, in accordance with his own statement, drafted the letter along lines "dictated or at least suggested" by Head; that Bidwell retained this draft, and in making the second or fair copy for Head he accidentally omitted the words later claimed to have been deleted; and that, owing to the stress of the moment, neither party then noticed the omission. The disputed words would occupy about one line of handwriting; the word "that" occurs twice in the controversial sentence; and if it occurred at the beginning of successive lines in the original draft, one complete line may have been omitted in making the fair copy. In any case it is probable that item 40 represents the true official letter.

For the reasons assigned by Sir F Head in his Despatch No. 96. of the 22nd August last, it seems doubtful whether the H. of Assembly will agree to any measure of that nature. but as the question has been mooted in an address from the Lt. Govr. to that House it seems import[ant] that it should be brought to issue by making to the Legislature some more definite proposition!

I take the liberty of adding that the earliest intimation to the Genl Comg. in Chief of your Lordship's pleasure that I should be appointed a Major Genl. on the Staff serving in U. Cana is very desirable in order that I may be enabled during the very short period before my embarkation, to confer with the authorities at the H. Gds upon that branch of the Public Service.

[An incomplete and cancelled paragraph here reads: "A subject of scarcely less moment than those to which I have adverted will I trust engage Your Lordship's early attention, and lead to the issue of your final instructions to me thereon. It is that of the Monetary policy of the Province as respects the port and".]

[42] JONAS JONES TO THOMAS RUNCHEY: L. 2p.

Dec. 11 *Government House, Toronto.* [Marked: "Duplicate".]

I am directed by His Excellency the Lieut. Governor to acknowledge the receipt of your letter of the 7th. instant and to express to you his Excellencys satisfaction at the loyal offer it contains[.]

His Excellency is pleased to accept the offer and to authorize you to proceed to raise and organize the men and concentrate them at or near St. Catherines—and to appoint or employ officers temporarily until His Excellencys pleasure respecting such officers can be made known[.]

You will make out a list of officers whom you will recommend for employment.

You will also make a Report with as little delay as possible of what steps you take in pursuance of this communication—and will hold yourself and men in readiness to obey any orders you may receive to march where your services may be required.— You are authorized to incur necessary expences.

[43] THO[MA]S RUNCHEY TO JONAS JONES: A.L.S.

Dec. 12 *York, Grand River, U.C.*

I beg to acknowledge receipt of your communication of yesterday's date, authorising me to form a Volunteer Corps of Coloured men,— and I beg to acquaint you, that I shall proceed forthwith to act upon that authority.

[44] GEO[RGE] RYKERT TO JA[ME]S FITZGIBBON: A.L.S. 3p.

Dec. 13 *St. Catharines.*

I commenced writing you two or three times during the past week, but owing to the great excitement, and frequent alarms, could not get time to finish a letter, and even now, cannot say much—as I expect every moment to be called upon again to turn out— Matters here since yesterday are a little more tranquil. A Report however reached us last night that McKenzie and his party had reached Buffalo, (of which I have no doubt) that a very large Meeting was assembled at that place on Monday night. They say from 1.500 to 2.000 were present, Doctor Chapin took the chair and apologized for Rolph & McKenzie not attending—that they would attend the next night to address them, and explain the grievances they had to complain of, Chapin then brandished a durk & called for "Six brave Sons of liberty" to guard McK—that he was then at his (Chapin's) House)— After the meeting dispersed a large number marched up to Chapins House and called for McK. A person came to the door and asked whether it was a mob coming to take him. On their saying No, he told them McK. was ill and in bed— I understand there is a strong feeling of "sympathy" as they state in Buffalo in favour of the "Canadian Patriots"— I am also aware that we have a desperate set here in our rear who are only awaiting the sound of the "tocsin" in some other quarter, to pounce upon us like hungry wolves—to pillage and plunder us— Undoubted information has been received that a considerable number of rebels have organized themselves into a body with Arms in the Short-Hills, ready to turn out in the rebel cause— I am not apprehensive that they will make any attack unless there is a rupture elsewhere—

I have been in favour of our turning out with sufficient force to disarm them, and bring the ringleaders to justice. A majority however of the Magistrates deemed it bad policy at this time, thinking it would create an unnecessary excitement—especially now that their party was so happily and gloriously defeated at Toronto— I am of opinion they will disperse, at same time I am not disposed to slumber at my post—

Disaffection I regret to say prevails to a great extent in the Southern Townships of this District— The Township of Palham has not more than 6 to 8 loyal men in it—Bertie, Willoughby, Arnland, & Humberstone are very little better— And I am persuaded that if the rebels had succeeded at Toronto, a large force would have been collected from those Townships against us—

It behoves us therefore in my opinion to be vigilent [*sic*] in this quarter, and follow up our glorious and timely victory—

There is little doubt of the Fugitives having passed through the front of our district on Friday last,—A boat with 5 persons landed along the Lake Shore a little above the 4 Mile Creek—where they were driven by the severe storm on that day—near where they landed there was a person burning Coal, from whom they enquired the way to Queenston stating they were going there after goods—they had no arms—nor anything with them except a bag containing a ps. of bread a few cold boil'd potatoes and 2 fishes which they warmed upon the Coals and ate— I examined the boat, and also took the description of the persons in writing, which answers to those of McK. & Son, Gibson, Lount and Fletcher, their clothes it was stated, seemed altogether inferior to the station of the individuals who wore them—they left the boat [with] the man, and proceeded towards St. Davids, they [were] tracked to within a short distance of St. Davids, where they crossed the road & went into the woods— And I have no hesitation in saying that in my opinion they were protected and forwarded from that neighbourhood[.] The two smaller ones had on grey clothes—and were subsequently seen with cloaks over them—

I am happy to find that we have a noble set of fellows in this quarter, ready to turn out in a moment in defence of their Country—on our receiving the first report from Toronto of the threatened attack they were called upon to turn out, to assist you, Mr Clark & myself started with nearly 100 volunteers, leaving Mr. Merritt to bring another lot the next morning— We embarked in the "Brittannia" [*sic*] on Thursday evening at Niagara with our good fellows but the weather was so boisterous that the Boat could not proceed with safety—and after going some 8 or 10 miles she was compelled to put about, and with difficulty got back— We were much annoyed that we could not get over—before we could start the second time, the "Transit" brought the glorious and welcome news of their defeat— Although I have great confidence in the Militia in this quarter, a very strong force can be collected here in a short time, I am sorry to find to[o] great a deficiency in Officers, we have not more than 8 or 10 who can be depended upon, the rest are really a disgrace to the battalion. In addressing an Officer of your experience I feel it unnecessary to comment upon the importance of having good officers to render the Regt. efficient and respectable— In the first place we are greatly deficient in the proper no. Secondly there are some 6 or 8 drinking fellows unfit for office, under whom the men do not like to serve—then again we have about as many disaffected ones who decline attending to their proper duty— You may perhaps deem it a little officious in me, but I do beg of you to take early steps to officer our Militia more efficiently, otherwise it will "go to the dogs", but in order to do so you will require to be exceedingly cautious to prevent ill feeling at this time— I understand there are a few young officious chaps who have been trying to "shove" themselves in, but I trust they may not succeed, as it will give very general dissatisfaction to the Regt—and create a great apathy in their duty— I was appointed to a commission by Sir J. Colborne some 5 or 6 yrs ago, but the commission having never issued, I declined acting as an officer until the late excitement, when I felt it my duty [to] act in any capacity where I could render the best service to my country— I therefore now beg to say that I have no particular desire to take a commission, but am willing nevertheless to act as an officer should His Excellency think proper to appoint me now, at the same time beg to say that at my time of life I would rather act as a private, than to commence as a subaltern—again I am of opinion that if the promotions are regularly made from the time of my appointment by Sir John, that I should now be entitled to a Captaincy—or at least a Senior Lieutenancy— However in this act as you deem best— I shall not be backward in times like the present in acting any part my Country may require—

Should you deem it proper to consult me, I shall be most happy to render you any assistance I can in the selection of proper Men to fill offices—

Steps will of course be taken to remove those who have refused to do their duty—or discouraged others—

Pray excuse this hasty scrawl. I have really not time to read it myself—I hope therefore you "will take the will for the deed".

[45] GEO[RGE] RYKERT TO C. A. HAGERMAN: A.L.S. 3p.

Dec. 14 *St. Catharines.*

Our district at present is all excitement owing to reports daily reaching us from the other [side] of the River— It seems to be the general opinion here that the fugitive rebels named in the Proclamation (and some other) are now in Buffalo, haranguing and inciting the American rabble to

Arms in the cause of the misnamed "Patriots" of the Canadas— On Monday night a meeting took place at the Theatre, where, I am very creditably informed not less than 2,000 persons attended, it was expected that McKenzie and Rolph would be present to address them— It seems however that the *celebrated* Doctor Chapin took the chair, and apologized for the absence of the two gentlemen (rebels) promising they would attend the next evening— He than brandished his durk and called for "6 *brave* sons of freedom" to guard McK. that night at his House. After the meeting dispersed a great number marched up to Chapins House, and called for McK, a person came to the door (whom I suppose to have been Gibson) and asked if there were a mob assembled to take him— A very knowing Jonathan replied—"you had better not apply the term mob to the people of this Country" (or in words to the same import)[.] They were then told McK. was much fatigued and unwell and had gone to bed— Of the result of their next meeting I have not received information upon which I fully rely— It was however reported last evening that a force of about 2,000 are preparing to cross our Frontier—if true, I hope we shall be prepared to receive them in "due form"— My greatest apprehensions however are from a set of rabble in our rear who I am persuaded are only waiting for movements in other parts to pounce upon us like so many wolves hungry for pillage and plunder,— There is no doubt of their having been frequently assembled with Arms, harangued and incited by some reckless villains of our own district to Arm themselves to assist the Papineau Cause[.]

An express has this moment arrived from Mr Merritt at Fort Erie dated yesterday (13th.) saying there is no doubt the Rabble of Buffalo and along the Frontier are arming themselves. that they succeeded yesterday in getting guns &c &c— He requested us to forward immediately all the Men, Arms, Ammunitions &c &c that we can muster here— Thus you see at once the state of things here, and there is no doubt in my mind the next brush will be on the Niagara Frontier— We *must* be prepared to meet them— I trust we shall have some assistance from the other side of the Lake, a few small pieces of Artillery would be of great use, on their attempting to land— When I comd. I intended saying more but the bustle at this moment prevents me— I have great fears that we shall be attacked in rear by the people in the Southern part of our district. . . .

P.S. Our Militia are generally true among us here; but require efficient officers— I hope no time may be lost in organizing them—really our officers are in many respects a disgrace to the Country—we have some 6 or 8 good ones the rest are either drunkards or disaffected—

[46] [A GROUP OF 88 INDIANS] TO W. J. KERR: L.S. 3p.

Dec. 14 *Brantford.*

Brother We would respectfully beg you will Supply us with 100 or 150 Guns for the use of our people as very many of our young Warriors are not provided with arms at the present time. . . [A list of 88 names of signatory Indians follows.]

[An Indian name, which apparently reads: "Thakawarentte", precedes Kerr's English name in the superscription.]

[47] [ARTHUR] TO GLENELG: Df.A.L. 2p.

Dec. 16 *London.*

[Replies to a letter of Nov. 20 asking for observations concerning an application by John W. Baker for a grant of land in Van Diemen's Land. Recalls Baker went there in 1824, returned to England, and went back again in 1835. Conditions and land values had greatly changed in the meantime. Has the highest respect for Baker; had made him a justice of the peace; commends him; but regrets the application cannot be conscientiously supported. Many claims have been refused on the same grounds.]

[48] GEORGE HAM TO ASSISTANT ADJUTANT GENERAL CAMERON: A.L.S.

Dec. 16 *Head Quarters, Chippewa.* [Marked: "No. 1."]

The moment the weather allowed of another inspection of Navy Island I again sent Major Boswell & Adjutant Pringle to observe— They have this moment returned & report that two armed sentries are parading on the North Shore of the Island & seven men are in a large scow busily employed with pails &c & axes bailing it & cutting out the ice. From every appearance there is a disposition to make an attack and I am making every preparation to be prepared for it[.]

I have communicated the purport of this despatch to the officer commanding at Lundy's lane[.]

[49] ARTHUR TO SIR GEORGE GREY: A.L.S. 2p.

Dec. 21 *London.*

With reference to the Letter which I had the honor to address to Lord Glenelg on the 15th inst., I beg you will be so good as to inform His Lordship that I have taken my passage in the Packet to sail from London on the 27th inst. and to request His Lordship will be pleased to recommend to the Lords Commissioners of His Majestys Treasury that the same allowance for passage money should be granted to me which has been authorised to Sir Francis Head.

The grounds on which I solicit this indulgence are submitted in my Letter to His Lordship to which I have alluded; and I trust the peculiar circumstances of the case will fully satisfy His Majestys Government that my application is quite reasonable—seeing that I am obliged to reequip— & to make provision for a double establishment whilst I am still without funds from the breaking up of my establishment in Van Diemen's Land.

[Endorsed: "Copy".]

[50] GLENELG TO ARTHUR: L.S. 4p.

Dec. 21 *Downing Street, [London.]* [Marked: "No. 1".]

I have the honor to transmit to you, herewith, copies of two confidential dispatches [marginal notes here read: "22 Septr" and "7th Octr"] from Sir Francis Head representing the necessity of an immediate increase in the Legislative Council of Upper Canada; and suggesting the names of various gentlemen to be added to that House. These dispatches reached me subsequently to the tender of Sir Francis Heads resignation, and I have therefore considered it my duty to abstain for the present from submitting to the Queen any advice respecting them:

As Sir Francis Head states that he has not communicated to any of the Gentlemen whom he has proposed for the Council his intentions in that respect, you will come to the consideration of their fitness unfettered by any considerations of a personal nature.

I have to request that you will take the whole subject into your early consideration and that you will report to me whether in your opinion it is necessary that the Legislative Council should be increased, & if so you will transmit to me the names of the Gentlemen whom you consider best qualified to be appointed to that Board—together with such information respecting them as may enable Her Majestys Government to judge of their fitness for the Office—

[Endorsed: "received in England"; further endorsed: "Mr Hugh Willson to be Clerk of the Gore District—John Law dissipated— Mr Willson Inc Militia".]

[*Enclosures:*]

[51] *1837*
Sep. 22

HEAD TO GLENELG: L.S. 6p.

Toronto. [Marked: "Private and confidential Duplicate".]

The subject of this despatch is to submit for Your Lordship's consideration the necessity which in my opinion exists for an increase to the Legislative Council of this Province, previous to the next meeting of the Legislature.

The Legislative Council is at present nominally composed of 29 members about 13 of whom can generally be assembled by a special summons, altho' there seldom attend more than 7 or 8.

Besides its' [*sic*] ex officio business, the Legislative Council has in this Province extraordinary duties to perform which I think it proper confidentially to explain to Your Lordship.

Your Lordship is aware that the House of Assembly of Upper Canada is composed of 62 members who represent the local interests of the various districts of the Province.

On the meeting of the Legislature each member has generally some particular isolated object which his constituents are desirous to attain, but in which the rest of the community probably feels little or no interest.

In order therefore to be successful, it has practically been found necessary for members to make arrangements among themselves for mutual support, and to such an extent has this practice been carried, that I have been credibly informed the immense undertaking of improving the navigation of the St. Lawrence, was in fact carried, not by the sincere advocates of that measure, but by the claimants for indemnity for war losses, who agreed to vote with the proposers of the Saint Lawrence expenditure (£300,000) if they in return would vote for the payment of the war losses!

Under a system of reciprocity of this nature, the members of the Assembly constantly find it necessary to give their votes in support of measures which they know, and even readily admit to be worse than inexpedient, but the common apology is "*Yes, but we knew quite well they would be thrown out by the Upper House!*"

The Legislative Council therefore, though it incurs much odium by apparently opposing the House of Assembly, yet in fact affords material assistance to its' individual members who relying on its veto, are enabled to vote with impunity to the Province in the way I have described.

The above reasons will I trust explain the necessity of making the Legislative Council efficient, which it is not at present, as it is often with difficulty that a quorum can be obtained.

As I expect I shall be relieved from the station I have now the honour to hold immediately before the meeting of the Legislature which should be assembled about the middle of January, I have deemed it adviseable not to apprize any of the individuals whose names I am about to mention, that I have recommended them to your Lordship. If therefore Your Lordship should deem it better that the selection should be delayed until my successor can become acquainted with the Province, there can be no possible objection on my part to such an arrangement.

The persons I have selected are generally speaking men who have considerable property *to lose*, and who on that account, form I think the best barrier to the members of the House of Assembly, whose constituents generally speaking have their fortunes *to make*.

I have generally selected old inhabitants of the Province; The Honble. Mr De Blaguière [*i.e.* Blaquière] however is an exception to this rule, but he is the brother of Lord de Blaguière, is a very intelligent man, a good speaker, and he is besides almost the only Irishman I can name.

(The Irish have complained and with reason that they have been neglected)[.]

To appoint many new comers to the Legislative Council would certainly be objectionable but now and then to infuse into the old mass a little good blood warm and fresh from the mother country has an invigorating effect.

I am of opinion that if the Legislature of this Province meets again without the Legislative Council being efficient great dissatisfaction will be felt and expressed throughout the country. . .

Names of persons recommended to be appointed to the Legislative Council of Upper Canada, previous to the next meeting of the Provincial Legislature.

F. Boyd—An English gentleman who has been three or four years in the Province possesses large property, is a sensible plain man of business and much respected by all political classes.

James [*i.e.* John] Simcoe Macaulay—A retired officer of Engineers possessing considerable property son of one of General Simcoe's first settlers—has leisure to attend. (A Canadian).

John Willson—Was very many years in the House of Assembly, of which he was speaker. (A Canadian.) [Marginal note in Arthur's handwriting here reads: "resides in Gore District Old."]

The Honble. P. de Blaguiere [*i.e.* Blaquière]—A settler who has but lately arrived in the Province— He is brother to Lord de Blaguiere, is an intelligent clever man of business and a good speaker. (An Irishman.) [Similar marginal note reads: "resides in County of Oxford at Woodstock recmds (?) for Lt Col: 3d Oxford vice Drew (?) 2 Sons in the Militia".]

Robert C. Wilkins of Prince Edward Island. A wealthy merchant highly respected; possesses great practical knowledge of the Province. (A Canadian)[.] [Similar marginal note reads: "appd Col of Prince Edward Reg".]

Adam Fergason [*i.e.* Fergusson] of East Flamboro'—A Scotch gentleman, author of a work on agriculture published in Scotland, possesses large property, is generally respected. (A Scotchman). [Similar marginal note reads: "Col of Militia", "Colonel Gore District".]

Isaac Fraser.—A magistrate highly respected; one of the oldest Settlers in the Province. [Similar marginal note reads: "Col. of one of the Addington Regts."]

Thomas Radcliffe [*i.e.* Radcliff]—Colonel of Militia—a British Officer on half pay, intelligent and respectable. (An Irishman.) [Similar marginal note reads: "Col. of one of the 4 Inc Regts (?) & now cmg the Western Rangers at Amersburg" (*sic*).]

David Campbell—A retired Major—possesses considerable property in the Province—a magistrate. (A Scotchman.) [Similar marginal note reads: "Township of Seymour commds 5th Northumberld".]

[52] *1837*
Oct. 7

HEAD TO GLENELG: L.S.

Toronto. [Marked "Private and confidential Duplicate".]

In my despatch of the 22nd. ultimo marked "private and confidential" I had the honor to submit for Your Lordships' consideration, the necessity which in my opinion existed for an increase of the Legislative Council of this Province, *previous to the next meeting of the Legislature.*

In addition to the names of the gentlemen I recommended to Your Lordship, I beg leave now to add that of Samuel Street Esqre. of Niagara Falls, who was inadvertently omitted.

Mr Street is considered to be the wealthiest person in Upper Canada, he has considerable influence and is very generally respected.

[53] F. CARPENTER TO ARTHUR: A.L.S. 4p.

Dec. 21 *Dorset Place*, [*London*.]

[States circumstances of distress and appeals for financial assistance.]

[54] THOMAS RUNCHEY TO JONAS JONES: A.L.S. 2p.

Dec. 21 *Niagara*.

I have the honor to acknowledge Your Despatch of the 11th. December, the subject matter it contains I have great pleasure in replying to.

I have proceeded so far as His Excellency has directed me and have met with surprising success[;] the number as yet I am hardly able to ascertain in consequence of Despatching men to different parts of the Country & not ascertaining accurately the number and there not being sufficient time to hear from them, however I shall be able in the course of a few days to report to His Excellency more fully on the subject[.] At present some proportion of my Volunteers are stationed at Niagara & Chippawa under the direction of Colonel Clark. I also beg to state that I found it necessary to purchase for some of them necessary wearing apparel at the lowest possible rate, in order to make the Men fit for service, it would also be very gratifying to me if His Excellency would recommend the furtherance of my object to the Magistrates of the District [.]

The Gentlemen whom I have chosen as Officers are both Sons of U.E. Loyalists and whose Fathers services entitle them to the consideration of Her Majestys Government[.] I have accordingly appointed as my Lieutenant Johnson Clench Esquire Clerk of the Niagara District Court he being as I am informed one of the first who volunteered his services to oppose the rebels from destroying the Citv of Toronto and was present at the affair at Mountgomeries[?] I have also appointed as my Ensign Mr. Johnson Stewart who is also a very active & Loyal subject to Her Majesty and who was highly recommended to me by Lieut Colonel Servos[.] I may add that those gentlemen have been in command of the Coloured Core [*sic*], previous to receiving my communication and they have kindly relinquished their claim to me and have consented to act under me[.]

[55] G. F. ANGAS TO ARTHUR: A.L.S. 2p.

Dec. 22 *Park House, Dawlish, Devon.*

I feel particularly obliged by your kind favour of the 11th Inst. written under your present pressing engagements. Instead of Canada I heartily wish you had been appointed to the Government of New South Wales, then, indeed, I am sure I should have ever found in you a true Friend to every benevolent effort to benefit the People in Australia whether English or Natives. But, the present state of Canada demands a Governor of your principles, firmness & long experience & Her Majesty has shown much discernment in the selection. My earnest prayer to God is that you may have strength & wisdom equal to your need, for in the present state of things there I need scarcely remark that it is the most difficult government of any in the Empire. I fear it will ever be so until Upper and Lower Canada are united under one Governor & the French Faction subdued. Alas! how few real Patriots are to be found! "All seek their own and not the things of Christ" is as true now as when Paul uttered the expression. I hope you will be able to mitigate the violence of religious party. I enclose you a Tract written by Revd. Baptist Noel. If Churchmen & Dissenters would adopt his views there would exist a fraternal Bond of Union amongst all Xtians. So long as the Shibboleth of a Party is considered of more importance than the vital principle of the Gospel and its moral obligations, peace must go far away from us. In the British Colonies where attempts are making to establish a dominant religion I am confident, the seeds of discord will grow luxuriant enough. It is impossible to be otherwise & on this account I consider the present policy of the Government in Australia to be wise & happy as I doubt not the consequences will show. I have no other connection with Canada, except that I hold 50 Shares in the British American Land Co—, am a member of the "Aborigines protection So." Comee—and was one of the Deputation which had the honour of a recent interview with Lord Glenelg on the subject of the removal of the Indians from the Wesleyan Settlement in Upper Canada into the back country by order of Sir F. Head & which I thought an inhuman & cruel measure to the poor Indians—but there was every reason to hope that Lord Glenelg would afford every redress in his power and mitigate their condition, if possible. . .

[Refers to South Australia; aborigines; trade. Sends wishes.]

[56] J. B. Askin to J[ohn] Joseph: A.L.S. 3p.

Dec. 22 *London, [U.C.]*

I have the honor to enclose you a Return of the Prisoners now in Gaol at London, some of whom are fully committed, and others in progress of Examination under charges of High Treason, Sedition and Treasonable practices; and to inform you that Col Radcliff with a detachment of 200 officers and men are doing duty—Guarding the Gaol, under the orders of Col McNabb [*sic*].

I am requested to report that this detachment left their homes without any preparation whatever to enable them to resist the severe cold at this season of the Year; and that they are now in want of many necessaries to keep themselves comfortable in doing the service which they perform, and without means to purchase or pay for many things they cannot well dispense with.

I beg leave to add that the magistrates with whom I am now acting desire me to request that you will lay this communication before His Excellency the Lieutenant Governor and to request that he will be pleased to take this matter into His consideration and Grant an Authority for the payment of Expences which have been, and are daily being incurred in the Service. . .

P.S. I beg to add, amongst those committed a number will be found, to have been induced under most plausable [*sic*], insiduous [*sic*], and false representations to take up Arms, and who, since appear most repentant and sorrey [*sic*]; and some few of less than 21 years of age, who I think have been completely beguiled into Error,—under such circumstances I would beg that His Excellency would be pleased to permit the Magistrates who act with me, to use such discretion as the particular circumstances of cases of the sort, which I represent may admit, and to allow such as are not most implicated to be allowed admitted to Bail for their Appearance to Answer at the next Court of Oyer and Terminer and General Gaol Delivery, such Charges as may be alledged against them[.]

[Enclosure lacking.]

[57] J. B. ASKIN TO JONAS JONES: A.L.S.

Dec. 22 *London*, [*U.C.*]

With this you will receive my report of the route and operations of the Volunteers from St. Thomas & its neighbourhood, which I am to request you will lay before His Excellency and obtain his sanction to our Acts during that service. I believe that the show of our Volunteers throughout its march has had a most salutary effect, in as much that it has displayed to the Radicals in the Country, that We can at all times thwart them without difficulty & it will I am sure deter them from acts of treason again;

[Enclosure is apparently item 58.]

[58] J. B. ASKIN TO JONAS JONES: A.L.S. 8p.

Dec. 22 *London*, [*U.C.*]

I have the honor to report for the information of His Excellency the Lieutenant Governor, that on the receipt of a communication from Her Majestys Attorney General on Monday Morning the 11th Inst. at 5 o Clock, to arrest the Editor of the "Liberal" Newspaper and such papers as might be found with him, I immediately consulted with Col Hamilton the High Sheriff, and upon consideration it was agreed between us, that I should wait till the following day, (tuesday the 12th.) having heard that morning that an attack was intended to be made on the town that night, at about 10 O Clock P.M. intelligence (which I had reason to believe could be relied on) reached me to prepare and to be on the alert at the same time giving me the signal intended to be used by the attacking party for assembling, which was the firing two Guns and to be immediately followed by the blowing of a Bugle, and their place of rendezvous the Scotch Church; this notice enabled me to rouse all the inhabitants that could be relied upon who instantly repaired to the Court House with all the Arms and Ammunition within their reach, in all about 200 strong, who soon put that building in a state of defence, capable of resistance for a period. I am fully satisfied now, that the Zeal displayed by the Loyalist on that night frustrated such plans as might have been in progress of maturity by the Rebels.

On Tuesday the 12th. I proceeded to St. Thomas to arrest John Talbot and found that he had left that place on the Afternoon of Sunday the 10th. at about 3 o Clock P.M. and subsequently heard that he had crossed the Detroit River on Tuesday afternoon the 12th. Inst.

On the Morning of Wednesday the 13th. after seizing the papers appertaining to the Establishment of the "Liberal" I heard that an Express had been received by Col Bostwick from Col Salmon stating that apprehentions were entertained that an Attack would be made by a Large Body of Rebels under Doctr. Duncombe and Eliakum [*sic*] Malcolm Assembled at Scotland, against Simcoe with a view of destroying the Court House there; and also that a large body of well armed Riflemen fully provided with ammunition and provissions [*sic*], had been met on Talbot Street on their march to join Duncomb[e]'s army and beating up for Volunteers: upon learning this I, immediately tendered my services to Col Bostwick, and requested permission to raise a Body of Volunteers, to pursue the Rebels and defeat them, that being granted me I instantly beat up for Volunteers and in less than three hours was on the march for Scotland (in the township of Oakland) which place I reached at about 12 o Clock noon on Thursday (about half an hour after Col

McNab [*sic*] and a very short time after Col Salmons [*sic*] from Long Point) with 260 Volunteers fully ready for action, having travelled a distance upwards of 60 miles within 23 hours, and found that the enemy had fled;—

I want words sufficiently strong to express the Zeal, ardour and patriotism evinced on this occasion by the Loyal Inhabitants of St. Thomas and its neighbourhood Who under every privation and difficulty incident to a turn out without timely notice, to prepare themselves for the Extreme severity of the Weather at this season of the Year, and I beg here to mention that Col Bostwick the Commanding Officer then at St. Thomas, and Assembling the Militia was most active and zealous in forwarding the Volunteers and provissions, in fact he ordered all that could, at the time be got to march instantly.

On the Afternoon of this day nine prisoners were taken by the Volunteers and surrendered to Col Mc.Nabb [*sic*].

On Friday the 15th. having received a General Order from Col Mc. Nabb I proceeded to Norwich and taking a position about a mile to the right of his Division, remained there on the Saturday, sending out parties to arrest the fugitives, who had fled from Scotland, on this day we captured 18 prisoners.— On Sunday the 17th. having been informed that a large Number of men who had been in Doctr. Duncomb[e]'s army were about to surrender, and throw themselves on the Mercy of the Government I remained there, till the afternoon, and moved to Cromwell's Mills on the Otter Creek in Norwich; on Monday the 18th. marched through Dereham, Scouring the Country and reached Richmond, on the Big Otter Creek on Talbot Street, taking several prisoners:—on Tuesday the 19th. marched up Talbot Street, through Bingham, Mallahide scouring the Country to New *Sarum*:—thence, turning to the Front of Yarmouth to Sparta a small village noted as a rendesvous or assemblage of Rebels— on Wednesday the 20th. marched to St. Thomas and dismissed the Volunteers, to enable them to return to their homes to provide for their families, leaving a strong guard over the prisoners;—this day the Prisoners taken by the Volunteers 38 in number were brought to this place and committed to Gaol.

In the performance of this service I beg to remark, that the Whole Country through which I had occasion to move (with the Exception of Norwich and the Village of Sparta,) appeared to me to be most Loyal and ready to serve wherever required by the Government—great numbers requesting to be furnished with Arms and Employed.

I beg to request that His Excellency the Lieutenant Governor will be pleased to give his sanction to this Act of Patriotism on the part of the Middlesex Volunteers and that he will in addition be pleased to grant some authority for the payment of the Expences incurred in the performance of this Service.

[The above is apparently the enclosure referred to in item 57.]

[59] J. B. Askin to Jonas Jones: A.L.S. 2p.

[*1837*] [*Place not stated.*]

[*c. Dec. 22*] I have the honor to submit for the consideration of His Excellency the Lieutenant Governor that the Regiment now on duty, under the command of Colonel Radcliff, are very badly provided with arms and ammunition, so much so, that several accidents have occurred in the use of arms the men are unacquainted with the management of (such as

Rifles, and Guns with Caps and percussion powder,) indeed, I may say, the whole body of Volunteers, as well as Militiamen from different sections of the Country who have turned out, were very ill provided with the means of being effective, from the want of arms and ammunition.

I send Capt Radcliff, who will present the actual situation of the men now on duty, and who is directed to take charge of such arms, ammunition, clothing, &c, as may be intrusted to him.—

I had the honor to submitting to Col McNab [*sic*], that it was absolutely necessary that a quantity of arms ammunition, blankets, and other necessaries, should be forwarded to the London district, which he promised should be done; so that we might at any moment equip one thousand men—(more than that number have tendered their services, and are ready to march to any point of the Province whenever required.)

I have to solicit that you will use your best endeavours with His Excellency the Lieutenant Governor, that he may be pleased to order, that one thousand stand of arms with ammunition and other necessaries may be forwarded, and also swords, pistols, and other implements, for the formation of a Troop of Cavalry of not less than one hundred men. . .

[P.S.] This letter I have shewn to Cols. Bostwick, Radcliff and to the Magistrates in which they fully concur[.]

[60] Arthur to Sir George Grey: Df.L. with emendations in Arthur's handwriting. 3p.

Dec. 25 *Oak House, Feltham.*

I have considered with much attention the question of the Clergy Reserves in Upper Canada, & the various interests therewith connected, & request you will do me the honor to submit the enclosed memorandum for Lord Glenelg's consideration.—

To hope for a satisfactory adjustment of this long debated subject, one point, as a preliminary, appears to be absolutely indispensible, viz the securing to each communion the full extent of aid which is at present afforded to it.—

Whether this aid be, under all circumstances, duly apportioned, depends upon various considerations, into any discussion of wh., however, it will be desirable not to enter, but rather to deal with the case, in this particular, just as it is.

Certainly, the aid derived by the Established Church of England far exceeds that enjoyed by any other communion; but, then, it is to be borne in mind, that in consideration of this very circumstance, under an arrangement with the Govt., the Society for the propogation [*sic*] of the Gospel largely contributed to the support of the Mission to New Brunswick—& further—it is undeniable that, whilst it is doubtful what the claims of the Church of Scotland may be, upon the Reserves—a most munificent provision, intended for the Church of England, is henceforth proposed to be shared by Her only in common with other Communions.

The Revenue, derived from the proceeds of the Reserves that have been sold, & from such as have been leased, amounts to no more than £6392 per annum. It is assumed if the sums of £68,953 now vested in the English Funds were transferred to the Province & there lent at even less than the usual rate of interest—the Purchase Money for Land sold, amounting to the sum of £1610.58 [*sic*] were paid up, & the Lands now leased, viz 361000 acres were sold & the proceeds vested in the Province—

that there would be ample Funds to meet all existing claims whilst large tracts of Land, would still remain to be disposed of in aid of Religious Instruction and Education—

[Enclosure is possibly item 17.]

[61] F. CARPENTER TO ARTHUR: A.L.S. 3p.

Dec. 25 [*London.*]

Although I took the liberty of addressing you last week—I cannot resist the feeling of happiness I have of congratulating you on the Appointment to Lower [*sic*] Canada. and the Rank of Major General—which must be so highly gratifying to your feelings as evincing so forcibly the high opinion entertained of your character in many points of view—and the great estimation in the highest Quarters, in which you cannot but be held. . . [Expresses the hope] that your character may ever rise in the opinion of the good and just public, as it has ever stood in the hearts of all who know you. . . [Recounts his own embarrassed circumstances.]

[62] J. B. ASKIN TO COL. MCNABB [*i.e.* A. N. MACNAB]: A.L.S. 3p.

Dec. 25 *London,* [*U.C.*]

Duncan McGrigor Esquire[1] is just this moment arrived from Chatham, he states that Hamilton & Douglass left that place on Friday Morng. at 5 o Clock (the 22d.) for Detroit, from the best information he had, he is fully of the opinion that the persons who were reported to be agitating the inhabitants in the City of Detroit with a view of exciting them to join the discontents from this Province who have taken refuge in the State of Michigan will totally fail in their attempts—he also adds, that Messrs. Prince, Elliott, and Mercer Magistrates in the Western District, had called upon Governor Mason of the State of Michigan who gave them every assurance that he would suppress any attempts made by the inhabitants of that State or others, to invade our Shores, as far as in his power.

Mr. McGrigor adds also that a very great number of persons have been observed passing through the Western District towards Detroit and has no doubt they were fugitives from Toronto and Scotland amongst it is reported that Duncomb[e]—and one of his Gallant Captains (Anderson) were of the lot, it is believed that Gibson and three or four others answering the description given of fugitives from Toronto, had crossed the St. Clair near Sarnia—

P.S. I hold *Ross Robertson* ready to move, the instant I hear from Col Hamilton—

[63] [ARTHUR] TO GLENELG: A.L. 3p.

Dec. 26 *London.*

On my proceeding to Upper Canada I have the honor to submit to Your Lordship, that, with reference to the present state of the Lower Province, one of the most important duties which will devolve upon me will be the immediate orginization [*sic*] of the Militia.

[1]Probably Duncan McGregor, of Raleigh, a magistrate in the Western District.

With this view, I have the honor to draw Your Lordship's attention to the great advantage which the public service would derive from the appointment of two or three able & efficient officers. And I would more especially urge upon your Lordship, that, one should at once go out with me as a Military Secretary; and such an appointment, being one almost in the usual course, will attract no particular observation.

I presume, without any declaration of such an intention, Her Majesty's Government will have no objection to its' [*sic*] being understood that there is a respectable Militia force in Upper Canada at command if there should be an *absolute necessity* to use it.

As I embark at Portsmouth on Sunday, and sail on Monday there is but barely time for an officer to prepare Himself for the voyage should my recommendation, as I trust it will, meet your Lordships approbation.

[64] ARTHUR TO SIR GEORGE GREY: Df.L. 2p.

Dec. 26 *London.*

I am exceedingly sorry further to intrude the subject of the Salary of the Lt. Governor of Upper Canada on the attention of the Secy of State; but, with reference to the concluding Paragraph of your letter of the 23rd. instant,—being in possession of the experience and opinion of Sir John Colborne, & knowing the pressing pecuniary difficulties of Sir Francis Head from this very cause—I feel it to be a duty wh. I owe to the Public Service, no less than to my own Family, to beg you will be good enough to express to Lord Glenelg my conviction, that the Salary at present allowed is quite insufficient to support the necessary expenditure of the office— I mean an expenditure that is essential to carrying on such a Government successfully[.]

[65] ARTHUR TO F. CARPENTER: Df.L. with emendations in Arthur's handwriting.

Dec. 26 *Brunswick House Hotel, Hanover Square,* [*London.*]

I assure you it has given me as much concern on receiving your letters, in not having it in my power to comply with the request they contained, as it could occasion you disappointment. To enter into explanation of the cause of, I hope, my temporary want of funds would be needless; but, I have acted very inconsiderately, and have suffered a good deal from having locked them up, which you may suppose must have deeply inconvenienced a man with eleven children!— I enclose you a check for £20 of which I request your acceptance.

[Redated from Dec. 4; address changed from *Oak House, Feltham.*]

[66] [SIR] GEO[RGE] GREY TO ARTHUR: L.S. 3p.

Dec. 26 *Downing Street,* [*London.*] [Marked: "Immediate".]

I am directed by Lord Glenelg to acknowledge your letter of the 21st Instant reporting that you have engaged your passage in a Vessel which leaves London for New York on the 27th Instant, and requesting that under the peculiar circumstances of your case you may receive the same amount of passage money which was granted to Sir Francis Head.

Lord Glenelg desires me to state that he will take an early opportunity of bringing under the notice of the Chancellor of the Exchequer your claim to an extra allowance of passage money, but in the mean time his Lordship has no power to direct the issue to you of more than the regulated sum.

His Lordship has accordingly directed a letter to be written to the Treasury requesting that the usual allowance of £300 may be issued to you.—

[67] H. F. FORSTER, WALTER BUCHANAN, W. H. HAMILTON TO ARTHUR: A.L.S. 3p.

[*1837*] *London.*

Dec. 26 Some months ago we were requested by Captain Moriarty R.N. and Roderick O'Connor Esqre., (acting on behalf of a numerous and respectable Body of their Fellow Colonists in Van Diemen's Land) to purchase, under your approval, a Service of Plate, and to present it to you as a mark of their high esteem and regard for your Publick and Private character. The sum remitted to us for this purpose amounted to Fifteen Hundred Pounds, which was raised in Van Diemen's Land by Voluntary Subscription.

It has afforded us Sincere Pleasure to have performed the first part of the Duty with which we were honoured; nor is that part, of which we are about to acquit ourselves, in completion of our Duty, less gratifying to our feelings.

We have now the honour to present to you a Service of Plate of the value of Fifteen Hundred Pounds. The Inscription upon the Chief Pieces of this Service was dictated by the Subscribers; and we doubt not that you will accept with proper pride and satisfaction this valuable testimonial of their sentiments, which appears to us to confer equal honour on the Donors and the Receiver.

[Misdated 1838.]

[68] [LORD] HILL TO ARTHUR: A.L.S. 3p.

Dec. 27 *Horse Guards, [London.]*

There is settled within your Government of Upper Canada a very old friend of mine Mr. Alison late paymaster of the 90th. Rgt. I believe him to be a highly respectable person but he has had a large family to provide for upon very slender means & I much fear you will find him in embarrassed circumstances—If you have any opportunity of befriending him or his Family I shall really feel much obliged— The last letter I had from Mr. Alison was dated from Warwick Upper Canada but his previous place or residence was Toronto[.]

[On the same sheet appears item 69.]

[69] ARTHUR TO [LORD HILL]: Df.L. 2p.

Dec. 28 [*Place not stated.*]

I have had the honor to receive yr. Lordship's note of last evening & shall take the earliest opportunity after my arrival in Upper Canada to find out Mr. Alison & hope to have the gratification of communicating to Yr. Lordship that it has been in your power to render him some essential service.

[The above appears on the same sheet as item 68.]

[70] JAMES HAMILTON TO A. N. MCNABB [*i.e.* MACNAB]: A.L.S. 3p.

Dec. 28 *Windsor.*

Since mine of the 25th. I have not much to communicate, further than having aroused the inhabitants from their apathy—and in some measure rather deadened the effects of the excitement on the opposite shore—by the demonstration on this—

I herewith send you a copy of a letter from the Governor of the State of Michigan which is in reply to one from the Magistrates of this District —this last I have not seen—

The reply appears satisfactory but I doubt its sincerity—see my mark θ in the accompanying newspaper of the same date—

Mr Prince writes me this evening that our present force is about 150— and from a deficiency of arms &ct ought not to be rated over 60 effective men—that he is in expectation of seeing here tomorrow abt 150 coloured men—principally armed—and that the Canadians generally refuse to turn out—

This evening through the exertions of Mr Dougal of this place we have been enabled to muster 75 stand of mixed arms—exclusive of those first mentioned— *We* have collected also (I ought to say *they*) about 25 Kegs of powder and more than sufficient Lead—

Permit me to recommend the sending from some other District from three to four hundred men fully equipped and for a determinate time— The french Canadians can not be relied on—

Be pleased to inform me more fully in what way I can be of more service or rather what you wish me to do further— From the little bickerings among the Magistracy and jealousy—my situation is not such as I could wish—without any definite object in view— Write me soon. . .

P.S. a Check on the Commissary will be acceptable—

[Enclosures lacking.]

[71] ARTHUR TO THE ADJUTANT GENERAL [SIR JOHN MACDONALD]: Df.L.S. 2p.

Dec. 29 *London.*

In reply to your letter of 26th. instant conveying to me by direction of the General Commanding in Chief Her Majesty's gracious pleasure in appointing me to serve as a Major General on the Staff in Canada, [the following words are here deleted: "but without Staff Pay;"] and requesting me to inform you of the date of my departure, I have the honor to acquaint you that I have taken my passage in the Packet Ship "Samson', for New York, and that it is my intention to proceed to Portsmouth on the 31st Inst. and to embark in that vessel on the 1st. January.

[72] SIR JOHN MACDONALD TO ARTHUR: A.L.S. 4p.

[*1837*] *Horse Guards*, [*London.*] [Marked: "Private".]

[*c. Dec. 29*] The Bearer the Honble. Lt. West of the 43d. Regt. has (in common with all officers now absent from Canada) received orders to return to his Regt. forthwith, and is anxious to go by the packet which takes you to New York— He is a remarkably fine young fellow, and Lord Fitzroy and I are particularly interested in him[.]

His father (Lord Delaware) wrote to me last night to say that he was very anxious that his son should go to New York with you, and begged that I would introduce him to you which I have great pleasure in doing, assured as I feel that you will like him exceedingly, and that, whilst you remain together you will shew him all the kindness in your power—

[73] J. B. ASKIN TO JONAS JONES: A.L.S.

Dec. 29 *London,* [*U.C.*]

I have the honor to enclose you a communication received from Col Radcliff in command of the detachment doing duty at this station on guard over the prisoners in Gaol which I am to request you will submit at your earliest convenience for His Excellency's consideration[.]

[Enclosure is probably item 74.]

[74] THO[MA]S RADCLIFF TO THE WORSHIPFUL THE MAGISTRATES OF LONDON: L.S.

Dec. 29 *London,* [*U.C.*]

I have the honor to submit for your consideration the enclosed Letter from Surgeon Phillips pointing out the prevalence of a Disease among the Men with his opinion that Great Coats should be provided for the Men on Guard as a preventative [marginal note here reads: "Number of Great Coats deemed necessary—*Fifty.*—"]— I also beg leave in the strongest Manner to draw your attention thereto and to recommend that the same may be supplied without delay as the Men are at present but very indif[f]erently provided with Clothing to protect them from the inclemency of the Weather on Night Duties[.]

I at the same time beg leave to Submit for consideration a rough Estimate of expense of converting into Temporary Barracks one of the empty Houses in the Village of London—a Measure which is most desireable [*sic*] as well for the better organization of the Troops as the convenience of the Inhabitants of the Village, and as far as can at present be ascertained, will be a saving to the Public.— Also in case of a threatened attack the Men would be in a body ready to repel it—

[The above is probably the enclosure referred to in item 73.]

[*Enclosures:*]

[75] *1837*
Dec. 29

THO[MA]S PHILLIPS TO COLONEL [THOMAS] RADCLIFF: A.L.S. 2p.

[*London, U.C.*]

As Surgeon Pegly has been kind enough to allow the use of a room to be occupied as a surgery for the sick of the Middlesex Light infantry I would beg leave to say that in consequence of there being no fire in it, it is altogether impossible to prescribe or compound Medicine in it[;] you would therefore oblige by making arrangements for a stove and a man to chop fire wood during the hours of attendance— It is also my opinion that there should be watch coats provided for the guard as the prevailing diaroha [*sic*] & colds may be chiefly attributed to exposure to the night air without su[i]table clothing[.]

[76] [1837]
[Dec. 29]

D. Mc. Pherson: A.D.S.

London, [*U.C.*]

Estimated Expence of Providing a Temporary Barrack for the Troops in the Village of London.

Rent of the House offered by Mr. Richardson for Six Months Capable of Containing one hundred and Forty Men		£ 15..—..—
Fifty Double Mattresses	@ 7/6 each	18..15..—
One hundred blankets	@ 15/. -	75..—..—
Fifty Rugs	@ 5/.	12..10..—
12½ Cwt. Straw		1..—..—
4 Deal Tables 12 feet x 3 feet		4..—..—
8 Deal Forms		2..—..—
		£128.. 5..

4 Chords of Fuel Wood is [*sic*] estimated as being sufficient for one week

Cooking utensils—say 6 small Boilers, will be sufficient

The expence of Billeting One hundred men for Six Months will amount to £270..—..—

D. Mc. Pherson
Q.Mr. Mx L. Iy.

[77] [Sir James?] McGrigor to Arthur: A.L.S.

Dec. 30 *St. James Place,* [*London.*]

The name of the Gentleman whom you yesterday permitted me to bring to your notice is Mr. Peter Lawrie [?] he is settled in Lawrieston [?] near Cobourg. in Upper Canada. . . [Sends wishes.]

[78] Jonas Jones to J. [B.] Askin: A.L. 2p.

Dec. 30 *Toronto.*

Since the receipt of your letter of the 22nd. I have been to the Niagara Frontier— His Excellency is much gratified with and fully approves of your proceedings as reported— Considering the Western District as a most important point of defence at the present time, His Excellency has ordered Col Radcliff to proceed thither with his Regt or using the most disposable force and directed you (see Genl. orders) to raise the necessary number of men to guard your Gaol— His Excellency trusts to your judt. [?] & discretion in using all necessary & proper means for your security having at the same time a due regard to economy[.]

I refer you to Col. Radcliff for particular information[.] We did all for you in our power—

[Endorsed: "Copy".]

[79] J. B. ASKIN TO A. N. MC.NABB [*i.e.* MACNAB]: A.L.S. 3p.

Dec. 30 *London*, [*U.C.*]

I forward a dispatch received this morning from Col Hamilton, by our friend John Stewart who has instructions to return from Brantford.

On Examination of prisoners in Gaol I find that several of the informations taken against them, have been given up to you, in such case will you cause them to be sent up here or will give your instructions how we shall proceed, in the mean time I shall order such as I represent to be committed for further Examination.

Nothing new here, all is going on very quiet indeed—Hall was not retaken by the last accounts from Oxford[.]

I have not done any thing yet with regard to the Independent Company— I wait for an answer from Toronto with respect to Arms and Ammunition sent for— The Boys at St. Thomas and this neighbourhood are all ready whenever wanted. . .

[P.S.] On being, informed of Elisha Halls escape, I immediately dispatched three persons one to Sandwich another to Bear Creek and one to Sarnia—neither of whom have as yet returned—

[Enclosure is possibly item 80.]

[80] JAMES HAMILTON TO J. B. ASKIN: L.

Dec. 30 *Windsor.* [Marked: "(Copy)".]

I have a few moments since heard a, Report at all events worth attending to—viz—

That there are about a thousand men organised and equipped and for some time training at Mount Clemens in the interior who intend crossing the Sinclair to penetrate as far as London— They have several peices [*sic*] of Cannon and well supplied with provision— Tomorrow we shall send a confidential person to that Quarter for Information— I detain Wm. Park until I hear more[.]

Prepare yourselves for this district cannot do more than guard its frontier and that only as a check to the Detroit Rabble— You had better have a constant communication with Duncan McGregor at Chatham—

Expresses here are too dilatory and the majority of the Magistrates afraid of doing their duty. . .

[P.S.] I shall meet the Magistrates tomorrow to concert plans ways & means—

[The above is possibly the enclosure referred to in item 79.]

[81] [STATE OF NEW YORK: MILITARY RETURN.]

[*1837*]
[*c. Dec. 30*] [A large printed broadside headed "Annual Return of the Infantry and Riflemen of the State of New-York, for the year 1837." and giving the "Total, commissioned, non-commissioned officers, musicians and privates, present & absent at inspection" as 164,034. The printed date is Dec. 30, 1837. The printed signature is cut out. Marginal comments in pencil, apparently of a later date than that here given, read: "hear is men enough to take Canada without any help from any other State or the Regulars"; "every Boy in the state is Practiceing with the Riffle". A comment on the reverse side, in the same handwriting, reads:

"Durham!!!

"how do you like to have your Steam Boat Burnt Drew or MacNab will git a Bowie knife in thair damd Hart when thay little think of such a thing

"What is the reason that navy Island was not taken if they was so fast for fighting no thay took good care to keep clear of that you would have had a small tast of New Orleans the is a scrap brewing in Newyork with your damd steam ships next thing thay will be Burnt

"God Dam the Queen

"Bill Johnson for Ever".]

[82] ARTHUR TO SIR G[EORGE] GREY: Df.L. with emendations in Arthur's handwriting. 2p.

Dec. 31 *Oak House, Feltham.*

On looking with attention into yr. letter of the 26th. instant respecting my extra passage allowance I observe Lord Glenelg has simply instructed you to inform me that He will bring my claim under the notice of the C[h]ancellor of the Exchequer & not that he will strongly or even favorably recommend it—. I do assure you that I believe His Ldship has little idea of the ruinous expense which has attended my removal from one Government to another.

For many years of my life I have prided myself upon being never in debt to any man but now I am forced to place myself under an obligation wh. really quite distresses me— I am sure you will concur with me that this ought not to be the case & that it cannot be required under the most rigid system of economy & I do hope you will do me the kindness to mention the subject again to Ld. Glenelg.

[On the same sheet appears item 85.]

[83] ARTHUR TO MAJOR GENERAL [SIR JOHN] GARDINER: Df.L. 9p.

Dec. 31 *Oak House, Feltham.*

I have the honor to acknowledge your letter, of the 7th Ultimo, with its enclosure, [marginal note here reads: "herewith returned"] informing me of the nature of the communication which the Genl. Commanding in Chief has received from the Secy. of State for the Colonial Department, on the expediency of measures being adopted for the promulgation throughout the service of the system of restraint & coercion to wh. Convicts are subjected in V. D. Land, and desiring me to state what are the Restrictions and Discipline by which they are controlled.

It is desirable that in the first place, the General Commanding in Chief should understand that a sentence of Transportation subjects the Culprit not only to be deported to one of the penal *Colonies*, but, when there, to be sent to a Penal *Settlement* (a place of especial punishment,) or to be employed at hard labor on the Roads, or on the Public Works, or to be assigned to the service of settlers, by whom they are employed in Agriculture, at their Trades, or as domestic servants, and amenable in these several conditions in case of misconduct to very severe penalties under an Act of the Imperial Parliament, and under Colonial Laws, enacted for the Special punishment of this unhappy class of the Community. In effect, a Convict is altogether deprived of his liberty, and is, to all intents and purposes, a Slave!

By every vessel conveying Convicts to the Colonies, there are forwarded from the Office of the Secretary of State, Lists of the names of all on board, and, in particular, of those whose characters are considered more than ordinarily bad, or whose crimes, in the opinion of Her Majesty's Government, merit more than ordinary severity;—and the latter are, accordingly, either at once removed to a Penal Settlement, or placed in the Road Gangs at hard labor.—

Lord Hill will readily perceive that *Assignment to Settlers* is the most advantageous to, and consonant with the wishes of the Convict; for, altho he is bound, as a Slave, to obey all the orders of his Master and to submit to all the caprices of his Mistress,—his mere animal wants of Food, Clothing and Bedding are amply supplied; while, independent of this condition being less wretched, it holds out a fairer prospect for the Reformation of the Offender.

Amongst this class, Military Convicts are ordinarily placed on their debarkation.— I do not recollect any instance in wh. specific Instructions have been sent out by the Secy. of State to inflict on them any particular degree of severity; and this exemption appears but reasonable and just, for it is to be borne in mind, that a Soldier is actually transported for a class of offences (such as striking a Noncommissioned officer) for which a Citizen would only incur a trifling penalty—

As Assignment, then, is the punishment to which Military Offenders are ordinarily subjected on being landed, it may be proper to remark on the objections that operate against it as a system.—vizt the unequal character and circumstances of the assignees, and the consequent unequal punishment of the Convicts.

If a Military Convict for instance should have been an Officer's Servant, the probability is that his New Master will employ him in Domestic affairs, &, then, his appearance in a good suit of clothing is, to the Eye, a considerable abatement of the degradation that is intended to form a part of his punishment;—whilst another Military Convict, and perhaps even of better character, is doomed to endure hardship on a Farm, with a Family who are obliged to exact the greatest possible amount of labour from their servants in order to maintain themselves and their Establishment.

It must be admitted that the position of these men is very different; but this inequality nevertheless extends, in point of fact, to the poorer class of life under all circumstances.— One man may fill the office of a Butler, at high wages and on good feeding, whilst his Brother, a better character perhaps in all respects, earns a scanty livelihood by Hedging or ditching.— This, in some measure, reconciles that seeming injustice of the fate of individual convicts. It is not possible to alter this state of things in common life, for who can make that straight wh. God hath made crooked? Again, it is to be remembered that the man who is in Livery today, may be, even "for disobedience of orders," in Irons Tomorrow;—and it is my conviction, that, Transportation, in its mildest form, is a full satisfaction to the offended Laws,—and that it involves as much degradation as is consistent with a prospect of reforming the Culprit,—a great & essential point to be kept steadily in view.— Besides, in reply to those who dwell upon this objection, it should be urged, that whilst one Military Convict is in Livery, ninety nine are at hard work in the Fields.— It would be severe, indeed unjust, to place the Military Convict in a worse condition than any other offender; but, of course, if a different view should be taken of the subject, by those in Authority, it may be prescribed that no Soldier shall on arrival, be assigned, and so the objection will be obviated. This course, however, will appear the less requisite when it is remembered, that insubordination, Drunkenness, & numerous other offences of the lesser grade at once remove the unhappy Culprit from Assignment to a Road party.—

Looking then at Transportation in its mildest aspect, I think the General Commanding in Chief will be of opinion, that, so far as fear of punishment can deter Soldiers from the Commission of Crime, Transportation is likely to have that effect; and in order that its full penalties may be thoroughly known to the Officer who awards & the Soldier who is to endure it, I submit that the publication of the 17th. and 18th. Clauses of the "Act to consolidate and amend certain of the Laws relating to the Courts of General Quarter Sessions, and to the more effectual punishment and control of Transported and other offenders," passed by the Legislature of Van Diemens Land, on the 4th. of August 1835, wd. be a most beneficial measure.—

It was my intention to have entered far more fully into this subject, but a pressure of business has prevented my devoting the time to it I could have wished. I therefore request you will do me the favor to communicate this circumstance to the General Commanding in Chief, and, at the same time, to mention that in the two letters addressed by me to the Arch Bishop of Dublin [marginal notes here read: "q I am not sure whether he *is Archbishop* W. H. H. Yes he is *Arch*bishop C. A:"], of wh. I had the honor to enclose copies to Colonel Egerton for His Lordship's perusal,—I have considered the subject very much in detail.—

[Endorsed: "sent in the 5th Jany. 38—"]

[The above is apparently the enclosure referred to in item 87.]

[84] [ARTHUR] TO MAJOR GENERAL [SIR JOHN] GARDINER: Df.L. mainly in Arthur's handwriting. 7p.

Dec. 31 *Oak House, Feltham.*

[An earlier draft of item 83, mainly in Arthur's handwriting. On the reverse side appears item 87.]

[85] [ARTHUR]: [RECIPIENT NOT STATED]: Df.L. with emendations in Arthur's handwriting.

Dec. 31 *Oak House, Feltham.*

I regret very much yr. absence from London has prevented my having the honor to see you prior to my embarkation on Monday Morng.—as I was very desirous indeed to have had a short conversation with you respectg. Canada[.] I enter upon the administration of the Upper Province under the most adverse circumstances in many particulars & I feel the weight of my responsibility to be very great, but I trust I shall fulfil the expectations of the Govt—you may be satisfied that I shall endeavour to do so!

I had the pleasure of an interview as you wished with Ld. John Russell respectg Transportation on Thursday last— I think you will concur that Sir W. Molesworth has used me exceedingly ill in drawing all the information he cd. from me—expressing himself in terms of high approbation to myself—& then reflecting bitterly upon me before Parliament [.]

[The above appears on the same sheet as item 82 and is cancelled by being scored through.]

[86] W. T. LYTTLETON TO ARTHUR: A.L.S.

Dec. 31 *45 Cambridge Terrace, [London.]*

[Sends good wishes, and hopes "that your exertions may be rewarded as they so much deserve, with entire success".]

[87] [CATHERINE ARTHUR ?] TO [W. H.] HAMILTON: Df.L.

[*1838*] [*Oak House, Feltham?*]

[*Jan. 1*] My dr. Papa dictated to me yesterday with a great mass of other Papers the dft . . . of a letter of wh. the enclosed is a copy wh. he begged me before I fairly transcribed it to send it to you . . . with the request that you wd. be so good as to revise & methodise it adding to or subtracting from it as you thought best— Wd. you be so good as to return it to me at yr. earliest convenience as I [am] anxious to send it as Papa desired. I will take care to send or go myself to the Sunbury Post for your answer[.]

[The above appears on the reverse side of item 84. Item 83 is apparently the enclosure referred to.]

[88] GEO[RGE] RYKERT TO A. N. MACNAB: A.L.S. 2p.

Jan. 1 *St. Catharines.*

A person by name of James H. Sears of this place has used much exertion to rally the Coloured population of this vicinity in defence of our cause, and succeeded in raising a Company for *permanent service,* (who have been on duty at and about Chippawa under him ever since the Rebels made a stand on Navy Island,) under the impression that he would be appointed to the command of a Company,—

He informed me today that a person by the name of Thomas Runchey who has been appointed by the Lieut Governor to the chief command of all the Coloured Corps—is about to take the Company from him, with the view of giving them to some favourite of his own—which under the circumstances appears to me to be exceedingly unjust— I am aware that Mr. Sears has been very zealous in the defence of the Country since the first Alarm—and has done more towards getting out the coloured people than any other individual in our district—and I trust will not be overlooked in confirming the appointments over the Colrd. Companies—

Mr. Sears will be perfectly satisfied if he could even succeed to the first Lieutenancy in the Company he raised which is now 40 strong.—

I should feel much obliged if you would use yr interest in getting Mr Sears appointed, either as Capt. or 1st. Lieut—as I am sure he justly merits it—

Mr. Runchey the *Commander in Chief* I know little of personally, but am informed he is ill qualified for the situation. Mr Sears is not a coloured man—but seems anxious to serve his Country in some way, and I think will be found to be a very efficient officer—

Pray has anything more been done respecting our St Catharines Troop— The gentlemen here who have done the duty seem anxious to learn what is to be the result of their application[.] If their Troop be not confirmed, they are desirous of attaching themselves in some other way—

I very much regret now that I consented to take the appointment—but having done so, I shall endeavour to discharge the duty to the best of my ability, provided the appointments are confirmed as we expect, and as in justice they should be— If not I shall be content to lay down my sword and shoulder the musket when occasion requires[.]

If I can get it I will send you a Keg of beer by first team from this—

As you made enquiry of me for a good saddle horse I have desired Mr Benham of this place to take up his— Should he please you in appearance and action, you will find him a very active Animal and I believe perfectly sound—

Mr. Merritt left today for Toronto, but does not I believe intend remaining to legislate—

I shall probably go over between this and the 15th. to attend to the Call on that day—

[89] H. Mittleberger to A. N. MacNab: A.L.S.

Jan. 1 *St. Catharines.*

Before His Excellency the Lt. Governor gave to Mr. Thomas Runchey the command of the entire of the Coloured Men in this District, the Bearer of this J. H. Sears was appointed Lt. pro: tem in command and as he has been active in collecting & keeping the men together—I would beg, after consulting with my Colleagues here, to recommend that he may be put Second in Command of the Cold. core [*sic*] if it can be done consistently—

I believe he will be found competant [*sic*] to discharge his duty faithfully, and if two companies is [*sic*] formed Mr. Sears had inducements held out that he would be second in command by Lt. Col. Clark, Mr. Runchey and the Magistrates—

[90] Head to Colonel [C. L. L.] Foster: L. initialled. 3p.

[*1838*] *Chippawa.*

Jan. 2

I have had a long consultation with Colonel McNab [*sic*], and the several halfpay officers who are here, on the state of the force here. It is composed of about 2000 Militia Men and a couple of Companies of the 24th Regt., one of which can shortly be dispensed with. The Militia appear deservedly attached to Colonel McNab, and I think he will be able to prevent their returning to their homes, which they are much disposed to do.

Under these circumstances I feel quite satisfied with the state of defense of this frontier, but I am I own uneasy at the unprotected situation of the Capital, where are not only deposited our public Documents, the Specie of our Banks, our Stores and the Fort, but where we are encumbered with the charge of 130 prisoners which many are apprehensive it is the intention of the Rebels to rescue.

Their approaching trial will cause very great excitement, and as the principal Body of the 24th Regt will as soon as it arrives at Kingston be there, I have no hesitation in saying that your services & presence at Toronto wd be of more service to me there than here.

At present you are aware that we have at the Capital (on which our maintanence [*sic*] of the Province depends) only one officer in the Army.

For the reasons above explained to you I think it wd be adviseable, and it is certainly my wish that you shd be so good as to keep your Hd Quarter for the present at Toronto.

[Misdated 1837.]

[91] GEO[RGE] RYKERT TO HON. COL [JONAS] JONES: A.L.S. 4p.

Jan. 3 *St. Catharines.*

In order to put His Excellency in possession of some facts relative to the raising of the St Catharines Troop of Cavalry, I am induced to drop a few lines, which I trust will not be deemed out of place at this time—

The gentlemen composing this Troop tendered their services under Mr Merritt, having first obtained his consent to take the command of them—

When the first report reached by express that we were threatened on our frontier by the rabble from the American side, they turned out to the number of from 40 to 50 and were accompanied by Mr Merritt, Col. Clark & myself— Mr McDonald also rode in company but was not considered as one of the number that originally volunteered under Mr Merritt—

At Niagara Mr Merritt & myself were required to Act with the Civil Authority there[;] during this time Mr McDonald *assumed* to himself the Command of the Troops, and on the arrival of Colonel Cameron— Mr Merritt (I think inadvertently) introduced him as Capt. McDonald which at once gave offence—and induced several of them to request that I would call upon Col. Cameron and undeceive him on this point, and state to him that they did not recognize Mr McDonald in their Troop at all, and that they were determined not to act under him—.

I waited upon Col. Cameron at Waterloo and communicated to him what they desired— Col. Cameron then told me that he would not recognize McDonald as their Captain, that if he required their services, he would address them as the "St Catharines Troop" with this they all seemed perfectly satisfied—

They then called a meeting of their members and requested Mr. Merritt to attend and inform them whether he still intended to continue in the command or not—they met and as I was since informed, while Mr Merritt was addressing them and giving his reasons for declining the command, Mr. McDonald entered the room with a gang of persons, unconnected with the Troop, and behaved in a most disgraceful manner, challenging and abusing every one, until he succeeded in breaking up the meeting—

The next evening they met at another place and unanimously agreed to continue the Troop provided I would consent to take the command, they waited upon me, and (contrary to my wishes) consented to do so— with the understanding however that it should be first sanctioned by the Head of the Government—

They afterwards informed me they had submitted the matter to His Excellency for approval and also advised Col. Cameron of what they had done—

Mr McDonald on hearing what had taken place, assembled his party and got himself elected Captain, and as we now learn was recommended by Col Cameron for confirmation—

I deem it quite unnecessary to comment now upon the stand hitherto taken by Mr McDonald or on the selection of his Troop, but whatever may be done, it would in my opinion be doing great injustice to those persons who so promptly tendered their services in the hour of danger to allow Mr McDonald now to step in and take the seniority— Indeed

I have every confidence that His Excellency upon learning the facts, will treat the matter justly—

I think it proper however further to remark that this Troop, has almost exclusively done the duty of carrying express to and from Head-quarters since the 11th. Ult. without any expense whatever to the Govt— they have not even been allowed provender for their horses.—

Under these circumstances I cannot think that Mr McDonald should be allowed to take seniority—

Should His Excellency be pleased to confirm our Troop, and allow the commissions to bear date before those of Mr McDonalds, I have no doubt the Troop will become a very respectable and efficient one— We now number 41—

I would beg leave to recommend James R. Benson as 1st. Lieut, Charles Robertson for 2d. do William May for Cornet and Samuel Haight for Qr. Master—

[92] J. H. Sears to Jonas Jones: A.L.S. 2p.

Jan. 3 *Chippawa.*

I beg to report; that upon the breaking out of the Rebellion I was appointed to the command of the coloured men in the vicinity of St. Catharines, and very shortly afterwards, I was solicited by Mr. Thos. Runch[e]y, through George Adams Essqr, to accept of a Lieut[en]ancy under him, and assist in raising a coloured volunteer corps under instructions from His Excellency the Lieut. Governour [*sic*]; I did accept the appointment, and have, up to the present time, used my best exertions to forward the intentions of His Excellency in regard to the raising of a volunteer coloured corps, and have enlisted forty men for six months service. Mr. Runch[e]y has, however, seen fit to annul my appointment, and for reasons to me entirely unknown. . . [Asks for an investigation of his own proceedings. His men are sincerely attached to him and extremely regret his displacement. A considerable portion enlisted only under the express condition that he was to be their lieutenant. As there are now sufficient coloured men enlisted for two companies, asks to retain command of the men he enlisted "together with the Militia under my charge by the authority of the Magistrates, until His Excellency's pleasure be made known."]

[93] Arthur to H. F. Forster, Walter Buchanan, W. H. Hamilton: Df.A.L.

Jan. 4 *Portsmouth.*

I have the honor to acknowledge your Letter of the 26 Ultimo, presenting to me, at the request of a numerous & respectable body of the Colonists of Van Diemen's Land, with a Service of Plate as a mark of their high esteem & regard for my Publick & Private Character—

It is most gratifying to me that my administration of the affairs of so anxious & difficult a Govern't has been satisfactory to so very large a portion of the community; and I accept this pledge of their kind feelings towards me with gratitude, & with a thankful recollection that it was by their cordial support that I was for so many years enabled so successfully to conduct the Public Affairs which resulted in a degree of prosperity almost without parallel.

Accept my sincere thanks for the trouble you have so readily undertaken & for the very kind manner in which you have carried into effect the wishes of your friends in Van Diemens Land.

[Endorsed in Arthur's handwriting: "Kate will be so good as to write this out fair on Letter Paper—addressed (*sic*) it on the inside to the three Genln & then put it under cover to Mr Hamilton for 3d Post—as soon as Possible"; further endorsed: "done 8th. Jany. 1838".]

[94] THOMAS RUNCHEY TO JONAS JONES: A.L.S.

Jan. 5 *Chippawa.*

I have the honor to state for the information of His Excellency the Lieutenant Governor that in obedience to a despatch directed to me dated Government Offise [*sic*] Toronto 11th December 1837—and signed Jonas Jones A.D.C. authorizing me to raise a coloured corps I have raised since the receipt of the despatch refer[r]ed to a corps consisting of Sixty Six effective Men... [Repeats the information concerning the appointment of officers as given in item 54.] I have also purchased clothing for some Fifteen or Sixteen who were absolutely destitute of common wearing apparel...

[95] J. [?] WELLESLEY TO ARTHUR: A.L.S. 3p.

Jan. 6 *Neuwied sur le Rhin.* [Marked: "Private".]

I hope this letter may reach you before you leave England; It is to recommend to your notice and protection Three missionaries of the Upper Canada Clergy Society, who are laboring among the Destitute settlers in Upper Canada— Their names are The Revd H. H. O Neill, who is employed in the Gore and Delaware[1] Districts, The Revd F. Osler, who is settled amongst the people in the Townships of Tecumseth and West Gwillembey [*sic*], and the Revd F. A. O Meara, who has lately left England to be, like Mr O Neill, a travelling Missionary— They are all three ordained Ministers of the Church of England, and, I trust, men of sound piety and learning— The labours of the two first, have I hope been already much blessed. The Secretary of the Society will forward to you with this, a few printed Documents, to shew the nature & aim of the Societies operations— Its formation was much approved by Sir John Colborne when he was Lieut Governor of Upper Canada, and I feel assured that the Committee will be happy to attend to any suggestions you may make for their future guidance, should you ever feel at leisure to remark upon their labours.

[96] JEREMIAH SMITH AND JOSEPH WALKER TO [HEAD]: 3p.

Jan. 12 *Toronto.*

A statement by Jeremiah Smith and Joseph Walker which they respectfully beg to call his Excellency's attention to. On Monday and Tuesday last we were travelling through King and Tecumseth, the general deportment of the people is any thing but quiet and we are seriously apprehensive that the Men will tumultuously assemble again[;] my servant lives in a Shantee on the tenth line and a general communication is kept up we fully think by this route and line of Country with the Pirates on Navy Island[;] how it is effected we cannot imagine still our conviction is that it is so, the Man says at night-fall Horsemen are

[1]Error for Niagara. *The Church* newspaper, Dec. 30, 1837, said that O'Neill was travelling missionary in the Gore and Niagara Districts.

passing his dwelling swiftly southward towards Albion at other times the way to Lloydtoun. The notorious Thomas Browne is returned to his home although he took so conspicuous a part in the last wicked plot; the rebels are leaving their homes[;] we called at many houses, and found no Men at them[;] we consider they contemplate another movement. Browne should be arrested, (with submission to your excellency) what but an assurance of protection by the rebels can make this audacious outlaw at home!! This party has assumed quite another air instead of the pitiful and abject mien they lately wore we now see the bold stare and insolent glance of defiance, and menace. On new year's day a group assembled in Lloydtown and the most serious apprehensions were entertained by the inhabitants: in our conviction these Men are on the eve of rising again, various meetings have been held by them one at Thomas Browne's another at James Doyle's in Tecumseth and a third it has been reported in Adjala. When the Group assembled in Lloydtown (about twenty men) they beat a poor fellow in the most brutal manner at Tyson Mill[;] he subsequently skreened him from further violence by secreting him behind sacks in the Mill, the party then paraded the Village, pulling off their hats twirling them in the air and hurraing for Mackenzie stating they were to be at the same nefarious business again that they had but so lately quitted in this notorious section of Country[;] we are left in the merciless hands of these despicable marauders, without the means of defence—the men disembodied: and many of them have volunteered, and are at this instant in the Garrison[;] these wretched Men are prowling about with feelings malignant and revengeful—thus unprotected having no civil power in the neighbourhood, or indeed any armed or Military force our situation is any thing but enviable and we implore your excellency in your wisdom dispassionately to consider this statement, and that your excellency will be pleased to devise a plan in this sad emergency to better our wretched, and defenceless condition[.]

Feb. 6 [J. B. Robinson] to Glenelg:

[See item 156.]

[97] Head to Arthur: A.L.S. 4p.

Feb. 9 *Toronto.* [Marked "Private".]

As we are all waiting for your arrival here with great anxiety, and as it has occurred t me that from the disturbances which have taken place in the Province you may possibly before you leave New York wish to know exactly how matters stand, I have ventured to write to you on the subject.

I am happy t be able to assure you that the Province is as tranquill [*sic*] as any part of England.

There still exists a deal of disreputable feeling in the United States but the crisis is over and the fever is subsiding—

Against me personally there is a a [*sic*] most malicious and revengeful hatred, and many people think it would be dangerous for me to attempt to traverse the country of our allies, but Lady Head my sister and my daughter left me three days ago to go to New York by Queenston and thro the United States, and I do not expect they will meet with any difficulty[.]

Towards *you* [the word "personally" is here deleted] there will be no angry feeling whatever, on the contrary those who dislike me will hail the arrival of my successor—

We are and shall be here in the greatest confusion untill you arrive, and I therefore hope you will proceed here with as little delay as possible.

The Steam-boats have stopped and you will therefore (if you come by Queenston) have to come round by Hamilton, but this will only add one day to your journey.

Hoping you may have left New-York before this reaches it. . .

[P.S.] When I came here from New-York I travelled as quickly and as quietly as possible, and I would recommend any one in your state to do the same.

[98] JAMES WHITE TO ARTHUR: A.L.S. 5p.

Feb. 17 *Plymouth.*

In the hope that ere the season of *planting* arrives in your Government, the sword will be turned or exchanged for the plough share, and that during the period of your absence from your native land, you will no more hear of war; I take the liberty of forwarding some Vittoria wheat from the Caraccas [*sic*], recently transmitted by Sir Robert Kerr [*sic*] Porter . . . believing from its rapid growth it may be worthy of trial in Upper Canada: in the month of April 1835 6th & 11th I sowed some of this wheat; both native & some which I had reared the previous year: the seed ripened and was gathered the 12 & 19th August. . . In No. 354. of the Penny Magazine, will be found some general account of this Wheat in a warmer climate from the pen of Dr Hamilton. . .

At Colchester Lake Erie, resides Major Robt. Lachlan, with his family . . . of his energy, & zeal, it is probably [*sic*] you may hear; by his endeavors to establish an Agricultural & Horticultural Society at Sandwich for the Western District. . . [Recounts Lachlan's experiences in India.]

At Maxwell Lake Huron resides, the family of my cousin Henry Jones; the brother of the Head of Exeter College[.] The three brothers I should expect energetic young men, & whose natural abilities, we had wished fostered in their native land . . . born at Bovey. . . Their parent took them to Scotland. . . The eldest, Henry, went to America at 17 . . . he must have traversed America from New Orleans to Upper Canada & now holds a public situation (for some years held) but whether a govermt. one I forget,—now located at Chatham where he is building a house in consequence.— He is known to & I have reason to believe much respected by Sir John & Lady Colbourne [*sic*]. . . His second brother John has a natural talent for ship or boat building, which he has exercised for his amusement if not combined with more advantageous pursuits. . . The youngest Robert is a the [*sic*] farmer; tho' John has been a cultivator of the Vittoria wheat— All are good shots, & Master Robt. gives due proof of his powers over the bold forresters, [*sic*] when within his range— No 3 bror is a cripple, and doubtless well cared for by his brothers and two sisters who reside on the farm. . . [Comments on weather, health, etc. Mentions two brothers of Jones. Sends wishes.]

[99] HEAD: A.D. 2p.

[*Mar.* ?] [*Place not stated.*] [Marked in Head's handwriting: "Confidential".]

Executive Councillors

The Honbl. R: B: Sullivan—great legal talent sound judgement particularly on financial questions but in danger timid

The Hon W [?] Allan—	An excellent honest honorable man of high character and sound principles, but not much talent or education; led a little by the Scotch.
Captain Baldwin	An honest English sailor, attached t British Principles, more in him than you would think
Captain Elmsley	A wrong headed man but brave as a lion, and devotedly attached t all that is British—
Solicitor General Draper—	Chairman of the Constitutional Society—a clever lawyer

The Chief Justice—the ablest and best man in the Colony, but cautious in giving his real opinion, but is said t be the head of the family compact.

Attorney General [*i.e.* C. A. Hagerman]	Able speaker loyal constitutionist but I have no very high opinion of his judgement. Sound, honest.

Judges.

Sherwood—	old
Macaulay—	most excellent—man & lawyer
Jones—	sound—brave—steady man.
Maclean—	was speaker—much respected no great lawyer

Strachan—

Vice Chancellor [*i.e.* R. S. Jameson] modest, able man.

Avoid Mr. Dunn.

[The succeeding page is headed: "Military", but no entry follows.]

[Endorsed in Arthur's handwriting: "Confidential Memorandum".]

[100] [Sir] J[ohn] Harvey to C. A. Hagerman: A.L.S. 6p.

Mar. 3 *Govt. House, Fredericton.*

An article in a New York Paper has just met my eye in which it is stated that Lady Head has met with incivility in her Journey to that Place and that something of the same kind would probably be attempted towards Sir Francis Head— Without offering any comments upon a transaction which must cause all decent Persons in the United States to blush with shame & confusion & must cover the Perpetrators with execration & indelible disgrace, I write merely to offer through you, to Sir Francis Head, the advice which I have already offered to Lord Gosford, vizt to adopt the Route of these Lower Provinces, vizt by Quebec, the Great Portage, Fredericton & Halifax—where he will be quite sure of finding either a *Ship of War* or one of *Her Majestys Packets* for his conveyance—& where, in the course of his *Journey*, he will be received with every mark of respect, instead of being Subjected to the possibility of indignity from the Citizens of a *Mob* Government.

For myself I shall be rejoiced to receive him & his Suite, (I hope *you* may be one) in a House in which their reception will expose us to no inconvenience.

I write hurriedly to have the Canada Post, or rather not to delay it.—

You will be glad to hear that I have been the means of getting a Post Communication established *twice* a Week (instead of once) betwixt Quebec & Halifax. . .

[P.S.] NB The distance betwixt Quebec & Boston & Quebec & *this Place* is, by the Kennebeck Road *exactly the same*, vizt 3 days from

Quebec to Bangor (State of Maine) & 3 days from Bangor to *Boston* or to Fredericton—from Boston to New York is also 3 days & from here to Halifax the same—the Route in one case laying wholly through Her Majesty's Dominions & in the other through a Country of which it mav be truly said the Reigning Power is the *Mob.*—

[101] [ARTHUR TO HEAD]: Df.A.L. 2p.

Mar. 8 *Samson off New York.* [Marked: "Private".]

As I cannot doubt you will be anxious to be in possession of the earliest intelligence I lose no time in apprising you, by forwarding this note to New York by the Pilot Boat of my arrival after a much protracted voyage of 63 days from Portsmouth—protracted, by extremely boisterous weather & constant downfalls. The rest of the Packets appear to have been quite as roughly handled & some are still due that sailed before the Samson.

I requested Mr Anderton to do me the favor to write to you two or three weeks before I sailed begging that you would not consider it necessary to put Lady Head to the least inconvenience on my acct—& I now beg to assure you that it will give me real concern if you do so, as a Ty[?] Qr. will answer every purpose for myself & aid de camp until the arrival of my Family *if they follow me!*

Having of course had the oppy. of reading yr correspondence with the Col: Office I can say sincerely that I most heartily & cordially concur in all yr political views & measures as far as I can collect them from that source & most anxiously desire to maintain them;

I stated as much frankly to Lord Glenelg without however referring to the particular point [marginal note here reads: "Mr Ridouts affair"] upon wh you are at issue with *the Dept* & I was delighted to find His L was disposed to do the utmost justice to yr services, & expressed great regret at your having found it to be yr duty to resign the Gov.— I beg not to be understood as having volunteered to fight yr Battle—it was not the case—but I thought it honest & straight forward that the Secy of State shd. distinctly understand before I was gazetted that if your policy was condemned mine wd. not be likely to give satisfaction—the result was the unequivocal declaration to which full expression is given in Despatch No 9 of the 29 Decr,[1] of wh. I hope you have received the duplicate[.]

Just before I sailed the information reached Engd. of the insurrection in Upper Canada & of yr decisive measures to suppress it. I shall deem it a privilege to give every continuance to those Individuals who may in yr estimation have distinguished themselves, being assured that those who have most cordially supported yr govt are most likely to support mine.

It is not my intention to remain more than two days at New York. . .

[P.S.] Having read—not only yr Despatches, but yr Publications I need scarcely add that I have at once addressed you—not as a stranger but as a friend to whom I am indebted for much information & amusement.

[Misdated 1837.]

---

[1]The despatch in which Glenelg commends Head, refers Arthur for guidance to the original instructions given to Head, and instructs him to imitate Head's example, promising him the cordial support of the home government.

[102] J[AME]S BUCHANAN TO [ARTHUR]: A.D.S. 8p.

Mar. 8 [*Place not stated.*]

Observations on Canada *1836*[.]

The following facts cannot be controverted first—

That whatever Measures have been adopted to retain the poeple [*sic*] in a friendly indentity [*sic*] with England have failed.—

That the population of Upper Canada partakes largely of those who were born and educated in the United Kingdom, and their feelings are truly Loyal or they would not have Selected Canada in preference to the United States.—

That the soil Climate and Natural Advantages of Upper Canada are more favorable for acquiring a Competency, and sustaining the respectability *of previous rank* in society than any part of the United States.—

That the Canadas have had the Advantage of large Annual Expenditure of British Capital, supporting the Army, Rideau Canal and other Public Works.

That they are Exempt from any tax for the support of Government, that the Customs are Applied to defray their Municiple [*sic*] Charges, Roads Bridges Administration of Justice &c &c[.]

That the province[s] enjoy the Exclusive advantage of trade with the Empire, while their imports are received fully 25 P Cent Cheaper as to taxation than in the United States[.]

Yet with all these Advantages, Lands in the adjoining States of the same quality, and in no wise possessing more favorable advantages as to trade, or Navigation, produce from three to 500 P Cent more.—

This Statement may be tested by Comparing the Lands *Equidistant* from the Lake Navigation in the adjoining States and in Canada[.]

These facts prov'd: *whence is this the Case*

All answer "the Government"[.]

Yet let it be borne in Mind, that all who are referred to, and are permitted to inform her Majesty['s] Government, and who represent those factions who complain, or require any Change; such persons will be found in one way or a nother either the promoters or Upholders of those who are Connected with the system of government as at present administered; and who have the preponderance of the Party in the province as their paramount object—their Loyalty being based upon the preservation of their influence and power over the Governor & Province—

The System has so interwoven family Connection, and so spread their influence into every department, that no Governor has been able to carry the poeple with him, hence the Governor is avoided by the few independent Gentlemen in the Province, as they find him always surrounded by the party, whom he has found in place, and Consequently these become his chief associates, and as may be Expected their influence daily encreases, and his Excellencys indifference towards those who will not Succumb [*sic*] to the party who thus surround him Necessarily encreases, so that their apparent want of Attendance on the Governor, is held forth to his Excellency, and is at length placed as opposition to the Sovereign and thereby the party rule triumphant— This has been Manifestly Exemplified in Sir Francis Head, on his arrival his first act was to place himself under the advice of one, if not the most independant Man in the Province, and Consequently the removal of Several of the family governing party and thereby hopes were raised of a Change, but in a short time, his Excellency Nominated to Office one Connected with the party, and Mr Baldwin remonstrated and retired, and from that hour Sir Francis Head has been led to regard opposition to his Measures as disloyalty to the Sovereign, and in his last Message upon the opening of Parliament he sums up Loyalty to the Queen in the poeple turning out as they did as Evidence of the poeples Approving his Excellencys Measures, yet it is proved that the turning out to resist Mackenzie was to protect their property, and avoid the burning of their houses, from his having burned D Hornes house—

[Marginal note here reads: "1838".] The only test by which her Majestys Government can come, at the real sentiments of the province, is to give a clear demonstration, that the *party* who have so long domineered in the Province, are not to Control the Governor as to the Patronage as they have done, and Call a New Parliament, holding forth that no Measure but such as is in agreement with the Principles of the British Constitution as acted on in England, shall Receive the Sanction of the Crown—that the Office of Sherriff [*sic*] shall be Amended so as to be Conformable to the British rule— The adjustment of the Clergy reserves upon the basis laid down by Sir Francis Head, the arrang[e]ment of the Legislative Assembly, so as to be a deliberative assembly, and not under the Control of the party as it is, and has been. Under such an administration her Majesty will find a truly Loyal and devoted poeple— The Expectations raised upon the arrival of Sir Francis Head having been defeated, by his Change of action and promoting the Very Men who defeated his Measures, places his Successor on More delicate ground,—a firm Mark'd determination alone will give Confidance [*sic*]— Men in power *rarely hear truth;* Evidence by actions will alone lead the poeple after the disap[p]ointment in Francis Head to give their confidance —Sir George Arthur by firmness of purpose, can render more important Service to the Crown than rarely falls to the Lott [*sic*] of Governors— Upper Canada is Loyal, to the Crown, and devoted to British connection —but they resist the dominant party which paralizes and has retarded the prosperity of the Province, and therefore they are denominated Rebels— Their discontent has led Mackenzie and some who are truly Rebels to take the part they did, but those Men who resist the family Compact—to a Man turned out to oppose the Rebels—yet Many of them have been, and are represented as Rebels by the party—should Sir George Arthur be drawn into the family nett [*sic*], the prosperity of the Colony is destroy'd, no prudent Man will settle in the Province, aware that it must one day or a nother become independent of England, if it is to become prosperous as the adjoining States,— Lands in the adjoining States are fully worth from 3 to 600 P Cent More Valuabl[e] than in Canada—previous to the late Rebellion but now Vast Numbers are determined to leave the Province and Many have done so—

[Cover sheet endorsed: "Upper Canada Observations, as to the Colony upon Sir George Arthurs entering upon the Government—first written in 1836—now Concluded—10th March 1838". The document is dated Mar. 8.]

[103] J[AME]s BUCHANAN TO ARTHUR: A.L.S. 3p.

Mar. 10 [*Place not stated.*] [Marked "private Confidential".]

I question whether my Loyalty would lead me to take this Liberty, yet did I regard British interests more than my private interests, I would run the risk, of speaking openly for where are [*sic*] your Excellency to look but to those deeply interested in the success of your Measures,—I have stated no man is more interested in the general prosperity—others have family interests to promote, others have office or power in View, all of these I disclaim but my firm Conviction is, that the Colony will be lost to the Empire, if the poeple [*sic*] are not led to believe that the Queen Governs, and and [*sic*] not—*the family*— Independent Men will keep alooft [*sic*] from your Excellency— You have all the tools to work with, which have too long prevail[e]d, and without appearing to oppose, they will thwart every act, which is not in accordance with the interests of those who pull the same rope— I feel in the duty I owe my Sover[e]ign and my family, I have done my duty in this Very frank statement; had I done less I might have reproached my self— I ventured to name Mr. Neilson he is too independent and will not obtrude upon your Excellency, but perhaps no other Man in Uppe[r] Canada stands so free from all parties—his determination is to leave the Province unless he sees[?] a change— I do not know who he is acquainted with at Toronto.—his address is The Honl. Robert Neilson Lake View Ston[e]y Creek near Hamilton,— If your Excellency wishes I would write to him to Visit Toronto—he wants no office, favor or Appointment for any, and if he leaves the province the Consequence will be that many will also withdraw[.]

Pardon Sir this letter— I shall never again presume to repeat these Sentiments— I feel I have done my duty,—and I pray your Excellency to pardon the Manner of doing it. . .

[P.S.] The family Compact

Robinsons Jones's McCauleys Bo[u]ltons Archdean Strachan	Majors
All men in office in the Province through the above influence Legislative Council Included—	Minors

[104] H. S. Fox to Head: A.L.S. 17p.

Mar. 11 *Washington.* [Marked: "Confidential".]

I have detained Mr: Boulton here for a long time, under the expectation that something might occur daily, which would require me to send a special messenger to Upper Canada; and I could not have found any one at this place, fit to be entrusted with such a commission.— I have now, after all,—fortunately,—very little of importance to communicate to you. The crisis of immediate danger is I think passing away; and there is less hazard of war than there has been; though the settling of accounts between Great Britain and America, for all that has passed, may yet give rise to discussions of the most extreme and critical importance. The last intelligence which we have received here from the Frontier, states, that the pirates embodied near Plattsburg, for the invasion of Lower Canada, had been dispersed, without fighting, and had surrendered their arms and ammunition to General Wool, within the American lines; also, that another piratical assemblage had been dispersed near Buffalo; and finally, that the armament from near Detroit had been discomfited by

Colonel Maitland's troops, after having actually entered Upper Canada at a point called "fighting island." It is believed here further, that this last mentioned body of pirates have been subsequently disarmed and dispersed by Colonel Worth and General Brady; but no positive accounts have been received.— It is to be hoped that these occurrences, at various points along the frontier, will put an end to the pirates for the present; but the safety of the Provinces from invasion by Americans from without, will continue all in all to depend upon the increasing evidence of political tranquillity within.— If rebellion or disorder shall again arise in Canada, there exists no power within the United States, capable of restraining the people from rushing in mass across the frontier, for the purposes of plunder and devastation. The United States have presented to us, during the last few months, the extraordinary and revolting spectacle of entire communities, in a state of boasted civilization, devoting themselves to the interests of gangs of outlaws, robbers, and assassins.— The President has no more power of controlling these piratical communities, than the Sultan at Constantinople has generally had over the States of Tripoli and Algiers. With respect to the individual United States Officers now upon the frontier, Generals Scott, Wool, and Brady, and Colonel Worth,—I believe, notwithstanding some suspicious appearances, that they are conscientiously doing their duty; and under circumstances of extreme difficulty and embarrassment. They are not only opposed, and resisted as public enemies, for doing their duty, by the great majority of their fellow citizens along the border; but they are impeded, more or less, by all the State Authorities, whose conduct has been infamous throughout.— The whole force of United States soldiers, which they have under their command, from Maine to Michigan, is under 400 men; and there can be no reinforcement; as there are not in fact any more U.S. soldiers in the service, excepting those employed in Florida.— The President and his Government are I think beginning to act with more honesty, and more vigour, for the restoration of order, than heretofore; but this favorable change again is owing, and wholly owing, to the increasing evidence of the hopelessness of the rebel cause in Canada; and to the noble and courageous front, which all of English origin, throughout the Provinces, have opposed both against domestic treason, and against foreign invasion. The "Neutrality Bill," after useless and vexatious discussion for many weeks, has at length passed through both Houses of Congress; and will I believe immediately receive the assent of the President.— I shall forward to you a copy of the act, when published.— If honestly carried into execution, it will afford much additional power to the Authorities, for preventing the conveyance of arms and ammunition from the United States to the rebels in Canada.— This may still be of considerable importance with respect to Lower Canada.— I hope that you will have safely received the letters which I wrote by Mr: Robinson,—chiefly upon the subject of the Steam Boat Caroline.— I have had no more correspondence upon that business with the United States Government, nor am I likely to have.— I am informed, however, that the President has lately received a large mass of additional depositions, collected at Buffalo and elsewhere, by the U.S. district officers, of course on their side of the question. I believe that the Government persist in their intention of demanding redress from Her Majesty's Government. The demand however will not be made through this Legation, but through the American Legation in London.— I hope that it will be met by an astounding answer. The opportunity ought not to be lost, of recording, in the refusal of redress, our opinions and feelings with respect to the conduct of the American population, and of the State Authorities, on the Canadian frontier.—

Since writing the above, I am informed that Sir George Arthur has already left New York on his way to Toronto.—If Mr: Boulton arrives at Toronto in time to deliver this letter to yourself, perhaps you will have the goodness, after reading, to hand it over for information to Sir George Arthur.— In the event of your embarking from New York, and having time and inclination to visit Washington, I should derive very great pleasure and satisfaction from seeing you: but I certainly do advise you, if you learn that there is any reason to apprêhend personal annoyance from the miscreants within the New York frontier, not to expose yourself to such annoyance. It might do much harm; and could do no good.— You might be molested, under pretence of legal process arising out of the Caroline affair, in a form for which the Government of the United States would be without power to offer redress or atonement. But whether there be any reason to expect such molestation, you will be better informed than I am. . . [Sends wishes.]

P.S. I find that the "Neutrality Bill" received the President's assent yesterday, and was published in the official newspaper of last night.— I forward an authentic copy under an accompanying cover.—

[Endorsed in Arthur's handwriting: "Read before the Executive Council 31 March 1838".]

[105] H. S. Fox to Head: A.L.S. 2p.

Mar. 11 *Washington.*

I have the honor herewith to inclose to your Excellency an authentic copy of a Bill, commonly called the "Neutrality Bill," which recently passed both Houses of Congress, and which has received the assent of the President of the United States; having for its object to enlarge and strengthen the power of the Executive Government of this Country, for the enforcement of the obligations of neutrality upon the frontier.—

[Endorsed in Arthur's handwriting: "Read before the Executive Council 31 March 1838".]

[Enclosure lacking.]

[106] Arthur to Colborne: L. 6p.

Mar. 13 *Albany.* [Marked: "Copy", "Private".]

I take the earliest opportunity to inform you that I am thus far on my way to Toronto having landed on Thursday at New York after a voyage of sixty one days from Portsmouth.

This morning I had an interview with the Governor of this State by whom I was informed that General Scott had returned last night from the Frontiers—that nothing had lately occurred of importance—that all was quite tranquil—and that it was his opinion there would be no further disturbance—

Much to the same effect I was informed by Mr. Dix the Secretary of this State! To my great surprize two or three hours afterwards the Montreal Gazette of the 9th. Instant arrived in which I found an account of Colonel Maitlands affair on the 4th Inst. at Point Pele Island, and the Governor and the Secretary, having very soon afterwards called upon me, I expressed to them my astonishment of their being unapprized of so important a conflict. Mr Secretary Dix, I really believe was, as he stated, altogether in ignorance of the affair, and looked to the Governor for explanation. The latter exceedingly confused, said that General Scott had certainly alluded "to the occurence" in a conversation last evening, but he had not understood it to be an affair of much importance, and would shew him Colonel Maitland's report if I would allow him to take the Paper—to which of course I readily consented.

Without entering into all the details of a pretty long conference or pushing far expressions which fell from Governor Marcy during a visit of ceremony I may venture to add—that the very worst impression has been made on my mind, and if all the unwarrantable proceedings that have transpired have not been openly countenanced by the Authorities it is my opinion that little has been done to prevent them. A merciful Providence has over-ruled their designs on the present occasion; but the understanding between the disaffected subjects in the Canadas and the Citizens of the United States can scarcely be questioned—

The Authorities of New York assured me that a warrant was out against McKenzie, and if he could be met with he would be apprehended and sent to Jail—but, what a farce! for McKenzie arrived in New York on Friday and the Mayor of the City told me that same evening that he had met him in a shop.—

I found on reaching New York a letter from Mr. Fox in which he expressed an earnest desire to see me, but as Lord Glenelg was so anxious that I should proceed to Toronto, I did not feel justified in going to Washington. From Lord Clarence Paget who had just arrived from Washington—ostensibly on pleasure, but, in reality to examine what was doing in the Dock Yard—I found that Mr. Fox's opinion was that our Government would be obliged to go to extremes to obtain satisfaction, and that in two months we might stand in a very different relation with the United States than one of amity— This was not given to me as a message from Mr Fox, but was the substance of his communication to Lord Paget, who had been dispatched by the Admiral for information.—

I have the pleasure to enclose the latest London Paper, and have much satisfaction in congratulating you on the well earned honour which is therein notified to have been conferred upon you by Her Majesty[.] With all my heart I wish it had not been accompanied by the notification of another appointment.—

I shall at all times have the utmost satisfaction in cooperating with you not only as a Matter of Duty on Military Subjects, but shall feel highly gratified by your opinion and advice on the civil affairs of the Colony, of which, no one can possess so much information founded on experience.

Mr. Bidwell called upon me this morning— I declined to express any opinion whatever upon his case, but acceded to hear a long statement from him—and never did I hear a weaker defence than he sets up.—

[On the same sheets appears item 109.]

[107] HEAD TO CHIEF JUSTICE [J. B. ROBINSON]: A.L. initialled.

Mar. 17 [*Place not stated.*]

I return to you two letters which passed between us some time ago—and which were endorsed by Henry at the time as you see—

It has never gone out of my private box, and has been seen by no one.

Whenever the matter again comes forward I leave it t you to clear me from having altogether neglected it.—

[Endorsed in Arthur's handwriting: "Chief Justice respecting his Brothers affairs".]

[108] HEAD TO ARTHUR: A.L.S. 4p.

Mar. 21 *Toronto.*

I have received and read with great satisfaction your kind letter to me written before you landed— I have not heard from you since, and as Mr. Moore told me you were t write I feel sure your letter has been stopped and opened.

I have been anxiously awaiting your arrival here for more than a month, but I write these few lines to tell you that the American *General* Sutherland (as he styles himself) is on trial here at this moment before a Court Martial.

In a moral point of view there can be no doubt whatever of his guilt, and under these circumstances the militia fully expect he will be executed—that fate [the word "sentence" is here deleted] however must depend not on public opinion but on the evidence brought before the Court, upon which together with the sentence of the Court the Lt. Govr must eventually decide.

Now whatever may be Sutherland's fate, I foresee it will not only throw great responsibility on the Lt. Govr. but tend considerably to embarrass him.

If the evidence should be deemed insufficient to execute Sutherland, the militia who see the case quite clearly, and who of course pay little attention to legal objections would be strongly excited against the Lt: Govr. if on the contrary the man were to be executed, I know quite well that the Americans would endeavour to make a second "Caroline outrage" of it and there are not wanting those in England who would be willing to support them—besides this the Lt: Govr. would for ever be exposed to the hatred of the party in this Province, and to the revengeful feelings of their accomplices in the United States.

Under these circumstances I feel convinced that for the good of the service the new Lt: Govr should be spared from commencing his government with this trouble, and I therefore my dear Sir George beg to submit for your consideration the propriety of your awaiting untill [*sic*] you again hear from me, before you proceed to this seat of Governt.—the thing must be over one way or other in a day or two, and you shall immediately hear from me, however pray do exactly as your better judgement may direct.

[109] ARTHUR TO HEAD: L. 2p.

Mar. 21 *Niagara.*

Thank you for your very obliging letter & I am truly sensible of the kind feeling which dictated it.

No one can possibly have less desire than I have to take any part in General Sutherland's affair and I shall be most delighted to have nothing to say to it,—especially as he is being tried before a Military Tribunal.

But having actually arrived within four hours sail of Toronto I do not see how I can stop short merely because a very disagreeable duty is pending. At the same time, although I should not feel justified in halting in order to avoid an unpleasant duty, I am sure I cannot do wrong in acting with the utmost courtesy towards an officer who has merited so highly the approbation of Her Majesty's Government, and under any circumstances I should have felt it proper to announce my arrival in the Province before I intruded myself personally upon you— My son will accordingly be the bearer of a note to you by the Steamer in the morning and I shall be most happy to be guided by your convenience.

This mode of proceeding will be more agreeable to me for other reasons which I will do myself the pleasure of personally explaining to you.

I am concerned to find you have not received a letter which I wrote to you from Albany— On no account would I wish it to fall into other hands—

[The above appears on the same sheets as item 106.]

[110] RICHARD BULLOCK: [RECIPIENT NOT STATED]: A.D.S.

Mar. 21 [*Place not stated.*]

Recommendation for promotion in the Queen's Rangers. 21 March 1838.

Lieutt. John. H. Cameron to be Captain vice Hurd, promoted.

Recommended by Colonel S. P. Jarvis Commanding the Regiment.

Approved & Recommended
Richard Bullock
Adjt. Genl
Militia[.]

[111] HEAD TO ARTHUR: A.L.S. 2p.

Mar. 22 *Toronto.*

I think you are *quite right* in the view you take of Sutherlands trial; and on reflection I admit that you decidedly *ought* to advance without delay to your post—

My note was hastily written from my heart instead of from my head, and it is not the first time the former has made me err— I must tell you that as soon as I had despatched the note, I thought I had done wrong, and before an hour I had determined to recall it, and not to send a duplicate to meet you on the road to Kingston, by which we all heard you were approaching.

You are welcome t Upper Canada, and I shall be delighted t see you tomorrow, at any hour you may find it most convenient to cross.

[112] J. B. ROBINSON TO HEAD: A.L.S. 4p.

Mar. 22 *Toronto.* [Marked: "Copy".]

I am much obliged by Your Excellency's kindness in returning to me the letter which I had written upon the subject of my poor brother's affairs. I shall take an early opportunity of laying it before Sir George Arthur, for my own sake, and then shall continue as I have done, to do whatever may be in my power for bringing things to a satisfactory close— And the Government of course, will interpose or not as they may feel to be right—

My brother's state of health makes it difficult and painful to me to force business upon his attention— Still I have managed to have all his accounts brought to a close & the apparent balances against him upon all except two, viz: the Clergy Reserves & the Surveyor General of Woods are paid up, leaving those two accounts still open. Upon one of these there stands against him an apparent balance of £4900, on the other £6700.

It has been the earnest desire of my brother to have these accounts thoroughly examined in the hope of detecting errors; and Mr. Ridout, Cashier of the Bank of Upper Canada, and Mr. Turquand of the Receiver General's Office, at my request undertook the duty and were about entering upon it when the confusion began here— Now that the Session of the Legislature is over, and every one is more at leisure, I hope to get them at the work, and I trust besides sums sunk in a manner that most probably will never be discovered, and which must of course be made good, they will find some error or errors in the entries that will materially lighten the difficulty; for I can not believe it possible but that the greatest part of the apparent deficiency is to be thus accounted for, if the truth can be made to appear—

I repeat for Your Excellency's satisfaction that the property owned by my brother before he received any of these offices is sufficient to cover much more than the sum which seems due—and I will answer for it's [*sic*] being faithfully applied—

He has lately sold one part of this property for £4000, but upon a credit for two years; and I have no fear but that he will be able with my assistance to discharge whatever may be found due, by the sale of his property, especially if peace and confidence are soon restored—

In the mean time I feel most grateful for Your Excellency's liberal forbearance; and I must say that I have been much struck with the delicacy shown on all hands, and which I hope and believe I may attribute to the prevailing conviction with all who know my brother's character, habits, and circumstances that he has derived no benefit from the loss which, for the time at least, seems to have been sustained by the public— I wish Your Excellency to keep this letter, in case you should be troubled with any inquiry hereafter.—

[113] COLBORNE TO ARTHUR: A.L.S. 8p.

Mar. 24 *Montreal.* [Marked: "Private".]

I beg to thank you for your letter of the 13th inst; I hoped to have had the pleasure of seeing you here en route to the Upper Province; could you have conveniently proceeded to your Government by crossing the St. Lawrence.

I have no doubt that the occurrences which have lately taken place on the frontier of the Provinces will alarm the Authorities of the United States, and induce them to adopt such measures to put an end to the incursions of the Brigands, as will ensure our remaining for some time undisturbed.

The Officers of the United States Army employed to check the movements of the Pirates on the frontier, have acted, I think, honestly and with great vigour and prudence, under very disadvantageous circumstances; having been opposed by the mass of the people of Vermont, and New York, and Michigan, and embarrassed in their duty by the States' Authorities. The American Government must be anxious to avoid a War; but if we should again have disturbances in either Province, we can only depend on our own force and exertions to defend the Colonies against the attacks which will be made on us by the people of the adjoining states. It is my intention to send two Regiments to the Upper Province as soon as our reinforcements arrive from Halifax.

You will then perhaps be enabled to relieve some of the Volunteer Corps, and send them home. We shall require a respectable regular force in the Western, London, Home and Midland Districts for some years.

I hear from Colonel Foster that much discontent prevails in the Western District, in consequence of the claims on the Military Chest, having remained for some months unsettled. I have been compelled to attend to the representations of the Commissary Genl respecting the irregular payments which have been made, and the danger of allowing the issue of warrants, without vouchers[.]

There is great difficulty in checking profusion and fraud, where the agents employed in making disbursements of the public money are not responsible to Government, and when the Troops are engaged in repelling sudden invasions of the frontier. I hope however that the cause of the complaints to which I advert may be speedily removed[.]

I shall have no hesitation in conveying to you full authority to issue warrants for the payment of all claims on the Military Chest, without reference to Head Quarters; and I think that by your appointing an experienced Assistant Military Secretary, assisted by an Officer of the Commissariat Department, the out-standing accounts might be examined and audited at Toronto, by your authority, and settled.

In the performing of my duties during the late critical period I have unfortunately been drawn into a most unpleasant correspondence with Sir Francis Head. I transmit to you a copy of a letter which I have forwarded to him, in reply to his attack on my conduct. I shall lay the whole of my Correspondence with him and the Commissary Genl, before the Secretary of State for the Colonies, relative to the military affairs of Upper Canada.

I believe you embarked with several of the Officers sent out by Government to Canada, to be placed at my disposal— I have directed some of them to proceed to the Upper Province, imagining that they may be employed as Inspectors of Volunteer Corps at Niagara, Toronto Kingston and the Western District.

There may however be impropriety in their being appointed to this duty, and a dislike on the part of the Officers of the Volunteers to submit to this interference. I shall be obliged by your informing me if you see any objection to the Officers lately arrived from England being thus disposed of:

I shall be at all times most ready to cooperate with you zealously and cordially; and have great pleasure in attending to your wishes and suggestions.

[Enclosure is obviously item 114.]

[114] COLBORNE TO HEAD: L.

Mar. 24 *Government House, Montreal.* [Marked: "Copy".]

I have the honor to acknowledge the receipt of your Letter of the 16th. Instant, with a copy of your Dispatch to the Secretary of State for the Colonies, and to acquaint you that, with a view of repelling your unjust charges against me, I shall take an early opportunity of transmitting to the Secretary of State my correspondence with you, the Commissary General, and Colonel Foster, connected with the Military Affairs of Upper Canada.—

[The above is obviously the enclosure referred to in item 113.]

[115] [ANONYMOUS]: TO ARTHUR: L. 2p.

[*1838*] [*Postmark: Toronto, Mar. 27, 1838.*]

[*Mar. 27*] The errors of your predecessors, and more particularly Sir Francis Bond Head, have all originated in holding to a certain party in this Province which has been its ruin. I pray that you may be able to discern that Party, and all other Parties, and avoid them, do equal justice to all act upon the broad Principles of impartiallity [*sic*] and you will make us a Contented People, and you will heal the sore wounds which have been inflicted upon this unfortunate Colony by Sir F. B. Head, Hagerman, Draper and Co— You will be surrounded by them, and their cunning devices to intrap you, Beware of them, they are unwise, and treacherous professors full of deceit. They are latent enemies of our enlightened ministry who have sent you here. The Chief Justice is at the head of what is called the Family Compact, which is as overbearing as it is wicked—. You have unsafe Executive Councellors [*sic*], Mr. Sullivan who is the first, is a man without character or influence, who has been amongst the Ranks of the worst of Radicals, elevated by Sir Francis Bond Head from the very dregs of Society, who should not have been any other than the trade of a Tallow Chandler, whose father was in a very small way not many years ago. The Comfort, and prosperity of us depends on you, and if you avoid The Shoals of the Family Compact, you will find your situation a happy one— Beware of the Smooth and Silvery tongue of the Chief Justice, Keep your eye on Hagerman, Draper, Robinson's and Boulton's. Pause, and look well before you act on their opinions, for on every case, rest assured they have their own purposes to serve.— The Chief Justice wrote the "*address to Sir Francis Head*" for the Legislative Council, on hearing of your appointment to this Government, and also the state of the Province, and Hagerman wrote the state of the Province for the Hous[e] of Assembly. Read these documents. In thruth [*sic*] these People plunged the Province into Rebellion, and Sir Francis Head has been a *Tool* in their hands. I warn you again to beware of them, and remember that you have Mr. Joseph about you Son in Law to this Mr. Hagerman. It is a misfortune which the Province hope and trust that you will remove. He is an unfit person for such a situation, all that transpires will be communicated to the Party.

I am in sincerity

Your well wisher and Subject.

[116] HEAD TO ARTHUR: A.L.S. 3p.

Mar. 29 *New York.*

I have taken my place in the Cambridge Packet which is to sail from here on the 1st April and long more than I can describe to be out of sight this land of liberty.

I shall watch with great interest and anxiety your progress, and I assure you it is a great satisfaction t me to reflect that I have left the Governt in your hands—

I hope you will be so good as to comply with my request respecting the little scrap of paper which I left with you—

This note will be delivered t you by Judge Jones who at my request attended me here—when we started he reminded me that he ought to have obtained your permission and I hope you will be so good as to excuse *my* neglect in not thinking of it—

He has been of great service t me and I really think that without him I should have got into trouble— He is a calm brave resolute man of sterling integrity of conduct—

I have got your despatches and private letter to Ly. Arthur both of which I will take especial care of, and if I find I can in any way be of service to Lady A it will give me sincere pleasure—

[117] J. S. MACAULAY TO ARTHUR: A.L.S. 4p.

Apr. 2 *Toronto.*

Recent events have sufficiently shewn the necessity of preparing this Country to become the Theatre of War, for though our neighbours may, for the present, abstain from further attempts to subjugate the Province, yet the fact of their having so readily seized, on the shallow pretext, afforded by the insurrection of the Constitutional Reformers under McKenzie, to attack us, leaves no reason to imagine, that they will have any higher regard for their national honour on any future occasion.

By an inspection of the Map of Canada it will at once be perceived, that the command of the lakes is essential to our protection. The Province, then, could only be entered by the St. Clair & Detroit Frontier on the west, or by the Niagara and Saint Lawrence on the South.

An attack on the extreme western frontier could not be successfully prosecuted, so long as we held possession of Lake Erie: the Niagara Frontier can only be crossed above the Falls, at Queenston or at Niagara: no very extensive system of Fortifications would therefore be required to close this passage into our country, while two or three small forts would sufficiently cover our western extremity.

Kingston is already partially fortified, sufficiently so, to render it safe against other than a regular attack.

On the line of the Saint Lawrence little danger exists, for if an enemy were to cross into the Johnstown or Eastern Districts, he could scarcely hope to maintain his position, open to attack both from the Midland District, and from Montreal.

It would appear then, that having fortified the western frontier, the Niagara, and Kingston, we have only to secure the command on the lakes, and then the inhabitants of this Country might feel themselves safe in the enjoyment of their property.

The description of naval armament best calculated for the service of the lakes would (as I think) be large gun boats armed with 10 Inch or 12 Inch guns for throwing shells. Such vessels might be passed through the Rideau Canal, and would be available for commercial purposes, when no longer required for war. Vessels of war of the above description might be built anywhere along the line of the Rideau, at Kingston, or at Toronto. There can therefore be no great difficulty in securing the command of lake Ontario.

The Port of Penetanguishene is of the first order, well placed to assure us the command of lakes Huron and Michigan. The expense of transporting naval stores to Penetanguishene would however be so enormous, that it would be well worth the while of the Government to proceed with and complete the projected rail road between this city and that port. That this road would not be altogether unproductive of a return for the money expended, may be assumed from the fact, that a private Company was formed with the expectation of undertaking that work, by whom all requisite Surveys Estimates &c. have been procured, and who have only abandoned their project, because of their lack of means to carry it into execution, the estimated cost being £200,000.

The Project of Messrs. Baird and Killaly for the permanent construction of the Welland Canal, submitted to the Legislature last session, and which embraces the construction of fine harbours on the Lakes connected by that canal, imperatively demands the notice of Her Majesty's Government—

The sum required to complete the project above mentioned is £290,000, a sum which would not I think be exceeded.

To appreciate the importance of this work we have only to consider that it would enable us to command both Lakes Erie and Ontario, with little more than the force required to maintain our superiority on one only. Vessels of the class before mentioned could be passed from one lake to the other in 24 Hours and all the naval force on both lakes could be brought to bear on any one point; an advantage of such great importance as already to have attracted the attention of our neighbours, who are, it is said, now collecting in force on the Niagara frontier with the avowed object of destroying the entrance to the Welland Canal.

If the American people are resolved to have war at all hazards, they could make no more important move, for there can be little doubt, that the Welland Canal even in its present imperfect condition will enable us to destroy all the shipping in the ports on Lake Erie, and command, where, were it not for that canal, we should be constrained to allow the Americans undisputed sway.

I have taken the liberty of bringing these projects under Your Excellency's consideration, in the hope that the attention of Her Majesty's Government being attracted thereto, they may be induced to lend the Province, such sum as may be required for the completion of the Welland Canal in a permanent manner, and thereby give assurance to all those who are proud of the distinction of being British subjects, that they shall in no part of this Province be left to the mercy of their Republican neighbours. . .

J. S. Macaulay
late a Capt in the Corps of Rl. Engrs.
and Professor of Fortn. at Woolwich.

[118] [A.] E. Ryerson to Arthur: A.L. 3p.

Apr. 4 *Kingston.*

The Rev E Ryerson presents his compts. to His Excellency Sir George Arthur, & takes the liberty to present, & respectfully begs His Excellency's acceptance of, the accompanying publications.

The plain discourses on "Wesleyan Methodism in Upper Canada" and "Civil Government," &c, contain a summary statement of the religious & political doctrines & sentiments which are inculcated by the Ministry of the Wesleyan Methodist Church in in [*sic*] U. Canada; &

which Mr R. believes, with scarcely any exceptions, obtain among the Members of that Church.

The documents printed by order of the House of Assembly, with the Appendix by the Editor of the Guardian, relative to the U.C. Academy, will fully acquaint His Excellency with circumstances respecting which His Excy. will doubtless wish to be informed.

The Letters on the "Affairs of the Canadas ["] were written by Mr R. in England in 1836-7 where he found much ignorance & many errors even in the best informed circles respecting the state of affairs in the Canadas. Mr R. believes these Letters will furnish His Excellency with a more impartial & correct sketch of the rise & progress of Canadian Agitations than is contained in a recent Report of the Select Committee of the House of Assembly. The Report of the House of Assembly does not admit that any acts of the Canadian Executives were ever in the least degree objectionable, & attributes *revolutionary* motives to *all* those who ever complained of the local Executives, & attacks the whole policy of the Imperial Government towards *this province*, as well as towards Lower Canada. A different view is given of these matters in the accompanying Letters, pp 9-14. These Letters were not written under the excitement of recent melancholy occurrences; and His Excellency will perceive from the "Preface," that the correctness of the views expressed in them has been endorsed by the constitutional press of the Canadas.

Mr R. begs most respectfully & cordially to congratulate His Excellency on his safe arrival as the Lt Governor of this Province, & earnestly prays that His Administration of the Government may be crowned with the Divine Blessing, & thus be rendered in the highest degree gratifying to His Excellency and beneficial to the inhabitants of Upper Canada.

[Enclosures lacking.]

[119] ARTHUR TO COLBORNE: LB.1, p. 1-8.

Apr. 5 *Toronto.* [Marked: "Private".]

I have had the very great pleasure to receive your letter of the 24th March and every day since it has been my intention to write to you; but I have been so much engaged throughout the past week that it really seems to me to have been one continued day containing 165 [*sic*] hours. I regretted much not having it in my power to proceed by way of Montreal; but I could not do so consistently with Lord Glenelg's urgent desire that I should reach Toronto without delay; and I was aware that he would be exceedingly disappointed at the length of my Passage.

With such a body of Prisoners in Jail, and such numbers out on bail; together with the embarrassment which arises from the terms of the Proclamation which have been issued; and the Act of the Provincial Parliament which has been passed—the strong desire of many that the severest punishment should be inflicted, and the wish of others that it should be mitigated—you may imagine that the commencement of my campaign here is at least troublesome and anxious.

After a week's anxious consideration in the Executive Council, I hope a Majority of Members are brought over to the opinion that it is possible, consistently with a due regard to Public justice, to extend Pardons very largely, and not to proceed to trial with the Multitude of cases which have been presented by the Grand Jury. In some cases, however, in which the Prisoners were actually parties to Murder and Arson, the Law must take its course, and two of the most guilty are now under sentence and will be executed on the 12th Inst.

General Sutherland has been tried before a General Militia Court Martial—it was assembled before my arrival and seems interminable, the defence I believe closed last night. It strikes me altogether to be an objectionable proceeding, and there will be so much difficulty in dealing with the case, if he is convicted that I sincerely hope he may be acquitted and then proceeded against for another offence by the Civil Power.

I am glad you think so favorably of the conduct of the Officers of the United States Army. That there was a good understanding between the *Authorities* in the State of New York and the disaffected in this Province I have no doubt. The scene I witnessed between Mr. Bidwell and Governor Marcy was quite convincing on the point to my mind.

I quite agree with you that the American Government must be anxious to avoid a war with us; but how are they to help it if the *People will?*—there are so many circumstances indicative of violent proceedings and agitation in the States generally, that although it may be warded off for a time, there must be an outbreak somewhere at no distant period—and if there be Her Majesty's Government will have cause to regret, I fear that this Province has been left in so defenceless a state as to fortifications.

There are daily reports made to me of the apprehension of fresh attacks as soon as the navigation is open on Lake Erie and a person who has been employed by Sir Francis Head for some months past to obtain information returned yesterday from the States with an account that further attacks are meditated. My impression however is that it is rather talked about by the Americans, than seriously intended at this moment. The only communication I place much dependence upon is one from Colonel Cameron (Late Major in the 79th Regt) who is a very sensible person and by no means an alarmist. He says, that there is a very bad spirit at Buffalo, Lewiston and Lockport, and that as soon as we withdraw the militia from the Frontier we may expect annoyance. In the district you name we certainly require a strong available regular force.

Sir Francis Head persuaded himself that there was a *general* loyal feeling here— Certainly there was a gratifying exhibition of Loyalty at the moment to put down that worthless creature McKenzie; and, no doubt there is a very considerable body of excellent persons well affected towards the Constitution—but, what has become of the Numbers who for years have been known as Reformers, and very disaffected ones too? Where are the persons who returned a Majority of Reformers to the House of Assembly, and elected McKenzie Mayor of Toronto? depend upon it if we ever get the worst of it with the Americans many a Reformer will resuscitate! I have not time, just now, to go into detail upon this subject, nor is it necessary to *you* as you must know the *constitution* of the People here much better than I do.

Colonel Foster has rightly informed you that there is much discontent in consequence of the claims on the Military Chest having remained for so many months unsettled. I am quite aware of the difficulty you labor under, and how important it is that every account should be accompanied with proper vouchers; but, really the distress which some persons, who have furnished supplies are suffering is, as regards their future good will, in cases of emergency—quite alarming! It must have occurred to you, I am sure, that the whole arrangements of the Commisst. Department in this Province is [*sic*] very objectionable.

There is no head of the Department in this Province—each Officer at the several Stations is a direct accountant with the Comy. General at Quebec, so that the Officer Comg. here can get no ready information either as regards expenditure or Supplies or Issues. Some years ago the same system was pursued in the Australian Colonies—but, as soon as it was pointed out to the Lords of the Treasury a district Commisst branch was formed at Van Diemens Land. Although both Colonies were blended in the same Military command. the two Departments of the Comt. were perfectly distinct—the head of each indeed corresponded, and they mutually assisted each other as the exigencies of the Service required—but nothing more! just in the same way the Ordnance branch was conducted—the board of respective Officers being quite distinct. They received their Authorities and Warrants on the spot, and their amounts were at once transmitted to England for final examination.

Subject to your approval I have put Captain Halkett Coldstream Guards in orders as Asst. Mily. Secy. to examine the Pay Lists. I have only appointed him provisionally—that is, in case Major M[a]cphail 98 Regt. does not come out to fill the situation from England— Lord Hill had approved of his accompanying me; but when I was on the point of embarking it was to late for him to make his arrangements.

Captain Halkett was Sir Francis Head's ADC; and as I shall be obliged to do away with some of my Predecessors appointments I shall be pleased at the opportunity of making this a kind of set off.

I am much obliged to you for allowing me to see a Copy of your letter to Sir Francis Head. I had read his correspondence with you, as well as Lord Gosfords upon the same subject. It was hoped in Downing St. that the code of "Instructions" which was prepared for the guidance of all parties in such cases would have prevented misunderstanding—but I was so satisfied such would not be the case that I refused to come out as Civil Governor only. I remember some years ago, when I was Depy Qr. Master Gl. in Jamaica, that the very same difficulty arose between the Duke of Manchester and the Commander of the Forces, as was agitated between Lord Gosford and yourself and I think it was on that occasion that the "Instructions" were framed by the King's Command to which I have alluded. The effect of clashing authority was very visible on my arrival here. Colonel Foster could furnish me with no return of the Militia Force. He could only guess he told me the strength of the Force employed. There was a want of cordiality between Sir Francis Head and himself—the Commissary would obey neither— Persons were handed from Office to Office with their Pay Lists and accounts and the Militia Authorities were half disposed to turn restive. As it is I find many expences have been incurred partly by the authority of Sir Francis and partly by the Authority of Colonel Foster—but, I suppose all will come out square at last.

With respect to the Officers who have arrived from England, I find some jealousy may be anticipated on the part of the Militia Officers. "Colonel McNab" and ["]the gallant Militia" have been so puffed up that I doubt if they think any Troops on Earth are to be compared with them, or that any Officers have the like experience of [*sic*] capacity. But this nonsense will I hope soon be got over—I mean the excess of it, for to a degree, it is most desirable; and I shall be happy to make the best disposition I can of any officers you may think proper to assign to the Upper Province. I wish it were possible to appoint one of them Adjt. Genl. of the Militia, for the Gentleman who was lately selected by my

Predecessor for that situation appears to me by no means competent. There should be a first rate man for it, and if I can contrive to persuade Colonel Bullock that he had better retire, do you think the vacancy in such times as these might be filled up by one of the new arrivals, and if so, would you kindly give me the Services of the most qualified Officer? The whole of the Militia Force requires to be reorganised.

In anticipation of the additional Regular Troops you propose sending into this Province, I should wish *at once* to proceed to reduce such of the Militia as can be got rid of under the engagement that was made with them when they were called out. Numbers are at this season of the year most anxious to get back to their homes, and if we do not get the seed into the ground we shall have no Harvest—and besides this Military life will have a bad moral effect upon the Yeomanry if too long continued; in carrying the measure of reduction into effect, will you have the goodness to let me know whether you wish me to have any reference to the State of Lower Canada— I mean whether you would desire me to keep on Service any number of Militia beyond what may be considered absolutely necessary for the defence of this Province. . .

[P.S.] I must have the pleasure of letting you know as I am sure it will be satisfactory to you if you do not know it already, that the long disputed point respecting the 57 endowed Rectories has been at length adjusted and pronounced to be legal. As soon as I read the despatches on the subject in England, I called upon the Archbishop of Canterbury and having known His Grace well for many years, he obliged me by cordially entering into the subject. So did the Bishop of London. Much depended upon Lord Ripons *Private* Letter to you, and as no Copy of it was in the Office, I went immediately to His Lordship and Mr Hay[?] and they furnished readily the information I required, and the question was again put to the Law Officers, and they then retracted the adverse opinion they had before given. Unfortunately on assuming this Govt. Sir Francis Head reported that the question of the Rectories was most embarrassing, and I really believe that was the cause of their endeavouring to throw it over in Downg. St.

As a Member of the Church of England I thank you most cordially; and although I do not wish to advance my own Church by the repression much less the extinction of others I sincerely wish that the number of Rectories secured had been double 57!

[120] R. A. TUCKER TO ARTHUR: A.L.S. 3p.

Apr. 6 *Kingston, Upper Canada.* [Marked "(Private)."]

An extreme solicitude to rescue me from a state of poverty & obscurity has, I find, induced my affectionate & too-anxious Sister, Mrs. Lauzan, to endeavour to interest you in my favor: & from her I also learn, that you were pleased to express a ready disposition to serve me, as far as your power of doing so might fairly extend.— I feel it therefore to be due to you, no less than to myself, to hasten to assure you, that *I am not a Candidate for public employment in this Province;* & in making this communication I shall take the liberty of briefly detailing some of the leading considerations which influence me on this head.—

Having held for more than *ten* years, the Office of Chief Judge of the Supreme Court of Newfoundland; & having twice, for a considerable period at each interval, discharged the functions of *Acting Governor* of that Colony, it is obvious, that there are very few, if any, Appointments under your Government of equal salary, rank, & importance, with those I formerly enjoyed: and you will easily understand, that a retrograde movement is always painful & humiliating.— But to such a mortification I cou'd bring myself, I believe, without much difficulty to submit, if I had merely to struggle against feelings of vanity & pride.— I trust, however, that I am guided by far better principles; & I confidently hope that no privations, or sufferings, to which I may be exposed, will ever tempt me to depart from the resolution I form'd—when a high sense of duty prompted me to *resign* my Official Situation—never to *solicit Office*, nor even to *accept it*, if spontaneously tender'd me, unless the offer of it were in every respect calculated to furnish both a distinct recognition, & an authoritative proof, of the rectitude & propriety of my conduct, as well during my *continuance* in Office, as also in the act of my *retirement* from it.— Of the former, I already have the most gratifying testimonials; in the strong & concurrent approbation of all the successive *Secretaries of State*, from Earl Bathurst to Earl Ripon inclusive, & in the almost universal & unanimous sentiment of attachment manifested towards me by the Inhabitants of Newfld: and, tho' I have reason to suppose, that the circumstances attending my *resignation* were—& probably still are—view'd in an unfavourable light at the Colonial Department, I can never regret a step—whatever its consequences to me may be—which was enter'd on under a sense of what seem'd to me right at the moment of adopting it, & which has since been fully sanction'd & approved by long reflection, & the calm sentence of a cool & dispassionate judgment.

In thus immediately & earnestly repudiating the Character of a *Suitor* for your *patronage*, with which my Sister's intense concern for my welfare has led her to invest me, I am most desirous to convey to you my best acknowledgments for your kind intentions towards me; & to reciprocate your wish to cultivate an acquaintance, if fate shall at any time bring us together.— And, remote as the probability is, that an opportunity of being useful to *you* will ever be afforded me, I will yet add, that it wou'd gladly be embraced by me shou'd it fortunately occur.

[In the original document, emphasis is apparently intended by the use of larger characters than those in the main body of the letter. The larger characters are here transcribed in italics.]

[121] ARTHUR TO THE ATTORNEY GENERAL [C. A. HAGERMAN]: LB.1, p. 8-9.

Apr. 7 *Government House, [Toronto.]*

I beg to transmit the proceedings of the General Militia Court Martial held for the trial of T. J. Sutherland for your perusal and consideration, and to request your opinion as to the legality of this conviction under the Statute: and also as to the sufficiency of the Charge against the Prisoner and the Evidence produced in support of it—

[122] R. B. SULLIVAN TO THE LIEUTENANT GOVERNOR [ARTHUR]: A.L.S. 10p.

Apr. 7 *Crown Lands Office, [Toronto.]*

With reference to the Militia recommendations which Your Excellency did me the honor to place in my hands this morning, I beg respectfully to make a few remarks[.]

I know of no objections to the promotions recommended sufficient to authorize a counter recommendation of my part. But serious objections strike me, as to the mode of making these recommendations[.]

1. The whole of the patronage of the militia is thrown into the hands of the Colonels. Yet the Government bears all the responsibility. The promotion in the sedentary militia seems at first view to be a matter of little moment. and perhaps in a military point of view it is really so. but it must be remembered that commissions in the militia—appointments as justices, & Commissioners of the Court of request and the like being open to the whole of the population above the degree of labourers, the jealousy and discontent produced by injudicious selections is much more formidable, than the out cry which is raised against the successful candidate for high office. where the competition and personal disappointment is confined to a few. The Colonel of militia however has all the praise of a judicious selection. all the personal thanks of the successful candidates. but all the slights and wrongs and forgetfulness of former services fall on the Government which hears for the *first time* how very badly it has behaved through the medium of a newspaper. I think therefore that the patronage as well as the odium should belong to Government.

2. In acceding to the recommendations of the Colonels of Militia Your E. knows who[m] you appoint as officers but sometimes, it is only at the *hustings* or in the *rebel camp* Your Excellency finds out who has been rejected: as the complainant says & thinks most tyrannically, cruelly and ungratefully. by a Government which in fact never heard of the names, or knew of the existence of the victim, whose mind is embittered whose life is rendered miserable whose political opinions are utterly changed by what is in reality the most difficult of all wrongs to bear with christian patience, *slight and neglect.*

I therefore think the Government should be made aware of the names of those who apply. but who are not fortunate enough to be recommended, as well as of those who meet with that favor.

The case of George A Clark who called upon Your Excellency at Buffalo. is an instance of the real importance to Government of Careful & judicious management in the appointments to situations of comparatively little individual consequence. That man was loyal, brave, attached to Government as were all his family. he was not perhaps the best fitted for the Magistracy, but he enjoyed the distinction of being a justice of the peace. Upon a false representation by a clergyman of his neighbourhood his name was omitted in a new commission of the peace. The man was prosperous wealthy in the enjoyment of every comfort otherwise. but this one slight drove him to madness and ruin. seperated [*sic*] him for ever from all his relations and from his native country—of which he has become if not an important, at least a bitter enemy.

The instances of discontent as respects militia appointments are innumerable. they must be numerous even if every thing were conducted rightly, but when well founded complaints are made the distrust in the Government and the discontent and insubordination thereby engendered. become truly formidable.

Whatever trouble the actual supervision of these matters may occasion, I think it must be encountered. a Government may from wrong or mistaken views inevitably fall into error. but it should not walk blindfold on difficult and dangerous ground.

Allow me to suggest most respectfully. that the Colonels of militia, should be commanded to acquaint the Government with all applications for commissions or would it not be well if these applications were made directly to the Adjutant General? The Colonels should be allowed to remark on the respective merits of the applicants, but they should have no power of keeping their names unknown.

As regards the active militia should such a force be considered proper to be continued. The appointment of Officers becomes of great consequence in a military point of view. all applications in my opinion should come directly to the Government and the patronage & power of making these appointments should be kept with the greatest jealousy from the commanders. The power of conferring favors on dependents and friends is a dangerous one, even in the hands of high officers of Government but the force of public opinion is a severe check to its exercise—in the hands of comparatively irresponsible persons. the temptation is too great to be generally withstood and if the recommendation be improper it is not the person who makes it but the Government which suffers.

I think that in the case of appointments to the active militia confirmation of the qualifications of candidates should be fully placed before Your Excellency. The responsibility of giving true information as to fact is a proper one to be incurred by subordinate officers. but that of judging, of the result of applications, & the power of absolutely conferring important favors is obviously not proper to be entrusted in such hands.

One officer in command may be a violent orangeman, another a bigoted catholic, or may be of an easy and conciliatory disposition another severe and unrelenting. one may think a mere difference of opinion in politics or religion a sufficient ground for persecution and disregard. another may overlook these distinctions. How then is it possible for the action of the Government to be uniform and consistent when it is directed by so many discordant influences?

As many evils may arise from hesitation and delay I am not desirous to press upon Your Exy. the adoption of the above course, in the cases now before the Govt. but I am not in possession of sufficient information to enable me to say that in acting upon the recommendations Your Excellency will always be doing justice to the Service, or to the claims of others.

[123] [Sir] John Macdonald to Arthur: A.L.S. 3p.

Apr. 9 *Horse Guards*, [*London.*] [Marked "Private"]

Allow me to recommend to your kind offices and protection the bearer hereof Mr. Henry Robarts whose family I have long been very intimate with, and whose father (the Head of the Banking firm of Robarts Curtis & Co. in Lombard Street) is my most particular friend.

This young man visits Canada as a traveller, and is accompanied by a friend of his Mr. Bland—a Yorkshire gentleman, with whom I am not personally acquainted, but for whom I must, nevertheless, likewise claim your protection[.]

The Bearer is a smart, intelligent little fellow who has travelled all over Europe, and devotes his whole time to travelling pursuits— I shall be grateful for any kindness you may show him, and his companion— I shall not enter, here, upon any other subject, it being uncertain when my young friend may have an opportunity of delivering this credential to you—

[124] A. J. WILLIAMSON TO ARTHUR: A.L.S. 4p.

Apr. 10 *Toronto.* [Marked "Private and Confidential."]

[Criticises, in high flown language and with theological allusions, Arthur's action concerning a pamphlet submitted by Williamson "with an intimation that I was *very poor.*" The reply courteously conveyed by "Lieutenant Arthur" had been that His Excellency "Had no funds for such a purpose." Williamson considers the action a reflection on his poverty.]

[125] ARTHUR TO THE ATTORNEY GENERAL [C. A. HAGERMAN]: LB. 1, p. 9-10

Apr. 13 *Government House, Toronto.*

At a time when you have so many important subjects pressed upon you, I regret much having occasion to trouble you further upon the case of the Prisoner Sutherland; but I am desirous that the proceedings of the Court Martial should not receive final confirmation until they have been most thoroughly sifted. I request therefore you will at your earliest convenience [furnish me] with your opinion upon the following points.

1—Is the Act under which Prisoner has been tried unconstitutional.

2. Does he in fact come clearly within the letter and spirit of it.

3—Is the charge sufficient—specifying neither day nor place of the Offence for which he was tried, and containing no averment that the traitors to whom he had joined himself, were on the 12th Jany. still trait[o]rously in arms against Her Majesty.

4. Does the Evidence make out each necessary point of proof.

5—Could the Court Martial properly sentence to transportation under this Act.

6—Is the sentence as to transportation properly passed.

7. Do the British Statutes and Orders in Council embrace such a case as to permit this convict to be sent and detained in V.D. Land.

8.—With what formalities must he be sent.—

9—Can the sentence be reconsidered— Can the Lieut: Governor change it.

10.—Has the Secretary of State or rather the Queen any over-ruling power as to confirming—of course She may pardon.—

[126] J. B. ROBINSON TO [ARTHUR]: A.L.S. 7p.

Apr. 16 *Toronto.*

An enquiry which you made this morning induces me to say a few words to you on a subject which is of some delicacy & of no little consequence to the successful and agreeable conduct of the Government. I have besides a personal reason for availing myself of a fair excuse for addressing some remarks to Your Excellency upon it. You asked me what had been the course usually pursued here in regard to references upon the various public matters that come under the consideration of the Government?—

There is no reason why any peculiar system should prevail in this Province; with regard to references or consultations— What is right in England, or in any other regularly conducted Government will be right here—and no deviation from the proper course can continue long without producing inconveniences and disadvantages of some kind— The Executive Council are of course the proper advisers on questions of policy and expediency; the Crown Officers on all matters that involve legal considerations—and all persons in charge of departments should be communicated with fully in all matters connected with their departments. When this is not done; they have not the opportunity which they should have, of stating objections; and fancying that they are not confided in they grow unfriendly, jealous, and suspicious—and there is much excuse for their becoming so, for it is a most uncomfortable thing to feel that they are held responsible by the public for measures and arrangements within their department upon the presumption that they must have been consulted, while in truth they may have heard nothing of the matter, and may have had no opportunity of making their wishes or opinions known— Whatever appearance you may have noticed of irregularity or confusion in this respect, you may be assured you will do wisely on every account to avoid it, for human nature in Upper Canada is like human nature every where else—

With regard to myself personally it is fair towards Your Excellency, and but justice to myself that I should leave no room for misapprehension— As Chief Justice I am, like my brother Judges liable to be called on for reports, and opinions and advice in those cases in which recourse would be had in England to the Judges, and in no others— I have no concern in the executive affairs of the Colony, and no claim or wish to be consulted in any of them, except where they have so direct a bearing upon the general administration of justice, as to make such a reference proper— And the more Your Excellency bears this in mind, the better I have no doubt it will be; for it is most desirable in public affairs that every thing should, as much as possible, be made to pass through its proper channel—

I had been 16 or 17 years Attorney General when Sir John Colborne came here, & in that capacity had necessarily & properly been in constant and confidential communication with the Lieutenant Governor— I continued in that office for some months after his arrival, and when I was made Chief Justice, I became (according to the Colonial system of that time,) President of the Executive Council, so that the habit of frequent reference to me was not interrupted. During his administration that system was changed, and I became, as I am now, merely C. Justice, & Speaker of the *Legislative* Council—having in neither capacity any thing to do with the Executive measures of the Government. Still Sir John Colborne did not seem always to bear in mind the distinction; and I was not surprised that he did not; for my long acquaintance with public business gave me of course a good deal of traditionary knowledge, which it was desirable the Government should have the advantage of— Most or all of the original officers of the Government, and members of the Council were off the stage, and I was a sort of a connecting link between the first, and second generations, having long acted with those whose experience was no longer available to the Government—

When Sir Francis Head came, I took an early opportunity of explaining to him the relation in which my office and duties placed me; but he had not had experience in Government, and therefore did not perhaps clearly perceive, nor constantly bear in mind distinctions of this kind which can nevertheless not be safely overlooked— It seemed to me that some one had impressed him, before he came, out, with the idea that it would be prudent for him generally to advise with me when he was in doubt,— In the last few months of his residence here the times were such that it was the plain duty of every one to be useful in all things to the utmost extent, & in the hurry & anxiety of the moment Sir Francis did not consult appearances as much as was desirable; at least I often thought and felt that he did not. In this he was very excusable, but it was nevertheless to be regretted—

I have troubled Your Excellency with this explanation because it may be useful to you, and can hardly be disagreeable; and I will take the liberty of adding that Your Excellency will meet with no difficulty as far as I am personally concerned—I do not affect to be without the common feeling of anxiety that all things may be done for the best in the Country I live in, & therefore, as well as from a feeling & principle of duty any information I possess upon public questions, and my opinions upon points not interfering with the free discharge of my judicial duties are at the service of the Representative of my Sovereign, when he may think proper to desire them—

But my wish is that any assistance of this kind should be sought & rendered in such a manner as shall give the least possible occasion of uneasiness or remark in any quarter.

And I beg Your Excellency to be assured that you need never let the apprehension cross your mind that it is necessary or expedient to refer to me for any other reason than because You wish it, on your own account, or for the public advantage—

I like my own range of duties, and shall always be satisfied in being left to find occupation within it— I desire no responsibility that does not belong to me; and shall take it for granted that Your Excellency will never think it necessary to refer to me, on my own account, except in those cases where it would be reasonably supposed that I must have been consulted, and where consequently I should share the responsibility of any erroneous decision—

I am sure Your Excellency's experience will prevent your misapprehending any thing I have stated, or my object in being thus explicit.

[127] ARTHUR TO THE CHIEF JUSTICE [J. B. ROBINSON]: LB. 1, p. 10-12.

Apr. 17 *Government House, [Toronto.]*

I had the pleasure to receive your letter of the 15th. Inst. although I have read it through two or three times I am not quite satisfied that I fully comprehend the depth and width of your meaning but I am sadly afraid you have misapprehended the observation you remark upon which I made to you, and must without delay express the hope that you did not for a moment imagine that I supposed *your* services had been unnecessarily called into activity in Executive matters. Nothing I do assure you was further from my thoughts, or, indeed, from the conviction of my mind, quite the reverse—!

A few minutes before I had the pleasure to see you a reference had been proposed to me to be made to a person for information who I thought had no more to do with the subject than the Secretary of State; and, it was therefore that I observed upon the strange manner of carrying on the public duty which had frequently attracted my attention. But as we are all too much in the habit of supposing that things cannot be right because they do not happen to fall in with our former habits and experience I have resolved not to be hasty in making any alterations, for it may be that what now seems to me to be crooked may soon appear quite straight.

I must say that I do like to see all the public officers discharging their own peculiar duties, and I think it most for the benefit of the Public

Service and most conductive to good feeling that reference should be made and information derived from its legitimate service—I mean, respectively, from the heads of departments concerned.

With regard to yourself however, from the office you fill, independant of your great experience and extensive information upon every subject connected with the Province—I cannot think there is a sensible person in the Country who would feel jealous or suspicious because you were consulted on any subject the political bearing of which might appear to me of more than ordinary importance to the interests of the Country. Neither the Members of the Executive Council nor Head of any department ought, I am sure, to feel it to be the slightest reflection—and if there be any person so unreasonable as to make it the subject of remark that the Lieutenant Governor was in the habit of confidentially consulting and conferring with the Chief Justice I must say it would give me very little concern.

In the colony I have lately left two near relatives of my own held the highest offices in the Government—they were remarkably able men and both were Members of the Executive and Legislative Councils; but neither they, nor any other Persons in the Colony ever felt hurt, to my knowledge at the well known fact that I seldom took any very important step without previously conferring with the Chief Justice on whose excellent judgment and information I placed the greatest reliance although I might not always follow his advice—

Having said thus much I will only add that if there are any circumstances peculiar to this Province which made it unpleasant to you to be consulted in matters that do not strictly come within the range of your official duties you may be assured—however much I may feel and regret it—that I can practice sufficient self-denial not to press the Matter.—

To say that the perusal of your letter has not given me much concern would be insincere, but I am quite satisfied you cannot intend any personal unkindness—especially at such a moment as the present when the Governor has to contend with more than ordinary difficulties and every assistance is consequently the more highly appreciated.

[128] [ARTHUR TO J. B. ROBINSON]: Df.A.L. 5p.

Apr. 17 *Government House, [Toronto.]*

[A draft copy of item 127 with slight variations. Following the third paragraph in item 127, there is a cancelled passage in this draft which reads: "I would not unnecessarily give uneasiness to any one, and I shall be happy to obtain your assistance if you will favor me with it in any manner which may be most agreeable to yourself—but I do hope you do not mean that it is not to be known that I am in the habit of confidentially conferring with & consulting you."]

[129] ARTHUR TO [A.] E. RYERSON: L.B. 1, p. 13-14.

Apr. 18 *Government House, Toronto.*

I beg to acknowledge your note of the 4th Inst. and to thank you for the publications which accompanied it. In the course of two or three days I hope to peruse the Discourses on Wesleyan Methodism in Upper Canada and Civil Governments—and, also the Documents printed by Order of the House of Assembly relative to the Upper Canada Academy.—

The "Letters" which first appeared in the London Journals, I read with the same respect for the Writer—with the same thankfulness for the information they contained—and with the same conviction of the excellent effect they were calculated to produce in the public mind, or rather I should say upon every unprejudiced mind—which were so generally entertained in England.

Accept my best thanks for your kind congratulations on my arrival, and allow me to hope, that in conjunction with all other Christian Ministers, you will strengthen my hands by inculcating Peace and kindly feeling. Allow me to request you will do me the favor to refer to its true cause my apparent inattention in delaying so long to acknowledge your communication—a very great pressure of business.—

[130] J. B. Robinson to Arthur: A.L.S. 3p.

Apr. 18 *Toronto.*

As my desire in writing to Your Excellency was to relieve you from all occasion for embarrassment so far as I was concerned, I am really sorry that I seem not to have made this as plain as I hoped I had, & that I have consequently rather added to your trouble at a most inconvenient moment— My wish was merely to enable Your Excellency to follow, without the least scruple or constraint your own inclination in availing Yourself of any information I might be supposed capable of affording, or in forbearing to do so.— And I thought I could best do this by assuring Your Excellency (as I did with the utmost sincerity,) that I am not one of those persons whom You need fear to make uncomfortable by adhering most rigidly to whatever You might think the proper course, in the matter of which You spoke to me— As to inclination of my own, I have none but to do all the good in my power, and to be as little as possible the occasion of difficulty to those whom it is my duty to serve with fidelity and zeal— It would give me great pain to think that Your Excellency retained an impression that there was any thing in my letter inconsiderate, or unfriendly—

It was suggested by feelings of the very opposite character— I must acknowledge however as my excuse for troubling You, that I wrote it under a misapprehension in some degree of Your Excellency's sentiments; and I shall take some opportunity, when I have the pleasure of seeing Your Excellency, of convincing You that I was far from intending to create a difficulty or to occasion the least unpleasant feeling.—

[131] [Anonymous]: to Arthur: L.

Apr. 18 *Washington.* [*Postmark: Kingston, Apr. 26.*]

To the Hon Sir George Arthur Lieut Gov &c &c Judge MacAuley Robinson & Others [.] Sirs [,] Since we Left the Upper Province we have had The pleasure of Consulting the Judge of Judges And am Authorised to say to you that the Mosaick Law is the true Law *Life for life Eye for Eye tooth for tooth*[.]

But the gost of uncle Sam sympathiser hung at Kingston says two for One in all cases of Reform[.]

Lount & Mathews[.]

[132] ARTHUR TO THE CHIEF JUSTICE [J. B. ROBINSON]: LB. 1, p. 12-13.

Apr. 19 *Government House, [Toronto.]*

I am much obliged to you for writing to me again, and assure you your letter is quite a relief to me. Although it is very possible to get through a stormy sea without a good Pilot, yet it is a very great comfort as well as satisfaction to have one. There is something very remarkable in my coming Here—it was much against my own inclination, and I would have avoided it if I could—but, being here, I will do my utmost, whilst I remain, to promote the prosperity of the Country and the welfare of the people: and for your unreserved and cordial assistance and zealous cooperation I shall feel very grateful. I do not mean merely on what are considered great matters and state occasions; the deprivation of comfort which many most respectable families who reside in the woods must daily endure until the earth is subdued and the country brought into better state is a subject to invite every one's warmest sympathy and I shall be glad always to be quietly on the watch to find out means for alleviating their condition; I say quietly because I know one must be discreet and very cautious in not appearing to go before or to overlook your great people in Parliament, and I shall always be very thankful for any observations or hints from you that may enable me with the least possible offence to use to the greatest advantage the little power that constitutionally [blank in MS.; item 133, here reads: "remains"] with the Governor.

[133] [ARTHUR TO J. B. ROBINSON]: D.A.L.

Apr. 19 *Government House.*

[A draft copy of item 132 with slight variations.]

[134] C. A. HAGERMAN TO THE LIEUTENANT GOVERNOR [ARTHUR]: A.L.S. 3p.

Apr. 19 *Toronto.*

I this morning transmitted to your Excellency my official Report in the case of Theller, and have—in it,—extended my observations to some points not strictly bearing upon the legality of his conviction—indeed with respects to that question there could be no necessity for saying much;—the Law being too plain to admit of the slightest controversy.—

The embarrassment created in your Excellencys mind arising from the necessity of considering the Policy of allowing the Sentence passed upon the Prisoner to be carried into effect, I am well aware must be very great—especially after receiving the Reports of the Chief Justice and the Executive Council:— With respect to myself it may be proper that I should explicitly state, that in my opinion *Law* and *Justice* require that Theller should be executed;—of the *Policy* of the Measure, it is not my province to offer any opinion beyond what my official Report contains—indeed it is a question that rests altogether with your Excellency and the Executive Council, and will probably be decided upon a consideration of what is most likely to be the view of the Home Government.— I cannot imagine however that, looking to the unprovoked aggressions that have been made upon us by Citizens of the United States for the last four months, Her Majesty will consider it right that persons standing in the situation of the Prisoner, should escape such punishment as may most effectually guard the people of the Province from a repetition of the lawless outrages of which he has been so clearly proved guilty. . .

P.S.— It cannot be necessary I imagine to require the Judges to give an opinion upon the Law of Thellers case—but your Excellency will find them probably as safe advisers as any you can select on the question of the *Policy* of his execution.—

[135] J. R. WRIGHT TO [SIR] C. [S.] GORE: A.L.S. 2p.

Apr. 19 *Royal Engineers Office, Quebec.*

As it appears from The Reports that I have lately received from The Western District Upper Canada, that a considerable expenditure has been incurred and is still going on in putting the Old Fort at Toronto and the old work at Mississagua Point, Niagara, in a state of Defence; I beg leave to suggest for the consideration of His Excellency The Commander of The Forces, that as the excitement which caused The Officer Commanding The Troops in Upper Canada to authorise the execution of those services has at present subsided, and the Works are of that nature to be unworthy of much expense being bestowed on them; whether it would not be adviseable that the further progress on them should be suspended, until an Estimate can be prepared for His Excellencys information; shewing the expense already incurred and the further expense that will be required to complete the services contemplated to be performed under the authority given by The Officer Commanding: in order that the whole expense to be incurred may be brought under His Excellency's consideration; As I am apprehensive that it may be found to be greater than he would consider adviseable to expend upon Works so constructed & capable of so little resistance[.]

Should this suggestion meet His Excellencys approbation it will be necessary that instructions to that effect should be given to The Officer Commanding in Upper Canada, and that Major Bonnycastle should be directed to prepare the necessary Estimates. . .

P.S. It appears that the sum of £1747 has been already expended on The old Fort at Toronto—I have not yet received any report of the expense incurred at Fort Mississagua—

[The above is probably the enclosure referred to in item 140.]

[136] PATRICK GALLAHER: D.S. 2p.

Apr. 19 *Toronto.*

Upper Canada The Queen v Edward Alexander Theller	Patrick Gallaher of the City of Toronto in the Home District

Gentleman maketh oath and saith that He this deponent was at the the City of Detroit in the State of Michigan one of the United States of America in the Autum[n] of one thousand eight hundred and thirty six that during his stay there he became acquainted with the above named Edward Alexander Theller, that at the time deponent was in Detroit as aforesaid an Election was holden for President of the United States, as well as for various State officers, that during the canvassing and election this deponent observed the said Edward Alexander Theller to be an active partisan, that he has every reason to believe that the said Theller was upon that occasion put in nomination for one of the offices then to be filled by election, as this deponent upon various occasions saw electors place the name of the said Edward Alexander Theller upon their ballot tickets— And this deponent further saith that from all he heard and saw during the stay of this deponent at the said City of Detroit he has every reason to believe that the said Edward Alexander Theller was deemed and taken to be, and to this deponents knowledge was received and accepted as a bonafide Citizen of the United States—

Sworn before me at Toronto this 19th day of April 1838. W. H. Coswell A Commr. in the Kings Bench Home District	Patrick Gallaher

[137] C. A. Hagerman to The Lieut. Governor [Arthur]: A.L.S.

Apr. 23 [*Place not stated.*]

The accompanying letter being on a very interesting subject I take the liberty of sending to your Excellency.—

I do not pretend to much knowledge of matters of finance but Mr MacAulay—(The Surveyor General,)—is a gentleman of much intelligence, and in whose opinions on subjects connected with Revenue former Governors reposed a good deal of confidence.—

[*Enclosure:*]

[138] *1838*
Apr. 21

Jno Macaulay to C. A. Hagerman: A.L.S. 10p.

Toronto.

I am confounded by the information I got a few days ago at Mr. Dunn's office, that the deficiency in the revenue of the current year will be swelled from £7000 as estimated by the Inspector General to upwards of £20,000—. We are indeed overtaken by the evils which I was sure would one day follow the incautious and uncalculating, I might almost say the reckless legislation of recent Parliaments, and especially of the present Parliament, much sooner than anyone could have anticipated— The first dip was clearly the rush vote of £350,000 for the St. Lawrence before any attempt had been made to ensure the cooperation of the Lower Province— This has entailed on us an expenditure of nearly £400,000 to improve the River at *one point* only, & an unavoidable permanent burthen of £24,000 of annual interest on a work which may never become productive—it being now admitted by the early enemies of the Rideau Canal that by that channel, the trade of the Province may pass with all needful convenience for the next half century— We no more required the work on the St. Lawrence for Upper Canadian trade, than your Coach requires a fifth wheel—(whatever may have been our once pleasing anticipations of alluring external trade to our waters), and the result therefore of the *unholy alliance* of the East & West, by which the War loss question was carried in connection with Saint Lawrence improvement is most disastrous. It was as I have said our first *dip*. By the legislation, the excessive and extravagant legislation of 1837, we made our great plunge into a sea of financial troubles— Being thus situated, however, our great consideration is how are we to get out, or how shall we provide ourselves with bladders or cork jackets so as to keep afloat— I am sure Sir George Arthur must have been amazed on his arrival here to discover the vast embarrassments with which he has to contend[.] I positively believe that he could have been appointed to no Government under the Crown more arduous than ours, but whatever may be His Excellency's opinions on the subject, it is some consolation for all the loyal people, that an officer of His Experience and, as we may infer from what he has already done, his tact and judgment in political affairs has been sent out at the present critical juncture to help the Province out of its difficulties. The question which presses with me is, what is to be done? How is the revenue to be raised to the expenditure, or the expenditure reduced to the level of the probably reduced revenue? One or the other object must be accomplished— Our state waggon is in the mud, & we are not sure that Hercules, alias John Bull, will come to our aid. Under any circumstances we are at any rate bound to put our shoulders to the wheel, resolutely, & at the same time appeal to generous John, & he may come to our relief.

It has occured to me in my dreams of last night, that relief may be had in three ways.

1st— I hope that we may depend on obtaining our proportion of the surplus Post office Revenue, as prayed for by the Legislature— There is no just ground for withholding it, and at our present moment of necessity, do you not think it would be advisable for Sir George, to urge the Home Government to a decision on the question— This would give us about £5000 a year—& would pay the interest on £100,000, borrowed in London to redeem some of the present debentures.

2nd— The Penitentiary continues a downright burthen on the Province revenue. This ought no longer to be suffered. The present year's appropriation is £5000. I would like to see the whole burthen taken off the Receiver General's chest, and thrown upon the District Treasuries. *Direct taxation* for the benefit of the *Provincial chest*, is an undertaking you will scarcely venture to recommend to the Lieutenant Governor, for whether it be called *ignorant* or not, there is here as in other countries a generally diffused "impatience of taxation" which we cannot venture to rouse by a direct tax, without ensuring the growth of discontent and disaffection[.]

The people, however, are accustomed to be assessed for local purposes, and therefore I conceive that they would not murmur if they were assessed for the support of the Convicts in the Penitentiary, either to the extent of the number sent from their respective Districts, or (as I think more equitably) to the extent of the whole number sent from the Districts in the Mass.

They know that formerly the burthen of their support fell on the several Districts, while the Convicts were confined in the respective Gaols—and cannot deny that there is some reason in their Districts funds being charged with their support while in the Penitentiary— It may indeed be objected that as the Sentences to the Penitentiary direct confinement for a longer term than was customary under the old system, the hardship is greater as respects the tax on the Districts but against this may be set off the chance of reform among the convicts, and the discouragement of crime afforded by the new system which benefits, so far as they may be realized, are a direct, and general public relief. It appears to me that you might devise for adoption at the ensuing session, a measure on this subject that would entirely relieve the Provincial chest from this burthen— And even if thrown upon the Districts, it cannot be long necessary that they should bear it. If the Justitutem is managed with due œconomy and judgment (of which by the way I am not over confident) it ought, as soon as the convicts double their present numbers to become a source of revenue, instead of a cause of expence— On this subject, I believe however, that your doctrines are somewhat *heretical* [.] If however you agree that it is practicable to tax the people by means of a District Assessment for the maintenance of the *Rogues' college* then, here is a relief for Mr Dunn's strong box to the annual extent of 4 or £5000—

3rd Now for my grand project— I have already said that (I fear *for ever*) we have to pay £24,000 per annum for the interest on the capital sunk in the Long Sau[l]t. That capital has been so sunk in an enterprise of equal promise as respects the commercial interests of both the Canadian Provinces—and it surely follows that, under all the circumstances, both should bear the burden— As the Constitution of Lower Canada has been suspended, our Parliament cannot negociate on the subject with the Lower Canada Parliament, & indeed during the virtual anarchy which has for years past reigned in that Colony negotiation must have been fruitless. But though Jean Baptiste cannot meet us through his favourite *Chambre*, and in no case, owing to his anti-commercial feelings, would be disposed to co-operate with us in the completion of the Saint Lawrence Canal from Lake Ontario to Lake Saint Peter, there is still a hope for us, since an eminent British Peer comes out to rule, with great powers, and in fact will be the Arbiter of our political destiny. Why should not an appeal be instantly made to that nobleman by the Government of this Province? Why should he not be informed of the efforts made by Upper Canada to overcome the impediments in the St Lawrence by a work of equal if not greater benefit to Lower Canada, and of the financial embarrassments to which in its prosecution, from causes which could not all be foreseen, we are now subjected? Would he not sympathise with the truly British spirit in which we embarked in our career of navigable improvement, & be induced to do whatever he might consider practicable to obtain relief for us? Now the relief I think we should suggest would be simply this—to provide a fund to pay the interest of the Saint Lawrence Debentures. This fund cannot be created here by ourselves in Canada, even if Lower Canada wished it, for the legislature of that Province exists not, or rather is dormant—and in the meanwhile our necessities are pressing— How then is the fund to be created? By an act of the British Parliament—grounded on its pure and plain necessity, & passed, if you please, for two years only, or until repealed by the Legislature of Lower Canada— It appears to me that the least oppressive impost would be an addition of 2½ per cent ad-valorem on the imported merchandise, which (unless the importing Merchants of Montreal could suggest something better) would yield more than the required sum by a few thousands—but there would be no harm in that. This fund should be specially raised & applied to the payment of the interest on the St Lawrence-canal-Debentures and to no other purpose whatever—and be considered as a fund expended on an object of common benefit to both Provinces— Now I cannot but think if this matter were ably urged upon the attention of Lord Durham by yourself & the Inspector General, he would consent to recommend the measure & that it might be adopted before the prorogation of the Imperial Parliament. And what a relief it would be!

This is the sum and substance of my last night's dreams—, which I give you currente calamo, while the subject is on my mind—& it is would be [*sic*] well if on a suitable occasion, you gave your own views of it to the Lieutenant Governor[.]

It is everyone's duty, so far as their ability may serve, to offer their suggestions in a moment of difficulty "ne quid detrimente respublica capiat"— I cannot imagine by what other means than I have adverted to, we can escape ultimate public insolvency—unless perhaps we fly to a remedy which may be even more disastrous. . .

[P.S.] In addition to any other retrenchments, or œconomical arrangements, I really wish we could adopt the suggestion made in a late Ministerial Pamphlet, in respect to the British Parliament. viz that we could put our Legislature *to sleep* for two or three years. The saving in money would be great, as well as in needless legislation. The propensity of the age is to *excessive law-making*.

[139] ARTHUR TO COLBORNE: LB. 1, p. 15-20.

Apr. 25 *Toronto.* [Marked "Private".]

When I addressed you officially on Monday last respecting the clamorous claimants for Payment for "Goods delivered and services performed"—I intended at the same time to have sent you a short explanatory private letter—but it was not in my power to do so as I was kept in the Council during the whole of two days upon the capital cases—

Allow me to assure you that nothing but the state of the Province, and the unceasing dunning of the Public Creditors—their increasing personal difficulties and consequent dissatisfaction could have led me to add to your responsibility on money matters.

As you were so good as to mention in your letter of the 24th ultimo, that you would empower me to issue Warrants[,] in the expectation of receiving that authority I put off the complaining parties from day to day until their increasing importunity and dissatisfaction obliged me to appeal to you in their behalf.

I think it highly possible, indeed, I am well convinced that much more expence was incurred than was necessary, and that there has been fraud and advantage taken of the public necessities—but still it is hard that the consequences should fall upon the Persons who furnished supplies or undertook to execute work or volunteered to serve upon certain conditions distinctly authorized by Sir Francis Head or Colonel Foster.

Although I have felt that the cases of the parties were really hard, I must honestly own that I urged the matter more upon your attention from apprehending that their services might be again called into action at no distant period. The Persons who have left this Province since December last are very numerous, and they have put themselves in connection with a large unprincipled class of Americans on the Frontier Towns, and have indicated more and more the intention of giving us further trouble.

My Predecessor before my arrival had deputed two or three Persons to obtain information in the States— All their accounts concur in stating that large quantities of arms and ammunition have been for some time collecting, and that a very considerable supply have been sent across the Lake and deposited in the Western District where the disaffected are very numerous.

These accounts have been strongly confirmed within the last two or three days from other Quarters.—

Colonel Salmon, whose testimony I am informed may be depended upon has hastened from Port Talbot in order to assure me that he is convinced from a variety of circumstances that another outbreak is intended in the Western District, and that the Reformers will be joined by a far more numerous force from the opposite shore than have yet taken part with the Patriots.—

An affidavit has been forwarded by Colonel Ratcliffe [*sic*] from the Gore District, where he commands made by a man of excellent reputation in which He states that a considerable force was moving from the London District towards Hamilton—that He had been in Company with some of the People who were well armed, and had ascertained that a formidable renewal of hostility against the Government was meditated.

Colonel Kirby who commands on the Niagara Frontier writes, that the communication which has been kept up between Queenston and Lewiston, and the Meetings which are constantly held at the latter place, together, with the information he has received of their proceedings convince him that some plan of operations is in Progress.

Last night a letter was laid before me from a highly respectable Person in Niagara in which He sketches out what the Plan of Operations is to be—namely, to cross in many small parties &c. I enclose you copy of his letter, and although I make no doubt matters are highly exaggerated, yet, it is remarkable, that most of the circumstances stated are corroborated by a Person who has for some time been in the secret service of this Colony—and by a respectable Female who keeps a boarding House at Buffalo—and who, having near Relatives in this Province has thought it worth while to bring the information of the Preparations which are in the progress, and which she has communicated to the Chief Justice to whom she is well known—

It is under these circumstances that I am more than ordinarily anxious that the monies which are justly due, and can be shewn to have been incurred under authority should be forthwith paid. We are, as it is, daily making our best friends our worst enemies!

In the letter which I had the pleasure to write to you on the 5th. Inst., I mentioned that I propose reducing some of our Militia force, provided, you did not think it necessary to retain it with reference to the State of the Lower Province.

The Men of some of the Companies which had not been called out for any fixed period, and were anxious to return home, were permitted to do so—but I paused in making any further reduction until I should have the pleasure to hear from you.

In the present state of things, of course, further reduction must be suspended, and, indeed I am very anxious for some additional regular Force in the Province. It would do much to quiet the Public mind; and a Regiment of the Line stationed on the Niagara Frontier would perhaps, tend to put an end to the intention of invasion at present, and, hereafter, I shall less regard it as I confidently hope to restore a better feeling in the Province. On the Niagara Frontier I am aware that desertion is always to be guarded against; but, under the late regulations, I should hope it need not be much apprehended in a Corps of high Character.

The Executive Council, the Chief Justice and Mr Justice Jones who were all in Sir Francis Head's confidence are now quite convinced that the disaffected feeling is far wider and deeper than my Predecessor supposed but of course it must be our policy in all our public transactions to regard the community as a Body of the most loyal subjects and to that very effect I am just going to issue a Proclamation.

It would be impossible to give you any just conception of the state of feeling here[;] for many years it was smothered, but the animosity now existing between Loyalists and Reformers is quite shocking.

What a stange mission Mr Vail has been sent upon[;] it is a very plain declaration of the sympathy of the Government of the United States;— The President is playing a deep game and I am surprised Mr Fox acceded to the Mission but as he did I have of course given Mr Vail a courteous reception.

Pray do not be offended at my suggesting whether the instructions under which the Officers from England who have been sent into this Province are acting are calculated to make their services work to the greatest advantage which I am very certain is your object.

For your immediate reference I enclose Copy of the Instructions which Major Anstruther presented to me yesterday.

Information may be obtained of the feeling of the people through other channels far more easily than by any stranger and especially that stranger a Military Officer. Without interfering with his Orders I have recommended by a letter from the Military Secretary to put himself in communication with the Commanding Officers of the Militia and to afford them all the advice and assistance in his power and at the same time I have communicated to them my hope that they will receive it as intended for the good of the Public Service. Experienced Military Officers if their services are not forced will I think be generally well received and if so the advantage will be great indeed.

I have not the pleasure of knowing Colonel Chichester, but if you could spare him for this Province I think he would from his character be a valuable acquisition in looking after our Militia.

Colonel Foster appears to have had a good deal of extra work without receiving any extra Pay, I do not know whether you consider him entitled to any extra allowance.

[Enclosures lacking.]

[140] T. L. GOLDIE TO ARTHUR: L.S.

Apr. 25 *Head Quarters, Montreal.*

I have the honor by the direction of the Commander of the Forces, to transmit to your Excellency, a copy of a communication from the Commanding Royal Engineer, in the Canadas, [marginal note here reads: "Quebec 19 April 1838"] on the subject of the great expence incurred, in repairing the Works in the Upper Province.

[Enclosure is probably item 135.]

[141] [SIR] J[OHN] GARDINER TO ARTHUR: A.L.S. 4p.

Apr. 25 *Horse Guards, [London.]* [Marked "Private".]

I was in great hopes of getting a line from you, on your landing at New York—my present object is merely to send you the enclosures, and if the Individuals they relate to, should come in your way I do hope and trust, that, you will give them the benefit of your countenance and protection— I am not further aware of their views, than, what is to be collected from the enclosures— Lt. Colonel Farquharson, who was always considered an active and intelligent officer, you may find useful. Mr. Welby, I am not personally known to, but his parents Sir W. and Lady Welby are neighbours of ours, and I really should be glad, if circumstances should admit, and the opportunity at any time offer, that, you will allow him to calculate upon your kind consideration of him — I have another request, which is to make known to you, if they should happen to come your way, Captain and Mrs. Daniell of the Coldstream Guards — His father, Col: Daniell, formerly of the Company's Service, is an old friend of mine, you may recollect his brother in the 49th. in Jersey—I do not see how the *Captain* is likely to get into your Govt, but in making the introduction I only fulfil the father's wishes—

I need scarcely say how gratified I shall be to hear from you and to learn, that, you do not find difficulties beyond what you contemplated— I will, when you are more at leisure give you some little history in regard to myself of occurrences [?] since we parted.

[Enclosure concerning Farquharson lacking.]

[*Enclosure:*]

[142] [*1838*]
[*c. Apr. 25*]

WILHELMINA WELBY TO LIEUTT. GENL. [*i.e.* MAJOR GENERAL SIR JOHN] GARDINER: A.L.S.

8, Belgrave Street, [London.]

[Asks that her son who "is extremely zealous in the loyal cause & ready at any time to volunteer any service he can render to it—" may be commended to Arthur. Refers to a letter to her son to be forwarded by Gardiner via Arthur.]

[143] HEAD TO LADY ARTHUR: A.L. 2p.

Apr. 25 *62 Park St., Grosvr. [Square, London.]*

Sir Francis Head has the pleasure of enclosing to Lady Arthur a letter which was entrusted t him by Sir George Arthur on the 23d of last month.

Sir F: Head takes this opportunity of assuring Lady Arthur that as nothing would afford him greater pleasure than to have it in his power t afford Lady Arthur any assistance or information, he hopes that her Ladyship will not hesitate to apply t him for either. and in case Lady Arthur should require any information respecting Toronto from Lady Head, Sir F: begs to say that a letter addressed t Lady Head 62 Park St. Grosvr. Square will be forwarded without delay—

Sir F: Head was happy to see Sir George Arthur and his Son in good health and spirits after their fatiguing journey.

[144] [ANONYMOUS]: TO ARTHUR: A.L.

[*1838*] [*Postmark: Toronto, Apr. 26, 1838.*]

[*Apr. 26*]

Revenge Revenge I Say
Bee gon Bee gon I Say
Or I Will Putt you in that
Place Whare you Will never return
you shall die a villains deth you
are marked out for mark that Shall
Bee onerd by a Pill Whitch Shall make
Hole in your body

I am
Sir
Your
Most Obedient
Friend[.]

[145] GLENELG TO ARTHUR: L.S. 2p.

Apr. 27 *London.*

I received your private letter of the 9th March from New York, announcing your long & distressing voyage, your arrival at that city, & the hospitable reception which awaited you there. I am much obliged to you for this unofficial communication. I have no doubt you judged rightly in not visiting Washington, altho' if your leisure had permitted you to enter into personal communication with the Chief Authorities of the United States, it would probably have promoted the future success of your administration. I shall at all times be happy to receive information of your proceedings & of your personal welfare, in the form of private letters, when you have leisure & the disposition to communicate with me in that manner.—

[146] COLBORNE TO ARTHUR: L.S. 6p.

Apr. 29 *Head Quarters, Montreal.*

In expectation of the arrival of the Commissary General I have delayed writing to Your Excellency upon the subject of the unsettled claims in Upper Canada, and the arrangements that it may be necessary to sanction for their immediate adjustment.

In reply to Your Excellency's letter of the 23rd inst which I received yesterday respecting these claims, and the causes which occasioned them, I have the honor to acquaint you that I think it appears obvious, that the whole of the charges for Pay and allowances authorized by Sir Francis Head, and the debts contracted by certain Officers, and Magistrates, in consequence of the sudden movements of the Militia and Volunteer Corps to the Niagara Frontier, and in the Southern and Western Districts, must be sanctioned however unreasonable and profuse the expenditure may have been; but, the Commissary General would certainly have neglected his duty, had he not called my attention to the irregularities he observed, and endeavoured to check the uncontrolled disbursements—

The Officers of his Department report that they have been requested to settle accounts to the amount of £50,000 in the Western District, and that in many instances no satisfactory vouchers can be produced by the irresponsible agents who demand payment for the expenses incurred— I have no doubt that it has become necessary to satisfy most of these demands under existing circumstances, and that many persons have just reason to complain of the delay which has taken place in settling their accounts—

I am persuaded however Your Excellency will concur with me, with reference to the shameful profusion that Colonel Maitland deemed it his duty to check, on his arrival in the Western District, and to the strong representations of the Commissary General respecting the constant and increasing expenditure, in several Districts, that I could not permit warrants to be issued without enquiry and adopting such means as would justify me in sanctioning the payments in question to be made from the Military Chest.

The Commissary General arrived in Montreal this morning, and I hope to be able to direct arrangements to be carried into effect with a view of settling, without further delay, the outstanding claims referred to in your letter[.]

[147] R. R. Davies: [recipient not stated]: A.L.S.

Apr. 30 *Longford.*

[Expresses thanks for interest taken in Mr. Sullivan, the eldest of eleven children, whose father was formerly a major in the 85th regiment. "I sincerely congratulate you on Sir G. Arthur's appointments— Such an appointment at such a time only proves how high his services are estimated at Downing Street—"]

[148] J. B. Robinson to [Arthur]: A.L.S.

[*1838*] *[Place not stated.]*

[*May ?*] I take it for granted that the Proclamation[1] which you spoke to me about is not intended to be issued until after the actual completion of your arrangements respecting the prisoners— I mean till the Cases are all determined upon & the gaols free, except of those whose cases are necessarily referred to England[.]

[1]Possibly the proclamation dated May 14, 1838 (*Upper Canada Gazette*, May 15, May 17, 1838.)

[149] R. B. SULLIVAN TO THE LIEUT GOVERNOR [ARTHUR]: A.L.S. 5p.

[*1838*] *Council Office, [Toronto.]*
[*May ?*] The Surveyor General showed me just now the accompanying letter which places the embarrassing question of the Saint Lawrence Canal in a still more perplexing position than ever inasmuch as it exposes in more detail the disadvantages of discontinuing the work.

The Canal is a very short one and only surmounts when finished some of the difficulties of the navigation. both above and below[;] expenditure to an enormous amount would be necessary to make this section available and even when a million of money would be spent in perfecting the line of Canal upon the Saint Lawrence we shall have merely established a rival canal to the Rideau[.]

On the other hand it will be most humiliating and perhaps destructive to the Provincial Credit if the works commenced are permitted to remain and go to ruin and to continue a perpetual monument of Legislative folly & extravagance.

Your Excellency will perceive that the Commissioners of the Canal are prepared to pursue a course which has already been taken by them and other Commissioners of Public works in this Province namely the raising money, or rather paying debts in their own debentures in the expectation of these being saved harmless by the House of Assembly. This seems to me to be most decidedly objectionable on many grounds and I am sure the assuming such a power will when the matter is explained at home meet with severe censure on the part of the Government. No men in England possess such a discretion as is here assumed by the Commissioners, & I fear that the Local Government which would permit such a course will not be held blameless.

Possibly Your Excellency may think it right to extend your Eastern journey as far as the Canal. much may be learned on the subject by personal inspection, and perhaps much further regret and embarrassment may be spared by the devoting a few days to the object.

[Enclosure lacking.]

[150] R. B. SULLIVAN TO THE LIEUT GOVERNOR [ARTHUR]: A.L.S. 2p.

[*1838*] *Council Chamber, [Toronto.]*
[*May ?*] I have called at the Atty Genls office to enquire into the state of the Kingston special Commission. he was not within but Mr. Strachan shewed me a letter which stated that the proceedings before the Special Commission were still going on.

Mr Cartwright puts the question to the Attorney General What is to be done with the Prisoners taken at Hickory Island?

As regards the Prisoners charged with High Treason it will perhaps be impossible to proceed satisfactorily until the Special Commission shall have risen. With respect to the Hickory Island prisoners If the Attorney General were to attend the Council tomorrow an order may be made disposing of them[.]

[151] R. I. ROUTH TO T. L. GOLDIE: L. 5p.

May 1 *Commissariat Canada, Montreal.* [Marked "Copy."]
I have the honor to bring the subject of the Commissariat Board of Claims under the further consideration of His Excellency the Commander of the Forces.

Depy Asst Comy Genl Thos. Wilson has laid before me, a variety of accounts which have been submitted to the Board from Sandwich and Amherstburgh, & upon these I am desirous of determining the principle, & course, by which these claims shall be collected and paid.

In the first place it is important to ascertain the Amount, in order to be prepared with the necessary funds.

To effect this, I wish the Board to proceed to Chatham, and London, and to remain there a few days, sufficient to afford to all, an opportunity of presenting their demands, and from thence to return to Toronto by way of Hamilton, so as to collect the Claims at that village, and its vicinity.— I propose, that at Toronto, these accounts should be classed into abstracts for each Post, and as they are Completed to be submitted to the Major General Commanding for his approval, & forwarded forthwith to the different Commissariat Posts for payment.

A Triplicate Abstract, of the sums so paid, will be sent to your office, for the Covering Warrant of the Commander of the Forces.

I propose to give power to the Board, if any errors or gross overcharges should be discovered in these claims to disallow them; leaving the parties to seek their own redress from the proper authorities, and to shew this, I shall cause two columns to be ruled in each abstract, exhibiting the sum claimed, and that paid[.]

There are large quantities of Provisions on the Amherstburgh Frontier, perhaps, of the Value of Three Thousand Pounds remaining on hand, which will require to be looked after, & deposited in safe Custody.—

This will be the particular duty of Asst Comy Genl Leggatt.

The Board will also direct their attention to the Imprests made to Mr. Anderton, and others under the Warrant of Colonel Foster, for which only a very partial account for a proportion of the sum has yet been rendered.

The Imprest to Mr Anderton alone, amounts to nearly £10,000 Currency.

His Excellency is of course aware that scarcely any of these accounts would be payable in the ordinary business of the Army, or, of this Department, and that the only principle, upon which this payment is now made, is to redeem the good faith of Her Majestys Government, which has been pledged under the Authority of His Excellency Sir Francis Head.

I therefore cannot propose to the Comr of the Forces to be responsible for this expenditure, and still less can I presume to undertake, that responsibility in my own person; but I apply to him for his Concurrence and authority, to relieve the Military Service from an embarrassment in which it has been involved, neither by His Excellencys acts nor mine, but by events which have been irresistible, and, which have controlled and borne down all the checks & regulations established by experience and good order.

I know that there is an outcry in the Upper Province that these accounts have not yet been paid, but Government, like an Individual, require time to examine a demand, & to collect its means of payment, & where many duties are to be performed by a small department, some must be the first and some last.— I shall be always ready on my part with the evidence, that no unnecessary time has been lost in any of these important avocations.

In the present advanced state of these transactions, I have reason to hope, that the larger proportion of them, will be settled in all the Month of May, & I shall place at the disposal of the Board a sum of Fifty Thousand Pounds Army Sterling for the despatch of this Service[.]

[The above is probably the enclosure referred to in item 154.]

[152] T. W. MAGRATH: [RECIPIENT NOT STATED]: A.L.S.

[*1838*] *May 1*

Brantford.

I send you a copy of my report to Colonel Maitland it will tell you the whole news of the neighbourhood. if you think his Excellency would think it worth reading you can give it to him. I have not been able yet to see a pair of horses that would answer[,] they are all too small, there is a very nice full dress cavalry bridle here for sale. I think it would suit his Excellency if he has not brought out one with him it was made in England & is quite new. the storekeeper that has it asks £2..10.. for it without a bit, it is real[l]y one of the nicest I have seen in the country, we have hard work of it here.

[Enclosure is probably item 153.]

[153] T. W. MAGRATH TO J[OHN] MAITLAND: A.L.S. 4p.

May 1

Brantford. [Marked "(Copy)".]

According to instructions received (verbally) from His Excellency The Lieut. Governor, I left this with twenty men and proceeded to Port Dover on the 29th. Inst. [*i.e.* ultimo], leaving two officers & thirty five men here ready to march if your orders arrived before my return.

At every tavern we halted we found the people extremely insolent and abusive, and it was with the greatest difficulty I prevented my men resenting it however I am happy to say no row occurred;

Numbers of persons met us at the different cross roads, and made use of the following expressions repeatedly. *we are getting ready for you:* our friends have only left this to *shew others the way here:* if *one* of *you* stay behind we will treat *him* as *you did Lount & Mathews:*

On my arrival in Simcoe I found the Company of your Regt: commanded by Capt: Markham there, several persons to whom I spoke in the village said we are *rebels* and *will* be *again* but what can any of you make of it.

From thence I marched to Pt: Dover 10 Miles. Capt: Markham came with me, on our arrival there we found the steam boat still aground, but 25 miles from the Port, not close to it, as had been represented by some of the Inhabitants at Toronto.

With very few exceptions they are all rebels there and I am confidant [*sic*] only wait for an opportunity to begin a row, in speaking to a fellow of the name of Herries, he said that did *their friends* come to Port Dover the red coats would not be a bit a piece for them as there were 1000 men between Scotland, Oakland, & there ready to turn out[.]

The Magistrates in general seem not to make that exertion that they ought, and I think a Magistrate ought to be sent there that would act. they all have property in the neighbourhood. & are evidently *afraid* of *those fellows,* I think it would be as well, as was done in Ireland repeatedly, to make all the officers in command Magistrates of the District in which they are stationed. I am confidant Capt: Markham would make an excellent one.

There is a guard of Twenty Men at Port Dover but they might just as well be in Toronto, they all go to bed at night and told me themselves if a landing was attempted they would run away as there would be no use in so few of them attempting to prevent it. There is not even a guard over an immense quantity of Arms placed in a room in a Tavern there. the same is the case at Brantford where they are only protected by a Pad lock, at Port Dover the room in which the arms are, opens into the street and there is nothing to prevent them being taken away in open day light by any one that wishes[;] the door was not even locked the night I slept there, I mentioned this to Capt: Markham who said he would have them taken care of.

I have placed a Sergt: Corpl: & three men under Capt: Markham's command at Simcoe, two men at Pt: Dover two at the village of Waterford, & two at Lowries Tavern, Oakland, which forms a line of communication between this and Port Dover 32 miles——

In consequence of their steam boats coming up to try to get the boat on shore off I halted a day at Pt Dover, they went away and said they would return with four to day.

Fearing that your order for me would arrive in my absence, I returned to-day and found on my return the people much more Insolent and abusive than before, one of my men whose horse got lamed I sent on before me and within a few miles of Brantford whilst leading his horse was attacked by four men and but for the assistance of some traveller who came up just at the time would in all probability be treated as they threatened, he knocked one of them down just as assistance came up and the fellows took to the woods[.] I will send you his deposition on oath if I can have it taken before the mail goes out if not by next Post.

If it was not taking a liberty I would beg leave to suggest that four of my men were stationed at Port Dover, four at the furnace, four at Ryersons Landing, a dispatch line from Simcoe to London and the remainder at Simcoe[;] this would prevent desertion at any of the Posts & in the event of any intention to land, communication could at once be sent to London & Simcoe.

I am not an alarmist nor do I think the fellows will attempt a landing, but did they do so, they have plenty of fellows from this part of the country with them and would be joined by hundreds on their arrival here which perhaps would only be for the purpose of burning the property of those who are obnoxious to them[.]

[The above is probably the enclosure referred to in item 152.]

[154] T. L. Goldie to Arthur: A.L.S. 2p.

May 2 *Head Quarters, Montreal.*

I have the honor by direction of the Commander of the Forces to transmit to Your Excellency the accompanying Copy of a Communication from the Commissary General relative to the settlement of the claims in Upper Canada, and to acquaint you that the arrangements proposed by the Commissary General for liquidating these claims have met with Sir John Colbornes approval and which he hopes will be satisfactory to Your Excellency[.]

[Enclosure is probably item 151.]

[155] J. B. Robinson to [Arthur]: A.L.S.

[*1838*] [*Place not stated.*]

[*c. May 3*] I send Your Excellency a Copy of my letter to Lord Glenelg, to which His Lordship alludes in his dispatch of 14 March—

[*Enclosure:*]

[156] *1838*

Feb. 6

[J. B. Robinson] to Glenelg: A.L. 2p.

Toronto. [Marked "Copy."]

I have been made aware that His Excellency Sir Francis Head, in a letter which he has lately written to Your Lordship, has been pleased to express himself favorably in regard to me, and to offer a suggestion which Your Lordship will probably bear in mind without my adverting to it more particularly—[1]

I can not but feel very grateful to Sir Francis Head for speaking kindly of my exertions in the discharge of my duty, since they have seemed to him to deserve it; but I hope the notice will not be taken of them which he has done me the honor to recommend— A distinction of that kind has never been coveted by me. If it had been usual here, as in the Eastern, and I believe the Southern Colonies, to confer it upon Judges generally, or upon the Chief Justice, I should not object, but it has not been, and I have no desire to form an exception, particularly as I can not but feel that my brother Chief Justice in Lower Canada, who is much my senior in office, is at least as worthy of it——

But of course I need not trouble Your Lordship with reasons; I beg rather to be excused for addressing Your Lordship on a subject so personal, and unimportant, and when it is probable I might with perfect safety have foreborne to do so—

[157] J. B. Robinson to [Arthur]: A.L.S. 3p.

May 3 *Toronto.*

I must beg You to believe that I am very thankful to Your Excellency for the terms in which You have been pleased to express Yourself in the *official* published in this day's gazette. It need hardly be said that this public declaration of Your Excellency is most gratifying; and it may some day or other be useful, if the chances of war or rebellion, or any other confusion should impel me to ask a favor.

I hope I have not appeared ungracious in not having adverted to that part of a note received from Your Excellency the other day in which you were so good as to allude to the same subject.— It is a subject not very easy for me to write or talk upon, and that must be my excuse— The truth is that I might have given other reasons to Lord Glenelg which weighed as much with me as those I did assign; but they were of a domestic nature, and I did not feel it to be necessary to trouble His Lordship with them— When I found that Mrs. Robinson's sentiments agreed entirely with my own I had no hesitation in declining— I considered that besides ourselves, our children only had any particular interest in the matter, and taking the liberty of judging for them I concluded that they were more likely to be injured than benefitted [*sic*] by it—

[1] *i.e.* the recommendation for a knighthood, along with A. N. MacNab.

[158] JOHN STRACHAN TO ARTHUR: A.L.S. 5p.

May 4 *Toronto.*

Allow me to leave with your Excellency a Memorandum of the communication, which I had the honor to make verbally last tuesday, in the hope, that after giving it due consideration your Excellency will take a Friendly interest in my favour, and promote the object I desire, if found to be just and reasonable—

Lord Bathurst in 1825 had some thoughts of dividing the Diocese of Quebec into two Bishoprics on the Death of the first Protestant Bishop Dr. Mountain, one for Upper, and one for Lower Canada— Had this division taken place at that time I have reason to believe, that his Lordship designed me for the Bishopric of this Province—

My Friend Sir Peregrine Maitland was Governor—and Sir Robt Wilmot Horton then under Secretary of State was favourable—

Lord Bathurst afterwards informed me, that the Division could not take place—as opposition was made to any diminution of the Salary on which the project of Division was based; for it was intended, that the first Bishops Salary of £3000 Sterlg should be equally divided allowing £1500 to each of the New Bishops—

The late Bishop Stewart had powerful Friends, who disliked any such Division of income—his Nephew Sir James Graham—the late Lord Darnl[e]y and others (as I understood) took a warm interest in the matter, and Lord Bathurst being unwilling to go to Parliament for a second Salary, the division of the Diocese was abandoned; and Dr: Stewart become Bishop of Quebec retain[in]g the whole Salary—

Lord Bathurst, feeling for my disappointment, did all in his power to sooth[e] it by conferring upon me the Archdeaconry of York—

The laborious duties of this immense Diocese soon affected Dr: Stewarts health, and he represented in the strongest terms the necessity of the division contemplated in 1825, and requested, that his duties might be confined to Upper Canada, which he preferred for the mildness of the climate, and that Dr: Mountain Archdeacon of Quebec (Son of the first Bishop) might be made his Suffragan for Lower Canada, frequently telling me, that if this arrangement took place it would secure the future Division of the Diocese of Quebec—that Dr Mountain would retain the Lower Province to which it would be inconvenient for me to go, while I as matter of course would succeed to that of Upper Canada—

On Bishop Stewarts death Dr Mountain urged upon Government the necessity of dividing the Diocese—freely stating, that the duties could not be discharged by one person however strong, and active, and, that they would be found very laborious even for two—

The Clergy of the Province have repeatedly petitioned the Imperial Government that it may be erected into a Bishopric—nor are our people less anxious to have their own Bishop— Fortunately the Arch Bishop of Canterbury has given his consent; the necessity being so clear, and from recent letters, I find, that Lord Glenelg is favourable to a division of the Diocese of Quebec— It is therefore likely to take place soon—

Now I think that it will be admitted by every intelligent man in this Colony, that, if it be made a Bishopric, no person has so strong a claim to the Office as I have, and did the appointment depend upon the Clergy and Church men of Upper Canada, there would be no difficulty—

I came to this Province in 1799 at the Invitation of our first Governor, General Simcoe to be the head of a collegiate institution—unfortunately the Governor had returned before I reached the Province, I was therefore disappointed, & the whole scheme of the College fell to the ground—I had left fair prospects behind me but I was ashamed to return—Sir John Campbell Her Majestys Attorney General and the Revd Dr Chalmers then my Friends appeared at the time to have no advantage over me except that I was a member of the Church of England, and which south of the Tweed would have turned to my favour— Friendless in a foreign land, I made my way silently & slowly and for more than a quarter of a Century I combined my Clerical duties, (the population being yet thin) with the education of youth— The result has been, that the leading men in every District in this Province besides many in Lower Canada have been my Pupils[.]

Four Judges out of five belonging to the Court of Queens Bench were my Scholars. The Speakers of both Branches of the Legislature, as well as a considerable number of the Members of both Houses—A great portion of the practising Barristers—of the Clergy, Merchants, and Land holders received their education at my Seminary; With what success and friendly attachment the Pamphlet, which accompanies this will sufficiently testify [Marginal note here reads: "No 1".]

I have been the Pastor of two Parishes—in one I remained nine years and was invited to the seat of Government twenty seven years ago by General Brock then Governor, and all the Principal Inhabitants of this City, who thought that here a greater Field was opened to my services than in any other part of the Province.

I left my first Parish in the best possible order, and, if the fruits of a Faithful attention to the duties of my charge are to be looked for in the number and Christian character of my continually increasing congregations—in the proportion of regular Communicants at the Altar, in the provision made through my exertions for the accommodation of the People in suitable places of public worship—in the relief afforded for the sick and destitute, and consolation offered to the afflicted I may safely appeal to them all—

The regard entertained for a Pastor will be found to be in proportion to these circumstances of his Flock and to the share which he is felt to bear in producing them, and I respectfully invite Your Excellencys examination of all these particulars—

Within a recent period this Parish has been twice afflicted with the Asiatic Cholera, a most appalling pestilence which cut off more at each time than 1/12 of our Population, and threw upon the Charity of the Survivors nearly two hundred widows and 700 Children Orphans, or Fatherless, or Motherless, and which required in its terrific progress the exertion of the utmost degree of that religious devotion, moral energy, and untiring attention to the claims of our suffering fellow Creatures which should distinguish a Christian Pastor— How I have acted during these two seasons of trial will best appear from the document annexed— [Marginal note here reads: "No 2".]

I have always lived on the most Friendly terms with Bishop McDonell the head of the Catholic Church, and with the late Mr Bethune, the head of the Presbyterians, and even amidst the disputes about the Clergy Reserves, I stand fair with all parties, and with the exception of one single Individual maintain the same Friendly relation with them as before— They do me the Justice to believe, that my opinion concerning the Church property is sincere, and has never changed—that I claim no privileges for the Established Church but those which the Constitution confers, and, that I freely admit that the Imperial Parliament can deal as it thinks fit with the Reserves, and that it will become our duty to submit[.]

I may safely say that my influence tho' perhaps greater than any other mans in the Province has ever been exerted for its benefit in preserving peace and tranquillity and a firm attachment to the Parent State—nor do I feel, that this influence diminishes, when I consider the number of Persons of all parties, religious and political, who come to me for direction and advice, or who apply to me to take trusts—to be Executor to estates—to protect Widows & look after the education of children—

Last Spring Dr Mountain Bishop of Montreal having at that time no Salary attached to his office and in the expectation of a Bishop being appointed for this Province postponed till late this summer visiting this part of the Diocese—with an expressed wish, that it might never be necessary for him to come to Upper Canada in his official capacity—On hearing this Sir Francis B Head without my knowledge recommended me strongly to Lord Glenelg, who is acquainted with my claims to be appointed Bishop of Upper Canada— His Excellency apprehended no difficulty whatever— In august he expected an answer, and thought I might go home and return, long before the time appointed for Bishop Mountains visitation—

Such an arrangement would have been very agreeable to me for I was exceedingly anxious as I still am to consult the Archbishop and the Bishop of London respecting the question of the Reserves, and how far for the sake of peace they are willing to concede—but no answer came—

In the mean time His Excellency sent in his resignation—then followed the insurrection—and every thing else seemed forgotten—But not so— Sir Francis B Head feeling as he declared, that my claims were such as could not be overlooked wrote again in January last—he said nothing of Salary because he desired the immediate services of a Bishop, and wished it to be kept in abeyance till the question of the Reserves was finally settled—observing that I could retain my present emoluments and appointments till the Church property was adjusted, and, that arrangements might be easily made to relieve me from all other duties than those belonging to the Bishopric to which I must be entirely devoted—

I confess that I was pleased with this kind and generous treatment and I felt that from my knowledge of the Country and people & my general influence I could do much more for the prosperity and extension of the Church than any other Person—but the result has only been, the cold letters, which Your Excellency had the kindness to shew me—

I feel, that I am trespassing on Your Excellencys patience and saying too much about myself— Yet believe me it is my misfortune— I am pleading for the last time— After nearly 40 years of useful and prominent exertions guided by a pious integrity—which has never been impeached and believing the Government pledged for many years in my favour it would be deeply mortifying to me to be superseded by a Stranger, for the best of men like to rise in their own profession—and he that is disappointed at my age can scarcely console himself with the hope of future promotion—

In regard to Salary or endowment that need offer no delay for in that respect I can remain as I am till the question of the Reserves is set at rest for tho' far from rich I am not avaricious & should be consoled & encouraged by the greater field of usefulness which my promotion to the Bishopric would open to my view[.]

I am deeply sensible to the great liberty I am taking in making this appeal to Your Excellency, but I feel from my correspondence with Lord Glenelg before it was resolved to divide the Diocese as well as from the answer to Sir Francis B Heads recommendation a coldness tho not a denial which satisfies me that unless Your Excellency takes up my case and that soon I have little to hope; for if nothing is done in my behalf till the Reserves are settled, and a Salary discovered a Person of influence at home will be placed over me—

When I look back on the exertions of a long life spent in the ardent discharge of the duties of a Christian Pastor and their happy results and call to mind my labours to unite our people and mitigate the miseries of hostile invasion during the last American war and for which as a token of Royal approbation I was made a Member of Government I cannot but feel that I merit Your Excellencys Friendly assistance on this occasion & that it will not be with[h]eld—

But whatever Your Excellencys determination may be, I owe it in justice to myself to declare that I shall still pursue the even tenor of my way—maintaining the character which I have ever supported in the Colony—and discharging with zeal and fidelity my various duties as I have hitherto done—nor shall I relax my exertions in promoting the interests of true religion and education and in calling forth the attachment of the people to the local Government to the Queen and the Parent State[.]

[159] [*Enclosures:*]

1833

Toronto. [Marked: "No. 1."]

[A printed pamphlet: *The Cornwall tribute: a piece of plate, presented to the Honourable and Venerable John Strachan, D.D. archdeacon of York, by forty-two of his former pupils, educated by him at Cornwall. Presented second July, MDCCCXXXIII. York . . . 1833.* p. 32.]

[160] *1835*
May 9

[A GROUP OF THE INHABITANTS OF YORK TO JOHN STRACHAN]: 2p.

Toronto. [Marked: "No. 2".]

Address[.]

Revd. Sir

During the prevalence of the Asiatic Cholera which on two occasions has raged virulently in this City, your Parishioners and others were so deeply impressed with a sense of your faithful and zealous discharge of the duties of a Christian minister, that many of them have since resolved to record permanently their feelings of gratitude and respect—

The measures for this purpose which were taken when the occasion was recent, have been carried into effect; and we now attend upon you with a request you will accept from us a token[1] of our affectionate remembrance of the fortitude, the Energy, the unwearied perseverance, and benevolence with which you devoted yourself to the duties of your sacred Profession, when surrounded by affliction danger and despondency,

In common with those whose sufferings you laboured to alleviate and whose distress awakened our warmest sympathy, we would express by this offering our thankfulness that amidst the mortality by which you were encompassed you have been spared for the farther exercise of those Christian Charities which we have seen you ever ready to extend without regard to considerations of personal danger or fatigue, looking only to the necessities which required your assistance and to the means which you had it in your power to apply to their relief.

[161] [COLBORNE TO ARTHUR]: L.

[*1838*] [*May 5*] [This letter is lacking, but a précis entry in item 578 reads:] On the 5th of May Sir John Colborne suggests that a "few Companies of Volunteers may be kept up for the defence of the Niagara and Western Frontiers."

[162] HEAD TO [ARTHUR]: A.L.S. 3p

May 7 *Athenaeum.* [*London.*]

It is my intention tomorrow to endeavour to have the pleasure of introducing myself to Lady Arthur on Board the Packet in which she and her family sail from London for New York— My slight acquaintance will perhaps prevent me from expressing to her how deeply I feel anxious that she may perform her tedious pilgrimage in safety, and I can enter I assure you in the feelings which you will entertain on that subject— I know by experience what those feelings must be, and it will give me very great pleasure to hear that she reaches Government House as prosperously as it pleased God to conduct my own family t that spot.

I intend to go on board with Sir Howard Elphinstone whose daughter Mrs. Anstruther is going to join her husband Major A. who is on duty at the Niagara frontier— It is not my intention often to trouble you with any recommendatn. but I have known this young person since she was an infant, and I need only say t you that I entertain towards her the same regard that I do for my own children to ensure from you (and thro you from Lady Arthur) some slight attention.

She has thro life conducted herself with very great propriety, and I believe I may say, has never given t her parents one moments anxiety. Much as I feel on this subject, I will not detain you any longer on it, but will venture to address this letter to Lady Arthur, who I trust will be so good as t excuse the liberty I have taken in doing so.

I saw Lord Glenelg yesterday yesterday [*sic*], and had some conversation with him respecting the execution of Lount & Matthews [*sic*]— I need not tell you what opinions I gave him, as I am sure you know what they must have been.—

You will not require, nor will it be in my power to offer t your administration of the Govnt of U. Canada much assistance, as I am but

[1]A massive and elaborate silver vase.

an humble individual, but you may depend on my allowing no opportunity to escape of giving you all the support in my power. . .

[P. S.] Pray remember me very kindly to my faithful friend Joseph, and permit me to thank you very sincerely for your kindness in providing for Colonel Halkett—

[Addressed to Lady Arthur.]

[163] JOHN STRACHAN TO [JOHN] JOSEPH: A.L.S.

May 7 *Toronto.*

I send you a heavy packet

1st The Despatches from Lord Glenelg respecting the Church property & Rectories

2d A report on one of these Despatches on which I should like to converse with His Excellency at some leisure moment after he has perused it

3rd A copy of a Bill on the Clergy Reserves adopted by the Legislative Council in 1836

4th A report on the religious state of the Indians within the Province

5th A copy of the Petition recently presented to the House of Lords by His Grace the Archbishop of Canterbury

6th A note to His Excellency[.]

[First enclosure lacking.]

[*Enclosures:*]

[164] *1838*
May 2

JOHN STRACHAN TO ARTHUR: A.L.S. 9p.

Toronto.

May it Please Your Excellency

Permit me to draw your Excellencys attention to the following remarks on the plan for the support of public worship suggested in Lord Glenelgs despatch dated the 26th Decr 1837 and which has, it is said, been recently pursued with much benefit in Van Diemens land and New South Wales—

My object in stating with some minuteness the probable difficulties with which a similar plan will be surrounded in this Province is that of bringing the subject in all its bearings at once under your Excellencys consideration in order to their remedy, and thus clearing the way for the settlement of a question, which I have so much at heart— No Person can be more desirous or has laboured so much as I have done to bring the question of the Reserves to a peaceable termination and I think, that I have arrived at what will appear to Your Excellency, as it does to me, the most probable and perhaps the most amicable and satisfactory method of its final adjustment—tho it may still require modifications and must after all depend almost exclusively on Your Excellency for its accomplishment—

These difficulties may be divided into General & Special[.]

1st General

1st This Province was set apart as an asylum for the Loyalists and their Children, who maintained their allegiance during the American Revolution and they became Inhabitants under a solemn pledge of receiving the same Constitution as that of the Mother Country—a Constitution which includes a decent provision for the due Ministration of the word and Sacraments according to the forms of the Church of England[.]

2d These pledges were solemnly redeemed by Statute 31st Geo 3d Chap 31 establishing the Government of the Province which provides for the support of a Protestant Clergy in a way that imposes no burthen upon any class of people or any disability upon those who profess a different Faith—

3 That the bulk of the population of this Province consists of two great classes 1st The Loyalists who took refuge after the American Revolution and 2d Emigrants from the Parent State—the more respectable of whom were induced to settle in the Colony because they felt secure that they and their Children would enjoy the inestimable privilege of worshipping their God and Saviour as their Fathers had done before them[.]

4 That the portion of the Inhabitants of the Province attached to the Established Church consider its ministrations their birth-right secured by the most solemn pledges and by the law of the land, and they feel that they are entitled to the same protection in regard to their religious principles as their Roman Catholic fellow subjects in Lower Canada to whom the pledges of the Imperial Government for the security of their form of worship and support of their Clergy are not stronger than those held by the adherents of the Church of England[.]

5 That any modification of the 31st Geo 3d Chap 31 that shall have for its object to place the National Church below that of the Roman Catholic Church in Lower Canada and upon a mere equality with other Protestant Denominations in this Province will be considered by a large portion of the most Loyal intelligent and influential People something like degradation and excite not a little discontent[.]

6 That a great number of the adherents of the Church of England sent out of late years have been Paupers from the Parishes and therefore to deprive the Established Church of any large portion of the Clergy Reserves or their proceeds will in a great measure force the abandonment of such poor and destitute Members for to carry the truths of the Gospel to the whole population of any country requires an Establishment directed and supported by the Government[.]

7 That during the American revolution as well as in the late insurrection Church people were almost to a man Loyal and it is a grave question for Government to determine whether they will sanction a religious Level which seems from experience certain to become a moral waste and a hotbed of sedition and discontent[.]

8 The first effect of such a levelling principle is virtually

to divorce the Established Church from the State and thus produce an organic change in the Constitution[.]

The Church thus seperated [*sic*] from the State will gradually become alien and in this manner will one of the strongest supports of Government be palsied or removed[.]

10 It must however in justice be admitted that if that part of the plan be rigidly adhered to by which Government gives assistance equal to that furnished by the denomination petitioning[,] the Church of England had it not Constitutional claims of a paramount nature would have no reason to complain for it cannot be denied that her Members are more able to contribute than any other denomination in the Colony[.]

11 In regard to the harmony of the plans operation one drawback of a general character may be mentioned as probable tho' I trust it will not go far—it is notorious that hitherto the Members of the Church of England have assisted all other Denominations in their religious purposes but a division of the proceeds of the Provision for the maintenance of a Protestant Clergy tends to seperate the different Sects of Christians—they will be apt to act more selfishly and to grudge every farthing given away because by so much will their claims upon Government by diminished[.]

2d Special Difficulties

We now proceed to notice some special difficulties in the way of adopting the proposed plan by the Provincial Parliament[.]

1st The Legislature of Upper Canada is empowered to make laws for the peace welfare and good Government of the Colony—such laws not being repugnant to the Constitutional Act—but to Legislate upon this plan is to provide for the Roman Catholic worship out of a maintenance expressly appropriated for the support of a Protestant Clergy in contradistinction to the Clergy of the Church of Rome who are liberally endowed in Lower Canada and entitled to tithes from their own people in both Provinces[.]

2 Any attempt therefore on the part of the Provincial Legislature to assist the Roman Catholic Church out of the Clergy Reserves would be directly repugnant to the Spirit and provisions of the 31st of Geo: 3rd Chap 31 and consequently a dead letter and altogether illegal[.]

3 The Power given to the Provincial Legislature by the 41st & 42nd Clauses of the 31st Geo 3d Chap 31 to vary or repeal &c is not retrospective and cannot affect what has been already done and while this power includes Clauses 35, 36, 38, & 39 it leaves clauses 37 & 40 wholly untouched—two clauses which are very important for they imply the continuance of the reservations already made and the permanence of the Established Church and her right to the Reserves so far as they are set apart[.]

4 The plan proposed recognises only three Denominations but in this Province so far as the House of Assembly is concerned a pledge has been held out to seven[,] for a resolution adopted by that Body on the 11th Jany 1837 recommends

the appropriation of the Clergy Reserves or proceeds among the following Churches

1st. The Church of England
2. The Presbyterians in connexion with the Church of Scotland
3. Presbyterians called the United Synod
4. Roman Catholics
5. British Wesleyan Methodists
6. Canadian Wesleyan Methodists
7. Baptists

It is apprehended that even this distribution will not produce content unless the following be added

8. Episcopal Methodists
9. Primitive Methodists
10. Lutherans
11. Independents
12. Congregationalists[.]

All these Denominations have the power of solemnising marriage by law and are therefore so far recognised by the Provincial Legislature that to omit any of them would produce as much perhaps more discontent than at present exists. Even difficulty will be found in confining assistance to these twelve Denominations because new Sects will be continually demanding admission a demand which the House of Assembly would find it no easy matter to resist[.]

5th Adverting to the Provision set apart for the maintenance of a Protestant Clergy it appears that it amounts to nearly 2½ Millions of acres of land which in a series of years may at a fair average price produce a Capital of one Million Sterling which placed in the Funds at home the only sure place of safety would at 3½ per Cent give an annual income of £35000—if this were equally divided among 12 Denominations it would give nearly £3000 each. but this only after the lapse of an indefinite period. Now before this period can arrive Clergymen of the Church of England will be required for three or four hundred Townships and for some of them more than one and perhaps three or four times the same number of Clergymen for other denominations—and what would £35000 be among so many? Hence it is evident that the Provision set apart for the maintenance of a Protestant Clergy which has been deemed so lavish is not sufficient to maintain one fourth of the Clergymen which the religious instruction of the Province will at no distant period employ. It is true that the interest arising from the Fund if placed in this Country might be nearly doubled and the Capital itself greatly increased by waiting till the lands fetch twenty instead of ten shillings per acre but to such delay there are serious objections—

6 If advantage were taken by the exertions of any one Denomination of the condition pledging the Government to give a sum equal to their contribution so as for a time to absorb the disposable part of the Fund as perhaps might be done, a general cry would be raised far more deep and bitter than any that has yet occurred[.]

7. The plan if it include so many denominations will not only be found to work unequally but in all probability it will operate as a premium to Dissent from the National Churches[.]

1st Many of these denominations may have four Teachers at the expence of one of our. Clergymen— Their Ministers are in general comparatively uneducated and being taken from a low class of Society they feel that their new Station elevates and gives them importance and is desirable to such persons almost without emolument hence it is an easy thing to multiply the number of Dissenting Teachers[.]

2nd Much the same remarks apply to the Roman Catholic Clergy— They have many ways of getting money from their people which we have not. They are single Men without families—and have in general been at little or no expence for their education[.]

8 On the whole it seems impossible to include so many denominations without reducing the assistance to a mere trifle, and yet it will be difficult for the Colonial Legislature to exclude any, and trifling as the assistance from Govt must be, irritation & angry rivalry will sometimes arise among so many Competitors— In Van Diemans[1] Land & New South Wales the plan contemplates only three denominations, and was adopted, when the population was small, and it might be considered to consist of only two classes; it will therefore work much easier in these Countries than in this Province where many applications for assistance may be made at the same time which cannot be satisfied— Besides the plan in the East is sustained by all the authority of the Home Government and the local administration in these Colonies is much stronger than in this Country— Moreover the Members of the Church of England in New South Wales & Van Diemens[1] Land do not see a regular Roman Catholic Establishment as we do in Lower Canada with no more right than we possess to so beneficial a distinction[.]

The Remedy

1st The only way left for the Legislature of this Province to deal with the Clergy Reserves is to resign the power given by the 41st and 42d Clauses of the 31st Geo 3d Chap 31 into Her Majestys hands for religious purposes within the Province and should this be found not strictly Constitutional or legal without a special enactment of the Imperial Parliament it would be easy for the Colonial Minister to get such enactment passed—

2 Such a measure re-investing the Crown with the Clergy Reserves for religious purposes within the Province may under the sanction of the Governor be carried through both branches of the Legislature— It is however a measure which I feel great difficulty in supporting but much ought to be done for the sake of peace and on this account I am willing to promote it to the utmost of my power[.]

3 By the passing of this enactment the Government in England would be enabled to adopt a plan similar to that recommended in the Despatch and now in operation in the

[1]Variants in spelling in the original.

Eastern Colonies and with far more effect than if established under the authority of the Provincial Legislature—

4th It will be much more easy to confine assistance to fewer denominations—the home Govt might at once declare that no deviation would be permitted in that respect from the practice of New South Wales and Van Diemans Land[.]

5th It would be in the power of the Government to modify matters so as to reserve portions of land for Glebes and small endowments for the Established Church if deemed expedient— The Bishop and Archdeacons might be supported out of the growing revenue— The Patronage of the Rectories established or hereafter to be established reserved to the Crown on the recommendation of the Bishop and thus a subdued Establishment might be maintained without giving just cause of offence to any and the attachment of a large portion of the people secured[,] for the Loyalty of Churchmen is an abiding principle[.]

6 Any other measure adopted by the Provincial Legislature than the one proposed would not be final but be made subject to judicial inquiry[,] for this far the Friends of the Established Church would feel themselves obliged to go— To the Colonial Legislature they will not submit in any distribution without appeal—but to the Imperial Govt they would feel it their duty to bow[.]

7 The details of the distribution if they are believed to be fixed at home will give far less umbrage than if determined by the Legislature of the Colony—and if the ratio should be made to depend on numbers that ratio ought to be taken from the population of the Mother country as in the Province which may be considered a reservoir for Emigrants from the United Kingdom the relative proportions are continually changing and it should farther depend upon the expence attending the Education and support of a Clergyman of each denomination respectively and also on the form of Ecclesiastical Govt.

8 Thus the Members of the Church of England in the United Kingdom may be taken at 12 Millions and the Roman Catholics at six—but to give the Roman Catholics half as much as the Established Church would be working injustice[.] First because their Clergy are single and without families[;] 2nd Because they have sources of emolument from their people unknown to our Church[;] 3rd Because they are entitled to tithes from their own People in both Provinces— 4 Because their Church Government is not so expensive as ours— All these particulars should form elements of the equation of distribution[.]

Again the Kirk has a population in the United Kingdom of two Millions and the Church of England twelve so that 1/6 would be the proportion of the Kirk and a full proportion because the form of her Ecclesiastical Government is equality & requires no provision for Dignitaries—

9 The leading principle of the plan that the Denomination petitioning receives assistance equal to its contribution might seem to supersede all reference to population and such perhaps

may be the case in New South Wales & Van Diemans land, but it is apprehended that some modification of this principle must take place with respect to destitute and back settlements otherwise it will be long before anything like the regular Ministrations of Christianity can reach them[.]

10 . Through the whole is taken for granted that the present establishment is to be kept up and extended in proportion to the contributions of Members of the Church of England and that the allowances to other Denominations will continue to be paid out of the Casual and Territorial revenue till such time as the growing income from the Reserves shall supply the means of covering them without interfering with existing rights[.]

11 In conclusion it seems evident to me that the plan cannot be dealt with in its details by the Provincial Legislature but that after that body has resigned its power over the Reserves to the Crown the authority and prevailing influence of the Imperial Government will be required to establish in a satisfactory manner the future disposition of the Clergy Reserve Fund—

12 A copy of a bill reinvesting the Clergy Reserves in Her Majesty for religious purposes within the Province which was adopted by the Legislative Council in 1836 & in favour of which a vote passed during last Session in the House of Assembly is annexed[.]

---

13 This paper might be considered incomplete were I not to remark that as some measure must pass the Imperial Parliament during next winter respecting Lower Canada two clauses might be introduced repealing the 41 & 42 Clauses of the 31st Geo 3d Chap 31 & causing the Clergy Reserves to revert to the Crown for religious purposes and such proceeding would be better received here than any measure of the Provincial Parliament[.]

14 The only difficulty in the way of this honest & straight forward course is the fear of interfering in local matters but every man who intends emigrating to this country has an interest in the Reserves because he has an interest in religion[;] it is therefore a question which more properly belongs to the Empire than the Province & ought to be settled by the Supreme Legislature[.]

15 I have only to add that it will give me great delight to render your Excellency every assistance in my power to bring the vexed question of the Clergy Reserves to a satisfactory result—it is a subject on which I feel strongly but I trust with every disposition to be just and reasonable and I have great pleasure in stating that from the short intercourse which I have had with your Excellency I begin to entertain a hope that the Church property will be satisfactorily adjusted under your wise discretion and experience[.]

[The numbering of the paragraphs is in the margins of the original.]

[165] *1836*

[UPPER CANADA. LEGISLATIVE COUNCIL.]

Toronto.

[A printed copy of a Legislative Council paper of 1836 headed: "Amendments made by the Legislative Council in and to the Bill sent up from the Commons House of Assembly entitled 'An Act for the Disposal of the Clergy Reserves in this Province for the purposes of General Education.' "]

[166] *1838*
May 7

JOHN STRACHAN: A.D.S. 6p.

Toronto.

Religious State of the Indians in Upper Canada.

Nations or Tribes	
Mohawks on The Grand River	These Indians are the remnant of the five nations so famous in American History—and still number upwards of two thousand Souls— They are distinguished among themselves as seperate [*sic*] tribes or nations viz Mohawks, Tuscaroras, Cayugas, Seneca's, Onondagoes— They have been for more than a century professed adherents of the Church of England, and during that time have had a Missionary of that Church resident among them. The whole of the Book of Common Prayer and a portion of the New Testament including St Marks Gospel have been translated into the Mohawk language and are used by the Indians— When the American rebellion broke out they were told by the Insurgents, that they would not be permitted as they desired to remain Neutral— On hearing this the vast majority chiefly through the influence of their Missionary joined the Royal Standard— On the peace of 1783 they retired into Upper Canada and had lands assigned them by the Government on the Grand River— A few years ago the expence of the Mission was assumed by the New England Society— Two Missionaries are now resident among them and are well supported by that Institution. Several Schoolmasters are employed in the education of their Children—and exertions are making to teach them the common

arts of life by means of a School of Industry. The result is said to be very favourable and highly creditable to the New England Society[.]

Mohawks in the Bay of Quinte

This is a small division of the same people numbering about three hundred and fifty— Owing to some difference among their Chiefs this party desired to have a seperate Settlement and chose the Bay of Quinte that they might be near their beloved Missionary the late Dr. Stuart of Kingston[.] They have a respectable Clergyman of the Church of England resident among them—and support themselves chiefly by agriculture as do their Brethren on the Grand River[.]

Chippaways of the River & Lake St Clair

This tribe consists of about four hundred Souls— The poverty of the Church prevented a Missionary from being established among them, but latterly a Methodist Preacher attends them —whether occasionally or permanently I cannot say—they still depend too much upon hunting and fishing for their subsistence[.]

Hurons Munseys and Chippaways near Amherstburgh

These are so very few in number as scarcely to count two hundred and at the same time so much scattered that little or no impression has yet been made upon them[.]

Munseys and Chippaways on the River Thames

These tribes number nearly eight hundred Souls— One portion profess to be Moravians and have a Missionary of that persuasion resident in their village— The other inhabiting a distinct village are attended by the Revd Richard Flood an English Clergyman settled near them and having a Mission among the Whites— He can only devote a portion of his time to the religious instruction of the Indians, but we have reason to believe, that his labours have been blessed with great success[.]

Chippaways of Lakes Huron & Simcoe

These Indians are upwards of five hundred in Number— A village has been built for a portion of them at the expence of Government at a place called Cold Water on the North East Shore of Lake Simcoe. A Missionary of the Church of England was sent to reside among them whose measure of success in gradually bringing them into order & in training their children was most encouraging but fiscal difficulties arose and he was withdrawn. Another Missionary of the Church appointed to travel through the Home District visits Coldwater occasionally and the Methodists have now established a Mission among them through the Assistance of Government[.]

Missasaguas [*sic*] of the River Credit

This tribe numbers about two hundred and twenty— His Excellency Sir Peregrine Maitland built a village for them on the River Credit with the view of placing a resident Missionary of the English Church among them— A Catechist was sent till a proper person could be found—but owing to some want of arrangement a delay intervened and in the meantime the Methodists got a footing and appeared to be doing so much good, that it has not been thought expedient to disturb them—

Mississaguas of Kingston & Grape Island

These Indians do not exceed two hundred. They are entirely under the guidance of the Methodists by whose exertions they have been very much improved both in a temporal and Spiritual point of view[.]

Mississaguas on Rice & Mud Lakes

This tribe consists of nearly three hundred—the New England Society has been assisting them and endeavouring to collect them into Villages. They are still erratic and very little religious impression has been yet made upon them— If any it has been by the Methodists, as the Church has no means to support a resident Missionary—

Indians on the North & West Shores of Lake Huron

These are numerous but scattered in families or small divisions over an immense tract— The Church of England sent Mr Cameron a Catechist & half Indian in 1830 to endeavour in the first instance to collect them together and form a Village at a place called La Closh [*sic*] but finding the Sault St Marie where the great Lakes Huron & Superior are connected by a strait and river afforded a better position for Missionary labours the Mission has been removed thither—and has since continued with great success. The present missionary The Revd Willm McMurray writes most encouragingly but here again the poverty of the Church intervenes for the Mission is supported by a private Society which is unable to give that assistance in School Masters, books &c which are required[.]

Indians on the Saguene[*sic*] and Sable Rivers

It was in contemplation to transfer these Indians not three hundred Souls and such families and small tribes as are scattered round the shores of Lake Huron not already noticed to the Manatoulin [*sic*] Islands and form a village and settlement— Some progress has been made in erecting a village and a Missionary of the Church of England was appointed but difficulties in regard to the settlement itself having arisen he was withdrawn after a short residence. Should these difficulties be removed and the proposed arrangements be completed another Clergyman will be appointed for the religious instruction of the natives according to the forms of the Established Church—

Sir Peregrine Maitland was very anxious during his administration of the Government to adopt and mature a general plan for the civilization and religious instruction of the Indians within the Province[.]

He found that almost all the different tribes had annual incomes of considerable value arising from their sales of lands to Government[.]

It was quite evident that they could no longer live by hunting as the settlements were extending through every part of the Province and unless something was done to induce them to alter their mode of life they must inevitably perish and this in a very short time for their annuities and presents were wasted and turned rather to their destruction than benefit[.]

The outline of the Plan was

1 To Collect each tribe or nation into a village or villages for so long as they continued erratic nothing could be done towards their real improvement[.]

2d The expence of erecting the Village might be defrayed by a deduction from their annuities and by allowing a portion of their presents to be paid in money—

3 To assign a reasonable portion of land to each family around their villages—

4 With a view to their civilization and religious instruction to establish in each Village one or more resident Missionaries Members of the Church of England—one Surgeon—one Blacksmith—one Carpenter—a practical Farmer with Schools of instruction and industry with proper Teachers—

5 It was believed that the whole might under good management be defrayed at much less expence than what the Indians now cost the Government[.]

6 Among the vast benefits which such arrangements would confer that of ensur[in]g the applicat[io]n of their presents & annuities to their real comfort was not one of the least— besides their spiritual comfort and happiness which are matters of infinitely more value—

Sir Peregrine likewise anticipated much relief to Government by having as it were a department in each village attached to and amenable to the Government—at the head of which was a Missionary of the Established Church— The Governor of the Province would be no longer molested or embarrassed by Persons interfer[in]g with the property of the Indians for such interference has been the source of great trouble and annoyance to every successive administration— nor has it been confined to Laymen— Insinuations have been frequently made to Indians by which their minds have been rendered uneasy and filled with suspicions against Government—and plots have been laid to acquire their property or at least the power of its appropriation by persons whose duty it was to confine their labours solely to their religious instruction. Nor did Sir Peregrine think that there was entire safety from intrigues of this nature but by some such plan as he proposed[.]

By placing a respectable Clergyman in each Village amenable to the Governor and the Bishop who had no other interest than the discharge of his duty all plots and conspiracies about the temporalities of the Indians would be prevented or timely notice given of their existence— Moreover Sir Peregrine wisely thought that if the Indians were to be instructed at the expence of the Government in the truths of Christianity it ought to be through the national Church over which Government has a just control and no other[.]

Sir Peregrine proceeded to act upon this plan but was not able to make much progress during the remainder of his administration and in the time of his Successor it was for some years lost sight of altho' some partial steps were taken respecting Cold Water & the Manatoulin [*sic*] Islands[.]

In 1830 the Lord Bishop of the Diocese Dr Stewart and his Clergy supported by the Friends and adherents of the Established Church seeing the Government lax or indifferent formed an Institution under the name of "The Society for converting and Civilising the Indians and Propagating the Gospel among Destitute Settlers[.]"

This Society is still in existence & is proceeding in promoting its objects with as much vigour as its limited means admit. It has received countenance & assistance from England and at the present moment contributes to the support of several travelling Missionaries whose duty it is to visit the Indians as well as the White population[.]

It has also one Mission entirely among the Indians at the Sault of St[e] Marie and it is not without hope of being enabled to establish one or two more at no distant period. At the same time it is much to be wished that the plan proposed by Sir Peregrine Maitland were carried into effect with such modifications as change of circumstances may render expedient[.]

Indeed humanity as well as religion requires something to be done for the Indians. They have now no hunting grounds for they have been purchased & taken by Government for settlement and without guidance they are wretched helpless and miserable— If much should not be effected with the grown up natives in the way of religious instruction their temporal existence may be made much more comfortable and as respects the children much might be done—

In truth the obstacles in the way of converting the Indians are not so great as with other Pagan nations, for their Paganism is of the mildest character— They believe in a future State of existence tho debased with corporeal associations— They retain among them the knowledge of the great principle of expiation & confide in a superintending Providence[.]

When spoken to on the subject of Christianity they ask if it be the religion of their great Father over the water, meaning the King & they are ready to receive it for it is a great recommendation as well as inducement to them to listen when this question can be answered in the affirmative[.]

[167] *1833*

[UPPER CANADA. CHURCH OF ENGLAND.] In Strachan's handwriting.

[*Toronto.*]

A copy of the Petition presented to the House of Lords by the Arch Bishop of Canterbury of the 9th of March—sent home by the Attorney General in 1833[.]

To the Righ[t] Honourable the Lords Spiritual & Temporal We his Majestys dutiful and Loyal subjects the Clergy and Members of the Church of England, in Upper Canada with other Inhabitants deeply interested in its prosperity, most humbly approach Your Right Honourable House on a subject of the utmost importance to the well being of this Colony—

Your Lordships humble Petitioners are composed of Loyalists and their Children who took refuge in Upper Canada after the American revolution, under a solemn pledge of receiving the same Constitution as that of the Mother Country; a Constitution which includes a decent provision for the due ministration of the word and Sacraments, according to the forms of the Church of England—

These pledges were fully redeemed by the Statute 31 Geo 3rd Cap 31 establishing the Government of the Province, which amidst many salutary enactments, provides for the support of a Protestant Clergy, in a way that imposes no burthen upon any class of people or any disability upon those who profess a different Faith——

Your Lordships faithful Petitioners consist also of Emigrants from the Parent State who have been more especially induced to leave their native land and to settle in this Colony because they felt secure that they and their Children would enjoy the inestimable privilege of worshipping their God and Saviour as their Fathers had done before them; since at the most earnest desire of our late King, communicated to his Parliament provision was made for the support of the Christian Religion in Upper Canada—

Your humble Petitioners desire to draw your Lordships attention to the Message of His Majesty Our late King of blessed Memory to His Parliament, and to the enactments in the Canada Act made in consequence of that wise and gracious recommendation, and they would further appeal to the Coronation Oath, which insures to His Majestys subjects the Royal favour and protection to the United Church of England and Ireland in every dependency of the British Empire and which we rejoice to see so amply confirmed by His Majesty's recent declaration to the Bishops on the 28th May last, expressing His Royal determination "to uphold the Church in the full enjoyment of all her rights and privileges, and that His Majesty considered the unimpaired prosperity of the Establishment in which you have been educated as essential alike to the spiritual and temporal welfare of the people[."]

We would most humbly represent to Your Lordships, that under all these circumstances we cannot but consider a Provision for the maintenance of a Protestant Clergy in this Province our birth right and guarranteed [*sic*] to us by the law of the land, as well as by the most solemn pledges; and we feel with deep concern the great injustice of the efforts now making to deprive us of this our vested right; nor can we suppress our indignation when such efforts are made to work this injury upon His Majesty['s] dutifųl Subjects who have done and suffered so much for their Loyal Acts and principles, chiefly by persons who have no comparative claim upon the British Crown and who are either ignorant of or insensible to the fundamental principles of our glorious Constitution[.]

On this occasion we do not appeal so much through your Lordships to His Majesty's well Known Grace, which at all other times we feel happy to acknowledge as to His Majestys Equity; we claim the continued security of our undoubted rights, that justice to which we are entitled—that regard to our religious privileges which is paid to those of our Lower Canadian Brethren of the Roman Catholic religion to whom the pledges of His Majestys Government for the protection of their form of worship and support of their Clergy are not stronger than those held by Your Lordships Petitioners[.]

Your Petitioners fully trust that Your Lordships will in your gracious wisdom maintain to them the advantage of a permanent provision for the support of public worship according to the National Church of England guaranteed to them by the most solemn pledges and by the law of the Land and of which they have been in possession more than forty years and that this tie which binds us to His Majesty's paternal Government and which we value more than life will not be rudely broken at the instigation of the enemies of their rights and of the prosperity of the British Crown—

Similar Petitions were sent to the King and the House of Commons[.]

[168] *1838*
May 7

JOHN STRACHAN TO ARTHUR: A.L.S. 3p.

Toronto.

Your Excellency will perceive that the measure which I require of the Provincial Legislature is abundantly simple—and may, I am confident, be carried through next Session with the exertion of that legitimate influence which necessarily belongs to Your Excellency, and which may be honourably exerted in procuring the passage of good laws—

After the Church Property is reinvested in the Crown for religious purposes the whole may be regulated by Your Excellency without giving any great trouble to the Home Government. A Scheme of management and distribution may be drawn up on the spot after mature deliberation, and sent home for adoption—then to be returned with the authority and sanction of Govt.

Such a scheme would I trust be more favourable to the Church than the plan suggested by Lord Glenelgs Despatch.

The great objections to this plan are that it requires too great a Sacrifice from the Established Church. That it proceeds upon the voluntary System or principle. And above all, that it seperates [*sic*] Church and State, which I consider Anti Christian— Moreover I am fully convinced that without an Established Church Monarchical Institutions cannot be long maintained in these Colonies—

Your Excellency will likewise perceive, that the plan proposed by Lord Glenelg keeps the Clergy Reserves under the management of the Provincial Govt: for an indefinite term, and will thus expose it, to be disturbed with incessant claims, and excitements, and keep the whole question alive—

Some plan which should have for its object the final and speedy settlement of the Reserves, and Fund, so that each party should have its share at once & for ever would perhaps be the most desirable, if it could be discovered—

The subject is the more perplexing as conscientious feelings and scruples are mixed up with it. The whole Sacrifice is to be made by the Church of England a result not to be contemplated without sorrow—and yet matters have been allowed to go so far, that concessions on her part are now become necessary— The subject however must be grappled with, and when Your Excellency has had leisure to examine it in all its bearings, I trust, that some plan will be found of which we can all approve[.]

Your Excellency may depend upon my zealous and active co-operation so far as a sense of duty will admit, and even should the principle adopted be such as I cannot fully approve, I will do my best when it is once settled to carry it out and make it work in the most satisfactory manner—

I have taken the liberty of sending a Report on the religious state of the Indians within the Province—in which I think Your Excellency will take great interest[.]

I likewise add a copy of the petition lately presented to the House of Lords by the Archbishop of Canterbury that Your Excellency may be acquainted with all our proceedings[.]

[169] OFIFNJBI HIJNOFZ TO ARTHUR: A.L.S.

[*1838*] *Ogdensburgh.* [*Postmark: Toronto, May 9, 1838.*]

[*May 9*] Information having been received that some Noble Patriot has made a glorious assa[u]lt uppon [*sic*] the Ignoble person of Sir George Arthur the Governor of Upper Canada with no other loss than that of the life of the latter, (It is to be feared that this report is not founded in truth,)

—should it prove to be so a suitable Monument will be furnished gratuitous on condition of the privaledge [*sic*] of composing the Epataph [*sic*]—Please direct your order to Ofifnjbi Hijnofz[1] Marble Mason Ogdensburgh St. Lawrence County York State[.]

[170] COLBORNE TO ARTHUR: A.L.S. 11p.

May 11 *Montreal.* [Marked "Private".]

I have so long delayed to thank you for your letters of the 5th and 25 Ult: that I can scarcely offer a sufficient apology for my silence. The Commissary General, whom I had requested to proceed to Montreal, was prevented by illness from leaving Quebec for some weeks. He however arrived here a few days since, and I hope the arrangements which he has made for the payments due in U. Canada will prove satisfactory— They will be completed, I believe, in the course of this month; but the Commy Genl must have time to provide means for supplying the large sums which he is called on unexpectedly to raise. Great allowance undoubtedly should be made for the events which have been the cause of the debts being contracted, and for the confusion and irregularity inseparable from the calling of Volunteers and Militia to the frontier, at a moment of much excitement and alarm. To prevent fraud and imposition on such occasions is impossible but when a public officer is called on to adjust claims finally, and finds that a sum of £15,000 has been issued to an irresponsible Agent, who can produce no voucher or satisfactory account for the greater portion of this sum which he was ordered to distribute, he cannot dispose of such affairs without strict enquiry, nor neglect to report that several Officers have been allowed to draw large sums without being checked or controlled by the Officer in Command in the Upper Province. Whatever discontent or clamour may prevail among the minor creditors, there is reason to believe that they will be easily satisfied when the Commissaries explain to them, the nature of the charges which have been brought against the public, and the enormous sums which appear to have been unnecessarily expended by the Agents to which I have adverted, and in settling the accounts of Tavern Keepers[.]

The arrival of a Deputy Commy Genl is daily expected; he will be stationed at Toronto and will have the superintendence of the Commissariat in the Upper Province—

The strong influential party in the United States averse to War, and whose interests are so much concerned in keeping things quiet will prevent a crusade against Canada, and check the sympathisers on the frontier. The United States I am persuaded cannot go to war. We have *also* rumours of hostile proceedings; it is said that the State of Maine has commenced a road through the disputed territory.

I am become so incredulous respecting the reports of the hostile disposition and preparations of our Neighbours, and the Patriots, that I give no credit whatever to the tribe of gentry employed in the Espionage, the system of falsehood adopted by them, or ill founded reports conveyed by them, sufficiently demonstrate that we cannot be too cautious in acting on their intelligence.

There are also many *Loyal people* much interested in keeping up

[1]These letters appear in the position of a signature. Regarding them as a cipher, and substituting the letter which immediately precedes each of them in the alphabet, the result is "Nehemiah Ghimney" which may or may not be the name of the writer.

the alarm of invasion. The only correct intelligence which I have received, has been derived from the statements of respectable merchants residing at Burlington and Platzburg [*sic*] and other Towns of the States of New York and Vermont, and of Priests settled in the United States. I hope our Government will persevere in their intention of sending out reinforcements to these Provinces; and that we shall be able to reduce nearly all the Volunteer Corps, and to dispense with the services of the Militia. A strong Corps of observation will put an end to the alarms in the London District, and restore confidence. We are only to have 7,000 men in this Command—If each Corps should muster 600 R & F; three Regiments will, I think, be a sufficient force for Upper Canada. I should suggest that each Corps should be kept together as much as possible—One Regiment at Kingston, one at Toronto, and another in the Western District, at London and Chatham[.] A Company of 100 R & F might be detached from the Regt at Toronto, to Niagara, and the same force from the Head Quarters of the Regt, in the London District to Amhers[t]-burg. By this arrangement we shall expose a small front to the temptation of desertion; while at the same time we should be able to bring 500 men against the Brigands or Rebels, in a few hours, or days at any point they may be inclined to try their fortune. A few Companies of Volunteers might probably be kept up on the Niagara Frontier and at Amhers[t]burg, if you think the companies of the regular force insufficient for the protection of the out-posts; but I think a corps collected at some distance from the frontier will be more formidable than nearer to our Neighbours of New York and Michigan. If you should require more Troops I will send you another Regiment when we have made our arrangements in this Province. The 34th Regiment, or the 71st. Regt, will relieve the 24th Regt— The 83d, I have moved to Kingston—and as soon as there are 600 men in the London District I wish the two companies of the 83d now at Amhers[t]burg to join the Head Quarters of their Corps at Kingston. The 24th Regt will proceed to By-Town and the Carillon as soon as they are relieved by the 34th. or 71st. The Guards arrived yesterday at Quebec— One Battn disembarked immediately, and the other will be in their Barracks tomorrow. The 15th Regt will move to Chambly, and the Head Quarters of the 88 Regt to Sorel; and the Companies of the 34th to Montreal. Should the 71st arrive in time, I should prefer sending that Corps to Toronto. I have requested Captain Sandon [*i.e.* Sandom] to communicate with you upon the subject of his boats, which I have authorised him to fit out at Kingston and to station at Long point, either at Port Stanley or Port Dover. His Flotilla probably may be of use in restoring confidence on the water frontier. He will have a Steam Boat, if he can engage one on reasonable terms.

With respect to the Officers sent out to be employed with the Militia. I have found some difficulty in disposing of all of them. Those stationed in Upper Canada are entirely at your service. They have, in fact, at present little duty to perform. I desired that the three Officers on the St Lawrence, should report direct to me sending you duplicates of their reports. The Officer at Niagara, who, I have been given to understand since his departure, is not ***always very sober***, will of course send his reports through you, and all Officers to the Westward of Kingston. Those now acting as Magistrates on the Richelieu are very active and useful—

You mentioned in your letter of the 5th. ult your wish to select an Adjutant Genl. from the Officers employed on a particular service. I should recommend Major Mackenzie Fraser in preference to any other— He I think would be glad to remain in the Country, and is very clever— He was some time Depty Adjutant Genl at the Mauritius. The Officer mentioned by you in your letter is, at present, at Nicollette— I am persuaded that he would not be approved of generally in the Upper Province[.]

I intend to leave this place on Monday for Quebec, to receive Lord Durham. I hope you have now no further anxiety respecting the trials—

I have been instructed to bring a certain number of the Prisoners accused of High Treason before the Ordinary Tribunals of the Province. This decision is I am persuaded so calculated to prove injurious, to our affairs, that I have determined not to act on the instructions which I have received— Lord Durham will be able to judge how far it is right or expedient to incur the risk of the whole of the Offenders being acquitted.

I understood that Colonel Foster had had some correspondence with Colonel Eden respecting his allowance while Commanding in the U. Province. I shall be very glad to sanction any charge for his additional daily pay that I have reason to believe will be approved of by the Secretary at War.

I beg you will make any arrangements which you may think best, either with respect to the instructions in possession of the Officers sent to the Upper Province, or any military affair or matter; and you may be assured that I shall neither be offended at your suggestions, [n]or disapprove your arrangements. Some of the intelligent Officers, selected for employment in U Canada, although strangers in the land, are more to be depended on, than persons not free from excitement. The reports of Major Young and of the Officers stationed on the St Lawrence and on our frontier are the best we have received[.]

[171] J. B. Robinson to [Arthur]: A.L.S. 4p.

May 16 [*Place not stated.*]

You will see by the act that the 4th. clause is correctly stated in the Report, & the language certainly is so comprehensive as to exclude nothing— It is clear that the Judicial Committee can advise the *Queen* upon the construction and effect of the Stat 31—Geo 3. upon a mere reference— It would be but an *opinion* to be sure, not a *Judgment*, but it would be the opinion of the best legal tribunal the Empire affords—and must have at least the effect of satisfying all reasonable men, and of making the obstinacy of unreasonable men unimportant— I have made one or two remarks in pencil on the draft— The only part of it, about which I should hesitate would be the last paragraph— & that not from any idea that an ecclesiastical jurisdiction would ever be applied, or that it would ever be desired to apply it in such a manner as the Presbyterians effect to apprehend— But merely because I am persuaded they press for this declaration for no other purpose than to obtain a recorded proof that the Church of England stands on no other ground in the Colonies, than the Church of Scotland—and it would certainly establish that point for them—contrary as I think to the plainest principles of the Constitution & the truth of history—

I should first have made them point out, what it was they were afraid of— Then as a lawyer I do not feel myself prepared to say on the sudden that so sweeping a declaration may not in a possible case lead to practical inconvenience as regards private rights & interests[.]

However the Secretary of State seems to have settled this concession —but like too many others, he has settled it without much thought— I fear—

[172] J[OHN] JOSEPH TO THE LIEUT. GOVERNOR [ARTHUR]: A.L.S. 6p.

[*1838*] [*Place not stated.*]

[*May 16*] I beg your Excellency will accept my thanks for the kind manner in which you have been pleased to convey to me your Intentions with respect to the office which, on your arrival, you were so obliging as to retain me in—on the express understanding however that it could be done without detriment to the public Service.

Your Excellency has been accustomed to have, in the office of Civil Secretary, a person intimately acquainted with the details of public business, and who could inform you on any Matters which might be brought under your Notice—without referring you to the department to which it more especially belongs: and I think Your Exceellency does no more than what is incumbent on you, to place in the office of Civil Secretary, a person so qualified. I only regret that it should have caused you any pain to announce to me my incompetency; since your Excellency does me injustice in supposing that I was not as sensible of it, as you could be. Had I held a different opinion of myself, it might have been a matter of Mortification to be made acquainted with it.

When Your Excellency was pleased to appoint me your Secretary, I considered at the time,—from the nature of the duties which you stated you should require from such an Officer—that I could only hold it until you should have leisure to find a more competent person. But you will, I trust, do me the justice to acquit me of any attempt or desire to deceive you. I mentioned to you at the time—that I did not write any of Sir Francis Head's despatches, except the mere routine ones: and on your stating to me what were the duties of the Secretary in Van Diemen's Land, I told your Excellency that in my opinion there was but one objection in this Colony to making that Officer a sort of Colonial Secretary of State:—namely, the jealousy that would be created of the influence which a person of talent and general ability might be supposed to possess over the Governor. But that objection I think is not worth much: And I think your Excellency acts wisely, as well as consciencіously, in making the arrangement you propose.

It only remains for me to thank your Excellency—as I do very sincerely—for the kind expression of your willingness to serve me. What I should prefer beyond any other appointment, is, to revert to the arrangement which Sir Francis Head had made for me. He appointed me to the first Clerkship in the provincial Secretary's office, in the room of Mr. Jarvis: and thereupon Mr. Cameron requested Sir Francis Head's permission to appoint me his deputy—(as he had appointed Mr. Jarvis)—which Sir Francis kindly acquiesced in. This arrangement was made on a clear understanding with Mr. Jarvis, that if his recent appointment to the Chief Superintendency of Indian affairs, should not eventually be confirmed to his satisfaction, that I should retire from his place in Mr. Cameron's office. On this understanding, I should be glad if your Excellency would be pleased to allow me now to accept that office. I have by me, the appointment—which I neglected to destroy; but which I will immediately place in your Excellency's hands to be destroyed, if you desire it.

This Situation would give me £300 a year: and the further arrangement was, that before I gave up my Secretaryship, I should appoint myself my own Agent for the Sale of Marriage Licenses in this City. My Agent is a Mr. Mercer—a person whom I never saw; but who is well off, and in no need of such Agency. The Civil Secretary appoints his own Agents throughout the Province, for the disposal of Licences: but of course I should not exercise this right in my own favour, unless with the approbation of your Excellency.

Whenever it may suit your Excellency that I should quit my present office, I shall be ready to do so: And if it shall please your Excellency to let that arrangement have effect which Sir Francis Head had made for me, I shall hold myself much bound in gratitude to your Excellency for a kindness on which I have no kind of Claim.

[173] ARTHUR TO JOHN JOSEPH: LB. 1, p. 21.

[*May 16*?] [*Place not stated.*]

I shall be most happy to confer upon you the office you name in succession to Mr Jarvis, With regard to the sale of Marriage Licenses I do not see how you can very well appoint yourself—but if the system be continued as at present, and I really do not know whether it ought or not, there can be no difficulty, I presume, in my arranging with your successor for your appointment provided the agency can with propriety be taken from Mr Mercer.

But, in place of this arrangement I hope eventually to have it in my power to offer you a more eligible appointment. I allude to that of Clerk of the Executive Council. I am not aware that there is any person, who, in succession, has a superior claim and, in the Australian Colonies, it is one of the most respectable offices—being filled in New South Wales by Sir Richard Bourke's Son in Law, and in Van Diemens Land by my Nephew.

[Misdated: "Thursday Morng—16th. May".]

[174] [ARTHUR TO JOHN] JOSEPH: Df.A.L. 2p.

[*1838*] [*Place not stated.*]
[*May 16*?] [Draft, apparently misdated the "15th.", of item 173 with some variations.]

[On the same sheet appears item 175.]

[175] [ARTHUR]: [RECIPIENT NOT STATED]: Df.A.L.

[*1838*] [*Place not stated.*] [Marked "Private".]
[*c. May 16*] By the enclosed Letter you will perceive that Mr Joseph is going to leave my office—not that He has said or done any thing to give me the slightest offence— As I am yet, as it were, a Stranger would you do me the favor to name say two or three competent, well informed Persons, possessing habits of business of whom I might select one— From what I have heard of Him & from what I have seen I think I should find Mr Macaulay the Surveyor Genl [The letter ends here.]

[The above appears on the same sheet as item 174.]

[Enclosure lacking.]

[176] C. A. HAGERMAN to ARTHUR: A.L.S. 2p.

May 22 *Toronto.*

I enclose herewith the draft of a letter such as in my very humble judgment may answer the purpose desired by Your Excellency. I am (I say it very sincerely) but an indifferent hand at *diplomatic* correspondence—but I have done my best.—

I beg respectfully to say that if during Your Excellencys absence there is any matter in which my services can be useful to your Excellency I trust you will command them.—

I have been the greater part of the day in Court, and the Vice Chancellor is now with me completing his report, or I would have sent you the accompanying earlier.—

Sincerely wishing you an agreeable trip—

[Enclosure is possibly item 177.]

[177] [ARTHUR ?] TO H. S. FOX: L. 3p.

May 22 *Toronto.*

I have had the greatest difficulty to bring myself to believe that the American Sympathisers would make another crusade to this territory: but I have received from such various quarters reports of the collection of arms, ammunition, and the cannon which General Scott could not recover in February last, that it would be wrong in me any longer to delay soliciting your interference with the Government of the United States, as it undoubtedly is nothing more than may reasonably be expected that decided measures should be adopted for putting down those proceedings which have a tendency to perpetuate irritated feelings, even if no attack be seriously meditated.— My own impression is that they will not rest quiet until they have had what they term their revenge for the affair of the Caroline, by destroying some one or more of our Vessels in our Harbours or on our Lakes.— This attempt of course, will be resisted, and it is impossible to foresee what the result may be.—

There are, so far as I can ascertain, about two thousand persons who have left this Province, and have taken up their residence in the frontier Towns on the American Side.— These people of course will continue to excite and agitate the lawless characters that are to be met with at Lockport, Rochester, Lewistown, Buffalo—and in the *neighbourhood* of these places. No force that they can collect will now make any serious impression upon us.— But as, I deeply lament to say—disaffection here, can only be considered to be smothered at present, every cause of excitement, it is my duty, by all possible means, to remove: and I therefore earnestly entreat your powerful interference.

[The above is possibly the enclosure referred to in item 176, and may not have been despatched until after Arthur's return from Kingston on May 26th; see item 178: "I have this moment written to Mr. Fox".]

[178] ARTHUR TO COLBORNE: L. 16p.

May [28 ?] *Toronto.*

I have had the pleasure to receive your letter of the 11th. inst. and thank you for the information it contains. All your suggestions and wishes upon Military points shall be fully acted upon except where unforseen circumstances require some temporary delay or partial alteration of which I shall of course immediately apprize you.

Every day for the last week I have intended to write to you; but every day I have postponed it, being still doubtful how far the information which has reached me might be depended on. But the storm now seems to be gathering so fast, that, although I have still the greatest difficulty to bring myself to believe that the runaway traitors and American Patriots will actually make an other crusade to this Province, yet, the tidings of their intention are brought from such various quarters that I can no longer safely oppose, on the mere grounds of its improbability, the general expectation that it is seriously meditated in pretty strong force.

Several letters have been intercepted by the Post Master at Toronto from some of the fugitives from this Province, and one in particular from a Mr. Ketchum, who was accountant to the Bank, to his Father is very confirmatory of the Reports received from various other sources that Doctor Rolph with Charles Duncombe and some others have been organizing a system of attack for many weeks past—they are both at Rochester—and it is impossible to suppose otherwise than that Bidwell, who is Doctor Rolph's particular friend, has a hand in the affair. They are two clever Rogues, whose abilities have come out with the times, and my Predecessor roused every bad feeling in their nature, and I believe they will retaliate upon the Queen's Government by attempting to inflict upon us all the mischief they can.

A letter which was forwarded to me by Colonel Maitland from Amherstburg states, upon what seems very good authority, that a considerable number of Patriots have within the last week made their appearance at Detroit—and it is rather strange that at the same time the *regular* American Troops have been removed from that Station.

On Wednesday last the Master of one of our Steamers from Rochester, who bears an excellent Character was brought to me by the Collector of the Customs. He stated that during the last three weeks he had seen such assemblages of Persons and other Proceedings at Rochester as convinced him that something was in agitation. He knew Doctor Rolph, and had a long conversation with him and never, he said, had he met with a person filled with more vindictive feelings. He added that within his personal knowledge a great quantity of arms had been collected.

The Steamer—Great Britain—the largest we have on the lakes belonging to Mr. Hamilton is (very improperly) commanded by an American Master.

It was rumoured that the people at Lewiston had attempted to seize her and that she had suddenly left the Port. I have this moment seen the Master myself. He says it is not true that an attempt was actually made to seize the Vessel, but that he was warned by a friend, on whom he could rely, of the intention and therefore would not stop at Lewiston.

There is no doubt, he added, that the Rebels and Patriots have collected a great quantity of arms and that many thousands have enrolled themselves to assist the "oppressed Canadians". We should, I believe, never have heard a word from this Person but that he has an interest in the Steamer.

About a fortnight ago I inspected the Niagara Frontier. It was remarkable that some few days before I went there a letter from a tradesman at Lockport to his son at Niagara was sent to me in which he stated amongst many other circumstances connected with the proceedings and plans of the refugees and Patriots, that they were going to send to the Western District several Spies, in disguise as soldiers who had deserted, whose object was to communicate with disaffected Persons in the London District and to corrupt our Soldiers. Sir Francis Head very much relied upon information given from the same person at Lockport in January last.

Accordingly I found from Colonel Kerby that, the very day before I arrived at Niagara, several of these reputed deserters had made their appearance—one of them got into some trouble, an examination took place and it appeared clearly enough that he was no Deserter—but as I had directed that there should be no restraint upon the usual intercourse across the River of course all persons may pass and repass as they please—so that the circumstance is of no other importance than as being confirmatory of the statements made by the same individual of preparations for invasion being in progress.

On Thursday last I inspected the 83rd. Regt. and the Militia at Kingston. Whilst I was there Major Bonnycastle received a letter from a merchant from whom he told me he had throughout the winter received very correct information, informing him that a considerable number of persons had been collecting under McLeod at French Creek and that they were to act in conjunction with Johnson [*i.e.* Johnston] in an attack that was simultaneously meditated at several different places along both Lakes. A respectable person named "Ewart" who was formerly a builder in Toronto, but who has I believe retired from business returned during the week from the States. He was last at Detroit & Buffalo. His information is that he is persuaded some attack is meditated but not until the month of July—the 4th. I have seen him since my return from Kingston and I should think him a person, from his manner, to be relied upon. He has no doubt that there is a movement in contemplation among the Persons who have left this Province and their connections who remain in it in conjunction with the Patriots—he relied a good deal upon the information given to him by a man who was apprehended in the London District during the revolt and was afterwards discharged and left the Province.

On my return to Toronto late on Saturday night I found Colonel Macaulay, the Commendant [*sic*] of the Militia, lately of the Royal Engineers very much alive to some Reports that had been received during my short absence— I will enclose his letter in an Official communication from the Civil Government as soon as I have written this.

Colonel Foster also had a whole catalogue of statements which coming from various quarters were certainly remarkably confirmatory of the report of projected invasion, and he entreated me at once to ask for another Regiment—

I requested the Assistant Adjutant General to condence [*sic*] his statement in a letter from himself which I will also transmit to you. I have this moment written to Mr. Fox calling his attention to what is going on amongst the people on the Frontier and requesting Him to represent the same to the American Government.

The Patriots have, no doubt, got possession of the Guns which General Scott could not recover during the winter, and there can be no question that a great many have banded together to do some mischief—but, probably, not to such an extent as Colonel Foster states although he is abundantly borne out by the statements from which he has derived his information.

If you can spare me another Regiment, I hope you will have the kindness to do so immediately, as I should rather deter the Banditti from undertaking the enterprize than have "the honour" of defeating them, for we are not yet in a very comfortable state *within our own Camp*.

Within the last three weeks I have allowed such men of the Militia as were enlisted until the 1st. July to return at once to their homes if they pleased. A great many have availed themselves of the permission, and it has been followed by the most animated remonstrances from all Quarters. Major Anstrothers [*i.e.* Anstruther's] correspondence is not very prudent on the occasion. He states, I observe, in a letter to the Military Secretary that his remonstrances against this reduction having failed he can no longer consider himself responsible for the security of the Frontier District, and that he has sent a Copy of his correspondence to Head Quarters—the fact is that he is not in command on the Frontier, but merely aiding and advising the Officer commanding.

He is a smart Officer, however, but, apparently, does not always exercise a *sober* judgement.

I need not say that as the responsibility rests with me I would have checked the decrease of the Militia force had it appeared *absolutely* necessary; *but up to this time*, I have not seen the necessity, and as the Militia were called out in a way that makes it unnecessarily expensive if it be found requisite to keep up *some* portion of that force, as now, I undoubtedly think it will be, I should prefer re-organizing it altogether.—

The Coloured Companies seem very useful men, & will be highly serviceable on the Frontier to prevent desertion. I have been endeavouring to put them in a good state. There ought if possible to be two Regiments in the Western District if you can spare another, I should propose sending it there, but removed away from the Frontier. Perhaps, Hamilton or Brantford you would approve? We ought, I think, to have a good Barrack either at the Short Hills or Burlington Heights.

I will as soon as possible, bring away the two 83rd companies from Amherstburgh but there is a general expectation that an attack will be made there to rescue the Point Pelê [*sic*] Prisoners, and to seize the Guns that are there— The Prisoners I have ordered to be removed, and propose proceeding to inspect the Western District next week if I can get away from Toronto.

All our State trials are now over with the exception of two or three unimportant cases at Kingston, and the juries here have done their duty upon the whole faithfully, but with less decision perhaps lately—and the Reformers who were silent are beginning to come forth again.

I have thought it better upon the whole to detain all the Prisoners in this Province until I receive the Secretary of State's answer, and propose sending them to Kingston.

I thank you very much for your willingness to give me an officer as Adjutant General of the Militia and Major Mackenzie Frazer, from your idea of his capacity would have been just the person—but, I find, I cannot get rid of the present incumbent very well. He is [a] worthy man, and a gallant soldier too I believe, but totally unfit for his office. Will you allow me to submit that an officer in the Quarter Master Genrl's Department is much wanting in this Province; it is impossible to say what may take place, and without proper Staff Officers the expence is exceedingly increased. If you can afford me this assistance I should consider it a particular favor if you would select a *very* intelligent hard working Officer of experience as I am not overburthened with aid of this sort—and my hands are so full just now that the head and time of a good Staff Officer would be a great relief to me—perhaps Major Frazer would do.

The Splinter Proofs they are fitting up for the Soldiers in the Barracks are really not wholesome[?];—it is too bad that the Home Govert have so long neglected this accommodation of the Troops. I have just been looking into your correspondence with the Secretary of State upon the subject, commenced in 1833, and have written to Lord Glenelg as strongly as I can with delicacy express myself. I enclose copy of my despatch upon the subject which will revive your recollection of facts—if you will be so good as to throw it into the fire after you have perused it—probably you have already reported the state of the Barracks to the H. Gds.—if not, there can be no doubt a short recommendation from you in that Quarter would ensure Success.

[Enclosure lacking.]

[179] JNO MACAULAY TO [ARTHUR ?]: A.D.S. 4p.

May 30 [*Place not stated.*]

Memorandum

The very important nature of the question as it respects myself, will perhaps be admitted as an apology for my submitting the following observations[:]

In the year 1836, I was residing at Kingston, where I had passed my life, in the possession of an income (independent of my private means) derived from two employments viz in the Post Office and a Bank Agency, of about £750 per annum, and had no intention or desire of removing from thence, when His Excellency, Sir Francis B. Head was pleased to propose to me the situation which I now occupy of Surveyor General of Lands, with a salary of £600 sterling a year and fees amounting together on an average to a trifle more than the emoluments I then enjoyed at Kingston—

After some deliberation, and not without considerable reluctance to sever those ties by which I was bound to my native town, I was induced to accept the honour offered me by Sir Francis B. Head; and I did so, not because I was intent on emolument only, for the difference in the expense of living, incurred by my change of residence turned somewhat to my disadvantage, but because I would when at Toronto find myself in direct intercourse with many of the most valued friends of my earlier days, and would also be advanced in rank, and by receiving the charge of an important Department, occupy a station of greater usefulness— On arriving at this City, I found that the office to which I had been appointed, had from various causes, fallen into disorder, and I saw the necessity of applying myself to a careful inquiry into the extent of labour and judgment that would be required for the purpose of bringing up the arrearages of work in each branch of duty, and re-establishing an exact and efficient system of business— I have since steadily pursued my plans of improvement, and have indulged in the hope that I might in the course of a reasonable period, reduce the affairs of the Department to a state of order and method that would reflect some credit on myself, and at the same time be satisfactory to the Government and the Country. In thus devoting my attention to these new duties, I must confess that a distaste for them was engendered by the condition in which I found the books, records &c, but this speedily gave way to the interest that was excited by the business in which I became engaged; and as a Despatch was addressed to the Lieutenant Governor, by the Right Honourable Secretary of State, within a few weeks after my appointment, conveying the gracious confirmation thereof by His late Majesty, I have at once surrendered my hold on the appointments at Kingston, and considering my destiny fixed by the assignment of an office of the first importance in the Province, neither anticipated nor desired a removal to any other place or station—

By the conversation with which I was recently honoured, His Excellency was pleased to observe that a person was required to discharge the duties of Private or Civil Secretary, and in expressing an opinion that I was qualified for that post, intimated on what terms it was desirable that I should hold it.

The impressions on my mind with regard to this proposed change of situation, I venture respectfully to note—

1st It appears to me that I should descend on the scale of rank, for in this Colony at least, the situation of Secretary to the Lieutenant Governor has never been accounted equal in rank to that of the Head Officer of a branch or department of Civil Administration— And as a person advances in years, it can seldom be found agreeable for him to retrograde in rank or station.

2nd There is this further consideration in my case:— While I should act in the capacity of Secretary, I could not with propriety occupy my seat in the Legislative Council, except perhaps once pro formâ during each Parliament[.] I clearly could take no part in the proceedings of that House.

3rd. The appointment of Secretary is *temporary*, and unless under some new arrangement, could only last during one administration. The average term of an administration is not, I believe much beyond six or seven years, and though I most sincerely hope that the present may extend beyond the most protracted one that is recorded in our annals, it yet must reach its close, and then will recur to mind the material difference between the Secretaryship, and an office that is usually retained by deserving occupants during life.

If these views be well founded, it would naturally follow that although there might be a superiority in point of emolument attending the change in question, I would find no permanent advantage result from it— I should be prepared for closer application, and more active exertions than are required by my present office—

Nevertheless if it should be conceived that I am capable of rendering the Government more useful services in the office of Secretary than in my present post, I shall hold myself ready to conform to its pleasure. But in relinquishing for that purpose the charge of an important Department, I hope I shall not be deemed unreasonable in being allowed to entertain the expectation of obtaining through His Excellency's interposition with Her Majesty's Government, a promise of the Reversion of the office of Provincial Secretary and Register on the next vacancy, and that in the event of His Excellency's requiring the immediate assumption of my new duties, my present office may in the mean while be kept in abeyance. By such a pledge from the Government I should be relieved from unpleasant solicitude with regard to the future, and be provided with a sure means of resuming my present rank in the Colony, when His Excellency might see fit to retire from its Government, or to dispense with my services as Private Secretary—

[180] ARTHUR TO COLBORNE: Df.L. with emendations in Arthur's handwriting. 8p.

May 31 *Government House, Toronto.*

I have the honor to represent to Your Excellency that, for some time past, but more especially within the last fortnight, rumours of an intended invasion by a combined force of Traitors who escaped from this Province, of disaffected persons, who hastily left it—and of a class of American Subjects, calling themselves "Patriots," have been gaining ground, and are certainly confirmed in a remarkable manner by statements from various persons, and from various and distant quarters.

Relying upon the preventive measures of the Government of the United States, I have proceeded with the reduction of the Militia force allowing all such men as had been enlisted until the 1st. July by Sir Francis Head to return to their Homes if they wished it—but, within the last few days, the Accounts from the Frontier are of a nature calculated to arrest this proceeding, and to require the most particular vigilance and attention.

Whether these people will put their threats of invasion into execution it is impossible to say;—but, as large sums of money have been subscribed, and arms and ammunition collected, it is not possible to doubt their intention—independant [*sic*] of the information to that effect derived from many intercepted letters.

On my return from visiting Kingston, where rumours of some intended acts of violence upon our Frontier were strongly entertained, I received a letter from Colonel Macaulay Commanding the Militia Force in Toronto, and one from Colonel Foster the Assistant Adjutant General, of which I have the honor to enclose copies—these letters contain the substance of the various reports of the proceedings and intentions of the Rebels & Patriots on the American side. The circumstance that most arrested my attention was—the danger which the Master of the Steamer "Great Britain" was warned by an American to avoid—that of having his vessel seized and burnt whilst laying at Lewiston, as part of a plan for destroying all the Canadian Steamers on the Lake!

Although an American subject, this report so alarmed the Master, Mr. Whitney, that he promptly hauled off from the Wharf, and there can now be no doubt thereby saved his vessel from immediate destruction.

By the depositions of several respectable persons it appears that on Tuesday morning about one oClock A.M. the very fine Steamer "Sir Robert Peel" was boarded by a band of American Citizens whilst laying along side the Wharf at "Wellesly [*i.e.* Wells] Island" in the St. Lawrence, and was utterly destroyed by fire—the Passengers, after having been robbed and plundered were sent ashore almost in a state of destitution.

Copies of the Depositions are enclosed. No doubt any longer remains on my mind, after this outrage, that the preparations so long represented to be in progress, may now be depended upon in the main as accurate; and it will be necessary to prepare for the result of them. At the same time, I have on this occasion considered it to be my duty to restrain, as far as possible, Her Majestys subjects from resorting to any acts of retaliation until we see what the American Government will do in this matter, and I have the honor to enclose a Copy of a Proclamation which was published this day as soon as the information reached Toronto.

I have despatched a messenger to Mr. Fox who will I hope demand satisfaction with firmness.

As the first brunt of this Affair will inevitably fall on the Upper Province, I shall be much releived [*sic*] to find it is in Your Excellency's power to send another Regiment into it at your earliest convenience; and I would propose keeping up four of the Regiments of the Militia which have been called out since December last— But, after the 1st. of July when their present engagement terminates, it would be right to place them altogether on a better footing, and I think it would be beneficial to engage their services for twelve months—not merely with a view of repelling any foreign invasion, but to produce an effect upon this Country, which is by no means in a satisfactory State.

[Enclosures lacking.]

[181] W. H. DRAPER TO [ARTHUR]: A.L.S.

[*1838*] [*Place not stated.*]
[*June ?*] I have requested Mr. Thorne to call upon your Excellency, as he has lately travelled thro' the state of New York and has just returned from Rochester where he remained three or four days[.]

His information may be satisfactory—

[182] J. B. ROBINSON TO THE LIEUTENANT GOVERNOR [ARTHUR]: A.L.S. 3p.

[*1838*] [*Place not stated.*]
[*June ?*] I have found it a very difficult task to reduce the number—No. 2. is the list I began with, but it much exceeds the limits— No. 1—contains I think the 25 worst names, but the difficulty is that of those omitted there are many whom it will not do to pardon, & whom it would be thought folly to banish— It is really a very perplexing business— I think it would not do to send home the bulky document herewith returned,[1] for it is not by any means in accordance with the views ultimately taken of the different cases—

On the whole I should be inclined to write to the Secretary of State placing the difficulties fairly before him, and saying that with the knowledge which you have acquired of the conduct of the parties & the sentiments of the Community in respect to them, You can not take the responsibility of relaxing further, but if on a view of the whole case Her Majesty shall think it proper to desire that the number to be transported shall be less, You will endeavour with the assistance of the Council to reduce it—

[*Enclosures:*]

[183] [J. B. ROBINSON]: A.D.

[*1838*]
[*June ?*]
[*Place not stated.*] [Marked: "1".]

[1]Possibly the report of the commissioners placed before the Executive Council on May 29, 1838.

Transportation for 14 years.

Walter Chace [Chase?]	William Alves
Stephen Brophy	Ira Anderson
John G. Parker	John Montgomery
Finlay Malcolm	John Stewart
Enoch Moore	William Stockdale
Horatio Hills	Wilson Reid [Read?]
Solomon Sly	Gilbert F Morden
Robert Walker	John Anderson
Thomas Shepherd [Shepard?]	Nathan Town
Michael Shepherd [Shepard?]	John Tufford
John Mavor	Charles P Walrath
Peter Milne	Paul Bedford
	Jay Cody

[184] [J. B. ROBINSON]: A.D. 2p.

[1838]
[June ?]

[*Place not stated.*] [Marked: "2."]

Transportation for 14 yrs.

Walter Chace [Chase?]	John Stewart
Michael Shepherd [Shepard?]	Finlay Malcolm
Solomon Sly	Horatio Hills
Leonard Watson	Nathan Town
Thomas Shepherd [Shepard?]	John Tufford
Robert Walker	Charles P. Walrath
John G Parker	Peter Malcolm
Gilbert Fields Morden	Harvey Bryant
John Montgomery	Enoch Moore
Randall Wixon	Jay Cody
Peter Milne	Ira Anderson
John Mavor	James Brown
Joseph Gould	Charles Chapin
William Stockdale	William Thompson
William Alves	Philip Henry
Stephen Brophy	Paul Bedford
John Anderson	James Hill
Wilson Reid [Read?]	John A. Tidy [Tidey?]
	John Kelly

[185] R. B. SULLIVAN TO THE LIEUT GOVERNOR [ARTHUR]: A.L.S. 3p.

[1838] *Crown Land Office*, [*Toronto.*]
[June ?]

The Receiver General called upon me just now, and stated that from a communication with *Dr O Grady* he had reason to believe that the disaffected to the Northwards. are ready to rise, Mr Dunn proposes the bringing the Indians into Town.

I think it necessary that Your Excellency should receive intelligence from the Receiver General himself and notwithstanding his objection to wait upon Your Excellency. (founded as it appears to me upon some little jealousy at not being spoken to [by] Your Excellency on the state of the Country) I think it my duty humbly to recommend to Your Excellency to require Mr Dunn's attendance so that Y. E. may learn the particulars from his own mouth—

I fear that the statement communicated by Y. E. to the Indians is not authentic[;] the *Extra* which arrived yesterday & the Montreal herald which I just now saw at the Attorney Generals give a somewhat different version of the affair, which appears very encouraging in itself although not quite so Chivalric as the first statement[.]

[186] ARTHUR TO COLBORNE: L. 3p.

June 1 *Government House, Toronto.* [Marked "Copy".]

Referring to my former correspondence respecting certain prisoners taken in arms against Her Majesty in this Province, I have the honour to inform Your Excellency that for reasons which are explained in the enclosed Order in Council. I have felt it necessary to transmit for safe-keeping at Quebec, the prisoners whose names are inserted in that Order.

As these prisoners were taken in arms against Her Majesty, engaged in hostile attempts against this Province, there can be no doubt that their offence is rather against the British Empire, than against the Municipal Laws of this Colony, and I have therefore no apprehension that any difficulty will be made with respect to their detention at Quebec. Their cases have been fully reported by me to Her Majesty's Secretary of State, and I have requested an early decision upon them. In the mean time, it is not without good grounds that I assure Your Excellency, of the expediency of making Quebec the place of their imprisonment, rather than any post in this Province.

It is I doubt not highly advisable for both Provinces that I should remove one powerful cause of that excitement which is at this moment agitating the American frontier, and deprive the ill-disposed portion of the American people of all hope of effecting one principle [*sic*] object of their hostile preparations which it is certain are now in progress.

[Enclosure lacking.]

[187] [R. B. SULLIVAN] TO THE LIEUTENANT GOVERNOR [ARTHUR]: A.L. 282p.

[*June 1*] [*Crown Lands Office, Toronto.*] [A torn cover sheet reads: "Mr. Sullivans Report on the State of the Province 1838 Original Manuscript".]

Your Excellency has kindly encouraged me to offer some remarks upon the present state of the Province and I have accordingly committed to paper my own reflections as they occurred to me in the intervals of other business—had I had more leisure I probably should have been able to give more information in fewer words but the manner in which I have been occupied has prevented me from spending the time with this paper necessary for proper condensation and arrangement.

Your Excellency will perceive that I have avoided both crimination and e[u]logium of particular persons. I have done so because it appears to me that the present situation of this Province has not been so much the result of the actions or policy of the few whose names might be introduced into the discussion as of a current of circumstances over which individuals had little control, or more strictly speaking not sufficient control to have made the results materially different, had most of the prominent actors been different men.

Were the Political state of these Provinces capable of being considered merely with reference to internal occurrences and opinions the inquiries to be made would have been comparatively simple, but this unhappily is not possible[.] The future safety and tranquillity of the Province must depend more upon External circumstances, over which this Government has no control, than upon the management of internal affairs. There are no mountains or seas, or differences of language to separate this Province from the United States, and this Province must be materially affected by the state of Politics and of the popular mind in the neighbouring republic.

Nothing could be more for the interest of this Colony than the practical success of the American theory of a purely representative Government[.] For if a settled state of the popular mind existed in the American republic. the quiet prevailing in our immediate neighbourhood would certainly promote the same state of feeling here. We should be under no fear of aggression from a moral and enlightened people. who acted upon principle and abhorred violence and wrong. The course of transactions between the two countries would shew a mutual interchange of benefits—and the relations which would in such case exist upon this continent between the two great powers who occupy it would shew a beautiful realization of the popular opinion— That the march of intellect and education had proceeded so far as to offer a prospect of universal peace and to preclude the probability of war or the necessity of defensive preparations. The interests of the people it has been said are best promoted by peace. The people are the best judges of what is conducive to their own welfare.[1] and the ambition of Emperors Kings, and aristocrats being removed. it would seem to follow. that the golden age. in which the hand of man would no longer be lifted against his brother was actually brought back to the earth, that a new political light had risen in America, which was to illuminate the nations, until the world would be one vast republic. in which justice peace and mercy would occupy the thrones now filled by earthly potentates[.]

But how very different has been the working of the American constitution[.] In the anxiety of the people to leave no power to do evil in the hands of Government, almost all power has been denied to it. It is true that no individual can be a tyrant, but the tyranny of a majority, is less responsible, and more unrelenting and universal in its application, every thing is referred directly to party, and from the highest to the lowest every functionary of the Government is dependant upon the will of majority for his continuance in office and in many parts of the union individuals can only be secure in personal safety, by following blindly the popular clamor of the day. The Bench of Justice is shamefully dependent on the same source of all power, Trial by Jury has become no better than investigation by public meetings. Law is a dead letter. punishment for outrages committed by the mob. is out of the question. The people that is the majority say we made the law and are consequently superior to it. in short the country is as nearly in a state of Anarchy, as a nation with the form of a Government can be.

Parties are so nearly balanced throughout the Union. that nothing is settled or likely to be so. The election of a constable or an officer of militia is looked upon as a demonstration of popular opinion which is to effect the next election of the President[;] individual votes are counted by Units, and the whole community is in the agitation of a continual election.

In such a state of things, when municipal law is trampled upon it is in vain to expect that treaties with foreign nations will be respected. It is of little avail to enquire if the Government are sincere in their expressions of amity, when they have no power to preserve amicable

[1]The punctuation throughout the transcript is Sullivan's. His use of periods cannot be regarded as a mere casual dropping of the pen by the writer.

relations and when an energetic attempt to do so compromizes the existence even of the name of the power, which [is] thus called into action. It is not therefore surprising to see the United States Government helplessly looking on, professing its desire for peace— While the great mass of the population, regard this country as a lawful prey, openly Scoff at all authority while mobs break open public arsenals take the artillery and munitions of war belonging to the nation. assemble and parade in the public Streets and publish in the very Newspapers their plans of aggression and carry them into effect by actual invasion.

The pirate, The Brigand The murderer and the plunderer cross the boundary line and invade this Province, the incursion is defeated. they are driven off at the expense of innocent lives, and with an enormous sacrifice of money. but they retreat behind their boundary again, and a Surveyors line becomes an impregnable fortification, from which they regard us with mockery, and cool[l]y prepare in perfect security for another attack. Their own Government will not and probably cannot restrain them, & We cannot follow them because we are nominally at peace with the United States—

In this country unfortunately the settlement of American citizens has been too much permitted and encouraged. and thus in the bosom of this community there exists a treacherous foe[.] The vicinity of the arena for the discussion of extreme political fantasies, infects this population, many of the natural born Subjects of the Crown are carried away by the plausibility of republican doctrines, and by the gratification to self conceit, which would be the consequence of every man being not merely a speculative but a practical statesman. personal disappointments disarrangement of private affairs. want of success in political intrigue, in short every Circumstance which does not fall out precisely as every man whether from good or bad motives desires, is made a ground for organic change in Government, a reason for revolution.

In such a state of things, It is not wonderful that a considerable portion of this community may be said to be disaffected and indeed it is much to the honor of the Upper Canadian people, that the great majority are truly loyal.

In all countries, and most emphatically it may be asserted in the United States a portion of the people are discontented. The misfortune of Upper Canada has been the apparent defencelessness of the Government, and the apparently more than adequate means for its destruction. This changes discontent into treason, and reform into rebellion.

If it were not for the vicinity of the United States. there can be no doubt, that in this Province the opposition to Government would scarcely ever be carried beyond what in a free country is wholesome and necessary. but with that vicinity opposition is dangerous. and may, should some even groundless cause of change in public sentiment prevail, become absolutely destructive.

It is not to be expected that any concessions to popular will, can produce universal content or that any measures of policy will unite the population. This Government has no right to deny a general assertion that grounds of complaint do exist. or to assert that the best measures are always pursued, but until the democracy of the United States exhibit a united people, and one not professing to labour under extreme grievances, it is useless to argue that an approximation to that form of Government will produce an effect which its complete adoption has utterly failed in bringing about, in the United States[.]

It is for the British Nation to judge whether it is for the interests of the empire to abandon this colony. or to give up its loyal inhabitants to the mercies of a demoralized American rabble. or its fair and fertile territory to the rapacity and avidity of American politicians[.] The Colonists may altogether overrate the importance of The American Provinces to England, and a balance Sheet may exhibit a yearly expenditure in maintaining their dependence upon the Crown, without a corresponding income[.] But The Americans, Government Legislature, and people of all parties, hardly conceal the hope, that England may consider as worthless, what they look upon as invaluable[.] Canada, Newfoundland New Brunswick, Nova Scotia, The West Indies The fisheries, The trade The ships, the timber The seamen are a property in which the American citizen is taught to believe he has a vested remainder, every hour that England holds it is thought an infringement of natural right, and when that property is brought into possession then the American looks upon rivalry with England and ultimate Superiority upon the ocean as the certain consequence.

It is said that The trade of the United States is more beneficial to England than the trade of the same Territories while they were Provinces of Great Britain and therefore it is usually argued, the commerce of an independent state is more profitable than that of a Colony.

The only position however which is actually proved, is simply this[:] a part of the trade of 15 millions, of people is more profitable than the whole trade of 3 millions. and before. the position can be made tenable that the trade of an independent country is superior in advantage to that of a colony it must be shewn that the relation of Colony and Parent State, actually prevents the natural increase of the human species or the influx of population from the overcrowded parts of the earth, into an extensive, fertile and unoccupied territory.

The commercial prosperity of the United States may however be traced to Sources perfectly independent of the form of Government existing therein.

The internal sou[r]ces of this prosperity may be stated as follows.

1st. The extent of unoccupied land which allowed the unrestrained spreading of the population and provided the easily attained means of subsistence, which made early marriage prudent and rendered an increasing family a source of wealth instead of an incumbrance even to the poorest classes[.]

2dly. In the climate of a part of the Union which permits the cultivation of the two great articles of American export, Tobacco & cotton[.]

Externally the great Sources of American prosperity may be Stated as follows—

First. In the connection with England and the colonization of the country by natives of the British Isles.

2d. To The valor and prowess, of Great Britain which gained for the Anglo-American race the uncontrolled possession of almost the whole continent of North America, and successfully established this Anglo American race thereon, in despite of the utmost exertions of one of the first military nations in the world, and to the exclusion of others of less importance[.]

Had the french dutch, Spaniards and Portug[u]ese, divided North America with the English race, the same progress would have been observed in the short period of American Existence which the History of Europe has always presented. namely continual warfare or preparation for war. confinement of the different sections of the population within defensible bounds, employment of the population in military affairs, and of the rescources [*sic*] of the respective communities in the raising and sustaining armies and the erection of fortifications, waste of human life must have taken place to an enormous extent, and in short had it not been for the complete conquest of the Country by England The subsequently rapid advance of the European race in North America would have been wholly impossible[.]

Thirdly. The great increase in the population of the British Isles. and the consequent necessity for Emigration[.]

Fourthly. The ingen[u]ity energy & enterprise of British manufacturers, which opened an almost unlimited market for the cotton of the Southern States. joined with the European taste for Tobacco.

Fift[h]ly The immense accumulation of monied capital in England and the employment of it in America.

The Northern Exports of wheat, flour, and Flaxseed. need only be mentioned at present, in connection with American Manufactories as they have been rapidly decreasing and must decrease, in proportion as the increase of an american manufacturing population excludes British goods, and makes a home market for these articles.

It seems very evident That none of these Sources internal or external were incompatible [*sic*] with colonial dependance upon England. and that without such dependance some of them could not have originally existed.

Unless the foregoing statements are altogether incorrect it would seem to follow that whatever England may have lost by American independence she has in fact gained nothing thereby. and also that by the separation of this country from from [*sic*] England there is nothing to be gained.

But it is yet to be enquired what loss would arise to the British Empire by a union of these Provinces with the American republic.

The exclusion of British manufactory from the United States, and the establishment of a great American trade upon the ruins of this English trade has been for a long time a favorite policy with the Northern States. extensive establishments for the fabrication of articles formerly imported from England have been set up, and maintained at the expence of high protecting duties upon English goods, This to the people of the Southern States is a total loss as they have no manufactories[.] The whole carrying trade of the South is monopolized by Northern vessells [*sic*], and the national dependence in a commercial point of view of the South, with England the principal consumer of its produce is forcibly destroyed. The South complains, remonstrates and threatens almost in vain, The Tyranny of a majority in congress, stimulated by the most unprincipled cupidity, is only bounded by its power of oppression and a slave population is not the one for armed resistance. The Northern Majority is not however quite complete. but let the British North American Colonies be once made Northern States of the union and the probability is that most articles of British fabrication will not only be made subject to heavy duties but will be absolutely contraband throughout the United States of America.

It may be argued on the other side that the United States are deeply interested in preserving the trade with England. It may be supposed that the principles of free trade would obtain if any where in a country which professes to be supereminently free. That the market which is open in England for the consumption of articles of American export is too valuable to be lightly thrown away. That the supply of population and the employment of British capital in the United States from the British Isles is so indispensable to America that she must retain them even at the expence of her manufacturing schemes. and it may be further added that British ingenuity, industry, enterprise and accumulated Capital and the immense artisan population of England places it beyond the reach of competition in America for ages yet to come.

As a whole the English trade is undoubtedly beneficial to the United States, and the benefits arising from this trade are fully appreciated by the Southern planters, & by The merchants and others engaged in the import & export trade throughout the Union. But unhappily universal suffrage or something very near it exists in all America amongst the white and free population and the consequence is that the Southern planters and the United States Merchants do not together form a majority. and the actual majority does not care for benefits which result to its rival, and on the contrary [is] decidedly hostile to the means by which that rival continues to be wealthy, and powerful even with smaller numbers and as a minority. The Government of General Jackson was sternly resisted by the Mercantile interests. The struggle resulted in the destruction of the United States Bank, and the passage of The tariff laws[;] the one measure directed against the introduction of British Capital, the other against the importation of British Manufactories. These measures have as yet but partially succeeded, but the carrying them out to the fullest extent has never for a moment been lost sight of by The United States Government and the democratic party[.] These measures have to a certain extent been struggled against, but the battle is still pending. The cry against, foreign influence foreign money. foreign imports, will always be popular in the United States, and the preponderance which a union of the Canadas would give to to [*sic*] Northern popular influence would prostrate all opposition, to the democratic party and annihilate the party which preserves to England any portion of the American trade.

Again. The principles of free trade, are not and cannot be those of of a country Governed by a numerical majority. The benefits to arise from it are too remote, and not sufficiently palpable to be appreciated by the mass of the population and accordingly we find that at the very time that Mr Huskis[s]on was promulgating the free trade system as undeniably right and any laws which would advance the interests of one portion of the community at the expense of another as antiquated and barbarous[,] The United States Government was urging with all its strength the war with foreign capital, invested in the United States Bank and with foreign imports by the establishment of The Tariff.

In the third place. The market for american produce, which England offers is beneficial to the minority. The Ultra American party, would much prefer the exportation of cotton from the South to the North, and its manufacture there, and the consumption of Northern products by the manufacturing population, in America to the export of either one or the other. And the Majority care nothing for the distress and ruin which would be caused to their rivals by the successive steps leading to this state of things.

Fourthly. As to british emigration, The people of the United States look upon foreigners with great jealousy. both parties partake of this feeling in Common. but Emigrants are endured because the poorer class have sided with the majority, and generally help to uphold the Government of the democracy. for the simple reason that they have little or no personal interest in assisting the mercantile body in the accumulation or preservation of wealth and they are flattered with the power which universal suffrage gives them, over a class which claims to be superior. It is probable that british Emigrants may for some time longer be permitted to settle in the United States and America will have the advantage of this means of increase to her population & rescources but it is evident that the exclusion of British trade from america can have no influence in preventing the emigration of the British people to America.

Fifthly. As regards the employment of British Capital in America.

This capital is employed, in the first place in loans to American Citizens and States to enable them to make rail roads, Canals and other public works to which American rescources would be inadequate[.]

On this subject it may be observed that while the British people, express their wonder at American Enterprize and industry when in fact the greater part of the money which paid for their improvement came from London, and the labourers who made them from Ireland leaving to America the very easy task of employing other people with other peoples money.

But it is very evident that neither the supply of money or of people would be cut off by an exclusion of British trade from America—

English Capital is also very largely employed in loans or advances to Americans, to enable their Merchants to import English and foreign goods.

The American statesman of the democratic side is an enemy to this extension of English credit, and when the late crisis in money and mercantile affairs took place which proved the course of trade carried on by this means to be ruinous to the English Merchant there was no pity on the part of the American democrat, he said it was England which encouraged the extravagance which led to the Bankruptcy of a great proportion of the American Merchants and let England take the consequences. Every measure which would tend to sustain the credit of the American merchant was accordingly rejected. And for a well founded reason as regarded party politics. The exclusion of British goods from the United States and The Monopoly of American Manufacturers in the North & the South, as far as their state of efficiency could enable them to supply america was materially advanced by the destruction of American credit in England, and the total restriction of the trade to America itself was brought nearer than ever, as a course of necessary protection and as one according with the popular feeling[.]

6thly. As regards the power of England by means of British industry ingenuity enterprize and accumulated capital and of her artisan population to overcome all opposition in America.

If the trade were left free and open there can be no doubt that nothing exists in America which could prevent the introduction of British goods, or the ascendancy of British fabrics over the domestic manufactured articles[.] But if the time should come when the democratic party in America can sustain American manufactures, to the exclusion of English goods, at the expence of the consumers by means of heavy import duties. The market will not be supplied by means of American Capital, or American Artisans but by the transfer of both from England to America[.] The manufacturer from Birmingham Sheffield or Manchester, can employ himself more profitably in America with a protecting duty of 50 per cent, than in England by supplying the same market in the face of that duty and when the British manufacturer finds trade dull, and foreign market inaccessible, at the very moment when activity and spirit is given to the domestic manufactories in America, he will emigrate, and by change of his position escape the effect of the exclusive american system, reap all its advantages, and give to a foreign country the profits, of the very same ingenuity enterprize and capital upon which England founds her hope of continued supremacy. America will fight her battle with English weapons. and instead of finding a foreign people to contend with England will be opposed to a portion of herself without any well founded hope of advantage in the contest. England will then be driven article by article out of the American market. and when this is accomplished the next step is competition in foreign countries, to which an European war, and as usual an American peace and a neutral flag will furnish the best means of success.

That this expectation of American rivalry with the manufacturing interests of England is not chimerical the fact that it has already succeeded, as regards the article of coarse cotton cloth in the South American and china market is a proof, and the advantage which the United States possess, in being untaxed comparatively with England offers a prospect of cheap production in America, of many fabrications, only obstructed at present by the want of monied capital, and of operative population, and these the transfer of money and population from England, and the substitution of machinery for manual labor is now gradually supplying, and in case of the exclusion of British manufactures from England will supply with rapidity proportioned to the demand.

America has successfully contended with England in the fisheries of Newfoundland and in the South Seas— She imports tea cheaper than the English Merchant and is gradually introducing her ships into the carrying trade, in most parts of the world, in all the splendid lines of Packets which carry on the communication between England and America there is not one British vessel: and with all the maritime superior[i]ty of England there are twenty American ships in the port of Liverpool for one English ship in the harbor of New York. Even the North Western fur trade of England has not escaped from American intrusion and though as yet it is preserved, and English Interests prevail, The American looks upon them with jealo[u]sy, and with a cupidity which is only restrained by want of power.

No American is blind to the fact that all the External trade of America at present exists at the will of England. or to the further fact that upon the maritime supremacy of England depends her possession of the West Indies, or to the further fact that The Eastern Empire of England depends for its existence upon undoubted, and unquestionable maritime supremacy, or to the further fact That in case of the destruction of the Dominion of England upon What has been termed her native Element. America is in the situation above all other nations, to take the lions share of the spoil.

This part of the subject of this report which confined as it is to the general statement of facts in the knowled[g]e of every man who has an opportunity of viewing closely the course of american politics is perhaps almost beyond the province of this paper, may be concluded by a short summary of what is humbly thought to be established by the foregoing statements.

1st. That whether for the interest of Americans generally or not, it is the policy of the democratic party to supersede the use of British manufactories in the United States; and to set up american manufactories in their stead.

2d. That the accomplishment of this object by means of protecting duties is directly contrary to the interests of the Southern planters and of the Merchants engaged in the import trade generally. but that these interests are not strong enough to contend with the democratic majority and the influence of the American Government.

3d. Were these Provinces joined to the United States the body of the population which would remain in this Province, the vast majority of lower canadians and probably the majority of the remaining inhabitants of the other colonies when universal suffrage shall be established in these Countries as American States, would be added to the ultra American democratic party.

4th. And it would follow that the beneficial trade of England with the United States, which even now is in danger would in case of the accession of the North American provinces to the United States be shortly at an end.

5th. And therefore that so far from the trade of America as an independent country being more beneficial to England than the trade of American Colonies no such beneficial trade would probably continue in case of the cession of these Provinces.

6th. That the exclusion of British manufactures from the United States would inevitably cause the setting up in their stead American manufactures.

7th. That this will cause the emigration of British artizans and Capitalists[.]

8th. That when this takes place to a considerable extent America will to the same extent rival England as an exporting country.

9th. The American Fisheries and the carrying trade are becoming highly important[.]

10th. That these can be held securely only by means of a Strong marine[.]

11. That a Warlike Marine can only be created and upheld, with the assistance of an extensive mercantile Navy. and therefore the increase of the interest to be protected, namely the Mercantile Navy is the best means of establishing the protecting power that is to say a Government Navy.

11[*sic*]. That the possession of the Canadas, the trade of the St Lawrence, the accession of Newfoundland and the Eastern colonies with the timber trade & fisheries, would place America suddenly in the desired position, of being a Naval power, of dangerous importance to England.

12. The possession of these colonies by America would make her unassailable by land, and enable her to turn her whole rescources and attention to the promotion of her Naval Strength and importance[.]

13. Were England to be thrown upon the North of Europe for her supplies of timber, the increase of price would probably make that article fully as dear to the consumer as at present, without the advantage to the public of the duties now levied upon the Baltic timber.

13[*sic*]. Were a coalition of the Northern European powers once more to take place, and were England to be excluded from the Baltic trade, and were America to join The supply of timber so essential to the English war and merchant Navy would be cut off. And these countries could to a certain extent dictate to England the terms on which she should be supplied.

14th. Although the Government of the United States is not in a condition to go to war at this moment it cannot restrain the Citizens of the United States from the expression of its views. or even from actual aggression on the frontier, it cannot force the State of Maine into a settlement of the Boundary question, and therefore it will not probably be able to wait until a European war enables America again treacherously to take advantage of British Embarrassments and to contend with a portion only of the power of England.

15. There can scarcely be a question that if The rebellion in the Canadas had been at all successful. The rebels would not have been without the aid of The American Government and the almost universal acclamation of the American people, would not only have forced America into war, but would have enabled her to sustain it.

16. The prompt suppression of the rebellion, prevented the open expression of this unanimity, and the prompt action of the American Government. so that the time of active and dangerous american aggression, will now probably depend upon the state of preparation for war, and the apparent means of resistance on our part.

16[*sic*]. And it would follow that the moral obligation to maintain the connection of the Colonies with England so long merely as the Colonists desire such connection, is not by any means the only ground for pre-serving that connection.

17. And that the colonies should be preserved to England even at a very considerable pecuniary expence—and even if such expence should be proved to exceed the immediate pecuniary advantage arising from colonial dependancy.

These considerations lead naturally to the enquiry as to the means by which these colonies can be held and particularly as relates to this Province.

The measures of conciliation pursued towards Upper and Lower Canada have no doubt been submitted to Your Excellency previously to Your assuming The Government of This province[.] They are also detailed in the able and elaborate reports of The two houses of the Provincial Legislature[.]

That of the Hon Legislative Council is particularly worthy of consideration as an accurate detail of facts particularly within the knowledge of some of the members of that body. It is also as dispassionate as a document drawn up under the very exciting circumstances of the Country well can be, and were it not that it is considered desirable that some points of vital importance should on the part of the Colonies be brought more prominently forward that report might be considered as superseding the necessity of these remarks.

It was thought fit by the Imperial Parliament to extend to these colonies a representative form of Government. And it is too late to argue that to small communities such a government is not always adapted or that when the interests of the Empire at large are to be considered of paramount importance such a form of Government would expose them to constant collision with local interests and sectional influence.

and produce on the part of the mother country concessions injurious to her supremacy, or in their place resistance, and consequent dissatisfaction.

In an independent country with a supreme legislature, there is very seldom a political change which destroys the form of Government, or a public wish to bring about organic alterations. The result of political agitation is generally in such case a change in the men who administer public affairs, and one set of men are generally forced by the current of circumstances to act very much as their opponents would do if they were in power[,] The constitution under which the respective parties act remaining nearly the same.

But in a colony the case if far different[.] The popular feeling is often opposed to the policy of the Empire and the Ambition of individuals meets with an insurmountable Check in considerations of justice policy and consistency by which the supreme Government must be guided. The consequence is that the severing the connection between the countries is the only course open to the ambitious leader of a party when the fiat goes forth "thus far shalt thou go and no further[.]" But if the question be conceded, that Legislatures are proper for subordinate governments, surely the form of constitution should distinctly limit the power given by the supreme authority. In some respects the limits have been defined, but what is the use of literal definitions when the power of assailing and overthrowing them is given.

The power of the British House of commons over the public revenue is the true foundation on which the practical supremacy of the people of England is based. and the functions of the Commons, at first confined to the mere granting money to the Crown, Now extend virtually to the making peace or war, the settling the prerogative of the Sovereign and the privileges of the Barons[.] At the voice of the House of Commons the machine of Government ceases to act. and if it be supported with any constancy by public sentiment every other power must be obedient. But is it right in itself, or just to a colony to put the same power into the hands of its legislature. to say to it You shall have the complete control over the public purse You shall have the power of staying the course of Government, and of reducing the country into a state of anarchy. but you must use it only for good or evil as we the supreme Government shall judge.

This concession is absolutely inconsistent with the relation of a colony to a parent state[.] In this colony the threat of stopping the supplies has often been denounced once it has actually been carried into effect. In this Province the public voice happily did not sustain the Assembly yet rebellion was so intimately connected in its nature with the measure that the project of revolt was then conceived, which was afterwards brought forth by the state of the Lower Province, and by American sympathy.

In Lower Canada the Popular voice sustained the House of Assembly. And there we find, accordingly deeply rooted disaffection and hatred to England and the great body of the people coerced into a sullen obedience. And the only practical remedy appears to be an undisguised, or a virtual breach of the constitution[.]

The Government on the one hand tells the Canadian elector You have no right to coerce us. The King's representative has the power of refusing to enact laws at Your dictation, You are even attempting to overthrow the constitution which gives you political power by the very means which that constitution places in your hands.

The answer is simple— Why did you give me the power to coerce the Government, why did you place in my hands the engine which is exercised for that purpose in England? Is not a debate on the subject of the Exclusion of Bishops from the House of Lords, as complete a breach of the British constitution as a motion in the Canadian Assembly, to abolish the Legislative Council or to make that Body elective, may not the one question be carried possibly so far in England as a stoppage of the supplies as well as the other has been in Canada.

There can be no question that with the exception of the sum necessary to secure the paramount consideration, namely the connection of the Colony with England and the carrying on the Government by payment of its functionaries. the surplus revenue raised from the people may in a colony be safely entrusted to themselves with the ordinary check of the Governor & Legislative Council. But revenue should never have been left in the hands of a provincial parliament to the extent of enabling it to coerce the Government in matters not properly relating to revenue, for the effect of conceding such power is to make two supreme powers, which is absurd. [The following passage is here deleted: "and the consequences of the attempt to exercise such power are improper concessions on the one hand, improper claims on the other, and collision and dispute without end between them both."]

In the Poem of the Thebaid, the Gods in Council, visited a country with vengeance by the introduction of two Kings who were to reign alternately but the divinities did not understand the modern refinement of creating two powers, which were to be coexistent contemporaneous and *co local*, separated merely by a few words in a statute, and some Utopian sentiments of moderation and mutual forbearance and concession.

On the original occupation of these colonies and on the granting them the boon of a representative form of Government, it cannot be maintained that this state of things was contemplated, because the principal expences of the Government of the Colony were defrayed by England. The first false step was the granting a representative form of Government, without a positive provision for the Executive expenditure. The next was the giving up the revenues arising from the duties levied under the Statute 14 Geo 3. without a full and adequate provision for the carrying on the Government. This however may be defended in a manner as the carrying out the British principle of the people having the expenditure of monies levied upon themselves[.] But the yielding up the hereditary revenue of the Crown can be defended upon no prinicple of safety utility or justice[;] it is wrong in principle as it will be found unfortunate in practice[.]

The lands of the Colonies belong to the British Crown, to the Sovereign, in the strict sense to the Sovereign for the people of the Empire; in the more modern and liberal acceptation of the term of Crown property the first 50,000 settlers have no more right to the ungranted lands of the Colony than the first settler, and the population of Upper Canada now have no more right to these lands than the first family of colonists had. The settlers have in fact generally received grants of land, and in some manner or other partaken of the bounty of the Crown, they have received their share, they are land owners. They can afford to pay taxes, they are represented in parliament[.] They lay out their own money as it pleases them. what claim have they then upon what remains, had the right of the first ten thousand colonists been asserted, and recognized to the remaining lands of the colony what would have become of those who have immigrated since. and if the same right be now recognized what will become of those who will yet immigrate[;] surely if any of Her Majestys subjects have a right to the lands of the Colony, yet ungranted or to the proceeds of them it is those who have lately come into the province, and who are coming who have as yet received nothing, and yet these people objects as they are of the Solicitude of Government, are unrepresented in the Provincial Parliament and have not any control over the expenditure of the province, or any interest with the Legislators.

To illustrate this position it is only necessary to enquire how the Provincial revenues have been generally expended and how our very heavy provincial debt has been accumulated.

Upwards of £400,000 has been expended on the Welland Canal. Upwards of £300,000, on the Saint Lawrence Canal and including these sums upwards of a million of pounds upon frontier improvements. The monies expended by Parliament upon the roads, Bridges and other improvements of the Province are naturally enough monopolized by the part of the community represented in parliament but no expenditure has taken place to make the wilderness accessible to the new settler, or to relieve him from any of the difficulties attending his settlement in the forest. on the contrary before he reaches his solitary destination he has to travel over thousands of acres of forest, granted improvidently to the old inhabitants, lying waste and uncultivated, until The industry of the New settlers shall make them saleable. The Government direct sales of public lands for the purpose of raising a revenue, but no money is expended to make these lands accessible[.] The Parliament have too much to think of in providing for the interest upon the public debt which has been incurred in the great frontier works[,] and the casual and territorial revenue is desired by the House of assembly now not for the purpose of being expended more prudently economically or beneficially than at present. but as a means of paying interest upon loans raised for public works, every one of which it was said would pay for itself and be a source of profit, a saying which however except the one small work at Burlington Beach, has that [*sic*] never been realized.

The Welland Canal was considered by its projectors as likely to be a most profitable speculation, it was supposed that a large revenue would be derived from it chiefly at the expence of Americans who would make use of it as a means of communication between the two lakes, That Canal has been in operation for some time[;] it is in a state of decay[;] it requires a further outlay of £300,000. it has never returned any income, and it is acknowledged on all hands that it is not probable that it will ever make a return of interest of the public money expended upon it[.]

The magnificent work the Rideau canal was made at the expence of the British Government. at the cost of upwards of a million of pounds sterling[.] Yet it was not completed when the Notion of a rival canal on the River Saint Lawrence was projected which will cost perhaps £500,000.— This latter expenditure was only justifiable as a good speculation and when it is considered that the success of it would be at the expence of the Rideau Canal, and that the trade which would occupy the one would in some measure be taken away from the other it is scarcely to be excused that one Government work should be erected to compete with another and to prevent the latter from being profitable.

It was entered into as a speculation however. and it is not now pretended that as a speculation it can succeed[;] it cannot pay the interest on the money expended which must be a burden upon the Provincial Revenues.

If the Provincial Parliament will enter into magnificent undertakings beyond the present rescources of the country, and beyond the wants of its present population The people who send the representatives to parliament ought justly to bear the expence as they would unquestionably be entitled to the profits should any arise. But it is too much to say That the Hereditary revenues of the Crown which are neither legally nor equitably the property of the Canadian people should be alienated from their legitimate uses either for the purpose of assisting an exhausted provincial Treasury, or to save the people from being taxed for the payment of interest on sums borrowed and expended by their representatives in Parliament.

The lands of this Province and the Crown revenues arising from them have hitherto been chiefly granted and expended in acts of royal munificence, a few of which it may be of use to allude to generally.

1. The opening this Province as a place of refuge for the Loyalists who joined the Royal Standard during the war of the American revolution and the assigning them lands as a free grant, was not only an act of Bounty but of Justice, indeed were it not for the possession of this Colony, it is difficult to say in what manner England could have provided for those who had fought for her and become exiles from their homes and property from feelings of unshaken loyalty, and it is hard to say how long this Province would have remained a mere hunting ground were it not that these exiles took up their abode in it and prepared the way for European Emigration. And although it is true that the promise of lands to the children of the U E. loyalists has in some measure impeded the settlement, of the Province from the fact that few of them when the time came for their procuring their respective grants were in a situation which made the attainment of wild land at a distance from the frontier an object of importance and therefore the rights which they held were sold to speculators at almost nominal prices, and the lands remain in a wild state. Yet this is an objection of little importance when taken in connection with the whole measure which was on the one hand an important relief to the Government and on the other of incalculable benefit to the Colony.

But it is very plain that if the principle now advocated in the Provinces, of the lands therein being politically the property of the Colonists and not of the Empire this act of bounty was an infringement of colonial right, according to the new theory these lands besides being purchased from the Indians ought to have been again purchased and the proceeds ought to have gone to the lower canadians—then the Colonists.

2d. The giving free grants of land to European Emigrants and thus opening the way to comfort and wealth to many who would have languished in poverty at home, was an act of Royal bounty not to the Colonists but to British subjects having theretofore no connection with the colony, and the lands given were granted not as the property of the Colonists, but as the property of the Crown, held for the benefit of the people of the Empire at large and the system was peculiarly adapted at least to the then existing circumstances of the Province, so much so, that it is not going too far to say that much of the prosperity of the colony has been owing to Emigration encouraged by the bounty of the Crown, or what is still a more strong expression That the safety of the

Province and its preservation against internal rebellion, and foreign invasion has been in a very great degree owing to the gallantry & devoted loyalty of these poor settlers in the back woods, who poured forth in thousands to the frontier during the late revolt and rallied round the Government in the hour of danger. and difficulty.

Third. The granting lands in the Province to military settlers officers and men. was an act of Royal munificence, and a reward for faithful service which in strictness had nothing to do with the Colonial rights, and was perfectly inconsistent with the notion that the settlers residing in the Colony and exercising political rights therein had any property in the ungranted lands of the Crown. Yet this very measure has been the means of introducing into the Province settlers of a most valuable class, in the men of education, and of liberal views, and Gentlemanly Character of the Officers. And to their presence and the steady loyalty of the Military settlers generally much of the Gallant spirit which pervaded this Province. during the revolt. and of the efficiency of the inhabitants of this Colony, in a military point of view. as compared with the enemies of England in the vicinity, may be justly attributed.

The munificent appropriation of one seventh of the lands of the Province for purposes of religion was the gracious bounty of a pious, and good King, it was it is true intended for the benefit of the Colonists, but it was not intended for those who should at any particular period inhabit the Country. but for the Colonists and their descendants, and for the benefit of subjects of the Crown from all parts of the Empire who might choose to take up their abode at any future time in the Colony.

It never could have been contemplated that the rights of the latter class should be wholly at the disposal of the former or that if it should chance that a party in the Province should at any time prevail who would desire to grasp at the inheritance of religion, that our most gracious Sovereign and the Imperial Parliament guardians of the rights and interests of all the subjects of the Crown would at any time be induced by mere sectional popular clamor to surrender that guardianship to those whose present pecuniary interests would inevitably lead them to the alienation of what it would be their duty to preserve. And yet there have not been wanting even in this loyal Province, many who have looked upon the professions of desire to accommodate the measures of Government in relation to this matter as much as possible to the popular will, as so many concessions of the right of the Crown, and who have built upon these professions the most unqualified declarations of right, to alienate the Clergy reserves in aid of revenue, or for the purpose of public improvements, and for other purposes totally inconsistent with the original bountiful intention of The Imperial Government. And indeed if the point be once conceded that the ungranted territory of the Crown, and the revenues arising therefrom, ought to be at the absolute disposal of the people of the Colony and of the local legislature it is difficult to draw any plain line of distinction between the conceded principle and the right to alienate the clergy reserves to any purpose, which the necessities, or the cupiditity [*sic*] of any Party in the Province who for the moment chance to possess popular ascendancy may point out.

The grant of 220.000 acres of land for the endowment of the University, is one in which the future interests of the province, are deeply concerned yet were it to be considered as subject to change or alienation, at the popular will, however convenient the present possession of the funds might prove, the future inhabitants of the Province would have good reason to lament the concession which for the sake of appeasing an Ephemeral faction sacrificed the deep and enduring rights of the Youth of the Colony, for ever.

The revenues arising from the property of the Crown, have been partly expended in aid of the public revenue, partly in Assisting in the support of the Ministers of religion, partly in providing a few pensions for old and worn out servants of the Govt. who must otherwise have been provided for at the expence of the Provincial revenue, or abandoned altogether after spending their youth & strength in the public service, partly in assisting destitute Emigrants to their places of settlement, in the relief of old soldiers & pensioners in the settlement of New Townships, in aid of the payments for war losses, and in many other objects of public utility and importance[;] every shilling that has been expended has been regularly accounted for to parliament[;] no money has been laid out in secret, if any has been expended injudiciously, the recurrence of such a circumstance may be avoided in future and much more easily than by a surrender to the Legislature, who cannot be said to be free from the charge of injudicious expenditure of their own or the peoples money. no matter which party had the control of that money from time to time.

The concession of the right to the revenues arising from the Crown Territory involves the right to the Territory itself for the parliament who look upon the Lands of the Crown as a source of revenue would never be satisfied to see them alienated for any other purpose and accordingly this principle has been so far carried out in the New Brunswick act which was proposed for the adoption of this Legislature that alienations of Crown Land unless with a direct view to revenue are actually made invalid, and although the same law does not yet exist in this Province, there is little question but that when the right to dispose of the revenue arising from Territory is given up the right of disposing of the Territory itself must go with it.

It is supposed by the advocates of concession to popular demands That when all that a people ask for is given they will be loyal and contented, and that when the Government have nothing more which ought to be conceded there will be a cessation of demands upon it. But it must be considered that concessions are generally required not by the whole people but by a party in the course of the perpetual struggle for power & preeminence, and that the measure which is popular today will probably be decried tomorrow. It must also be remembered that there are concessions which cannot under any circumstances be made, with any regard to the preservation of colonial dependence, and that a Colonial Legislature is not supreme, but stands in a position in which it may and ought sometimes to be resisted. For the purpose therefore of offering an effectual resistance when it is proper to use it the Government ought to possess a certain degree of power and independence of temporary popular will, and the utter prostration of the legal power of the local government, can only lead to violent and illegal breaches of the constitution and to fatal collisions upon vital questions which if possible ought never to be discussed.

For instance the demand for a responsible executive Council had it been acceded to, would have placed the whole local Government with the exception of the Lieutenant Governor himself at the control of the prevailing party in the assembly, and had he unfortunately found himself alone in the advocacy of or resistance to any measure of vital importance, the next step of the popular party would naturally be to demand a Governor appointed by themselves. the object of the popular party of completely controlling the whole Government and making itself supreme would not be attained without it. If the Colonists were permitted to have a voice in the selection of the Governor, The next result would be collision with the Home Government. The next rebellion civil war and slavish subjection or complete independence.

The demand for an Elective Legislative council, is also full of the same tendency. perhaps the Chief use of that body is that it offers a field for fair discussion of public measures, independently of the prevailing popular party[;] were that body elective it [would] only add to a power already too strong for the safety of the colony. and instead of the fair discussion & contest now open, The Governor would be found upon some unhappy occasions either swayed about by every breath of opinion, in a small community in which change of opinion is necessarily frequent, and produced by causes which ought to be inadequate, or on the other hand he would appear in silent and sullen opposition to the whole legislature, to his Executive Council, to the officers of His Government who would naturally lean to the strongest side. And the result would be insubordination revolt and subjection by force of arms or independence.

The Election of juries is a favorite measure, as also their blind and chance selection from the populace according to certain lottery schemes. The natural result of this concession would be, the impossibility of procuring the legal conviction of any person charged with a crime of a political nature, This is felt in the United States so much that a popular man is above the law, and forgery fraud riot outrage and even murder, have often been committed with Impunity when there was any thing connected with the crime in accordance with the popular clamor of the day. In a colony this state of things would not be borne, but the remedy would be infraction of the constitution[,] martial law, and the end would be armed resistance.

But of all the concessions which have been the subjects of Political debate and agitation the Placing the Government completely in the power of a subordinate legislature with respect to revenue, is the most likely to induce discussion and agitation respecting the original principles of Government, and to bring organic changes always within view. The Imperial Government responsible to the Imperial Parliament, through the representative of the Sovereign in the Colony ought to have at least a supreme negative voice in all measures which relate to the interests of the Empire generally, and particularly as these measures are connected with the continuance of the connection of the Colony with the Parent State. The Imperial Government ought also to exercise its Constitutional Power in preventing a colony from falling into financial embarrassments which cannot fail to be injurious to the credit honor and character of the Empire. And generally it ought to exercise mildly prudently and carefully a controlling power over measures of internal policy, with a view of preserving throughout the dominions of the sovereign some degree of system and uniformity of laws and institutions, but when the subordinate legislature has the power of retaliating upon any resistance to its will by a refusal of the supplies necessary for the conducting the Government, It is too much to expect from any Colonial executive steadiness of purpose or consistency of action, for if these be exercised the result is the refusal of the supplies, the consequence in the end is infraction of the constitution, agitation insurrection & civil war.

Unless upon a review of the lists of grievances which from time to time have emanated from discontented Colonists it is hardly possible to conceive the trifling and unworthy causes which may lead to serious disagreements and final separation. when the means of coercing the Executive are so readily at hand. The people of Lower Canada did not become actual rebels, because of their disappointment respecting the success of the ninety two resolutions, but they refused the supplies, It became necessary therefore to break in upon their constitution, every man was alive to the change which was produced in his political state, when the constitution was invaded, and it was easy afterwards for an ambitious demagogue or a foreign emissary to argue him into rebellion. In Upper Canada, rebellion was not caused by any particular measure, but by the facility which the House of assembly possessed of resorting to the extreme measure of denying the means of carrying on the Government. This made a dissolution of Parliament necessary, and though the party which refused the supplies was in a manner prostrated by the result of the elections it still thought itself strong enough, to resort to arms, and hoped with foreign aid to reestablish its power.

While the possession of the means of carrying on the Government for a time in opposition to the popular voice seems essential to the preservation of colonial relations, There is not the same danger to the civil & political liberties of the subject, which the possession of such means in the supreme Government would induce because the people of the Colony are under the Guardianship of the Imperial Legislature—a body which has no interest in oppressive measures towards the Colonists, but on the contrary whose best interests are concerned in preserving the inhabitants of the dependencies of the crown in peace contentment & tranquillity.

In the absence of any adequate and certain provision for the carrying on the Government The casual & Territorial revenue would have been were it partly husbanded for that purpose a most convenient rescource against temporary disagreement with the legislature. Popular excitement is generally brief and often without any grave foundation. had the Government the means of retreating for a time upon its own rescources. it is very probable that the resort would seldom be had by the assembly to the measure of refusing the supplies. because it would not in such case produce immediate distress, and coercion at a distant point of time would not effect the immediate and temporary object. the public mind would have time to return to a healthy and tranquil state, and violent infringement of the constitution would not be necessary.

Immigration from the British isles is at once the great and indispensible [*sic*] source of the prosperity and safety of this Province. And no expenditure could be more judicious that that [*sic*] made in the promotion of this great object. at the time when this Province was most prosperous thousands of Emigrants landed every week at the different ports upon the Upper Canada lakes, many of them brought money and other wealth, some were rich, some were poor and sick. and these latter became the care of Government[.] The Casual and Territorial revenue the property of their Sovereign was expended in their relief and in enabling them to settle in the Country. The reward has been an industrious useful and loyal population with their condition infinitely improved, and many of them in a state to acquire comfort and comparative wealth & independence.

But this revenue is to be given up. And when it is sunk in the vortex of a public debt, and disappears in some expensive public work or is bound and pledged to the public Creditor, it is painful to contemplate the scenes which must ensue, should the emigration so necessary to the safety and well being of the Province again be renewed on an extensive scale. It may be said The Provincial Parliament will furnish the means of relief and sometimes it is true it may do so. but it must be considered that the Province is heavily in debt, and the people unaccustomed and utterly averse to taxation. and there is a party which is almost as much opposed to immigration and who until lately affected to despise and treat as strangers and aliens the subjects of the Crown. coming into the Country. This rescource for the relief of the poor & sick emigrants would therefore be most precarious and scanty. Their numbers and necessities are too great for private Charity and these people who with seasonable assistance would become a valuable portion of the population must either be excluded from the colony or perhaps left to perish when they come into it. They poor creatures will have no sectional influence, no representatives in parliament, and most probably from thence no efficient sympathy or assistance— But according to the present constitution of the Colony, they have as just a right to partake of the hereditary revenue of the Crown, and of the royal bounty as the people represented in the assembly. and a more urgent claim for they are her majestys subjects coming to settle upon improve, and make valuable Her Majestys Territory. and are therefore proper objects of Her Majestys royal protection and bounty.

A considerable portion of the casual and territorial revenue ought to be expended in the parts of the Province from which it is raised or expected to be raised. In the early settlement of the Province when the inhabitants took possession of their lands they chose them in the vicinity of the frontier waters, and those who settled at any distance from these means of communication were materially assisted by the Government and Parliament in the formation of roads and now being inhabitants of thickly settled neighbourhoods they have weight and influence in the Legislature. but the parts of The Province which are now in the hands of Government and open for sale and location, actually require considerable expenditure to make them accessible or habitable. the few persons who have taken up their abode in these remote settlements have to encounter hardships and difficulties almost insuperable, and yet so little has their situation engaged the attention of Parliament that while hundreds of thousands of pounds have been expended in speculations from which money was promised if not expected to flow into the treasury, it has not been uncommon to see the backwoodsman bearing his sack of wheat upon his back for ten or twenty miles through the woods, because a few hundred dollars could not be spared to make a bridge over a stream or a log causeway over a swamp. upon which his ox cart could travel. It is in vain to require the local Government to sell the lands of the Crown while they are not trusted with the power of expending a shilling in the building a mill or the making a road or a bridge[.] It is in vain to grant to an officer a number of acres of forest when to occupy it he would have to expend three times its value to open a communication with his estate. The consequence of this state of things is that the back country remains almost a wilderness, while those who would occupy it are driven to seek a residence in the United States, or to return impoverished and despairing to Europe, abusing the country when the country was not to blame, and when the fault rested in the want of confidence in the local government, and in the gratuitous assumption that its power of expending the revenues of the crown was always indiscreetly or corruptly exercised, and in the still more unfounded reliance on the infallibility of the local Legislature.

It has been a melancholy duty to read the petitions from the settlers in the rear parts of the Province setting forth their difficulties and praying for some comparatively trifling expenditure for their relief[;] it is a discouraging and pitiable answer to these petitions, that there is no power in the local government to assist the petitioners[.] It would not have been surprising if these men had been foremost in the ranks of rebellion but none were more forward in the defence of the Government.

A considerable portion of the Territorial revenue ought to have been expended on the formation of slides and channels on the Ottawa and its tributaries for the purpose of making the transit of timber from which a considerable portion of the revenue is derived more safe and expeditious as well as less expensive. The loss of property for want of such improvements has been immense, and another evil of a most injurious tendency has arisen in the granting privileges to individuals of erecting works at Private expence and charging extravagant tolls on the passage of timber. These circumstances cause the timber to be taken to market at considerable risk and expence and added to the length of the voyage, and the want of a navigable channel for deeply laden vessels through Lake Saint Peter to Montreal form the causes why The Canadian timber cannot compete with that from the North of Europe in cheapness[.] Nothing can be more evident however than that the reduction in the Price of Canadian timber which would arise from the lessening the expence of procuring it would be of more importance to the Canadian Provinces, with a view to trade and Policy than the whole of the Casual & Territorial revenues.

Were the Crown revenues of sufficient amount, there is no object in which they could be better expended than in the promotion of Education or in the direction of Education in a proper Channel. The evils arising from the want of Government superintendence in this respect are incalculable[.] Sums of money have been from time to time granted by The Parliament but these are frittered away in insignificant sums through the country and no general or uniform system has been attempted. in many parts of the Province the teachers are Americans, for the sake of obtaining employment they have swallowed the oath of allegiance which agrees so ill with them that the rest of their lives is spent in attempts to disgorge it. These men are utterly ignorant of every thing English and could not if they tried instruct their pupils in any of the duties which the connection of the Province With England casts upon them. The books they use are all American filled with inflated accounts of American independence and the glorious wars with England. The exploits of General Jackson and the heroes of 76. fill the youthful mind to the exclusion of every thing glorious or interesting in English history[.] The young man grows up without a single preposs[ess]ion in favor of his country, he looks upon a british soldier as a person whom it would be honorable and glorious to oppose with the rifle. The British Government in his mind is a chimerical monster 4000 miles off, which notwithstanding that it has been beaten all to nothing by American prowess, and excelled in every thing by American ingenuity still drags on an antiquated existence, which it holds almost at the will of the United States. The boy gains a smattering of Geography out of an American compilation in which the state of Rhode island occupies as much detail as the Eastern hemisphere and in which England appears a pitiful little island filled with tyrannical Landlords and very fat clergymen, and a great number of squalid tenants and labourers. Ireland is a joyless land of bogs, pigs and catholics, and Scotland an out of the way place in which the mountains and the men have a national and barbarious prejudice against decent covering.

It is impossible that the young man so educated can become a good subject of the Crown of great Britain[;] he cannot be brought to think colonial connection with England either an honor or an advantage. all his noble and good sentiments are enlisted on the side of revolution and independence and his mind is only accessible to motives of adherence to the Government by means of terror and coercion, or through the equally base channel of personal & pecuniary advantage.

It is strange to observe that while in the state of New York, the course of instruction and the books which are used are under the strictest surveillance and direction of the Government, all this in Upper Canada is left to the care of a few illiterate ignorant and sometimes disloyal local Township trustees.

To this and to the want of a respectable resident and educated Clergy, belonging to the really respectable Churches which prevail in the British Isles, and to the presence of ignorant sectarians from the United States much of the bad feeling which exists amongst the old inhabitants of the Province and their children may fairly be attributed[;] much has been done to check the progress of these evils by the assistance afforded out of the Crown revenues and lands to the Churches of England Scotland and Rome, as well as by the introduction of British Wesleyan Methodism. but what has been done is small in proportion to what the Province required.

It is perhaps a useless and invidious task to dwell upon this subject. The concession of the Crown revenues has been offered, and will be accepted and the means of doing good and promoting the moral religious and permanent Interests of the country once in the hands of Government after being held back controlled and inactive for years. is now to be given up. It will however disappear in a single session, and be appropriated for the present and for the future in some object of immediate pecuniary interest, and the Casual & Territorial revenues of the Crown will be heard of no more.

After offering these observations and statements, which contain no new fangled doctrines or reference to obscure or doubtful facts or charges against individuals for what naturally fell out in the current of circumstances— It will be right to advert to the course of Politics for the last few years and to account for the state of the public mind which led to the late revolt.

United States citizens who have been permitted to settle in this Province, and their children form a considerable portion of the inhabitants of the Province. These people were formerly quiet and orderly, as many of them are at present but they never had as a body any active principle of loyalty or attachment to England. on the contrary their education & prejudices naturally lead them the other way.

All that can fairly be expected from them is a grateful sense of the protection and privileges they have been permitted to enjoy under the British Government and a consequent forbearance from any attempt to destroy British institutions.

Many of them it is fair to admit carried their sense of duty still further during the late war, for they fought against their own countrymen when they attempted to invade the Province.

They did not do this however because they preferred British institutions, but because they had nothing to complain of and they did not like to be interfered with by their own countrymen or any others, some of this good feeling also rose from the spirited and successful manner in which the enemy were met, at the commencement of that contest. when blood is spilt and battles won the absorbing interest of war for the time left little room for other feelings, and the war was one of National aggression and defence and not a war of opinion[.]

When This Province became the arena of Political contest and when opinions affecting the institutions of the country became subjects of discussion it is not surprising to find The American settlers and their Children taking the side in Politics which tended most towards their favorite republican institutions. It is very probable that if the Imperial Government had in a very decided manner declared that questions which affected the relations of the Province with the Mother Country and the monarchical constitution granted to the Province were not open for Colonial discussion many of the well disposed amongst the American settlers would not have felt at liberty to urge their opinions at the risk of being considered disaffected to the British Crown. But when discussion was permitted, negociations entered into, and admissions made by British Statesmen of the ill working of The Provincial constitution, it became a kind of duty in these people to advance their own notions, They had in their immediate neighbourhood the country from whence their opinions came. They had a violent democratic American Press to furnish them with argument, and a successful revolution, the theme of eulogium on every hand as an example. They knew that however conservative or restricted the views of an English Politician were respecting his own country, That the American constitution and its success, was either lauded in terms, or tacitly admitted as points upon which liberality of opinion and generosity of feeling might be safely exhibited. They saw the Government and institutions of the Colony violently attacked in the House of Commons, and but feebly if at all defended And they naturally enough thought that they were not acting criminally in endeavouring to substitute institutions which could only exist with safety in a republic, for those which were compatible with Monarchical Government. The Independence and strength of The Colonial Executive The appointment of the Legislative Council, The non extension of the elective system to all details of Government were only advocated with vigour in the Colony. The Governors of the colony looked for support and assistance from their own officers, and from the intelligent and sober minded classes of the community who plainly saw to what end the public advocacy of democratic opinions was tending. The officers being interested in the maintenance of the Government fell under the charge of corruption and the exclusion of the violent democratic party from office was said to be partiality and oppression. In this manner have things gone on, until it was found necessary to destroy at once some of the hopes long and fondly cherished and to declare that *every thing* could not be conceded to popular will. Men could not be suddenly stayed in what had theretofore appeared a successful campaign against the constitution of the Province, opinions could not be suddenly wrenched out of their course by late and sudden declarations of adherence to principle, hope founded upon agitation within the letter of the law was at an end, and in the weak & unsupported state of the Province, and with the vicinity of Lower Canada and the United States, this hope did not change its direction and object, but its foundation, and what reliance it once placed upon popular clamor & political agitation was easily transferred to Physical force and armed resistance.

The first settlers in the Province, that is to say The U E. Loyalists although through danger suffering and deprivation, they adhered to the British Crown. yet had still many points of similarity in habits and education with the Americans who revolted. And this similarity of manners when the revolutionary war was at an end made the amalgamation of the American citizen with his more loyal countrymen & his descendents an operation of great facility, and to this admixture and the want of proper means of education, may be attributed in some measure the adherence of some of the descendents of the U E. Loyalists to republican principles and even to rebellion.

There were not wanting moreover to this republican party men from the british Isles and their descendants who if they were not absolutely enamoured of republicanism or disaffected towards monarchy caught the spirit which pervaded a portion and a very considerable one of the British population, at home. Every abuse real or imaginary which was an object of hostility to English reformers found a paralell [*sic*] in Upper Canada. Parliamentary reform was said to be and probably was wanting in England. And as a matter of course there must be a Parliamentary reform in Upper Canada. and accordingly the most unfounded and impossible charges have been made against the Government for exercising an influence over elections, which they did not exercise because they in fact never possessed it. Whenever an election was lost by the reformers they were loud in their complaints against the Government, as if it was bound constitutionally to transfer its functions to the complainants, and as if the friends and adherents of the Government were obliged to assist in every plan for its amendment whether they liked it or not. No officer of Government however circumscribed his connection with the Executive or with Politics might be could set up for a member of the House of assembly, could be active at an election in favor of the conservative party (using the term in a Provincial sense) or could vote at an election, without becoming an object of reproach to the reformers and without being said to exercise an unconstitutional influence. This Proscription from Political rights extended not only to the heads of departments and the Crown lawyers but also to their Clerks[,] to District treasurers[,] Clerks of the Peace, and even militia officers[;] even their children and relations were not exempt from suspicion and reproach. on the alleged ground of their dependence upon Government[.] The moment a man acquired the confidence of the Government and became a public Officer he was expected to forfeit all his political privileges. and even the common right of self defence. No matter how false and bitter the accusations and denunciations of the popular orators or the public press might be whenever an attempt at resistance or defence was made it was considered an interference with popular rights, which the Government ought to prevent. The absurd extent to which this notion of non interference on the part of Government has been carried by the reform party in this Province is not only contrary to the practice in England where the ministers of the Crown and the Officers of the Government act as if they felt it to be a due deference to popular opinion to set themselves and their measures in a right point of view before the public but it is diametrically opposite to the course taken in the american republic, where *all* appointments & even continuances in office are made and permitted with a direct and avowed view to party purposes. The doctrine set up is also repugnant to all just notions of legal and constitutional right, for a man should not be held to forfeit his elective franchise, or his right to direct or persuade popular opinion[;] he should not be silent and inactive, and his friends supine and indifferent, merely because the Government of his country thought him worthy of distinction of confidence and employment. some of the reformers have not been so extravagant as others in their desire to exclude all connection between popular rights and Government but the limitation of the desires of an individual were of little effect. When elections were to be won by popular outcry candidates do not look very scrupulously to the rectitude or constitutionality of the doctrines which appear to influence the public mind and the mental reservation or faintly expressed opinion of a popular leader to the effect that he desired only constitutional reform was of little avail, when his whole talents, exertions and influence, were freely given to support a party, and advance its march to power and predominancy, and when that party or at least the great Majority of its members held and advanced principles, utterly at variance with the British constitution or the continuance of colonial connection.

[The following paragraph is here deleted: "The wealth of the English and Irish established churches, and the alleged oppression arising out of the levying of tithes, has for a long time been the subject of angry declamation amongst English reformers and".]

It is not extraordinary therefore to find half pay officers stigmatized as the bribed pensionaries of a corrupt Government, while they were merely enjoying in a British Colony the reward of long services, and exercising their rights as freemen, or to find British Emigrants spoken of in the House of Assembly as foreign paupers intruding upon the political rights, and territorial inheritance of the American settler or the children of the Soil. The settlement of discharged soldiers in the Province upon the *national* demesne. has been spoken of as the introduction of bribed and demoralized ruffians, by whose assistance the cause of Freedom was to be controlled, and its advocates murdered at the expence of the *Province*[.] All these topics through the Vehement declamation of rebellious demagogues, and the equally hurtful tacit acquiesence of Constitutional reformers, have been used against the Government[.] And the Imperial Government as contradistinguished from the local Government has vainly imagined that it was gaining golden opinions when one by one the land granting system, The right of The Sovereign to dispose of the territories of the Crown, and the revenues arising therefrom were yielded up as concessions of just claims advanced on the part of an oppressed people.

A digression from the immediate subject of this part of the report it is hoped may be excused for the purpose of advancing or reiterating summarily two or three doctrines as to colonial policy which do not appear to be easily controvertible when applied to the British North american Colonies and when their vicinity to a hostile nation is considered.

1. The ungranted lands in the Province belong to the Empire not to the Colonists—

2. They should be disposed of for the interests of the Empire primarily and secondarily for the interests of the Colonists.

3. The policy of the Romans in establishing military settlements of the discharged Legionaries upon their frontiers has never been successfully impeached and is well worthy of imitation.

4 In this Province no ancient possessors. or at least users of the soil need be dispossessed and therefore justice & Christian principle do not interfere with the policy of Military Colonization.

5 The same policy respecting territory and revenue which is applicable to distinct and insular colonies does not apply to continental possessions divided by extensive and easily invaded boundaries and the measures of defence which in the former are not necessary are of primary importance in continental possessions which must be held by means of military efficiency or not at all.

6. If soldiers were to be allowed to retire from the army and to settle in the Colonies at an age when they would be capable of enduring labor, service in the army of England would become honorable and desirable even to the private soldiery.

7. The Colonies were won by the valor of the army of England, and the acquired territories cannot be more justly used or appropriated than in the reward and provision for soldiers.

8 The Colonies cannot better be defended than by military colonization—had this object been held in view instead of the realization of a paltry revenue. This Canadian frontier might now have been bris[t]ling in arms. a terror to our enemies instead of being a weak point for their attack & conquest.

9. Military Colonization in America cannot therefore be too strongly recommended provided it shall consist principally of officers and men capable of enduring the labors hardships & privations attendant upon settlement in a northern region.

But to return to the immediate subject under discussion namely the means by which the public mind has been brought to weigh against the Government and the effect which the agitation of questions of reform in England has had upon the affairs of this Province. The question of religious establishments next forces itself for consideration.

The wealth of the English and Irish Established Churches and the alleged grievances and oppressions arising from the levying of tithes, and even the disputes between the Scottish establishment and the dissenters have been favorite themes of declamation and agitation in England and the appropriation of the Clergy reserves in this province was made the occasion of introducing all the topics of discussion into Upper Canada which cotemporaneously [*sic*] agitated England Ireland and Scotland, and in proportion to the heat of contest in the mother country, the acrimony of religious dispute prevailed in the Colony.

On reading the Provisions relating to the Clergy Reserves in the act which visited this Province with a constitution there can scarcely be a doubt but that the provision for the Church of England, without expence to the Colonists was what was contemplated. This view is not only accordant with the words of the act but with the policy of

England from the reformation downwards. The exclusive appropriation of the reserves to the Church of England may now be considered as a ceded question, and it is not of value to enter into the controversy as to the rights of the Church though it may be of vital consequence to review the effect which the discussion of that right and the contending claims of other churches, sects, and of the colonists who disclaimed all but voluntary support of congregations to religious teachers, have had upon the Political affairs of the Province.

For a number of years the Church of England in the Province was supported by annual grants made by Parliament. The Clergy reserves were unproductive and the limited population of the Colony, and the want of immediate pecuniary interest, did not allow of the setting up of claims as points of conscience and principle, against what was then the acknowledged right of the Sovereign and the avowed policy of the Empire.

In process of time however the Clergy reserves began to yield a small income, and it was thought proper to leave the Church to rest upon its then and now inadequate provincial rescources. Questions relating to Church establishments became of more frequent discussion in England, and however sternly vested rights were upheld there the same unbending regard to them was not expected to be exercised in a distant Colony. The Scottish Church began to examine the act of Parliament by which the Church of England was established in the Colony and adverting to the only ambiguous term in the Statute that is to say a *protestant Clergy*, and the recognition of the Presbyterian establishment by the act of Union, set up its claims to equal participation in the benefit of the Clergy reserves and to the dignity of a Church Establishment in the Colony.

The Scottish Church could not for a moment have sustained its side of the question upon its own claim right or comparative importance. But it was strong when used as a destructive engine of warfare against the Church of England because in in [*sic*] that warfare it found itself united with people of all religions some of whom were no doubt entitled to the favor & protection of the Government. and with people of no religion[,] with those who were looking for a share when the spoil came to be divided, and with those who in the extremity of their democratic zeal considered it irreligious for the sovereign of England to contribute towards the advancement of religion at all, who not only declined assistance themselves but with true sectarian intolerance, would deprive others of the support which their religious tenets permitted them to receive with gratitude to their Sovereign and to Providence which provided the means of religious instruction to a scattered and poor community which its private rescources could not furnish.

If the disturbance produced by the agitation of this question were not of deep and serious consequence to the tranquillity and prosperity of the Colony It would be most amusing to listen to the heterogeneous arguments, The confused doctrines, and the discordant clamor which distinguishes the debates upon the question of the Clergy reserves, It appears as if we were erecting a New Tower of Babel, instead of laying a foundation for religious instruction.

It is not for its own sake that the question of the clergy reserves is so fiercely contested. but because it offers a field for agitation which is peculiarly open for the introduction of the most exciting and inflam[m]able topics. If it is of no use to insist That the Term Dominant

Church is actually unmeaning in a country wherein no church attempts to exercise Ecclesiastical jurisdiction[.] When the Church of England Clergyman is mentioned in debate it is not the needy and threadbare incumbent of a parsonage that is presented to view but a tyrannical overbearing monster seeking what he may devour. It is useless to reiterate that when the Clergy reserves shall be disposed of and the proceeds funded there will not be sufficient to maintain on the most moderate terms the increasing wants even of one Church[.] The Clergy reserves figure in the debate and the newspaper as one seventh of the Landed estate of the Province. although the lands of a single Town or a populous District would sell for more than all the Clergy reserves in the Province. Tithes, Church rates, persecutions of times past. popular grievances and popular rights all dragged in to the discussion of a question with which they have nothing to do. & Thus the munificent intentions of the British Crown & Parliament are defeated, and the Gift for the maintenance of religion without expence to the people is a source of unending discord and evil. It is like the Box of Pandora without Hope at the bottom—

It may be worth enquiry if all this could have been avoided, and it appears to many reflecting persons in the Province that it might[.] If the Donor, that is to say The Sovereign and the Imperial Parliament had settled the question decisively. In such case one advantage would have been secured, namely purity of motive, secured by want of the most remote influence of personal interest. In the next place whether the decision were satisfactory or not the Question would be set at rest. and all hope of disturbing it again being removed, attempts to agitate would naturally cease. It is not the object of this report to recommend any plan for the arrangement of the distribution of the reserves which would be an assumption of a function in a colonial body which the same body deny the propriety of investing in any but the Imperial Government, but it is respectfully urged for Your Excellencys consideration, that there is much more probability of a just and equitable decision in England. than in the Colony where so many conflicting interests stand in the way. and also that even if the decision be not perfectly in accordance with the views of the Colonist no satisfactory decision can be arrived at here and further that it is better that an adjustment should be attained objectionable in itself. than that the question mooted should remain an unceasing cause of discord and agitation.

When the question shall be decided in the Colony if it ever is decided here it is vain to hope that the matter will be at an end, it having been settled by a Colonial Assembly will be a sufficient reason for its being opened again by the same authority when a new election changes the majority, the former majority will be declared not to have expressed the will of the people. and even if the Government should determine upon acceding to no application for a new arrangement it cannot avoid receiving addresses and remonstrances without end. with the risk of quarrel, stoppage of supplies and its attendant evils. Whereas if the question be decided not upon the presumption of its being settled according to popular sentiment, but as a right on the part of Her Majesty in Parliament to dispose of the Crown demesne as seems best for the good of the Empire. and as seems just towards the claimants, the foundation for clamor & discussion will be at an end. And although some may be disappointed, and may complain, the loyal will be loyal still, and the disaffected no worse than they were before[;] they cannot take the preliminary steps to produce agitation, for the matter being finally disposed of in another country the hope of *peaceful agitation* which always precedes insurrection will as far as regards this topic be taken away.

No topic of agitation and discontent has been more successfully urged than that of the extravagance of the Government, perhaps there is no country where it is not so more or less, but in this Colony it has been particularly and successfully urged.

It is not generally known or considered that a republican Government is naturally an expensive one. We have been accustomed continually to hear the economy of the American republic extolled beyond all praise, though in reality while a parsimony which excludes from high office the most able and efficient men. marks the policy of the United States. The multitude of half employed functionaries of Government which the ramifications of their complicated system requires renders the system one of great expence and little efficiency.

The greater concentration which the monarchical form of Government requires, brings before the public view the whole expences of the state, and the sum appears extravagant. In the United States we find the federal Government, the State Governments, and the subdivisions of Township Governments as they may be called all employing officers. most of the subordinate ones highly paid in proportion to their services. The amount of expenditure in the administration of the laws, and conducting public affairs in Salaries & fees of Office is large though not easily discovered. The most prominent offices are accordingly badly paid, while the multitude of subordinates pass without observation.

The true way of comparing the relative extravagance or economy of a concentric with an excentric Government is to be found in the amount of taxes paid by each individual—and if this mode of comparison be resorted to the Colony will be found to have infinitely the advantage over the republic. In the United States between import duties, state and municipal taxes the citizen really feels, that he is taxed to an inconvenient though perhaps to a necessary amount. In this Colony taxation is too trifling to be felt at all.

To illustrate this position we may recur to the effect of an approach to republicanism which took place during the Parliament dissolved by Sir Francis Head. The assembly chose to appoint its own Commissioners. its township officers were to be elected. the consequence was that the duty of one or two public officers was discharged by numerous boards & township committees, each individual receiving so much per diem. while employed, and he was to be employed at his own discretion or as many days as he could find any thing to do[.] The persons appointed or elected were only controlled by the letter of the law, breach of that law only exposed them to legal prosecution, and it is needless to say that the working of the plan to the small extent to which it was carried into effect, was without system uniformity or control, expensive and inefficient[.]

[The following paragraph is here deleted: "But the appointment of Officers responsible to the people, was a favorite theme for declamation. and unreflecting men could not see that while the head of a department is watched in every movement with jealousy and controlled by powers to which he is continually accountable, he has ten times the responsibility to public opinion which numerous".] It is worthy of remark that if any extravagance has been committed in this Colony it has proceeded from the popular branch of the Legislature[.] A natural desire to cause the construction of public works, and to bring it about during the period for which the members were elected so that the credit and popularity of the measure might attach to the members who devised it, while the difficulties attending public embarrassment would remain for future parliaments, and the Government. as well as less worthy motives of pecuniary interest which were felt by those who expected to reap advantage from the expenditure of large sums of money, and by the construction of public works in their neighbourhood. has caused the rescources of the Province to be anticipated, and works to be undertaken far beyond the means or necessities of the present population of the Province[.] The consequence of premature undertakings has naturally been want of success in their completion and want of utility or profit commensurate with the expenditure when the works have been carried into operation. another result of the attempt to do more than was conveniently in the power of the Legislature in the way of great undertakings has been the neglect of common and ordinary improvements within the reach of the present population, and of actual present necessity for its convenience and comfort. This has given rise to conflicting opinions and parties, and has had much influence in bringing about the various changes in the majority of the Assembly which have distracted the Province of late years.

Mercantile men. those possessing large landed property which they wished to make productive. speculators in land and others interested in money transactions have naturally been most forward in urging what is called public improvement, they have also been the most active supporters of the Government. and the most opposed to theoretical and organic changes for the sake of mere political abstract principle. They consequently formed a portion of the Government party. and in the public view became identified with it[.] This naturally forced the republican party into the opposite course, and although nothing could be more opposed to the American Character than economy of expenditure in speculative improvement, The apparent anomoly [*sic*] was created. of the persons most opposed to british institutions, advocating prudence and economy. in public expenditure and anticipating taxes and Bankruptcy. while the Government party were promising golden harvests, and urging on the career of American speculation.

Disappointment in the results of this speculation helped to give the republican party a temporary ascendancy. And it will be shewn hereafter how consistency to their own, or at least their adopted principles of prudence and economy helped to overthrow them.

A desire to usurp the Executive functions of the Government in the appointment of Officers has been generally entertained by a considerable portion of the people. those who happened to hold office, or to expect Government favor. were of course satisfied with things as they were. while those who were unworthy of trust or unfit for employment or who found themselves excluded for want of a sufficient number of offices to employ all who conceived themselves fit. were led to seek their ends, by a change of system. and to look to popular favor for what they failed in procuring otherwise[.]

The elective system of the United States was before their eyes in full operation, they read its praises in every American Newspaper. Its evils numerous as they were they found ascribed to mere accidental causes. and what a practical statesman would call its defects appeared to be its greatest recommendation.

This party could not or would not see that while the head of a department appointed by the Government is watched with jealousy in every movement and controlled by powers to which he is continually accountable he has in reality more responsibility to public opinion than a number of individuals exercising the same functions & elected either directly or through the medium of the Legislature are under, who while they possess influence in the Assembly, or in the neighbourhood from whence they are chosen may hold at defiance general public opinion, and the executive Government.

The theory of direct accountability to the people is so very plausible and so congenial to the best popular sentiments. that the opposite practice is in most countries rather tolerated than approved, persons intimate with the working of Government, see a practical necessity for an executive head, by whom public functionaries shall be appointed, and by whom they must be directed. They see that when officers are elected either directly or indirectly, the individual opinions of the officers, are substituted in the place of public opinion, and of the opinion of Government. that these individual opinions are swayed by individual interests, and that neither are under any necessity of giving way to the general public opinion or to the public interest. particularly during the short periods for which for which [*sic*] the functionaries are appointed by popular election. In short it appears to be plain that if uniform and systematic subservience to the public interests, or to public opinion is an object of search it is only to be found with public servants who are appointed by & required to be obedient to an executive head. which on its own own part acts in general conformity with public opinion because it is more interested in preserving public favor than in pleasing or serving its own creatures.

What would be said in England were the Lord Lieutenant of Ireland to write a despatch to the Secretary of state telling him in the most quiet manner and without the air of saying any thing of extraordinary import that he would in a certain contingency of the Government protecting a part of the community from the rapacity of another part find it necessary to have recourse to arms. and to fight her Majestys troops. if they presumed to interfere? Yet a circumstance precisely similar has occurred within a few days in the State of Georgia. from whence the Governor threatened the President of the United States with armed resistance if he persisted in protecting the Cherokee indians from popular violence. and forcible expulsion. This is nevertheless only one of thousands of instances of what we should call insubordination or treason. almost of daily occurrence. at present The United States President professes to be at peace with England. The Magistrates of Oswego (qy) are really so, The authorities of Buffalo and lockport on the contrary subscribe to patriot funds and assist the invaders of the Province. Governor Mason sympathises, and Governor Marcy favors them. In fact neither we [n]or they know whether peace or war exists. The Congress pass laws to be executed by local Magistrates[.] The local magistrates are elected and they hold the laws in contempt break them themselves and refuse to punish others who may infringe them.

From this short statement of facts it may be proved that public opinion does not practically *prevail* in the United States.

The President is elected by the whole people, and may therefore be said to be a representative of the popular will.

The Congress of the United States are elected by the whole people and may therefore be said to be representatives of the popular will.

These have concurred in enacting a law making it criminal to commit aggressions upon the neighbouring Provinces of Great Britain.

The will of the People of the United States may therefore be said to have declared such aggressions criminal.

The law is broken in a thousand instances under the eye of the public authorities yet in no one case has punishment followed. It follows therefore that public opinion does not prevail in the United States democracy.

And it may be argued that it cannot prevail when public servants, are independent of the Government and of each other. and liable to account to the electors only for their actions[.]

Plain as these deductions may be the doctrine of subservience and obedience to the public will as expressed by those appointed to make and execute the laws is no where actually popular. those who see its truth are silent respecting it when they seek the suffrages of the people, and those who most loudly decry it and who bring the exercise of executive power nearest in prospect within the grasp of the sectional portions of the populace which he [*sic*] addresses, has a great chance of being the favorite candidate.

It may be thought in England that great influence is exercised by the Colonial Government in the Assembly, and at elections[.] The fact however is not so. The state of the Colony in not possessing the classes of landlord and tenant, employers with numbers of employed or other dependent relations prevents individuals from possessing influence, Men seem for the moment to lead the popular mind, but it is only while some favorite object is to be gained, to which the candidate must sacrifice individual opinion and political honesty. but the influence is ephemeral and is more likely to end in popular reprobation than to grow stronger with its continuance. It is only by means of Individuals of influence, that Government influence can be gained[.] these Individuals are not found. or if one appears, who is apparently a popular favorite and is selected for advancement he is soon found to have forfeited his claim to be a popular leader. The man who at a public meeting or in his place in the assembly puts forth extravagant claims for his constituents, or for the Province upon the Legislature the Government or the mother country in the full knowledge that he ought not to succeed and without the desire to do so may for the time be popular, but when he is placed in high office under the Government he is under the necessity of acting instead of talking. he has to a certain extent to be moderate prudent and just. he discovers that what he would have urged in debate, or triumphed in accomplishing when he was in no respect the judge and with only the responsibility of an advocate, is not a measure to which he can assent when he is has [*sic*] seriously [to] advise the decision of the question.

Hence arises the difficulty of satisfying public expectation by the Government. in appointments to office, and in the formation of the Legislative Council. or the conciliation of a party by the advancement of its leaders. the individual ceases to be dependent upon his party and he loses his popularity.

Thus Lord Gosford thought he was gaining golden opinions by the advancement of some of the French canadian leaders. he gained nothing with the canadians[,] he made the men he advanced unpopular, and he offended the whole British population[.] The British saw in the act a leaning towards principles inimical to their prosperity[.] The french saw themselves no nearer the domination they sought for, the new officers were silenced and became insignificant.

When Sir Francis Head arrived in the Colony. He found a House of Assembly which had been elected by a considerable popular Majority[.] This House was chosen on the ground that reform was wanting[,] that the country was full of abuses, and the Government of corruption. which they were affecting to remedy by an increase of their own powers. and by assuming all the functions of Government.

Those who saw in the pretensions of the Assembly principles fatal to the connection of the Colony with England were discouraged and looked on in gloomy silence[.] They found that the most extravagant charges had been received in England against them, and had made an impression which they saw little hope of removing. They saw that an opinion was gradually gaining ground that the Colonies were burdensome and unprofitable to England and in every admission whether tacit or expressed of the alleged grievances of the Colonists, of the bad working of Colonial institutions, and of the necessity of change, a new step towards separation. attachment which is not valued and loyalty which is contemned are cold and cheerless sentiments. and it is not too much to say that indifference to the tendency of the public measures of a colony and to the result even if it should be separation, are the surest means of accelerating that event, and much more rapid in their effect than those usually received as the active causes of revolt[,] that is to say bad and oppressive government.

The Legislative Council were weary of interposing their prudence firmness and moderation between the dangerous and unconstitutional measures of the Assembly and the Government[.] they found they were not thanked their motives were impugned they were attacked in the British Parliament and scarcely met with one to defend or vindicate them.

The Assembly for the purpose of consolidating their power demanded the whole revenue at the disposal of the Government. The justice of the demand was conceded with the charge of a small civil list. which proposal was not accepted because they wished to have the Government at their mercy completely which could not be accomplished so long as a permanent provision for its maintenance existed.

All the measures of the Assembly, relating to the expenditure of public money, were framed with a view of consolidating & continuing their own power. They appointed their political emissaries to expend money on the roads. for the important works which were carried on they appointed their own members commissioners and directors.

They lavished the public money on the support of a worthless seditious and unprincipled press they paid agents to proceed to England to slander the Colonial Governor and they charged all this to the contingencies of the House.

They demanded that the Executive Council should be rendered responsible to themselves[,] that is to say bound to follow out the Policy of the Assembly in all things. The Assembly were to rule the Council The Council the Governor. who was to be relieved from all responsibility as well as of all independent action.

The interference of the Ministers of the Crown was decried, as Downing Street Tyranny. and the baneful domination of the Mother Country[.]

The abolition or reform of the Legislative Council, was sought for so as to make that body completely subservient to the views of the Assembly.

It is evident that when these things should be accomplished The Assembly would possess a power superior to that of the House of Commons, The House of representatives or any political body we know of short of despotic authority. They would also possess the means of influencing and insuring their own elections, The British Govt. The Governor, The Legislative Council The Ex. Council The Offices of Govt. all would be mere workers of the will of the Assembly.

In short The Assembly claimed to exercise all the functions of an Independent National Government except the burdensome one of providing for its defence. and of finding exclusive markets for colonial produce. These they were inclined to leave with the Home Government[.]

It is said perhaps with truth that the reformers would not have become rebels were their claims all conceded[.] They in fact would have no interest in procuring a union with the United States. because they would thus as a Colony exercise a power and domination which if the Colony were made one of the United States they could not enjoy.

In this state Sir Francis Head found the Province. He was thought to have been sent out to carry on reform principles. He was expected to do exactly as he was told by the Assembly. and his coming and the removal of Sir John Colborne was hailed by the reform party with delight by the Majority of the Assembly and its partizans.

Sir Francis Head, desiring that every opportunity should be given for the removal of abuses which were said to exist, and supposing he would be best assisted by the presence of reform Executive Councillors appointed two who were known to entertain reform principles to a great extent. Mr Dunn the Receiver General who was popular with the reformers, because he was not connected with any of the families, whose members were Officers of the local Government was also appointed—

Sir Francis appears to have desired the discussion in the Council of the claims of the reformers. he could scarcely have expected unanimity or that the decisions of the Council should be final. He rather wished by means of the Council to have understood clearly the questions discussed so that they might be fully and impartially considered by himself and the ministers of the Crown. He accordingly invited discussion and awaited the time for the decision of the points which should be raised.

It so happened however That his views as well as those of the Government in England were misapprehended by the Councillors. for the old ones as well as the new, asserted to its full extent the right of the House of assembly. to control the Government. and to make the Council dependent upon the Majority of the Assembly.

Sir Francis Head on the other hand did not understand what the Council were aiming at. He no doubt expected inquiry into grievances in detail which he intended to investigate with the impartiality which his position as the representative of the King whose sole interest was the welfare & peace of the Colony would enable him.

In short he hoped to govern the Colony without reference to party[,] yielding to none, and doing justice to all[.]

This must always be the hope and object of a supreme Government, and its conscientious representative. for although the Majority of electors and the prevalence of party may prevent impartiality, and secure the interests of the prevailing party to the exclusion of those of the losing one at home. Yet it may be presumed that no Government in England would see injustice done to, a minority in a colony. or allow the rights of the subjects of the Crown to be invaded, or their just claims denied merely because a prevailing party in the province desired it.

That Sir Francis Head sincerely desired to administer the Government with justice and impartiality is evident from his refusing on the one hand to oppress the tories as they were called by dismissals from Office without reason. He shewed his desire on the other hand to relieve the reformers from their exclusion from Office and power, by calling them into his Council and by recommending the Speaker of the Assembly a leading reformer to a seat on the Bench.

Sir Francis and his Council were mutually surprised at the result of his endeavours[.] He found the Council declaring as their unalterable conviction principles of Government which he had no authority to admit and which with his conviction of their incompatibility with the relation of a colony to a parent state it would have been treason in him to have recommend[ed] for adoption.

The Council on the other hand were surprised to find that their views which they truly stated to be in accordance with those of the Assembly. and the success of which only could secure the Cooperation of that Body with the Government declared by the Lieutenant Governor totally inadmissible.

Thus without a single difference of opinion on any practical measure of Government It became apparent that a separation must take place between the Governor and his council[.]

Had the Council gone on silently entertaining the principles they expressed and giving weight to the opinions of the Assembly, And if the Assembly finding the Governor disposed to act with deference to their opinions forborne extravagant measures which originated in a desire to embarrass the Government[,] It is probable that the affairs of the Province would have been conducted for some time with apparent peace and cordiality[.]

It was fortunate that this did not take place—the practical domination of the Assembly. which though moderate at first would have by degrees become intolerable. Concessions made by the ruler, to the governed are scarcely possible to be revoked. and every day that the functions of the Government and of the Assembly, and the line which divided them remained undefined, The former would be losing ground which could not be regained without violence.

The resignation of the Councillors was the signal for hostility on the part of the Assembly. They found from Sir Francis Heads instructions that he could not. and from his disagreement with the Council that he did not desire to accede to the pretensions of the Assembly, and war was declared accordingly. The Governor was insulted in the most opprobrious terms he was in a manner put upon his trial the business of the country was at a stand and the eyes of the people were turned upon a contest which it was plain must end either in the removal of the Lieut Governor. or the downfall of the Majority in the House.

The Assembly in their rage, and disappointment lost all discretion. Had they been temperate in the assertion of their claims, and contented themselves with insisting calmly upon them, they might possibly have secured the public confidence, and finally have succeeded with the Home Government. But they depended too much upon popular support, and were blind to the loss they were daily sustaining in popular favor.

It happened that at this period the emigration from the eastern to the western states was in full operation[.] The rage for public improvements extravagant loans gambling speculations in land, laying out what have been significantly called lithographic cities in the wilderness. prevailed in the Neighbouring States to a most unprecedented extent[.] The people of Upper Canada are just as fond as their neighbours. of Magnificent undertakings, of paper money, and paper Cities. But alas for Upper Canada her legislature were talking of popular rights, and grievances and abstract politics just at the very time when these topics were completely absorbed in the desire for wealth and the apparent ease with which it was gratified upon our frontiers[.] A properous people never think of their rights. when men are making money they have no grievances[.] Even the reformers themselves began to think that their representatives would be better employed in borrowing money. increasing the circulating medium and the value of property, than in quarrelling with the Government about barren principles, which they could neither understand [n]or explain. This want of tact in the Assembly is sufficient in itself to explain the result of the late elections which seemed to astonish the Assembly as well as the Government. and which set the reformers seeking for some occult and hidden corruption on the part of Government, as a means to account for so strange a Phenomenon.

For a little time it was amusing to the reformers to find the Governor and his officials outraged and insulted. It gratified their pride of independence and equality. But when they saw That Political agitation did not invite settlers, that Emigrants shunned a country declared by the representatives to be suffering under tyranny & oppression[,] to be upon the eve of a revolution. and that capitalists were not likely to invest money, in a province said to be ruined by its Government— [sentence is incomplete.]

In considering the result of the late elections while the want of policy in the assembly is so apparent This great cause of their downfall must not be lost sight of. nor should their overthrow be considered final or the ascendancy of British principles calculated upon with too much certainty at future elections. change of circumstances may produce change of popular opinion[.] The enemies of Government may not always be so blinded or choose their time so badly. The American bubble is now burst. perhaps it is happy for us that it continued to float so long.

On Sir Francis Head declaring his unalterable determination to preserve the const[it]ution of the Colony unimpaired those really attached to it became inspired with new life hope & activity. They had looked upon their case as almost desperate, they had sought in vain for encouragement from England. but there they found the Government the Parliament and Public Opinion poisoned by the declarations of their enemies[.] They read the opinions expressed by statesmen as well as demagogues that the time for independence must shortly come:

And they knew that if such was to be the case, the sooner they were relieved from the invidious situation in which they stood the better; but when Sir Francis Head published his instructions, and declared his intentions. They came with a noble spirit. And prayed for a dissolution of Parliament so that their influence might be constitutionally felt.

Another cause of the result of the elections arose from the fact that many of the Emigrants who at the previous election had not procured their titles and therefore had not voted now had gradually become entitled to demand their deeds, and in the anticipation of an election they urged their completion with the greatest avidity. These people were almost universally attached to the Government, and in their activity in endeavouring to obtain the elective franchise to which they were legally entitled is to be seen the foundation of the Charge against the Government of issuing Patents for the purpose of fabricating votes—

The Lieutenant Governor with consum[m]ate policy watched the progress of these causes upon public opinion. he occasionally assisted them by spirited answers to addresses praying for a dissolution of Parliament[;] he bore with Patience the insults of the House of assembly. by which they were destroying themselves. and furnishing his justification for the step he was about to take; irritated at his patience and ascribing his not dissolving them to apprehension of the displeasure of Government They thought to complete his downfall by the stoppage of the supplies. even this did not force him to anticipate the time for action. he first decided upon reserving the Royal assent to the money bills passed by the Assembly. he refused to accede to the address of the house to pay their contingencies[.] In these bills, and in the way the money applied for in the shape of contingencies The Assembly had exposed themselves to well merited reproach. and assisted in their own destruction.

Finally at the very crisis of public impatience The Lieutenant Governor in Council on the Kings birth day. and as it happened when the Royal Salute was firing, declared the assembly dissolved and issued writs for a new election. The result of which proved to be a constitutional House of Assembly.

The truth of the above remarks upon the influence of the American speculation fever. upon the people of the Colony and upon the result of the elections, is fully borne out by the proceedings of the new house. Bills for the establishment of numerous Banks. and for appropriations to a very great amount for public works. were immediately passed. The merits of these measures are variously estimated and it is not intended to discuss them at present[;] there can be no doubt however But that the members were elected with a view to these measures, and were only carrying out the wishes of their constituents. and that the want of like measures on the part of the members of the last House of Assembly was one great cause of their unpopularity.

For a time the reformers contented themselves with charging the Government with corruption and undue influence at the elections and persisted in declaring themselves the great majority of the people. gradually however those who were really disaffected began to act with the direct object of obtaining independence. Their time was now well chosen and they were sanguine of success.

It is unnecessary at this time to state the progress of disaffection in Lower Canada. it is sufficient to say that it had proceeded so far as to threaten immediate revolt. and that the disaffected leaders were in active communication with those in Lower Canada [Lower Canada is queried for Upper Canada in the MS.].

The American speculations ended in Bankruptcy of the speculators[;] Business was to a great degree suspended on the American frontier which was filled with Idle vagabonds. ready to sympathize with and to assist in rebellion.

The Province although it had scarcely time to enter into the spirit of american enterprize since the new elections, suffered severely by the pressure on business and although the depression was not felt here to the same extent as in the United States. The excitement produced by the promise of prosperity to arise from increased expenditure was stayed. Emigrants had been deterred from coming to the Province by the late Political agitation. The Banks were not in a condition to afford facilities to trade by furnishing Capital. and the debtors to the Banks were not in a condition to pay them.

The Government confiding in the Pacific declarations of the U.S Government, and in the apparently pacific conduct of the American people since the late war. had gradually reduced the military force until in this Province it was but a name. The few forts were dismantled the arms were removed. and the Province may be said to have been without military strength.

The first symptoms of disaffection in the Colony appeared in the increased virulence of the Reform press. it became seditious and even traitorous. The question is now asked why was not the law put in force against the press. this is not said merely by constitutionalists but also by rebels taken in arms—they have said continually We were misled by the Newspapers, why were they allowed by the Government to deceive us, without punishment[;] when we saw statements in the Newspapers against the Govt. issue without legal prosecution we were forced to the conclusion that they were legal and true, and that if they were otherwise the law would have been enforced against them.

It is very doubtful however whether any means taken for the punishment of seditious editors would have been effectual. The people are excessively jealous of what they call the liberty of the press and prosecutions for political libel. have too often proved ineffectual, and attended with mischievous results to permit of their being resorted to with expectation of benefit[.]

Had McKenzie been arrested as a libeller. he would have been treated by the reformers as a martyr to liberty. He would have thereby gained partizans[,] he would most probably have been acquitted by any jury impartially chosen and if rebellion succeeded, his arrest and prosecution would have been set down as one of the causes of revolt[.]

The American plan of restraining the licentiousness of the *opposition* or *minority* press is a more effectual one than can be adopted in a British Colony. Had McKenzie in the United States dared to publish statements so inimical to the opinions of the majority of the people as his denunciations of the loyalists were in this Province, his house would have been burned and he would have been murdered by a mob. and the murderers would not have been punished.— The fact stands thus McKenzie in his treason was protected by a Government which would permit no other than legal means for the suppression of crime, and it was more than doubtful whether these legal means would have been effectual for good while the evils necessarily attending upon them were certain and apparent.

When the designs of the disaffected became more undisguised and the loyalists were awakened to a sense of danger. prosecutions might have been effectual. and had the outbreak been delayed for twenty four hours McKenzie would have been arrested. but this measure would not have been a preventive one as far as related to the alienation of the minds of the reformers from their allegiance which had been produced previously[.] If the prosecution had taken place previously he would have denied the existence of the conspiracy[;] he would have professed his loyalty. loyalists would have viewed him as a disappointed and desperate politician[;] his own political adherents not actually in the plot would have looked upon him as a persecuted man. and his arrest would probably have made many reformers rebels. who have never forfeited their allegiance to this hour.

Another mark of the progress of disaffection was the establishment of reform associations, the enrollment [*sic*] of reformers in bands of 40 each and for a short time before the outbreak the meeting of these bands for the purpose of shooting at a mark, and for drill.

It is charged against Sir Francis Head, that he did not cause these meetings to be dispersed. and the persons concerned in them arrested. In Sir Francis Heads dispatches he lays himself open to censure which has been liberally dealt out to him both in England & in the Province by making statements true in themselves but which perhaps ought not to have been made without the concurrent and qualifying circumstances which accompanied his measures[.]

Sir Francis Head states that he was aware of the design to revolt. and that he calmly awaited the result.

From this statement it might be supposed that H. E. had positive legal information sufficient to disclose in a Court of Justice the plan of the conspiracy and the names of the traitors so as to have caused their being brought to punishment. But the fact really was that the Lieut Governor only knew that meetings were taking place, of persons armed with rifles for a supposed traitorous purpose. The greatest pains were taken to reduce the supposition to legal certainty and the only way of accounting for the want of success which attended these endeavours is the probability, which after investigation has confirmed that no plan of rising in arms was formed until very shortly before the outbreak and that until the very moment of the rising very few persons were aware of the intentions of the chief conspirators.

Affairs were evidently tending towards rebellion but the information before the Government was of the most vague and unsatisfactory character. and scarcely ever amounting to sufficient legal ground for the committal of an individual[.]

Had the Lieut Governor therefore ordered the arrest of persons for attending seditious meetings or for assembling in arms. the great probability was that the persons arrested would be innocent of every thing but inclination or desire to overthrow the Government[;] that no actual plan to do so was formed by them or if actually arranged that it could not be legally proved.

Sir Francis Head was acting under the ordinary law of the land, and he knew that however vehement his suspicion and belief might be, they formed no legal ground for imprisonment and conviction of the parties charged with treason. arrests of innocent persons or of persons who could not be proved to be guilty, in the absence of actual revolt would undoubtedly have added to the numbers of the disaffected, and would most probably have been censured by H M. Government[.]

Had the rebel leaders taken time to organise a really dangerous plan of insurrection there can be no doubt that it would have been discovered and the leaders would have been arrested and punished but the fact was that little was discovered because there was little to discover. the state of affairs in lower canada. and the vigilance of this Government hurried McKenzie and his adherents into a premature rising the danger of which has been magnified to an extraordinary degree. It is true that great danger was apprehended at the time of the outbreak because sensible men were not prepared to ascribe absolute insanity to their enemies, But if the same opinion of the want of preparation and rescources on the part of the rebels had been persisted in, which was entertained but the day before the rebellion the rebels would have been justly and truly considered as an insignificant body of misguided men. without numbers, plan, arms, munitions of war, design or resolution to fight, which was the precise estimate of their force before the meeting at Montgomerys.

What was that meeting after all that has been said & written about it.

In a country accustomed to peace and tranquillity in which there was no police and no military force. two or three hundred young ignorant men were suddenly called together on the 4th. December. under the most false and unfounded pretences. they were told that there would be no resistance, that Lower Canada was in the hands of the Patriots—that the principal functionaries of the Government in this Province had joined the same cause. that all they had to do was to step forward and seize the country[:] that he who was foremost would be promoted and he who remained behind treated as an enemy.

It is true that these men assembled at midnight within five miles of the City, but it was after forced marches of from ten to thirty five miles in a canadian winter,. they lay wearied and exhausted on the floors, they had to procure provisions[,] in many instances arms[,] to cast bullets, to procure Gunpowder[,] to learn the state of the City and to make up their minds to attack it.

Had two hundred or even one hundred resolute men, accustomed to scenes of blood and violence made a sudden descent upon an unprepared city, Had this place been in a similar situation to a city upon the Spanish main, with a buc[c]aneer ship entering the harbour in the dead of night the danger would have been imminent[;] as it was, the rebels were on monday night in much more danger of being taken by the city, than the city of being taken by them. and so they felt it themselves for from the moment of their assembling the camp was a scene of insubordination mutual distrust and reproach[.]

The rebels owed their safety to their sudden assemblage and their not having made previous preparation, and to the consequent ignorance of the Government of a plan which was put into execution as soon as conceived. The little information which arrived in the City of the rebel force exaggerated it beyond all measure. The Government not conceiving it possible that men would be so infatuated as to make such an attempt with such means. was forced to give the enemy credit for previous plan, military organization, importation of arms and ammunition[,] a cooperating force in town, a simultaneous exertion throughout the Province and the enlistment of foreign aid. all which appeared the more formidable from the apparent secrecy with which the whole was in the most unaccountable manner brought to maturity[;] preparations were therefore made to contend with a formidable enemy, not to capture a few disheartened criminals.

The numbers of the enemy increased on tuesday and Wednesday. The force was however continually changing[,] those who had joined being discouraged and alarmed at the want of adequate means for attack or defence, and those who had not joined being encouraged by the forbearance of the loyalists whose means and spirit they consequently underrated.

The illusion on both sides was not completely dispelled until Thursday. when the rebels were surprised by the advance of a very superior body of the Loyalist militia from Town. and the Loyalists on the other hand to find little or no resistance and that the enemy were flying in all directions. on their approach.

Sir Francis Head has been blamed for consenting to the withdrawal of the military force to Lower Canada. He accounts for his doing so by his desire of producing the moral effect which would be the consequence of the Loyalists finding they they must depend upon their own courage & conduct for the maintenance of the principles to which they were attached, and also in their feeling that the Government fully trusted in their ability to preserve the Province without military assistance. but there were other reasons which Sir Francis did not put forward in his own justification which were cogent enough to make his policy almost of actual necessity.

Amongst these was the state of the neighbouring province in which the loyalists were infinitely outnumbered, and in which previous symptoms of dangerous rebellion had appeared. which made the presence of not only the regular troops become necessary there, but which also made it appear advisable to afford the Loyalists of Lower Canada all the assistance otherwise, which could possibly be spared.

Add to this that the numbers of regular troops which Sir Francis Head could have been permitted to retain in the Province, amounted only to a few men to be used for a guard, to post sentinels at Govt House according to the usual form. but which would have been utterly useless as a force wherewith to prevent or suppress a rebellion, such as success of the traitors in Lower Canada would have occasioned. The fact is, that Sir Francis Head sacrificed nothing and he gained much by allowing the troops to be withdrawn[,] for without losing any means of resistance to rebellion, he did what was much wanting in the Province and in England[,] that is to say he proved that under the most alarming circumstances, with a rebellion raging in Lower Canada. & without the prospect of military aid for months to come. the loyalists were able in themselves to maintain British power in the Province, against the utmost endeavours of the disaffected.

Sir Francis Head has been censured in the Province for not calling out the militia and for not putting arms in their hands for the defence of the Province in anticipation of the revolt.

Those who blame the late Lieut Governor for this omission, do not know or consider the difficulties under which he was placed and it may be well to mention some of them.

The commencing an expensive system of military defence was a measure for which the local Government had no authority. from home and no pecuniary means at its disposal, here. it is said that the calling out a militia force would have prevented rebellion. but this would have required a larger force than has been found necessary for its suppression. to have garrisoned so extensive a country would have required a large body of men. to have posted a few here and there. would have exasperated without intimidating the disaffected and it would have exposed the parts of the Province in which there would be no armed force to violence and outrage. a small force in the City of Toronto might have put off the attack upon the City, for a season. but it would only have made it more formidable better arranged and more dangerous when it would happen. The rebels would have laughed to scorn the preparations for defence. The very fact of the assemblage of an armed force would have been represented as a tyrannical attempt to trample upon reformers. and this would have gained the cause of rebellion many an adherent which as things have happened remained passive if not loyal. a small force could not have suppressed seditious meetings[;] it could not have prevented treasonable communications with the U.S. frontier. its employment would in short have had all the moral effect of declaring the country in a state of revolt, without producing the physical means of preventing or suppressing it.

The raising large bodies of loyalists, might have had the effect of preventing to a great extent any actual armed revolt within the Province. but the necessity for such a measure would never have been apparent and its justification would have been impossible. there would have been nothing to prevent the reformers from continuing their peac[e]able declarations. To this day nothing has been proved or discovered to shew any actual preconcerted plan of formidable rebellion. and had such plan been anticipated and rebellion prevented by formidable means, how could the use of these means, and the expence attending it have been afterwards justified? hôw could charges of extravagance on the part of the local Government. and alleged intention of establishing an armed tyranny have been met, when brought forward in the Imperial & local parliaments. And where was the evidence beyond mere supposition in the hands of Government?

Again had the loyal inhabitants of the Province been called from their homes and had the reformers remained passive or confined themselves merely to sedition and libel. is it to be supposed that the country could have been aroused by the really noble and active spirit which the treacherous attempt made by the rebels has brought forth. It is in vain to expect that a population can be called from their homes. their peaceable & profitable pursuits, on a mere supposition or anticipation of danger[;] the loyalists of the country judged for themselves. and offered to take up arms not because they were commanded to do so but because the enemy was in the field. actually in arms threatening the destruction of their lives and properties[;] had the Government summoned them from their homes, upon the evidence of intention of revolt in its possession, they might have assembled, they might have taken up arms in the expectation that Government had good reason for summoning them[.] But it would have been vain to expect on a mere supposition of rebellious intentions which some would believe and some would not the same alacrity, & ardent feeling which the loyalists exhibited on learning that the enemy was actually in arms[.] Had a call been made upon the militia without its being promptly and enthusiastically responded to, the moral effect would have been most injurious, and yet it is evident that the degree of readiness on the part of the loyalists to take up arms, depended much upon the opinions individuals entertained respecting the necessity of doing so. It was for the rebels by their preparations to make that necessity apparent. but they seeing that each step on their part was closely watched and that if they delayed a week or even a day. they would have been met by an armed force, determined on anticipating the calling together of the militia and surprising the Town & Garrison. They assembled in haste determined to make the attempt but finding themselves without considerable numbers and resources. of any kind equal to the enterprize they waited until the loyalists had time to make ample preparation and to attack them.

Had there been any regular force of importance in the Colony. of course it would have been well to dispose of it in such a manner as to prevent or defeat attack from the supposed rebels. but the calling out a militia and arming volunteers, appointing officers, incurring expence— all upon suppositions founded perhaps upon empty boasting of the disaffected was a very different measure. from using in the best manner a force already raised.

Had a large muster of militia been called, and armed. it would have caused much excitement and alarm and if it had for the time intimidated the rebel party there would have been nothing to prevent McKenzie & his associates from denying any intention to revolt. in such case it is much to be feared that men who were called out under excitement & who supposed they were to meet actual opposition would have returned home with very different feelings from those which actuated them on their coming out. They or many of them would have blamed the Government for their being brought from their homes in the depth of winter without necessity, and when actual necessity afterwards arrived the same alacrity would not have been found.

The militia law of the Province, directs the calling out of militia in a particular manner[;] the militia man is enrolled according to the section of of [*sic*] country to which he belongs without any regard to his loyalty or desire to fight in defence of the Country, the law only contemplating foreign warfare in which every man is supposed to join, and not internal insurrection in which men must of necessity be divided.

Indiscriminate calling out and arming a militia regiment according to law would have been to furnish both sides with arms and ammunition so that they might fight the battle on equal terms, which was by no means a prudent or admissible course.

The raising soldiers upon the simple authority of the Lieut Governor could only be justified by actual rebellion, in the strict sense it is illegal and unconstitutional at all times. and had the Lieut Governor chosen to take the responsibility and had no rebellion ensued who was to bear the expences or to answer for the illegal act and had those troops been used in dispersing meetings, or arresting suspected individuals who was to answer for the acts of men thus illegally employed. as soldiers. Sir Francis Head was thus in a manner forced into the course he took as well by the law of the land as by motives of common prudence. Had he been proved to have permitted extensive and dangerous preparation for attack, and revolt to be made in the Province without interruption he would have been subject to blame. all that he can be charged with at present is that he was not prepared for an attack which did not require preparation to withstand it.

The premature assemblage of the rebels had a very great effect upon the disaffected in the country generally. all who had not committed themselves, seeing the total want of means and rescources of the rebels forbore to join them. whereas they never could have discovered the weakness of their own course in any other way than by the actual attempt. this has no doubt been the means of preventing the implication of thousands in the conspiracy, and it is not improbable has caused many to join the loyalists and do their duty as good subjects.

The only measure not adopted, which would under the circumstances have been prudent, and which had the Lieut. Governor been persuaded of the possibility of a sudden assemblage of a body of men with the intention of attacking the Town and Garrison was the providing adequate means of defence for the arms and ammunition so as to prevent their sudden capture. Sir Francis Head however is justified by the result in his supposition that the rebels had neither numbers or resolution at the moment to make an actual attack, before the Citizens would have had time to prepare to resist. In the mean time a small guard was left at the Garrison, and some special constables at the City Hall rather as a watch than a guard. Sir Francis desired no more notice of the movements of the disaffected than the intelligence of their advance and he did not suppose it possible that many men armed could come together from different parts of the neighbourhood without being discovered or that they could have marched upon the Town without previous discovery. upon that discovery the rallying of the citizens was reckoned upon with certainty and the advance of a few hundred men, into a city of 10000 inhabitants with arms to oppose them was not considered as a project likely to be entertained[.]

Still there is no doubt but that a force of perhaps two hundred men. considering the absence of regular troops would at least have given confidence to the citizens because it would have put the arms upon which they depended in positive safety, and much of the confusion and alarm which ensued might have been spared by this measure.

The Terms in which Sir Francis Head admits that he was surprised are very strong and unqualified, and the motives for this unqualified admission are not always appreciated. Sir Francis in fact was always ready to place in the strongest point of view the merits of H M. loyal subjects on whose attachment & assistance he so fully relied. but unless an actual attack had been made or something accomplished on the part of the rebels, by their assemblage. Sir Francis Head cannot be said to have been surprised by them. he heard *suddenly* and *unexpectedly* of the gathering at Montgomerys. but he had previously thought that the Citizens were sufficient on any alarm to repel such an attack. The result proved that he was right. for the enemy were not assembled in numbers before the City was alarmed and no attack upon it was actually made.

It is not necessary to enter into any details respecting the short progress and the suppression of the rebellion. Its course and the energy and spirit of the Loyal subjects of the Crown in the putting down the revolt as well as the measures adopted towards the unhappy persons concerned in it are all detailed in the despatches of the Government or the proceedings of the Courts and Council. The disaffected have learned that the overthrow of the Government of even a distant and exposed Colony is not so easily accomplished as they imagined. The British people find that it is not in the power of those who claimed in the Colony to be exclusively the people. to overthrow British institutions, and that these are valued not the less in America (Canada?) because Republicanism is at our door and the good and evil which it produces exposed to our close inspection. The true danger to which these Colonies are exposed from American aggression has also been clearly shewn and time given to oppose it before it could come against us with fatal effect[;] and English liberal politicians it is hoped have learned that it is no light matter to advise British Colonists to revolt. and to encourage them in rebellion by assurances of passive submission to American patriots and domestic traitors[.] It now therefore only remains to offer a few suggestions as to the different measures proposed for the settlement of Political Questions in the Canadas, and if these Colonies shall be really considered of value either as regards their intrinsic worth or their relative position as regards the American States[,] to represent the necessity of defensive and protective military measures.

Questions of vital consequence to the future preservation and prosperity of The American Provinces are now opened for discussion. and plans are proposed for the settlement of the Canada question which may possibly succeed in the restoration of tranquillity or which may make any further attempts to retain the Provinces desperate & impossible[.]

Extensive sudden organic changes are always dangerous. their consequences are not possible to be altogether foreseen, and steps taken of this nature cannot be retraced.

They are however almost always popular. the public mind is generally sanguine because each individual hopes for some undefined good result while he trusts to his own ingenuity and prudence for avoiding evil consequences.

It is not therefore because a proposed alteration in a constitution is very popular that it is very advisable and proposed measures of change ought to be estimated by their intrinsic value rather than by popular favor. There scarcely exists a people on earth who if invited to make political changes in their institutions. would not seize upon the opportunity with avidity, and the almost total want of ancient and local prejudice, of ties of interest, property, and the influence of religious establishments render the countervailing conservative principle. which would maintain settled institutions much weaker in all parts of America than in Europe.

The different plans proposed on the side of the loyalists. and which are said to be under consideration by the Government for the Union of the Provinces deserve and require the fullest and most cautious consideration[.]

The evils suffered by the British inhabitants of lower Canada and particularly by the mercantile Body of that Province from the anti commercial spirit of the french population and the complete cessation of any beneficial action of the Legislature and Government of that Province, naturally forces upon the loyal & enterprising colonists the necessity of seeking some change which would set the machine of Government once more at work. and furnish the power wherewith to bring into active operation the latent rescources of that extensive province. It is not to be wondered at that the the [*sic*] mercantile population of lower Canada are sanguine as to the success of any scheme which would tend to relieve them from their present condition. The Legislative union of Upper and Lower Canda is therefore a favorite measure as well as the federal union of all the North American Provinces.

The dispassionate observer of the state of Politics in Lower Canada will easily trace the principal cause of the condition of that Province in the existence of two separate and distinct races of men therein, one of them having a foreign language. adhering to foreign laws, and foreign habits. these races come into constant collision with each other],] the line of demarcation becoming continually more marked and distinct as the numbers become greater and the opposing interests more formidable.

When Lower Canada was first conquered and the French power was prostrated in America, it would have been merciful and Kind immediately to have commenced the amalgamation of the French colonists with the British subjects of the Empire. The french canadians were then accustomed to arbitrary rule. Their numbers were comparatively few and they were wholly in the Power of the British Government[.] It was not for their sake that canada was conquered. And they had no right to expect that the future interests of a Colony which was to be inhabited by millions of British subjects should be sacrificed to preserve french laws language & institutions[,] and the prejudices or attachments of the inhabitants to them ought to have weighed but little when the future prospects of so important a province were considered.

Had the English language been at once introduced into the courts of justice and the proceedings of the Provincial Councils and had English law regarding property and civil rights at once prevailed these would have been regarded as necessary consequences of the conquest, and there would now probably have been as few traces of french institutions in Lower Canada, as there are of those of Holland in the State of New York.

But the preservation of French laws and language has been one of the most irritating causes of dispute[.] The french laws were not made for a commercial people. and the language was not necessary in a country in the midst of a British people. and carrying on all its foreign trade with England.

The continuance of french law and language has however kept up the distinction of races and since the numbers of the British population have increased the struggle for predominance between them has been severe and unremitting[.]

The french race has been preserved distinct, by artificial means that is to say by the protecting power of the Government. without this the race would long since have disappeared at least as to any political effect. in the British population coming from home, and from the neighbouring colonies.

Successive administrations have endeavoured to promote peace and contentment by doing justice between the contending parties. but they were contending for predominance and not for justice. And therefore the exertions of Government met with little success.

A constitution was bestowed on the Province with a representative Assembly. so that they might Govern themselves but this only set them loose upon each other. in an interminable contest. because there was a superior power in the Government which prevented one from completely suppressing the other.

The numbers of the french party being the greater they always have had a majority in the popular branch of the Legislature. but the British interests were naturally at least passively protected by the Government, and the Legislative Council being appointed by the Crown the opinions of the British minority prevailed in that Body. and in the Councils of the Government.

Thus neither party had the power of enacting laws without the consent of the other. their situation became intolerable to both[;] one naturally inclined towards the Government. while the other in its desperation sought for assistance from the neighbouring republicans although it is well known that their habits manners and institutions were more different from those of the canadians, than the habits manners and institutions which the British party desired to establish ever were, or were likely to be[.]

Had the attempt to bring about revolution in the Colony been successful. there is little doubt but there would have been a speedy end to the Grande Nation Canadienne and its existence as a distinct french race, would have immediately been on the decline. The lands which the Canadians desire as they say to preserve for their children would soon be occupied by American squatters, who even now cannot be kept at their own side of the boundary. The anti commercial laws which throw almost insuperable difficulties in the way of transfer of real estate, and have a direct tendency to prevent improvements upon it, would not be allowed to stand in the way of American speculations nor would american enterprize suffer itself to be impeded for the want of Canals rail roads, and a public debt. republican Majorities do not pretend to the delicacy, and forbearance of Monarchical Government[;] the influence which protects the Canadians would be at an end, and they would as a race with all their ancient laws prejudices and attachments sink overwhelmed beneath the superior, and overpowering interests of the Anglo American race.

But a discontented and disappointed party will seek for triumph and revenge in any quarter even at the risk of self destruction.

The ancient Britons called in the Saxons to their assistance, they were enslaved & became extinct. The ancient Irish invoked English interference in their domestic quarrels. and it led to their speedy subjugation[.] The Dutch, Swiss, Spaniards and italians asked the french republic for liberty and received military de[s]potism. all ages and periods of history shew that faction, has no view to the future, that it sacrifices every thing to the immediate qualification of its present desires.

Such being the present result of popular contest in lower Canada. will the proposed union between the Provinces prove a remedy for existing evils?

It is said by the advocates of the Union, that the measure would give a decided preponderance to the British party in the Legislature.

Supposing this object already attained. It is scarcely to be expected that the french canadians will be more contented than they are at present. or better pleased under the active rule of a majority of an inimical interested party than under the mild sway of a protecting Government. Can it be supposed that they will be better pleased to lose their laws, language & institutions, by the vote of their enemies, than by the enactments of the Imperial Parliament[;] will they be better pleased at seeing their money spent and debt incurred for the interest of the Merchants and Upper Canadians, in the erection of public works which their own anti commercial spirit, and want of enterprize prevent their using or profiting by? will they like to have their religious establishment made the object of daily attack and furious debate. in a united

Legislature, in the same manner as the members of the Church of England have suffered in Upper Canada. will they be pleased at hearing their priests vilified[,] the dues paid to them claimed for secular purposes[,] their schools remodelled[,] their inconvenient vehicles subjected to Parliamentary measurement. all for the empty name of a constitution and the form of self Government which they must feel & know to be a hollow mockery as respects them.

They would therefore most probably become more desperate and discontented than at present. In the mean time the act of union would not remove the American boundary, or place republican influence more out of reach. The Canada Question might be settled, but so would not be the public mind in Lower Canada.

The proposition for a union of the Provinces is moreover founded upon a fallacy. a supposed unanimity of purpose amongst the whole British population. But the fact is otherwise, The population of Upper Canada is divided into political parties. it is not all even loyal. The neighbourhood of American political agitation has infected many of them with republicanism, and with notions of politics inconsistent with Colonial dependence, though perhaps all that entertain them are not positively aware of their tendency, These people are quite in sufficient numbers to have some influence in the Upper Canada Legislature. Late events have prostrated them for a moment. but questions of policy are continually arising which have a tendency to revive their influence. the reformers and the disaffected will go certain lengths together and if the latter are restrained from actual rebellion, the former will by the party connection be carried further in their measures and votes than they would individually desire. If then this democratic party were to have even partial success in the Upper Canada Elections there would be two contending parties amongst the British representation in the United Legislature.

The french canadians have shewn that they are united as a party, by religion, language, mutual ignorance. peculiarity of manners and habits. They have their own views to forward[,] their own objects to gain and they will unquestionably unite themselves with the one of the British parties which will undertake the most for them. The democratic party being the weakest in the British representation will unquestionably undertake any thing for the sake of gaining french support[;] there will be no question no hesitation in their united measures. which will all be directed to the overthrow of their enemies. and it has been seen too plainly that their measures even where the parties were separate have gone so far as refusal of the supplies necessary for the Government. The suspension of the Constitution in one Colony and open rebellion in both.

When the subject of the Union of the Provinces is mentioned in the reports of the Legislative Council, & the House of Assembly. and in the address of the Constitutional Society of Montreal, all these bodies seem to argue upon the assumption of the union of the whole population not french, whether Americans, old Canadian settlers native Canadians or old Country men. but were the question asked as to the result of a general election two or more years hence, no member of these bodies would say that he did not look upon that probable result with much anxiety. it is true that he might confidently believe that a a [*sic*] majority attached to British interests and the Unity of the

Empire would be elected. but no man will stake his credit as a politician in an assertion that all will be so inclined.

It is not necessary to argue that those who are likely to be of the democratic party will be all traitors or inclined to be so. what is here asserted is that some and in considerable numbers too, will be advocates for principles inconsistent with the connection with England. that for the purpose of obtaining their end they will act with those really inimical to England and that both will act with the Franco Canadians, and that together they will probably form a majority in the United Legislature.

The Union of the Legislatures is no doubt intended as a permanent measure to remain in operation for an indefinite number of years. If then it is impossible to be assured against a democratic majority of the united french members and reformers. even at the first election who can answer for the result of elections which are to take place ten or twenty years hence.

If then unfortunately unity of purpose and action should be established between the democratic anglo canadian and the french canadian parties, if these parties should command a majority in the assembly. and if that majority should insist as they no doubt would insist upon the concession of points now denied, if they should refuse to act with the Government[,] refuse the supplies, refuse to act as a legislative body, pass resolutions tantamount to a declaration of independence[,] where would relief or remedy be sought for? would the Upper Canadians remain for years virtually without a legislature? would not double the number of H M. subjects be involved in the misfortune, double the number disfranchised, by suspension or breach of the constitution? would not a united house of assembly be a more formidable body to manage or oppose than the separate assemblies, with separate views, different interests, and different alleged grievances.

So long as the Colonies possess legislatures nearly supreme in their powers and functions so long it is reasonably and calmly to be expected, that periods will arrive when these legislatures acting for their constituents, will be claiming advantages and concessions which ought not to be granted, in such cases the real points of dispute and discontent seldom occupy a prominent place in the discussion[;] they may be of a religious, legal or merely personal nature, but they are invariably made the ground for claims of concession to popular or legislative power or in other words they are used by the majority as further steps towards supremacy & independence. The demands are not to remedy this evil, or to redress that specific grievance. but they say if we had supreme control such an evil or grievance would not have occurred, therefore give us more power, forbear to act to think or interfere in our concerns, you are 4000 miles off. leave every thing to us but our expences.

Can any one fail to see that small colonies are more easily managed in detail than if united into nations. Why should Upper Canada be agitated about signor[i]al rights or Jesuits estates of Lower Canada. or about Quarrels between the merchants and fishermen of Newfoundland. why should lower Canada or Newfoundland feel the agitation of the Clergy reserve question which shakes this Province to its centre.

The Union of the Provinces even if the party favorable to British interests and connection should have a majority brought about by framing a constitution particularly with that view and by the introduction of members from a distance into the local legislature, may coerce the french canadians into political submission but it will not make them more contented or better subjects.

The measures of such a majority will not probably be of a conciliatory character or more likely to produce content or submission in Lower Canada.

But if unfortunately by a union of the French and democratic parties, measures should be adopted in the United Assembly. and the same state of things produced in both Provinces, which now only affect one it is impossible but to see that the connection of these Provinces with the mother country would be in very great danger of dissolution.

But it is said that the two provinces are by their position so intimately connected in interest, that they ought not to be separated[.]

It will be found however that this seperation [*sic*] has little if any thing to do with the discontents which have existed in both Provinces or with the state of the public mind in either.

Danger in a political sense, may be produced to both Provinces by a Legislative union, but the measure does not promise to produce peace or contentment in either.

It is obviously convenient that local laws and regulations should be left as much as possible to the people themselves. members of an assembly brought together from such distant points as would be comprised in the United Provinces would scarcely legislate satisfactorily for either.

The expences of the Legislature are already found to be a severe burden upon this Province. this evil must of course be aggravated by the removal of the seat of Government to a greater distance, and the attendance upon Parliament would produce additional inconvenience to members.

The represent[at]ive of the Sovereign, being within the reach of and accessible to the people is of much beneficial effect. The power and patronage of the Government such as it is is exercised with a view to public opinion, and with better information in separate Governments, than in large Unions of territory.

The having two executives and but one Legislature, would be found if not altogether impracticable, at least very inconvenient. The Governor of Upper Canada. or the Governor of lower Canada may act so as to please his own people but probably but one of them could please the United Legislative body. one Governor would find himself working against another, or he must be so completely subservient as to be a mere useless pageant[.]

General laws applying to the two provinces can scarcely be framed on the multitude of domestic matters which occupy the local Legislatures. and the representatives of one portion of the United colony would not understand or be fit to legislate upon the necessities or wants of another.

It is only in a commercial point of view these two colonies have any concern each with the affairs of the other[.] The evils arising from the relative position of these Provinces as regards trade can be avoided without a legislative union, without its danger or its evil effects and inconveniences.

These remarks will to a considerable extent apply to the proposed measure of a federal union between the North American Provinces.

It is difficult to imagine moreover what connection these Provinces have naturally with each other, or what would be the functions assigned to the Federal Legislatures.

The trade of New Brunswick Nova Scotia Newfoundland and lower Canada, are either directly with England, the United States or the West Indies. with each of which they have communication & common or contending interests. but they have little or none of these with each other.

The Province of Upper Canada has to pass its commerce through lower Canada, but with the Exception of Montreal which is virtually an Upper Canada port. there is not, or at least there will not be any direct trade or community of interests. The products of the soil are nearly the same, Upper Canada imports no lower Canada produce. Lower Canada for its own use imports little from Upper Canada. and there appears little but the want of a seaport, and access to the sea to require a United or Federal Legislature.

Then as to the functions of a federal Legislature.

The Congress of the United States has the regulation of the foreign relations, the foreign commerce of the Union. and it has to provide for the means of war and defence, but its powers are almost limited to these few matters.

It is to be hoped that it is not contemplated to vest any of these functions in a colonial federal legislature. they are not desired or required by the Colonists, and their exercise would be totally inconsistent with Colonial relations.

Is this federal legislature to frame municipal laws to expend money, to levy taxes. and regulate the internal affairs of the several colonies.

If so the local legislatures will be superseded in all their functions. they are found fully competent however to their exercise. and much more likely to execute them to the satisfaction of their respective constituents than any general legislature can be.

Is this new body to be a legislature of appeal from the local Legislatures or from the different branches composing them.

This would be the usurpation of a power which ought only to be exercised by the Imperial Parliament for in that body the decision of all Questions must ultimately rest. and there is no reason for any intermediate power because the Imperial Parliament is more immediately interested in matters affecting the welfare & good Govt. of each colony than the several colonies can possibly be in the welfare & Good Government of each other.

Unless it is for the purpose of enabling the Colonies to combine against the domination of England or to negotiate with England in the manner of *an independent nation* for the extension of commercial privileges, or as *United Colonies* for the extension of *Political privileges*. to the detriment of the rights claimed by the Mother country—it is difficult to understand what the use of a federal Legislature can be, and how far this could be useful and how far detrimental. it is not difficult to prognosticate.

It ought to be tolerably well understood at this time what the relative rights of Colonies and the Parent state are, and how far political rights can be extended with due regard to the continuance of any degree of subordination on the part of the Colony. There appears always to have been a disposition on the part of the British Government to make concessions to the verge of what may be considered safe, and to cause the full and favorable consideration of Colonial claims, nothing has been necessary but addresses from the legislatures of the Colonies, and even private and unaccredited individuals have been attended to and the most serious and elaborate inquiries entered into upon these representations. The Colonists can desire no extension of facility in the urging or discussing their claims, and no greater attention on the part of the Home Government to these claims than has hitherto been afforded.

The Imperial Government must always be the judge of the justice of these claims, and the safety of making the desired concessions. there can be no arbitrator between the Colony and the parent state. no appeal from the judgment of the latter unless to arms.

If then there must be a judge upon one side and a claimant upon the other—the more powerful the one is in comparison with the other the more final and complete will be the decision, and the less probable will be the resort to force.

When two nations negociate upon equal terms if they disagree, war is the only means of settling the dispute. The more nearly therefore the colony is made to approximate to the condition of a nation the nearer will be the probability of the same result.

If there be constituted a federal Legislature of the Colonies however unconnected they may naturally be. the Legislature cannot meet without agreeing upon some points. or without taking upon themselves to adjudge the justice of the claims of any one of the colonies to which the attention of the federal Legislature may be claimed. If the demand of the colony be just, or the concession required safe. it is only requisite that its justice and safety should be shewn. and it will be granted. But one colony can state and prove a fact and contend as fully for the justice of a political principle affecting itself as many can do: and therefore no good can result from the Union. But if the demand be unjust, or its concession unsafe or injurious to the interests of the Empire It cannot be denied that the power of enforcing it is infinitely increased by the Federal union of the Colonies and the probability of a general rupture is brought much nearer.

If England desiring to preserve to itself the dominion of the sea. to assert the rights of blockade and search, the right of Navigating the entrance to the Black sea, the right of holding Gibralter [*sic*] and Malta. were to find those asserted rights. disputed by other nations having opposing interests, would it not be more advantageous to discuss the questions separately with the several powers interested, than with a combination of the maratime [*sic*] powers of Europe and america in a general congress of their Governments, particularly if they were pledged to assist each other in obtaining their respective ends.

If there be any weight in these observations it would follow that the Federal Union of the Provinces is a measure fraught with danger, and that it is one for which no necessity exists. that the functions of such a body could be defined with *extreme difficulty*, and that it could be confined within these functions with *extreme difficulty*. and that any good to result from the measure is very contingent and uncertain.

A representative from the Colonies in the Imperial Parliament is spoken of favorably. and it may have the good effect of affording a pretext to the British Government for interfering more frequently and effectually in the internal affairs of the Colonies. But it will have the effect of placing the Governors of the Colonies in a very difficult and invidious position. The members for the purpose of sustaining their popularity will feel themselves under a continual necessity of doing something for their constituents, and for that purpose of encouraging and inventing colonial claims[;] their numbers it is true will not entitle them to much influence. But The patronage of the Crown must be placed in their hands to a considerable extent. and their measures must be received with deference and consideration even in opposition to those of the Governors of the Colonies. they will of necessity be rival powers exercising to a certain extent the same functions. and it is impossible not to foresee that The Queens representative must either give up his independence of judgment to the Colonial members, or be liable to come into constant collision with them. One source of information on which to found colonial measures will be the despatches of The Lieutenant Governor responsible for the opinions he offers and the facts which he states. the other will be the correspondence of the Member of Parliament with his constituents who will be responsible for neither. The difficulties of Government will be thus infinitely increased insomuch that it is very questionable whether high minded men sincerely desirous of doing their duty to the Queens Government, will be found willing to undertake the office of a colonial Governor stripped as he would be of political power, his due influence transferred into other hands and his office passed by, in the consideration of public measures. at the same time he will be exposed to continual collision with the colonial members. and be placed in the position of a political Partizan instead of that of an administrator of the Government.

It is therefore very questionable whether any good can arise from the proposed measure to counterbalance these probable evils.

So long as the Queens Government are sincerely desirous of doing justice to the Colonies there seems little occasion for organic changes. Questions the decision of which properly come within the functions of the Imperial Government and Legislature should be settled with as little delay as is consistent with due deliberation and with as little reference to the Colonial Legislatures as possible. they engender party spirit and animosity, and the hatred and opposition which arises out of the popular agitation of questions which divide the public mind are not unfrequently transferred from the parties against whom they are at first directed to the Government and institutions of the Country.

For the settlement of the colonial question the first point of actual necessity which prevents [*sic*] itself is the placing the possibility of successful revolt by means of American interference as much at rest as possible.

The United States are interested to an enormous degree in obtaining possession of the Canadas. and the other American Colonies. Their intentions can only be defeated by measures of military defence. these will involve very considerable expenditure which the Colonies are not able to meet. The first question is therefore whether the Colonies are of such value to England either for the profits of trade[,] the employment of English shipping sailors and Capital or as a means of checking the growing and dangerous power of the American Union to warrant that expence.

The policy of England in engaging in extensive warfare for the purpose of preserving the balance of Power in Europe would seem to be in principle directed to the present state of America with the greater force, because her own possessions and her own trade, as well with these possessions as with the United States are directly involved in the question. And also because it is the aggrandizement of a naval power which claims rivalry with England which is the event desired to be avoided.

In this point of view the expenditure necessary for the preservation of the colonies, becomes trifling in proportion to the object to be attained. In this view The count[r]ies in question are emphatically British possessons and not the territory of the Colonists. and political measures inconsistent with the dependence of the colonies are infinitely magnified in importance.

If on the contrary the colonies are considered a burden to England. If it be for the sake of the Colonists they are preserved[;] if the loss of territory will be no loss to England. The expenditure necessary for their preservation is a positive injustice to the English people. The principle of self Government should in this case be extended as far as possible. and the measures of Government should be directed altogether to the satisfying the popular will[;] allegiance should not be considered a virtue as far as England is concerned, or rebellion a crime. against the British crown. In short the accomplishment of the peac[e]-able independence of the Colonies ought to be as much an object with the Government as with the disaffected populace.

These questions must be discussed and decided in *England.* If the Colonies should be considered of value they will be efficiently defended and properly Governed. And if not it is in vain for the loyal inhabitants to expect that the English people will for a long time continue the sympathy and protection now held out to the colonists[;] in the mean time the unsettled state of the country and the prospect of change will continue to depress the value of property and to limit the trade of the country to such an extent that the inhabitants will be visited with ruin, and their situation will become intolerable.

Continental possessions cannot be held in Europe without armies and fortifications nor is there any difference in this respect in america. The United States seem destined before long to become the scenes of Civil commotion. which must be the more fearful because there exists in that country no controlling power[;] should these commotions continue for any time this Province if undefended cannot be at Peace. and if they should end in the formation of a standing army and a Strong Government The danger of conquest is still more imminent.

Supposing these colonies to be placed in a position to look forward to a settled state of things there remain two or three points which require the attention and in which the Colonists require the interference of the Imperial Government.

The strongest reason for the Union of Upper and Lower Canada is the want of a sea port to the former. This is felt in the consequent want of power in Upper Canada to raise revenue by way of duties. and in the difficulties of just division of the duties received at the common Port of Entry[.]

Inconvenience to a great extent has also been felt, in the want of enterprize and public spirit in Lower Canada. In its not participating in the expences of Canals and improvements in communication which the Upper Canadians deem necessary for the purposes of trade.

Ships from the sea come to the City of Montreal. and that city although situate in Lower Canada, is sustained by the Upper Canada trade and derives all the profits of being the importing and exporting mart for Upper Canada.

The only obstacle to the navigation to Montreal is the want of depth in Lake Saint Peters [*sic*]. which prevents deeply laden ships from going through. to Montreal.

The timber exported from Upper Canada is therefore floated down that lake in rafts at great expence and with a considerable yearly loss of life and property[.] It has been ascertained that this lake can be made navigable for deeply laden timber ships at an expence, of no great amount considering the advantages which would be consequent upon the improvement.

It is not surprising that the Lower Canadians have not contributed to this object, or to the important works in Upper Canada because with the exception of Montreal which is the depot of trade Lower Canada has not the slightest interest in the success of the undertakings. indeed their interests as respects the improvement of Lake Saint Peters are directly opposed. to the success of the work because if it were completed The timber trade which is now centred at Quebec would come up to Montreal or at all events to the head of Lake Saint Peters.

It would be unjust to make the canadians below Montreal or at least those below lake Saint Peters, pay for public works above them in which they have no interest, or an opposing interest.

It is unjust towards Upper Canada that its great commercial depot should be in another Province, and that Upper Canada should have no share in the wealth and rescources accumulated there.

These facts do not point out the Union of the Provinces as a desirable or proper measure. they rather show that so great a separation of interests exists, as to make it necessary that a territorial division should be made which would make that part of Lower Canada sustained by, and interested in Upper Canada a part of the latter Province. and that where the separation of Interests commences there should be the boundary line.

If the Island of Montreal and the District of Three rivers, bordering on Lake Saint Peters, together with the lake, and the river Ottawa were united to Upper Canada. she would have direct communication with the ocean. she could carry on her whole commerce within herself[;] she could not be interfered with by the lower canadians or require their assistance in matters in which the vast majority of them would have no interest.

This would bring the British settlers in the Eastern Townships within the Province of Upper Canada where they could neither injure or be oppressed by the Lower canadians.

After this division the Lower Canadians may safely be permitted as large a share of self Government as is consistent with colonial dependence, they may have a legislative council appointed principally of their own members, most of the Officers of Government may probably be appointed out of their own body. The Government need seldom find itself in opposition to them. they may enjoy bad laws, bad roads bad sleighs, bad food and ignorant legislation in peace and quietness, injuring no others and not being interfered with themselves.

Were they in this state they would speedily split into parties, and if there should be Lower Canadian rebels, there would be Loyal Lower canadians to keep them quiet. if they are left to themselves they will not be unanimous or united.

The other important point in which the assistance of the British Government is required is in the settlement of the finances of Upper Canada.

The principal rescources of Upper Canada are derived from the duties levied at Quebec. Upper Canada has perhaps to too great an extent anticipated these rescources. and there are present difficulties of a serious nature to be met and settled, or else the consequences to this Province will be of incalculable injury.

This expenditure has been principally occasioned by the construction of public works of great magnitude, The importance of which however may be easily estimated on reference to the Geographical position of the Province.

The Country is extremely fertile and productive, but most of its products are bulky and heavy in proportion to their value.

The noble rivers and lakes which flow by and through the Province offer facilities of transport. without which export would be impracticable, and the settlement of the country impossible.

To open this superb inland Navigation completely it was found necessary to undertake such works as the Welland Canal, to enable vessels to ascend and descend the difference of elevation between the Lakes Erie and Ontario. The Rideau Canal to avoid the rapids of the Saint Lawrence, and the Saint Lawrence canal to overcome them.

The Rideau Canal was made as a military communication at the expence of the British Government. at the recommendation of the Duke of Wellington. It is however incomplete—on account of the obstruction offered by the Saint Anne Rapids.

It is not wonderful that in Undertakings generally of such necessity and importance the probable expences should have been underrated and the immediate profits overrated. or that The Province finds itself unable to meet the interest on the public debt thereby occasioned.

It is but just however that the Province should pay that debt. and it is highly expedient that such of the works as are of manifest and immediate utility and importance should be finished.

This can only be done by increase of revenue. and the only practicable way of raising revenue is by the increase of import duties. which can only be accomplished by giving this Province a Port of entry from the sea. at Montreal[.]

These duties are at present so trifling that that [*sic*] they may be very materially increased without injury to trade and without any perceptable [*sic*] burden to the people.

The security for the repayment of the Public debt is therefore unquestionable.

But the present Political state of the Province renders it impossible to procure further credit unless upon disadvantageous terms.

The money which has been already raised, has been lent at an interest very much above that paid by the British Government.

If the British Government were to lend its credit to the Province to the amount of a million Sterling. the interest on the public Debt would be very materially reduced by the redemption of the debentures. and placing the amount upon the New loan. The repayment of the money may be secured upon the revenues to be received at Montreal, and the recurrence of a like application might be prevented by the Government looking with more caution upon Colonial Enterprize, and by not sanctioning any further loans without its express approbation or the expenditure of money on Public works unless by Officers of ability appointed by itself and not liable to be affected by local interests, or popular influence.

The improvement of the Ottawa river for the purpose of assisting the timber trade, and the deepening lake Saint Peters for the same purpose may be accomplished by means of a loan, and the interest upon that loan may be provided for out of the dues upon Crown timber.

The expence and risk of conveying timber to the sea would be much lessened and the English people would have less reason to complain of the Protecting duties upon the Baltic Timber.

These measures would have a very great effect in tranquillizing the public mind. and would cause an incalculable flow of prosperity into the Province[;] they would give confidence to the people[,] induce immigration, raise the value of lands. make the public works productive. and tend more to the restoration of this Province to its former happy & tranquil state than any abstract political measures which can possibly be [de]vised. But unless means are taken to induce people of property to come to this Colony instead of the United States. and to restore the public confidence and the trade of the country. The People will continue poor and distressed, and will therefore be unhappy & discontented.

[Marginal precis headings to the first portion are not here transcribed.

A copy preserved in the Canadian Archives (see *Report of the Public Archives for the year 1923*, p. 173) is in three handwritings, probably clerical, but is signed by Sullivan. It has a contemporary wrapper which reads:

"For the Right Honble. The Earl of Durham G.C.B.

When Sir Geo Arthur assumed the administration of the Province He requested the members of the Executive Council to furnish Him with a Report on its actual State, & condition—

That request has not been complied with; but, Mr Sullivan, the President of the Council, presented the enclosed Statement of his own opinions.—

The Earl of Durham will probably, during his Journey to the Lower Province find time to peruse the Document.

Toronto
16 July 1838".

The Canadian Archives copy lacks the marginal precis headings, has different pagination, and embodies occasional slight verbal changes as well as the emendations marked on the above copy.]

[188] PRICE[?] BLACKWOOD TO [ARTHUR]: A.L.S. 8p.

June 3 *19 Grosvenor St. [London.]*

I cannot allow Lady Arthur to leave England without sending by her these few lines, thanking you for your kind recollection of me at the moment of your embarking for Canada, & to assure you that I look forward with great interest, but no anxiety, to your career in your present Government; & that you have with you my warmest wishes for your continued happiness & welfare; in spite of whatever sens[e]less attacks may be made on your public conduct by the Humes & the Duncombes. Your brother Richard was kind enough to call on me the other day—He is here for the purpose of embarking your family, & will accompany them to Portsmouth. He tells me he is applying for a command, in which I sincerely trust he will succeed. His former service ought to insure him one immediately . . . [Refers to Dr. Annesley's retirement from the Madras service; to Ireland, O'Connell, the Corporation bill, the ministry, and to a reported parliamentary vacancy.]

I fear I have but little hopes of getting a command at present, but should such good fortune befall me, it would be infinitely gratifying to me to be employed where you hold so distinguished a command . . . [Sends remembrances.]

[189] [ADMIRAL] E[DWARD] HAWKER TO ARTHUR: A.L.S. 5p.

June 4 *Norton's [?] Hotel.*

I cannot let your dear wife & family leave England without sending you my greetings, & expressing my hopes that you are comfortably settled in your Government, I hope you will by God's blessing have a happy meeting with your family, they are going on board the best of the American Packets that I have seen, with a *smart looking* Captain, & looking to the *Great Pilot* there is nothing to fear. I have been busily employed fitting out my third Son James to go out with my Christian friend Coll. Gawler, who goes Governor to South Australia, This Colony appears promising & the population appears to increase immensely. I am sending out another agent a Mr. Bell (Surgeon of the Navy) to *supersede* the old agent at New St. Wales— With regard to news, the ministry are going on as *usual,* striving by every means to keep their places, & the other party are not strong enough yet to form a Ministry with a majority in the Hs. of Commons to keep them in. The most alarming thing to my mind is the supineness of England with regard to foreign powers, who are arming to an extraordinary degree. Russia goes on steadily pursuing her schemes whatever they may be, she has now about 50 sail of the line in commission & numerous Frigats, & might take the command of the *ocean* when she likes, & not only that but actually might burn London & all our shipping at pleasure in our present state, & especially since *you* have taken *all* our troops away, for we have now neither soldiers [n]or sailors, [n]or ships in any state of readiness[;] the infatuation of our rulers is extraordinary to leave this Country without a Navy, while France & Russia have actually nearly 70 sail of the line in commission!— Well my dear friend, we know the Lord (the Rock of Ages) reigneth & no harm can eventually come to them who love him, I bless God that although I see what ought not to be, that is that England is reduced to the most defenceless state & unless something is done in the way of defence, that we shall be open to the plunder of any power who chooses to kick us. Yet I know nothing can come by chance, & I do not feel anxious or at least *over* anxious. Our little Queen does not go on I fear as well as at first, she is constantly at the Theatre seeing *Don Giovanni* or other vile performances. If you have time give me an acct. of yourself & how you like yr. Govt. May the Lord bless you & yours[.]

[190] ARTHUR TO GLENELG: A.L.S.[?] 15p.

June 5 *Government House, Toronto.*

I write unofficially to Your Lordship because the subject of this Letter is one of peculiar delicacy, and, because it is my wish to proceed in such a manner as may be least inconvenient and embarrassing to Her Majesty's Government.

Your Lordship's "Circular" has just reached me, transmitting for my information a copy of Your Lordship's Letter to the Earl of Durham dated the 3rd day of April last in which I find the following Passages.

"As Lower Canada is that part of British America in which the necessity of Your Lordship's presence will be chiefly felt, your residence will be principally fixed in that Province. But it will probably be convenient, if not indispensible, that you should occasionally resort to all or to some of the adjoining Provinces. As often as such an occasion shall arise, and Your Lordship shall pass into Upper Canada, New Brunswick, Nova Scotia, or Prince Edward's Island you will, by virtue of the Commissions there awaiting your arrival assume the administration of the Government of the Province in which you may be, and retain it during your residence in such Province—during that period the functions of the Lieut. Governor will be altogether suspended." . . . ."It will therefore be the duty of each Lieut. Governor to enter into a free and confidential Correspondence with Your Lordship on every topic in which you may invite such communications; and to obey any instruction, not in itself unlawful, which you may address to Him. But it will be desirable to limit such correspondence to questions of general and permanent interest. Nor will you address any positive instruction to any of those officers without fully weighing every representation which he may have made, or may wish to make on the subject of it."

Your Lordship will not, I think, be surprised at my stating that I have read those parts of Your Lordship's Dispatch with the greatest disappointment and concern.

I am sure I shall not desire in vain to recall to Your Lordship's recollection the confidential conversation in which Your Lordship was so kind as to intimate to me, before my acceptance of this Government, the possibility that it might be thought expedient to invest the successor of Lord Gosford with a power of interfering more directly and particularly in the administration of the Government of Upper Canada than any former Governor General had been authorised to do.

I am persuaded, also, that the explanations which followed were too particular and explicit to have escaped from Your Lordship's recollection, for they were not of a nature to be confounded with the ordinary occurrences of Official business.

Your Lordship will not fail to remember that—in answer to the question considerately put to me, in presence of Your under Secretary—whether, I should feel any objection to such an arrangement—that I did at once, respectfully, but distinctly state to Your Lordship that I had experienced the practical working of such an arrangement, whilst Van Diemen's Land was a dependency upon New South Wales, to be most embarrassing. That I was satisfied the feeling of the People in Upper Canada would be still more opposed to it than they were in Van Diemen's Land—and that, under it, the difficulty of managing a Province, so peculiarly circumstanced, would be so much encreased that I must decline undertaking it. That Your Lordship was then pleased to say—that it was a measure only thought of, by no means decided upon; and that you would see Lord Melbourne upon it—and it was not until I afterwards received Your Lordship's assurance that no change in this respect would be made that I consented to come to Upper Canada.

This is so strongly fixed upon my mind, and must, I am satisfied, remain so clearly impressed upon Your Lordships, that I venture with confidence to ask—whether, Your Lordship is not convinced that I was led to assume this Government by the direct assurance that I should not be subjected to any such interference on the part of the Governor General as Your Lordship's Despatch now authorizes?

Under such circumstances, I cannot incur the risque of offending Your Lordship by venturing to speak plainly. It is no vain jealousy on personal grounds of the control of a Superior that makes me look with extreme concern upon this innovation in Colonial policy in these Provinces which Your Lordship has announced. It is because I see and feel very clearly that upon such a system it will not be possible to conduct this Government with advantage to the public service, or with credit to myself.

My experience in other colonies was sufficient to convince me of this; but when I look around upon the numerous and varied population which it is my duty to govern, and the delicate questions to which local circumstances and personal interests daily give rise—and consider how much the difficulty would be encreased by my having to cooperate with a Legislature which must have a reasonable degree of confidence in my power to act in Unison with them, and to fulfil my Professions—I entertain not the slightest doubt that I shall be unable to maintain the proper efficiency of my Station if measures within my Government are to be directed from the Province of Lower Canada.

Your Lordship will have it in recollection that Sir John Colborne had the utmost difficulty to maintain such an influence over the Province as was necessary to enable Him efficiently to administer the Executive.

Sir Francis Head in several of his Despatches distinctly stated to Your Lordship that the Executive had not sufficient influence in his hands. "Governor after Governor", he observes in his private and confidential Letter to Your Lordship of the 5th February 1836, "has practically found his influence insufficient. A successor must be young and careless to undertake the situation with diminished means"—and down to the day of his departure, he urged the same argument.

The Report of both Houses of the Legislature at the close of the last Session clearly point to the injurious effect of the control *then* exercised over the local administration—and, now, Your Lordship has directed a measure that, in the nature of things, must lower the Station of Her Majesty's Representative in this Province, and go far to deprive Him of all Official influence whatever—and *that* at a period the most critical Upper Canada has ever known.

I shall have, I assure Your Lordship, the most sincere inclination to correspond or consult freely with Lord Durham upon any and every measure of this Government upon which His Lordship may desire to be informed, or upon which His Lordship may be willing to afford me the benefit of his assistance or advice. I am quite aware that the present posture of affairs in these Colonies makes such a disposition proper, and, at all times, and without any such necessity, I believe, I should be found to entertain it.

But, I am constrained to say, as I now do with much earnestness, to Your Lordship, that, in all matters of Government within the Province, the *decision* and the responsibility must rest with the Queen's Representative Here— That no other arrangement can maintain permanent tranquillity and confidence—and that upon the first occasion in which any Act of Government within this Colony is understood to proceed from orders of the Governor General, I shall feel that—no longer representing the Royal Authority—it will be impossible to render that service for which I was sent here.

Rebellion in arms had certainly been put down when I arrived on the 23 March last—but I found the Province in a most distracted state. and I must say it has appeared to me that Disaffection to the existing form of Government had taken deeper root, and had far more widely extended itself, than my Predecessor could bring Himself to allow.

The Public Mind seemed held, as it were, in suspense. There was no confidence in the stability of the form of Government—a very numerous body, perhaps [the word "certainly" is here deleted] a Majority, of the Inhabitants having been most artfully, and wickedly misled, still seemed to wish for democratic Institutions.

Within the Province was a subdued, but numerous and dissatisfied Republican Party; & a party of opposite Politics not less excited & stronger in point of character, Property & personal influence [a cancelled phrase here reads: "and a still stronger, highly excited, and, in my opinion, a far more dangerous Ultra Loyalist Party"] which it will be found extremely difficult to restrain within those barriers which are essential to the Public Peace[.] Without the Province, on the American frontier, was a restless & inflamed Mob of Rebels and Patriots, "American Patriots" eager for mischief of any kind, & most anxious by acts of violence and insult to provoke measures of retaliation in order to bring on War between the two Countries.

The Jails were full of Traitors and captured "Patriots". Religious differences were running very high, whilst Religious Institutions & Education were very low. The Province struggling under a heavy debt. Large Engagements for Public Works entered into, without any apparent means of meeting them—a declining Revenue, and public credit totally prostrated!

The Troops without proper Barrack accommodation, in a Country where, from the high inducements to desertion, the most comfortable Quarters should have been provided—and, except the small Fortress at Kingston, not one work of defence, in a Province open to a jealous Rival, and the Invasion of which is as certain, sooner or later, as that the nature of man leads him to aggrandisement.

This is no highly colored description, but plain matter of fact—and, still further, the Reports of the Committees of the two Houses, at the close of the last Session, which were adopted, shew that those bodies were in many important particulars much opposed to the policy of the Department over which Your Lordship presides.

By exerting with unwearied diligence the Powers, which, either Constitutionally or by Prescription, the Lieut. Governor is supposed to possess, and looking with confidence to Your Lordship for all the support and countenance which might reasonably be expected under such circumstances, I did hope, under the blessing of God, to have removed what I sincerely believe to be the most injurious prejudices, and to have seen that tranquillity and prosperity restored to Upper Canada which I know your Lordship has much at Heart; but, with diminished personal influence the prospect of success is almost entirely taken away!

Will Your Lordship allow me to explain this by referring only to one circumstance. Since I assumed this Government, I have scarcely passed a day without carrying forward, either directly or indirectly, my design for adjusting at the next meeting of the Legislative the Clergy Reserve Question. I have personally discussed the matter in an amicable spirit with the leading Members of various Communions; and upon a distinct understanding of the manner in which I proposed to carry out the measure I had no doubt that I should succeed in getting that all important question passed through the Legislature with a large Majority. But, who will henceforth confide in the professions of a functionary whose pledges may be made void, and whose intentions may be overruled?

Your Lordship will not suppose that I have overlooked the several expressions in the "Circular" which are impliedly designed to qualify the power intended to be conveyed, and to reconcile the Lieutenant Governors of the respective Colonies to changes which it is said are not intended to impair their authority.

The consequences which I apprehend from any direct interposition I look upon as inevitable in Upper Canada. They will be found, I am persuaded, inseparable from the measure itself, and cannot be counteracted or mitigated by declarations or expressions as to the intention with which the act is done.

I know from a high minded Nobleman like the Earl of Durham, that I shall suffer nothing personally—but the very means that have been adopted to throw all possible power and influence into his Lordship's hands, shew that Her Majesty's Government are conscious what the political consequences must be where power and influence are taken away.

[191] JA[ME]S HYDE TO ARTHUR: A.L.S. 2p.

June 5 *London.* [Marked "Private".]

[Regrets having communicated to his son George Hyde a statement by Arthur that a certain action by Colonel Alexander Macdonald at Omoa had been considered too violent by the colonial office. George Hyde had passed the statement on to Macdonald.]

[*Enclosures:*]

[192] *1838*
Mar. 22

[ALEXANDER MACDONALD TO JAMES HYDE]: L.

[*Government House, Honduras.*]

["Extract", recounting the above, denying the suggestion, and sending a copy of a letter from Glenelg approving the action.]

[On the same sheet appears item 193.]

[193] *1838*
May 30

JAMES HYDE TO ALEX[ANDE]R MACDONALD: L.

London. [Marked "Copy Private."]

[States that Arthur's allusion to the matter had been the contrary of unfriendly. Will send Arthur a copy of Glenelg's letter.]

[The above appears on the same sheet as item 192.]

[194] *1837*
Aug. 19

GLENELG TO A[LEXANDER] MACDONALD: L. 3p.
Downing Street, [*London.*] [Marked "No 25".]
[Expresses approval of Macdonald's action on the occasion concerned.]

[195] J. B. ROBINSON TO [ARTHUR]: A.L.S. 2p.

[*1838*]
June 6

[*Place not stated.*]
I think the proposed Militia order will answer exceedingly well— The danger of retaliation I hope has pretty well gone by, but it is well to take every possible precaution—

I know your Revd. Correspondent very well— He is a right minded person—but feels warmly—& I fear is getting into difficulty with some of his flock by his manner of proceeding.— If it were not for the evil of desertion, I should think the employment of regular troops at Brockville very desirable[.]

The statements in the letter are evidently made under the influence of strongly excited feeling, but I am sure they are by no means unfounded[.]

[196] W. B. JARVIS TO LT COL [R. H.] BONNYCASTLE: A.L.S. 2p.

[*1838*]
June 6

By Town.
In compliance with your suggestion I have taken the opportunity of the return Boat to say that I have thus far arrived with my prisoners. We arrived last evening and not finding the Shannon, which was detained by the 85th—I prevailed upon the Captain of our Boat to pass the locks and run down the River a few miles when we came to anchor. We returned this morning when the 85 came up and are now on the eve of again leaving this place.

There are reports in circulation that the disaffected intend doing some injury to the Canal and have chosen the *white fish dam,* as the scene of operation. I have often thought that some attempt would be made to injure the navigation by this route, which could be most easily effected by these vagabonds in a few hours.

I have mentioned the report to Captain Boulton at this Post, who informs me that he had made a communication on the subject to Sir John Colborne.

[197] F. EDWARDS TO [ARTHUR]: A.L.S. 3p.

June 7

13 Park Place, Regents Park, [*London.*]
[Regrets not having seen Arthur before departure. Offers wishes. Commends George Grange, a connection of the Baring family, a magistrate at Guelph. "I was present the other day at the Colonial Dinner to Sir F. Head but I thought it rather a failure—"]

[198] COLBORNE TO ARTHUR: L.S.

June 8

Kingston.
With reference to your letter of the 1st. instant, which reached me at Montreal on the 5th, I have the honor to acquaint you that I im-

mediately forwarded instructions to the Commandant of Quebec to prepare accommodation in the Citadel at that place for the ten Prisoners who had been taken in Arms against Her Majesty in Upper Canada.

[199] COLBORNE TO [ARTHUR]: A.L.S. 2p.

June 9 *Kingston.*

I hope to pay my respects to you at Toronto on Monday.

We embark at 7 oclock this morning on board the Cobourg, with the intention of proceeding to Niagara. I shall be most happy to have a few hours conversation with you, respecting our affairs and military arrangements.

[200] C. B. BROWNING TO ARTHUR: A.L.S. 4p.

June 12 *Her Majesty's Ship Hercules, Quebec Harbour.* [Marked: "Private".]

I had the honor of addressing your Excellency through Sir Colin Campbell's private secretary, on our arrival at Halifax about the 27th. March last. We sailed for England on the 4th. April, Embarked Troops at Plymo. sailed on the 5th. May, and arrived here this morning, after being a whole week, & more, detained in the St. Lawrence. Besides Colonel & Mrs. Airey of the 34th. we have brought Detachts. of the 1st. Royals, the 32d and the 43 Regts. Amounting, *in all*, to 583.— We have been very crowded, but very fortunately the weather, generally speaking, has been favorable. The circumstance of a considerable number of the Ship's Company being compelled to sleep on Main deck under Hatchings, & so exposed to cold & wet, has, of course, increased my sick List. But, as last trip, we have had no deaths, for which I desire to feel thankful to the Author of Life & of health— We debark the Troops immedly. and I have hastened to my Cabin to write these few hurried lines with the view of intrusting them either to the Honble. Capt. Spencer or the Hbl. Lieut. Plunkett who, I think, proceed to the seat of your Government.—

I have examined every newspaper which has fallen in my way, in expectation of seeing something respecting your Excellency;—but, hitherto, my search has been unsuccessful.— I sincerely trust, however, that the Gracious and Merciful God whom I believe you habitually study to serve & to glorify, has been, & continues to be with you, to guide, to comfort, & to bless you in your person, & family, & government . . .

[Mentions having written to Lady Arthur concerning his present appointment; Divine Providence has placed him in a ship of war instead of in a convict ship that he might have leisure to reflect on his shortcomings and religious convictions.]

My duties in the *Hercules* are purely professional,—and as I have two well educated Assistants,—the *details* of duty devolve not upon me.—*prescribing* is almost my only professional exercise,—having attention to the general state of the ship, crew, weather &c. and writing official reports.—

We have a Chaplain on board; but divine service has not been performed once on the Hercules since I joined her beginning of last Feby.— I have offered to collect the sick in my Hospital for the Chaplain when he pleases, but my offer has not yet been acted upon.— I read the Scriptures, in consequence, to those who are in my "Sick Berth," myself, on the Lord's day;—& endeavour to encourage the reading of the Scriptures by the Convalescents. I have I believe witnessed one instance of decided conversion to God . . . I have not recd. from Sir Wm. Burnett any reply to my letter. I intend taking no further notice of the matter— Admiral Hawker thinks I had better let it rest, & assures me that my Lords Commission[er]s are favorably disposed towards me, particularly the head of my own department Capt. Berkeley.

[201] W[ILLIA]M ROWAN TO ARTHUR: L.S. 3p.

June 12 *Toronto.*

I have had the honour to submit to the Commander of the Forces your letter of this date transmitting several Pay Lists and returns for Lodging and Horse Allowances for His Excellency's consideration, and I am commanded to acquaint you in reply, that as it appears these allowances were authorized by Sir Francis Head, and Your Excellency having recommended their immediate payment, the Commander of the Forces cannot withhold his approval; and the necessary instructions shall be issued to the Commissariat for the payment of these claims, as soon as they have been approved by Your Excellency.

With reference, however, to the rate established by Sir Francis Head, of 4/- Currency a day, for the use of a horse & horse furniture for the Volunteer Cavalry, in addition to their Pay and other allowances, I have been desired to state, that as that Sum greatly exceeds the remuneration granted in other parts of the Command, Sir John Colborne suggests to Your Excellency the expediency of reducing or discontinuing that force at the expiration of the period for which they were enlisted by Sir Francis Head.

[202] J. B. ROBINSON TO ARTHUR: A.L.S. 5p.

June 13 *Toronto.*

By the death of the late Grant Powell Esquire the office of Clerk of the Legislative Council has become vacant. It is worth, I believe, about £400 a year & ought to be filled by a Gentleman of education, and considerable talent—

There will be many applicants I dare say, indeed some have already addressed themselves to me, upon the supposition that as the Speaker of the Legve. Council, I may have it in my power to promote their views— On the part of the family of the late Mr. Powell, I have not yet been spoken to, but if I can be of any service to them upon this occasion, it is so much my desire, that I shall trouble Your Excellency with no application except in behalf of Mr. William Dummer Powell the eldest son of the late Mr. Powell—

I am afraid he is not quite of age, but I believe he is very nearly so, and may be of age perhaps before he would be required to enter upon the discharge of the duty—

He has been liberally educated at the Upper Canada College, and I think his capacity is good, & that his character & morals are in no respect exceptionable—

Your Excellency's connexion with this Province is so recent that I may be excused for mentioning some circumstances that are familiarly known to those who have lived longer here— The late Mr. Powell was appointed Clerk of the House of Assembly in 1813, and after serving in that office about twelve years, was made Clerk of the Legislative Council— In both capacities he served most creditably, being a Gentleman of much more than ordinary intelligence, and knowledge— He has left behind him a widow and five children, who so far as I know are unprovided for, and I much fear that their present circumstances are such as press for particular consideration—

Mr. Powell was the last surviving son of a former Chief Justice of this Province, a Gentleman who for nearly forty years discharged the duties of a Judge, and of other highly responsible offices with eminent ability—& his connection with the earliest history of this Colony was such as ought to make it painful to it's [*sic*] inhabitants that his descendants should by misfortune be left to struggle with difficulties which they may find it absolutely impossible to surmount— If the Young Gentleman whom I now recommend were three or four years older, I think this feeling would be found to prevail so generally, as to leave Your Excellency no reason to doubt of the propriety of appointing him— And I trust his youth may not be thought a decisive objection to his apointment, for I believe he is not a year younger than I was when by the unsolicited recommendation of his Grand father I was made Attorney General of this Province. The public service I hope received no injury, on that occasion, from what may have appeared to be a hazardous step; and it would be a particular personal gratification to myself to be able at this distance of time to repay in some sort an act of friendship which must have materially influenced my success in life—

I can not urge this matter further, for I am persuaded that considering the relation in which I stand to the Legislative Council, it will be the inclination of Your Excellency to comply with the wish which I have expressed—if you feel it not improper to do so.—

[203] ARTHUR TO GLENELG: Df.L. 19p.

June 15 *Upper Canada, Toronto.* [Marked "Private & Confidential".]

I had the honor to receive yesterday Your Lordship's Note of the 7th. May enclosing a sealed packet addressed to the Revd. Egerton Ryerson, which has been this day forwarded to that Gentleman's residence at Kingston agreeably to Your Lordship's request.

Mr. Ryerson has lately published in the journals of this Province, three letters, which, it appears, he addressed to Your Lordship on 23rd March 1836 and 27th. March 1838, with an explanatory note, and a Postcript dated 3rd April.

The subject of these letters is the case of Mr. Bidwell, which Mr. Ryerson appears to have espoused very warmly, and I observe he alludes therein to certain original letters which he had transmitted to Your Lordship with the request that they might be returned to him; and, probably, these are the papers contained in the packet which I have just received and sent to Mr. Ryerson.

In his letter of the 27th. March, Mr. Ryerson says, "I believe Mr. Bidwell has fallen an unconscious victim of Sir Francis Head's adroitness and ambition, and that he is excluded from this Province upon grounds both unconstitutional and unjust["]—and having been so much consulted by Your Lordship as he states and by Mr Stephen respecting the judicial appointments, he is "induced, in justice to Your Lordship, to himself, and to Mr. Bidwell, to furnish Your Lordship with all the facts of the case, *as your Lordship is not likely to get an impartial statement from any other quarter.*"

The conversations which Mr. Ryerson represents himself to have had with Your Lordship, and with Mr. Stephen—the enquiries which were made of him, and the expression of his own opinion and recommendations of persons, he cannot be unconscious must have been of a confidential nature, and that the publication of them is a breach of confidence.

As I write solely from a sense of duty towards your Lordship, I trust I shall not give offence in venturing to intimate in a confidential manner that the Reverend Gentleman is in my opinion a very dangerous correspondent. The publication of these letters at all events has called forth very remarkable excitement, and I have no doubt the subject will be taken up warmly by the Constitutional party when the House of Assembly meets.

I have no disposition to enter into any controversy with Mr. Ryerson; but I happen to know, positively, that his story about Sir Francis Head's treatment of Mr. Bidwell, is utterly untrue; and in order to prevent Your Lordship's falling into any error, through Mr. Ryerson's representations, I am desirous of explaining how this has come to my knowledge.

During my journey to Upper Canada, travelling in the midst of night in bad roads, in the Winter, I met with a severe accident which detained me two days at Albany.

The morning after my arrival, the Secretary of state of New York, Mr. Dix, called upon me, and accompanied me on a visit to Governor Marcy, with whom I wished to confer, and to enter into a treaty of good understanding.

Whilst I was with the Governor, the door was opened, without any announcement by a person who seemed "quite at home", and who walked familiarly up to Marcy to shake him by the hand.

The Governor half rose from his chair—exceedingly confused, coloured high, and hesitated whether to accept the offered hand.—

The stranger now on his part drew up—seemed not to understand his friend's coldness, looked round the room, then enquiringly in Governor Marcy's face—then in mine—in fact there was a scene worthy of the pencil of Hogarth— At length, the unwelcome visitor moved towards Mr. Secretary Dix. They retired towards a Window—a few words passed between them— The stranger once more glanced his eye upon me and, then, hastily retired!

It was impossible not to be exceedingly struck with all this. When I left the Governor Mr. Dix accompanied me, and, in place of leaving the building, I crossed the Hall in order to inspect some of the Apartments, and again unexpectedly came upon the mysterious stranger. As he threw his cloak around him and walked away, I could not refrain from asking Mr. Dix who the person was, and, then, all the Shuffling I had seen in the Governor's room was explained—it was Mr. Bidwell—late of Toronto!

In the course of the day Mr. Dix again called upon me at the request of Mr. Bidwell, who was particularly anxious for an interview, which he hoped I would not refuse *as he was a voluntary exile, and had parted on the most friendly and cordial terms with Sir Francis Head.*

Upon this distinct understanding, the interview was acceded to; and when Mr. Bidwell was announced, he repeated the same to me in still stronger terms.

He stated that at a moment of peculiar anxiety and suspense, he had experienced the utmost kindness and consideration from Sir Francis Head, who had acted towards him in the most friendly manner. That he had no complaint to make, but was anxious to explain his conduct on some particulars in which he was aware that appearances were much against him.

My impression at the time was that the explanation was a complete failure. Mr. Bidwell was, I have no doubt, adverse to the rising *on the day* it took place, and so was Doctor Rolph. McKenzie and Lount had been premature, and anticipated the general intended rise by some days, which was the means used by the Providence of God to destroy their wicked scheme.

I need not trouble your Lordship with all that passed. It will be sufficient for my present purpose to say that Mr. Bidwell assured me over and over, that Sir Francis Head's conduct towards him had been generous and benevolent in the extreme and that he should ever feel grateful to him.— This Your Lordship will observe was more than three Months after Bidwell had left the Province!—

Another remarkable incident occurred whilst I was at Albany into the details of which I will not trouble Your Lordship by entering— but, will simply observe, that before I left the City I was strongly impressed with the idea that McKenzie who was more bold and daring than his employers, was a mere tool in the hands of Rolph and Bidwell, who had *for years* been meditating the overthrow of the Government of the Province, and had lately received the cordial support and co-operation of Governor Marcy; and the mass of information that I have since acquired confirms strongly the opinion I then formed.—

I am not, My Lord, urging this in defence of Sir Francis Head's general Government; for I will not disguise from Your Lordship that I disapprove of much connected with the rebellion— That calamity though readily suppressed, but most awful in its [the word "ruinous' is here deleted] consequences, might, and ought, as I think, to have been altogether prevented,—and by not doing so, amongst many other sad results a party has been brought forward— I allude principally to the Orange Association—who are much more dangerous than the disaffected whom they contributed to overthrow; and who in their turn must be put down with *a very cautious*, but firm and decided hand— Still, in this case of Mr. Bidwell, I think Sir Francis Head has been most unjustly calumniated by Mr. Ryerson.

I could gain a victory over the Refugees and Patriots with half the trouble it occasions me to endeavor to keep them from actual invasion; and the disaffected might be suppressed, if in arms, with far less pains than it requires to keep them quiet; but, however successful the result against Patriots or Traitors might prove—there are elements in existence here which it will be well at this moment not to agitate, if it can be avoided, and Mr. Ryerson is an agitator to whom I would recommend Your Lordship to give no encouragement.

[The following passage is here deleted: "He has done Mr. Bidwells cause much injury,—his own political character has been such as to destroy all confidence in him, and he has thereby greatly lost caste with his own Communion, and is not, I believe, trusted by any party."]

A number of the more moderate and influential persons in this Province have long suspected that Mr. Ryerson had an undue influence in your Lordship's Office whilst in England, and that they have by that means been misrepresented,—and he has just now had the imprudence to publish just so much as leads them to suspect a great deal more.

Whatever may have formerly been the sentiments entertained by Mr. Ryerson with respect to Mr. Bidwell, I think that he has been evidently less guided in his recent proceedings by his friendship for that Individual, than by a deep feeling of resentment against Sir Francis Head—originating in the disappointment which he felt on his returning from England, where he had received so much attention, to find that his services were not here appreciated according to his own estimate of their value.— This feeling was I think rendered inveterate by the discussion which subsequently arose respecting the advance of money which Your Lordship had authorised in behalf of the Wesleyan Academy at Cobourg, but which was not obtained from this Government precisely in the manner desired by Mr. Ryerson.—

I hope your Lordship will kindly receive this confidential communication in the spirit in which it is addressed to You—under the impression that if Your Lordship takes up Mr. Bidwell's case upon any reliance you may place in Mr. Ryerson's statement, it will do much mischief, and Your Lordship will have cause to regret it exceedingly on that account.—

[The following passages are here deleted: "I am not insensible to the merits of Mr. Ryerson's publications in England relating to Canadian Affairs, which I perused with satisfaction before I came to this Country—nor to the fact that he has exhibited an inclination to support my Administration.

Yet I cannot forbear from expressing my opinion that I cannot implicitly rely on the Revd. Gentleman's professions or feel assured that he has not some ulterior object of very questionable policy concealed behind his present exhibition of an affected zeal for the cause of justice and the Constitutional rights of British subjects."] . . .

P. S. Mr Ryersons acknowledgmt of the Package I have only this day received which has caused the detention of this letter. I have in the mean time received your Lordships Officials upon the subject; it is my present impression that it will be more prudent to await Your Lordships reconsideration of the subject than to take any step whatever until Mr Bidwell shall himself apply either to your Lordship or to this Government.

Mr Ryerson has called forth the most bitter controversy, which has been taken up by all the Papers for many weeks, and even if the case were a good one, which it is not, there could not be a more unfavourable moment for entering into any enquiry.

[204] ARTHUR TO THE CHIEF JUSTICE [ROBINSON]: LB.1, p. 30-31.

June 15 *Government House, Toronto.*

I have had the pleasure to receive your letter of the 13th. Inst. recommending Mr William Powell to succeed to the vacancy occasioned by the death of his Father to the Office of Clerk of the Legislative Council.

This young Gentleman has called upon me, and personally requested that the appointment might be conferred upon him.

It is impossible to read your letter without feeling the most sincere desire to accede to a wish proceeding from feelings so natural and from resolutions so truly characteristic of an humane and grateful mind;

moreover, the valuable services you have rendered to the Legislative Council gives [*sic*] a weight and force to any recommendation from you which I feel and admit fully.

Nevertheless, independant [*sic*] of the objection which is made in almost every community to what appears an hereditary occupation of any public Office, I must say that Mr William Powell is too young to be placed in such a situation—an opinion I do assure you which I am obliged to express with much regret and great concern.

[205] ARTHUR: D.S.

June 16 *Toronto.*

Good to John H Dunn for Fifteen Hundred Pounds Currency
Toronto 16th. June 1838.

[Endorsed in Arthur's handwriting: "received this back from Mr Dunn & issued another good this day 4 July G A".]

[206] ARTHUR TO COLBORNE: LB.1, p. 22.

June 16 *Government House, Toronto.*

I have the honor to inform your Excellency that I find my Personal Staff quite inadequate, with the utmost exertion, to perform the various duties of this Command and request you will be so good as to allow me to appoint another Aide De Camp—

Although I have for some time found such assistance much required, I have declined to ask for it until compelled by necessity.

[207] J. T. JONES TO ARTHUR: A.L.S. 2p.

June 16 *Albany.*

On my arrival at Syracuse on Thursday evening I found myself quite unexpectedly under the same roof with Govr. Marcy & through the medium of my friend Capn Bloodgood of the U.S. Army procured an introduction for the purpose of communicating the substance of the conversation I had with your Excellency when you did me the honor to favor me with an interview on Wednesday last[.]

I informed Govr. Marcy of your desire to cooperate with him for the apprehension of the parties concerned in the burning of the Sir Robt. Peel & of your willingness either to meet him at Oswego or at Govt. House, also acquainted him of your not having received any acknowledgement of the letter you addressed to him shortly after your arrival at Toronto, to which he replied that he had received said letter, but he was afraid that in the hurry of the business which accumulated on his hands at the close of the session of the Assembly he had forgotten to render a due acknowledgement of the same; I presume from the manner in which the communication was received that he felt gratified & that he will address your Excellency forthwith; he mentioned to me that he had caused his receipt of a friendly letter from you to be inserted in the newspaper at the time of its receipt. I informed Govr. Marcy that I was in no way connected with the British Government but merely communicated to him the subject of a conversation held with your Excellency on a call at Govt. House & I hope I may not have exceeded your wishes in what I have done[.]

Your Messenger Mr. Phipps leaves here this evening for N. York; I have given him my address in New York & it will afford me much pleasure if I can render him any assistance on the arrival of Lady Arthur.

June 16 H. S. Fox to Durham.

See item 222.

[208] Arthur to Colborne: LB. 1, p. 23-27.

June 17 *Government House, Toronto.*

I have felt much disappointed at not having received the Memorandum from you before you left Toronto, as to your final recommendation respecting the Militia, and the positions to be occupied by the Troops; because, whatever Militia Force is to be kept up, the men ought to have been reenlisted before this time, as the period of Service of the Force now engaged expires on the 30th Instant.

It is difficult to decide upon what enemy, numerically, we may have to contend against, and the question is open to much difference of opinion. So, also, it is doubtful, and difficult to determine with what earnestness the American Authorities are really endeavouring to suppress the proceedings of the rebels and Patriots—but, there can be no question, that there is a large ungovernable body of ruffians along the Frontier, threatening to invade us, and within the Province (who would immediately rise if we sustained any reverse) a considerable number of very disaffected Persons.

In this state of things great excitement exists amongst all classes of this Community!—

Since your departure I have continued to receive reports of the intention of making descents upon various parts of this Province. The people of Amherstburg and Sandwich have actually been daily expecting the Patriots to cross.

Colonel Maitland,—who has shewn great discrimination, and been quite alive to the interested feelings even of our friends—had hitherto felt no apprehension, but within the last fortnight *he* seems to be of opinion that there is some cause for alarm. In his letter of the 11th. Instant, he says, "It is only the presence of armed men being stationed at Sandwich and Amherstburg that the public feeling for some time to come will be allowed repose from the unpleasant excitement which is constantly alive on the Frontier. I would beg to suggest that two incorporated Corps of Militia, under practical officers, should be at these two posts of 400 or 500 men each."

I forward his letter, with its enclosure, for your perusal.

With the view of reducing the Force, so far as I recollected the substance of the Draft Memorandum I directed the Military Secretary to desire Colonel Townshend to state what force He actually required for the protection of the Frontier, and what possible grounds there were for apprehending an attack. He replies—"from the general corroborative tenor of the whole of the Reports together with the acknowledgments of the American Authorities that they are congregating and meeting secretly for some vile purpose, I feel assured that acts of piracy and aggres[s]ion will take place in the unprotected parts of our Coast. I am of opinion that a force somewhat equal to that at present embodied" (900 men) (on the Niagara Frontier he means) "would be desirable not only for its security, but to inspire confidence into the peaceable and well disposed.["]

I also enclose Copy of Colonel Townswend's [*sic*] letter, together with some Reports the latest dated yesterday, by which you will perceive that Colonel Creighton reports that a considerable body of these Brigands have got [?] upon Grand Island, which is no doubt quite correct—and that *many* have already secretly made their way into the Interior—this I do not believe—a *few* may have done so.

Upon the whole—not only with reference to the excitement which does exist beyond all controversy—to the mass of lawless characters who have especially within the last three years been filling up the west and north west Country—to the numbers of inflamed refugees on the Frontier—to the very possible consequence of the Earl of Durham's presence in these provinces—especially as, happily, he is a man of ability and determination and will carry through with a high hand what he has undertaken, it is my deliberate opinion that independent of the coloured companies we should at once incorporate on new terms four Regiments at least of the sedentary Militia consisting of from 4 to 500 men each according to circumstances, upon a much better footing[,] that is I mean upon a better defined understanding and better officered to serve for twelve months certain. Much as I regret the necessity of this measure I have not a doubt it will be found economy in the end at once to adopt it.

Notwithstanding Sir Francis Head's extraordinary reports to the contrary, it is in vain to attempt to deny the fact that this Country is full of disaffected persons—I will not say positively that they preponderate, but I think so!

Major Bonnycastle has not arrived to commence upon the Barracks, and I fear Winter will steal upon us—furnish the Brigands with a Bridge of Ice and find us still unprepared.

A large supply of arms is much needed—those in possession of the Militia are very bad, and were so when issued— 20,000 stand should be furnished for the use of the Province, 10,000 to be deposited within the Fortress at Kingston, 5,000 at Toronto, and 5000 in the Western District where small armouries should be constructed.

Carriages for the six pounders are also much needed.

Bedsteads and Blankets, and in fact every article of Barrack furniture is greatly needed. All these matters have of course been reported through the proper Channel, but nothing will move the *respective* Officers so quickly as a word from you.

You were so good as to say that you would replace the 85th Regt as soon as I withdrew that Corps from Kingston. I am now very desirous to bring them up immediately. No risk ought to be run. We have force enough to crush rebellion or to repel Invasion; but certainly by no means enough to prevent either from being attempted, which is of great confidence [*sic*].

Confidence cannot be restored until security is felt.

What has become of Captain Sandom he ought to have some force on Lake Erie[.]

Major Webbe [?] of the Queens Niagara Regiment crossed over from Fort Erie to Buffalo last week, in a plain Coat to dine with some friend. Immediately on landing he was mobbed and most grossly insulted and in so much danger as to be obliged to decamp by the rail road dinnerless. Being very intimate with Major Young of the United States Army the affair has been taken up by the authorities in rather a spirited manner. A Special inquest was held the following day, and the jurors have expressed how strongly they *disapprobate* such conduct; but, poor Creatures, they all seem powerless against the people . . .

[P. S.] I propose to visit the Western Frontier forthwith.

[Enclosures lacking.]

[209] J. B. ROBINSON TO [ARTHUR]: A.L.S. 3p.

[*1838*] [*Place not stated.*]
[*June 18?*] I have just received Your Excellency's letter, & a Note from Mr. Joseph telling me that he is to be the Clerk to the Legve. Council— Since you could not patronize my young friend, I am happy that you have made the appointment you have, & I am sincerely of opinion that Mr. Joseph will be found a very acceptable & satisfactory officer— Among the applicants there is none I should have preferred to him & I am particularly thankful that Your Excellency has put a speedy end to suspense among the several expectants—

While on this subject I take the liberty, (since I am not able to call) of adding that another office which is said to be shaking in the wind is, in my view, of vast importance to the Governt.— I mean the Inspr. General's—& I do most anxiously hope that the best man the Province will afford may be placed in it— I think it above all things desirable that Mr Macaulay should occupy precisely that post with a seat in the Council—

[210] J. B. ROBINSON TO [JOHN JOSEPH]: A.L.S. 3p.

[*1838*] [*Place not stated.*]
June 18 Having made an application in behalf of Mr. Wm. D. Powell, which His Excellency has thought it inexpedient to give effect to, I have of course nothing further to say in respect to the office— It is unnecessary I trust to assure you that your appointment can not be otherwise than agreeable to me— Indeed I am persuaded that you will be found well suited to the office, and though the time may come when like other crusty old Gentlemen, I may contrive to annoy you a little by way of variety, I have no doubt we shall get on for some time "to our mutual satisfaction—"

[211] J. B. ROBINSON TO [ARTHUR]: A.L.S.

[*1838*] [*Place not stated.*]
[*c. June 22*] I like the draft of the Proclamation much & see nothing in it that should be altered.

I do hope that a *hue & cry* will be raised with spirit & should like to join it— The fellows should not have a moment's rest.

[212] ARTHUR TO COLBORNE: LB. 1, p. 28-29.

June 22 *Toronto.*

With reference to my letter to you of the 17th June Inst [*sic*]; I beg to enclose a Report, just received from Colonel Townshend by which you will find, with regret, that a body of these vagabonds have crossed and planted themselves in the neighbourhood of the Short Hills. They surrounded a small detachment of the Lancers, and at length set fire to the Building and so captured and plundered them and then let them go.

Whether these people have actually crossed the River or whether they are disaffected persons who have taken up arms does not clearly appear—perhaps both.

I also enclose you another letter from Colonel Townshend with a memorandum of information obtained from General Brady who evidently expects something serious in a few days. The part of Genl Brady's information that concerns me much is the intimation of some of our Militia Officers being disaffected— This I have heard for some time before, but, all along my impression has been that disaffection had taken deeper root and had far more widely extended itself than was supposed. I have now no doubt of it.

We shall have a sharp attack I apprehend from Detroit; or Brady would not notice it in the manner he does.

On the 17th I wrote for the 85 Regt to be sent on from Kingston, but they have not yet arrived—probably, Colonel Dundas has no certain information of the departure of the Corps from Montreal to relieve them. I hope and trust you will be able to spare six Regts for the U. Province two to be stationed at Kingston, two at Toronto and two in the Western District. I do not at all like the 32nd Regt being so far away unsupported!

I am convinced the whole of that Country is full of disaffected persons.

Pray do not think me troublesome in again pointing out our want of arms Blankets &c[.] Nothing has yet been done about the Barracks in the Interior.

Capt Sandom is waiting for this and I am therefore not able to write to you as fully as I could wish[.]

[Enclosures lacking.]

[213] Arthur to Lieut Col. [Henry] Dundas: LB. 1, p. 31-33.

June 22 *Toronto.*

During the last four or five days the rumour of some of the Rebels having crossed the river and got to the rear of Colonel Townshend's position on the Niagara has gained ground, still from the extreme improbability of it the rumour was not believed. From two or three corroborating circumstances however I was led to think there was some truth in the statement and therefore I sent off three Companies of the Regular Troops to Niagara and two Companies to Hamilton; and directed the 85th to be forwarded to replace them as Sir John Colborne assured me that he would be prepared to send another Regt to Kingston immediately, and that I might withdraw the 85th. directly if I thought it necessary.

Ten days ago I ordered Colonel Clark commanding one of the Regiments of Militia on the Frontier to send a Detachment to a place in his rear called Short Hills (where the Duke of Wellington proposed to have a Military Work) but in reply he begged the Adjutant General not to send a force there as he knew the Country thoroughly and it was his own[:] no part of the Province was more loyal and sending Troops there would rather give offence.

Colonel Townshend, however did send a small party of the Cavalry to St Johns, close by the Short Hills to examine the Country.

I have just received a report from Colonel Townshend informing me that on the night of the 20th or rather at two oClock A.M. this day (21st) the party consisting of a Sergeant and nine men had been surrounded in their Quarters by a gang of two hundred men having white ribbons in their hats and an eagle on the side— The cavalry behaved exceedingly well, resisted them for some time until the rebels set fire to the house and they were then captured and plundered.

The Military Secretary will also enclose you a statement, which has been sent to me by the American General Brady, who has begged however that his name may not be mentioned. You will perceive what Johnson's [*i.e.* Johnston's] plan is said to be, and where he is said to resort. I do not know that implicit confidence is to be placed in this report, but it ought not to be disregarded.

I am quite satisfied that your zeal for the Service will be guided by prudence, and that you will not incur any expence that can be avoided or call out more of the Militia than is absolutely necessary,—and therefore I repeat what I said to you at Kingston that you will adopt any measures you deem essential on my responsibility—only let me know through the Military Secretary what you do[.] I am certain that in all warfare of this kind, it is economy, great economy in the end to adopt at first vigorous measures.

I took the precaution to write to General Clitherow, and as Sir John told me he left always discretionary power with him I hope you have been reinforced and that the 85th are now on their way up.

[Enclosure lacking.]

[214] COLBORNE TO ARTHUR: A.L.S. 7p.

June 23 *Quebec.*

Before I received your letter of the 14th instant, I had mentioned to Lord Durham the substance of your conversation with me in regard to the inconvenience which you had some reason to apprehend might be experienced should the Administration of the Government of the Upper Province be actually assumed by the Governor General on his arrival at Toronto.

His Lordship has authorised me to acquaint you that he has no intention to interfere with your Government in any respect whatever; and that his sole view in visiting your Province would be, to procure correct information, as to the opinions of the different parties how far the projected scheme of Government may be carried into effect with benefit to these Colonies; and to enable him to judge of the difficulties that he may encounter in developing his plans— In availing himself of his Commissions of Governor of the the [*sic*] several N. American Provinces, he has no doubt that his assumption of the Government in every Province while he remains in it, will give him the great advantages, of obtaining information speedily; and he mentioned that he would not have accepted his appointment without the power of ever using this authority.

He is most anxious that his views should be explained to you, and to consult with you on every measure he may propose to adopt, and in fact to work through you, in the Upper Province.

He has read your letter of the 14th instt, and with reference to it requests that you may be informed that he intends to leave Quebec on the 4th; and to proceed direct to Niagara. He will probably not arrive there before the 11th or 12th. He is of opinion that your contemplated changes in the Executive Council &c, should rather be commenced, or completed previously to his arrival at Toronto than afterwards, as otherwise it might be supposed that he had exerted an influence in your affairs. He begs that you will give yourself no trouble respecting his residing at Government House. He never had the least intention of occupying it or disturbing you. If he should be in it, he hopes you will receive him as your Guest— He said much more, and appeared to be inclined to meet your wishes fully; but this is I believe the substance of his conversation with me.

Lady Durham and his family will take up their residence at the Falls. I understand from him that there is no intention of abridging the powers of the Provincial local Legislatures; but that such extensive authority and control will be conferred on the General Legislature or Govrnt. for the N. American Colonies to be assembled, (at Montreal perhaps,) as will protect the enterprizing spirit of the British Population, and secure the grand interests of all the Provinces, and prevent the interference of the Lower Province in certain cases with the rights of Upper Canada—

With many thanks for your kind reception at Toronto,

[215] JAMES ENGLAND TO [ARTHUR] A.L.S. 8p.

June 24 *8, Portland Place, Bath.*

[Regrets his return to Europe was too late for him to congratulate Arthur "upon The Triumphs you achieved over your Ennemies (*sic*) and Slanderers here" which were so completely shown by the copies of the correspondence with the Horse Guards sent by Arthur to Colonel Logan at Madras. Would like to serve on the staff under Arthur. Sends wishes. "I have been led into this Interruption of Your More Valuable time which I hope is not so Much Engrossed as at Hobarton, by the Grateful Recollection I shall ever entertain of past Obligations, and the Gratification of expressing Myself to an officer to whom I look up with real Attachment."]

June 24 H. S. FOX TO PALMERSTON.

See item 221.

[216] [ARTHUR] TO [JAMES] STEPHEN: A.L. 3p.

June 25 *Toronto.* [Marked "Private & Confidential".]

When I came out Here Mr Wilberforce & yourself took a kind interest in behalf of Mr Joseph who accompanied Sir Francis Head as his Private Secretary and I accordingly continued Him on yr recommendation in the same capacity[.]

I hope you will not think that I have been indifferent to yr wishes in this matter when I tell you that on a vacancy occurring in the Office of Clerk of the Legislative Council I thought it proper to transfer Mr Joseph to that situation.

Several circumstances led me to consider this arrangt. as necessary & without recording all my reasons it may be enough to say that I do not see many things in the same light with my Predecessor (whose Character & Proceedings by the bye an Offl. directs me, after 24 years

Col: Service to make my guide &c.) and as Mr Joseph was entirely in his confidence I found it productive of inconvenience & of some unpleasantry [the word "perplexity" is here deleted.]

I much wish a change could have been made without Mr Joseph's suffering so much in point of Salary for he has always been very civil & obliging—but I really felt it to be an unavoidable measure although it is most probable that I shall not continue more than a few months in the administration of this Province[.]

I have had a busy time of it since I came Here & have many anxious cares upon my mind just now—but I refrain from touching upon any of them as I know yr objection to Private correspondence— I have seen affairs Here, of course, at their worst, but I do not find the People so difficult to deal with as I expected although undoubtedly there is a strong Exhibition of feeling in more parties *than one* & no System for carrying on the Govt seems ever to have been established . . .

[P.S.] Take a confidential hint from me—

Be cautious of any private correspondence with the Gov Genls Staff. You have not been fairly used by some Person on that Establist.! I expect Lord Durham Here in the course of ten days.

[217] COLBORNE TO ARTHUR: A.L.S. 6p.

June 25 *Quebec.*

I received your letter of the 17th instant yesterday— On my return to Quebec I directed the Commanding Engineer to lose not a moment in sending Officers of his department to carry into effect the arrangements proposed in the accompanying instructions to Lt Colonel Wright, for establishing a line of posts on the St Lawrence and Niagara frontiers and in the London and Western Districts— A Detachment of Sappers and miners under the command of Capt MacKenzie will proceed to the Upper Province, and two Officers of Engineers, to be employed on this service.

I have examined attentively all the reports from the Niagara frontier and the Western District, which you forwarded with your letter of the 17th instant. The whole of them are, I think, loose and vague, and many of them absurd: but they must be acted on as there can be no doubt that the panic in Upper Canada will continue till the population generally are confident that the Pirates and Rebels can be effectually opposed, and repulsed, should any efiort be really made from the United States to sustain them, or disturb the Province. I still suspect that the alarm is encouraged by interested individuals.

The people of Norfolk Middlesex and of many of the Townships of the Niagara and Western Districts are natives of the United States. If they are disaffected and prepared for insurrection, a well organized police could probably be established to keep you informed of their proceedings. To attempt to protect the whole frontier from the St Clair to the mouth of the Grand River and Fort Erie, from piratical incursions, would be useless, and divide our force, which when united and stationed at the Bar[r]acks proposed to be built in charge of arms and ammunition to supply the Sedentary Militia, appears sufficient to prevent any serious disaster—

I suggest for your consideration whether four companies of Volunteers could not be formed immediately, and organized, and placed under the orders of old Officers of the Line— These might take the duty from

Chippewa to Fort Erie; and the same number for the duty of Amherstburg and Sandwich.— For the duty of the St Lawrence I propose that three companies of Col. Macdonnells Glengarry Regt, may be taken on pay, and stationed at Prescott, Gannanoque [*sic*] and Lancaster; and that a company should be raised at Cornwall of the inhabitants of that village and neighbourhood, to be stationed at the Depot about to be established there. The 32d Regt, 580 R & F, will occupy Chatham and London. Two Companies of the 34th, Niagara and the Falls. You will have the whole of the 85th at Toronto, and 4 Companies of the 34th Regt. I wish the three Companies of the 24th Regt sent to Kingston, if you can spare them[.] These Companies require to be reequipped—they have had hard duty, and should be brought to Head Quarters. I am however compelled to keep them in your Province for some time longer; and should the alarm continue, it will be better to retain them, than not to disembody the Militia.

Captain Sandom will order two schooners to Long point as soon as possible, and hire a Steam boat. We will also fit out boats to cruise near the 1000 Islands; and cooperate with the American Authorities who are disposed to assist us in protecting the water frontier. Lt Colonel Cox you will probably order to Niagara instead of Major Anstruther. Major Towns[h]end of the 24th Regt. will be required to do duty with his Regiment—

[Enclosure lacking.]

[218] W[ILLIA]M ROWAN TO ARTHUR: A.L.S. 2p.

June 25 *Mily. Secys. Office, Quebec.*

With reference to your letter of the 16 Instant representing that your present personal Staff is quite inadequate to perform the various duties required of them & requesting permission to appoint another Aide de Camp, The Commander of the Forces has directed me to acquaint you that he has no objection to your selecting an Officer to act as Extra Aide de Camp, but His Excellency regrets that he cannot authorize the issue of any pay or allowances.

It is His Excellency's intention however to station an officer of the Quarter Master Generals Department at Toronto, and also to order one of the officers who are employed on a Special Service, to repair to Toronto and to place himself under Your Excellencys Orders[.]

[219] ARTHUR TO COLBORNE: L.B.1, p. 34-38.

June 26 *Drummondville.*

I wrote to you from Hamilton, and hope my letter found its way to you. Enough has taken place to make me anxious, but I hope nothing serious is now to be apprehended. We have been before hand with the disaffected, and I trust have completely deranged all their plans—there is at least every reason to hope so, in my opinion, notwithstanding the exaggerated statements which are current on all sides[.]

The account which had reached me when I wrote to you was, that considerable numbers of the Refugees had crossed over, and had taken themselves to the Short Hills—the Narrows, and the Swamps and Marshes near Wainfleet. It was represented to Colonel Townshend from the American Authorities that they could not prevent the expedition, and the best service they could render was to give information and an assurance that a large force of Canadian Refugees was in Motion.

This information corroborated by General Brady's communication which I have already conveyed to you, & the reports though vague daily brought in to Colonel Townshend left no doubt that some of these people had got into the Country and that they were to be followed by others.

I sent orders immediately therefore for calling out the Sedentary Militia in this District to search the Interior, and directed Colonel Townshend not to remove his Troops from the Frontier—except a few parties to reconnoitre. At 2 oClock on Friday morning a small Cavalry Post was attacked by a body of armed Ruffians and taken Prisoners after a very gallant defence, by superior numbers—two houses of very loyal persons were at the same time plundered of about 1,500 dollars.

On receiving this intelligence I proceeded first to Hamilton taking with me Colonel Chichester and placing him in charge of the direction of the Militia called out by Sir A. Macnab, who felt less jealous of the interference, than I expected, in fact, who felt no jealousy at all, but readily and heartily entered into all my arrangements. In a few hours we had the Militia in motion, and as the Indians had already been prepared for seeing me on my way to London; they were also soon put in motion down the Grand River—the Bridges over which were occupied on Saturday night and during the same night I came on to Niagara[,] issued a Proclamation offering a Reward of £500 for the apprehension of a person calling himself "Colonel" Morreau, and warning all persons of the consequences of aiding and assisting the Brigands, and then taking with me a few Cavalry I set off for the disaffected Districts of Pelham and Gainsborough.

The consequence was just what I expected—the worst people became the most busy and officious, and the whole country was soon in motion—sixteen of the Invaders were apprehended by twelve oClock yesterday—and amongst the number a man who it is supposed, is the Colonel Morreau but I do not think so myself. This man is a Canadian of the name of Wait a remarkably [blank in MS.] person, bold and intelligent. There was found upon him the flag of Liberty, ready to be hoisted—and Returns of the Patriot Force under Colonel Morreau with some useful correspondence. He was examined yesterday, but made no disclosures. His companion who was confoundedly alarmed was more communicative— According to his account not more than fifty have crossed over— McLeod with about 300 men are to follow (or rather *were* to follow, for I think they will scarcely venture now) in a few days[.]

They crossed from Grand Island where McLeod now is, Johnson [*i.e.* Johnston] or his eldest son is at Detroit plotting further mischief from that Quarter, where I am morally certain another expedition upon rather an extensive scale is in the course of preparation. I have however taken care of that part of the Province and have no anxiety as to the result but it is heart rending to see how the families of the loyal People of this Province are harrassed [*sic*]. It is more than men can bear quietly and cost what it may, this state of things must be put down, or those who are loyal now will turn their arms another way. I retain the opinion firmly, which I suggested when I had the pleasure of seeing you respecting the Militia. There ought to be a force that will give confidence to the Community for at least twelve Months— We have abundance to beat any enemy but that is not enough.— However whatever you determine upon, I am sure will be the result of great experience and much information.

Toronto 29th June 1838.

I was prevented from closing this letter whilst at Drummondville[.] We have now succeeded in taking about forty persons engaged in the late Crusade; including, so far as we know all the leaders and a few of the Parties who joined them after landing.

I have ordered the sedentary Militia to return to their homes, and enclose copies of the Proclamations and of the Militia General Order. Of course, a great many have escaped who joined these vagabonds; but we have more Prisoners already than I know what to do with, and I shall be glad if all the rest find their way back to the States, or return quietly to their homes. it is impossible to punish such Masses of People—the Ringleaders must be punished with severity, and the rest of them made loyal subjects if it be possible.

I send off Colonel Cox with a Despatch to Lord Durham requesting His Lordship's advice how to deal with the Banditti who have been captured. Lord Glenelg seems averse to any Capital Punishment.

[Enclosures lacking.]

[220] H. S. FOX TO ARTHUR: A.L.S. 24p.

June 26 *Washington.* [Marked "Private".]

I am afraid that I must have appeared very inattentive, in so long omitting to acknowledge, and to thank you for several important and interesting communications. The fact is, that being at present, and for some time past, without any secretary, or writing assistance, and having much correspondence to carry on, I am frequently a good deal pressed for time.— I shall endeavour, for the future, to be a more regular correspondent, and hope that you will not deprive me of the advantage and satisfaction of often hearing from you.— I herewith enclose to you, confidentially, extracts of despatches which I have addressed to Lord Palmerston, and to Lord Durham, since the affair of the "Sir Robert Peel," and the recommencement of the border disturbances.— I certainly was not prepared for so early a recommencement of those troubles: I had considered the danger as passed for the present summer; and had only looked forward to a recurrence of the danger, and a consequent necessity for great vigilance and precaution, during the ensuing autumn and winter, when the bands of vagabonds upon the frontier will be out of employment, and the Canadian territory more assailable by reason of the freezing of the Lakes and Rivers.— You will, I doubt not, have been informed, before this reaches you, of the principal measures which have now been adopted by the United States Government, with the view of cooperating with H. M. Authorities, to quell the piratical warfare which the border Americans and Canadian refugees are waging, and threatening to wage, along the frontier.— Two armed steam boats, manned and officered by U. S. regular troops, are to be employed in scouring the lakes and rivers. General Macomb, the Commander in Chief of the Army, has been sent to the frontier to superintend the operations, and every disposable reinforcement of regular troops that the Country can furnish, will be sent to join him.— These reinforcements, however, cannot amount to more than two hundred men, until Congress think proper to pass a law, long since pending before them, upon the recommendation of the Government, for the increase of the army.— If the law passes, the Secretary of War assures me, that two regiments at least shall be sent to the frontier before the autumn.

I believe, as I have said in my public letters inclosed, that the U. S. Government are now, more than at any previous period, sincere in their desire to perform the duties of neutrality, and alive to the danger which exists of a national war ensuing:—which they are, assuredly, neither desirous of, nor prepared for.— Their sincerity, however, must always be believed in with large grains of allowance. If the efforts and strength displayed on our side, and the loyalty and courage of our English Canadians, were to relax for an instant, the neutrality of the U. S. Government would be at an end at once.— Whatever might be the real wish of the President, and of the more respectable American Statesmen, the torrent of the popular will would then be too strong for them.— All Americans have been born and bred up in the expectation, that the Canadas were necessarily destined to belong, sooner or later, to them: and they are, now only, slowly recovering from their surprize, at the astounding contradiction given to this notion by the events of the last six months.—

I do not believe that the President, and his Government, are intentionally playing a double game; but a sort of double game, that is to say a game in which they might win and cannot lose, is by the force of circumstances thrown into their hands.— They will neither risk a war, nor commit a great political crime, in order to better their chance of one day possessing Canada; but we cannot suppose that they would in their hearts regret the event, if, without their interference, Canada were to fall off from Great Britain. The secret wishes, of even the most honest Americans, *must* be against us, in every struggle between the Authority of the Mother Country and the People of the Provinces—

Mr: Vail was much gratified by Your Excellency's attention and kindness to him. The result of his mission has been, fully to satisfy the Govt: here, that their citizens in confinement for public crimes in Canada, had no just cause of complaint.— I was aware of the inconvenience, which you justly mentioned as liable to follow from Mr: Vail's mission; but I found the Govt. determined, either to adopt that measure, or to demand information officially through me. If I had consented to become the official channel of obtaining that information for them from you, it would have been difficult to avoid (the correspondence being liable to be published)—giving them a pretext for throwing upon *me* the burthen of appearing to doubt the purity of the administration of justice in Canada.—

Lord Palmerston communicated to me, some time since, the copy of a confidential letter from Ld. Glenelg to yourself, containing the first opinion of the Law Officers of the Crown, in justification of the capture and destruction of the Steam Boat "Caroline". I have heard nothing further from home, upon that subject. I duly received your obliging letter from New York: it was forwarded to me by the Consul, Ld. C. Paget having left it behind.— I should have had great pleasure, on many accounts, in seeing you here; but I was not at all surprized at your haste to reach your post in Canada.— I have detained Mr: Macdonell many days longer than I had at first intended, and I have availed myself of his services to convey to New York some important despatches for England, to be forwarded by the Steam Ship the "Great Western."— He proceeded from hence to New York, accordingly, on the 24th. I despatch the present letter, and letters for Lower Canada, to overtake him at New York, from whence he will finally start for Canada on the 28th.— I beg to assure you how happy I shall be, to have the advantage of a continuance of your correspondence; and how desirous I am to cooperate with you, to the best of my power, in all things which may tend to the benefit of H. M. Service, and to the success of your anxious and difficult government.—

[Enclosures:]

[221] *1838*
June 24

H. S. Fox to Palmerston: A.L.S. 15p.

Washington. [Marked "Extract".]

"I lament to have to report to Your Lordship, that the troubles upon the Canadian frontier have lately recommenced to an alarming extent.— Large bodies of Canadian refugees, joined by bands of lawless American citizens, are gathering together at various points within the American border; drilling, arming, and equipping themselves for fresh piratical assaults upon H. M. Provinces; and evading, or violently overruling, the efforts made to subdue them by the Civil and Military Authorities of the United States.—

Intelligence, in a detailed and authentic form, of the destruction of the British Steam Boat "Sir Robert Peel," at an American Island in Lake Ontario, together with the proclamations and other public papers, having reference to that atrocious act, will have been transmitted to H. M. Government, by the respective British Authorities in Lower and Upper Canada. The destruction of the Steam Boat was, in itself, a violent act of crime: and it becomes of still more serious importance, when regarded, as I am afraid it must be, not as an isolated outrage, but as part of an extended system of offence against the peace of H. M. Provinces, organized by lawless men within the jurisdiction of the U. States, and which it surpasses the means at present possessed by the Government of the United States, to defeat—.

Shortly after the Earl of Durham's arrival in Canada, and immediately after the outrage upon the Steam Boat "Sir Robert Peel," His Lordship adopted the very judicious and sensible measure, of despatching Lt. Col. the Honble. Charles Grey to Washington, for the purpose, both of conferring with myself, and also of communicating, personally, to the President of the U.S., and to his Ministers, the feelings and views of Ld. Durham, in relation to the present anxious state of affairs upon the frontier.— Col. Grey fulfilled the objects of his mission, with ability and discretion; and the result, as Your Lordship will judge from the papers which I shall have the honor to forward with the present despatch, has been of material advantage to the interests of H. M. Service.— I believe that the President, and his Government, are now, more than at any former period, sincere in their desire to suppress the border disturbances; and more alive to the danger which exists, that a continuance of the piratical conduct of their citizens may involve the Two Countries irrevocably in war.—

But notwithstanding the opinion which I here express, I feel that the present crisis is one of extreme anxiety and peril. The question of the more or less absolute sincerity of the President, and of his Ministers, is, morally, of the highest importance; but with a view to immediate practical effect, the question is almost immaterial: for, whatever may now, or might afterwards, be the real feeling and desire of the U. S. Govt:, of Congress, and of the respectable part of American society, all would be equally impotent to prevent a general piratical rush of American citizens into Canada, if a new rebellion should break in H. M. Provinces, with any apparent prospect of success.— I believe that the U. S. Authorities are now sincere in their desire to perform the obligations of neutrality; but their means are lamentably insufficient; and I cannot avoid also bearing in mind, that the course of their neutrality has along kept exact pace with the evidence afforded of the strength of the British resources, and of the fixed resolution of H. M. Govt:, and of the British People, to defend at all hazards the Honor of H. Majesty's Crown in North America.—

Under all the circumstances now existing, I would conjure H. M. Govt: to send still further reinforcements, during the present summer, to North America.— All the reasons which now present themselves, for anxiety and alarm, will be materially increased during the ensuing seasons of autumn and winter, when reinforcements can no longer arrive.— It is by a formidable, and an imposing, and by what careless lookers on will perhaps reckon a superfluous display of military force in Canada, that the best chance will be attained, of eventually saving the English and the American People from the calamities of a general war."—

[222] *1838*
June 16

H. S. Fox to Durham: A.L.S. 8p.

Washington. [Marked "Extract".]

"I have the honor to acknowledge the receipt of Your Lordship's despatch of the 5th: instant, which was delivered to me by Lt: Col. the Honble: Charles Grey.— The mission of Colonel Grey has been highly satisfactory to me; and will, I believe, have been productive of material advantage to the interests of H. Majesty's Service.— Col. Grey has had interviews with the President, and with the Secretary of State Mr. Forsyth, and also with Mr. Poinsett the Secretary of War, under the immediate direction of whose department, the operations of the U. S. Govt: on the frontier are conducted.— The result of these interviews and conversations, of which Colonel Grey will make to Your Lordship a detailed report, is, to a considerable extent, satisfactory.— The President's Government appear to be now fully alive to the extreme danger which exists, that a continuance of the piratical conduct of their frontier citizens may involve the Two Countries irrevocably in war; and I believe that they will sincerely exert themselves to abate the evil.— But unfortunately, the means possessed by the Supreme Government of this Republick, for enforcing the laws, and for performing the duties of neutrality towards foreign nations, are lamentably insufficient; and I should be betraying Your Lordship if I did not seize this first opportunity of earnestly expressing to you, that it is not to any efficient exercise of authority on the part of the U. S. Government,—however sincerely we may believe them to be well disposed,—but that it is to the well known sagacity and vigour of your own character, to the zeal and discipline of H. M. Troops now under your command, and to the courage and loyalty of the great mass of Her Majesty's Canadian subjects of British origin, that we must look, for repressing the system of piratical violence which has so long disgraced the American frontier, and for thereby taking the best chance of eventually saving the Two Countries from the calamities of a general war."—

[223] H. S. Fox to Arthur: A.L.S. 3p.

June 26 *Washington.*

I have the honor herewith to inclose to Your Excellency, the copy of a message transmitted by the President of the United States to Congress on the 21st; instant, with a report from the Department of War annexed, upon the subject of the border disturbances.— The latter part, especially, of the President's Message is important and satisfactory; and places the present extraordinary situation of things upon the Canadian Frontier in the true and proper light.—

[Enclosures lacking.]

[224] Colborne to [Arthur]: A.L.S. 2p.

June 28 *Quebec.*

I have but this moment received your letter of the 22d inst. with the information respecting the affair at the Short Hills; and the menaced attacks of the Rebels.

I have directed the 43d Regt to move to Kingston without the least delay. I shall leave this tomorrow, for Montreal, on my route to the Upper Province.

[225] Arthur to Colborne: LB.1, p. 39-41.

June 30 *Toronto.*

Two expresses from Colonel Maitland announce the Landing of a considerable force—numbers not stated—of rebels and Patriots at Nugents Inn River St Clair—and that further parties are preparing to cross over; indeed are in the act of doing so. Some parties of rebels well armed have made their appearance in several parts of the London District and the day before yesterday they attacked some constables who were conveying Doctor Wilson to the London Jail and rescued him[.]

Most of these men who joined in the attack were rebels who were pardoned in January last.

Colonel Maitland, who has all along been too unbelieving and rejecting the reports which now appear but too well founded, begs to be reinforced with another Regiment immediately. A week ago I forwarded two Companies of the 34th Regt to Hamilton, I have now ordered them forthwith on to London and the remainder of the Regiment will proceed at day light tomorrow morning for the same destination.

This leaves Toronto and Kingston with only one Regiment each, as I do not find that the 85 Regt has been replaced as you intended at Kingston.

Our artillery is in a most inefficient state. The two Nine Pounders with Colonel Maitland, he says, "are hardly in a fit state to be moved to any distance besides which I have neither horses nor Harness.["]

Copies of his letters are enclosed.

We much require more six pounders in the Province, and, as I have before communicated we are *much* in want of arms for the Militia.

I enclose a memorandum from Major Jackson shewing what the orders are that he has received.

To crown my difficulties just at this moment the Militia are dissatisfied at being required to serve another month[;] they consider that they should either be sent home at once or engaged for a longer period.

I have ordered the half Battery to be sent up at once from Kingston which I hope you will approve.

[Enclosures lacking.]

[226] ARTHUR TO COLBORNE: LB.1, p. 50-51.

June 30 *Govt. House, Toronto.*

I had the pleasure to receive during the night, by Lieutenant Jones 43d Regt your letters of the 23d and 25th Instant. Under the circumstances of this Country, it became absolutely necessary to keep up some Militia and not having receeived [*sic*] your Memorandum upon this subjec, I directed that the force now employed and whose service expires this day should be continued for one month longer—but I find the men do not like remaining for so short a period and a great falling is the consequence.

You appear to think the reports which I sent to you are "loose and vague and some of them absurd" but it appeared to me that they were rather [more] circumstantial than such reports usually are— An officer who has just arrived from Sandwich informs me that just before he left that post, General Brady had given notice to Colonel Reid at Sandwich that a very considerable force of the Canadian Refugees and Patriots were preparing to make a descent upon some part of the Western Coast, which it was out of his power to prevent— A report also reached me last night from Cleveland to the effect that a considerable expedition is preparing to make a descent from thence upon this Province.

It is difficult to suppose that so many refugees have for so many months been hanging upon the Frontier without some serious design. I am glad to find that you have approved of the Depot of arms and that other necessary arrangements are positively ordered.

With regard to the Militia force, of course I will accede to your recommendation, but I must say I do not think it adequate.

But, upon these Matters I will do myself the pleasure to write to you again in a few days.

[227] W[ILLIA]M ROWAN TO [ARTHUR?]: A.L.S.

June 30 *Quebec.*

[Forwards "copy of a letter to the Commissary General"; this is apparently item 228.]

[228] W[ILLIA]M ROWAN TO [R. I. ROUTH]: L.

June 30 *Military Secretary's Office, Quebec.*

Copy of a Letter addressed by desire of the Commander of the Forces to the Commissary General . . .

Adverting to my letter of the 18th. Instant addressed to the Senior Officer of the Commissariat, at Toronto, I have the honor to acquaint you that the Commander of the Forces will issue covering Warrants for such sums as His Excellency Sir George Arthur may approve of being paid to the Staff Officers of Militia in Upper Canada, with reference to any Appointments Authorized by the Lieutenant Governor of that Province.

I request you will have the goodness to communicate the substance of this Letter to the Officers of the Commissariat in Upper Canada.

[229] J. B. ROBINSON TO [ARTHUR]: A.L.S. 3p.

[*1838*] [*Place not stated.*]
[*July ?*]

I had a letter this morning from Col Jarvis of the Queen's Rangers, which I should like to enclose to You, but I have it not with me at present—

He says the men oppressed with their winter coats & out at elbows, are very impatient, as their term of enlistment has expired—that they cheerfully went over upon the late alarm but now that the danger seems over it seems very desirable that they should be enabled to part with credit, rather than in ill humour, It is impossible to keep them as they are, & it would be a pity that they should melt away disreputably & go grumbling home—

Can not some final step be now taken with them?

[230] [WRITER AND RECIPIENT NOT STATED]:

[*1838*] [*Place not stated.*]
[*July ?*]

On the arrival of His Excellency M. General Sir George Arthur, the Militia Staff in Toronto consisted of the following Officers:

1 Adjutant General
1 Asst Do. and a Clerk.
1 Asst. Quarter Master Genl. & a Clerk.
1 Military Secretary
1 Asst. Do.
1 Asst Inspector of Hospitals
1 Colonel Commandant of the Garrison
1 Staff Adjutant.

[231] [ARTHUR TO COLBORNE]: L.

[*1838*]
[*July 1*]

[The letter is lacking, but a précis entry in item 578 reads:] Sir G. A 26th June[,] 30[,] 1st July[,] 5[,] Recommends a force for *12 months* (3 or 4 Regiments) & does not think the Companies proposed by Sir J. C. adequate to the desired end. is obliged to keep on the existing force for a month longer, to their great discontent, as final arrangements had not been agreed upon.

[232] ARTHUR TO GLENELG: L. 3p.

July 2 [*Place not stated.*] [Marked "Confidential".]

Your Lordship's Despatch of the 21st. December 1837 respecting appointments to be made to the Legislative Council should not have been so long unanswered; but Yr. Lordship is aware that I could not satisfactorily make any recommendation until time permitted me to acquire that knowledge of persons & of the state of the Province, which would enable me to act with safety.

Having given to this very important & delicate subject the best consideration in my power, & having had it continually on my mind, I now transmit to Yr. Lordship a list of Twenty six names, all of whom I can venture to say will be eligible and satisfactory appointments.

I send Yr. Lordship a short description of the circumstances of each Gentleman. The number may appear large, but under the present circumstances of the Country I do not consider that to be an objection. They are all gentlemen of good steady character, well attached to the Government, & in general possessing extensive influence in their respective districts; and from the consideration that the expense of their attendance during the Legislative Session here, is unremunerated, the proportion of Members actually present is in general so small that I am convinced the House would very rarely contain more than thirty Members.

I consider it so important that this increase should take place without delay that I trust Yr. Lordship will find no obstacle on account of the small fee due on each Commission.

I will see that the amount is remitted as soon as I am made acquainted with it.

I have numbered the names in the order in wh. I think they should stand if Yr Lordship will not concur with me to the full extent, which, however, I hope you will.

I think such a measure would be found to give very general satisfaction.—

There are many highly eligible individuals whose names I have omitted, because they are Members of the House of Assembly, and I consider it injudicious to withdraw any gentleman of influence from their seats in that House— Amongst those I would instance Sir Allen [*sic*] Macnab and Mr. Prince whose services to the Country during the late outbreak deserves [*sic*] such a mark of the approbation of the Crown.

It must not be understood by Your Lordship, that in proposing to add so largely to the number of Members of the Legislative Council, or, indeed in proposing an addition to any extent, I am influenced by an impression, that that Branch of the Legislature, as it is now constituted has in any degree failed to discharge its important duties either as regards the Crown or the people of this Province.

On the Contrary, the result of every inquiry I have made, has convinced me that the judgment, firmness, & discretion, with which the proceedings of the Legislative Council have been hitherto conducted, and sometimes under circumstances of peculiar difficulty, have been of incalculable advantage to this Colony— I only venture to recommend so large an addition to the Numbers of the Council, in the hope that it will enable them to pursue with encreased confidence, and better public effect, the same honorable course, which has hitherto distinguished them, and to which it is my belief that the British Govt. have been, on more than one occasion, much indebted for the safety of this Colony.

[Enclosure lacking; but see item 270 which begins on the reverse side of the same sheet. The whole, together with item 310, appears to have been detached from an official letter book.]

[233] ARTHUR TO DURHAM: LB.1, p. 52-54.

July 4 *Govrnt. House, Toronto.*

From your Lordship's Despatch of the 25 Ultimo I find it is Your Lordships present intention to be at Toronto on the 16th. and by a letter from Sir John Colborne, I understand your Lordship proposes to go direct to Niagara where the Countess of Durham will remain.

Will Your Lordship permit me to suggest whether this arrangement just at present is altogether desirable for Her Ladyship. There is and has for some time been great excitement in the Niagara District; and until we see [?] exactly what turn the present unpleasant agitation throughout the Province will take I would certainly recommend that the Countess of Durham should not reside at Niagara.

Your Lordship if it were necessary I am persuaded would rough in the field as well as any of us; but this is not exactly the moment for successfully entering upon the grand object of Your Mission. Your Lordship could not, and I am satisfied would not expect Gentlemen to leave their Homes to pay their respects to you at Toronto, whilst their families were so full of apprehension, and yet I must say it is most desirable that Your Lordship should see them, so as to be enabled to extend your enquiries beyond the Public Officers and Residents of Toronto.

Every precaution I can devise has been taken to prevent another general outbreak and if unhappily it cannot be altogether averted I trust it will be limited. After men are *detected* traitors it is difficult to deal with them in such numbers, and there is a numerous and very troublesomely disposed class of persons in this Province—Orangemen—who consider lenity of any kind under such circumstances to be an insult to their order.

These Orangemen as a body are fine brave fellows, but they are under very bad direction—and although it cannot be attempted just now, I am resolved to clip the Wings of the Leaders of this Party as soon as it can be done prudently.

My Establishment has not yet arrived from England so that I cannot make your Lordship and the Countess of Durham by any means as comfortable as I could wish, but the best that can be done is in progress and when some repairs are completed which the Architect *promises* shall be the case in the course of a fortnight the House though small and unappropriate will be just habitable for your Lordships family. Still I must say, I wish the times were more quiet for Your Lordships visit, because the people generally will be unavoidably prevented from receiving Your Lordship as they would otherwise I am sure desire to do.

I have just heard that one of the Brigands whom we took last week in the woods in the Niagara District has been identified as being one of the party who burnt and plundered the Sir Robert Peel— His name is Reynolds.

[234] J. B. ROBINSON TO [ARTHUR]: A.L.S. 6 .

July 4 *Toronto.*

Under present circumstances it has only been in my power to read Mr. Sullivan's proposed report[1], with a view to it's [*sic*] general tendency and the results to which it is calculated to lead— I have derived much pleasure and satisfaction from the perusal— The sentiments throughout are just; at least I recollect none that did not appear to me to be so; and several topics upon which a Legislative Assembly, from various causes, can only be prevailed upon to press lightly, are treated in it with clearness and force, and pursued with much effect to their legitimate conclusions—

Among the measures recommended in this report there are one or two upon which, following my individual judgment I would concur only to a certain extent; but this part of the paper is of the least consequence, since I take it to be exceedingly unlikely that Lord Durham would consent to derive his notions of remedies from any official authority in the Colonies— The principle most consistently acted upon for ten years past—is to look upon residence in a Colony as disqualifying a person from exercising a sound judgment upon any point relating to it's interests— This objection is strengthened if official employment has been added to residence— The suspicion of impure motives seems then to amount to conviction— Nothing but a notorious factious opposition to Government, in the adviser is acknowledged as giving any value to colonial opinions— A sound recommendation from the Executive Council may drive a Commissioner from the right course, but is by no means likely to lead him into it—

If this report is to be presented, merely in confidence for the private consideration of Lord Durham, it's present shape, & style are perhaps the best; but if likely to be published as an official document, there are some passages that should be considered, with a view to make them in keeping with the peculiar character of the board from which it would be known to have emanated— Considered as the free expression of the opinions of an individual, the paper is better as it is, because more natural & forcible. Indeed I am sure it would be generally admired, & be thought to reflect much credit upon the writer of it— It's tone is liberally conservative, as *liberal* as any man who combines common sense with common honesty would desire it to be—

No two persons who think for themselves would concur exactly in so long a train of reasoning— Some arguments I think are too much relied on, while others might with advantage be pressed more forcibly—

For instance with respect to the control of the Assembly over the expences of the Government;—it has never been plainly enough stated that the English House of Commons has not, and never had, nor has any other legislative body on earth ever had that absolute power over the ordinary public expenditure which was thrown into the hands of the Assembly in Lower Canada, and in a great measure here also—

Stopping the supplies in England never could have interfered with the payment of the kind of charges which are here made to depend on the annual vote of the Assembly—

Again as to the measures in agitation respecting the surrender of the casual and territorial revenue, I do not consider that "they have naturally fallen out in the current of circumstances"— They are, so far as I have observed, the mere consequences of the ruinous influence

[1]See item 187.

of an unsound heart in the Colonial Department,—they are the suggestions of some mind that is governed by no fixed principle—which deals with effects rather than with causes, and which is willing to sacrifice all chance of permanent good government in the Colonial possessions of the Crown to the ambition of establish'g a reputation for what is absurdly called liberality—

In speaking of events here, in the 50th. sheet, I think the issue of patents to new settlers, before and during the elections (which was simply done in the ordinary and rightful course of public business,) is mentioned in terms that may convey an erroneous impression. The people pushed for their deeds most naturally, because they were anxious to vote— They had a right to them, and to have withheld them or delayed their issue would have been a positive wrong—

But they did not in any an instance amount to such a number as to turn the scale—

In most, if not all cases, their issuing was a matter of evident and utter insignificance as to the result.—

[235] J. B. ROBINSON TO [ARTHUR]: A.L.S. 5p.

July 4 *Toronto.*

Col. Hill of whom I have several times spoken to Your Excellency has sent me some papers (*personal*) which he much wishes you would do him the favor to peruse— Will you be so kind as to look over them & place them in a drawer, that I may receive them again—

I should be sorry that he were overlooked while absent on an anxious & very responsible service, the guarding a remote, & exposed frontier with a very small force— He is I think an officer that combines the necessary qualities for a militia command—exactness in the business concerns of his Corps—with a cool & determined spirit—strict enforcement of duty, with conciliating manners in his general intercourse with officers & men— He is a man who will, under no circumstances disgrace himself—

Col Adamson—is desirous of raising—or rather enrolling a Corps & keeping them in readiness for any call of duty, without expence until called out— He has I dare say explained his plans— I can only say that I think he is second to no officer in the Province in experience, & knowledge of military arrangements—& he is certainly a highly honorable & respectable Gentleman— His object seems not to be emolument, so much as to be of service—

Capt. Edward Davis of Lake Simcoe, formerly in the 8th. Regt. has just arrived from England, & would like much to be on service in command of a Corps—

If Your Excellency has seen him, I am sure you have been favorably impressed—for he is a fine manly, intelligent person— He is Colonel of a Regiment of Militia & if he had not happened to be absent during our disturbances in December last, he would unquestionably have been admitted to be the proper person to have taken the lead in the Northern part of this District from whence so many fine loyal fellows come—

[Enclosures lacking.]

[236] R. B. SULLIVAN TO MR. SECY. [JOHN] MACAULAY: A.L.S. 3p.

July 4 *Crown Land Office*, [*Toronto.*]

I was directed by His Excellency Sir Francis Head. to make some enquiries relative to the claim of the Wesleyan Methodist Missionary Society for support out of the Casual & Territorial revenue.

In the course of this enquiry I called upon the Venble Archdeacon for the purpose of learning from him the state of the Indians as to religious Instruction. upon which occasion Dr Strachan was kind enough to say that he would draw up a short report upon the subject.

As it did not however enter directly into the question I was ordered to investigate I did not delay my report until I should receive a communication from the archdeacon. which has only come to me this day.

His Excellency I am sure takes a lively interest in the religious condition of the Indians. and I therefore beg of you to submit the archdeacons report. for H.E.s consideration.

It is difficult to say how far the distracted state of the Colony as regards religious opinions. and parties will permit the Government to pursue a course calculated to advance the religious Interests even of the Indians who are emphatically under the guardianship of the Crown with a sole view to these Interests. But at all events the question is one of justice and benevolence, and is worthy of great consideration. and I therefore transmit the Archdeacons report.

[The enclosure referred to is possibly item 38, of which item 166 appears to be a revised copy. See also item 262.]

[237] ARTHUR TO COLBORNE: LB.1, p. 41-44.

July 5 *Government House, Toronto.*

It will gratify you to hear that Colonel Maitlands report of yesterdays date is more satisfactory—the reports of the number of Pirates and others have been exaggerated.— Only six have been taken Prisoners, and reluctant as I have been to adopt that mode of proceeding, I have come to the determination to try these Ruffians by a General Militia Court Martial; Colonel Maitland adds "the disaffected in every direction received great encouragement about here by these Reports, and are only kept back from rushing to open violence and renewed rebellion by the presence of the Troops".

I am much obliged and most grateful for your having put the means within my power of deterring the people from going into Rebellion, whereby some hundreds would again have subjected themselves to capital punishment, and our jails would have been full of Traitors. Finding their efforts hopeless I do trust they will now abandon their wicked intentions.

There can be no doubt there was to have been a General rise th[r]oughout the Province on this day and tomorrow, but, in every district such Militia as have arms were promptly turned out by their Commanding Officers and have assumed an attitude that has answered every purpose.

I could not have supposed it possible that such a panic could have been so universally felt. This will be prevented for the future if the arms were sent into the Province which you have authorized for the various Stations, and a respectable body of Militia kept up for at least twelve Months.

I do not consider the affair to be quite over; but it is to be hoped we have had the worst of it.

These villains must be disappointed that the People have not joined them i.e. to the extent they expected either at Niagara or at the London District.

With respect to the Militia force I will do myself the pleasure to write to you officially either this night or tomorrow morning.

I ordered the Demi-Battery up from Kingston; but, in the present posture [?] of affairs I do not think it necessary to detain the Guns or to send them on with the Militia assembled at Hamilton—and shall return them to Kingston fort[h]with.

I regret to say we have had no effective Artillery as yet, but, I trust we shall do better in this respect hereafter. I have been obliged to express myself very strongly to Major Jackson upon the subject. The Ordnance and Commissariat Departments are certainly by no means efficient in this Province. The system is bad and its effects bad.

In my letter to you this morning I adverted to Sir Allan Macnab's expectations—in a note which he addressed to a friend at Toronto, I find, he says alluding to Colonel Chichesters having the Command of the District in which were troops of the Line as well as the Militia. "Sir John Colborne said to me, that if the militia were again called out I should have the command of them[.]"

I conclude it was not your intention he should take precedence of other Militia Colonels or that an officer of the Line with the rank of Lieut: Colonel in the army should act subordinate to Sir Allan.

The people on the West side have however very earnestly begged for Colonel Chichester's services and Colonel Maitland has requested that he should be stationed at Chatham. . .

P.S. I have just received a report from Colonel Townshend of this date.

He had felt it necessary from the demonstrations on the other side to call out the Sedentary Militia for two or three days, but I am pretty confident all will be quiet again soon[.]

[238] ARTHUR TO SIR A. N. MACNAB: LB.1, p. 45-48.

July 5 *Govt. House, Toronto.*

Colonel Maitlands letter of last evening, with its enclosures, convey[s] the satisfactory assurance that the alarm felt on the Western Frontier has abated and that the Reports were much exaggerated.

I had also last night the pleasure to receive a letter from Captain Sandom—informing me that one of the Gun boats well manned and armed was half way through the Welland Canal, and that two others would follow as last night, and that the Steamer purchased from Genrl Porter would be employed in Lake Erie with the Gun boats.

Under these circumstances justice to the people of England upon whom the expence of our defence falls requires me to decrease the force that has so promptly answered to my call with the least possible delay. I request therefore you will be so good as to express to the Gallant Fellows both Officers and men, who have flocked to your Standard how highly I appreciate their zeal and how truly thankful I am for the Service they have rendered to their Country in suppressing this Rebellion—and knowing how very important their attendance upon their domestic concerns is—they may at once be permitted to return to their Farms with the exception of 70 men who should be left in charge of the Posts under the Command of a Sturdy Captain and two Subalterns for a few days.

There is the less danger from adopting this course in consequence of my being reinforced by another Regiment of the Line from Montreal.

The 43d one of the finest in the British Army—the head Quarters of which arrived at Kingston on the 2d Instant; General Clitherow having forthwith acted upon my requisition without waiting to send down to Sir John Colborne.

The Half Battery also arrived last night, but I send their Guns back to Kingston, without landing them, hoping the worst of our difficulties are over but it would not surprize me were Rebellion to burst out again.

I sent a positive instruction last night to Colonel Foster to put in Orders your being in Command of the Militia at Hamilton, if he had not done so upon the order I had already given[;] his hesitation I find has been from the desire to explain to me that the Lords of the Treasury had directed the Commissariat Officers not to recognize any signature of any officers but those of the regular Troops as authority for expenditure[;] of course their Lordships object is rigid economy but as I feel convinced you have given the strictest attention to this important particular I have required the order should be issued and the accounts passed upon your requisition and signature, and I will explain to the Lords of the Treasury that I have no desire to contravene their regulations but simply to promote the good of the Queens service.

An Officer of the Commt Department has made enquiry this mrng whether I had authorized the hiring of a number of teams at Hamilton which on reflection leads me to fear that an observation I made in a letter to you of which I have no Copy has possibly been misunderstood—if so pray correct it at once for although it was highly desirable to make arrangements for obtaining Waggons so as to be ready at the shortest notice as is so often done here yet it would not be proper to engage them unless they were actually required.

Accept yourself my best thanks for the zeal with which you have acted on this occasion and for the good feeling and exertions you have made to second my wishes which have been founded on the desire to afford protection to the Country and to deter the disaffected from rising so that not being exposed as detected traitors they might yet become loyal Traitors [? *sic.*]

[239] GLENELG TO ARTHUR: L.S. 4p.

July 5 *London.*

Mr. Stephen has addressed to me a letter of which I send you a copy. It will apprize you that he has thought it his duty to place in my hands your letter to him of the 2nd. of June.—

I most sincerely lament the misapprehension into which we mutually appear to have fallen of each other's meaning respecting the appointment of a Governor General of British North America. You will require no assurance from me of my conviction that you understood me precisely in the sense which your letter ascribes to my language.

Unfortunately however you mistook the sense which I intended to convey not less than I must have misconceived that which it was your design to express.—

When I first made to you the offer of the Government of Upper Canada, I stated that it was probable that a Governor General of British North America might be nominated. You urged upon me the objections to that arrangement,—to which I listened with all the respect & attention due to your opinion. I expressed no final determination on the subject, because in truth it was then very doubtful whether the plan of appointing such an officer would ever take effect. I certainly did not understand you as stating that the abandonment of the design was the only condition on which you could accept the Government. I find that in this respect Mr. Stephen's impression was the same as mine, and that his memory confirms my own.—

Almost immediately after my first interview with you, Lord Durham intimated to Her Majesty's Government his resolution to decline the offer of Governor General. Consequently when I met you the second time, I offered to you the Government of Upper Canada on the usual terms,—because I had at that time no reason to anticipate any departure from them. I certainly entered into no guarantee that under no conceivable change of circumstances the Government would revert to the plan which was at that time abandoned.—

But after your leaving England the aspect of the whole subject underwent a most essential alteration. The revolt in Upper Canada was alike unknown & unexpected, when you quitted this country. In this new state of affairs Lord Durham altered the view which he had formerly taken of the proposals made to him & was prepared to assume the general Government. I did not feel myself precluded by any thing which had passed with you from availing myself of the offer of his Lordship's services to Her Majesty in that capacity. The other Lieut. Governors of the British Provinces had precisely the same reason to complain of being superseded in their functions. They accepted their places precisely on the same conditions with yourself, but from none of them has any complaint reached me.—

I trust that this explanation will convince you that you have no just ground of remonstrance. I cannot suppose that you really think that I was deliberately wanting in the frankness & plain dealing which I owed to you & to myself on the occasions to which your letter refers. It was I am aware not written for my inspection, but being addressed to one of my Under Secretaries, it was inevitable that it should meet my own eye, & therefore I have not scrupled to answer it as distinctly as if it had been addressed to me.—

[*Enclosure:*]

[240] *1838*
July 5

JA[MES] STEPHEN TO GLENELG: L. 2p.

London. [Marked "Copy".]

I have received from Sir George Arthur a letter dated the 2nd. of June, which tho' it be marked "private" I think myself bound to place in your hands.

Sir George Arthur states that "you suggested to him the contemplation of such powers being given to Lord Gosford's successor, & that he immediately & decidedly, in my presence declined to accept the government under such arrangement".— and further that "two days afterwards you distinctly informed him that this purpose was abandoned".—

My recollection of the two interviews in question is distinct & differs from that of Sir George Arthur. On the first occasion you told him of the probability of a Governor General being appointed, to whom he would be subordinate. He strongly pointed out the inconveniences of such an arrangement, but as my memory assures me, did *not* decline to accept the office on these terms. On the second occasion you informed him that you could then offer him the government on the usual terms; but nothing was then said as to any power of subsequently changing that resolution. No guarantee on the subject was ever entered into in my presence nor did I ever understand that Sir G. Arthur's acceptance or rejection of the Office depended on his being the Supreme & independent Governor of the Province.

[241] GLENELG TO ARTHUR: L.S. 8p.

July 5 *Downing Street*, [*London*.]

[Another copy of item 239, marked "Duplicate. Private." with slight variations.]

[*Enclosure:*]

[242] *1838*
July 5

J[AMES] STEPHEN TO GLENELG: L. 4p.

London. [Marked "(Copy)".]

[Another copy of item 240 with slight variations.]

[243] COUTTS & CO. TO ARTHUR: L.S.

July 5 *London*.

We have the pleasure to inform You that Your Account Book with Us, and a similar Account Book with the Derwent Bank, together with Five Bills—Duplicates—the other parts of which we appear to have received on Your Account—have been placed in our hands by Mr John Borthwick. that Gentleman states having found them in the Lodgings he now occupies in Harley Street and has sent Us the accompanying Explanatory Letter to be forwarded to You—

[*Enclosure:*]

[244] *1838*
July 4

JOHN BORTHWICK TO ARTHUR: A.L. 2p.

21 Harley Street, London.

Mr. Borthwick presents his compliments to Sir George Arthur, & begs to inform him, that as the successor of Lady Arthur in these lodgings here, there were found by him in one of the beds 2 account books in one of which were contained bills to the amount of £3104.10/- Mr Borthwick thought it advisiable [*sic*] to take these books & bills under his own special charge, & that the best course he could follow, in order speedily & safely to have them restored to Sir George was to deposite [*sic*] them with Messrs. Coutts & Co; who now accordingly have them. The bills appear to be duplicates, and to have been paid.— Mr. Borthwick shall feel happy if he has been the means of restoring to the proper owners these books & papers, tho', now, of perhaps little consequence. Mr. Borthwick returns immediately to Scotland, where his address is "J. B. Esq., of Crookston, 28 Queen St Edinburgh."

[245] COLBORNE TO ARTHUR: A.L.S. 4p.

July 6 *Kingston.* [Marked "Private".]

I have to thank you for your interesting communications of the 30th Ult. and of the 4th inst. It was the intention of Lord Durham, on my departure from Quebec to be in Montreal on the 5th instant. and to remain there till he might receive information from me as to the best route and his future movements towards your Capital. I had recommended him to meet you at Kingston; but I have acquainted him since my arrival here, that I think it will be more convenient to you, with reference to the occurrences which are taking place in the Western Districts, to receive him at Niagara, and that I would write to you upon this subject and propose to you to meet him there next week. If he proceeds as I have suggested, he will leave La Chine early on Tuesday Morning, sleep at Cornwall, and reach Kingston on Wednesday Evening— On Thursday he will embark in the Cobourg and arrive on Friday, or Saturday Morning the 14th inst. at Niagara; where he will expect to meet you, and arrange for his visit to Toronto. I hope this plan will be agreeable to you.

With respect to the appointment of Capt Power to the D. Qr. Mr. Genl's Department, I shall be glad to confirm it, if another arrangement which I have sanctioned should not take place; but Capt Brockman of the 34th cannot be attached to the Adjutant Genls Dept, the number of Officers allowed for that Dept, having been already nominated. I have directed Major MacKenzie Fraser to proceed to Toronto to place himself under your orders. He can do duty in the Adjutant Genl's Dept till further orders. You will find him very useful, should Col Foster be ordered to Montreal. Have the goodness to desire Major Jackson of the R Artillery to meet me at Niagara on Monday next.

[246] COLBORNE TO ARTHUR: L.S 10p.

July 6 *Kingston, Upper Canada*

I have had the honor to receive Your Excellency's communications of the 30 ultimo and of the 2nd and 4th. inst acquainting me with the attacks menaced by the Brigands in the London and Western Districts.

The intelligence which you receive must be so far credited and acted on, however exaggerated the reports may be, that the extensive frontier population may be convinced that they have no cause for apprehension, and that every arrangement has been made for the protection of the several Districts as far as the nature of the incursions of the Marauders will admit of protection being afforded. But it must be also recollected in defending the Upper Province from insult that we have Lower Canada to attend to; a Province which is but slowly recovering from the effect of a serious revolt.

I have already communicated to Your Excellency my suggestions with regard to the protection of Upper Canada; and the Posts and Depots of

Arms which are to be established, and in fact which are now being carried into effect. And I must again refer to the very improvident manner in which the arms ammunition and stores which were forwarded to the Upper Province last winter have been distributed— More than 13,000. Stand of Arms it appears have been issued to the Militia, and I have never been able to learn in whose possession they are at present[.] Your Excellency will agree with me that if such a system of delivering arms be continued, the Depots in the Lower Province will soon be again exhausted— Although there are not more than 9000 Stand of Arms remaining in the Stores at Quebec, 3000 have been ordered to be forwarded to the Upper Province, and will be at Kingston in a few days, 1500 of them will be sent to Toronto and 1500 to Niagara to be conveyed if you think proper to the Western Districts by Lake Erie— I trust that when the regular Forces are satisfactorily posted, and the Volunteer Provincial Corps organized, and the Township Guards also organized, and the Depots of arms established, that the Militia will not be called out on every alarm— If confidence can not be speedily restored by the presence of the Force now in the Province, and by the defensible Posts, it will be certainly necessary to recommend that further reinforcements should be sent to these Colonies, for the calling out of the Militia, if frequently repeated, will be both ruinous to the Mother Country and injurious to the Colony— The Stores, Barrack furniture, and Camp equipage intended for the Upper Province were forwarded the moment they could be disembarked. 20,000 Stand of Arms have been demanded from home and I have desired that 10,000 may be sent to Kingston[,] 5000 to Toronto, and 4000 distributed in the District Depots—

With respect to the dissatisfaction that prevails all over the Province at the delay which has taken place in the settlement of just accounts, I am without information from the Commissary General as to the circumstances which still cause the delay adverted to by your Excellency, but, that he has made arrangements for satisfying every claim that he can consistently settle.

If however there are still claims which your Excellency would recommend to be discharged, it will be better that the Government should not require the usual vouchers, and lose by imposition than that the excitement should continue[.] I will therefore authorize all claims to be settled which Your Excellency may be of opinion ought to be paid— I can not understand from the Memorandum of Major Jackson why the Demi Battery in the London District has not been rendered fit for service long since— Colonel Campbell ordered the 6 Pounder Battery to be attached to the 32nd Regt, and the heavier Guns to remain at Amherstburgh in charge of the Militia and Volunteers— The 32nd. Regt consisting of 580 rank and file can have nothing to apprehend, whatever distance that Corps may be from support— The Copy of the memorial of Dr. Dunlop was not to be found among the enclosures transmitted to me by Your Excellency. I intend to move this Evening with the 43rd Regt— This Corps will be encamped near the Falls, and will be in readiness to be conveyed on any alarm to the Western District in the Steam boat purchased by Captain Sandom— Colonel Booth one of the most active and intelligent Officers in the Province will Command on the Niagara Frontier— One squadron of the 1st. Dragoon Guards will probably arrive here this Evening and move to Niagara tomorrow, a Company of Sappers and Miners are also on their route to Fort George and will be employed in repairing Fort Missisagua[.]

[247] [ARTHUR TO COLBORNE]: L.

[*1838*] [The letter is lacking, but précis entries in item 578 read:] Sir J. C.
[*July 8*] 6th July Mentions "Volunteer Provincial Corps and Township Guards." Sir G. A. 8 July Remarks on those expressions, and forwards the proceedings of a Board of Officers, who recommend that *3 Regts* should be raised according to the Militia laws.

[248] ARTHUR TO DURHAM: LB.1, p. 55-56.

July 8 *Govermt. House, Toronto.*

By a letter which I have received from Sir John Colborne, I find that he has arranged that I should meet your Lordship at Niagara on Friday or Saturday next.

I beg to be permitted to say, that unless the state of affairs to the Westward rendered it improper for me to go to the Eastward, it has always been my intention to have the honor to receive Your Lordship at Kingston, but as Sir John Colborne has made another arrangement I shall of course govern myself accordingly.

The results of the last two or three weeks have altogether placed the province in a better position, and even without the protection of the 43rd Regt the Countess of Durham might now be free from all apprehension at the Falls.—

All I wished for Your Lordship's accommodation at this Residence is not completed, but I have with pleasure done my best to make it habitable. I wish it were better.

May I be permitted to express the hope that your Lordship would defer receiving any Address from the Inhabitants of Kingston until Your Lordship's return. It ought to be as numerously signed as possible, and I am sure many will be disappointed who reside at a distance if their names do not appear to an Address.

I have not heard from Sir John Colborne what your Lordships plans are; but, as many highly respectable persons reside in the Western District, it would be very advantageous if your Lordship could arrange to pass through that part of Upper Canada—and if the long intended measure of constructing a Fortress in the Western District were on this occasion determined upon, so far as may be, and the first stone of Fort Durham laid it would be one of the greatest boons your Lordship could confer on the loyal inhabitants of Upper Canada.

[249] COLBORNE TO [ARTHUR]: A.L.S. 3p.

July 8 *Niagara.*

We have now so large a force near the falls, the *sooner* the Militia are suffered to return to their homes the better. I wish only that 40 or 50 men should be retained to perform the duty at the landing places at Niagara and Queenston; and to furnish small guards to prevent desertion.

I hope the arrangements which I have in contemplation, will not render it necessary again to call out the Militia, an expense which our Govrnt cannot bear if it be too often repeated, particularly as it really appears there has been no necessity for such a measure, with reference to the projects of our unseen Enemy[.]

[250] C. A. HAGERMAN TO ARTHUR: A.L.S.

July 8 *Toronto.*

I send your Excellency Mr Buchanans letter to Lord Durham— On the title page you will perceive that it was sent to me by "*My sincere friend!*"—

I have not been able to trace the Conversation with Mr Radenhurst— but I am quite confident Mr. McAulay could obtain a correct account of it either from Mr Radenhurst himself, or Mr. R's brother-in-law— Mr Ridout Cashier of the Bank—

[Enclosure lacking.]

[251] C. A. HAGERMAN TO THE LIEUTENANT GOVERNOR [ARTHUR]: A.L.S. 3p.

[*1838*] [*Toronto.*]
[*July 9?*]

I have this moment seen Sir Allan McNab—he says that Mr. Buchanans conversation and remarks on the public affairs of this Province when at Hamilton, were so very offensive that he treated him with the utmost coolness—and as plainly as he could shewed that he did not desire to hear any thing further from him.—

Sir Allan among other things states that a Mr. Forsyth who lives at a place called St Johns in the Niagara District told him that Mr. Buchanan on board the Steam boat on his way up from Quebec, and in the presence of all the passengers [said] that your Excellency was to be recalled;—And to Sir Allan himself, Mr. Buchanan stated that the people living in the neighbourhood of his Sons residence in the District of London, were willing to fight for The Queen but not for the faction.—

In order to get rid of him Sir Allan called into the room several of the labourers and common people with whom he had business, and began a Settlement of his accounts with them:— And in this way he got rid of the presence of the Gentleman.—

[252] ARTHUR TO DURHAM: L. 16p.

July 9 *Government House, Toronto.* [Marked "Copy Separate".]

I think it proper Your Lordship should be put in possession of every circumstance that can in any way effect the object of your Lordship's mission—and, therefore, I have the honor to submit the following observations.

Your Lordship naturally wishes to possess all the information that is to be had; and by Yourself and your secretaries many enquiries are directed, and observations of course invited to that end.

Amongst those who have been contributing their quota of intelligence, as I collected on Saturday from himself, is Mr. Buchanan.

It so happened, my Lord, when I landed at New York Mr. Buchanan gave me, what he was pleased to call, an insight into men and parties in this Province; and, of all things, pressed upon me the danger of any alliance with a party which he designated the Family Compact; and, in order to impress the matter more strongly upon my mind, he subsequently addressed a confidential letter to me upon the subject.[1]

The family Compact, & other persons proscribed by Mr. Buchanan, include the most able men in the Legislative Council, and some of the most prominent public Officers. So that, the recommendation was to

[1]See item 103.

exclude myself from the services, and to regard with suspicion, the most influential & powerful party in the Province, by whom mainly Sir Francis Head had been enabled to overthrow the knot of disaffected men composing the last House of Assembly, of whom Mackenzie, Bidwell, and Rolph were, in fact, the leaders.

Her Majesty's Government urged upon me, before I left London, in a very energetic Dispatch, that I should pursue the Policy and the measures of Sir F. Head, and it was considered a point of some importance that it should be known in the Province that it was my intention to do so— A Despatch of such a nature, however, written at a distance of 4,000 miles and without the Ministers having an accurate knowledge of all the underworking which goes on in every community must leave much to the discretion of the Officer to whom it is addressed, and I have seen reason for acting upon it only to a very limited extent. But Mr. Buchanan's recommendations were quite of an opposite character, being nothing more or less than to resuscitate a faction that was all but politically extinct, and to commence my Government by giving great Offence to the Constitutional and most powerful section of the Community. During the three months I have administered the affairs of this Province, perceiving they were not times for agitation, I have not entered upon one controversial question, except, that I have amicably discussed, with the leaders of each denomination the long contested Clergy Reserve question and have intimated to them my intention of bringing in a Bill to re-invest those lands in the Crown, if better means cannot be devised; and I have every reason to hope I shall at length successfully carry the measure through the Provincial Parliament.

Under these circumstances I have identified myself with no party, but have seen enough to convince me that Mr. Buchanan's statements are incorrect—that his opinions are valueless, that his invectives against the Family Compact are most unjust—and that his meddling at all at this time is most mischievous.

Mr. Buchanan read to me I remember, whilst I was at New York the Copies of two letters which he had addressed to Lord Glenelg upon the affairs of this Province—unless his Lordship well knows Mr. Buchanan, the communications were calculated however unintentional[ly], to mislead the Minister to whom they were addressed! He is now doing a double mischief, first by endeavouring to prejudice Your Lordship's mind against some of the most respectable and most highly esteemed men in the Province, and secondly in exciting bad feelings amongst an influential party, by making his advice, and Your Lordship's intentions the subject of conversation.

Having heard of the impolitic course he was thus pursuing, I requested an interview with Mr. Buchanan on Saturday, and said to him much more than I have expressed in this letter to Your Lordship. He deals wholly in generalities—I could not extract from him one single fact on which he could rest his assertions; and such I am persuaded Your Lordship will find to be the case with the contents of the letter which he says he has addressed to your Lordship.

When Sir Francis Head was at New York on his way to succeed Sir John Colborne, Mr. Buchanan urged upon him successfully the arguments which he used with me, and Mr. Baldwin, brother to Mr. Buchanan's son-in-law, and some other reformers were in consequence admitted to the Executive Council. The result is a matter of history. They immediately began by disputing for powers which the Constitution has never given to Members of the Executive Council. A rupture took place, and the whole of the reformed party, the real object of the leaders of which was the subversion of the Government was overthrown, and and [*sic*] to their struggle to regain influence, the Rebellion in December last, is to be referred, with all the lamentable train of consequences which are still agitating the Country.

Mr. Buchanan, in conversation with me, after passing the highest eulogium on his character, adverted to the great influence of the Chief Justice, as the Head of the Family Compact, and to the ultra Tory views of that gentleman. This is just the language that has been used by interested parties to the Colonial Department for years, until, at length, the Individual, who for integrity and ability stands the highest in the estimation of *all men of all parties*, there is reason to fear, must be regarded with apprehension by the Secretary of State.

In this Colony, as in other countries, respectable station, united with superior talents, and good conduct gives a certain degree of influence which is natural and salutary, and it would, indeed, be of all things ungracious and discouraging, as well as impolitic, if the Government were to manifest a jealousy of an influence so honorably acquired. It is, so far as I have been enabled to judge most unobtrusively exercised, and I am satisfied, from what I have experienced, that so far as he can conscientiously do so, Your Lordship will have the most cordial co-operation of the Chief Justice, and of all the Family Compact in all its ramifications throughout the Province.

Mr. Buchanan has not considered, that, what the Family Compact have for years fought against has been the introduction of measures tending to republicanism and the countenance given to individuals who were at least strongly impregnated with republican principles, so that all their views and all their predilections must be deeply interested in the success of your Lordship's measures, which are destined to strengthen the bond of union between Great Britain and the Canadas.

Not only have the Americans for years looked upon the Canadian Provinces as their own eventually, but many residents in this Province have regarded it almost as a matter of course. But your Lordship's arrival in North America, and the measures adopted by Her Majesty's Government within the last six months have given an extraordinary contradiction to this notion, and diffused the highest gratification amongst the loyal part of the community, whilst others are only slowly recovering from their surprize and disappointment.

The ideal, therefore, that any Tory Party is being formed for the purpose of opposing Your Lordship's measures, as Mr. Buchanan asserts to be the case, is so improbable that I can only refer such a rumour to some ignorant or very mischievous person.

Whilst passing through such a crisis as the present, the Province of Upper Canada must feel more or less convulsed for the next year, but *I am quite certain* that British connection and British Institutions being secured to them, which every man ought to regard as the grand object of your Lordship's mission across the Atlantic, Your Lordship will encounter no opposition from the Constitutional Party of the Province, and I am convinced that the settlement of this grand point will tend to the settlement of all others—and in achieving it, Your Lordship in place of being met with coldness will be regarded as the warmest friend Canada has ever known.

[Endorsed in pencil: "Intended for His Exy Sir John Colborne".]

[253] COLBORNE TO ARTHUR: L.S. 5p.

July 11 *Head Quarters, Niagara Falls.*

I have had the honor to receive Your Excellency's letter of the 8th Inst. I beg to assure you, that whether the disaffection in this Province has arrived at the Extent to which you are persuaded it has reached, or that the numbers connected with the refugees and the American adventurers in the United States are inconsiderable and less formidable than the information communicated in Your Excellency's letter would lead us to believe, I am fully convinced that not a moment should be lost in adopting such Military precautionary measures as will afford protection to the population on the frontier most exposed to the sudden incursions of the Lawless American Gangs in correspondence with the disaffected, and as will restore confidence to the Western District.

I have already stated to Her Majesty's Govt. the necessity of stationing a large regular force in these Provinces; and that such a precautionary measure will be more economical in the end than employing the militia, and render it unnecessary to resort to the ruinous expedient of calling out Volunteers from the Militia on every alarm and under circumstances which will occasion the same unchecked extravagance which prevailed last winter, while the pirates and rebels were assembled on the frontier at the time the Province was altogether unguarded, and unprepared for an attack or insult, on the part of our neighbours[.]

It is to avoid the recurrence of the confusion and improvidence of last year, and the rush of an unmanageable Mass of Volunteers to the points of attack; in whose efforts few of my acquaintances and friends at Toronto had confidence; that I should recommend Volunteer preparations on a moderate scale but in every respect adapted to the existing circumstances of the Province.

I need only advert to the expensive, useless militia staff which was established at every station where troops were posted and the undue proportion of officers attached to every Corps, to prove to Your Excellency that the Home Govt will not where there is time to organise a force on a more economical system approve of any expensive formation of Volunteer Corps.

If it is intended that the corps of Militia which Your Excellency has determined to arm should be paid by the province, as in New Brunswick, that arrangement would I think be highly approved of by the Home Govt— But any provincial force that is to be paid from the Military Chest to be raised for the temporary defence of the Frontier and to act immediately in conjunction with the regular force should, I am of opinion, be chiefly confined to the raising of independent companies which may be stationed on the St. Lawrence, Niagara, and Western District Frontier[.]

This description of force might be speedily armed and raised on a more economical plan than any other, and without leading many of the young men of this Province into a mode of life and habits destructive to their future prospects[.]

I should not consider myself justified, while I am in this command, to sign warrants for corps proposed to be raised on an expensive scale— Sedentary Volunteer Companies from the militia might also I think be formed, with great advantage to the province, at Toronto, Niagara, Kingston Amherstburg Brockville Cornwall, and in all the large Towns[.]

These would be selected from the Loyal Population which has taken so conspicuous a part in the late occurrences, and would be prepared to act with such Volunteer companies of the militia of every county, which probably could now be selected, in the first instance, in the same manner from the Militia of many of the townships of the London[,] Gore, Home, Newcastle and Eastern Districts[.]

After reading many reports from several districts and examining the information received from the American frontier I cannot think that the projects of the American Adventurers or of the disaffected in any district are on so extensive a scale, or are so formidable as Your Excellency is led to believe; but I entertain no doubt that it will be necessary to station a regular force of not less than 4000 men in this Province for some years—

[254] COLBORNE TO ARTHUR: A.L.S. 4p.

July 11 *Niagara Falls.* [Marked "Private".]

I should have paid you a visit, en passant; but as our movements in this quarter may have a good effect both on the American side; and in this District and in the Western part of the Province; I considered it better to lose no time in shewing our force on the Niagara frontier and making arrangements for conveying troops and arms to any part of the London district; by Lake Erie[.]

I hope I shall have the pleasure of seeing you on Friday at Niagara—

Buchanan is so well known to be a great fool, that I cannot think that anything he has said will make an impression on Lord Durham. Buchanan's conversation must have been with Mr. C Buller, I rather think, a Gentleman more susceptible of taking erroneous views than his master. . .

[P.S.] The enclosures are from Gibson the Surveyor, and Colonel Campbell respecting his artillery arrangements. Have the goodness to return the Memoranda from the latter[.]

[Enclosures lacking.]

[255] GLENELG TO ARTHUR: A.L.S. 3p.

July 11 *London.*

There is a gentleman in Upper Canada in whom I take an interest—Mr. Tucker, formerly Chief Justice of Newfoundland. You are, I understand, acquainted with him, and so well esteem his talents & character as to have intimated a wish to make use of him in the public service. This overture he declined, on some scruple of punctilious honor. That difficulty I believe is now removed—and I trouble you with a line to say that I should be glad to hear of any thing to his advantage—I know well how careful and circumspect you must be in selection for Offices—both as to the merits of the person selected, and as to the effect of every appointment on the public mind. Therefore it is that I desire to leave to you the fullest discretion as to every nomination & to leave to you also the whole responsibility— But in reference to what has passed respecting Mr. Tucker, I only beg to say that if in your own judgment you are inclined to place him in Office for which he is qualified & without injustice to others, you will find me quite disposed to regard the choice favorably—

[256] [ARTHUR TO COLBORNE]: L.

[*1838*] [*July 12*] [The letter is lacking, but a précis entry in item 578 reads:] Sir G. A. 12th July In consequence of Sir J. C's letter (8th. July) reduces the Niagara force to the desired small detachments & sends orders to Colonel Maitland to embody 4 Companies for 12 months for the Western Frontier—which orders he suspends, not knowing that Sir J. C. will agree to the terms.

[257] GLENELG TO ARTHUR: L.S. 4p.

July 12 *Downing Street,* [*London.*] [Marked "Private."]

I have received your private Letter of the 5th. of June. It is very agreeable to me to perceive in it a proof that you are prepared to discuss with me on the confidential and friendly terms which ought to be maintained between us, every part of my official conduct which you may think open to exception. I am most anxious to avail myself of the same channel of private Correspondence for removing, if possible, from your mind, any painful or erroneous impression under which you may appear to me to labor. The interests at stake are of such extreme moment, that I am convinced we shall both feel it to be nothing less than a sacred duty to act together in the spirit of mutual confidence, and to construe favorably whatever may appear on either side to admit of a more or less indulgent interpretation.

On the subject of what passed between us respecting the appointment of a Governor General, I have already written to you in my private Letter of the 5th. Instant. I can now only repeat, that neither I, nor Mr Stephen, correctly understood the meaning which it is clear that you intended to convey to me in his presence. Your strong disinclination to act under a Governor General was expressed in terms which we both distinctly recollect. Your absolute determination not to act at all under such a Superior must have been declared because such is your own statement of the fact. But neither he nor I understood you as announcing that determination. It is our common recollection that the conversation terminated without any decision being expressed on my part whether a Governor General would be appointed or not, or on your part, whether if such an appointment were made, you would or would not accept the Office of Lieutenant Governor.

I have already explained to you, that after your departure from England the Government were induced to resume the intention which when you quitted us had been abandoned. If I had considered that any pledge had been given to you that a Governor General should not be appointed under any circumstances, I should have applied to you to relieve me from it. But such a supposition never occurred to me until I read your Letter to Mr Stephen.

I yet indulge the hope that since the date of your Letter of the 5th. of June, your views on the subject of the effects of Lord Durham's appointment have undergone a material change. The correspondence between his Lordship and yourself, of which he has transmitted Copies for my perusal, is conducted on both sides in a spirit which promises the best understanding and the most friendly co-operation between you. It has apprised you that it is not Lord Durham's intention, nor that of Her Majesty's Government that he should interfere in the ordinary administration of the Affairs of Upper Canada, but that his interference will be confined, during his residence in British North America, to those subjects in which the whole of that part of Her Majesty's Dominions has a common interest. At a date considerably later than that of your Letter to me, I find that you expressed yourself to his Lordship on the subject in such terms as induce me to hope that when the real state of the case became known to you your objections to the arrangement were greatly diminished, if indeed they did not entirely cease: I cannot but think that, if this change of opinion has not already occurred, your mind will be open to it on further reflection and experience. I am of course well aware of the views entertained and expressed by the two Houses of Provincial Legislature on the subject of the differences of opinion which existed between myself and your immediate Predecessors, and that so long as a Lieutenant Governor has the support of a majority of those Houses, they will desire and expect that he should be supported with at least equal decision by the Home Government under which he serves. Without entering into a retrospect to which it would be impossible to do justice within any short space, I must deny that I have ever failed to satisfy the reasonable expectations of the Council and Assembly on this head; and I am happy to see that while quoting their Reports, you do me the justice to rely on my support of yourself. In Lord Durham's appointment it appears to me, and I hope by this time to you also, that much has been done to sustain your authority, and nothing which can really impair it.

It is impossible that any general principles could be maintained at the present crisis of British North American Affairs without concert between the Governors of five different Provinces, or that any such concert could really be established without some degree of subordination. A Nobleman justly occupying a very high station in the public confidence, has been appointed to exercise this authority, probably for a short period, and with a view to enable all the different Governments to act together for the promotion of one common object. Possessing the entire confidence of Her Majesty's Advisers, Lord Durham instead of fettering you by an additional authority will have the power, as he certainly will have the inclination, to assist you by anticipating many decisions which must otherwise have been expected from this Country, while your close vicinity to each other may, in many cases of importance enable you to communicate with him, either personally or by Letter, with a facility unattainable in your intercourse with me. He is far too conversant with the theory and the practice of Government, not to feel the necessity of strengthening your hands, both by abstaining from all needless interference, and by affording you all the relief and support in his power.

The account which you have given me of the state of affairs within the Province, painful as it is in some respects, corroborates my previous conviction of the indispensable necessity of bringing the whole of the affairs of British North America, so far as the Executive Government is concerned, under the temporary control of a power common to them all. To deal with them as so many detached and isolated States is no longer possible. They have so many conflicting interests to be reconciled, and so many common interests to be promoted, that the attempt would be equally dangerous and futile. Formidable as was the aspect of affairs when I had last the pleasure of seeing you, they became incomparably more so afterwards. If we view this subject in somewhat different lights it is probably because we are compelled to regard it from different positions—you from the Seat of Government in Upper Canada, and I from the Seat of the Imperial Government in this Country. It may be very difficult or impossible for us to enter completely into each others difficulties, but it is my most earnest and anxious hope that you will make for mine the allowance, which you would wish me to make for your own, and that you would give me credit for the deep solicitude which I really feel, to secure your cordial co-operation with Her Majestys Government, and to promote to the utmost of my power your personal honor and comfort, as well as the success of your administration. Permit me most respectfully to request that you would dismiss from your mind any distrust which circumstances may have induced you to cherish towards me, and that in the cause of Our Sovereign and Country you would accept my co-operation in the spirit of friendship and confidence in which it is tendered.

[258] GLENELG TO ARTHUR: L.S. 10p.

July 12 *Downing Street.* [Marked "Duplicate Private".]
[Another copy of item 257.]

[259] J. S. MACAULAY TO ARTHUR: A.D.S. 2p.

July 12 *Toronto.*

Assuming that the Province of Upper Canada is to be fortified it appears desirable—

1. That the Fortifications should be so contructed as to afford complete protection to large bodies of Troops, requiring at the same time but few to defend them.

2. That they should be sufficiently imposing, to deter even a daring foe from attacking them, otherwise than by the ordinary process of a siege.

3. They should be as little costly as possible.

To effect these objects, let the sites to be fortified, be occupied with casemated redoubts, connected with Carnot walls.

Avoid enclosing towns, or villages, within the precincts of the Fortifications.

As regards the Niagara Frontier, if the ground near Fort Erie, and in the neighbourhood of Niagara were so occupied; a small fort were built on the triangular piece of land off by the Chippawa cut, a tower at the Grand River and a redoubt with one or two batteries to protect the harbour at Port Colborne, that frontier might be considered as sufficiently fortified.

Instead of occupying The Short Hills, might not Port Dalhousie, be made the great depot of arms, for that section of country?

It is in the immediate vicinity of the Main route from Niagara to Hamilton, is one of the entrances to the Welland Canal, and can at all times receive assistance by water, it could not therefore be neglected by an enemy entering the country on that side.

In combination with the fortifications before mentioned, it would further, secure the Welland Canal to our use, and consequently enable us to compete with the Americans on Lake Erie, and reinforce our western frontier when necessary.

The Burlington heights have been spoken of as a place of arms. Could not a garrison be easily shut up there? Cannot the communication by water be easily impeded or rendered insecure? These questions have occurred to me as requiring investigation, before any permanent occupation of that site be resolved on.

It is true that a depôt of arms is required at Hamilton, but it would perhaps be better to erect our principal Fortresses near to the Fontiers, and if any where else, the seat of Government must be the most important point.

All of which is respectfully submitted[.]

[260] N[ATHANIEL] YOUNG TO ARTHUR: A.L.S.

July 12 *Headquarters, Niagara Frontier, Buffalo, N.Y.*

The day after I had the honor of seeing you at the Falls, I addressed a letter to Maj: General Macomb, who is now at Sacketts Harbour, on the subject of the expected arrival of your Family at Oswego.— I have now the pleasure to inform Your Excellency, that by a letter received last Night from the Maj: General, I am directed to assure you that every attention will be shown Lady Arthur and Family, on their arrival; and with that view Lieutenant Temple of the U S Army, is now at Oswego, awaiting the arrival of her Ladyship, and will not only do all in his power to make your Family comfortable whilst there, but if agreeable to Lady Arthur, will accompany her to Toronto . . . .

N. Young
Maj: U S. Army[.]

[261] M. S. BIDWELL TO FRANCIS HINCKS: L. 4p.

July 12 *New York.* [Marked "Copy".]

I have seen today Mr. Bronson who informs me that a law was passed to establish a territorial Government in Ioway. The limits of the territory are extensive; but the Indian Title is extinguished only to a tract of land about 300 Miles in length and 80 in breadth,—so that the Settlers will have the Courts &c. at their very doors.

Two land Offices are opened West of the Mississippi River. He thinks these circumstances will afford additional inducements to emigrants to resort to that Country. Upon that account I have thought they might be interesting to you.

I am rejoiced to hear there is again an independent Newspaper in Upper Canada.— I hope it will effect wonders.— It appears to me a critical time in the history of the Province. What an opportunity Lord Durham has to be honoured and beloved through all Succeeding Ages? What an opportunity to do good; to establish free institutions? but I confess my fears are much greater than my hopes! If he allows Sir George Arthur to remain, there is an end, of course, to all reasonable grounds of hope.

I understand that there is some prospect of the Settlement of the Clergy Reserve question—in a satisfactory manner. To find these expectations realized would give me the most sincere pleasure; for the policy of the dominant party on that Subject has been in my opinion unjust and has undoubtedly given great dissatisfaction. It is not, however, by any means the Sole evil or the cause of the troubles in that Country.— The System in which the Government has been administered—that of disregarding the opinions and wishes of the people generally, and of advancing and sustaining and rewarding those and those only who adopted that Course, is at the foundation of all the troubles,—and while that System Continues, it is of Comparatively little importance what is done with the Clergy Reserves. I should not trouble you to read my opinion on the subject, if I did not believe that it was of immense importance at the present moment that Lord Durham should not be misinformed on this subject.

Please to give my respects to Mrs. Hincks, and remember me to all my friends. I hope to get settled here before long and if I can do anything for you I shall be glad to do it.

[Endorsed: "Copy Intercepted Letter M. S. Bidwell to Francis Hincks."]

[The above is possibly the enclosure referred to in item 267.]

[262] JOHN STRACHAN TO JOHN MACAULAY: A.L.S.

July 12 *Toronto.*

Permit me to draw His Excellencys attention to a Report on the religious State of the Indians in Upper Canada, which I had the honor of presenting in May last—[1]

My reasons for troubling the Lieut. Governor at this time are, 1st. That His Excellency will have an opportunity of conferring with Sir John Colborne on the subject of converting and civilizing the Indians, and becoming acquainted with his plans for that purpose, and which in my humble opinion were liberal, extensive, and efficient— Unfortunately His Excellency Sir John Colborne was recalled before it was possible to put them fully into operation, and his Successor adopted different views with which it was impossible for me to concur. And even after the settlement on the Manatoulin [*sic*] Island had been commenced, and a Missionary stationed there with the Indian Superintendant, they were withdrawn, and the farther prosecution of the design postponed— 2nd. That the Revd Chas Brough a Gentleman of excellent attainments & in my opinion every way qualified seems inclined to undertake the Mission on the Manatoulin Island should it be now established, and I have no doubt, but that his piety and zeal assisted as he will be by an experienced School Master will be blessed with a great measure of success— The hearts of the Parents will be reached through their Children and their improved temporal comforts will become the Harbinger to their spiritual advancement—

Persuaded that His Excellency Sir George Arthur is equally anxious with His Excellency Sir John Colborne to ameliorate the condition of the poor Indians and that a conference between them on the subject must lead to their substantial benefit, I most respectfully hope, that this note of remembrance will not be considered unreasonable[.]

[Endorsed in Arthur's handwriting: "Dispatch 8 Novr 1832".]

[263] [LORD] FITZROY [J. H.] SOMERSET TO ARTHUR: A.L.S. 2p.

July 16 *Horse Guards,* [*London.*]

I have received your very interesting letter of the 9th. Ultimo and having communicated it to Lord Hill, I beg to thank you in His Lordship's name and my own for the information it contains. I am also much obliged to you for mentioning the state of the Barracks in Upper Canada upon which I will immediately write to the Ordnance.

[1]See item 166.

[264] ARTHUR TO COLONEL [GEORGE] COWPER [*i.e.* COUPER]: L. 2p.

July 17 *Government House, [Toronto.]*

I wrote to you last night to explain that the alteration in the plan proposed for Lord Durham's movements—by which His Lordship was to arrive at Toronto at 7 o clock in the Evening of Wednesday, in place of at 4 oclock as before settled—would lead to so much disappointment, that I trusted the proposed the proposed [*sic*] alteration would be abandoned, and that his Lordship would adhere to his original intention, of receiving the address of the inhabitants of Toronto & its vicinity at 4 oclock. In fact, all that part of the arrangement I considered to be fixed—it was his Lordship's further progress Eastward that remained open for further consideration.

If by any mischance my letter of last night should not have reached you, pray let me hear from you in answer to this by the Queen Victoria Steamer, which leaves Niagara early tomorrow morning.

I omitted, with my letter last evening, to send the copies of two addresses intended to be presented to the Earl of Durham on Thursday Morning— The omission is now supplied. . .

[P.S.] I have sent the necessary orders to Kingston, respecting the Governor Generals movements—

[Enclosures lacking.]

[265] COLBORNE TO [ARTHUR]: A.L.S. 3p.

[*1838*] *Niagara Falls.*
July 17

I did not receive your note till late last Evening.

The Lancers will be with you today.

Lord Durham leaves Niagara at 10, tomorrow, he will probably not arrive at Hamilton before 2 P.M; You cannot therefore see him at Toronto till ½ past 8 or 9—on Wednesday Evening.

He intends to embark on the Cobourg on Thursday about 3 P M. so that he may reach Kingston early on Friday, and arrive at Prescott the same night.

[266] COLBORNE TO ARTHUR: L. 2p.

July 19 *Head Quarters, Falls of Niagara.* [Marked "Copy".]

With reference to Your Exy's letter of the 12th. Inst. upon the subject of the Volunteer force of the Militia required to be embodied, in which you request farther information respecting the details of the precautionary measures to which I have already adverted, I think it necessary to state that the force under my command being intended for the defence of the Upper & Lower province, I must be guided in the location and disposition of the troops by the reports which I may from time to time receive of the projects of the disaffected, and the extent of the distrust or panic which the movements of the American Marauders may occasion in particular districts.

The troops which have been brought to this frontier, will, I am persuaded tend greatly to restore confidence in the Niagara and London districts, and I am not apprehensive that any serious affair can occur in the Western part of the province while the Steam Boat now stationed on Lake Erie can be employed in the conveyance of troops—

Nine volunteer companies from the Militia of 60 rank and file each, will I think be a sufficient force to be employed on the detached duties on the St. Lawrence, Niagara and Western frontiers.

4. 6 pounders equipped at Quebec, 5000 stand of arms & 500 barrels of powder in addition to that quantity formerly ordered, have been transhipped at Montreal for Kingston.

In fact the preparations for the defence of a disaffected province depending as to their extent and continuance on vague and loose reports of inexperienced Officers, will occasion a constant enormous expense. if confidence in every district can not be speedily restored—

In regard to the Militia being called out on every alarm, instructions should be immediately circulated to the Senior Colonel residing in each County upon that subject. The case of Colonel Jones of Brockville [marginal note here reads "Young's Mills—"] has been I understand laid before Yr. Excy; He was only authorised by me to assemble a company for the protection of his Mills till a detachment of the 71st. Regt. might arrive. . .

P.S. I understand that many of the militia still remaining on duty on this frontier under the command of Colonel Kingsmill, Major Warner and Captain Egan, are desirous of being employed. . .

A true copy.

F. A. Mackenzie Fraser

Asst. Q. M. Genl.

[To the above are attached items 280 and 286.]

[267] C. A. Hagerman to The Lieut. Governor [Arthur]: A.L.S. 2p.

[*1838*] *Toronto.*

July 19 I return your Excellency Mr. Bidwell's letter.— It bears the stamp of hypocrisy—no man that sincerely venerates the Christian Regligion [*sic*], or that possesses the humanity and charity it enjoins would write of utter strangers as he has done.— It moreover contains untruths which he knew to be such at the time he wrote—and there would be no great difficulty in proving (at least I think not) that the persons he would denounce, are those, he and his friends are most indebted to for acts of kindness.

The person to whom the letter is addressed, is I apprehend a discontented, if not a disaffected man.—he most probably is concerned in the new paper—(The Examiner—) recently established in this City, and Mr. Bidwells chief object in writing to him, is to give him a few hints as to the proper manner of conducting it—at least such is my opinion.—

[Enclosure is possibly item 261.]

[268] Colborne to Arthur: A.L.S. 4p.

July 20 *Niagara Falls.* [Marked "Private".]

We intend to embark at Gravelly Bay this morning; and proceed to Long Point, Port Stanley, and Amherstburg. On my arrival at those stations I may find it necessary to move some of the Companies of the 32d and 34th. Regiments. Mr. Henry Jones was the person to whom you alluded, I think, in mentioning your intention to appoint a private secretary. You would find him useful in your office. I do not however know whether he is qualified for the portion of the work, which you would be desirous of giving him.

I promised to mention to you the son of Mrs Muttlleberry [*i.e.* Muttlebury]. I believe She is very anxious to obtain employment for him. I also was requested by Capt Davis of Lake Simcoe, an old Officer, and a good Settler, to inform you that he had returned to his farm. You will find him a clever intelligent Settler, that may be made very useful in his District[.]

[269] HEAD TO ARTHUR: A.L.S. 4p.

July 20 *Athenaeum*, [*London.*]

I received from Lord Glenelg about the latter end of April a despatch dated 25th April a copy of which I was informed would be sent to you with a despatch of the same date, a copy of which was given t me—

By these communications it appeared t me that the Legislature of U C might be given t understand that the subject of my remuneration or rather non-remuneration formed "a prominent feature" in the correspondence which ended in my resignation of the Govrt of the Upper Province—

I immediately called Lord Glenelg's attention t this, and it was *at once* agreed at the Colonial Office that my objection should be removed, and the despatch sent t you on the 25th April should be replaced by another commn.

This however was delayed, untill [*sic*] I yesterday read in the newspapers that you had convened the Legislature on the 2nd of August—

I accordingly went this morning t the Colonial Office t complain of their having delayed to do what had been promised— I saw Mr. Stephen who promised me *most faithfully* that the despatch to you recalling and replacing the despatch of the 25th of April should be sent t you this evening by the great Western Steamboat, by which conveyance it would probably reach you before you had communicated with the legislature on the subject—

I am however afraid that the promised letter t you may not be ready, and my object therefore in troubling you is (in case it should not arrive by the great Western) t beg you to wait a while for it—

You of course know what was the real reason of my leaving U C. and I need not add that nothing would give me so much satisfaction as that it should be known here and in U C. but having on principle preserved a strict silence on the subject, I think it unfair that any false impression should be circulated by the Govrt. directly or indirectly, and that they should give no part unless they chose t give the whole—

You have authority t pay t me out of the Casual and Territorial revenues the sum of one thousand Pounds— I should feel obliged t you if you would be so good as to transmit it to me with as little delay as possible. I could sign any receipt at the Colonial Office thro which it might be sent[.]

Adieu my dear Sir George, I need hardly say that I watch your progress with anxiety and that my best wishes I may almost say prayers attend you and the welfare of U C[.]

[270] ARTHUR TO GLENELG: L. 7p.

July 23 *Govt. House, Toronto.* [Marked "Confidential".]

With my Despatch marked "Confidential" of the 2nd. Instant, I transmitted to Your Lordship the names of Twenty Six Gentlemen whom I recommended to be appointed Members of the Legislative Council, and I stated that I had numbered them in the order in which I thought they ought to stand.

Although the List was previously for two months continually before me, and was revised over and over as information opened out to me; yet, after despatching it, I regretted the order in which I had placed two of the names, fearful Your Lordship might not approve of all.—

In transmitting the Duplicate, herewith, I have therefore revised the order in which the names stand in the Original List and I have added the name of Mr. Robert Neilson, who was formerly a Member of the Council at Trinidad—and is a gentleman of considerable ability, possessing very extensive property in this Province.

The more I have reflected upon this subject, the more I am convinced that a large accession of Members to the Legislative Council will be in many respects a desirable and acceptable measure. . .

Revised List of Twenty-seven Gentlemen recommended as Members to the Legislative Council of Upper Canada.—

---

1. Robert Simpson Jameson
Vice Chancellor.

---

2. Robert Baldwin Sullivan
President of the Executive Council—a Barrister—Commissioner of Crown Lands &c.

---

3. John Wil[l]son.
Of the District of Gore—many years Member of the Assembly and formerly Speaker— A Canadian.

---

4. Isaac Fraser.
Of the Midland District—a highly respectable farmer—formerly member of the Assembly— A Canadian.—

---

5. Robert Charles Wilkins.
a wealthy Merchant, and extensive Land-owner of the District of Prince Edward— A Canadian.—

---

6. Adam Fergusson.
a gentleman from Scotland, highly respectable and intelligent—resides in the District of Gore, where he has a large Property.—

---

7. John Macdonald,
(Of Gananoque) has resided in the District of Johnstone [*sic*] for many years, has an interest in Mills and other valuable property at Gananoque.

---

8. David Campbell.
a Major of the Army on half Pay—a Scotch Gentleman, some years settled in the District of Newcastle—a very respectable man.—

---

9. Thomas Radcliffe [*i.e.* Radcliff].
A retired Officer of the Army, who emigrated some years ago from Ireland—a very respectable person, and leader of an extensive settlement in the District of London.—

10. Samuel Street.—
A very wealthy Merchant— A Canadian long resident in the district of Niagara—possessed of large property and of highly honorable character —partner of the late Honble. Thomas Clark.—

11.— Alexander Fraser,
a Quarter Master of the Army on half Pay—a Scotch Gentleman long resident in the Eastern District—a farmer and possessed of large real estate.—

---

12. Robert Dickson,
a Barrister retired from Business, a gentleman of independant [*sic*] fortune,—a Native of Canada— Son of the Honble. Willm. Dickson, a member of the Lege. Council, who from age and infirmity is little likely to attend.

---

13. Robert Neilson,
A Gent. from Trinidad, in the West Indies, & formerly of the Council there, now resides in the Gore District—highly respectable & intelligent & possessed of wealth & property.

14.— John Simcoe Macaulay
A retired Capt. of the Royal Engineers—a Canadian possessed of valuable property.—

---

15. John Ogilvie Hatt,
A Barrister living in the District of Gore—a Son of the late Richard Hatt, formerly one of the most wealthy and respectable Inhabitants of the Province.

---

16. Francis Boyd
An English gent. of highly respectable character—has been for some years resident in the Home District—a Farmer.—

---

17. James Sampson
An Irish gent. highly respectable for intelligence and character—living in the Midland District—formerly a Surgeon in the Army—now a practising Physician.

---

18. Henry Graham.
An Irish Gentleman long resident in the District of Bathurst, and of large Property—a Merchant.—

---

19. Henry Vansittart.
a Rear Admiral in H. M. Navy—has resided in the District of London for 3 or 4 years, & possesses a large property there—is rather advanced in years. It is conceived that his rank makes it proper to appoint him.

---

20. Peter Boyle De Blaquière [*sic*],
a brother of Lord De Blaquière, who has been but a short time in this Province, but a highly respectable gent. living in the District of London.—

21. James Cotter
A Canadian residing in the District of Prince Edward—formerly a Member of the House of Assembly—a farmer much respected in the District.—

---

22. John Mc.Gillivray.
A Scotch Gent., formerly a partner in the North West Company, long resident in the Eastern District.—

---

23. Justus Sherwood Merwin.
A Canadian, resident in the District of Johnstown a highly respectable person—a Merchant—much esteemed in the neighbourhood.—

---

24. Edward Favell Davis.
A Capt. of the Army on Half Pay resident at Lake Simcoe—a respectable gent. and possessed of good property—there is no Member from that part of the Province.

---

25. Thomas Matthew Whyte.
From Jamaica—formerly of the Council there—now President of the Gore Bank at Hamilton.

---

26. Duncan Campbel[l]
Of Yonge Street, formerly Lt. Colonel of the 79th. Regt.—retired from the Service—now settled a few miles from Toronto on Yonge Street.—

---

27. Thomas Mercer Jones.
A Commissioner of the Canada Company.—

[The above begins on the reverse side of item 232.]

[271] J. B. ROBINSON TO [ARTHUR]: A.L.S. 3p.

July 27 *Toronto.*

I have, as nearly as my memory would serve me made the same notes upon your Copy of "the Scheme" as upon Lord Durham's and in about as legible a hand—

His Lordship, I fear, is losing much valuable time—by abstaining from discussing & considering any other than this one project, which I do not think it likely will be carried upon any principle, & which if carried upon the principles proposed, would assuredly be ruinous to these Colonies—

I wish he could be persuaded to apply his mind to some *alternative*, in case he should find his scheme impraecticable [*sic*].— I am satisfied the most rational course would be to extend the limits of Upper Canada so as to embrace the Island of Montreal & to govern what would remain of Lower Canada by a Legislative Council, well constituted (partly elective) & with full power to do all that a Legislature ought to do— I should like to see this tried for ten years at any rate, & I doubt whether the good people of Lower Canada would sue for a restoration of the blessings of an Assembly—

[The document referred to is apparently item 272.]

[272] [*1838*]
[*July ?*]

[DURHAM ?]: 27p.

[*Place not stated.*] [Marginal comments in pencil in Chief Justice Robinson's handwriting are here transcribed in quotation marks within square brackets.][1]

The object is to form a Government for the British Colonies in North America which whilst it maintains the supremacy of the Mother Country, and protects the common interests of all the Colonies, shall leave to each the arrangement of their own peculiar affairs, and at the same time have in view the formation of new Commun[ities] out of the present Wastes on one comprehensive plan which as population and settlements spread shall give to such Communities—Laws, protection and definite limits as separate Provinces, providing for the future as well as the present by embodying (in the federative Union) [these parentheses are inserted in pencil] not merely the existing Provinces, but all such future Provinces as may arise in British North America. ["It is not probable that any new Provinces will be formed, unless by subdividing the present, which may not be found necessary—"]

To have any chance of success in this object it is necessary to limit and control our views by what may be considered likely to be sanctioned and adopted at home.

The Colonies which are contemplated as those which should be placed under this arrangement in the first instance are Upper and Lower Canada, and subsequently at *their*

[1]Another copy of this document in different handwriting is in the possession of the Canadian Archives. It is endorsed: "This is a summary but with some additions and variations of the document entitled 'A Plan for the Government of British North America.'—The annotations in the margin of this document are in the handwriting of Lord Durham. W. D. LeS[ueur]. 27 Feby 1907". Correspondingly, the *Dominion of Canada, report of the Public archives for the year 1923*, (*The Durham papers*), pp. 209-210, states: "this summary has many marginal comments made by Durham . . . Durham criticized the plan freely."

As against this view, first, the critical comments in the margins both of the Archives copy and of item 272 are in Chief Justice Robinson's handwriting, not Durham's.

Secondly, item 272 is endorsed: "Copy from Earl of Durham Send C[hief] J[ustice]", and in item 271 Robinson says to Arthur: "I have, as nearly as my memory would serve me made the same notes upon your Copy of 'The Scheme' as upon Lord Durham's and in about as legible a hand."

Durham had been in Toronto on July 25th, and Robinson, writing in Toronto, made the above statement to Arthur on July 27th. Robinson was therefore repeating for Arthur the comments he had made for Durham one or two days earlier. There is a close approximation between the two sets of comments; they cover substantially the same points and appear practically in the same places in the two copies.

Thirdly, amongst the most serious of the marginal criticisms are those dealing with the proposed discontinuance of the legislative councils; the vesting of a semi-legislative function in the executive councils; and the constitution of a general legislative body by means of the provincial assemblies each appointing five members. These are exactly the proposals which Durham later announced himself to Robinson as having abandoned (item 316).

Contrary to Mr. Le Sueur's conclusion, therefore, it would appear that item 272 and the Archives copy originated with Durham; that Durham submitted copies of this document to both Robinson and Arthur; that the Archives copy is the one which Robinson refers to as "Lord Durham's," and that item 272 is Arthur's copy.

Consequently, we probably here have Durham's early plan for federation. Indeed, in view of the date of Durham's letter to Robinson announcing his modifications (Sept. 6, 1838, item 316) this plan together with those modifications not improbably represents what Durham still had in mind when he left Canada six weeks later on November 1st, 1838.

See also items 309, 315, 333, 338.

option Nova Scotia New Brunswick, Prince Edward's Island and Newfoundland. ["If an option be left & Nova Scotia & New Brunswick should decline then the measure wd. result in the Union of the Canadas only, which would on several accounts be unwise—"]

It is proposed

1st To give such a special Government for each Colony or Province as will enable the Inhabitants thereof exclusively to control their own peculiar or local affairs.

2— To create such a General Government for all the Provinces in British North America, present or future, as will control and regulate all such Matters as may be common to all or to some two or more of them.

3— To maintain the supremacy of the Mother Country by means of a Governor appointed by the Crown for each separate Colony, and also one appointed by the same authority for the General Government. Such Governors to form integral parts of the separate Legislatures, local or general, over which they preside, and to have a veto upon all Legislative Acts.

Provincial Government

Administrative:

The Government of each Province will consist of,

1st. A Governor appointed as before mentioned, who when Bills shall have been passed by the House of Assembly and revised or altered or considered by the Executive Council, shall give or withhold the assent of the Crown necessary to make them Laws. ["The substitution of the Executive for the Legislative Council as a branch of the Legislature would be approved of in no respectable quarter—"]

2nd. The Executive Council to consist of not more than five Councillors, all of whom shall be appointed by each successive Governor and removeable by him. ["It is not expedient to limit the number absolutely to five—the Governor should do no more than nominate—the appointment shd. rest as at present with the Sovn.—"]

Whatever Salaries shall be payable to the Governor or Executive Council by the Province shall be fixed by the Provincial Legislatures for Periods of six years, not subject to reduction or increase for that period. ["I see no good reason for this limitation of a civil list to six years but many obvious objections—"]

Legislative:

The Legislative Government of each Province shall consist of,

The Governor,

Who may convoke the Meetings of the Legislative Body, and without cause assigned allow or disallow any Bills presented by the Legislative Body, or reserve them for the pleasure of the Crown, and at the request of the House of Assembly may prorogue it before the period of its Annual termination, ["There is no period appointed by law for the termination of the annual session— It depends on the prerogative & no change in this respect is desired"] and may by speech or Message state his views as to the State servants[1] of the Province, and give such information as the House may require.

The Executive Council,

Who shall have the right merely to revise alter and amend Bills when sent from the assembly, but not to reject any, merely returning them (within a time to be fixed) altered amended or untouched as the Council may deem necessary, to the Assembly for further consideration. ["This is in effect having but one Legislative Assembly an experiment that has been tried & signally failed, & upon which the Americans in forming their constitution did not think it safe to venture The project of abolishing the Legislative Council is most unwise & I am convinced will be generally disapproved of by all who desire the continuance of our dependence on the Crown—"]

A House of Assembly,

which shall be chosen and constituted as at present until a new arrangement shall be made of the places which return Members if found that a more fair arrangement can be made.

The whole Provincial Revenue to be under the control of the Provincial Assembly, subject to the Civil List only being open every six years to revision. ["I see no good but much mischief in this. Even the Democ(r)atic States of America avoid having their Govemt in so abject a state of dependence—"]

The Elections to be triennial on the 20th. September every third year commencing on the 20th. September 1840. ["No one desires that elections shd. be more frequent—it wd. be no improvement—"]

The Government not to have the power of dissolution. ["This is a clear prerogative of the Crown & shd. not be abandoned—"]

The session to commence on the 1st. November and terminate the 1st. of May, if the House should not be prorogued or continued by the Governor at the request of the House. ["This is better on its' (*sic*) present footing & I am satisfied no change is desired—"]

The Provincial Legislative Body to possess all powers not expressly conferred on the General Government, or General Legislature, and the Local or Provincial Government to be supreme in its own limits, ["This general language will not do— The power of each must be specified"] so far as it shall not be controlled by the Government at home with which the Provincial Governor should correspond direct, merely acquainting the General Government of what acts are passed or measures adopted for the information of the

[1]The word "servants" is apparently a copyist's error; in the Archives copy it is deleted and amended to read: "and wants".

General Government, but not for the purpose of the latter exercising any control.

And as no Law can pass without the assent of an Officer of the Crown in any Province, or in the General Government, the supremacy of the Crown of England will be preserved as inviolate as now.

Judiciary.

The Judges in each province to be paid by the Province a fixed Salary not subject to be encreased or diminished except in stated periods of ten years. And at those periods the same salary to be fixed for all Judges of the same grade throughout the Province. ["The footing on which the Judges Commissns. & incomes rest in England is the most proper— to make their salaries temporary is inconsistent with the independent discharge of their duties— The Legislature of Upper Canada have lately passed an act upon the principle that prevails in England".] Each Judge to send in his resignation upon attaining the age of [blank in MS.] years, and to be eligible to be reappointed for any term of years with the assent of the Assembly on message from the Governor, ["This is not worthy to be copied as it evidently is from the constitution of some of the United States— All intelligent persons there condemn it—"] and all Judges to be appointed by the Crown or Governor, and to hold their Office during good behaviour, removeable on Address if the Governor should think fit. All Judges and other Provincial Officers to be open to impeachment by the Local Assemblies before the General Assembly ["Impeachment before an assembly elected by the popular voice is not English, & not proper—".] Local and Circuit— Provincial Courts to be established of which the Judges whether appointed by the Inhabitants or the Crown, shall be removeable on petition by a Majority of the Inhabitants of the Districts where such Judges act. ["There needs no separate appoint. of circuit Judges In Upper Canada, as in England, the Judges who compose the superior Courts go the circuits— In L C. it is otherwise from the different nature of their laws— No Judges should be removed by the people in a British Province—"]

The General Government of the combined Provinces to consist of

1st. A Governor General appointed by the Crown with an Executive Council.

2nd. A Legislative Body nominated by the Provincial Assemblies of the Separate Provinces and elected as hereinafter mentioned.

3rd. A Judiciary appointed jointly by the Governor General and the Legislative Assembly. ["I do not see clearly the necessity for this proposed Judiciary—"]

The Governor General's power as respects the General Government will be similar to that of the Provincial Governors in the respective Provinces so as in no degree to clash with or override them. ["This general direction will not avail, they must be so framed as not to clash & therein consists the main difficulty of the measure—"] The Executive Council also of the Governor General to be appointed in like manner, and to act in a similar way, and to similar extents with relation to the General Government as those in the Provincial Governments towards the Latter.

So also should the General Legislative Assembly act so as to the preparation, discussing and passing of Bills with the assent of the Governor General after being subject to the revision of the General Executive Council, and will also try Impeachments of Provincial Officers and Judges on the prosecution of the Provincial Assemblies.

The General Legislative Assemblies to be appointed by each separate Province will make it unnecessary to continue the present Legislative Councils. ["This is a change that I believe no intelligent person desires—"]

Whether the separate Provinces may be great or small, populous or thinly inhabited, the General Legislative Assembly to be formed in manner following:

Five Members to be named and appointed by each of the Provincial Assemblies. ["This would give too small a number— The Assembly shd. contain from 45 to 60 members—and they should be chosen by elections independent of the others—& for a larger circle of territory—"] If Members of their own Body are named their seats in the Provincial Assembly to be vacated by acceptance of seats in the general Assembly. A census of the population of each Province to be taken every five years, and for each (say) 50,000 or 100,000 Inhabitants an additional Member to be sent to the General Assembly to be elected by the People as hereinafter determined. ["I would fix the number finally at once—"]

The General Government is not to possess any power not expressly conferred on it—and its object is to settle affairs in which one or more of the Provinces of the Union have a common interest and those only. But for this purpose to act by Officers of its own, not by those of the Provinces.

All matters relating to peace and War belong exclusively to the Crown, and therefore cannot be interfered with by the General Government any more than they could be by the Provincial Governments. But the defence of the Combined Provinces so far as the Militia or any Provincial Troops or forces may be concerned, and as may not interfere with the Prerogative of the Crown, to be with the General Government, and for that purpose the Government to have the power of levying, and paying troops for defence against foreign aggression or internal commotion or common enemies. ["This will require to be carefully considered to provide for exigencies—"]

Besides this, subject to the Prerogative of the Crown, the following subjects to be brought under the control of the General Government.

The Coin and Circulating Medium, Banking Operations extending beyond the limits of one Province; ["Qu".] The Laws of General external and internal commerce, and all laws affecting the regulations of the Provinces or any of them with Foreign Powers—whether such relations are commercial or political;

All boundary questions whether between the Provinces or between any one or more of them and Foreign States: ["The King & Privy Council is the proper tribunal for such questions".]

All duties on Articles imported from Foreign States or by Sea:

The Laws of Bankruptcy and Insolvency extending in their operation beyond the limits of any one Province:

All intercommunications between the Provinces or into Foreign States, or to the limits of the Combined Provinces whether by Rail Roads or Common or other Roads or by water natural or artificial—and to make and repair all such intercommunications, roads, Canals, and improvements in any navigable or other waters as the General Government may think fit, and may by any Act declare to be general, or to belong to the intercommunication between the Provinces, and, as connected with this, the Post Office: ["This distribution of powers & duties will require long & careful consideration".]

All questions relating to the Vice Admiralty Jurisdiction or Offences upon the Lakes if made of the nature of the high seas by any future Law, to remain or to be made subject to the Vice Admiralty Jurisdiction which will be maintained, but should offences on the Lakes remain or be made punishable as Offences merely on Navigable Waters, such Offences will be cognizable before the Courts of the General Government as all other offences committed in places within their control and governance will be: ["This not applicable to the state of the Law in Upper Canada".]

All original grants and the management of the Waste or Crown Lands or Domains of the Crown will be submitted to the control, so far as the Crown may consent to part with any portion of its prerogative to the General Government—["I doubt the expediency of this".] But, where any such lands shall be once granted, they will be subject to the Courts of the Province in which they are situated except so far as any rent or other duty may be reserved thereout or charged thereon for the Crown in or by such Original grant. ["I see no reason why each Province should not have jurisdiction in these cases".]

The General Judiciary to be composed of a Supreme Court of (say) Four Judges, ["I do not see that such a Court would be required"] and such number of other Courts and Judges as may be found requisite throughout the Combined Provinces, such inferior Courts subject and subordinate to the Supreme Courts.

The Supreme Court would try:

Disputes between the Provinces; ["I can think of none which the united Parliament would not most conveniently settle".]

All invasions of Provincial Rights by the General Government or of those of the General Government by the Provinces;

Appeals from the Provinces, and the several inferior Courts;

Piracy;

Treason; ["should be tried in the Courts of the Province in which committed".]

All offences against Laws or Matters made subject to the control of the General Government and the Judges would assist for matters of Law on impeachments before the General Assembly.

[Endorsed: "Copy from Earl of Durham Send CJ."]

[273] HEAD TO [ARTHUR]: A.L.S.

July 28 *62 Park St. Grovr. Square,* [*London.*]

Mr Tuffnel [*i.e.* Tufnell] Lord Mintos Private Secy. has requested me t give a letter of introduction t you in favor of Mr. Samuel Bawtree who he informs me is going out t Upper Canada as a settler with a capital of £3000— Mr Tuffnell is interested in this gentlemans welfare, and is very anxious that he should succeed.

[274] [ARTHUR] TO [COLBORNE]: L.

[*1838*] [The letter is lacking, but a précis entry in item 578 reads:]

[*July 29*] Sir G. A 29th July Adverts to a letter from Sir J. C (19th July *lost*) in which he recommends nine Companies of Volunteers (60 men each) for the General defence of the Frontiers, but without mentioning on what terms they are to be raised, or what number of companies are intended for each frontier.— *Sir G. A.* will wait for more particular instructions.— with reference to his knowledge of Sir J. C's wishes has authorized *2 Companies* for the Western District.—has reduced the force of the Niagara Frontier to 2 small detachments, one at Queenston & one at Fort George.—it appears from at [*sic*] letter to the Adjt. Genr the [*sic*] Sir J. C. himself had partly checked the reductions on the Niagara Frontier.

[The letter referred to as "lost" is apparently item 266.]

[275] [SIR] R. [J]. W. HORTON TO ARTHUR: A.L.S. 2p.

July 29 *Brighton,* [*England.*]

My Son-in Law Mr Tufnell, Private Secretary to Lord Minto has requested me to give Mr Samuel Bawtree a note of Introduction to you. I understand he is going out as a Settler to Upper Canada with an adequate Capital— Any attention that you can shew him will oblige me[.]

[276] J. B. ROBINSON TO [ARTHUR]: A.L.S. 2p.

[*1838*] [*Place not stated.*]

July 30 I intend accompanying my brother William to Niagara to morrow, and to return on Friday—& during that time I shall endeavour to meet Sir John Colborne, as he has expressed a wish to see me—

Can I do, or say any thing for Your Excellency?— On Wednesday next I shall proceed to Niagara to open the Special Commission—in the meantime I shall have a communication to make to Your Excellency on the subject of my late brother's affairs—

[277] J. B. ROBINSON TO [ARTHUR]: A.L.S. 2p.

1838] [*Place not stated.*]

July 31 The bearer of this note, Mr. Strange has just returned to this Country after visiting England.

He brought out a particular introduction when he came some years ago, to Sir John Colborne from Lord Fitzroy Somerset—& wishes me to say to Your Excellency that I have known him for some years— He has resided at Guelph, where he has a large property acquired by purchase[.]

Your Excellency will find him an intelligent, Gentleman—& perfectly well disposed.

[Endorsed in Arthur's handwriting: "was formerly in the Commission of the Peace Henry Strange".]

[278] MARIA DICKINSON TO ARTHUR: A.L.S. 3p.

Aug. 2 *London.*

[The wife of Captain Dickinson of the 86th regiment, being the daughter of John Gray "to whom you were kind enough to bestow the Office of Treasurer at Honduras during your administration in that Colony, and to whose infant family you continued your patronage after his death", appeals on behalf of her brother, Henry Gray, for any public office he may be qualified to hold. Henry Gray has been "Assistant Clerk of the Courts & Keeper of Records at Honduras for several years," but has no chance of advancement. "Our hopes are therefore naturally directed towards one who so kindly interested himself in us during our Infancy."]

[279] ARTHUR TO THE REVND. DR [J. H.] HARRIS: LB. 1, p. 57-58.

[*1838*] *Government House, Toronto.*

Aug. 4 Before your departure from Toronto I addressed the Archbishop of Canterbury respecting your Successor, and enclosed the memorandum with which you favored me— My letter was retained until the meeting of the College Council on the 9th of May; and from a circumstance that has now occurred, I have reason to fear that it has not been forwarded at all—there having been some confusion in my office—or,—rather, that misunderstanding respecting Papers, which is I believe inevitable when there is a change of Secretaries.—

I enclose a copy of the public letter which I have addressed to His Grace—in addition to which, I have written a long private letter to the Archbishop.— Vexed I am beyond measure at this occurrence, but it is unavailing to be so—the best I can do is to entreat your immediate interference and kind assistance in remedying the mischeif [*sic*], and I trust you may already have in your eye some well qualified Clergyman to bring under his Grace's notice.—

Since your departure we have had constant excitement, but I do now trust that the worst is over.—

Have the kindness to offer my best remembrances to Mrs. Harris, and with every wish that you may have reached your destination in safety.

[Enclosure lacking. The private letter referred to is probably item 282.]

[280] COLBORNE TO ARTHUR: L. 3p.

Aug. 6 *Head Quarters, Niagara.* [Marked " 'Copy.' "]

I have the honor to acquaint you, with reference to your Excellency's letter of the 29th. Ulto. respecting the formation of Volunteer Companies for the protection of the frontier, that the two Companies which you have Authorized to be raised in the Western and London Districts, will, I think be found a sufficient guard, with the regular force stationed at Amherstburgh, Sandwich, and Chatham, to prevent a repetition of the piratical incursions to which that section of the Country has been exposed, and that one Company of 80 Rank & file, placed under the orders of Colonel Booth, would be able to take the detached duties from Fort Erie to Niagara.— With respect to the terms on which the Volunteer Companies are to be raised, and the period of Service for which they should be engaged, these points should I think be determined by your Excellency. I beg to defer offering any further opinion in regard to the Companies necessary for the protection of the Townships on the St. Lawrence till I have passed along that frontier on my route to Montreal— I should recommend one light Gun Boat to be stationed at Sarnia and another at Sandwich and one Volunteer Company to be posted at Windsor and small detachments to be placed at Plympton, Sarnia, and Sutherland's Wharf to relieve the settlers from the duty which they now perform—

Several old and excellent Officers who have been lately in Command on this frontier are anxious to be employed and I shall take an early opportunity of mentioning their claims to your Excellency. . .

"A True Copy."

F. A. Mackenzie Fraser
Asst. Q. M. Genl.

[The above is attached to items 266 and 287.]

[281] [ARTHUR] TO GLENELG: Df.A.L. 2p.

Aug. 11 *Govt. House, Toronto.*

I have the honor to acknw.,—exactly one month from its' [*sic*] date, such is now the wonderful rapidity of intercourse with England—Your Lords. private letter of the 11 Ultimo expressing your sentiments & kind disposition towards Mr Tucker.

I am on the eve of setting off on a tour of inspection to Kingston & will make it a point to see Mr Tucker & ascertain from Himself what can be done for Him— [The following passage is here deleted: "Having held such an office as He once filled he expressed at the only interview I have ever had with Him some difficulty on this point".] He expressed at my last interview with Him some difficulty on this point, in reference to the important office he once filled.—

I have no doubt He is an honorable, & competent, Person & wd. make a valuable public servant, but If He looks for a superior office, I fear he may have to wait for some time—

[282] [ARTHUR] TO THE ARCHBISHOP OF CANTERBURY [WILLIAM HOWLEY]: L. 16p.

Aug. 11 *Government House, Toronto.* [Marked "Duplicate".]

When I left London Your Grace, in the kindest manner, permitted me to address a letter to you—in a manner, indeed, which has made a lasting impression on my mind and affections, and to which I have often recurred, as a pleasing relief, amidst the very anxious cares, and extraordinary and painful occurrences which met me on the very day of my entering upon this Government and have since continued with almost unabated pressure.—

The Jails, I found, in every part of the Province were full of Persons committed for Treason, others, for the same crime, were on Bail and new arrests were being daily made.

The Mischief of a Civil War is—that, every step taken to arrest the evil has a tendency to increase it, and the apprehension of every disloyal man lays the foundation for fresh strife and additional Excitement— Brother is arrayed against Brother and Parents are influenced against their Children for the Political opinions they entertain— Of all this, the most painful instances have occurred.

Two Ringleaders of the Rebellion suffered capitally shortly after I entered upon the administration of the Government, and to all others the door of mercy was at the same time thrown as widely open as circumstances would admit which at once relieved our overburdened prisons and checked the alacrity of those who had been but too ready to testify their Ultra Loyalty or to gratify bad passions by giving information against Persons *suspected* of treasonable Practices.—

As soon as the progress of Rebellion was stayed, about two, or perhaps, three thousand Persons who had shewn their disloyal Colors, fled to the United States, and being joined by the demoralized and ungovernable Mob of Citizens that disgrace the Frontier American Towns, the Excitement of invasion was kept up for several months and at length terminated by the descent upon this province of about a hundred of these People who had the hardihood and wickedness to attempt once more to raise the standard of Rebellion—but, they were all speedily Captured and their leader has been executed.

This brief account will afford Your Grace at a glance an idea of what has been transpiring in this Province since the Month of December last and how that excitement has really been kept up which is variously accounted for in the public journals according to the Political or interested views of the Writers.

I fear I must in truth add—that our own Militia have rather, to an extent fanned the flame they were originally called out to quench not being overanxious to lay down their arms with the accompaniments of pay and Rations from the Queen's Stores and return to their homes.

With regard to the cause of Rebellion in this Province, it is easily accounted for— In the first place a great number of American Citizens were injudiciously invited to settled [*sic*] in the fertile soil of Canada and having wormed themselves into very fair possessions avowing a temporary allegiance, they soon began with their accumulated wealth to desire democratic institutions.— With this view they seduced others to unite with them in gradually seeking those changes in the cons[t]itution of this Province as most verged towards their Republican notions. Some clever, but bad and disappointed men availed themselves of this party to extend their general influence— Grievances were then thought of—the dominant church, as they called the Church of England, was a fruitful source of agitation—then came in aid of this cause the speeches and writings of Mr. Hume and others of his way of thinking, and what was worse than all, some of the most peaceful men of all parties at Home spoke of the separation of the Colonies from Great Britain as a measure that might indeed be protracted but seemed inevitable—the consequence of this was, as might be expected, the defection or rather the concurrence of some men who only thought that if the change must take place the sooner the better and I have no doubt that they really did expect that the objects would be effected almost without opposition and certainly without bloodshed.

The withdrawal of all the Queen's Troops from this Province was the signal seized upon by the Chief Leaders in the revolt to bring about the desired change and it may be hoped that, the *decided feeling* of attachment to monarchical institutions which has been manifested by the great body of the People on the occasion together with the decisive measures of the Parliament of Great Britain has rectified erroneous impressions and under Providence tended to strengthen the connexion between the Canadas and the Mother Country.

The Clergy Reserve question is still an unsettled one of increasing excitement—there is not one acre of Land in that Reserve more than is required to provide an adequate support for the Clergy of the Established Church of England, but matters have gone too far now to shut out other denominations of Christians from participating and all we can do is to make the best terms circumstances will allow.

One of two plans is open and either I think might be carried through the provincial Legislature—either to introduce the plan which has succeeded so well, giving a decided preponderance to the Church of England as in the Australian Colonies—or, simply to reinvest the Lands in the Crown for Religious purposes to be appropriated by the Imperial Parliament as the Legislature may think proper.

Should I ask too great a favor to solicit your Grace's opinion on this point?

The Australian plan, I could explain in case your Grace should not happen to possess a copy of the New South Wales Act but one could easily be procured from the Colonial Office—is simply this— That where any body of Christians in connexion with the Church of England or the Church of Scotland or the Church of Rome or the Wesleyans contributes a sum of money for building a Church or Chapel or, for the support of a Minister a like sum is voted out of the Church Reserve for the same purpose— No communion has been able to stand any thing like a competition with the Church of England on these terms in Australia—and I think they would not do so in this Province—but I am apprehensive of committing myself upon a point of so much importance.

Our want of Ministers and of small Churches is great beyond description; but, I shall not at present intrude this subject upon your Grace because I am upon the point of setting out upon a tour of inspection through the Province and shall be able upon my return, in a more satisfactory manner to bring the subject under the attention of the Government and under your Grace's review through some [blank in MS.] Channel.

By this opportunity I have at the express desire of the Council of the College of Upper Canada solicited from your Grace the very special favor of your nominating a Principal for the Upper Canada College. It is an institution in close connexion with the Church of England, which has been most unmercifully attacked by all other denominations and the appointment of a Principal of sound learning and sound religious Principles is of the utmost conceivable importance as regards the future Religious and Moral state of this noble Country— Will your Grace therefore pardon the great freedom I have used in suggesting to the Council that, to allay the differences as to the appointment which exists [*sic*] even amongst those who are most interested in the success of the College, the nomination of the Principal should be made by your Grace. The appointment is understood to rest with the Lieutenant Governor of the Province as Chancellor so that there can be no disrespectful omission towards the Secretary of State and I feel persuaded that nothing will gratify Lord Glenelg so much as to find the office is filled in a manner satisfactory to the Community.

[283] [ARTHUR] TO THE ARCHBISHOP OF CANTERBURY [WILLIAM HOWLEY]: L. 4p.

Aug. 11 *Government House, Toronto.* [Marked "Duplicate".]
[Another copy of the first portion of item 282.]

[284] [ARTHUR] TO [THE ARCHBISHOP OF CANTERBURY: WILLIAM HOWLEY] Df.A.L. 4p.

Aug. 11 [*Place not stated.*]
[A draft copy of the first portion of item 282.]

[285] W[ILLIA]M ROWAN TO ARTHUR: L.S.

Aug. 15 *Mily. Secy's. office, Quebec.*

I have the honor to acquaint you in reply to Your Excellency's letter of the 6th Ultimo, that the Commander of the Forces regrets he cannot comply with your request to sanction the employment of a Clerk in the Assistant Military Secretary's office at Toronto, with the pay of 7/ a day and allowances— His Excellency will, however, authorize the temporary employment of a Military Clerk, with the usual allowance of 1s/5d per diem.

[286] COLBORNE TO ARTHUR: L.S. 9p.

Aug. 16 *Head Quarters, Sorel.*

With reference to my communications to Your Excellency upon the subject of the Troops that may be considered necessary for the occupation of certain Districts, in consequence of the extent of the supposed disaffection in Upper Canada, and the menaces of the Refugees in the United States, I have the honor to acquaint you that if the information I have acquired can be depended on, I am of opinion that it will be for the advantage of Her Majesty's Service, and for the Province to reduce every description of Militia Force, with the exception of the Companies which I have recommended to be formed for the frontier duties of the St Lawrence, and the Niagara, and Western Districts—

The Townships on the Western frontier having been so frequently menaced, it may be difficult to prevent occasional alarms in the settlements on the St Clair, exposed to the sudden incursions of American Marauders associated with the Canadian Refugees in Michigan— I have therefore ordered five Companies of the 34th. Regt to remain at Amherstburgh, from which Corps, a Detachment will be sent to Sandwich under the Command of a Subaltern Officer; and I have requested Captain Sandom to station a Gun Boat at Windsor, or Sandwich with two Pinnaces attached to that Vessel, for the service of the water frontier of the St Clair and Detroit—

The two Companies which you directed to be formed for the protection of the Western frontier, I think should be placed under the control of Colonel Airey, and stationed at Amherstburgh; Sandwich, Windsor, and in the Townships of the St Clair at Plympton, Sarnia, and Sutherlands Wharf—

In all these Townships the Settlers are much dispersed, but so able and willing to protect themselves that I should recommend arms to be given to them— I have directed the Old Fort at Amherstburgh to be repaired, and armed for the reception of the Militia, on an emergency; and Barracks to be built; and a Company of 100 rank & file of the 34th. Regt to be stationed at Chatham where Barracks will be built for that number of Men—

The Troops stationed in the Niagara District, with the Company of Volunteers to which I have alluded in a former letter for the duties of the Ferries, will I have no doubt be found a sufficient guard in all cases which it is probable may occur on that frontier. The locks of the Rideau Canal, and dams, which could be injured without incurring any great risk by gangs of Marauders from the St Lawrence might be protected by posts occupied by small Guards from the regular force stationed at Kingston, Brockville, or By-Town[.] I have directed the Commanding Engineer to prepare block Houses, without incurring any great expense at Kingston Mills, Jones Falls and at the White fish dam. [In item 287 these three places are numbered consecutively in pencil in the text, and a marginal pencil note reads:

	"Cap.	sub.	Sgts	Rf
x	1 .	1 .	3 .	35
2			1 .	12
3			1 .	8."]

The Company which Colonel Turner formed, with my sanction, at Cornwall at the period of great alarm, after the burning of the Sir Robert Peel appears in very good order. I should recommend that Company to be kept on permanent duty for the posts on the St Lawrence; and with the Glengarry Company now at Prescott, or any other Company which might be raised, should I think occupy the detached posts of Gannanoqui [*sic*], Prescott, and Cornwall— Every other description of Militia Force that may be now on duty on the St Lawrence should be disembodied— Brockville will be occupied till further orders by a Detachment of the 71st. Regt.

The Buildings, which I understand have been hired, at Hamilton, will not be required, nor any Houses not mentioned in the return of the Respective Officers as intended for permanent Quarters. . .

[P.S.] The objection which has been made to employing independent Companies as respects their discipline, might be removed by placing them under the control, and constant superintendence of the Field Officers of the Line stationed on the frontier.

The merit and claims of Colonel Kingsmil[l], and Colonel Hill, and their wishes are so well known to Your Excellency, that, I shall only mention that I am most anxious to promote their interests; and recommend their cases to your favorable consideration, should any opportunity occur of employing them; but I hope I succeeded in persuading them, that, the public could reap no advantage from raising the Militia Corps, which were at one time intended to be formed, nor their interests be essentially advanced by retaining them in a temporary Command.

[287] COLBORNE TO ARTHUR: L. 4p.

Aug. 16 *Head Quarters, Sorel.* [Marked "Copy—"]

[Another copy of item 286, attached to items 266 and 280.]

[288] G[EORGE] COUPER TO ARTHUR: A.L.S. 2p.

Aug. 16 *Quebec.*

This will be conveyed to Your Excellency by the Wife of Benjamin Waite [*i.e.* Wait], and the daughter of Samuel Chandler, two of the prisoners condemned to death, for High Treason, in Upper Canada.

These women have come to Quebec to supplicate Mercy for those Prisoners, and a despatch upon their cases will be forwarded, this Night, by Special Messenger, from the Governor General to Your Excellency, to request that no Executions shall take place upon the late convictions for High Treason, in Upper Canada, without from [*sic*] His Lordship—

[289] G[EORGE] COUPER TO ARTHUR: A.L.S. 2p.

Aug. 16 *Quebec.*

[Another copy of item 288, but with the final phrase altered to read: "without further communication from His Lordship—" Concerning this correction and the substitution of this copy of the letter for item 288, see items 291 and 292.]

[290] W[ILLIA]M ROWAN TO ARTHUR: L.S. 2p.

Aug. 17 *Mily. Secys. Office, Quebec.*

I have the honor by direction of the Commander of the Forces, to acquaint you, that he cannot sanction the appointments to which Your Excellency refers in your letter of the 2d. Instant; nor the issue of Pay, or Allowances to any officer, not authorized by The Secretary at War, except to the Assistant Military Secretary, who was appointed with a View of hastening the payment of the Militia Claimants, but who must necessarily be discontinued as soon as possible, the appointment not being provided for in the List of Staff Officers furnished by The Secretary at War, for the twelve months, ending 31st March 1839.

[291] [F. L. ARTHUR][1] TO [GEORGE COUPER]: Df.L. with emendations in Arthur's handwriting. 2p.

Aug. 19 *Cornwall, Upper Canada.*

The Lieutenant Governor who is just now pressingly engaged has desired me to acknowledge your letter of the 16th. Inst. which was presented to him this morning by the wife of Benjamin Waite [*i.e.* Wait].

[1]This unsigned and unaddressed draft letter is obviously in reply to item 288. It is in the handwriting of F. L. Arthur, Sir George Arthur's aide de camp. It was probably sent

[The following paragraph is here deleted: "His Excellency being exceedingly occupied this evening and desirous you should obtain an answer to your communication as speedily as possible has directed me to reply to it."]

From the tenor of yr communication His Excellency scarcely knows whether to consider it as a private or official letter [the following passages are here deleted: "or to acknowledge it as an official communication.

The Lieutenant Governor is inclined to think from the style in which you have commenced yr letter that you have wished to address him privately at the request of Mrs. Waite, but at the conclusion of your letter you state 'that His E. the Gr. Gl has directed that no further execution is to take place in U.C . without from his Lordship' the expression of which is very different from and much stronger than the tenor of His Lds. Despatch to the Lt Governor which His E. has received this day from His L. respecting the cases of Waite and Chandler—

Considering it therefore as a private communication His Excellency has not adverted to your letter in his reply to the Govr. Genls. Despathe (*sic*) on this subject.

On a reperusal of your (*sic*) you have inadvertently left out a word"] if the latter the word which has been evidently omitted by mistake is important & He will be much obliged to you to supply it—moreover the whole of the last passage conveys an intimation beyond any expression included in the official despatch from the Govr Genl[;] perhaps it was intended as a private note, but, if so, the L Govr cannot exactly catch your object in addressing Him merely to say that an official Letter had been forwarded to Him by the same oppy—

I enclose you an exact Copy of your letter wh. you will observe commences as a private note & terminates officially—[2]

The Lt Govr defers answering Lord Durham's Dispatch until He reaches Prescott when He expects to find some Letters from Toronto.

The Lieut Governor is now prosecuting his tour of the Eastern part of the Province and intends proceeding to the Western Frontier after remaining a few days at Toronto.

[292] G[EORGE] COUPER TO COLONEL [FREDERICK] HALKETT: A.L.S. 4p.

Aug. 20 *Montreal.*

I hasten to acknowledge your Note of yesterday, & to remedy the inexcusable omissions of my letter to Sir George Arthur of the 16th. Instant.— Lord Durham's Official despatch of that date entered fully into His Lordship's views of the subject of my letter, and it is therefore to be considered of a private Nature— It was in fact given to the two

as coming from him. It did not go from Halkett, Arthur's military secretary, because item 306 (in the same handwriting) refers to "your note addressed to Colonel Halkett in reply to my letter."

The question of authorship is not without interest. Arthur has elsewhere shown some sign of his regard for the observance of the proper channels for official communications (item 306).

What appears to have happened is that when an important communication like item 288, involving a direct instruction on high policy, came from Couper, Durham's military secretary, and not from Durham himself, and when the document was conveyed by a woman and delivered to Arthur by her, Arthur then deliberately replied to Couper through his aide de camp. Couper in return replies not to the aide de camp, but to Halkett, Arthur's military secretary (item 292).

[2]It begins "My dear Sir" and terminates "I have the Honor to be Sir Your Excellencys Most obedient Humble Servant G. Couper." In the revised copy (item 289) Couper changed "I have the Honor to be Sir" to read: "I have the Honour to be My dear Sir".

women, who took charge of it, chiefly with a view to satisfy them, as it would not have been expedient to entrust them with any more official document.—

I should feel obliged by Sir George Arthur permitting the enclosure to be substituted for its erroneous original—

We moved here this morning with Sir Colin Campbell and Sir Charles FitzRoy, and I believe we shall return to Quebec tomorrow Night[.]

We passed yesterday at Sorel with Sir John Colborne, who will return to England in about 6 weeks, in H M Ship Inconstant. . .

[P.S.] I address this to His Excellency that he may read it should you be out of the way.

[Cover wrapper endorsed in Couper's handwriting: "Should Colonel Halket(t) be out of the way, Colonel Couper requests that Sir George Arthur will do him the favour to peruse the enclosure".]

[Enclosure first referred to is apparently item 289, intended to be substituted for item 288.]

[293] CHA[RLE]S BULLER TO [ARTHUR ?]: A.L.S. 4p.

Aug. 21 *Quebec.* [Marked "Private".]

I beg to acknowledge the receipt of your letter of the 13th. & to return you Col. Kingsmill's letter, which you enclosed to me. It is indeed most Satisfactory. Ld. Durham continues to receive representations of the mischief of Orangeism & of the irritation aroused among the Catholics by it. Whatever may be the object of Mr. Gowan, the effect must be to produce such irritation. And I do not think his actions very much in accordance with his words. If the Institution be not designed to keep up religious animosities why assume a false bad name? If the Reformers were to call themselves Jacobins, nobody would attach much credit to their private assurances that they meant not Revolution but Reform.

But whatever the object of the Orangemen the organization of their Society is equally condemnable & mischievous. It would be wrong to seek the best public objects by affiliated Societies, & secret oaths. A Temperance Society so constituted would be a public nuisance.

Ld. Durham is at the Montreal races, whence he returns on Thursday or Friday; so that you will not be very far from each other. I am quite re-established, except being still weak.

[294] ARTHUR TO COLBORNE: LB.1, p. 58-61.

Aug. 22 *Kingston.*

I have had the pleasure to receive your letter of the 17th. Instant with its enclosure from Major Webbe,—it will give me great satisfaction to attend to your wishes respecting this officer, or in any other way—but Major Webbe has not stated the case distinctly— Your recommendation is that one Company should be kept up on the Niagara Frontier, and the question is, who shall command that company?

Before you went to the Westward it was your request that Captain Egan's company should be retained on duty at Fort Erie—therefore orders were issued accordingly, although, I believe Captain Eagan [*sic*] to be by no means a well qualified officer, and consequently, I directed that it should be distinctly understood that the appointment should only be temporary.

After your return from Niagara, Major Webbe called upon me, and strongly urged upon me, that it was your kind wish towards him, that if no Field officer were employed, he should have command of a Company; in reply, I told him if a Field Officer were employed no person would I was persuaded perform the duty better than himself—but, it scarcely appeared to me just, that he should have a company to the prejudice of the Captains,—nevertheless, if it were your desire, I would readily accede to it, especially, as it appeared Colonel Booth took an interest in the matter. This, then, is the true point which Major Webbe should have proposed in his letter to you. The next applicant is Captain Palmer, and he strongly urged upon me your kind intentions towards him. He is I believe an attentive and very good officer, and with reference to former services has the strongest claim if Major Webbe's rank be considered a decided objection.

The only doubt I have with respect to the appointment of either is the new disposition you have made of the Troops; and if the 43rd and 34th. Regiments continue in their present positions, which I most earnestly and fervently pray they may not from the great moral evil desertion entails upon the Province it may not be necessary to keep the two militia companies on the Western Frontier—and, in this case, one of them might hereafter be removed to Niagara.

My present opinion is that a very great change has taken place in the public mind, and, although I have no confidence whatever that the disloyal section will become reconciled to British Institutions, or, that the Americans will cease to pursue the game they have so long had in view, yet the firmness of the Loyal Inhabitants can no longer be doubted, and their majority is quite triumphant.

I experienced the greatest disappointment in your having left the Upper Province without paying me your promised visit—there were many subjects which I was most anxious to have conferred with you upon—and this I feel the more since I learn from Colonel Phil[l]potts that it is your determination to leave Canada in a few weeks; which I sincerely believe to be a very great public calamity, and moreover personally, I lament it most deeply.—

I am on the point of proceeding through the Interior to Peterborough and on my arrival at Toronto on Monday next, I will reply to your official letters.

[295] [Arthur] to Colborne: LB. 1, p. 49.

Aug. 22 *Kingston.*

[Another copy of the first portion of item 294, cancelled by being scored through.]

[296] Colborne to Arthur: A.L.S. 4p.

Aug. 22 *Sorel.*

Notwithstanding my determination not to embarrass you with petitions for employment, I cannot refuse to bring before you the claims of several of my old friends and acquaintances residing in your Province.

I have already taken the liberty of mentioning to you the services of Colonels Kingsmill and Hill, and Major Webbe, and Captain Creighton. These Officers, and Major Browne of Cobourg, are all desirous of military employment, if they could obtain it in the Militia Corps, that they understood were to be raised for the protection of the frontier,—and I believe were amongst the first who came forward at the commencement of the disturbances in Upper Canada, with Volunteers in aid of the Government.

I think, however, from my conversation at Niagara with Colonel Kingsmill, that he appeared convinced that his being placed in the command of a Corps would prove ultimately disadvantageous to his interests; but he hopes you will have an opportunity of removing him from the Collectorship of Port Hope, and giving him a more agreeable appointment. I am confident that you will find him an active and useful Officer in any situation you may be able to place him— I promised Major Magrath of the Lancers, to mention his name to you. He and his Brother have been always zealous supporters of the local government since they have been in this Country.

I have received several applications from Colonel Hartwell of Brockville to be employed— He was the first Officer of Militia who offered to march to Lower Canada with his Regiment.

With many apologies for this intrusive letter of recommendations[.]

[297] [ANONYMOUS]: TO ARTHUR:

[*1838*] [*Postmark: Queenston.*] [Wrapper marked: "Johnsons Creek Augt 24".]

[*Aug. 24*] [A sheet of crude, coloured drawings intended to represent "A Chart of the Tirents doom in Upper Canada to take place in 1838". The drawings have as inscriptions: "the Radical Glory and Vitory Gained"; "Yanky power that will spoil and distrow peticoat Goverment within three years"; "Governor G Arthur quartered and food for dogs"; "descected for the Hogs"; "the Judges that Killed Lont & Mathew stretching Hemp"; "Governors Son In Chains"; "Jail and Cort House Set on Fire by the Rath of God"; etc.]

[298] W[ILLIA]M ROWAN TO ARTHUR: L.S. 2p.

Aug. 27 *Mily. Secys. Office, Quebec.*

Having had the honor to submit to the Commander of the Forces Your Excellency's letter of the 9th. Instant, with its enclosures, relating to a claim for Pay as a temporary Provincial Commissariat Officer preferred against the Government by Mr. Holland of Sandwich, I am directed to acquaint you that His Excellency thinks, that all demands for remuneration made by persons who held temporary appointments authorized last winter by the Lieutenant Governor of Upper Canada, must be decided on by the local Government, and paid from the proceeds of the Provincial Crown Revenue, or, referred to the Lords Commissioners of Her Majestys Treasury, for their Lordships decision.

Mr Holland's letter is returned herewith.

[Enclosure lacking.]

[299] E[DWARD] HAWKER TO ARTHUR: A.L.S. 6p.

Aug. 28 *Ashford, Petersfield, [England.]*

It is a good while since I wrote to you, but you have not been long out of my mind, or your dear family, who I hope have all joined you safe & well. The state of Upper Canada was quite different to what was expected when you sailed, & I conclude you have incessant employment & some anxiety, but not equal to what would be experienced by a *worldly* man; you know where to look at *all times* & *under all circumstances*; Affairs have a warlike appearance in your quarter still, but the fear is the *greatest* of a rupture between America & us upon the question of the boundary line, & a war would be disastrous to this Country in our *utterly helpless* state. The abandonment of our Navy will then be felt in its full force, for the United States would fit out their Navy, and man them quicker than we can ours; & chiefly with *our seamen* from the prospect of the *golden* harvest of prize money they wd. have; they wd. strew the Ocean with their privateers & might come into our Channel before we have any thing to oppose them so utterly destitute are we of every kind of force; besides the immense fleet Russia has in the Baltic, France is increasing her Navy fast & can put a very superior Navy into commission to ours; with all this we do not add to our Navy at all, & we have a miserable force every where in comparison to other powers. The infatuation of our Govt. & of the whole country seems extraordinary, we are preparing, as it were, to be *soundly beaten*, & are almost tempting other powers to go to war with us; & if war were to arise what would England say or do? Well! I hope it will please God to do for us more than we are *doing for ourselves*, while we know him to be an [*sic*] merciful God & Saviour, we know no harm can happen to his people eventually although they may be *tried*. I hope you will be able to keep Jonathan quiet & peaceable *near you*. but if it should be otherwise I feel assured that if we heard of a war with the U. States, we should hear *very soon* after of *Halifax being* taken by a couple of American line of battle ships & some smaller ships running into the harbor & just [?] landing troops; for there is *nothing* of consequence to prevent them, we ought not to be without a couple of 74s in *that* harbor not ships *without* their *lower deck guns*!!! England is in a complete *pickle* if a war were to take place! & so I will drop this unpleasant subject. There is a very respectable gentleman who farms a very large Estate near the Bayles's [?] Mr. King[;] we all feel an interest in him & his family[;] his brother Mr. Walter King lives at Mr. Hennings, Bognor Lodge, Guelph, in Upper Canada. I have told the Bayles's & Mr. King I wd. recommend this young man to you, if therefore you could promote his interest in any way it would gratify us, & we should be thankful if he had a commission in the Militia, if they were called out perhaps this might be of use to him. There is another person (to whose sister a Mrs. Wright a nice pious woman) I said I wd. mention him to you for *your Excellency's* notice. the name of the Gentleman *is Mr. James Watson* Commercial Bank Toronto... [Refers to a son going out with Col. Gawler; the prosperity of South Australia; the purchase of some land there.] I hope the climate of Canada agrees with you & yours, I shall enclose a note to Miss Leech. I hope she continues to give you satisfaction... [Sends remembrances and regards. Mentions Sir E. Williams going out to India.]

[300] [ARTHUR] TO DURHAM: L. 22p.

Aug. 29 *Government House, Toronto.*

In my communication of the 20th. Instant, marked "separate", I had the honor to acknowledge Your Lordship's Despatch No. 7 of the 16 Instant.

On considering that Despatch, my impression was, that the power of extending the Royal Clemency to a convict, of whatever offence proved to have been guilty, was distinctly vested in the Officer actually administering the Government; and it seemed to me, that Your Lordship's assuming that power, whilst Your Lordship was absent from the Province, was virtually depriving Upper Canada of Her Government; and that it would have the tendency of weakening, materially, the Executive authority in the Province; which, in times like the present, and particularly with reference to the crime of Treason, would be full of danger. Moreover, I contemplated the possibility of a difference of opinion in any particular case, either in favor of mercy or otherwise, which could not fail to produce great embarrassment, or painful consequences.—

These considerations, together with a reference to what must be expected to be the feeling of the Legislative Bodies with whom I have to act, and who would not fail to enquire with great strictness into any innovation upon the Constitution of the Province, and, most particularly, in respect to the administration of justice, induced me—whilst I informed Your Lordship that the sentence of death upon the convicts Chandler and Wait (the representation of whose cases had apparently been the occasion on which Your Lordship thought it necessary to communicate with me) had been ordered to be respited before I left Toronto—to request Your Lordship would excuse my delaying to reply to Your Lordship's Despatch until my return.—

I took the liberty of remarking what would be the effect of Your Lordship's interposition in this matter—that it indeed appears to deprive the Officer administering the Government of Upper Canada of a most important power expressly given under the Royal Commission—and I submitted to Your Lordship, that, from the whole tenor of the Correspondence of Her Majesty's Secretary of State with me, I was under the impression that Your Lordship had misapprehended those parts of Lord Glenelg's Instructions to which my attention was called by Your Lordship—in which I was the more confirmed by remarking, in the very passage of Lord Glenelg's Despatch which Your Lordship quoted, that, whilst Your Lordship was enjoined to pursue a certain line of Policy, the Secretary of State observed that the same course had been pointed out to the authorities in Upper Canada.—

In addressing my "separate" Despatch to Your Lordship, I confess I felt also that, to a certain extent, Your Lordship was practically (though I was sure unintentionally) encouraging complaints and endless appeals from this Province,—and it occurred to me, that it was possible, upon a full reconsideration of the subject, Your Lordship might not continue to be under the impression that you were obliged to interpose your decision, "in particular cases," and, I entertained the hope that Your Lordship might be induced to withdraw the instruction which I thought it possible had been induced by feelings of kindness and humanity towards the petitioners, without fully estimating the want of confidence it implied—the power it suspended—and the prejudice it worked in taking from the Officer administering this Government the uncontrolled exercise of the prerogative of Mercy, which is of particular importance at this moment.

The receipt, on my return to Toronto on Saturday the 25th. Instant, of Your Lordship's Despatch No. 8 of the 21st. Instant, dissipated this expectation; and, therefore, early on Monday the 27th. Instant, I convened the Executive Council to take into consideration the Report of Mr. Justice Jones on the prisoners who had been tried at Niagara, and, at the same time, I laid on the Council Table Your Lordship's Despatches Nos. 7 and 8 of the 16 and 21st August.—

After considering the cases of all the Convicts reported, and discussing the whole subjects at great length, the members agreed upon the advice which they thought it their duty to give; and the Council adjourned until this day, and then gave the opinion and advice embodied in the accompanying Minute.

Your Lordship will perceive, that, after considering the advice given, I directed that the sentences passed upon all the prisoners should be respited until the 1st. October, which will afford Your Lordship time to consider their cases.— The Report of Mr Justice Jones, and the petitions in favor of the prisoners, with such other information as is before the Council in these cases, which are the most pressing for decision, has been directed to be prepared to accompany this Despatch; and, as some of the Papers are original and important Documents, Your Lordship will I hope excuse my having detained Your Lordship's messenger to be the bearer of them.—

Upon the cases of the prisoners implicated in the original Revolt, who have not been unconditionally pardoned, I would beg to remark, that, on reporting them to Her Majesty's Government—, I suggested that it should be left in the power of this Government to exercise their discretion, so that up to the last moment of the Convicts remaining in this Province, a mitigation of sentence might be extended. This suggestion was necessary, because, at that time, I was not acting under Your Lordship's Commission, which enables the Officer administering the Government, in Your Lordship's absence, to pardon, even in cases of Treason—and, secondly, because the Act of the Provincial Legislature which has received the Royal approval, authorized the Lieutenant Governor to extend Mercy to petitioning prisoners, *only* with the advice of the Executive Council—and the Members (whose anxiety and desire to do what they considered was their duty in justice towards the Country, and in Mercy towards the Prisoners, I cannot too highly commend.) could not, with reference to the safety and tranquillity of the Province, at that time, bring themselves to advise any further extension of Clemency.—

Notwithstanding the Terms of the Provincial Act, to which I have alluded, I have no doubt the Officer administering the Government might extend pardon independently of the Council; but, when it is considered that they are all Gentlemen of great experience in the Canadas, and are extensively informed, as to its political relations, I have considered it prudent, that my proceedings should, if possible, be, in every important particular, supported by their unanimous advice.—

In my despatches of the 18th. and 27th. June Nos. 3 and 5, I stated to Your Lordship what my views and intentions were, respecting an extension of Mercy to a great number of prisoners— Continuing to entertain the same sentiments, I have endeavoured gradually to reconcile the Public Mind to that view of the subject, and where applications for pardons have been made to me, I have generally suggested, that, in order to warrant the Government in extending its Clemency, it would be desirable to procure the interposition of respectable and loyal persons in their behalf.—

On the receipt, therefore, of Lord Glenelg's Despatch No. 111 of the 12th. July last, I intimated to the Executive Council my desire again to go through all the cases of the prisoners under sentence, and requested their attention to the subject during my absence on a tour of Inspection; and, whilst I was recently at Kingston, I visited all the prisoners in the Fort, and in the Jail of that Town, and, indeed, in the Jails generally, in the Eastern Districts, and afforded each one of them an opportunity of bringing forward any additional favorable features in his case, with the view of fully preparing myself to carry into effect to the utmost, the wishes of Her Majesty's Government, so far, as it can be done with safety, and without giving occasion for strong remonstrances of dissatisfaction in the Province.—

I have not yet gone through the list of names which have in consequence, been under consideration in the Executive Council—and, although I think it proper to allude to the circumstance, I take it for granted that Your Lordship does not desire to restrain my powers of action in this proceeding, upon which Her Majesty's Secretary of State, has conveyed to me distinct authority.—

Your Lordship is already in possession of My Despatches of the 30th. of May and 7th. of June, to the Secretary of State, a copy of His Lordship's answer to them I have the honor to enclose, and I would simply observe upon it, that, even if it be possible that I am mistaken in the opinion I have formed, that it never was intended to take out of the hands of this Government the decision of such cases as those of Wait and Chandler; yet, Your Lordship will I am sure be disposed to admit, that the view I entertain, and have expressed in my Despatch marked "separate," might well be drawn from the Secretary of State's reasoning and instructions.—

[Enclosures lacking.]

[301] J. B. ROBINSON TO [ARTHUR]: A.L.S. 3p.

[*1838*] *Aug. 29*

[*Place not stated.*]

I am not sure that in considering the various applications for the vacant office below, the fact passed through your mind, that the place to be disposed of is that of "Register *for the County of Leeds*", and that Morris & Gowan both members representing the *County of Leeds* join in soliciting it for Jones—[1] I do not mean to intimate that as a matter of course such an interposition should prevail—but where the Members for the County are respectable in their public conduct, that is when they forbear giving a factious opposition to the Government I think it should have weight—upon the principle that their representing the County argues that they have the confidence of the people & are acquainted with the comparative merits & claims of their constituents generally— I am only afraid that you might regret not having given distinct consideration to this circumstance— I forget who is the third signer of the letter in favor of Jones.

[302] W[ILLIA]M ROWAN TO ARTHUR: L.S.

Aug. 29

Mily. Secys. Office, Quebec.

I have the honor to acquaint you, with reference to Your Excellency's letter of the 26th. Ultimo transmitting accounts from Mr. Lasher [?], and Mr. W Stewart of Brockville, that the Commander of the Forces

[1]David Jones, appointed Sep. 22, 1838.

recommends, that these claims (which are returned herewith) and any other of a similar nature, may be referred to the officers of the Commissariat, who are to be appointed to investigate, & report upon such claims, against the Government.

[Endorsed in Arthur's handwriting: "The My. Secy will attend to this 10 Sepr 38 GA".]

[Enclosures lacking.]

[303] W[ILLIA]M ROWAN TO ARTHUR: L.S. 2p.

Aug. 30 *Mily. Secys. Office, Quebec.*

Having had the honor to submit to the Commander of the Forces, your Excellencys letter of the 30th. Ultimo enclosing a Pay List for the Quarter Master General's Department attached to the Militia Force under the Command of Colonel A N MacNab, I am directed to acquaint you, that His Excellency does not think himself warranted in sanctioning the payment of this claim from the Military Chest—the appointments being temporary, & made under the Authority of the Civil Government.

The Pay list is herewith returned.

[Enclosure lacking.]

[Endorsed in Arthur's handwriting: "My. Secrty I thought that other appointments made under similar circumstances had been already paid under the authority of the Comdr of the Forces— I wish to know exactly how the matter stands—& I hope what I have all along wished has been attended to—viz—that no Staff Pay or Allowances have passed under my approval that have not been sanctioned by the Comdr of the Forces— 5 Sepr. GA".]

[304] J. B. ROBINSON TO [ARTHUR]: A.L.S. 3p.

[*1838*] [*Place not stated.*]

[*c. Aug. 31*] I think I should have preferred sending but one dispatch, & shd. have endeavored to make that exceed in length as little as possible the last letter of Ld. Durham— The Report of the Council reasons the Case, & a letter accompanying it might have touched shortly on those points on which Your Excellency wished to intimate expressly your concurrence in the report, leaving the other topics to stand as they do in the Report—

But perhaps your dispatches going more into particulars may be more satisfactory— I have ventured to suggest some changes in expression chiefly from the consideration that all these things seem destined to find their way into the Columns of the Newspapers, and one must therefore consider the probable effect of them on the multitude here— A single sentence or expression may serve as a text for illnatured & mischievous articles—

[The above probably concerns Arthur's despatches to Durham dated August 31st. See the *Dominion of Canada, report of the Public archives for the year 1923*, (*The Durham papers*), pp. 113-114.]

[305] J. B. ROBINSON TO [ARTHUR]: A.L.S.

[*1838*] [*Place not stated.*]

Sep. 3 I think it would be well to notice particularly the dispatch of 3d April—either in the report, where I have placed what I would suggest, or in one of Your Excellency's dispatches—

The dispatches of 3 Apl. & 12 July are only capable of being reconciled by giving to the former such a construction—.

[306] [F. L. ARTHUR] TO COLONEL [GEORGE] COUPER: Df.L. 2p.

Sep. 3 *Toronto.*

The Lieutenant Governor has desired me to acknowledge your note addressed to Colonel Halkett in reply to my letter and enclosing your revised letter respecting the cases of Waite [*i.e.* Wait] and Chandler, and which His Excellency will be most happy to substitute for the original which was presented to Mrs. Waite— These men have with all the other prisoners been respited till the 31st. Inst.

[307] W[ILLIA]M COX TO ARTHUR: A.L.S. 4p.

Sep. 5 *Toronto.*

I Have the Honor to Acquaint you, that from my residence at Whitby during the last six weeks, I have been enabled to observe that there is a very great want of that feeling of Loyalty that is to be desired.

It is evinced in various ways which perhaps trifling in themselves, are sufficiently indicatory of that bad feeling towards the Government that I have no doubt would be expressed more unequivocally were there an opportunity of displaying it.

The people of known Loyalty are annoyed in various petty ways, by injury to their property, such as pullg down small Huts [?] Offices, Gates, Fences &c, And in one instance within the last week, of maiming and cutting the Tail of a Horse belonging to Mr. Heathcote an English Gentleman residing at Whitby.

The Magistrates are averse (tho' instigated by me to do so) to take Any Active Measures to repress this Conduct, fearful that they themselves may be sufferers, they observe "they have no Assistance they can rely on" and there are no Constables in the Country.

This place, Also, from its facility of communication with the United States by the Harbour of Windsor requires the presence of a Military force of some kind, And I should beg to observe, that in my opinion, a force of at least twenty five Men, should be stationed here, under an officer having Magisterial Powers.

[308] ARTHUR TO [COLBORNE]: L. 6p.

Sep. 6 *Toronto.*

Have the kindness to excuse my apparent inattention in not having earlier replied to your private Letters.

Nothing can be more natural than that Persons residing in this Province should be desirous to ask for your support and patronage, and nothing more in unison with your universally esteemed kindly—I was going to say—"sympathising" but that is a word that will not do now adays—character than to assist those who so long served under your Government. Of course you know how limited are the opportunities of providing for the numerous applicants for Government Situations, but, you may rely on it, that I will not forget the claim of any Person whom you have recommended, and shall be most happy if it be in my power to be useful to them. I consider Mrs. Muttlebury's Sons to be the first on your list and have much regretted that I have never yet had an opportunity of doing anything for any of them. They stand first on my List for such offices as they can fill— The Son who was in the Army I propose to appoint to the Company serving on the Niagara Frontier if He will accept a Lieutenancy, but, I fear, He looks higher.

There has been a struggle for the Under Mastership of Upper Canada College, and I must say the qualifications of the applicants were very equal. Your recommendation in favor of Mr Henry Scadding turned the Scale on his side, and I have no doubt he will make a very valuable Master. As soon as I get over these present busy times, which entirely occupy Mind and Time, you may be satisfied that I will not forget the Interest you took in the College nor that which you have now expressed for the Under Master. I have heard him preach twice, and am far better pleased with his Sermons than some others I have heard in the same Church. Captain E [blank in MS. Name intended was probably Egan] company was first retained because you named it on the Niagara Frontier but he has been informed it is only pro tempore and I hope to be able to appoint Major Webbe according to your wish but I can scarcely say that I am quite satisfied it is right towards the Captains. If Webbe does not get it, then Captain Palmer, who was the next on your List, will succeed.

Of Colonels [blank in MS. Name omitted was probably Kingsmill], Hill, and Crighton [*i.e.* Creighton] all I can say is—that I shall be ever ready to admit their claims founded on your good opinion of them—& so I shall particularly of Major Magrath who is a most zealous Person, but, I fear, He is very angry with me about his pay and allowances and thinks if I would have recommended it you would have kept up his troop. These gentlemen have, of course, no notion of our responsibilities and make it a point to look a[t] every thing through another medium.

I regret much Mr. [blank in MS.] misfortunes but I do not know what I am to do for him.

Respecting Major [blank in MS.] & Major [blank in MS.] I make no promise.

Having disposed of your List I will only add—that in every case into which I have gone, referring to olden times, I find so much reason to regard your high principles of justice, with a[n] earnest desire to promote the best interests of the Province—that I do trust that the Legislature at their next meeting will communicate the same by a vote of a handsome Service of Plate—it is a tribute they owe you, which at least I shall take care shall not be forgotten. I am sorry I have not had the pleasure of more personal intercourse with you & will only add, that, in common with every other Soldier in the command, I sincerely regret your departure.

An unpleasantry has arisen respecting the Prisoners engaged in the late incursion and insurrection on the Niagara Frontier. You will recollect, I daresay, the first conversation I ever had with Lord Durham in your presence when he expressed his regret that the Banditti, as He called them, had not been punished in a more summary manner—they ought to have been put to death upon the spot &c &c. A few weeks appear to have made a great change in His Lordship's mind, & on the application of the families of "Chandler" & "Waite [*i.e.* Wait]," the Governor General wrote to me to say—that these were cases, he thought, of a political nature into which he was required to look and to decide upon by his Commission & Instructions. Knowing what will be the angry feelings of the House of Assembly & the Legislative Council upon this kind of interference with the administration of justice, &, in fact, upon the constitution of the Upper Province, I endeavoured to dfvert the blow which I am persuaded will give me a great deal of trouble hereafter; but, in vain, & rather than any controversy should be oi public notoriety between the Governor General and myself, I have sent all the cases to him & I sadly fear it will be the beginning of a boisterous Session. Ld. Durham has fallen into a like error with regard to to [*sic*] the Land question, having issued a Commission Himself & appointing Commissioners sent it to this Province to have the Seal affixed by his direction. I hear that these interferences have given great offence, especially, as the Home Government have so very recently placed all the Lands at the disposal of the Legislature of the Province & as the course pursued in both these matters is regarded as both illegal & unconstitutional on me, I suppose, will fall all the ire of our warmest Politicians. The Governor General possessing such extraordinary powers, & so much personal influence is not able to understand the difficulties which other men have to encounter & I am persuaded can scarcely make the allowances which are necessary in dealing with such a Legislature as I have to deal with—but enough of this!

I am very apprehensive, from all I hear, that we shall have further trouble again in the winter; but I think it will henceforth be attended with less confusion than heretofore with respect to our Militia arrangements— I propose revising the Militia Act, & preventing the Colonels from calling out their Men as they have authority to do at present.

Under your last recommendations I directed the reduction of all the Militia except the Companies which you named. Colonel Maitland & Colonel Chichester appear to think that there has been a misapprehension of your intentions & that it was your determination to keep up the Men enlisted by Colonel Maitland (about 100 men) in addition to the two Companies to be placed under Colonel Airey's orders at Amherstburgh— I have addressed an Official to you upon the subject.

I have inspected the 83rd. & 85th. Regts & on Tuesday I am going to inspect the 43rd. upon these I will report at once. I fear it will be impossible for me to inspect the 34th. Regt before I receive Lord Durham's answer respecting the Capital cases: but as soon afterwards as possible. You are not to leave us, I understand, for three weeks.

I need scarcely say that I have been obliged to write this with the pressure of business upon me that has left me but little time.

[The above is attached with items 232 and 270.]

[309] [J. B. Robinson] to [Durham]: A.L. 3p.

Sep. 6 *Toronto.*

In consequence of a most serious illness I have found it necessary upon the recommendation of the physicians who attended me to apply for Six Months leave of absence from my official duties; and His Excellency the Lieut. Govr. finding it so strongly pressed upon me as indispensible to my future health, has been so kind as to grant it—

It is my intention to proceed to England with part of my family in the Great Western Steamer on her next voyage[.]

I regret much on several accounts that a necessity for my absence should have arisen at this moment, as I should have been happy to have availed myself of the opportunity which it was your Lordship's intention to afford me of considering & discussing the measures to be proposed for the future Govt. of these Colonies & more particularly of Lower Canada.— I shall be in Toronto until the 26th. inst., and if I can in any way render service in promoting the objects of Your Lordships Mission it will give me much pleasure to do so—

I trust that upon further consideration Your Lordship has determined not to press those parts of the proposed measure which it is certain would be looked upon by the best informed persons in these Provinces with alarm & repugnance— To such changes in our Constitution I am convinced it will be impossible for the most intelligent & best disposed portion of the population ever to reconcile themselves, because they will feel no doubt that they must prove ruinous to the security & tranquillity of these Colonies—

I allude now to those points on which I took the liberty of remarking when Your Lordship did me the honor to refer to me—

It appears to me that if these are pressed they will lead to great excitement & perplexity, & will make it very improbable that any satisfactory result will be attained—

Your Lordship did not seem by any means resolved to adhere to them, & I sincerely trust that in these respects the scheme will be modified—

I should not have taken the liberty of troubling Your Lordship with these remarks but for the kindness shown by Your Lordship in explaining your views to me—

If my opinion is of any value it is but right I should acquaint Your Lordship that upon these points it continues to be the same as I have already stated it to be—

I repeat that if I can be useful to Your Lordship in any way in the arduous mission in which you are engaged I shall be happy to render the service—

[310] COLBORNE TO ARTHUR: A.L.S. 8p.

Sep. 7 *Sorel.*

I beg to thank you for your letter of the 22d Ult. I am aware that few of the number of applicants who have been recommended by me can receive any benefit from my patronage. As to their degrees of merit it is most difficult and embarrassing to decide on their relative claims on the local Government. But although I am convinced that not many of the Candidates for military, or civil employments can be provided for, you will concur with me in thinking that nearly all the Officers who have called for my aid in obtaining employment for them have a right to calculate on my good offices both as Soldiers and Settlers; with whom I have been long acquainted, and whose exertions zeal, and distresses, disappointments, and *very* bad circumstances are well known to me. With respect to the applications of Major Webbe, Palmer, Creighton, Ratcliff, and Warren; I understood that they all wished to be employed either as Field Officers or Captains of independent Companies. When at Fort Erie I mentioned to Dr. Egan that as many of his men who were inclined to volunteer to remain on duty, would probably be engaged as part of the force to be kept up on that frontier. No arrangement in respect to the Regiments or Companies had at that time been decided on, nor was I to suppose that he as a Medical Practitioner would be inclined to inlist—permanently— I am still of opinion that it is most desirable, and an arrangement almost indispensable, to station a Regiment of the line at Niagara, or Queenston, or at the Falls, and also another at Amhertsburg. If the Commanding Officers are active and can have the constant assistance of a Volunteer company from the Militia to look out for deserters and to watch the ferries, the desertions will not, after the worst characters have bolted, be more numerous than they are, or have been, at Kingston Toronto and Chambly. The 34th Regt lost 7 men at St Thoma's [*sic*]; and the 83rd suffer as much by desertion at Kingston as they did in the Western District. The 15th Regt I believe lost two hundred men in the Upper Province, chiefly from Toronto. Regular Troops on the frontier inspire more confidence, and are in fact much more efficient, moveable than Volunteers from the Militia good as they may be. The moral effect, as it concerns these Provinces I agree with you, is bad and lamentable, but it is an evil to which they have long been accustomed, 1600 men having deserted from six Regiments since 1830, and about, 5000 since 1815.— The Secretary at War has proposed a scheme of forming Battalions of Veterans composed of men who have served more than fourteen years; which I think will be immediately adopted.

I regret that I did not see you en passant. I should have enjoyed to have communicated all that I heard, and saw; but I must tell you that although I enjoyed my visit to the Upper Province, and received sincere pleasure from a renewal of my acquaintance with many persons for whom I have a regard, I was on many accounts glad to get out of your Province. The Inconstant, I expect from Bermuda in about three weeks to take me and mine home.

I feel obliged to you for your very kind expressions in reference to my departure from this land in which I have experienced so much to be pleased with, and to be disgusted.

I regret that circumstances compel me to give up this command; I think however I act *wisely* and prudently in making my escape from these Provinces in whose affairs and interests I am so deeply involved; that I can scarcely be denominated a Military Character free from political considerations—

If the Legislative Councils are to be abolished, or even that subject discussed, the effect in both Provinces will be ruinous—

In your application to the Colonial Office for a separate Commissariat you have alluded to my correspondence with Lord Gosford and Sir F. Head; and I can assure you the annoyance and the injustice I experienced from the selfish pertinacity of the one and the absurdity and measureless vanity of the other, and the apprehension of similar collisions with Governors who are, I believe, fully as sensitive as I am, touching military command would be reasons sufficiently strong to induce me to relinquish this command.

I have desired Colonel Rowan to send you my reply to the Treasury respecting the separate Commissariat establishment in Upper Canada; upon which subject I disagree with you. I hope you and my successor will be better able to decide on our rights and privileges than we are, without appeal.

I am confident that everyone that will take the trouble to examine my letters to Sir F Head will be persuaded that the military state of the Province, and the danger of the moment demanded my interference.

I rejoice to hear that the accounts of the health of the Chief Justice are very favorable. I shall hear with regret that he is obliged to go to England; at this time. He is the most able, and decidedly the *most honest* person in office on this side of the Atlantic; and a Gentleman whose talents and influence will be called into play more than they have been, before the projects for the future Government of these Colonies are carried into effect.

[311] W[ILLIA]M ROWAN TO ARTHUR: L.S. 3p.

Sep. 7 *Mily. Secys. Office, Quebec.*

As the exigency no longer exists which induced the Commander of the Forces, to assume the responsibility of authorizing the temporary employment of an Assistant Military Secretary, to facilitate the payment of the Militia and Volunteers of Upper Canada, & other outstanding claims, which had caused much discontent in that Province; and, a great portion of those claims being now adjusted, & the remainder in the course of settlement by Boards of Commissariat officers, & the persons attached to the Mily. Secys. office at Head Quarters, I have the honor to acquaint you, that His Excellency Sir John Colborne, does not feel warranted, under present circumstances, in continuing an appointment which is not included in the List of Staff Officers provided for, upon the Establishment of this Command, for the twelve months ending the 31st. of March 1839, which has been received lately from The Secretary at War— I am directed to request therefore, that Your Excellency will have the goodness to inform Captain Halkett, that the Commander of the Forces regrets, it will not be in his power to avail himself of his services as Assistant Military Secretary after the 30th of September instant.—

[312] [ARTHUR] TO [COLBORNE]: L.

[*1838*] [*Sep. 8*] [The letter is lacking, but a précis entry in item 578 reads:] Sir G. A. 8 Septbr. Recommends a Subaltern's detachment at Whitby.— small detmts. for Simcoe & St. Thoma's [*sic*].— Wishes that a larger Militia Force had been kept on the Niagara & Western Frontiers.—

[313] [LORD] BLOOMFIELD TO ARTHUR: A.L.S. 2p.

Sep. 10 *Woolwich,* [*England.*]

Doctor O Brien, the Son of one of my oldest comrades & a particular friend, has fixed his tent at Thornhill, near Toronto. If you can render him Service by your protection & notice, I am sure you will— He is well spoken of in his Profession & indeed in every way.

I trust & hope that Lady Arthur and your Children have safely reached you & that your Career may each day be of satisfaction & prosperity. I should be a Monster if I did not love an Arthur; *Bygone times are not forgotten.*

[314] [LORD] BLOOMFIELD TO ARTHUR: A.L.S. 2p.

Sep. 10 *Woolwich,* [*England.*]

Mr. Ed. O Brien, the son of an old Comrade & one of my oldest friends too, being settled on Kempenfelts [*sic*] Bay Lake Simcoe I would ask your notice of him: He is an old Officer, of long Service in both the East & West Indies. I have this day written to you in behalf of his Brother an M.D. My wishes, and anxious ones they are, follow you in all Climes & in all your Undertakings.

[315] DURHAM TO ARTHUR: A.L.S. 4p.

Sep. 16 *Quebec.* [Marked "Confidential".]

I enclose open my answer to the Chief Justice, that you may read it, & be aware of the alteration which I have made in my original plan, in compliance with what seems to be generally wished.

I have stated the scheme thus amended to the Deputations from Nova Scotia & Prince Edward's Island, & have received their warm assent. I expect the Deputation from New Brunswick the end of this week.

I beg you to be kind enough to seal up the enclosed letter, after you have perused it, & direct it to be forwarded to the Chief Justice.

Its contents of course may be *confidentially* communicated to whomsoever you please.

When the plan is fully drawn out I will forward Your Excellency a copy to be then *made public* in any way you may deem most advisable[.]

[Enclosure is apparently the original of item 316.]

[316] DURHAM TO J. B. ROBINSON: L. 4p.

Sep. 16 *Castle of St. Lewis.* [Marked "Confidential".]

I regret extremely to find that I shall be deprived of your highly valuable assistance in the preparation of the important measures for the future government of the North American Colonies, which I am commissioned to submit to the consideration of Her Ms Ministers, and more specially from the cause which occasions your absence.

I sincerely hope you will derive every possible benefit to your health from your excursion to Europe.

It is not my intention to propose any change in the Provincial Constitutions. The Legislative Councils therefore in each Colony will remain as at present. All therefore will be gain to them—they will have the additional privileges of sending ten Members to the General Assembly and two to the Imperial Parliament. I should propose also that the Members of the General Assembly should be elected by the constituent body, under proper regulations, and *not* by the Provincial Legislatures.

You will see that I have not pressed any of the points to which you apprehended objection and that I have sufficiently shown my desire not to force my own opinions against the settled conviction of those who from their position have a right to command respect and consideration.

[Endorsed "Copy . . ."]

[317] DURHAM TO J. B. ROBINSON: L. 2p. In Robinson's handwriting.

Sep. 16 *Castle of St. Lewis.*

[Another copy of item 316.]

[318] JOHN EDEN TO ARTHUR: L.S.

Sep. 18 *Deputy Adjutant General's Office, Quebec.*

I have the honor to inform your Excellency that as the services of Lieut. Griffin D.A. Adjt. Genl. will be required in Lower Canada, it is the wish of the Commander of the Forces that he should proceed to Montreal, as soon as he has made the arrangements which have required his return to Toronto.—

[On the reverse side appears item 330.]

[319] [ARTHUR] TO [COLBORNE]: Df.A.L. 4p.

[*1838*] [*Place not stated.*]
[*c. Sep. 20*] Your Excellencys Mily Secretary has forwarded to me, by your command, copy [of] a Letter which you had addressed to the Secretary of the Treasury in reply to a reference made to Yr Excellency by the Lords Commssrs of Her Majesty's Treasury upon a communication wh., as Lieut. Governor of Upper Canada I had addressed to the Secy of State upon the subject of the Commisst. Department[.]

Your Excellency from your long acquaintance with Colonial business is of course aware that the Standing Regulations for the guidance of Governors of Colonolies [*sic*] require that the Officer administering a Govt shall address the Secretary of State upon every important subject to whatever Depart of Govt. that subject may refer. The extreme mischief which I had daily before my eyes with reference to the Militia & to the adjustment of the accounts of Civilians led me therefore to suggest to the Secy of State what appeared to me to be a remedy for that mischief.

I do not doubt that during the peaceable period of Sir John Colborne's administration of this Govt that no inconvenience or disadvantage was found to exist from the System on wh. the Commisst Depart was carried on; but, at a more stirring period, I beg to assure His Excy that the utmost inconvenience to the Public Service resulted from there being no superior officer of the Commsst. Deprt. in charge at Toronto & from the necessity of all the delay incident to constant reference to an officer stationed at a distance of between 4 & 500 Miles from the Scene of operations.

His Excellency, I am persuaded after one moments reflection [sentence incomplete.]

When His Excellency reflects that for the last five months I have been in the Constant habit of carrying into execution His orders & instructions; and that I have been equally in the habit of referring for his authority all directions upon the minutest points of Military duty, He will make some allowance for the surprize I feel that His Excellency shd. have stated to the Lords of the Treasury that I have supposed myself to have been appd. to an independent Military command.

Certainly on being sent out to administer the Civil Govt. of this Province Her Majestys Govt were pleased to recommend to the Genl Cmdg in Chief that I shd. be appd. a Major General on the Staff for the purpose of commanding the Troops in Upper Canada; but, on this account, I never doubted for one moment that, on all Mily points, I was under the orders of the Comr of the Forces, and I request you will do me the favor to assure Sir John Colborne that it gives me deep & unaffected concern that he shd. have entertained Himself or felt it necessary to convey a different impression to the Lords Cmr of H M. Treasury.

When Lord Durham was in Upper Canada I have a recollection that I mentioned to His Excy that I had recommended a separation of the Comist. Depart. to the Secy of State but I beg you will assure the Cdr of the Forces that I have never made any appeal to the Govr. Genl upon the Subject.

[Endorsed: "Dft to Sir John Colborne".][1]

[1]It is no part of the purpose of the present publication to attempt to gather together contemporary documents outside the *Arthur papers*. Nevertheless the commissariat question looms so large in the *Papers*, and, to Arthur, had such far-reaching influences upon the militia

[320] [Arthur] to [Colborne]: Df.A.L. 4p.

[*1838*] [*Place not stated.*]

[*c. Sep. 20*] I can scarcely convey to you how much it has distressed me to perceive from the Official Letter wh. I have received from your Mily Secy with its enclosure to the Treasury & from your private Letter to myself that you are hurt to [*sic*] my having submitted to the Secty of State my views respecting the Comsst Dept[.]

On reflection, I hope you will see that, deeply involved as the interests of so many Individuals in this Colony were at the state in which I found things on my arrival in the Province, that I could not do otherwise than submit to the Secty of State where much of the evil lay according to my view of it—and which view, right or wrong, I entertain as strongly as ever. But I have looked at it as it regards Colonial & Public interests & not as a mere Military question, & if I were disposed to be tenacious which I can truly say I am not, I might certainly take an exception to a communication originating in a Dispatch to the Secy of State being so forwarded to me through your Mly Secy[.]

---

turn-out, that it seems very inadequate to let the above document stand alone. This document may have been a first draft of an "official" to Colborne, later dated September 20th, 1838. But the ultimate despatch is so much more comprehensive that an exception seems justified in reproducing it here by courtesy of the Dominion Archivist, along with Colborne's despatch to the Treasury dated August 31st, 1838, which gave rise to it.

1838
Aug. 31

Colborne to A. Y. Spearman.

Head Quarters, Sorel. [Marked "*Copy* No. 118".]

With reference to your letter of the 30th. of May, upon the subject of a Separate Commissariat Establishment for Upper Canada for which Sir George Arthur has applied, I have the honor to acquaint you, for the information of the Lords Commissioners of Her Majesty's Treasury, that, having been nearly eight years Lieutenant Governor of Upper Canada, and during that period a Major General on the Staff, I am enabled to assure you, from my experience, that no inconvenience or disadvantage whatever, resulted from one Commissariat Establishment only being authorized in Canada; and that I entertain no doubt that the irregularities and confusion that occurred last Winter in the Commissariat arrangements of the Upper Province, originated in the temporary suspension of the Control of the Commissary General, when the local Government necessarily called on the Assistant Commissary General at Toronto to make imprests from the Military Chest on his own responsibility.

My correspondence with Lord Gosford and Sir Francis Head, alluded to in the extract of Sir George Arthur's Despatch to Lord Glenelg, had reference to the relative duties of Civil Governors, and the Commander of the Troops; but, Sir George Arthur, in his capacity of an Officer serving under my immediate orders, solicits Her Majesty's Government to establish a separate Commissariat in Upper Canada. It appears, therefore, that he has fallen into the error of supposing that he has been appointed to an independent Military Command. and I am confirmed in this opinion, from the appeal upon this subject which I understand he has made to Lord Durham.

The inconvenience which might result from adopting Sir George Arthur's proposition will become more evident by my Stating, that, should the menaces of attack on the frontier, which have occasioned lately so much alarm, be renewed, the Commander of the Forces in Canada would probably fix his Head Quarters in the Upper Province, or find it necessary to order a General Officer from Montreal with reinforcements to proceed to the Western Districts.— In either of these cases a separate Commissariat, or another direct Accountant, would render the business of that Department more complicated.—

With respect to the Individuals who, in a moment of exigency, furnished supplies and transport, you will learn from Colonel Foster's Communications, that the Complaints, that their demands remained unpaid, were strongly

When you addressed the Secy of State upon the subject of the B[arrac]ks in this Province, I am certain it never entered your mind that you were unduly interfering with the Genl Officer Commdg in Canada and yet the cases are quite parallel[.]

Most of all, it concerns me that you shd. have fancied that I have been setting up for an independent command, because I can truly & sincerely say that I have made it my study [the words "most scrupulously" are here deleted] not only to obey all yr orders as a matter of duty but as a source of pleasure to myself, and until I perused your Letter to the Treasury wh. upon this point is, I must say, much calculated to mislead their Lordships my apprehension was that you wd. think not that I had set up for Mily independence but that I had pestered you too much upon Military points which ought to have been acted upon without troubling you. Upon this point I have been so scrupulous having even hesitated to act upon the general authority which you gave me in one or two of your Letters that I shd have supposed it impossible I could have been open to such a misconstruction of feeling

---

represented, before the Commissary General interfered with the disbursements of the local Government, or attempted to check the expenditure by demanding proper Vouchers.—

In fact, the transition from perfect tranquility to disturbance and revolt was so sudden, that the defective arrangements could not have been remedied by a separate Commissariat.—

Boards were formed at an early period, to investigate the claims to which Sir George Arthur adverts, and I believe that most of the demands that could with justice be allowed, have been liquidated.—

The rush of volunteers from the interior of the several Districts to the Water Frontier continued for some weeks, and on their arrival at the several stations, they were generally supplied by irresponsible Commissaries, appointed by the Magistrates; and Tavern Keepers and Farmers on the road were called upon to furnish them with provisions and transport without limitation.— Accounts of such a description cannot be speedily settled; but boards of Claims have been constantly employed in settling the outstanding charges, and the Officers of the Commissariat who have been appointed to the unthankful and laborious office of examining those Accounts Vouchers, have performed their duty with zeal and diligence.—

1838
Sept. 20

ARTHUR TO COLBORNE.

Government House, Toronto.

The Military Secretary has transmitted to me a Copy of a letter which Your Excellency has addressed to the Lords Commissioners of Her Majesty's Treasury, in reply to a Communication from their Lordships founded upon a Dispatch which I addressed to the Secretary of State in March last, recommending a separate Commissariat Establishment for Upper Canada.—

As I made that Communication to Her Majesty's Government as the Lieutenant Governor of this Province, according to the Rules and regulations for the guidance of Governors, &c, under the head "Correspondence" [marginal note here reads "See Page 83".], Your Excellency will, perhaps, concur with me that the observations which I wish to make upon the subject will most properly be addressed to yourself.

Your Excellency, if I understand your communication to the Treasury Correctly, conveys the opinion—that as no inconvenience nor disadvantage whatever, resulted from one Commissariat Establishment only being Authorized in Canada during the eight years your Excellency administered the Government, there can be no occasion for the alteration which I have recommended, and from my having done so, it appears that I have fallen into the error of supposing that I have been appointed to an independent Military Command—in which opinion your Excellency expresses yourself to be Confirmed, from the appeal which you understand I have made upon the subject to Lord Durham.

or intention. Upon reflection I hope you will think I do not deserve the imputation. Certainly on being appointed [sentence incomplete.] I have no conception to what you allude respecting my having appealed to Lord Durham [the words "respecting the Commst" are here deleted]— I have made no appeal whatever to His Lrdp.— When He was Here Lord Durham enquired of me whether there were any arrangts. He could facilitate that I wished to have carried into effect, & amongst some other subjects I then alluded to the troubles & endless claims that existed & wh. I attributed to the Constitution of the Comisst. there being no Head of the Dept in this Province & mentioned that I had suggested an alteration to the Secy of State & there the subject dropped. I made no appeal to His Lrdp & if I had it wd. only prove that I was not merely looking at it as a Military question, but as one involving as it does in fact the general interests of the Province.

It is true I cannot bring myself to entertain the same opinion you have formed with regard to occupying the Niagara & Western Frontiers. I have discussed the matter with respectful deference although if any thing serious should result wh. I dread every day much of the responsibility will rest with me as administrator of the Govrt & I dread almost

---

Will Your Excellency permit me, in my own justification, to explain, that, because the system was not inconvenient nor disadvantageous during the period of profound peace, whilst Your Excellency administered this Government, it does not follow, that, in a state of things totally reversed the consequences might not be just such as I have represented.—

It would seem unnecessary to set about establishing this by many arguments, for it is apparent in almost every aspect of our affairs.— I will allude, therefore only to one— In one of Your Excellency's letters to Sir Francis Head in November last, when you thought it expedient to withdraw the 24th Regiment from Upper Canada, you remarked that "he did not incur the least risk or responsibility in trusting to the good feeling of the Province",—whilst, Your Excellency in a letter addressed to me on the 24th of March immediately after my arrival, remarks, "We shall require a respectable Regular Force in the Western, London, Home, and Midland Districts for some years",—and, again. on the 11th of July—"I entertain no doubt that it will be necessary to station a regular force of not less than four thousand men in this Province for some years".—

I do not mean to imply that there is the least inconsistency in these opposite opinions, but that a change of Circumstances may render a change of measures not only desirable but necessary.—

Of Course, I never intended to refer to the period to which Your Excellency alludes. I have looked at the working of the Commissariat Department just as I have found it within my own experience. The first Circumstance that struck me was, that, whilst such a mass of persons were so clamorous to be paid their various accounts for Teaming, Supplies, &c, Mr. Wilson who had been sent up by Mr Routh to proceed with the investigation of the Accounts, was checked at the very ou[t]set for want of Instructions, and obliged to proceed from the Western District all the way back to the Lower Province to Confer with Mr. Routh, and to get his Instructions enlarged; and this in the spring of the year when the navigation of the lakes was still closed, and the Roads were all but impassable.—

The consequence was, as Your Excellency observed in your letter to me of the 24th March, that "much discontent prevailed in the Western District in consequence of the claims on the Military Chest having remained for some months unsettled."—

The Officer in charge at Toronto, Mr. Foot, I found had been totally paralyzed in his operations and I can say with confidence, that I have not met one officer of the Commissariat Department who has not complained of the difficulty and embarrassment that frequently results [*sic*] from the delay of reference to the head of the Department—and, so far as the Public are Concerned, to this hour the utmost dissatisfaction exists, not only at individuals having been so long kept out of their money, but at the manner in which the accounts have been adjusted, which they consider most unjust.—

every day that there will be some unpleasant collision by the Americans tampering with our men to desert.

I have inspected the 83—85 & 43—& tomorrow I shall see the 32nd Rgt. Colonel Booth is doing every thing that is possible to prevent desertion. I have recommended His giving up the American Boat wh. He had seized, as, although it was no doubt engaged in a smuggling expedition there was no legal proof. Some of the Dragoons behaved extremely well in an endeavour to capture some Americans who crossed in the middle of the night on Tuesday to take off two men whom they had enticed to desert—one American was supposed to have been shot in the affair, but there was no certain information when I left Niagara.

The Barracks which was fitted up for 100 Men had been completed & handed over to the Barrack Master & immedly afterwards before the Military occupied it it was set fire to & burn[ed] to the Ground. Colonel Booth had no doubt it was intentionally distroyed [*sic*].— I intend to return to Niagara & see the Rgt again in the course of ten days, and at the same time I shall arrange with the Colonels of the three Militia Regs to select 200 Men from each Rgt to act, if occasion requires it, without the confusion & expense that has hitherto existed in turning out. I proceed to London to inspect the 32nd Rgt Tomorrow.

Their claims, they contend, should have been left to a Board or Boards equitably formed, and not to the sole decision of any Commissariat Officers.—

The extent which the feelings of the Loyal Inhabitants have been hereby estranged, is most painful, and if we have any further Military Operations in this Country, may be severely felt.—

Heavy, I am aware, has been the expenditure upon the Military Chest; but it has been nothing compared to the ruinous losses which have fallen upon the Public of all classes in the Province.—

When Your Excellency was penning your letter to the Secretary of the Treasury, it could not, I am sure have occurred to you, that the works which are now in progress in various parts of this Province are done by contract, and that at every stage almost, some reference is necessary under the existing system, to Commissary General Routh by the Officer of his Department, and I can state positively, that this is frequently accompanied with all the inconvenience and all the disadvantage which attends upon delay.—

With regard to the difficulty which your Excellency contemplated should the Commander of the Forces fix his Head Quarters in Upper Canada, I do not see how it can possibly arise.— All I urge is, that there should be a distinct Head of the Department in Upper Canada, who should give Instructions, and receive the Reports of the subordinate Officers in the Department in this Province, and I cannot perceive how a measure of this kind can produce any inconvenience whatever—on the contrary, the benefit which I Contemplate the Public interest, Colonial and Military, would derive, the Commander of the Forces would himself participate in under such circumstances.—

Your Excellency's representation to the Treasury, that I must suppose myself to be appointed to an independent Military Command, I am at a loss to understand.— The representation is certainly not consistent with the almost daily communications which I have been making to Your Excellency upon Military subjects, through the Military Departments, since my arrival in the Command, in which I have referred matters of ordinary detail for your consideration, and sought your Instructions and commands, from which I have in no instance deviated, to my knowledge;— Your Excellency, I am persuaded cannot have intended to convey the obvious meaning of the terms you have used.— Certainly, when the Civil Government was conferred upon me, I was appointed a Major General upon the Staff for the express purpose of Commanding the Troops in the Upper Province, but I never for a moment doubted, that I was subservient to the orders of the Commander of the Forces according to the spirit of the service, in all Military detail, whenever it did not clash with the higher Appointment which Her Majesty has been pleased to confer upon me.—

[321] [COLBORNE (?)] TO [ARTHUR]: L.

[*1838*]
[*Sep. 21*] [There is no letter of Colborne of this date. A précis entry in item 578 reads:] Sir J.C. 21st Sept. Suggests small guards for the Water Frontier of Plympton—Sarnia—Moore &c. [The entry probably refers to item 323, from Rowan.]

[322] W[ILLIA]M ROWAN TO ARTHUR: L.S. 2p.

Sep. 21 *Mily. Secy's. Office, Quebec.*

I have the honor to acquaint you with reference to your Excellency's letter of the 8th. Instant, that the Commander of the Forces still thinks that there can be no difficulty in disposing favorably of the claims of Officers who were authorized to act in any Department with the understanding that they were to receive Pay, provided that the Pay List is approved by Your Excellency, but Sir John Colborne objects to decide on any claims for remuneration, in cases, in which appointments have been made or continued without the sanction of the Lieutenant Governor of the Province.

The Claim of the officers of the Militia Qr. Master General's Department, is for Staff pay from the 9th. of December to the 31 of May 1838, without proper authority, or, the case would not have been submitted for the decision of the Commander of the Forces.

When the Earl of Durham was in this Province, his Lordship kindly enquired whether there were any difficulties in the working of my Government in which he could render me assistance. I remember in reply, amongst one or two other circumstances, adverting to the Commissariat, And mentioning to Lord Durham, that I had recommended that an Officer should be placed in charge of that Department in the Upper Province, which I thought would be attended with great facility and convenience to the Public Service; but I made no appeal whatever to his Lordship, although I do not doubt that had the Earl of Durham administered this Government only for one fortnight that he would have seen the practical inconvenience, not to the Troops only, but to this Community, to which I adverted, and would have concurred in my suggestion.—

There is no Officer whether in the administration of a Colony, or in the command of Troops, who does not know the value of the relief of having a Commissariat Officer of experience at hand, in whom the Lords of the Treasury repose Confidence, to Confer with on all points of difficulty, connected with expenditure of every kind—especially if it be of a mixed kind,—and the want of such assistance I have felt from the day I entered upon this Government down to the present hour. In the arrangement I proposed, I sought the good of the Public service in it's [*sic*] largest sense, in the administration of this Government— It never entered my mind to interfere with Your Excellency's Authority, any more than your Excellency, in addressing the Secretary of State upon the subject of the Barracks, intended to interfere with the Military Authority of the Senior Officer then commanding in Canada, or to cast the least imputation upon the zeal and ability of Commissary General Routh of whose talents I have the highest opinion, and believe, if any person could make the present system work, he would do it—but I am still persuaded the good of the Queen's service requires that an Officer of the Commissariat should be in charge of the Department in the Upper Province, whether his accounts are forwarded for examination to the Commissary General or direct to the Treasury.—

Arthur, in self defence, sent a copy of his despatch to the Treasury. The Treasury concurred in the desirability of "the most unreserved Communication on all subjects" with the government at home, and emphasized that there was no "reproof" of Arthur because his channel of approach had not been via Colborne. But Colborne's point of view was sustained, as that of the senior officer. There was to be no separate commissariat for Upper Canada. But see item 399.

[323] W[ILLIA]M ROWAN TO CAPT. [FREDERICK] HALKETT: L.S. 2p.

Sep. 21 *Mily. Secys. Office, Quebec.*

I am directed by the Commander of the Forces to acquaint you, for the information of Sir George Arthur, in reference to your Communication of the 9th. Instant, that His Excellency is of opinion, that small detachments of Volunteers will be required to be employed as Guards on the Water frontier of the Townships of Moore, Sarnia, and Plympton, to give confidence to the Settlers, and to relieve them from the necessity which they imagine exists of establishing Posts on the River St. Clair.

Colonel Chichester will be the best judge, from his being in that vicinity, what number of Volunteers may be required.

If the Settlers of those Townships retain their Arms and Capt Sandom has stationed a gun boat at Sutherland Wharf, it appears that we need not apprehend incursions from the Marauders.

[324] [ARTHUR] TO [COLBORNE]: L.

[*1838*]
[*Sep. 22*] [The letter is lacking, but a précis entry in item 578 reads:] 22nd Wishes for a second Company at Niagara.—

[325] ARTHUR TO DURHAM: LB.1, p. 61-63.

Sep. 22 *Government House, Toronto.*

Your Lordship has I am aware such a pressure of business upon you that I most reluctantly trouble you with a private note; but, conscious as I am of the depth of anxiety which you have manifested in the great objects which have induced you to undertake the Government of Her Majesty's North American Possessions, and of the solicitude which your Lordship has felt to restore stability and security to these tottering Provinces, I cannot see you so unjustly assailed as you have been by Lord Brougham without expressing the deep concern I feel, in common I believe with all classes of Persons on the occasion.

It is not possible to read Lord Broughams speeches without at once detecting that he is influenced—not by that ardent love of public justice and that anxious solicitude for the Liberty of the subject, of which he speaks—but by personal jealousy if not animosity towards Your Lordship.

There was not, I will be bound to say, one individual in these Provinces who ever thought for one moment that it was Your Lordship's intention to visit Papineau or any of his Gang with death—every one saw distinctly the end Your Lordship had in view, and the difficulty you had in accomplishing it, and were disposed to look at Your Lordships ordinance accordingly— The silence of the whole Press is a remarkable proof of this.

The first impulse of Your Lordships high spirit will be to resign; but I do trust you will not yield to it. The people in both Provinces ought immediately from every district to send in Addresses to Your Lordship, and, I hope that the Citizens of Toronto, will at once lead the way, upon which subject I have just been speaking to Mr Ellice. A Measure of this kind is very necessary to remove the injurious impression that may be made upon the disaffected Portion of the Community by the disallowance of the Ordinance.

It is not to be disguised that we are in a very critical position.

[326] ARTHUR TO DURHAM: LB. 6, p. 4-5.

Sep. 22 *Govt. House, Toronto.* [Marked "Private".]
[Another copy of item 325.]

[327] ARTHUR TO COLBORNE: LB. 1, p. 63-65.

Sep. 23 *Government House, Toronto.*

Your private letter of the 7th instant I received whilst I was on a tour of inspection, and perused it with great pain, for I perceived that you labour under the impression that I have been unnecessarily sensitive upon Military subjects. Upon the point of the stationing of the Troops on the Frontier, I have felt anxiety, and considered it to be a duty in the Administrater [*sic*] of the Government, to express the opinion I formed; but, I do assure you, I have not in any other respect felt sensitive upon the subject.— It is evidently difficult to decide where the exact line between the Military and Civil Authority should be run, and my earnest wish has been, to keep as wide of it as possible, and in bidding you adieu, I am anxious to assure you, that I would not intentionally have given you the slightest vexation or annoyance on my account.—

Upon the subject of the Commissariat, and I might add, the Ordnance Department also, I am confident you cannot be aware of the extent of inconvenience and delay that has taken place.— I could state instances without number, to prove the objection of the present system, and why the Lords of the Treasury have sent a Deputy Commissary General here, to do the duty which might equally be well done by a Deputy Assistant Commissary General, I cannot imagine.— If we have employment in both Provinces this Winter, as I believe will be the case, I have no doubt the result will make all I have said apparent enough.—

The worst of excitement has begun again on the Frontier— Many letters have reached me upon the subject, and there can be no doubt, I think, that a great quantity of arms have been collected at the Westward.— Mr Ellice, who has just come in from the States, confirms the statements which have been made from other quarters, of the general expectation of further troubles.—

The parties who were pardoned, and are retained in the country, have shewn no sense of gratitude whatever.— I have just received a Deputation from Sarnia, where the people are in a sad fright again, and threaten to leave the Country.— Another Company of Militia would have been very useful in that quarter—the people, it is evident want confidence, and the account Captain Vidal gives is really distressing.—

The Cheif [*sic*] Justice is obliged to return to England and leaves Toronto tomorrow, the loss of his assistance I shall feel exceedingly.—

[328] COLBORNE TO [ARTHUR]: A.L.S. 8p.

Sep. 23 *Sorel.* [Marked "Private".]

I must confess that I am undeserving of your very kind and considerate letter of the 6th inst. You have entered more warmly into the cases recommended by me, than I had reason to expect, with reference to the host of applicants with which you are surrounded. I am much obliged for the countenance you have given Scadding. He is a very good young man, but wants, I believe, energy—

With respect to the defence of the frontier, although I was desirous of seeing reduced a force raised in a storm, and which appeared to me rather calculated to create alarm than to allay excitement; I am aware that we are not in a state of security, and that we ought to employ the time allowed us by the present lull to prepare for future troubles. I still think that the occupation of the Niagara frontier by the 43d. Regt will keep you more quiet, than any other military arrangement or distribution of Troops. If you are of opinion that the Militia Companies should be gradually increased, so that all the detached duties may be taken by them easily; and that they may form a respectable Corps on the frontier, in case of a sudden move being necessary to the Eastward or Westward; I request that you will give such orders as you may think expedient. They could be probably soon increased to 200 R & F., or additional companies might be formed. In this Province affairs are not looking favorably. Lord Durham's determination to return home, (if he adheres to it,) will cause great excitement and afford the Rebels a new point of departure; and I think we shall be placed in a much worse state than we were in some months since—

I offer you my best thanks for all that you have so kindly expressed in regard to my proceedings in your Province. I can assure you, with the greatest sincerity, that I detest all Addresses and the marks of approbation to which you allude. They embarrass me, and can produce no advantage, and I am quite satisfied in having acquired the many firm friends among those with whom I lived for so many years.

Lord Durham, I imagine, has received despatches since his interview with you, which convinces him of the anxiety of Ministers to avoid severe or extreme punishments. This may account for the change to which you advert in his opinions.

I mentioned to you, verbatim, what he expressed to me, and I recollect his repeating nearly in the same terms to you his view of the treatment which the Marauders should experience; and "that they ought to be tried and hung up to the nearest Tree"[.]

You have a difficult part to perform between the interference of a Governor sent out with the extraordinary powers possessed by Lord Durham, and the wishes and fears of the most respectable inhabitants of the Province, who have a large stake and interest depending on the result of the proceedings of the ensuing six months. The House of Assembly will not listen to any interference on the part of the Governor Genl, with the laws of the Province; you may therefore expect to be censured, when the Legislature meets, for having permitted it.

I have received letters from Lord Glenelg and Lord Hill in which they acquaint me that it is the Queen's desire and wish that I should not relinquish my command; and they express themselves so warmly and kindly in respect to my continuing in this country for a further period that I have *given in my adhesion* and have consented to retain my command. I shall fix my Head Quarters at Montreal for the winter, as soon as I can move from Sorel conveniently.

I should have great pleasure in having an interview with you, *half way*, before the Winter— Our arrangements cannot be too cautious, I hope we shall be able to hasten them and take the lead[.]

[*329*] J. B. Robinson to [Arthur]: A.L.S. 2p.

[*1838*] [*Toronto.*]

[*c. Sep. 24*] I need not say that we should all have been most happy to avail ourselves of Your Excellency's kind proposition conveyed in your note of this morning, but I have been unexpectedly confined again to the house for these two days past, & I am warned by this second attack that I must be more than ordinarily prudent for some time to come— This cross event has rather thrown us back in our arrangements and Mrs. Robinson with very great regret finds herself as decidedly frustrated as I am from accepting any invitation between this time & the day of our departure which I think will not be later than Thursday— As soon as I leave the house I shall call upon Your Excellency.

[330] ARTHUR TO [JOHN EDEN]: Df.A.L. initialled.

[1838] *[Place not stated.]*
Sep. 24 I have the honor to acknowd your Letter of the 18th inst. informing me [blank in M.S.] in reply, I beg to state for the information of the Cmdr of the Forces, that Lit. Griffin being already at Montreal will proceed from thence to Quebec. May I entreat you will submit to His Exy, that, although I shd. exceedingly regret to put the public to the least expense that can be avoided, it will not be possible to conduct the military detail, as I could wish it to be conducted, with such very limited assistance as His Excellency has assigned for Upper Canada.

[The above appears on the reverse side of 318.]

[331] ARTHUR TO [BROWNE ?] WILLIS: LB.6, p. 1.

Sep. 25 *Toronto.*

I received yr. letter of the 4th. Augt. yesterday, & as I am just closing a Bag for the Secy. of State I will answer it at once—I mean that part wh. is, no doubt, most interesting to yourself— I allude of course to your observations respecting yr. son. My advice is this— By all means let him get his Commission—then, if possible, let him be appointed to a Company in these Provinces—the Upper Province if possible— And we shall have the double chance of my being able to do something for him either in the Military or Civil Line. In the mean time I recommend strongly his habituating himself to compose with facility, & to write with despatch. I cannot ask you to remember me to any one, for I must have fallen into disgrace with all my friends from my apparent neglect in writing. but as I intend to redeem my character soon, pray say a kind word for me if you can . . . [Sends regards to "Aunt Betsey & all yr. family".]

[332] R. B. SULLIVAN TO MR SECRY. [JOHN] MACAULAY: A.L.S. 6p.

[*1838*] *[Place not stated.]*
[*Sep. 25 ?*] I am happy that His Excellency has determined not again to refer the case of Beamer to the Council. as in all probability they must have adhered to their opinion. The pardon will now rest where it ought principally on the responsibility of the Governor General.

I fear very much that the deliberations of the Council on the general amnesty will only have the effect of producing useless discussion with His Lordship. the Govr General[.] His Lordship is evidently determined on his measure[;] a protest from the Council will not prevent his insisting on it, it is an odious task to oppose the granting of mercy. If the Council approve of the amnesty all the credit, which the measure may deserve will attach to His Lordship. If they do not approve they cannot prevent it, but will perhaps unnecessarily embarrass His Lordship. and induce him to enter into a vindictive contest with this Government which cannot but produce much evil to the Province & not a little to the parties concerned[;] it is evident that Lord Durham does not like the course of submitting his measures to this Council and indeed when His Lordship has once decided that a measure falls within the range of his functions. the advice of a body in which His Lordship has no confidence and who are not the constitutional advisers of His Lordship seems vain & anomalous.

In fact the whole jurisdiction of His Lordship tends to produce anomaly. & so will every intermediate power between the local government & the Crown—whether in the shape of a federal Governor or otherwise—but it seems to me that by the dispatches, Lord Durham is the director, or at least the adviser assigned to H. E. in all matters coming within his instructions. he has the power of enforcing his recommendations and the advice of the Council cannot aid but may embarrass him and the Government. The responsibility of Lord Durhams acts ought to rest with himself[;] he cannot in fact freely exercise or be responsible for the exercise of his powers as to general measures if he be opposed by the council and if his Lordship should fail in the mission with which he was entrusted it would be mortifying were he afterwards to point at the Ex Council of Upper Canada as having thwarted him & caused his failure.

I mention these views not with any intention of acting on them in Council but to put His Excellency in possession of my private opinion. I shall most cheerfully undertake the consideration of any question referred by H. Excy.

[333] ARTHUR TO DURHAM: LB.6, p. 6-7.

Sep. 26 *Govt. House, Toronto.* [Marked "Confidential".]

I have had the honor to receive Your Lordship's note marked "Confidential" of the 16th Instt., with its enclosure for the Chief Justice wh. I forwarded to him without delay.— It gives me the sincerest gratification to find that Your Lordship has made the alteration wh. you mention in your original plan. it will I feel convinced remove the difficulty contemplated by all those whom I have heard speak upon the subject & I am much obliged to you for allowing me confidentially to use it.

The Chief Justice continues to suffer a good deal—his health appears much broken down & he proceeds for New York Tomorrow Morng. on his way to England.

I avail myself of the opportunity to enclose Copy of the Resolutions to be proposed at the public Meeting this day, with a Copy of the proposed Address— I hope it will be quite satisfactory to Your Lordship.—

Mr. Draper being the Member for Toronto & also a Member of the Executive Council would be the most proper person to form one of the Deputation to proceed with it to Quebec, but he is, unfortunately, on Circuit.

I also enclose Copy of the Resolutions on wh. an Address is proposed to be framed at Cob[o]urg. It is not so entirely acceptable as the one from Toronto wh. I hope will be generally adopted in all the other Townships.—

[Enclosures lacking.]

[334] J. B. ROBINSON TO [ARTHUR]: A.L.S.

Sep. 26 [*Toronto.*]

I set off to walk down with the inclosed paper, but found it necessary to return— I should like to have it back & with it the two printed papers on the Union—

I was quite well this morning & shd. have continued so, if I could have indulged in a little rest.

[Enclosure lacking.]

[335] W[ILLIA]M ROWAN TO CAPTAIN [FREDERICK] HALKETT: L.S.

Sep. 26 *Military Secretary's Office, Quebec.*

With reference to your letter of the 28th. Ulto. covering an Application for a Months Pay for the Quarter Master of the late Queen's Rangers, for Services rendered by him since that Corps was disembodied, I am directed to acquaint you for the information of His Excellency Sir George Arthur, that for the reasons stated in My Letter of the 13th. Instant, The Commander of the Forces does not feel justified in deciding on the Merits of this Claim[.]

[336] COLBORNE TO ARTHUR: L.S. 14p.

Sep. 28 *Sorel.* [Marked "Confidential".]

I beg to thank your Excellency for your letter of the 9th. Inst., in which you acquaint me with your intention of directing the arrangements, to be completed which have been proposed by me in regard to the Militia—

With reference to your suggestion of stationing a detachment of Militia, at Whitby, I have no doubt from the character of a portion of the Settlers of Whitby, Reach, and Pickering, that those Townships should be closely watched; and there can be no objection to a Subaltern's Detachment of Militia being stationed at Windsor if you think the disaffected can be kept in order or their designs counteracted by a small Guard at that Post, and that such a precaution would prevent the Americans from landing. If they were determined to risk an incursion in that neighbourhood; it must be recollected however, that Baldwin's Creek, Duffin's Creek and River Rouge are also points that would serve the purpose of the Marauders as landing places— If the Americans disembark at any point between Port Hope and the Highlands the invasion would be made, in expectation of being joined by a large proportion of the Townships on the Ontario and I should suggest that it would be better to establish an armed police in Whitby, Darlington and Pickering and to form a certain number of Companies of the Sedentary Militia in the Townships near Port Hope and Toronto with a view of having them ready to march with the regular Troops at a short notice— I am anxious that whatever preparations may be considered by you necessary to give confidence to that part of the the [*sic*] Province and any other, in which it may be suspected that the Rebels and Americans might find encouragement and protection, should be completed without the least delay—that in case of an alarm we may have arms conveni[e]ntly distributed in the vicinity of the Companies of the Sedentary Militia—that are ready & willing to be employed[.]

I do not think that the Brigands are sufficiently organized to incur the risk of disembarking on any part of the shores of Lake Ontario or any of the Great Lakes, from which they would find it difficult to make their escape in the event of a failure—

The Townships on the St. Lawrence, Detroit, & St. Clair, can never prudently be left without some Companies of Volunteer Militia, raised for permanent duty—as we are aware, from experience, that alarms & excitement, may be continued by the landing of a small number of persons, who can easily return to the American side, after communicating with their friends in the Interior— We shall have a great advantage this Winter in keeping the country quiet if the Regular Troops are well concentrated, & kept together, in hand— I request therefore that the Regiments of the Line may send out no detatchments [*sic*] whatever when the duties can be performed by Militia Companies—that they may have no harassing or frequent night duty. and that the men, in regard to beds and bedding &c, may be made as comfortable as circumstances will admit of—

If we can assemble a regular force of 1200 men ready to be conveyed to any point that may be menaced in two or three days, we need not apprehend any great danger in having particular Towns & Districts unprotected for a short time— Neither Toronto [n]or Kingston could be left with less than 300 Men, but I should apprehend no danger, on an emergency, from reinforcing the Troops in the Niagara District from Toronto, or drawing Troops from Kingston to Toronto— The Niagara frontier is well protected by the 43d., Regt. 1st. Dragoon Guards & the Staff Corps. I should not think it advisable to draw any Troops from that Quarter unless other points are attacked—

It is of no importance whether the 43d. are in Barracks at Drummondville or at the Town of Niagara; but they should be kept together and have little duty— The Militia Companies should be completed as soon as possible, and ordered to take all the detatched duties and particularly those of the Wharfs, & Ferries, & Quays— In case the 43d. should be ordered to march against the disaffected or marauders, the Sedentary Militia should be prepared to occupy Fort Messissaaga [*sic*]— I have already stated to your Excellency that I am well aware of the extent of the moral evil of Desertion in regard to the circumstances of the Province, but the regular Troops cannot be withdrawn from the Frontier without producing a great want of confidence in the Frontier population— There are few stations from which men inclined to pass over to the States do not attempt to desert. We have lost more men from Toronto Kingston & Montreal than from several frontier posts. I hope therefore both at Niagara and Amherstburg by the exertions of the Comdg. Officers, with the assistance of the Companies of Militia on Permanent Duty, desertion will be greatly checked & confined to young men who come out to this Country determined to make their escape the first opportunity[.]

The whole of the 32d. & 34th. Regts., and the half battery of Artillery at London should be considered disposable and ready to concentrate either in the Interior or on the Frontier in case of necessity— The 34th. I should also recommend to be kept together at Amherstburg— I hope you will not find it necessary to detatch from that Corps to Penatanguashine [*sic*] and that you will be able to have the whole of the service Companies at Head Quarters, except a party of 25 R & F at Sandwich & about 80 R & F at Chatham— One Company of the Militia Volunteers will take the Wharf Duties at Amherstburg & the Company formed for that Frontier should be stationed at Windsor &

Sandwich— In case the 34th. should be required to march suddenly the Sedentary Militia of Malden, Colchester & Gosfield should be prepared to occupy the Fort. The Townships of Sarnia Plympton & Moore I think require small guards to be stationed on the water frontier to give confidence to the settlers & relieve them from the duty which they have voluntarily taken to prevent the landing of small parties—

The Company raised by Col: Maitland's orders, will of course be selected for this service; & Col: Chichester shall be directed to visit the detatchments from time to time— The Roads from all the Townships on the Sinclair & Lake Huron are almost impracticable, therefore any sudden successful invasion, at any season need not be apprehended[.] The Depot of Arms at London, Chatham, and Amherstburg, may be so arranged that they may be delivered without confusion to the Companies of sedentary Militia destined to be the first called out on duty[.]

I hope Captain Sandom has stationed your Gun-boats at Sutherlands Wharf or Sarnia, at Sandwich & at port Dover & I beg you will have the goodness to request that he will direct a Gun-boat to be stationed at Whitby. From these suggestions you will perceive that I am persuaded that we should look on the greater part of our regular force in the Upper & Lower Provinces as disposable and to be marched freely on any emergency to any section of the Province that may be seriously threatened—and that a certain number of Companies from the Militia Corps should be prepared to take the stationary duties of large Towns or disturbed Districts— I cannot see any great necessity for having a Compy. of the 32d. Regt. at Simcoe, many of the gentlemen in that neighbourhood are however much alarmed for their safety with reference to the disaffection supposed to exist in Norwich, Oakland, &c— Whether the 32d. Compy. or a Militia Volunteer, are stationed at Simcoe, the Barracks should be repaired & the men made comfortable for the Winter[.] St. Thoma's [*sic*] being only 28 miles from London there appears no objection to a Compy. of the 32d. being stationed at that place & your Excellency may authorize the Barracks to be repaired & improved— I have stationed a detatchment of the 71st. at Brockville in consequence of the great alarm at that Town, and the disputes which occurred last winter between the Militia and the political parties of the neighbourhood—but as it is impossible to prevent the desertion at that post to any extent, and communication with the large number of deserters on the opposite side, I intend to withdraw the 71st Detatchment as soon as it can be replaced without injuring the character of the Corps—

I beg you will increase the Compy. at Prescott or Cornwall or raise a Compy. of Pensioners, as soon as possible, and station them at Brockville under a half-pay Officer, and Major Young's Inspection— The state of this Province and the movements & activity of the Refugees on this frontier and the reports that a large quantity of arms have been brought in by the Missisqu[o]i Townships make it necessary that we should be, in fact, in in [*sic*] position and prepared to act in every case likely to occur in reference to the organization & schemes said to be in progress on the part of the Refugees & the friends with whom they are in constant communication[.]

[Endorsed: "Read in Council 18th. October 1838".]

[A précis entry referring to the above appears in item 578, where, following the sentence: "I am anxious that whatever preparations . . .

should be completed without the least delay", an interpolation reads: "The preceding refers more particularly to depots of arms for Sedentary Militia.—"]

[337] [ARTHUR] TO GLENELG: L. 5p.

Sep. 29 *Government House, Toronto.*

I have had the honor to receive your Lordships private letters respecting the misunderstanding on which I came to this Colony, in regard to the powers to be given to the Governor General.

I thank Your Lordship very sincerely for the trouble you have taken in saying so much upon the subject.

I am persuaded if Mr. Stephen were to reflect upon the conversation I had with him after my third interview with your Lordship, that he would feel it due to me to qualify the observations he has made in the letter of which your Lordship has been pleased to enclose me a copy; but, my Lord it would neither be proper nor respectful in me to add any thing more upon the subject.

All the mischief, which I anticipated from the interference, I feel practically in its fullest force. Your Lordship must not however suppose that there is any misunderstanding between the Governor General and myself.

It is far from being the case—from the Earl of Durham I have received the utmost personal courtesy, but, unfortunately, His Lordship feeling his own perfect independence requires me to cooperate in Measures, which, with the Legislature to deal with; I cannot accede to without the certainty of involving myself with the Provincial Parliament, and most probably, bringing no small future trouble upon my administration.— I am, in fact, just as I expected, required to act upon the opinion of others, and not according to my own Judgment—and placed between two fires, from which it will be difficult, if possible, to escape without being wounded.

Your Lordship will hear with great regret from my official Despatch of this Date that the Patriot cause is reviving on the Frontier, and that combinations for another descent upon this Province are again going forward upon rather an extensive scale all along the coast.

The late proceedings in Parliament will I fear have a very bad effect in the Canadas, and the expected resignation of the Governor General has occasioned great excitement amongst all classes.

[Endorsed: "Copy".]

[338] ARTHUR TO GLENELG: LB.6, p. 8-11.

Sep. 29 *Govt. House,* [*Toronto.*] [Marked "Private."]

I did myself the honour to intimate to Your Lordship in a private note that the Earl of Durham had contemplated the discontinuance of the Legislative Council. This proposition of His Lordships so clashed with my suggestions for augmenting the Number of Members for that Council in Upper Canada that I thought it my duty to make the communication to Yr. Lordship wh. I hope has been duly received.

By the accompanying note from the Governor General to Mr. Chief Justice Robinson with whom his Lordship largely communicated upon his scheme, whilst in this Province, it seems that the Earl of Durham has now abandoned all intention of getting rid of the Legislative Councils—a proposition, indeed, which no one person of any politics, professing a knowledge of the Country, favored in any way— I revert therefore to my official recommendation of the immediate appointment of some additional Members, as a matter of urgent necessity.

I have shewn my List to Mr. Robinson, & he thinks it judicious—nevertheless, should Yr. Lordship doubt whether the number I have included be not too great, or wish for further information, I know no person more capable of affording it than our Chief Justice—at the same time from Deaths & other casualties, the House is so reduced, that I quite concur with Sir Francis Head that an augmentation should immediately take place— Indeed it is most urgently required before the next session of the Legislature when I fear that there may frequently be a difficulty in forming a Quoram [*sic*] in the Council,—there will be just sufficient time to provide agt. that inconvenience if despatch be used.

I have deeply to lament the absence of Mr. Robinson at the ensuing session. He is so talented; has so extensive a knowledge of the country; is so practical and consistent in his views; and his opinion has so much weight with men of all parties, that I am aware I shall very much feel the want of his assistance—especially upon the Clergy Reserve question, in wh. his moderation, as a Member of the Church of England, and disposition to conciliate, would be of the utmost importance—

Whilst alluding to this Gentleman I cannot avoid submitting to Your Lordship that some mark of distinction wd. not only be most deservedly conferred on Mr. Robinson, but that it wd. be most politic to confer it—and, whether he be disposed to accept it or not, I wd. strongly recommend such a mark of grace spontaneously springing from Yr. Lordship, as soon as possible after his arrival. I think Yr. Lordship wd. thereby conciliate a very influential party and strengthen my hands at the coming session of the Provincial Parliament—the assembling of wh. I intend to defer as long as possible, in accordance with the wish of the Earl of Durham.

The Chief Justice, I am aware, declined any thing of the kind when Sir Francis Head recommended it, and I think he did so, wisely and properly—but it wd. be a different matter, if the compliment sprung at once from Yr. Lordship.—

I think it right, however, to mention that I have not given Mr. Robinson, the most distant hint of this suggestion, so that if Yr. Lordship differs with me upon it, no personal offence can be given[.]

[Enclosure is probably a copy of item 316.]

[339] ARTHUR TO GLENELG: LB.5, p. 252-253.

Sep. 29 *Toronto.* [Marked "Separate".]

I have the honor to submit to your Lordship, that, as Colonel on the Staff in Van Diemen's Land, during a period of twelve years, I received no pay, but was authorized throughout the whole period to draw the usual allowances of Fuel, Forage &c.

On my appointment as Major General on the Staff in Upper Canada, I was quite aware that I was not to draw any pay as Major General; but the allowances, I concluded as a matter of course, would be granted to me. As, however, it is not expressly authorized in my letter of Service, I have declined to draw any allowances, until I submitted the case to Her Majesty's Government; but, from an extreme pressure of Public Business, I have not had it in my power to request your Lordship would be pleased to recommend the same to the Lord's Commissioners of Her Majesty's Treasury.

In common with all my Predecessors, I find it utterly impossible to support the necessary expenses of my office upon the Salary allowed me in this very expensive Command; and I beg to add that, from the existing circumstances of the Country, the Circle of Visitors and Residents, Civil as well as Military, to be entertained, has very considerably encreased.

Should the House of Assembly concur in granting me the salary of £3,500 Cury per annum, I shall be in the receipt of an income much less than Sir John Colborne received when holding the same offices.

There is nothing more painful than urging one's own suit, but I am satisfied my application in this matter is most reasonable under the circumstances on which it is founded.

[340] W[illia]m Rowan to Arthur: L.S.

Sep. 29 *Military Secretary's Office, Quebec.*

I have had the honor to submit to the Commander of the Forces your Excellency's letter of the 15th instant, representing, with reference to my communication of the 7th of September, that it would be attended with the most serious inconvenience to the public service, if the appointment of Assistant Military Secretary at Toronto was discontinued before the Militia and Volunteer accounts are finally closed, which, certainly, cannot be the case by the 30th instant, the period mentioned in my letter.— Under these circumstances I am directed to acquaint you that His Excellency has been pleased to approve of Captain Halkett being continued as Assistant Military Secretary to the 31st of December next.—

[341] C. A. Hagerman to [Arthur]: A.L.S. 3p.

[*1838*] [*Place not stated.*]

Sep. 30 I received a note from Mr MacAulay last night informing me that your Excellency had decided that I should proceed to Quebec— I shall do so with great cheerfulness, and I humbly hope that my seeing Lord Durham before he leaves the Country *may* be productive of some good.— At all events His Lordship cannot but feel gratified that your Excellency should notice his departure by a special communication.—

I mentioned to your Excellency yesterday that the Assizes commenced at Cobourg tomorrow—it was my intention to have conducted the Crown business there myself if public duty had not required my presence elsewhere,—and as the time is barely sufficient to give instructions to Mr. Cartwright to whom I have written to come to Cobourg, I think of leaving for that place in the morning and will wait your Excellencys despatches there, with which I will immediately proceed to Quebec, and will be quite ready to leave Cobourg on tuesday Night or Wednesday Morning.—

If your Excellency should prefer any other arrangement I of course will adopt it, but the one I mention will probably be most convenient to meet *all* arrangements.—

[342] JONAS JONES TO [ARTHUR]: A.L.S. 2p.

[*1838*] [*Place not stated.*]
[*Oct. ?*]

I last evening received the accompanying note from Mr. Bethune—I shall probably have some thing more from him respecting the President elect of the State of Upper Canada; if I do I will immediately communicate it—

[Enclosure lacking.]

[343] ARTHUR TO DURHAM: LB.1. p.65-66.

Oct. 1 *Government House, Toronto.*

By Your Lordship's answer to the Deputation from the Provinces I perceive Your Lordship has determined to proceed to England. I dreaded and most deeply lament this determination for the consequences I am persuaded will be most injurious to the interests of the Colonies.

I shall hasten to Quebec tomorrow to pay my respects to Your Lordship before your embarkation, and after a short conference I hope at once to determine upon such an amnesty as will meet your wishes and prove that you have actually effected in both Provinces all that could be effected consistently with the Public Interests.

[344] COLBORNE TO [ARTHUR]: A.L.S. 9p.

Oct. 1 *Sorel.* [Marked "Private and Confidential".]

That I am much gratified and pleased with the contents of your late private letters, in reference to my concerns and intentions, you will learn from my private letter of the 28th inst [*sic*], which I hope you will receive before this reaches Toronto. I assure you, that when I have adverted to our doubtful powers relating to military matters, and to our being apt to be a little sensitive on such points, I intended to explain my desire and opinion, That the right and power of the Commander of the Forces should be so far established, in time of trouble, that there should exist no ground for appeal from his authority, nor doubt that he is the Commanding Officer and the only one in these Provinces—

But it was not my intention to contend that a General Officer at a distance from Head Quarters; ought not to have *full swing*, and have power to direct all Commissaries in his District, or Province, to comply promptly with his orders; and Ordnance Officers also, provided he reports his proceedings regularly to the Chief in Command. I am inclined to believe, that whatever hesitation took place in forwarding supplies last winter on the part of the Ordnance Department, was caused by the unprepared state of every Department for a *breeze*, the contradictory orders which were given to the Eastward and Westward, when we are equally pressed on both sides of Kingston, and also by the uncertainty as to the time of arrival of arms and ammunition; the *inefficiency* of *many* of the Heads of Departments at Niagara, Toronto, and Kingston; and the want of method in delivering out Arms. It is with reference to the confusion of last Winter that I have transmitted to you my long public essays of the 28th inst, respecting the defence of the Province, in order that we may take into consideration the cases which we suppose may occur the ensuing Winter, and provide for them, by having arms &c ready for the willing and Loyal Militia, at certain points; without exposing our stores and Arms to be taken possession of by the disaffected, should the Rebels obtain any temporary advantage.

I have within these few days received such intelligence from Canadians, who have from the commencement of the Revolt, been made aware of all the designs and intrigues of the disaffected Leaders, and who are still in a situation to discover from time to time their proceedings, that it becomes no longer possible to defer making every preparation in our power to preserve peace. We shal lhave so much to occupy our attention in Lower Canada, that we shall be much perplexed, if we are obliged to detach from Montreal on every alarm in the Upper Province[.]

I shall lose no time in requesting Sir Colin Campbell, with the sanction of of [*sic*] Lord Durham, to send us another Battalion from Halifax, and a supply of Arms. Should we receive this reinforcement I shall direct another Regiment to proceed to Kingston; and suggest that that [*sic*] *three* companies of that Corps should be stationed at Toronto. So that one Regiment at Toronto may be considered as disposable to act in the Home or Erie District, and one Regt, at Kingston disposable, to act on the St Lawrence or in the Bay of Quinté. I have already mentioned in a former letter that the 43d Regt must be also considered disposable, and kept well together, and that the 34th, and 32d Regiment may have occasions to form a junction and act on any part of the Shore of Lake Erie—

Now for the Militia— I so far recant, that I conclude you are the best judge of the extent of disaffection in your own Province, on the frontier, or in the interior; and from your direct and constant communication, that you must know more of your winter prospects than we can. Therefore, with reference to the Military Chest, you have my full authority to raise and organize such companies or Corps of Militia as you may think it expedient to form. Any state will be preferable to the renewal of alarm which prevailed a few months since; and which the Patriots and Refugees will have the power of keeping up. Although I suspect that the whole tribe of Contractors, on both sides, and Volunteers in bad circumstances are desirous of turning alarm to their own account, I cannot, with this persuasion, permit any risk to be incurred. We have a sufficient quantity of arms in the Upper Province for our immediate preparations. Sarnia, and the Neighbouring Townships are again in full cry, that nothing has been done for their protection[.] The Company raised by Colonel Maitland has I hope been completed. If it be not, I request that you will direct at least 100 men to be raised without delay and stationed at Sarnia and Moore &c, or such force as will give confidence.

The settlers in that quarter are generally loyal; and the roads through Plympton, Warwick and Adelaide so bad that regular troops can neither be sent to them, nor could the Americans make any rapid movement towards London, on the main road between Chatham and London.

But if the settlers are armed from London, and the companies required to assist them are placed on permanent duty, it may be presumed that no serious misfortune can happen in that District.

Captain Sandom has stationed a Gun boat at Sarnia, and the sooner the Militia company arrives or part of it, the better.— Have the goodness to acquaint Capt Sandom that as the Navigation will probably not close to the Westward, before the middle of January I think that the *Toronto* Steamer ought to be stationed at Amherstburg, and to ply between that place and Sarnia, and to be placed at the disposal of Colonel Airey to convey Troops or stores from one station to another.

I request that a sufficient number of companies may be raised as soon as possible, to assist Colonel Airey in guarding the Western frontier, and to defend the Fort, Malden, in case the 34th should be obliged to act at a distance from Malden. I request also that Colonel Booth may be reinforced with 200 Militia Volunteers, or as many as you may think necessary to keep a good look out at Fort Erie, and Chippewa, and to occupy Fort Misissaga in case the 43d are obliged to act at a distance from Niagara. I am convinced that if we can command on an emergency a respectable force on the St Lawrence Niagara and Detroit, we need not fear for the interior.

Captain Sandom will I conclude take care of the St Lawrence and direct the Steam Vessel Experiment to ply from Kingston to Prescott frequently, with his gun boats.

[345] H. S. Fox to Arthur: A.L.S. 17p.

Oct. 4 *Washington.* [Marked "Confidential".]

Several confidential reports, of an alarming nature, have been received within the last few days by the Department of the Treasury at Washington, from the United States Collectors of Customs at different stations along the Canadian frontier,—and have been communicated to me by Mr: Forsyth.— The Collectors at Rochester and at Oswego, in the State of New York, state their belief, that a secret combination, of vast extent, and possessed of great resources in money and in warlike provisions, has been formed, or is now in the course of being formed, along the whole line of the Canadian frontier, and principally on the shores of the Lakes Ontario and Erie, for the purpose of again invading Her Majesty's Provinces, during the approaching season of autumn or winter.— The Collectors believe, that this unlawful combination includes already as many as Forty Thousand persons, American citizens of the different States, with a few, but apparently only a very few, Canadian refugees.— It is believed that these men communicate with each other by secret masonic signs; that they hold frequent private meetings; have a regular organization, with military assumed rank and commissions; and are under the general direction of delegates from the several States whose citizens have entered into the conspiracy.— The informants further declare their belief, that the leaders of the Conspiracy carry on a continual intercourse and correspondence, in spite of the Authorities on either side of the line, with the disaffected party both in Upper and in Lower Canada.— They do not profess to have ascertained, or divined, whether it be the design of the conspirators to invade Canada, on their own account, from the American side; or whether only—(and this would appear to be the most probable conjecture)—to hold themselves in readiness for joining some new treasonable movement, which it is evident they expect will be attempted within the Canadian Provinces.—

I hope, and believe, that the above reports, from the Collectors of Customs, will be found, by the result, to have greatly exaggerated the danger; but at the same time, I cannot doubt that they contain a considerable portion of truth.—In defending ourselves against secret combinations, we must of course be prepared for frequent exaggeration of the danger; but it would be most imprudent to disbelieve in its existence altogether.— The Town of Cleveland, in Ohio, is represented to be the principal centre or focus of the present conspiracy; and it is suspected that large quantities of arms are concealed in that neighbourhood.— The same Collectors of Customs, who give the above information, distinctly state their opinion to the Government, that the great mass of the American population, along the whole line, would be in favor of any movement against Canada; and that neither the independent citizens, nor the subordinate local civil Authorities, could be relied upon, in any emergency, for aiding in the enforcement of the laws of the Country for the preservation of neutrality.— The regular military force is the only valid assistance upon which the Government can rely.— General Macomb has now between Two and Three Thousand men (regulars) under his command; but although this is considered a large military force in the United States, it is manifestly inadequate for preserving order along a frontier of 800 miles, from Maine to Michigan.— It appears from the language of the same informants, that both they themselves, and the American population generally on the frontier, are obstinately persuaded with the belief, that a majority of the inhabitants of Upper Canada, as well as of Lower Canada, are ripe for revolt against the British Authority: and such belief is of course diligently inculcated by the Canadian refugees.— The most active of these is stated to be a person of the name of "Macleod", a refugee I believe from Upper Canada.—

In consequence of the above intelligence, urgent instructions have without loss of time been addressed from the Departments at Washington, to the United States Chief Civil and Military Officers on the frontier, directing the utmost efforts to be made, both for discovering the truth, and for preventing the machinations of the conspirators.— But after all that we have before witnessed, I cannot profess to anticipate much effectual succour from the American Authorities, for the prevention of outrage against Her Majesty's Possessions,—however honest and sincere may be the intentions of the Supreme Government.—

The letters and reports, from which the above intelligence is taken, were shown to me in confidence by Mr: Forsyth. The writers are apparently in great terror of being compromised in their own immediate neighbourhood, if known to be employed in seeking for information.

I write to communicate the intelligence contained in this despatch, to the Earl of Durham, as well as to Your Excellency; and I will not fail to convey to you any further information, which I may obtain upon the same subject.—

[Endorsed: "Received and Read in Council 18th. October 1838."]

[346] J. B. Robinson to Arthur: A.L.S. 5p.

Oct. 4 *New York.*

We arrived here last evening after an exceedingly pleasant journey, spending the Sunday in Montreal—and we are so fortunate as to find that births [*sic*] are retained for us in the Steamer, which we were rather in doubt about, since I would not venture to engage them absolutely.

Mr. Moore gave me some letters last night which Mr. Macaulay had forwarded, but as there are no public letters among them, & none from Your Excellency I infer that whatever you had to send has been sent in the ordinary way by the Great Western—

At Montreal I found very confident rumors that Lord Durham had been so *particularly* urged to remain, that his resolution would probably be shaken, but this must have been all conjecture, for the last arrival from his Lordship at Montreal was that of Mr. Cavendish who crossed on the way the letters going to Ld. D. from the Great Western, so that their purport could not be known— Mr. Cavendish states positively that he takes home Ld. Ds. absolute resignation—that he is convinced nothing will make him recall it, & that he intends to embark soon at New York— Upon this point, your Excellency is probably by this time better informed— Considering the very special nature of Ld. Durham's mission I do not see how he can relinquish it without the express or implied assent of the Queen's Government— Sir John it seems undoubtedly remains—

If in the midst of the unhappy confusion & distraction of counsels upon Canadian affairs I can render any public service, I shall not be wanting in the necessary exertion, but I have little faith— When I arrive I shall write fully to Your Excellency—

Mrs. Robinson & all our party (not by any means excepting myself) are in good case for the voyage— The weather is most delightful— I fear we shall find the Steamer disagreeably crowded, but the prospect of a 13 days passage will reconcile one to a good deal—

I can not take my departure without most sincerely thanking Your Excellency for the great kindness which I have received at your hands from the first moment of your accession to the Government— I assure Your Excellency that during a long course of public service nothing more gratifying has occurred to me than to find the full & unreserved confidence which was so readily reposed in me— I owe in return for it my best exertions in forwarding the objects which Your Excellency has in view—the happiness & prosperity of Canada— I earnestly hope that things may proceed successfully & as agreeably as can reasonably be looked for—

[347] ARTHUR TO COLONEL [HENRY] BOOTH: LB. 1,p. 73-74.

Oct. 5 *Montreal.*

Before I left Toronto I desired that a letter might be addressed to you by the Military Secretary to the effect that I should be glad if further information could be desired from the Person, who had already communicated with my Aide De Camp and Lieutenant Jones of the 43rd Regt.

I am quite satisfied that you will act with your usual prudence in the matter; but, still I am anxious to say, that I would rather remain without intelligence, than any officers should incur the least personal risk. I shall return to Toronto in a few days, and shall be glad to hear from you upon this subject.

The extent of anxious feeling in this Province has quite surprised me, that we shall have a troublesome time of it; and that soon, appears to be a very general expectation.

I am quite sure you will put and keep your Frontier in the best state circumstances will admit.

[Superscription reads: "Colonel Booth. Comg 43d Regt.—"]

[348] H. S. Fox to Arthur: A.L.S. 7p.

Oct. 5 *Washington.* [Marked "Private".]

I should be sorry to be the means of giving unnecessary alarm, but I think the circumstances stated in the accompanying despatch are deserving of serious consideration.— I shall feel anxious to hear, whether the reports of the U.S. Collectors agree with any other information which you may have received upon the same subject.— Probably, if peace is preserved through the winter, *within* Canada, all this conspiracy will end in nothing more than foolish threats of invasion: but if there should arise any rebellious movement in either Province, such an organized combination to succour the rebels from this side of the line, would undoubtedly much increase the mischief.— It is *Upper* Canada, more than Lower Canada, that is, and always will be, the object of attraction and ambition to the Americans. And I can perceive, from the language of the people here, that it is their settled policy to believe, or profess to believe, that the disaffection in Upper Canada is more extensive and more serious than we are aware of, or like to acknowledge. As soon as I can learn what are General Macomb's reports to his Govt:, upon the subject of the present alarm, I will let you know.— I feel sure, that in any intercourse or communication which you may have with General Macomb, you may rely upon his honesty, and cordial desire to do his duty.— Indeed, I must say, in justice to the Superior Officers of the United States' regular army, that through all the troubles of last winter, and ever since, I have observed both their conduct and language to be perfectly honest and straitforward—but their means are wholly inadequate to repress the lawless propensities of their fellow citizens.— I hope that you received a long letter which I wrote to you in June, by Mr. Macdonnel.—

[Endorsed: "Read in Council 18th. October 1838".]
[Enclosure referred to is probably item 345.]

[349] T. L. Goldie to Arthur: A.L.S. 4p.

Oct. 5 *Sorel.*

I am directed by the Commander of the Forces to acquaint you, with reference to your letter of the 24th ultimo, enclosing a Communication from Colonel Maitland of the 12th. that he has always considered it the duty of a General Officer Commanding a District, to interfere in any urgent case, in which the public service is concerned, in respect to the Comfort of the Troops under his immediate charge, or in providing accommodation for them, without waiting for the permission of the Commander of the Forces to sanction the work required. In these cases it is his duty to report the outlay which he may authorize, and to procure regular estimates for approval; but when he thinks that Her Majestys Service requires his interference, in order to ensure a speedy result, he can not properly refrain from assuming the responsibility. The Commander of the Forces adverts only to such cases in which the public service would be injured by delay—

I am also desired to state, that, as it has been understood that there has been great delay in carrying into effect orders respecting certain buildings, the Officer in Command should have lost no time in reporting to you the circumstances which occasioned the delay, so that you might have sooner interposed. I am further desired to request that you will have the goodness to direct Major Bonny Castle, the senior Officer of Engineers, to visit all the works, and Barracks which have been authorized, and in course of being erected and undergoing repair; and to send in a report of the progress which is making, and likewise state his opinion as to the cause of the delay complained of by Colonel Maitland in his letter of the 12th. ultimo.

[350] [SIR] J[OHN] HARVEY TO ARTHUR: A.L.S. 3p.
Oct. 6 *Government House, Fredericton.*

I have the honor to acknowledge Your Excellency's Communication of the 3d Ultimo in answer to mine of the 21 July.

Upper Canada, as the Colony of the North American Group, in which the greatest quantity of exportable Grain & flour is produced & manufactured, has always appeared to me to be the most directly interested in the Completion of an undertaking which, in connexion with the works in progress for the improvement of the Navigation of the St Lawrence, must place at the doors & Wharves of its Merchants, the power of commanding the Markets of the West Indies, as well as the intermediate ones of the United States & of these Lower Provinces;—the object therefore of connecting the Waters of the Bay of Fundy with the Gulph of St Lawrence by a *Ship* Canal, must be regarded as any thing but *remote* as respects Upper Canada, & I am happy that, seeing it in that light, Your Excellency will bring the subject under the favorable consideration of its Legislature.—

[351] [COLBORNE] TO [ARTHUR]: M. 8p.
Oct. 10 *Sorel.*

Memoranda.

Assuming that the greatest part of the population are loyal and determined to support the Government, but that most of the settlers in the London District, being natives of the United States, would join the rebels if they were successful, and that there are many disaffected persons scattered through the Province ready to assist the American Brigands, should they invade in any force. It becomes necessary from the reports lately received of the preparations making in the United States, to consider the cases that may occur during the winter, both Provinces being menaced with attack.

The Patriots, if they disembark in any number, will probably attempt to cross by the new Townships on the St. Clair, by the Niagara frontier, or by the St Lawrence frontier, in order that should they not be successful, they may easily return.

All our care should be directed to the Frontier, and we should be prepared instantly to crush any armed parties that may land. It is not probable that any considerable movement will originate in the interior, nor that any American Brigands will risk a landing on the shores of Lake Erie, or Ontario.

They may land at Sarnia or Sombra[;] they could not easily penetrate by any tolerable road to the direct road from Chatham, to London, but, they might wish to reach Eakfrid [*i.e.* Ekfrid] and Mosa where there are many disaffected persons—

To prepare for such an invasion, the Militia of the Townships of Adelaide should be immediately organized, and arms and ammunition distributed to them at the shortest notice, they could watch the roads from the new Townships to London. The loyal settlers of the Townships of Moore, Sarnia, and Plym[p]ton, should be armed—and the Compy. raised by Colonel Maitland ordered to take the Guards at Sarnia, Sutherlands Wharf,etc.

It is not probable that the American Brigands will attempt to land near Amherstburg or Sandwich while the 34th Regt occupy Amherstburg supported by two Companies of Volunteers.

If we imagine the Americans to disembark at any place between Port Talbot and the Township of Gosfield, the 34th would follow their movements acting with the 32nd. from London, and the Militia and Volunteer Companies would immediately occupy the Fort, and protect the frontier.

If a landing should be effected at Port Dover, or in that neighbourhood, the 32nd Regt should move to attack them. Captain Sandom, I think should order the Toronto Steamer to Amherstburg where that vessel should remain during the winter, assisted by the Gun boats,

The Niagara Frontier will be protected by the 43rd. Regt, Dragoons, Sappers and Miners, and two Companies of Volunteers which will be completed it is concluded as soon as possible.

Should the 43rd. Regt. be called to act at a distance from Niagara the Volunteer Companies, and the Sedentary Militia will protect the frontier— Any disturbance in the Interior not of a serious nature the Militia will probably be able to put down.

Two Battalions of the Line will be always available for any operations between Toronto and Kingston.

On the St Lawrence it is proposed to station three Companies of Volunteers viz—Gannanoqui [*sic*], Brockville, Prescott and Cornwall. If the Americans land in that neighbourhood it is supposed that the Garrison of Kingston and the Loyal Militia of Leeds will be in force sufficient to repel any attack.

The Glengarry Men have offered their services permanently which of course can not be accepted without consultation with the Home Government—but as they have arms enquiry should be made whether the two Corps which volunteered can not be reorganized, and prepared to march in case of emergency either for the defence of the St Lawrence or to Lower Canada—

Companies to be raised—

Three Companies on the St Lawrence sufficiently strong to enable them to protect the principal frontier Towns, and the Rideau Canal.

Two Companies for Sandwich and Amherstburg.

One Company for the new Townships of Sarnia, Plym[p]ton and Moore[;] 2. Companies at Niagara[.]

The Militia Company at Simcoe it is supposed can not be of any use whatever.

[Endorsed: "Read in Council 18th. Oct. 1838."]

[352] ARNOLD BURROWES TO THE ADJUTNT GENRL. of MILITIA [RICHARD BULLOCK]: A.L.S. 2p.

Oct. 10 *Strathmore, Brantford.*

I beg you would tender to His Excellency the Major Genrl. my resignation of the command of the 10 Gore Regt of Militia[.]

My reasons for this earnest request, are,

First, my conviction of the great proportion of disaffected Men, not to be trusted with arms—

Second The impossibility under the present System of making an efficient Corps out of such materials[.]
Third. The Expense imposed principally on the Comdg Officer without remuneration—
Fourth Having served actively in the regulars on foreign Service I desire to be at rest having three sons in the service—

Disreguarding [*sic*] any other Motive but the good of the service it has been my good fortune to be able to form a most respectable—active & efficient corps of Officers to the 10th Gore—

[Endorsed: "Read in Council 18. October 1838".]

[353] ARTHUR TO COLBORNE: LB. 1,p. 66-68.

Oct. 11 *Montreal.*

I have the honor to inform your Excellency that I have been in communication with the Earl of Durham upon the subject of granting an amnesty to the Parties, in the Upper Province who are implicated in the charge of Treason.

As a means of carrying this measure into effect, I have proposed to the Governor General—

First. That the proclamation which is required by law should be forthwith published preparatory to the outlawing of those persons who have been indicted for treason, and who have fled from the Province.—None of these persons are to be permitted to return to Upper Canada except upon Petition, and giving security for their future good behaviour.

Second. That the most guilty and dangerous of the Traitors concerned in the Rebellion in December last, and whom the Council will not recommend for any further remission—about ten in number—should be forthwith removed to England for the purpose of being transported to New South Wales or Van Diemen's Land.

Third. That in like manner the convicts who were tried and convicted for being concerned in the incursion and insurrection in the Niagara and Western Districts, in the month of June last, whom the Council will not recommend for any further remission of their sentences—about 13 in number—shall also be removed to England forthwith, for transportation.

Your Excellency is fully aware of the strong feeling amongst all the Loyal Population of Upper Canada—Canadians as well as British—against further lenity—and that they almost unanimously call out for the punishment of the traitors,—but, I think if the measure of severity be carried into effect which I have described, that—that [*sic*] a General Amnesty may be extended to all other persons, and that it may have a good effect—

The Earl of Durham has expressed his entire concurrence in this proceeding, and having at his Lordship's request, conferred with Mr. Secretary Buller upon it—I was happy to find that he also considered it a proceeding well adapted to the exigency of our present position.—

Still—as the effect of this measure may, in one way or another, produce an immediate and striking effect upon the Public Mind, I shall feel much obliged—without wishing to be relieved from the slightest responsibility—if Your Excellency will favor me with your opinion upon the measure—it can of course be delayed, if you think at the present crisis, delay important—

[354] ARTHUR TO DURHAM: LB. 1,p. 69-70.

Oct. 11 *Montreal.*

It has occurred to me that if your correspondence with Lord Glenelg be not forwarded to me confidentially, that the best use to be made of it will be its production before our House of Assembly—and—then an address would in all probability follow from both Houses to Her Majesty expressive of the feelings of the Legislature towards Your Lordship.

My course in such a case will necessarily be—whilst every measure is taken to manifest the high confidence reposed in your Lordship, and the great regret felt at your departure—to take the utmost care that there be no reflection cast upon the Government under which I am serving. There will be no difficulty, I think, in arranging this—or—I should make it a point, that my sincere desire to be useful to Your Lordship should give place to my duty to the Ministers.— It would have a good effect, perhaps, that such addresses as I have alluded to should reach England just before Parliament meets.—

Sincerely hoping that the Countess of Durham and yourself may have a prosperous voyage.

[355] ARTHUR TO HOWICK: LB. 1,p. 70-73.

Oct. 11 *Montreal.*

I have always borne a most grateful recollection of your kindness to me when I was so bitterly assailed in the House of Commons; and, although I by no means wish to cancel the obligation, I am very desirous to avail myself of any opportunity to offer some proof, however trifling, that I am sincerely sensible of your support on that occasion. As soon, therefore, as I found that Lord Durham had positively made up his mind to return to England, I hastened to Quebec to take my leave of him, and to place my humble services at his disposal if they could be useful in any way.— My visit to the Governor General has, I believe, at this moment been acceptable to himself, and therefore will, I am sure, be gratifying to your Lordship.—

It would be neither discreet nor proper in me to express any opinion to you upon the course of events that have determined Lord Durham to return to England; but, I may venture to say to Your Lordship that the consequence will be largely to increase our difficulties in both Provinces, if not, to peril their security!.

The French Party in the Lower Province, and the American Party in the Upper Province, consider the disallowance of the ordinance and the act of indemnity as a triumph; and, assuredly they needed no such exhilarating support! They seem all alive, and so do their sympathizing friends on the opposite shores, amongst whom Lodges have been formed, to aid the Canadian Cause, along the whole Frontier, from the St Lawrence to Lake Huron, so that there can be little doubt we shall have a very disturbed Winter of it.—

Lord Durham has a mass of information which no Governor General ever before collected, and he must be convinced that McKenzie and Papineau had the same object in view—separation from Great Britain! I do trust His Lordship will be able to convince Her Majesty's Government of this fact, and in that case, in place of any longer wasting time in the vain attempt to conciliate people so irreclaimably disaffected, it may be hoped that there will be at once bold Legislation, to maintain British supremacy.—

To prepare for coming events would it be possible to revive emigration during the next season, which has fallen off almost to nothing— Without it, it will be almost impossible for any length of time to retain these Provinces, without an enormous expenditure for Military protection.—

I should prefer Immigrants from England or Ireland. The Scotch make excellent settlers elsewhere,— but their form of Church Government is a little too Republican for this part of the world—for men are too much disposed to think that what is beneficial for their spiritual interests, may also be beneficial to advance their temporal concerns.—

The outline of the views which Your Lordship mentioned to me, you entertained respecting Military Immigration would answer admirably well in Upper Canada, and I should be delighted to hear that it was to [be] attempted on a large scale.—

The accompanying packet which I have taken the liberty of putting under Your Lordship's cover, Lord Durham is very anxious to have forwarded, with the least possible delay to Mr Robinson, the Chief Justice of the Upper Province, who has lately returned to England for the recovery of his health, and this, in truth is the direct occasion of my taking up my pen to address your Lordship.

Will Your Lordship be pleased to direct the packet to be forwarded as soon as possible to Mr Robinson.—

[356] ARTHUR TO LORD FITZROY [J. H.] SOMERSET: LB. 1,p. 79-83.

Oct 12 *Kingston.*

Your Lordship will naturally be extremely anxious to know how we are affected in the Canadas by the late discussions in Parliament, and by Ld. Durham's consequent determination to return to England, which was communicated to the Government by the Great Western on the 4th instant— I avail myself therefore of a spare moment whilst returning from Quebec, where I have been paying a short visit to Lord Durham, to give Your Lordship a brief sketch of our present position.—

But first I must thank your Lordship for your obliging interference about our barracks, which, notwithstanding the answer you received from the Ordnance, has been of the greatest service,—or, if not, it is rather a remarkable coincidence that I have since received a dispatch from the Secretary of State, which affords a better promise of comfortable accommodation, for the Troops at Toronto, than Sir John Colborne or myself were before able to extract.—

Yesterday Ld Durham published the Proclamation which is required by the indemnity act, together with another very remarkable explanatory proclamation, which Your Lordship will find in the accompanying Gazette— The French Party in the one, and the American Party in the other Province, consider the disallowance of the ordinance to be a triumph, and we have the whole American Frontier again alive with the Patriot Lodges, and it is almost universally expected that we shall have the work of the Last Winter over again, and perhaps something worse,—

Coming out with all the mistaken notions by which the leading men of all parties have been so completely misled for some years, Ld Durham laid himself out to conciliate the French Party, by [*sic*] happily he early discovered the error, and I believe returns to England convinced of what others years ago ought to have been convinced of—that they are not to be conciliated— The true object of the French Party, it cannot be doubted, has been to get rid of British rule, and, rather than submit to it, they would throw themselves on the Americans. The truth is— men have been the same in all countries, and in all ages; and when their blood is up, and their passions excited, there is nothing they will not do in homage to the demon, whom they, for the time blindly worship— The Roman Catholic Canadian must from his heart abhor the whole American polity, religious and civil; and yet to be avenged of the British Party, I have not a doubt that he would turn Republican if he could, to get rid of British rule—

The British Party, on the other hand, seem quite resolved not to suffer their energies to be any longer repressed by their ill associated French connexion, and they now no longer suppress the expression of their wish, that the Canadas were free states, rather than continue in their present feverish state.— The fate of Lord Durham's mission must bring matters to a crisis, and I must confess that I am well pleased, that there can be no further trimming.— It has been tried until the Provinces are on the very verge of being lost.— Both Parties, from the most opposite views and feelings, are becoming more and more prepared for American amalgamation, though I believe the British Party will be faithful, if they be not driven to despair.—

The 23rd Regiment are sent from Halifax, and Sir John Colborne has requested me to call out some companies of Militia, and to prepare one or two Corps to support him in the Lower Province if required.— It is not possible any longer to disregard the preparations making by the "Patriots", who evidently expect to be joined by their Friends if they can but get a footing in the Provinces—

[357] ARTHUR TO COLBORNE: LB. 1,p. 83-89.

Oct. 14 *Kingston.*

On my arrival here this morning, I found your official, and two private letters.— I will answer all the points in them to which you would wish me to refer, as soon as I reach Toronto—the present being the time for action—and it would appear there is none to be lost.—

There is much excitement here in consequence of the various accounts which have been received of the forward preparations on the other side.— As usual, no doubt, there is, on this occasion, some exaggeration, but enough remains to shew that no time should be lost in making immediate arrangements for the defence of the Province, which may possibly prevent attacks.—

I enclose copies of the statements &c, I have received this day.—

The Deposition made by Daly, is a very remarkable corroboration of the whole of the statement given by Stewart at Youn[g]stown to my Aide de Camp, And also by an American gentleman to Captain Eyre of the 73rd. whose letter I enclose.

I know you have hitherto been slow to credit the accounts from the other side, but I do think it is time to give good heed to them—

My opinion has been throughout that the Americans have acted with bad faith— All the People of the Northern States, it cannot be otherwise, would wish to see the Canadas Republican States: and altho Respectable Citizens would not perhaps take an active part in subverting our Monarchical Institutions, still they will do but little, if any thing, to prevent the aggressions of that class of persons who would pour in upon us as they did upon the Texas.—

Captain De Rottenberg's [*sic*] letter is so very important, that I have determined to proceed to Belleville to-morrow, and see the Magistrates, and I hope to get them in good humour again,—but, as I have before mentioned to you, there is very general dissatisfaction in this Province in consequence as it is asserted, of delay and ultimate injustice, in settling the accounts after the last outbreak.

I approach this subject with regret, because it is one in which I am so unfortunate as to differ with you in opinion—but—I am more and more convinced, that the present system of the Commissariat is practically most inconvenient to the Public Service, and calculated to occasion the repetition of annoyances— The Upper Province forms a Military District, and if the Deputy Commissary General were in charge of it as a District, and the officers serving in it received and executed their orders under him, there would be more Despatch and facility in carrying on the duties of that important department.

So, with regard to the Ordnance, we are not at all in the state of preparation which I am sure you wish and expect—the most valuable time has been lost in references, which ought not to have been necessary, after once your own orders had been issued.—

If these two departments have proper prudence of action, there will be, I am confident, no additional expense, but the very reverse, and you could not, I am persuaded, more effectually restore confidence in the Upper Province than by acquiescing in this arrangement.

I have inspected the stations at Cornwall and Prescot[t], and ordered the two companies there, to be augmented to one hundred men each, and directed a Company of a hundred men to be stationed at Brockville, but there seems great difficulty in getting men.—

Colonel Turner will immediately inspect the Glengarry Militia, and I have ordered one Regiment of them to be warned to [be] ready to assist in the Lower Province if required.— only be so good as to give me timely notice.—

I have seen Colonel Macdonal [*i.e.* Macdonell], and warned him that, in case of need, he will again have the honor of marching into the Lower Province.

There should be a depot at once, of arms at Cornwall and at Prescott, and I have directed 500 stand to be sent to each.—

Do you not think it would be proper to place a force in the works at Coteau du Lac— I will raise a company of the Glengarries for that Service, if you wish.— It is certainly an important point.

I have ordered one company of a hundred men to be raised for the service of this Town, so as to relieve the Regular Troops of some of the duty, according to the wish expressed in your official letter.

There will be, of course, expenses incurred in all these arrangements, in preparing Barracks, clothing, and various incidental items—pray let there be a formal authority in orders for this, that the Militia may see at once, that it is intended they shall be taken as good care of as the Regular Troops, and this may tend to bring about a better feeling both amongst Officers and men of that description of Force.—

It is of great importance to keep up appearances as much as possible at Toronto, as the Country will always take its tone, in a great measure, from thence— I would therefore recommend that the Headquarters of the 23rd. should be posted there.

Were it not that I think you would object to divide the squadron—I would also particularly recommend that one of the Troops of the

Dragoon Guards should remove to Hamilton—we have accommodation there for one Troop— The Gore Militia might be quickly called out, if required, and with the Troop might promptly reinforce Colonel Maitland.—

I would also reembody Major Magrath's Troop of Lancers to watch Young [*i.e.* Yonge] Street, if required.—

From all I hear, the Country about Belleville and along the Ontario—Whitby—Pickering—&c &c—is the most disaffected *East* of Toronto, a company of Militia at each will be quite essential.

I shall not remain at Toronto more than two or three days before I proceed to the Westward, but I may hope a few lines from you may reach me before my departure.—

It will be better, I am confident, to spend a few thousand pounds in suppressing either invasion or a rising, than to let either gain head, and I wish with all my heart, that we had three good Militia Regiments embodied.

The Arms at many of the stations are quite unserviceable. The Ordnance, under the usual regulations, require them to be sent to Kingston for repair, but if you will give authority in the emergency, for their being repaired at the several stations, it might be done for less expense, I believe, than would be the cost of carriage—and it would be done in half the time—

It is of the utmost importance that neither Patriots nor Insurgents should gain any temporary advantage, which induces me to wish that every thing that can be done should be done off hand.

[Enclosures lacking.]

[358] Arthur to Col. [C. L. L.] Foster: A.M. initialled.

[*1838*] [*Place not stated.*]
[*c. Oct. 14*] Col: Foster

Will address a Letter to Montreal, informing Sir J. Colborne that there are about 1500 Stand of Arms at Niagara delivered in by the Militia which require cleaning & some require repair—

Colonel Booth is desirous that these Arms shd. not be removed to Kingston & He will send his Armourer to Clean & put them into a good serviceable state if the Comdr. of the Forces will approve—

I wish this to go as soon as possible—

[359] Durham to Arthur: A.L.S. 2p.

Oct. 15 *Quebec.* [Marked "Private & Confidential".]

There can be no doubt that I have communicated the correspondence to you officially, & not confidentially, for the purpose of accounting to you & all the other Lieut Governors, for my absence from the General Government.

I should imagine therefore that there could be no objection to the Legislature of any Province, that calls for Explanation, being made acquainted with it.

Of course it should not be made the groundwork of any censure on the Ministry—

[360] T. L. Goldie to Arthur: A.L.S.
Oct. 15 *Sorel.*

I have the honor by the direction of the Commander of the Forces to transmit to Your Excellency the enclosed Copy of a letter [marginal note here reads: "15th. October"] which he has this day written to Captain Sandom Comr. on the Canadian Lakes.

[Enclosure is apparently item 361.]

[361] Colborne to Captain [Williams] Sandom: L. 4p.
Oct. 15 *Sorel.* [Marked "Copy—"]

I have to thank you for your letter of the 24th. ultimo, acquainting me that the small vessels intended for the protection of the Western Frontier of Upper Canada have been some time stationed at Sandwich, and Sarnia— With reference to the Communication from Lieut McClure Commanding the Schooner Brock, and to the reports, and information received by the Lieut Governor of the Province, respecting the intentions of the Refugees and American Marauders, and the preparations which it is said, they are now making to recommence their incursions in the Townships on the St Lawrence, and in those on the Western frontier, from Michigan. I beg to state to you, that I am of opinion that the schemes and operations of the Invaders would be greatly impeded, and perhaps frustrated by your ordering the Toronto Steam boat to be stationed during the winter at the Port of Amherstburg— The navigation of the Detroit, and St Clair may probably remain open till the end of January; and in that case, the Steam boat would be available either for the transport of Troops, or for towing Gun boats. The appearance of a flotilla in that quarter would give great confidence to the population. This arrangement would I think afford more protection to the London, and Western Districts, than stationing the Toronto at the Grand River a very unhealthy Port—

If the "Experiment," and such Gun boats as you may be able to equip at Kingston, occosionally [*sic*] cruise between Gannanoqui [*sic*] and Prescott, from this time to the close of the navigation, that Frontier with the aid of the Troops quartered in the Midland, and Johnston Districts will be tolerably secure—

Whitby on Lake Ontario, and Port Dover on Lake Erie should also be protected by Gun boats—

[362] Arthur to Colborne: LB. 1,p. 77-79.
Oct. 17 *Cobourg.*

In consequence of the information which I received at Kingston, I proceeded as intimated in my letter to you I would do, to Hastings, and had a meeting of all the Magistrates at Belleville.

Baron de Rottenburgs statement, I found was not overdrawn; There was great discontent and great excitement. I took with me Mr Cartwright from Kingston, who, I thought might act as peacemaker.

The discontent proceeds from some non-adjusted accounts of expences incurred in turning out the Militia last winter. These Accounts were rendered some time since to the Commissariat, many items were disallowed, and even the residue has not been paid. I will call upon Mr Clark the Comt Officer for explanation, as the accounts have been, it would appear, rendered to him. If the statement of the Magistrates be entirely correct, there is cause for remonstrance no doubt, but none for *disaffection*. From the trials which took place at Kingston, there cannot be a question that there were well grounded apprehensions entertained that the disloyal people in Hastings would go to great extremes, and the Magistrates were fully borne out in adopting the measures they did—the expenses ought therefore to have been defrayed.

The existing alarm is occasioned by the information received of *the doings* on the American side. Every Magistrate, I found, had heard something which he considered conclusive.

Frequent communication was kept up with the States and several meetings had recently taken place amongst known disaffected people. "The menaces of these people and the revenge they felt towards them by whom they had been arrested last winter were matters of notoriety; and, yet the Government had done nothing for their protection". The conference lasted about two hours and a half, during which time I was overwhelmed with all sorts of fears and grievances.

Some weeks ago, I had heard from Mr. Boswell a professional Person, who certainly *has been* very much in the confidence of the Reformers in this Province, that he had no doubt the disloyal feeling extended far and wide in December last,—and in a conversation with Him today he told me that the extremes to which the disaffected had determined to go "was quite appalling to think of." He defended the Traitors who were tried at Kingston, and thereby got into their secrets, and he assured me that he had no doubt they were acting in concert with a great body of persons on the American Frontiers with whom they had conspired to attack and seize upon Kingston— It is his opinion that a very considerable number of persons are still residing in Hastings, who would take up arms against the Government, if they saw any prospect of success. There is not, that I have been able to discover, any sufficient cause for the feeling of dissatisfaction which so generally prevails, but that it does prevail, I have no doubt, and we must look well to it.

I have mentioned Mr. Boswell's name in perfect confidence to you. . .

P.S. I think much more must be done than your Memorandum specifies, but I will officially write to you at length when I get to Toronto. No time should be lost I am of opinion in calling out a much larger force.

[363] R. B. SULLIVAN TO THE LIEUT GOVERNOR [ARTHUR]: A.L.S.

[1838] [*Place not stated.*]

[*Oct. 18?*] I send herewith the deposition of W. J. Kent who I believe to be a true man & that his information is of a most valuable kind[.] I have directed him to come to me tomorrow.

[Enclosure lacking.]

[364] ARTHUR TO THE BISHOP OF REGIOPOLIS [ALEXANDER MACDONELL]: LB. 2, p. 172-173.

Oct. 19 *Government House, Toronto.*

I have to acknowledge the receipt of your favor of the 6th. Inst communicating your intention to induce the Catholics of Upper Canada to relinquish their claims to a share of the Clergy Reserves of this Province provided they get a Grant of the Property formerly belonging to the Jesuits in Lower Canada, and further that you had called an aggregate meeting of the Catholics of this Province for the purpose of petitioning Her Majesty on this subject.

I have also learned that the contemplated meeting has taken place, and that Resolutions were adopted at it in accordance with the views expressed in Your Lordships letter to me.

I am highly gratified in perceiving in these Proceedings a plain indication that the Catholics in this Province are desirous, so far as in them lies, of removing any obstacle that their claims to be considered by the Government might present to a satisfactory adjustment of the long agitated question of the Clergy Reserves.

A stranger, on my arrival in the Province, to the conflicting opinions which existed on the subject, I have felt it my duty to examine into it's [*sic*] various bearings in order that I might, as a disinterested umpire between all parties interested, endeavor to offer some principle of satisfactory adjustment which should provide to the utmost extent possible for the Religious Instruction of the People of this Province.

The ecclesiastical Jurisdiction and authority which the late creation of Rectories was stated to give to the respective Incumbents was among the first matters that attracted my particular enquiry. I took for granted that each Rectory embraced an extensive circle within which many persons, not members of the Episcopal Church, were resident, who had reason to believe they had in consequence become in Law the parishioners of the Incumbent. But I have recently had my attention drawn to the fact that these Rectories are confined to limits not extending generally beyond the Church and Church Yard. In some cases, an acre or two of Land adjoining is included on which the Parsonage House is or may be built.— As, therefore, the Ecclesiastical Authority of the Rector extends only over persons residing within the limits of his Rectory, the conscientious alarms and scruples that have been entertained and expressed on this point prove to be entirely groundless.

Deeply conscious that no country can long flourish in which religion and piety are not cultivated by the People, it seems to me to be one of the first duties of a Government to make provision for so important a purpose—and by keeping this great object steadily in view in the discussion of the Clergy Reserve Question, and meeting the difficulties which are found to environ it, in a spirit of Christian Charity, and sincere determination to promote the general good, I cannot but hope that, at the next Session of the Legislature, a plan may be presented and adopted, which shall secure to the People of Upper Canada, the inestimable advantage of religious Instruction.

[365] R. B. SULLIVAN AND W. H. DRAPER TO [ARTHUR ?]: A.M.S. 2p.

Oct. 19 *Council Chamber*, [*Toronto.*]

Mr Draper & Mr Sullivan are of opinion that the proposal of Sparks as now made, namely to receive from time to time an amount not in the whole to exceed four or five hundred dollars, and, that his further remuneration should depend on the value of his information is very reasonable and may readily be acceded to. Mr Jones may further be authorized to communicate that any persons who may be induced to join with Sparks in bringing any vessell [*sic*] of which he may be placed in charge by the enemy within the power of this Government would receive a reward proportionate to the service rendered.

[The above is in Sullivan's handwriting but is signed by both Draper and himself.]

[366] ARTHUR TO COLONEL [HENRY] BOOTH: LB. 1,p. 74-76.

Oct. 20 *Toronto.*

I intended to have written to you in some detail this morning but I have so much upon my hands and so many persons waiting in the Ante Room that it is not possible.

It occasions me much concern to hear that you have been so unwell, and I am apprehensive that you take a little too much to heart the desertion of your men.

No prudence nor precaution can circumstanced as your Regiment is, provide against such occurrences even in the very best regulated Corps; and, therefore we must be resigned to such consequences, and encounter them as evils that are unavoidable and to be endured accordingly.

I do not entirely meet your views with respect to the Sergeant; as he *had* returned, it would have been better to have kept him as a Prisoner, until he could have heard the decision of the Commander of the Forces.

I am much obliged to you for affording me the services just now of Lieutenant Jones, and I propose despatching Him with a letter to General Macomb.

The accounts the Government has received concur in the information that there are serious preparations making all along the Frontier. I have a "confidential" communication from Mr Fox from Washington in which He tells me that the American Government seriously apprehend that large numbers of these "Patriots" will attempt to cross over in defiance of all their measures to prevent it.

I wish General Macomb to take steps to prevent the arms being plundered from the Public Depots, if he can help it. Nevertheless, whether they get them or not, we shall give a good account of these Pirates, I am sure, if they do attempt invasion.

I am just going to transport all the Batch that were captured at Niagara in June last, and that measure will, most probably, bring matters to an issue one way or another.

I will immediately notify Captain Swan's appointment as Major; and propose reinforcing you with another Militia Company, or perhaps two Companies, so that I may have your Regt disposable—for at Niagara they will never cross I think whilst the 43d are posted there.

Any suggestions you will offer me I shall receive thankfully and with every disposition to render you all the assistance in my power.

Wherever these people land, if they do attempt it, we must be at them *immediately.*

[367] ARTHUR TO COLONEL [HENRY] BOOTH: LB. 1,p. 89-90.

Oct. 21 *Toronto.*

From the person who has come from Cleveland, who passed through Niagara, and saw you I believe, I have received such a confirmation of the Reports which had been already made to me, as to leave no doubt of the intended attacks in a few days on this Province— It does not appear that Niagara is to be one of the points of attack—but the most serious attempt is to be made upon Fort Malden (Amherstberg) [*sic.*] I shall thank you therefore to send off the accompanying Letter by some confidential Person—to warn Colonel Airey of his danger— The Persons he has been employing to work in the Fort, are Spies—and they fully expect to take him by surprise.—

Upon the whole it will be better, perhaps, to send an Officer in whom you can confide, and desire him not to lose a moment in reaching Amherstberg.—

Pray lose no time in getting all the arms at Niagara in the best possible order—let your Armourer get any assistance—he requires.

I am rather inclined to the opinion, that if the Dragoon Guards were moved from Niagara to Brantford & replaced immediately by a draft of 200 men from the sedentary Militia, that it might be advantageous— In that case you might call out one of the Troops of Sedentary Militia to patrol and carry Despatches.—

I wish very much that I could get another good Steamer for the Service, on Lake Erie.

[Superscription reads: "Colonel Booth Comg 43d Regt".]

[Enclosure lacking.]

[368] COLBORNE TO ARTHUR: L.S. 14p.

Oct. 21 *Canada Steam boat.*

We have not a moment to lose in preparing on an extensive scale to repel the attack which our neighbours, it appears from the information we have received from all parts of the United States, are determined to make on our long line of Frontier—

You will have heard from Mr. Fox that the Washington Government have no doubt that an alarming organization exists in the States of Vermont, New York, Ohio, Illinois, and Michigan, and that the Collectors at the different Ports all concur in their reports as to the extent of the sympathising societies, and of the preparation for an invasion.

In Lower Canada Arms have been for some time passing the Frontier, and I regret to add have been distributed in some of the Seigniories. It must be decided this winter, whether our Colonists will submit to be kept in a perpetual state of suspense and alarm: We must therefore at any outlay or expense show that we can protect them— I am already at work to complete our chain of Posts and Reserves, I transmit to you Copies of the regulations and orders which I intend to establish for the guidance of the Volunteer Corps on permanent duty, and those in reserve called Sedentary— I wish that the Corps in Upper Canada may be organized on the same terms. If however you can not obtain them on the terms on which we raise them, either as to the extent of their services, or their pay and allowances, we can not afford time to hesitate, therefore you will proceed as you may think it expedient or necessary— I think that the ten shillings per month, to be paid after their service, is a better plan than giving them two pounds enlistment money, to get drunk with at the time they enlist— I wish the Corps or Companies to be raised not to be considered as Militia. I think we shall find some inconvenience on active service in permitting the Militia laws to interfere with us— Now for the Posts we are to occupy, and the force required on permanent duty, and in reserve.

I beg you will permit Colonel Donald Macdonell to raise, 600, six hundred men, immediately in Glengarry, they have all their arms and accoutrements— I wish this Corps to be placed on permanent duty, two Companies to be placed at the Coteau du Lac, two in Lancaster and two in the neighbourhood— Another Corps must be raised by Colonel Fraser, I suppose, to be in reserve, to be called out and drilled once a week, Clothed and paid at the rate of 2s/6d per diem, when they are called out— This Corps will be held ready to march at the shortest notice— At Cornwall Colonel VanKoughnett [*sic*] will raise 400 men to be placed on permanent duty and ready to march— Two Companies to be raised for Brockville and two for Prescott— Colonel McMillan perhaps will be able and willing to raise a Corps at Perth, and march to Ganonoqui [*sic*] and Kingston— I wish Colonel Marshall to be stationed at Gananoqui and to have charge of that post and vicinity and Beverly—

A Corps should be raised at Peterborough to be stationed at Port Hope and Cobourg, ready to march to Whitby[.]

We require two volunteer Corps on permanent duty for the protection of the frontier from Chippewa to Fort Erie, and from Fort Erie to Gravelly Bay— At Hamilton a Battalion might be placed in Reserve *but not on* permanent duty— We must also have a Corps for the detached duties in the London District at Simcoe, St Thomas &c—

The Adelaide and Warwick Volunteers would probably be well placed under Colonel Radcliff in their own Townships ready to march, they could guard the roads from Sarnia and the Western frontier[.]

In addition to the Force you may think required for the Western frontier Townships of Moore, Sarnia, and Plympton, a Reserve Corps should be formed Composed of the Settlers of those Townships—

Two Corps should be raised for the protection of Sandwich, Windsor, and Chatham, and the Inhabitants formed into Corps of Reserves. The Townships of Malden Gosfield, Colchester should be organized and supplied with arms, and mustered occasionally. By these arrangements we should be able to keep the Regiments of the Line together— The whole of the 34th Regiment should be stationed at Amherstburg when the Posts of Chatham, and Sandwich can be strongly occupied by Volunteer Corps; and the whole of the 32nd Regt should be at London— The Penetanguishine detachment of the 34th Regt should be ordered to join their Head Quarters when they can be relieved[.]

There can be no objection to Major Magraths Lancers being embodied to keep Yonge Street in order—

I beg you will not divide the 1st. Dragoon Guards, nor take them from Niagara[.] They will be very useful at that Station and will probably act on the Erie Frontier,— Hamilton will be always well guarded, and can be reinforced easily from Toronto— We must be vigilant on the front, particularly between Fort Erie and Port Colborne. The 23rd or some other Corps will in the first instance be ordered to Kingston, You may then move the Head Quarters and three Companies to Toronto—

We must always have a strong Corps of the Line ready to leave Kingston, and march on the St Lawrence if required— It is said that 6000—Patriots are ready to invade Upper Canada, and 3000 to enter the Lower Province— If several points are invaded simultaneously, we must endeavour to bring our principal force on any body of Patriots that can be easily destroyed, so that the Invaders may be completely defeated and destroyed, whatever progress they may be making at other points—

Captain Graham's Perth Artillery may probably be brought down from Perth to Kingston— The Commissary General acquaints me that he has made arrangements for all accounts at Belleville to be paid— The other difficulties to which you advert in your letter of the 14th. respecting the Ordnance Department and Commissariat shall be met by my authorizing you to approve of all Estimates etc—and directing the heads of Departments to carry into effect your orders, without waiting for the sanction of their Chiefs—

Every Corps raised by you must be notified in General Orders—You will have the goodness to keep the Adjutant General and Military Secretary regularly informed as you proceed. That no time may be lost I have authorized Major Phillpotts to notify the Officers on the St Lawrence my intention with your sanction to authorize the forming of the Corps which I have mentioned. . .

P.S. All the Officers stationed on the Water frontier will of course assist in forming the Volunteer Corps and have the Command of their respective Districts—

A few Dragoons may be raised for the purpose of carrying Despatches on the line of the St Lawrence—

[369] H. S. Fox to Arthur: A.L.S. 15p.

Oct. 21 *Washington.* [Marked "Confidential".]

The Treasury Department at Washington continues to receive reports, from the United States Collectors of Customs at different stations on the Canadian frontier, in which those officers, (the collectors especially at Oswego, Rochester, and Cape Vincent,) reiterate,—to the full extent stated in my former letter to you of the 5th: of this month,—their belief in the existence of a secret conspiracy or combination, formed within the jurisdiction of the United States, for the purpose of future offence and aggression against the peace of Her Majesty's Provinces. Neither the Collectors, however, nor the United States district attorneys and marshals, who are specially charged to seek for information, appear to have obtained as yet any positive or accurate insight, into the plans and state of preparation of the members of the conspiracy.—

The Minister of War, Mr: Poinsett, on the other hand, has communicated to me the reports which he has received from General Macomb, the Military Commander in Chief on the frontier.— General Macomb does not believe in the existence of an organized secret combination, as described and denounced by the Civil officers of the Government; although he appears to consider the state of things, within his command, to be such as will require the utmost energy and vigilance on the part of the Authorities, to prevent, during the approaching season, a renewal of those acts of violence which disturbed the Canadian frontier in the winter and spring of this last year.—

I should be inclined to believe, that the truth will be found to rest between the two above statements of information.— In such emergencies as the present, the risk will of course always occur, of believing too much, or believing too little.— I must remark, however, that the Collectors of Customs in this Country, from their peculiar and extensive intercourse with the people, are probably the class of public officers the most likely to possess good information, with respect to dangerous and secret machinations carrying on within their districts.—

A small deposit of arms, consisting of muskets and rifles newly repaired, has been seized, under the new act of the 10th: of last March, by the United States Authorities at French Creek.— It appears that the Authorities have intelligence of a large illegal deposit of arms at Massillon, a town I believe in the State of Ohio.

The reports received, since I last addressed you, from several of the

Collectors, and which are dated from the 6th: to the 12th: of this month, contain some very remarkable particulars, in relation to the supposed conspiracy, which they state to have been communicated to them by private emissaries in their employment.— It is really most difficult to calculate, how far these alleged particulars partake of truth, exaggeration, or falsehood.— It is affirmed, in the information given to the Collectors, that the regular organization is completed, of a pretended Provisional State Government for Upper Canada, to be proclaimed at the breaking out of the anticipated rebellion: that the President elect of this, so called, Provisional Government, is a Canadian refugee of the name of Smith; and the Vice President, Mr:———, of ——— [marginal footnote reads: "see the accompanying private letter." [1]] in Upper Canada. It is added, however, by the same informants, that they doubt whether this last gentleman's name has not been used entirely without his own consent, or even knowledge.— It is further affirmed, that a national State Bank, to be so called, of Upper Canada, has been organized; to be established when the Country is revolutionized; the Crown Lands being to be pledged for the redemption of the notes of the Bank: that these notes are already engraved; and many of them in the secret possession of persons at Buffalo.— The chief contrivers of this part of the plot are stated to be, Grant a Canadian refugee, and Ebenezer Johnston, formerly Mayor of Buffalo.— This last individual is, I understand, well known in that part of the Country, a bankrupt, and of notoriously bad character.— All these strange stories may certainly be pure inventions, palmed upon the credulity of the United States Collectors; but the truth of them is very positively asserted; and equally so from divers quarters: and although I entertain no doubt that the denunciations are greatly exaggerated, I acknowledge that I remain of opinion, considering the many extraordinary occurrences which we witnessed on the Canadian frontier during the past year,—that it would be most hazardous altogether to disbelieve them.—

[370] H. S. Fox to Arthur: A.L.S. 4p.

Oct. 21 *Washington.* [Marked "Private".]

The name left in blank, in the accompanying confidential despatch[2], is "William Hamilton Merritt, of St. Catherine's [*sic*] Upper Canada."— I hope that the mention of this Gentleman's name is only a stupid calumny. I have understood that he is a most respectable man, enjoying the confidence of the Provincial Government.— It appears to me that nothing is more probable, than that the Canadian refugee rebels should endeavour, by similar inventions, to involve men of loyalty and influence in suspicion with the Authorities of the Colony.— You will however be a better judge upon this subject, than I can [*sic*].—

I do not write upon the present occasion to Lord Durham, as I believe my letter would find him already departed from Canada, and his functions as Governor General ceased.— I leave it to your discretion, to forward, if you judge expedient, the information contained in my despatch, to the administration of the Lower Province, or to the Commander in Chief.— The whole of the supposed machinations, however, seem to me to point to Upper Canada, and not Lower Canada.

[1] *i.e.* item 370.
[2] *i.e.* item 369.

[371] ARTHUR TO GLENELG: LB. 1,p. 98-100.

Oct. 22 *Government House, Toronto.*

I am well aware what your Lordship's anxiety will be after reading my Despatch of this date, from what I know it was last Winter.

After the affair of the invasion on the Niagara and Western Frontiers in July last, which was suddenly put down, we had a most deceitful lull for some time; but, now affairs seem more serious than ever.

The whole frontier is overrun with Patriots or Hunters, as they call themselves, and the American Government cannot, or they say they cannot, put them down.—

As it is impossible to determine what force is coming against us, I do not like to be over sanguine; but, if these Brigands do cross, which I suppose they will, unless they shall be deterred by our present preparations, I think they will be signally defeated in in [*sic*] their enterprize; and if matters go tolerably well in the Lower Province, I think we shall make a good stand of it here.—

The worst part of the story is—that the Militia do not seem disposed to turn out with any alacrity.— Our defences also are in an unfinished state, and we want many necessary supplies for the comfort of the Militia.

Arms,—Blankets, Clothing—Shoes &c will be much wanting, I fear; and altho I will not address Your Lordship officially, and thereby place myself under the fire of the Treasury again, for interfering with Military Matters, yet, I hope you will permit me, in this private note to say, that if it be not too late in the season, all the stores applied for, should yet, by all means, be sent out immediately[.]

[372] ARTHUR TO JOHN MAITLAND: LB. 1,p. 91-92.

Oct. 22 *Government House, Toronto.*

I send off Captain Markham to you to give you the information that an attack upon an extended scale may be expected *very suddenly*— I have already sent a letter to you to the same effect viâ Lake Erie.

The information I have obtained leads me to expect that [the attack] will be made at the same time upon Fort Malden, Port Stanley and Port Dover—but, mainly, I think upon Fort Malden—the day fixed upon is the 27th. Instant, but, I doubt if the plan will be sufficiently organized by that time. However, not an hour should be lost in getting together whatever force can be collected, and making all your arrangements to move against the Enemy. Let Him have no time, but land where he may let him be assailed at once.

Colonel Airey should assemble whatever force he can to strengthen his position and so should Colonel Chichester. It may be well for you to embody also some Volunteers to be attached to your own Corps, so that if you march you may leave a good force to protect your Stores &c &c in London.

Chatham should be a point well looked to. I will look in the morning to what arms and ammunition you have, and will send a further supply if it appear necessary—so that you may reinforce Colonel Airey if he should stand in need of arms or ammunition.

I rely upon your deriving great assistance from Colonel Chichester, and you may employ some of the Mounted Militia to keep up your communication with him if you find it necessary.

The Steam Boat "Toronto" should at once proceed to Amherstburg— She is, I hope well manned and armed.

All the loyal People I am satisfied will readily assemble around you.

[373] [Sir] A. N. MacNab and W[illia]m Kingsmill to Arthur: L.S. 6p.

Oct. 22 *Toronto.*

In reference to the conversation which we had the honor of holding this day with Your Excellency on the subject of raising Provincial Troops in order to reinforce and assist those of the Line in repelling the threatened invasion of this Province by "Brigands" now assembling on the American Frontier— We beg respectfully to state that in our opinion the Militia will not turn out with the same degree of alacrity which they evinced on a former occasion, the causes of which it is not necessary at present to advert to;

To ensure a sufficient number of Volunteers it would be necessary to extend the time of their service to as lengthened a period as possible, *and the terms* upon which thesese [*sic*] men are to be embodied should be communicated with the least possible delay to those Officers to whom Your Excellency may think proper to entrust the Command, calling upon them at the same time for such remarks as they may deem it proper to offer, for the consideration of the Major General Commanding. As it must necessarily take some time before Regiments raised under such circumstances can be brought into an efficient state, we deem it proper to suggest that each Corps should be concentrated at its Head Quarters, and not detached at least for some weeks unless under a very pressing emergency, and in order to facilitate this object, and render the men upon joining as comfortable as possible, we are further of opinion that a certain portion of Clothing, Bedding, Blankets, Cooking Utensils &c &c should be forthwith procured, and placed in store, subject to the orders of the respective Commanding Officers of Corps.

From the experience which we have already had we deem it absolutely necessary that means should forthwith be taken to place the Arms and Accoutrements in a thorough state of repair previously to issuing them to the men—after which the Armourers of the different Corps can preserve them in order.

As it appears in consequence of recent information to be Your Excellency's intention to reinforce Malden, and the Western Frontier, we beg to suggest the propriety of your Excellency calling upon Colonel Prince an influential Magistrate, to organize as large a Militia force as he can procure, calling at the same time upon Colonels Askin and Elliott to cooperate in carrying this measure into effect—it would also be advisable to obtain as quickly as possible from that quarter, a return of Arms, Accoutrements, Ammunition, Stores &c which may be disposable—

In conclusion, we beg respectfully to suggest the propriety of calling upon the Officers in Command of Regiments of Militia, to send a return to Head Quarters, of the number of men of their respective Corps, who can be depended upon to turn out at any moment, that their services may be required, and such men, should be apprized of the necessity of holding themselves in readiness to take the field, at a very early period[.]

Colonel Cameron being still absent from Toronto, we deemed it prudent to comply with Your Excellency's instructions without waiting for the arrival of that Officer . . .

Allan N MacNab
Col: 3rd. Gore M.

Wm Kingsmill
Col 1st. Durham.

[374] COLBORNE TO MAJOR [GEORGE] PHILLPOTTS: A.M.S. 2p.

Oct. 22[?] *Sorel.*

Memoranda for Major Phillpotts.

Major Phillpotts will deliver the accompanying letter to Sir George Arthur, and explain to him my intentions with respect to the Corps proposed to be raised on the S Lawrence. He will convey such instructions to the Officers on his route to Toronto as he may think necessary in order to hasten the completion of the Corps— He will explain to the Colonels of Regts and others the regulations by which they are to be guided, and acquaint them they are authorised to raise these Corps without delay, as there can be no doubt Sir George Arthur will concur with Sir John Colborne in sanctioning the proposed arrangements[.]

[The letter referred to is probably item 368.]

[375] ARTHUR TO COLBORNE: LB. 1, p. 92-97.

Oct. 24 *Government House, Toronto.*

I have the honor to acquaint your Excellency that the security of this Province requires, and the good feeling of the community can only be roused by the immediate employment of a very considerable augmentation of the Military force.

In my letter of yesterday which you will receive with this communication, I transmitted to Your Excellency a copy of the Minutes of the Executive Council, in which, for the reasons set forth in much detail, the Members strongly advise, that at least 5.000 men should be at once embodied.

I now beg to enclose, for your perusal, the statement on oath made by Mr. Kent, [marginal note here reads: "I regret that this paper cannot be prepared in time for this conveyance, but will be transmitted tomorrow."] who arrived on Monday from Cleveland, and has proceeded to Washington to give the ample information which he possesses, to the American Government, and to the British Minister Mr Fox— Mr Kent considers that the American Government have it not in their power to put down this intended conspiracy for the invasion of Canada—but I have thought it prudent, notwithstanding, that he should proceed to Washington.

I have seen Mr Hamilton who is deeply interested in the Steamers on Lake Ontario. Last winter he had no apprehension; but, now, he is much alarmed at the threatening aspect of affairs.—

There prevails, in fact, a general expectation that we shall be assailed from *without* and from *within*.— I therefore, last night, came to the determination, that it was my duty to call out, and arm at least 5.000 Militia, and upon that scale I propose at once to proceed.— It exceeds much the force which your Excellency has recommended, but, then, our situation is far more perilous than was anticipated when I had the pleasure to confer with you on the [blank in MS.] Instant.—

The recruiting of the Companies already directed to be formed goes on very slowly indeed—there is an apathy, an indifference, about that part of the Population by whom the greatest zeal was displayed last Winter, which is very distressing—they do not appear anxious to come forward.— I augur worse from what I have observed about the Conservative Party, than of anything else that has occurred since I have been in the Province.

It will be a greater inducement, it is represented to me, for men to volunteer for the embodied Militia, if their services are engaged for a longer period than has heretofore been the case, and I have therefore approved of receiving men for eighteen months, a period which will embrace two Winters. I wish much it were in my power to engage them to serve for five years, and I earnestly hope your Excellency will concur with me in recommending that measure to Her Majesty's Government— There will be no confidence in the stability of the Government after what has occurred, for many years to come.—

This will have a good effect in some other respects—and I hope my expectation may not be disappointed—for, I cannot deny that I have now a far worse opinion of our situation, than I have ever before entertained.— The Loyal people are disheartened and deeply dissatisfied with the policy which has been pursued—the lenity shown to others they consider as a punishment to them, and there is none of that lively exciting determination to support the Government, which one would wish to see exhibited at such a moment.—

I do not despond—but the most active measures must be adopted, for nothing else I think will prevent another outbreak under the expectation that there will be prompt and effectual assistance from the Brigands.

I have caused the Steamer "Traveller" to be engaged according to the recommendation of Mr. Routh, and I only wait the arrival of Captain Sandom for whom I have sent to engage another Steamer for Lake Erie.—

I fear it will be out of Your Excellency's power to spare *two* additional Regiments for this Province—but it would be most important to me if it could be affected [*sic*]. I should wish of all things to have a Regiment of the Line at Brantford.

It is my wish to avoid the expense that took place last Winter in the appointment of Militia Staff officers—with Your Excellency's concurrence, therefore, I should be glad to employ the Regular Staff with any temporary assistance that may be unavoidably required.— In this case it will be just and most reasonable that Major Frazer [*i.e.* Fraser] who is in charge of the Quarter Master Generals Department should receive the pay and allowances of an Assistant Quarter Master General.

With Your Excellency's sanction I have also an officer of the 85th. Regiment, Ensign Domvile serving on my staff, as an Extra Aide-de-Camp, but without any pay or allowances—it will—I trust, appear to you necessary to allow this officer to receive at least the allowances of the appointment if the pay cannot be permitted, as I can truly state, that his employment has hitherto been laborious on many occasions—and now is likely to be much more so—

[376] ARTHUR TO COLBORNE: LB. 1, p. 97-98.

Oct. 24 *Government House, Toronto.*

Mr. Kent whose deposition I transmit by the present opportunity, stated to me, that the Head Quarters of the *first* Division of the Army of the intended Republic of Canada would be fixed at St. Albans in Vermont. In this deposition he has stated that Cleveland was the Head Quarters of the second Division.—

It would therefore appear that the First Division must be intended principally to act against the Lower Province. The Town of St. Albans being on the Eastern side of Lake Champlain, is too remote from Upper Canada, to induce me to consider that any demonstration will be made from thence against the Eastern District.—

I mention this just as it has occurred to me in order that you may cause the movements in Vermont &c. especially at St Albans to be watched with particular care at the present very critical emergency[.]

[Enclosure lacking.]

[377] ARTHUR TO COLBORNE: LB. 1, p. 100-103.

Oct. 24 *Government House, Toronto.* [Marked "Private".]

The information coming in from all quarters, affords the fullest corroboration of the advanced state of the preparations made by the Brigands—and of the assistance they are likely to receive in the Province.— The most unbelieving are now convinced that the extent of disaffected feeling in this Province, is much greater than was supposed—in fact—having had with me persons from every portion of the Province, I feel fully justified in stating, that from various causes, there exists a great alienation of the affections of the people toward Great Britain.—

The Militia evince great hesitation in coming forward, and it now seems evident, that so far from their keeping up excitement for the purpose of being kept in the Queen's employment, that most of them were desirous of returning to their Homes, which they were reluctant to leave.— This is further accounted for, from Immigration having been checked, and the price of labour consequently enhanced.—

In the report laid before me, I was sorry to observe, that at this moment, when an attack is hourly threatened upon Fort Malden, two soldiers of the 34th Regiment have deserted! Mr. Kent, the gentleman who has come from Cleveland, and has proceeded to give information to the Government of the United States at Washington, assured me that great efforts had been made to seduce our soldiers to desert, and that constant communication was kept up with them.

There ought undoubtedly to be a difference made with regard to soldiers serving in the Canadas— Numbers of them have their Fathers, Brothers, and Sisters, and other Relations residing in the States, who continually press them to join their families— Could it not be ventured upon to give them the Rations free, as we do the Militia, and so put an end to the invidious distinction, which is certainly felt by our Soldiers? This would be worth a couple of Regiments— I have mentioned it to Lord Durham, who would be perhaps good enough to take the responsibility of the measure upon himself.

I hope you will spare me what arms you can and by all means enable me to arm some of the Cavalry of the Country.— It seems to me a great pity to keep the Dragoon Guards pent up in a corner of the Niagara Frontier.— I could well supply their place with a hundred or two of the Sedentary Militia, and give Colonel Booth the benefits of a Troop of Sedentary Cavalry to carry Despatches, and then avail myself of the Dragoon Guards as a check upon the Western Country, to act with Troops raised in Hamilton—Brantford &c.—

This measure would be of great benefit, but I am most reluctant to interfere with the disposition of the Troops which you made yourself—although the circumstances of the Country are so much altered, that, were you present, I am almost certain you would wish it.—

Major Jackson's place had better perhaps be filled by Major Mc.Bean from Kingston.—

If we can deter these Ruffians from crossing, and the disaffected from rising, it is better than any victory over them—for then the misery of filling our Jails with Criminals will be obviated, with all its attendant sympathy . . .

P:S:. At what a moment you are called upon to assume the administration of the Lower Province!

[378] GLENELG TO ARTHUR: L.S. 2p.

Oct. 24 *Downing Street*, [*London*.] [Marked "Duplicate No. 156".]

I have received your Despatch of the 29th. September marked Separate, requesting me to recommend to the Lords of the Treasury that you should be permitted to draw the allowances of a Major General on the Staff.

On referring to my Despatch No 7, dated the 28th. December 1837 of which you were the bearer to the Colony, you will perceive that the ground on which Her Majesty's Government consented to recommend to the Legislature an addition of £500 to your Salary as Lieutenant Governor was the fact that you did not receive any other remuneration from the Public than the Civil Salary attached to the Office.

I have therefore not thought it expedient to submit your application to the Lords of the Treasury[.]

[379] J. B. ROBINSON TO ARTHUR: A.L.S. 4p.

Oct. 24 *Cheltenham, 7 Lansdown Place.*

We had a very agreeable & exceedingly expeditious passage in the Great Western—12. days & 12 hours from the Quay at New York to the Mooring in King's Road, being six hours shorter than the remarkable passage made by her in the summer— On my arrival at Clifton I wrote a short letter to Ld. Glenelg reporting my arrival & stating that as soon as I had placed my family at Cheltenham, I intended to go up to London, when I should have the honor of calling upon him— I had not then looked at any English paper & was not aware of Sir Robert Grant's death, or I should have addressed my note to Mr. Stephen instead—

The next post brought me a letter from Mr. Stephen—very civil—accounting for Ld. Glenelgs not writing himself, & expressing his wish to see me as soon as I could come without inconvenience to my health. I have been obliged to delay going to town for some days, & have written to say so— The day we landed I was all the day on my feet, as under such circumstances most people are, & I found myself much the worse for it— The drive to Cheltenham aggravated a local inconvenience which I felt, & I have been obliged to act discreetly & take some days rest for fear of bringing on a more serious illness— I am now almost free from pain, & early next week I hope to be in London— So far as I can gather from the London papers, great anxiety is felt by Ministers on the subject of Ld. Durham's probable return— The "Globe" affirms that he has been written to by the Liverpool Steamer to urge his remaining at his post, & that it depends upon the timely arrival of those despatches whether he will continue in his Government or not— One rumor is that Lord Normanby is to succeed him, & that the Duke of

Sussex, or Duke of Richmond is to go to Ireland in his place— It is very clear that Ld. Durham's return is expected and deprecated by the Government—that they know no more than any one else does whether he will return or not, and that in the mean time they are in a very uncomfortable & embarrassing state of suspense— When I get to London, and find that I can communicate any thing that all the World does not know, I shall write again to Your Excellency— In the mean time you will be pleased, I am sure to hear that Mrs. Robinson and the young travellers have reached their journey's end in perfectly good health, & find themselves most comfortably housed, near kind friends who are made very happy by the meeting— The weather is fair & mild, & I need not tell you that those who have never been in England, or who have been absent from it for a long time must find a great deal to delight them—

Sir Francis Head resides at Atherstone in Warwickshire, & has been very kind in his notice of us since our arrival—

If it should happen that Ld Glenelg declines to add to the Legislative Council, those members who can attend ought to be regularly at their post & I hope the Archdeacon, on account of the Church & indeed on all accounts will make a point of being present as often as he can— I am sure he would, if Your Excellency were to express a wish to that effect, he has for some years past attended but seldom—

I found my poor old Neighbour, Mc.Donell about the time of my departure very much troubled & disappointed at his apparently bad chance of success in an application he had made to have his son substituted for him as Inspector of Licences— He is a most worthy, old Gentleman, & one whom I am sure the Government would on many accounts take pleasure in gratifying, for I believe his connection with the Province is of older date than that of any other man in it—& his conduct & character have been always most unexceptionable— I have no doubt as to the ground of your Excellency's hesitation, & shall not presume to argue about it, but I believe those scruples might be as safely laid aside in this instance as they cd. be in any—

I have neither seen nor heard any thing interesting in the way of public intelligence since my arrival—

Mrs Robinson joins me in kind regards to Lady Arthur[.]

[380] [George, Baron] de Rottenburg to Dep[ut]y Com[missar]y Gen[era]l [F. E.] Knowles: LB. 4,p. 1.

Oct. 24 *Government House, Toronto.*

I am directed by His Excellency the Major General Commanding to request you will immediately cause Depots of Coals in sufficient quantities to be established at the undermentioned places viz at Port Colborne at Kingston & at Toronto & at such other places as may be necessary for the supply of the Government Steamers on the lakes.— That to be established at Kingston will also be required for the use of the Troops there & at Fort Henry: With regard to Toronto a depot must either be established there, or the Steam boats chartered by the Government must be required to provide their own Coals at that place—

[381] [GEORGE, BARON] DE ROTTENBURG TO J. S. MACAUL[A]Y: LB. 4,p. 1-2.

Oct. 24 *Government House, Toronto.*

His Excellency the Lieut Governor having given directions for the establishment of a Depôt of Coals for the use of the Government Steamers at Port Colborne requests that you will have the goodness to take immediate steps towards fortifying the Mill at that place, to effect this loop-holes should be pierced in all places from whence the wharf & canal gates can be defended[.] Platforms must be made to enable the men stationed for its defence to fire through, & such other means as may appear to be necessary to render the post tenable & capable of a sufficient resistance[.] His Excellency desires me further to state that all reasonable expenses incurred in effecting these objects will be defrayed by the Government.—

[382] W[ILLIA]M ROWAN TO CAPTAIN [FREDERICK] HALKETT: L.S. 2p.

Oct. 24 *Mil. Secy's. Office, Quebec.*

I have the honor to acknowledge the receipt of your letter of the 29th Ultimo, transmitting accounts of Travelling Expenses incurred by His Excellency Major General Sir George Arthur, on a tour of Military Inspection through Upper Canada, & I am directed to acquaint you, that with reference to the 2d. Article of the Treasury Regulations page 21 of Condensed Schedules, the Commander of the Forces has forwarded these accounts for the Consideration of the Lords Commissioners of Her Majesty's Treasury.

[383] [GEORGE, BARON] DE ROTTENBURG TO COLONEL [RICHARD] AIREY: LB. 4,p. 3.

Oct. 25 *Government House, Toronto.* [Marked "Immediate".]

With reference to your letter of the 17th. Sept 1838 addressed to His Excellency The Major Genl Comdg I have the honor to inform you that instructions have been received from the Commander of the Forces dated 17th Octr 1838 sanctioning the discontinuance of the working parties hitherto furnished by the Regt under your command: I am also directed by His Excellency Sir George Arthur to acquaint you that there will be no objection to Militia Soldiers being employed as labourers, provided the consent of their Commanding Officer can be obtained, but it must be understood that this is not to interfere with their drill: The working money to which they will become entitled will enable them to purchase such articles of Necessaries as they may be most in need of.

[Superscription reads: "Colonel Airey Comng 34th Regt Amherstburg".]

[384] [GEORGE, BARON] DE ROTTENBURG TO COL [HENRY] BOOTH: LB. 4,p. 3-4.

Oct. 25 *Government House, Toronto.*

I have the honor to enclose a Copy of a communication addressed to His Excellency the Major Genl Commanding conveying the approbation of the Commander of the Forces of the conduct of the Detachment King's Dragoon Guards stationed at Fort George Niagara under the command of Captn. Martin: I am directed by His Excellency to request you will have the goodness to obtain from Capt Martin a list of the names of the men whom he considers deserving of the pecuniary reward which the Commander of the Forces approves being given to these men & also to state what amount should be paid to each[.]

[Superscription reads: "Col Booth . . . Comg Drummondville".]

[Enclosure lacking.]

[385] [George, Baron] de Rottenburg to Colonel [Henry] Booth: LB. 4, p. 5.

Oct. 25 *Government House, Toronto.*

I am directed by His Excellency the Major Genl Commdg. to express to you his regret at the delay which has occurred in receiving an answer to the application which was made to the Comr. of the Forces upon the subject of placing the Wesleyan Methodist Chapel at Drummondville in a proper state of repair for the performance of divine service for the troops stationed there[.]

The answer was only received this day & His Excellency desires me to say that to insure the placing of the building in a comfortable state of repair he applied for the sum of Twenty pounds which has been sanctioned by the Comr: of the Forces, & instructions have been sent to the Commanding Royal Engineer at Niagara to carry the same into effect.

[386] [George, Baron] de Rottenburg to Capt [Colin] McKenzie [*i.e.* MacKenzie]: LB. 4, p. 2.

Oct. 25 *Government House, Toronto.* [Marked "Immediate".]

I have the honor to enclose for your information a Copy of a letter received by His Excellency the Major Genl Comng from the Commander of the Forces dated Quebec 17th: Octr 1838 approving of the discontinuance of Working parties being furnished by the 34th Regt & authorizing Capt Biscoe to hire labourers[.] I also enclose a Copy of His Excellency's instructions to Col Airey Comg 34 Regt upon the same subject & I am directed by His Excellency to request you will without delay communicate with Capt Biscoe, in order that immediate steps may be taken to carry His Excellency's directions into effect.—

[Superscription reads: "Capt McKenzie Comg Royal Engineers Niagara."]

[First enclosure lacking. Second enclosure is apparently a copy of item 383.]

[387] [George, Baron] de Rottenburg to The Offr. Comg. Royal Engineers Niagara [Colin MacKenzie ?]: LB. 4, p. 4-5.

Oct. 25 *Government House, Toronto.*

I have the honor to enclose for your information a copy of a letter addressed by His Excellency the Major Genl Comg of the 24th Sept. 1838 relative to placing the Wesleyan Methodist Chapel at Drummondville in a proper state for the performance of divine Service to the troops stationed there, & also a Copy of the answer received from Col Rowan containing the decision of the Commander of the Forces thereon[.] I am directed by His Excellency Sir George Arthur to request that you will in conformity with these instructions take steps for carrying the same into effect at an expense not exceeding the sum of Twenty Pounds—

[Enclosures lacking.]

[388] JOSEPH HUME TO THE EDITOR OF THE EXAMINER TORONTO [FRANCIS HINCKS]: A.L.S. 2p.

Oct. 25 *Bryanston Square, [London.]* [Marked "Private".]

I received your letter some time ago, but cannot now refer to it as it is in the Country; & I cannot longer delay its acknowledgment.

I take as warm an interest as ever in the Affairs of the Canadas, and shall be ready, (whenever I think my services can be of use), to give them willingly to promote the wellfare [*sic*] of the people of those provinces: But I am sorry to observe the same family Compact & tory Orange party as yet continue to mar the destinies of that People.

The sufferings of the Canadas have been mainly produced—at any rate they were brought to a Crisis in Upper Canada by the unjust & tyrannical Conduct of Sir Francis Head which, by his misrepresentations to an idle & inefficient Minister in Downing Street, were supported & even approved of—!!

I am pleased to see that Sir Geo Arthur gives, by his dispatches, the lie to Sir Francis Head's reports: But notwithstanding all this, Downing Street will support Ogle Owen [*i.e.* Gowan ?] & all the abettors of Arbitrary Govt in that Province.!! I ask, when will they learn wisdom from their past misrule? The public mind here is much occupied with the reported resignation of Lord Durham. I am sorry for it as the Houses of Parlt, having abolished all law, & crushed the liberties of the Canadas, it was foolish in the highest degree, to quarrel with the first acts of the *Dictator*, without having his reasons for such acts. I think Lord D, acted wisely in sparing the effusion of Blood, & I shall be happy to hear that he will remain & continue & complete his plans for ultimate settlement of the Country. My own opinion still continues, that compleat self Govt. in unison with & under a Governor from England to keep up the British Connection, (but not such aristocratic Domination as heretofore) can alone satisfy the Canadians.

I am anxious to see how the Upper Province will provide, by local taxes for the increased expenditure & Govt of Sir Francis Head, which in the present state of the Province must press heavy.

I have been pleased to see the bold & effective manner in which you give the public news & your able reasoning on them: & I shall be pleased to receive the Examiner regularly that I may see what is going on: &, if I can send you any documents that can be of use to you in your labours, let me know & they shall be sent.

[389] COLBORNE TO ARTHUR: L.S. 14p.

Oct. 26 *Montreal.*

With reference to your letters of the 20th. and 22nd. inst which I have just received, I may observe that I am fully aware of your difficulties, and those of the Lower Province also. It is therefore only necessary to adopt every measure that may enable us to prepare for the storm as soon as possible.

In regard to the unsettled accounts upon which you appear to place so much importance, I think the persons who have been most forward in drawing your attention to the cruelty of Government in not paying every iniquitous demand, as well as reasonable claims have little reason to complain— I believe the just accounts unpaid are very limited—

I had formerly a better opinion than I now have of the Croaking Officer at Kingston who has with great perseverance from an early period encouraged the Complaints respecting the non payment of teamsters, and Tavern Keepers, as if Government are not entitled to have the credit, and time to make payments which every individual expects in private transactions.

It can not be denied that gross impositions have taken place in the dealings of those who have brought in claims against Government, nor that it is the duty of public servants to resist unjust claims, notwithstanding the outcry and clamor of individuals who take special care to hold out the menace of withdrawing their support in the time of alarm— I am confident that the Clamour is confined to persons who are more intent on acquiring popularity, then anxious to protect the interests of the Claimants whose cause they have undertaken with so much activity. I hope this matter is nearly set at rest, and that the bulk of the loyal people will not be influenced by the pretended ill treatment which the Volunteers received after their services of last winter— If affairs are not managed with greater regularity and economy than they were during the last Rebel Campaign, the Commissary General will have great difficulty to furnish money—

The terms which you have offered are I think higher than was necessary and, that if they are continued the Volunteer will receive a greater allowance than he requires to render him fit for service, or contented— We shall be able to raise men in this Province at the rate mentioned in the regulations forwarded to you, but if persons who are inclined to enlist find better terms in the Upper Province, than in the Lower, they will of course proceed to the best market— The information which we have lately received is now of such a nature that we are compelled to act on it with promptitude, and make every exertion in our power by a steady preparation without alarm, to repel the invasion[.]

In endeavouring to repress the Military spirit of the last summer, and to discountenance the absurd idle rumours of a danger which did not exist at that time, the true interests of the Province were consulted, as no plague could be more injurious to their welfare, than perpetual excitement; and no more probable remedy for the virulence exhibited by our neighbours than the return of the Militia to their usual occupations— It may be satisfactory to the officers of Militia to be called out, but the best men if they are long kept from their homes inactive, will become disgusted. If proper means are adopted to bring forward the Militia, or to prepare them to march, in the Western, New Castle, and Bathurst Districts and in Leeds, a sufficient number of Militia may be organized in time to meet the sympathisers, if they give us ten days more; and I can not think that their arrangements are so far advanced, that, they can combine their attack with a prospect of success before the middle of next month[.]

If you have information that can be relied on that an immediate attack is intended, the Militia will in several districts hold themselves in readiness to march, and some of the best of them will probably come forward to assist in protecting the Detroit Niagara and St Lawrence frontiers—

I request that no time may be lost in collecting the 34th Regt at Amherstburg, and the 32nd at London, and that they may be prepared to act together under certain circumstances—

If Colonel Maitland is not able to take the Command an active Field Officer must be ordered immediately to the London District to supply his place.

I have for some time heard of the misfortunes of the 43d Regt alluded to in your letter, but Colonel Booth must recollect that he has not lost more men than other Regiments stationed in Upper or Lower Canada, and that if it be evident that he has done all in his power to prevent desertion, no blame can be attached to him, or more disgrace attach to his Regt than to other Corps exposed in similar situations, this must not interfere with the very responsible duty which he has at present to perform in the Niagara District, and I hope in future neither your time [n]or mine will be consumed in reading long reports on desertion which offer no remedy for the desease [*sic.*]

If the Province is to be invaded on the magnificent scale as reported in several Communications, two or three Battalions which were proposed to be raised last year would not have prevented the Menaced Crusade from Ohio, and Michigan, but of whatever use they might have been the local Governments with the Force sent out for the protection of these Provinces were not required to raise Regiments on the appearance of four hundred vagabonds on the American frontier—

The 93rd. Regt will probably be at Quebec in a few days. I shall send them to Kingston as soon as possible— This reinforcement will be equal to several thousands of sympathisers—

I should regret to be compelled to divide such a Regiment, You will however draw three Companies to Toronto either of this Corps or of the 83rd. but Colonel Dundas and the Head Quarters of the 83rd will remain at Kingston[.]

I have desired Colonel Fraser of Glengar[r]y to place his Volunteers also on permanent pay—with your sanction— I have promised Lord Durham to be at Quebec the day before he takes his departure— As soon as I am declared Administrator I shall return to Montreal—

Our prospects here are not brilliant but we are arming with all our might— The habitans are also on the alert, and their leaders are preparing them to assemble when the attack of the Americans takes place— The secret Oath which they take, it is said, binds them to assemble when called on to act, and a ticket indicating the place of Assembly is given to each person in the bonne Cause— This organization I believe extends from this District to Gaspé— It is probable that attacks will be made on the New York frontier of Lower Canada, and on the St Lawrence; so we must endeavour to turn our force against one Corps of the invaders to destroy it, and not to allow our attention to be diverted from the principal object of attack by any partial success of the invaders— It is supposed at New York, that, if the Sympathisers can once make head, that they will soon be joined by a large body of recruits— I read the public and private letters of Mr. Fox to Lord Durham when I was at Quebec.

[Endorsed: "Copy sent to the Secretary of State in Despatch No 78—30th Oct. 1838—"]

[390] [George, Baron] de Rottenburg to Asst. Com[missar]y General [C. A.] Clarke: LB.4,p. 6.

Oct. 26 *Government House, Toronto.*

I have the honor to forward a report addressed to His Excellency The Major Genl Comg upon the subject of the unsettled claims of the Inhabitants of Belleville & its vicinity & I am directed by His Excellency to convey to you his peremptory orders that you take immediate steps to settle the same provided that no error exists in the accounts—

[391] [George, Baron] de Rottenburg to The Collector H M Customs Port Colborne [W. B. Sheehan]: LB.4,p. 6.

Oct. 26 *Government House, Toronto.*

His Excellency The Lieut Governor having given directions that a depot of Coals for the use of the Government Steamers should forthwith be established at Port Colborne, & as no military force is at present established there, I am commanded by His Excellency to request you will have the goodness to take charge of this Depot as public property until other arrangements are made[.]

[392] Arthur to Colborne: LB.1,p. 106-110.

Oct. 27 *Government House, Toronto.*

I hasten to answer your letter and memoranda, which I received from Col. Phil[l]potts, who, on his way up here made the different posts acquainted with your instructions— The information which I continue to receive, more than confirms Mr. Fox's statements— I forward, for your perusal, two depositions which have been lately sworn to.— From all the concurrent testimony, of which I have received abundance, no doubt can possibly exist, that invasion on a most formidable scale, is intended, aided by a serious outbreak in both Provinces— I sent an Officer with a letter to General Brady (yesterday) of the United States Army, of which I enclose a copy.— I have this day received information which can be relied on, that some of the Cheif [*sic*] Movers of the Conspiracy (American Citizens) are now in this Province—. They have mixed themselves with the Inhabitants; but, unfortunately, so much secrecy is observed by all implicated, and there is such a total want of any Police establishment, that the parties cannot be got at.—

I have ascertained, beyond all question, that the disaffection, formerly believed to exist in so many parts of the Province, is now clearly and satisfactorily established and borne out.—

My orders relative to the formation of Corps and Companies had been promulgated, and to a certain degree, acted upon, before I received your communication.— There will be found great difficulty in acting upon your terms here—. At this moment, the men who are called upon to Volunteer, do so, with considerable reluctance, and I find myself obliged, in the state of emergency in which I am placed, to get men upon the best terms I can— The plan I am obliged to adopt is not the one I would choose, and in taking another course from the one which you have adopted, I have been actuated solely by the necessity of the case, and the recommendation of a Board of Officers whom I assembled for the purpose.— I have sent orders by Colonel Phillpot[t]s, to carry into effect your instructions, relative to sending 600 men under Colonel Donald McDonald [*i.e.* Macdonell], to be disposed according to your wishes.— The Corps, under Colonel Frazer [*i.e.* Fraser] will be formed in Reserve, and I will endeavour to get these men under the terms which you have laid down, but I am compelled to say, that I am not very sanguine as to prospects of success in this respect, or indeed, as regards the other reserve Battalions to be incorporated in different parts of the Province—

It will require considerable inducements of pay and allowances, to tempt the Militia to come forward, and the distances that many of them will have to travel, would, I fear, far more than counterbalance the allowance of 2s-6d per diem.—

I have also given directions to form a Corps of 400 men under Colonel Van Koughnet, and to carry into execution your instructions relative to Brockville Prescott &c.—

All your recommendations relative to the defence of these parts, as well as the Western and other Districts will, from the further information received, be much exceeded, but I have not time now, to issue the District General order upon the subject.— This, however will be ready this night or tomorrow, and shall be sent to you by the first opportunity.—

I have directed the Detachments of the 34th. Regiment at Sandwich, and Chatham & Penetanguishine, to be relieved by Militia, and those of the 32nd Regiment in like manner, and will hold these two Corps concentrated at Amherstburg and London.—

Since the time that you administered the Government in this Province, I fear that a material change has taken place in the sentiments of many of the Inhabitants of Hamilton, where you do not think an embodied Force necessary— There are, no doubt, a great many very loyal men there, but at the same time, I find, from the best authority, a great number of disaffected.—

Ancaster abounds with disaffected.— These, with the People who were in arms at Norwich, last year, formed a plan to seize Hamilton & hold it, and the Brigands who are now preparing to invade the Province, have a similar scheme, and will, if they can, seize and fortify it.—

London is the centre of the Western County, Hamilton and Chatham the flanks of that extended position.— I have great pleasure in observing, that you intend to give instructions to to [*sic*] the Ordnance and Commissariat Departments, to carry my orders into immediate effect, without any further communication with their respective Cheifs.— This will much facilitate my future operations.— I cannot but think that in many respects we are in a very backward state, owing to the delays which have occurred in transacting business with these Departments; However I now trust that these have been overcome, and that in future, the Public Service, as regards these necessary military bodies, will be carried on in that prompt and energetic manner, which can alone ensure success.— Colonel Phil[l]potts on his way up (as I have already stated) left your orders with the several posts.— Such modifications as were absolutely necessary I have sent down by him, but I think that no serious inconvenience will arise from this circumstance[.]

[Enclosures lacking.]

[393] [ARTHUR] TO [COLBORNE]: Df.L. 8p

1838 *Government House, Toronto.*
Oct. 27 [Draft copy of item 392 with slight variations.]

[394] COLBORNE TO ARTHUR: A.L.S. 4p

Oct. 27 *Montreal.*

With reference to the information brought by Mr. Kent, communicated in your letter of the 22d inst; you will have the goodness to consider the substance of my letter of yesterday not applicable to the supposed pressing difficulties of this moment—

You will now of course call out 10,000 Militia if you can get them to move[.]

Brantford should be occupied with a strong Reserve of 2000 men. The Gore District Militia can be assembled at Hamilton. The Adelaide and Warwick Lads, might probably be pushed on to Sandwich or Chatham, if the Townships of Sarnia and Moore are protected.

I shall order the 93d to Toronto as soon as they make their appearance, as we may presume that the militia on the St Lawrence will turn out well. If you should apprehend an immediate attack, the 71st Regt shall be prepared to proceed to Toronto without waiting for the 93d Regt[.]

[395] T. L. GOLDIE TO ARTHUR: A.L.S.

Oct. 27 *Montreal.*

I have the honor by the direction of the Commander of the Forces to transmit to Your Excellency the enclosed Copy of a Communication addressed by His Excellencys desire to the several Officers named in the Margin on the subject of raising Volunteers [Marginal entry reads: "Major Carmichael Colonel Turner Colonel Young".]

[Endorsed in Arthur's handwriting: "The Asst Adjt Genl had better forward to the Dy Adjt Genl at Montreal copy of the Gnrl Militia order by wh the Cmr of the Forces will see what Force has been called out GA".]

[Enclosure is apparently item 398.]

[396] [GEORGE, BARON] DE ROTTENBURG TO DEP[UT]Y COM[MISSAR]Y GEN[ERA]L [F. E.] KNOWLES: LB.4,p. 7.

Oct. 27 *Government House, Toronto.*

With reference to your letter of the 25th. inst. I have the honor to inform you that instructions have been sent to the Collector of Her Majesty's Customs at Port Colborne to take charge of the depot of Coals (to be established there) for the present[.]

[397] [GEORGE, BARON] DE ROTTENBURG TO THE RESPECTIVE OFFICERS H. M. ORDNANCE, KINGSTON: LB.4,p. 7-8.

Oct. 27 *Government House, Toronto.* [Marked "Immediate".]

I have the honor to enclose the return of Arms, &c in Store at Kingston & the several other posts in Upper Canada, which has been furnished from the Office of Ordnance at Kingston[.] I am directed by His Excellency the Major Genl Commanding to request you will have the goodness to state whether the Musquets, Ammunition &c stated at the foot of this return as "to be forwarded to London, Brockville & Chatham" respectively are included in the general total of those returned as being in Store or *not* & whether also these arms &c have *already* been sent to those posts— His Excellency also wishes to have a return sent without delay of the number of Arms, accoutrements, ammunition &c at this moment in the several Stores: His Excellency further commands me to say that One Million of Musquet Ball Cartridges should forthwith be procured from Quebec to complete the Magazines in this Command.

[Enclosure lacking.]

[398] F. J. GRIFFIN TO MAJOR [LEWIS] CARMICHAEL, COLONEL [C. B.] TURNER, AND COLONEL [PLOMER] YOUNG: L.S. 2p.

[*1838*] *Oct. 27*

Head Quarters, Montreal. [Marked "Copy".]

I have the honor by direction of The Commander of The Forces to acquaint you, that as the dangers which threaten the Peace and tranquillity of the two Provinces seem imminent, and pressing:— His Excellency hereby authorizes you to raise, and embody as large a Volunteer, Force in your neighbourhood, and District; as can be made available and that *as soon as possible*;—you may either add to the numbers of the Battallions [*sic*] already ordered to be raised or embody other Battalions, His Excellency relies on your exertions, and discretion, and begs there may be as little confusion as possible also that you will report progress.

The Commander Of The Forces authorizes these measures relying from his communications with Sir George Arthur that His Excellency will sanction them. . .

One copy of this letter sent to
Major Carmichael at Coteau du Lac
One to
Colonel Turner at Cornwall
and one to
Colonel Young at Prescott.
[Misdated 1837.]
[The above is apparently the enclosure referred to in item 395.]

[399] ARTHUR TO CHIEF JUSTICE [J. B. ROBINSON]: LB.6,p. 12-16.

Oct. 28

Toronto. [Marked "Private".]

I have desired Mr. Macaul[a]y to send you Copies of the various Statements which have been lately received respecting the movements of the "Patriots" in connection with the disaffected in this Province. By Mr. Fox's letters and Sir John Colborne's you will perceive that they consider it almost certain that we shall shortly be assailed. Sir John, you will recollect, was long most incredulous, & in spite of all I could urge, he would not consent to the Militia Battalions. Now he deeply regrets the valuable time that has been lost. I have been making the best use of the time allowed. Four Militia Regts. I have ordered to be raised for eighteen months—for which, I suppose, they will not thank me in Downing Street—but it seems to my mind the duty of the Govt. to shew something like permanence of purpose in their measures, & not to be defending the Country by fits & starts & on every occasion of threatened invasion to be calling out the Militia. The Colonels of these Corps are Sir Allan Macnab—Cameron—Kingsmill—& Hill— I am also preparing a still larger force to take the field for six months & am making other preparations—in all of which arrangements I have *often* wished for your experience and friendly advice for I have found no one to take your place.

The evidence from various quarters is very strong in establishing that an organized system of invasion has long been going forward, & it is impossible to doubt the wicked disposition of these people, & I shall be really glad that the Government so far takes the alarm as to come into my recommendation for placing this Province in a proper state of defence by the erection of some good fortification—but, on carefully considering all the statements, I must say, I incline to the opinion that there will be no such formidable invasion as is apprehended. This is but mere opinion, & those who have seen all the papers & are as capable of judging as I am, entertain not a doubt that we shall be assailed in a very formidable manner. I thought so too at first! Lord Durham sails, or rather I should say, states that He will sail on the 1st. You will have received my letter with the Copies of his Despatches long before his arrival in England. He will, I trust, retain his intention of putting himself a good deal in your hands—but, all will depend upon the turn of his own political station what course he pursues— Politicians never have, I believe, but one end sincerely in view—their own interest! Montreal ought *at once* to be added to this Province; it cannot go on without it: we have no funds nor can they be raised unless we have a Port, & can lay on an impost on imported goods. Were this done we should beat the State of New York in prosperity, &, without it the Colony must languish. Nothing would gratify me more than to see this accomplished before I leave the Colony.

The Law Officers of the Crown after giving me so much trouble & anxiety, appear to have made a miserable defence of the opinion they gave respecting Foreign Invaders.

I have desired Maccauly [*i.e.* Macaulay] to send you their last report to the Secretary of State which can only be considered an abandonment of their former opinion— I have carried my point at length against the Commisst. system— Sir John has been obliged to come into my view & He ought to thank me for relieving Him of what He could not manage Himself.

Mr. Routh *has had* too much influence— He will be very angry no doubt at the orders I have issued today in which I have directed the Commisst. Officers to report to the Dy. Commy. General who is stationed at Toronto & to take their instructions *from him*!

I have equally succeeded in relieving this command from the incubus of the Quebec "Board of Ordnance". Colonel Wright is no doubt, I believe, a good man—but, oh! the delays & difficulties in getting anything through his office.

Lord Glenelg will now, I hope, deliver me from all responsibility to Lord Durham's successor. It has sadly interfered with what ought to have been done here. No one would suppose from this long private letter that my table is *loaded* with official Papers of considerable urgency. .

[P.S.] Thank you for your letter from New York.

[400] H. S. Fox to Arthur: A.L.S. 4p.

Oct. 28 *Washington*. [Marked "Private".]

I write this by the post,—to acknowledge the receipt of your letters of the 22d:, which were brought to me yesterday by Capt: Roxburgh, in a remarkably short space of time from Toronto.— I shall write to you fully in a few days, by the return of Captain Roxburgh.— In the mean while, you will have received a letter from me of the 21st:, containing some details which tally remarkably, and alarmingly, with the information that has reached you through other channels.— I will do all that I can here: but that all will be very little.— In this Country, it is not the Govt: that governs,—as we have already sufficiently witnessed. How they are eventually to keep themselves out of a war with Great Britain, I hardly see. For the people of England will not always continue to be as complaisant as their Government.— I hear from Ld. Durham, that he will sail for England direct, about the 1st: of the month.— I hope he may be able to awaken the Authorities at home.— I wish to Heaven it might end, in his occupying the Colonial Office.—

[401] ARTHUR TO J. [*i.e.* W.] M. HARVARD: LB.1,p. 103-106.

Oct. 29 *Government House, Toronto.*

I fear you will consider me very negligent in having so long delayed to answer your letter of the 14th of September, and to return the paper which accompanied it.—

Unfortunately, as I personally explained to you, on proceeding to Quebec I omitted to take that paper with me, and since my return, the expectation of invasion and insurrection has been such, that every moment of my time has been occupied, and now I can say but a few words, not having a moment at my own command in the midst of those arrangements, which are required to provide for the Public Peace, and for the security of the Province.—

I thank you for your kind attention in allowing me to peruse the Paper— It would have given me great pleasure, had you taken the view of it, that, amidst the strife and contention that has been created in the Province, the reinvestment of the Lands in the Crown, and the future disposal of them by the calm deliberation of the Imperial Parliament, for religious purposes would have been the best means of terminating the question.

The Wesleyan Methodists in our own native land, when the Church of England was assailed, a few years ago, by the contemplated measures in Parliament, stood forth most manfully in her defence; and, as I believe, by some very specious persons here, the same plot is laid against her in this colony. I look to you, My Dear Sir, and to Ministers and men like you, to come forth in the spirit of the great founder of your communion, and throw yourself in the Van, to oppose this wicked intention of strife and dissension.—

This subject, I see clearly, is made a handle for the worst purposes— even to effect the separation of these Provinces from the Crown of Great Britain—.

The "Christian Guardian" has treated this subject in a bad spirit indeed, and is altogether conducted in a way which no true Wesleyan can approve.—

I write, by this opportunity, to Her Majesty's Government, to beg that the Reverend Mr Alder may be requested to come out immediately— He will be of great service in many respects, and, more especially, in aiding me to dispose of the many questions connected with the Indians.—

I do not deny that in the writings of the Defenders of the Church of England, there is much to disapprove—but—then—it should be recollected, that no legal doubt exists, that if not all, at least the great portion of the Church Lands is admitted, on all hands, to have been intended for her—and, that to conscientious men, it is hard to give up what has once been assigned to the Church.—

I cannot conclude, without correcting an error into which you had fallen, respecting a Journal which you term "an understood organ of the Government"— The only Press which I use, is the Upper Canada Gazette.

[Superscription reads: "The Revnd J: M: Harvard Mission House— Quebec."]

[402] COLBORNE TO ARTHUR: A.L.S. 5p.

Oct. 29 *Sorel.*

I have received some important information from a Mr Ferguson lately arrived from England, and now at New York— He has been strongly recommended to Lord Durham by Colonel Yorke, Lord Mulgrave's secretary.

Mr Ferguson has found out an old acquaintance by the name of Baird, who has been employed by the Patriots in conveying arms into Lower Canada.

This Baird formerly was a Servant of Ferguson's, and afterwards a Sergeant in the 17th Lancers—

Ferguson is persuaded that he can obtain from Baird further facts that may lead to a discovery of the plans of the Conspirators, and also of the names of principal leaders of the conspiracy in *England*, and in the United States. I shall therefore direct Ferguson to follow Baird to Buffalo, to which City he has lately proceeded from New York, with his Principals; and direct him to be informed that you will send a confidential Officer to communicate with him as soon as he may acquaint you where he resides. . .

[P.S. on separate slip.] *D. H. Ferguson*, formerly a Reporter of debates in Parliament; left England for New York in the expectation of finding employment in some Printing Establishment—

[403] COLBORNE TO ARTHUR: L.S. 11p.

Oct. 29 *Sorel.*

In my letters of the 22nd and 26th. inst I have so fully entered into your views of the state of these Provinces that your Communications of the 24th. scarcely require any reply. I beg however to mention that I concur with you in the opinion that at least 5000 men should be raised in Upper Canada, and I recommend your Calling out 10,000 men if you can by your exertions, and by rousing the spirit of the Loyal Districts obtain their services. For I am confident that our Colonists can no longer submit to live in a perpetual harrassing [*sic*] state of suspense and danger, and that we must prove to the Mother Country by the extent of the population that are willing to come forward at this moment, and during the winter that they are ready to make any sacrifices provided they are powerfully supported from home—

The organization of the Rebels in this Province is proceeding so rapidly that I fear to create alarm by moving a Regt till the arrival of the 93rd—but I shall send a Regiment to Toronto at any rate in a few days[.] With respect to the general defence of your Province, with reference to the supposed disaffection I can only imagine the cases which are likely to occur— I have dispersed the Regular force, because I think that at Amherstburg; on the Niagara frontier and on [the] St Lawrence are the points at which it is most probable the Invaders would attempt to cross in the absence of a regular force, and that a Regiment of the Line is the best force to repel the first attack— Whether however you can assemble 1200 men or a 1000 must be decided by circumstances. All that I intended in my former Communication on the defence of the Province was, to impress on you the necessity of concentrating the regular force, if you can, the moment any of the Invaders have landed[.] In the London District the 32nd Regt must not be confined to London, but prepared to unite with the 34th—and trust the interior and perhaps the Western frontier also to the Militia and Volunteers—

Have the goodness to send an Officer immediately to look at the road from the Mouth of the Grand River, to Woodehouse [*sic*]; and I authorize you to form rafts, or a bridge of boats across the Grand River; and to employ three or four thousand labour[er]s at any wages, to make the Coast roads practicable for Troops, and Artillery, from the Grand River through Rainham and Walpole to Port Dover, and Woodehouse—

When you have placed two Thousand Militia on the Niagara frontier, the 43rd Regt may be disposable for the London District, and may be marched if necessary from Port Robinson, by the Canal to Dunnville, by the Coast road to Port Dover— Engage as many Steamers as you can hire on Lake Erie— Order Fort Mississagua [*sic*], and Fort Malden to be strengthened; and concentrate the regular force whenever you are able, without reference to internal disaffection— Penetanguishine is very vulnerable, but, I doubt that an attempt will be made at that point from Cleveland; The population of Oro, and Orill[i]a might be probably called out for the defence of that Post, and their section of the Country— As you have published your terms it appears to be impossible to retreat, or alter them, therefore I authorize you to notify to all the Officers employed on the St Lawrence, and in other parts of the Province, to offer your terms, should they experience any difficulty in enlisting men on mine— I beg that the 1st. Dragoon Guards may not be moved till the Invaders have crossed; you will then act according to circumstances—

Raise as many Corps of Cavalry as you may think can be brought forward to act immediately to check the projects of the disaffected, and to prevent them from uniting— All the arms that we have in Store at Quebec and at Montreal viz 4000 are on the route to Kingston—

10,000 more shall be forwarded as soon as the ships laden with the 30,000 stand, expected daily at Quebec, may arrive—

The soldiers of our Regular force are contented with their pay and rations— Paying the Volunteers at a high rate may create some discontent, but no increase of pay or rations will check desertion or prevent a Sergeant or Private from passing into the United States who is anxious for his liberty, or who has relatives inviting him to settle with them on advantageous terms, 6 men of the 85th Regt have deserted from Toronto lately[.]

I have particularly mentioned the Coast road of Rainham because there was another Communication opened some years ago for the Inhabitants settled near the Grand River which can not be made useful for the Military purposes which we have in view. . .

[P.S. on separate sheet.] Memorandum of Articles shipped from Quebec per Canada Steam Boat for Kingston by the Commissary General.

1772 Blankets.
1878 yards of Pilot Cloth.
3406½ " Grey Do— for Trowsers[.]
1624¼ " Serge for lining.
106¾ " Scarlet Cloth for facings.

A further quantity of grey could be purchased at Quebec, and some white Kersey.

There are no Bayonet Scabbards, nor Pouches, nor Belts with the Arms sent from England.

There are no Pistols nor Sabres nor other Cavalry Appointments at Quebec.

[404] COLBORNE TO ARTHUR: L.S. 2p.

Oct. 29 *Sorel.*

With reference to your application from Major Frazer [*i.e.* Fraser], I request you will inform that officer, that I had already acquainted Colonel Gore, before his incessant importunities for additional pay were forwarded, that an arrangement, was under consideration, for issuing pay to the officers employed on a particular service, and, that he must have patience, till the general order, upon that subject can be issued.

Ensign Domville's [*sic*] appointment, as your Extra Aide de Camp, shall appear in General Orders immediately.

[Endorsed in Arthur's handwriting: "Transmit to Colonel Frazer the extract of Sir J. Colborne's Letter—enclose it simply with the observation that you are desired so to do. G A"; further endorsed: "Done Mly Secy".]

[405] [BISHOP] ALEX[ANDE]R MACDONELL TO ARTHUR: A.L.S. 3p.

Oct. 29 *Kingston.*

As your Excellency has been pleased to say that my stay might be of some use to the Province during the impending invasion I have put off my departure for England for the present; I unhesitatingly advise your Excellency, in order to form impenetrable ramparts against the enemy, to select men for the commanders of corps in whom the people have confidence, & who exercise a powerful influence over them. In this number I consider the bearer of this Mr. Macdonell of Peterboro who commands the 2d Regit. of Northumberland Militia. he has been for the period of thirteen years dispensing the Govert. bounty in lands to Emigrants in that District, & superintending their set[t]lement & has rendered himself extrem[e]ly popular among them, & useful to Govert. His services have been acknowledged by Your Excellencys predecessors. In consideration of his great exertion in set[t]ling twelve townships, & the heavy expenses he had been at in accomodating & entertaining strangers & Emigrants before public houses were established in that part of the country a valuable town Lot has been given to him in Peterboro as a remuneration altho the Patent Deed be not yet issued.

Should your Excellency determine to raise a Corps of Irish Roman Catholics under the Command of Coll Baldwin of the Gore of Toronto I would pledge my life that Your Excellency cannot muster a more Loyal, more Gallant or a more effecient [*sic*] corps in in [*sic*] this or any other Province, & old & stiff as I am Im willing & ready to go to Toronto to attend them if they require my presence[.]

I am given to understand that a corps is to be raised in the County of Glengarry. two Corps of 5 or 600 men each might be raised between that & Stormont without injury to the agriculture of the country but they would not be disposed to rise for less a period than twelve or eighteen months except on the event of an actual Invasion.

aware of my warm & ardent zeal for the safety and prosperity of the Province I hope your Excellency will pardon the freedom I have taken in expressing my sentiments thus so unreservedly[.]

[406] ARTHUR TO LORD FITZROY [J. H.] SOMERSET: LB.1,p. 117-121.

Oct. 30 *Government House, Toronto.* [Marked "Private & Confidential."]

I do not wish to be intrusive, much less disposed to report upon military details in an official form, which more properly belong to my

Cheif [*sic*] Sir John, with whom I am on the most friendly terms—but, as information of the latest dates must, in the present state of things be acceptable to Lord Hill, and as your Lordship will be anxious to know what you may have to prepare for in this Province, I shall continue to address you privately, provided your Lordship will consent to accept my unpremeditated thoughts, as they move at the moment.

A few days after my return from Kingston, from whence I wrote to you on the 12th. instant—I received from Mr. Fox the letter of which I enclose you a copy,—its contents are alarming enough— Other communications followed, confirming, in a very remarkable manner, the information which through other channels had been conveyed to the American Government—of these I enclose three of the most important.—

The Government of the United States affect to be suddenly alarmed; but I have not a doubt that they have known long enough what the state of things has been on the Frontier, and that Unions have been forming ever since January, to overrun this Province, after the manner of the Texas.— The Government to take no part—to appear to discountenance such proceedings, but privately to further them.— We know well enough in the Army, that an Officer may significantly tell a few smart soldiers, on no account to jump upon some troublesome fellow who intrudes into the Barrack Yard, and at the same time, be morally certain that he will be well ducked the next time he ventures to enter it.—

It is impossible to suppose but that the United States authorities have known all that has passed during the last six months, and have clandestinely furthered all that has been doing.— This I cannot prove, but I sincerely believe it.—

In the first place a large number of Canadians Collected upon Grand Island in arms, and remained undisturbed by the United States' Government as long as they pleased.— Then they assembled on Point Pelée Island, faced the 32nd. Regiment, and when defeated, none of them were apprehended by the American Government, or, if they were, we have never heard that any of them were punished— The Sir Robert Peel was next destroyed, we made a great fuss about it at the time, large rewards were offered, and some parties deeply implicated, were apprehended in the States, but, in the face of the strongest evidence, the Prisoners were acquitted, and others were set at liberty without any trial— Again in June last, a number of Citizens, about 300 at least, made a demonstration to cross over at Niagara—but their unlawful assembling was never noticed, that we have heard of, by the States Authorities— Another party actually crossed over, we captured some of them, they were tried and convicted, and then followed Petitions from all parts of the States, that we should deal tenderly with them.— In favor of one man, who had been the most mischievous, there were no less than 3.560 signatures.

An arrangement was entered into between General Macomb and Captain Sandom, who commands Her Majesty's Vessels on the Lakes for combined search of the Islands, and if Johns[t]on or any of his gang were found on a British Island, they were to be handed over to us for trial—if on an American Island, they were to be handed over to the American Authorities.

The search accordingly commenced— Johns[t]on escaped, but two of his gang were taken by an officer of the Royal Navy, with a number of arms. According to the agreement, they were delivered up to the American Authorities, and Captain Sandom informed General

Macomb, that an officer and some of his men would be ready to appear and give evidence.— To his utter astonishment, he soon afterwards ascertained that the Prisoners had been discharged without being brought to trial, and the General informed him that so great was the excitement of the American Citizens, that he was obliged to make void this agreement. And that Unions have been formed all over the Frontier, and that 160,000 people have entered into a conspiracy to overrun the Province, of whom 40,000 have bound themselves to be the actual Invaders—in the expectation of another insurrection to further the Republican cause.—

The Americans are without a Government unless they can control their population, and, if they can control them, they are acting in violation of the law of nations, and should be compelled to keep faith with us—I say this—altho if it can be avoided, we ought not to go to War with them at present on any account.—

In speaking of the American Authorities, I have not intended to include the officers of the U:S: Army, for, with the exception of General Scott, I have a good opinion of them.—

At present, I have ordered 12,000 of the Militia to be called out, but we want arms, clothing and bedding for them. The most loyal people in the County, and those who would make the best troops, are the Provincial Cavalry, and they are all well mounted, but for them we have no equipments whatever.—

If it be determined that the Canadas shall be retained, they must be fortified, and large depots of stores of all kinds formed for promptly taking the Field when necessary—

[First enclosure is possibly a copy of item 369. Other enclosures lacking.]

[407] [GEORGE, BARON] DE ROTTENBURG TO COL [WILLIAM] ROWAN: LB.4, p. 8-9.

Oct. 30 *Government House, Toronto.*

I have the honor to enclose a Copy of a communication, received from Colonel Booth Comg at Niagara, containing the names of men of the detachment King's Dragoon Guards stationed at Fort George who are recommended by Capt Martin Comg the detachment to receive a pecuniary reward for their Conduct on a late occasion, & which has been notified by instructions from the Depy Adjt General dated Quebec 17th Octr. 1838. I am directed by His Excellency Major General Sir George Arthur to say that as Capt Martin has not named what amount should be paid to each man, & as the question is one of pecuniary reward to be conferred by the Commander of the Forces the Major General has referred the point for His Excellency's decision—

[Enclosure lacking.]

Oct. 30 H. C. [*i.e.* ALEXANDER] MACOMB TO THE OFFICERS COMMANDING THE TROOPS AND POSTS ON THE CANADIAN FRONTIER:

[See item 421.]

[408] ARTHUR TO H. S. FOX: LB.1, p. 111-113.

Oct. 31 *Government House, Toronto.* [Marked "Private".]

I thank you for your private letter of the 21st. Inst., which I received yesterday. Mr Wm. Hamilton Merritt, is, I believe a perfectly Loyal

Person. He is a member of the Legislative Council, and although a little speculative, quite a respectable person.

It was a fancy with Mackenzie and others last winter to call into question the loyalty of many of the most respectable Inhabitants, and it certainly answered their purpose by deluding many weak persons.

The proceedings of the Patriots appear to gather strength—their intention to invade the Province is now a matter of notoriety all along the Border of the States.

They seem not to desire that it should be a secret.

There must be an understanding that the Government will not effectually oppose them; and I am persuaded when they raise their Standard, they will meet with no serious opposition from the authorities Civil or Military. Major General Macomb is very probably desirous to do what is right; but, it is generally understood that he is easily imposed upon.

The Governors of New York and Michigan there cannot be a doubt wish well to the "Patriot" cause.—

The Statement to which I have alluded in the postscript of my official confidential comes from a person who may [be] entirely depended upon. He is an American, who has been employed for about two years in this Province, and is much respected.

I have sent a copy of your last confidential to Sir John Colborne; the scheme no doubt is to attack both Provinces, in conjunction with the disaffected, at the same time.

I forward my present Despatch to you by Mr Bewes an officer of the 85th. Regt., who takes charge of my Despatch bag to New York. I shall be very anxious to hear that you have successfully negotiated respecting our proceedings on the Lakes.

If the American Governmt would only now at the eleventh hour, shew decision and energy, I do not think it would be too late to arrest the progress of the Conspirators— There is no time for a remonstrance from our Governmt.— We can only look to your firmness and decisive tone.

I think even more seriously of Mr Wilkinson's Statement than of Mr Kents.

He knows the American Government and people thoroughly and is well acquainted with the Private Springs, which induce many to desire the separation of the Canadas from Great Britain.

You will remark that he lays much stress upon the general impression in the States, that our Government would not make the aggressions upon the Canadas a subject for War!

They ought certainly to be disabused of this error.—

[409] ARTHUR TO [W. H.] HAMILTON: LB.6. p. 17-21.

Oct. 31 *Govt. House, Toronto.*

It must seem strange to you, indeed, that I have so long been silent, but the cares and anxieties that have pressed upon me daily have actually not left me one disposable moment to attend to any private affairs—&, now, as you will perceive by the Public Journals, we are on the eve of Invasion from without & another Insurrection.—

One hundred & sixty thousand Persons are said to have joined the Unions in the States agt. this Province—they have formed these Unions upon the plan of Masonic Lodges, &, of that number, 40,000 have pledged themselves to be parties to the actual Invasion— Of these proceedings we have long had rumours, but no Person believed them, &, unfortunately, least of all Sir J. C. who wd. make no preparations— but, on the contrary, ordered all the Militia to be disbanded three or 4 months ago. I have now called out thirteen thousand Militia—& we have 6 good Regts. in the command. This would be abundant defence if we could depend on our own People, but, alas! that is not the case.— Disaffection has spread far & wide, & the worst is—we know not the extent of it. There can be no question that we shall have a busy & anxious Winter of it.—

I recd. about a month ago long letters from Montagu, with an account of my affairs into wh. I have never been able to look with the slightest attention. But I observed, that, the Interest wh. he stated I might annually draw exceeded what he had mentioned in a former letter—*viz* £3900 a year—independent of Cottage Green & some other Properties that had not been disposed of. But, I observe, that their money matters were not in a good State & that they were feeling the shock of the bad times you had in London last year. If the price of wool keeps up all will be right again Mr. O'Connor says in a later letter to me than Montagues [*sic*]. It has been a disappointment to me that, in place of remitting me the interest Montagu embarked £3500 in a Speculation at Pt. Phillip tho' it seems to be turning out extremely well— I feel this only, however, because I had mentioned to Messrs. Coutts that they would regularly receive remittances to the extent of about £3000 a year.—

I brought a letter of credit with me from Coutts for £2000; but, I have hitherto only drawn upon them for small sums & shall not have occasion to draw more from hence. I remitted to them lately an order to receive from the Treasury £500 on my account & I begged them to sell the £200 or £300 wh. I have in 3 per Cents—this will put them in funds—but, I draw upon them for £280 in favor of Sir F. Head.— I have now earnestly to beg of you to Settle for my dear Boys Schooling wh. is due to Mr. Walton for the last half year & another half year is at hand.— Upon the Authority wh. I left with you in England, I believe you can draw for £300 more from Montagu, &, if so, that will be more than enough for the present. I enclose a letter to Coutts left open for yr. perusal.

Mr. Hyde has written to me for Letters of Introduction in favor of his son Mr. George Hyde, who is on his way to V. D. Land to settle from Honduras, where he was born. It occurs to me that this Gent. wd. be very glad of yr. Bill on Montagu on my account, & I think it wd. be as well to provide for contingencies if you were to give him a Bill for a £1,000 & place it to my acct. at Coutts'.—

I was beginning very anxiously to wish for you out with me—the Private Secretary's Appt. turns out to be worth at least £1200 a year— but, *now*, I wd. not recommend you to come on any account.— I annex Mr. Walton's address & Mr. Hyde's— Remember me most kindly to Mrs. Hamilton. . .

W. Walton Esqr.
Hampton.
James Hyde Esqr.
46 Montagu Square.

P.S. I am indebted to Mr. Hyde for shipping all my Goods &c.— I wish you wd. discharge the debt for me as soon as you can draw upon Montagu.

[Enclosures lacking.]

[410] ARTHUR TO [JAMES] HYDE: L. 3p.

Oct. 31 *Govt. House, Toronto.*

If I could convey to you any idea of the pressure of business which I have had upon me for months past you would, I am sure forgive my apparent neglect in not writing to you; but, I can say truly, that I have not had one disposable moment, and now, for reasons which I will presently assign, I am more engrossed with difficulties than ever.

For two months I have been chiefly engaged in travelling all through the Province and it was whilst I was on one of those excursions, that I received your letter requesting an introduction for your son. The delay in this matter I lament particularly but it has been unavoidable. I now enclose a letter to Mr. Montagu, my nephew, who is the Colonial Secretary of the Province, and he will I am sure shew your son Mr George Hyde, any attention in his power, and be useful to him if he can in any way. I have mentioned to my friend Mr Hamilton, whom you saw with me in London—Oxford Terrace—that Mr George Hyde was going out and no person can give him more information, or be of greater service to him as Mr Hamilton has a large property and large connexions in the Province. If Mr George Hyde wishes for Bills upon the Colony, Mr Hamilton can draw upon Mr Montagu upon my account. I have requested Mr Hamilton will be so good as to settle the balance which I am in your debt.—

The troubles in this Province are again commencing with the commencement of Winter. 200,000 Citizens of the States are said to have joined in the conspiracy to free this Province from the yoke of Great Britain as they call it, of these, 40,000 have pledged themselves by oath to invade us during the Winter and they expect to be joined by large numbers of disloyal persons.

I am now calling out a large Militia Force, and expect to be surrounded by difficulties and anxieties of every kind. But, I endeavour to look to the Almighty to deliver the Province from the impending calamities. Make my best regards to Mrs. Hyde.

[Enclosure lacking.]

[411] ARTHUR TO COUTTS & CO.: LB.6, p. 21-23.

Oct. 31 *Govt. House, Toronto.* [Marked "Private."]

I wrote to you lately—informed you that I had drawn upon you in favor of Sir F. Head for £280—& enclosed the Copy of a Despatch, authorizing my receivg. £500 additional passage Money from the Treasury, and requested you to apply for the same. I also begged you wd. dispose of the small sum I had in the 3 per Cents, so that you might be in funds to meet some demands wh. I had to discharge. My friend Mr. Hamilton will call at yr. house with this Letter, & he will provide, on my acct. further funds if they are required.

When I left V. D. Land I arranged that the Interest of the Property wh. I left there sd. be regularly remitted—but, unfortunately, there has been a misunderstandg.—& Mr. Montagu—(the Coll. Secy who kindly undertook the managemt. of my affairs) has been tempted to invest a large Sum in the purchase of Sheep & Land at Port Phillip. I say, unfortunate, because it has been attended with some temporary inconvenience, but, I understand, the speculation—or investmt. is a most desirable one. Henceforth I trust he will regularly remit about £4000 a year & I will hereafter say how I wish it to be invested.

I have troubled you with this history of my affairs by way of explanation, as it will appear strange to you that no remittance has been made from V D Land on my acct..

I enclose another Copy of the Secy. of State's Despatch in case the one I have already forwarded has not reached you—&, further, I must advise that I have this day drawn upon you in favor of Major Willis for £50.

You will perceive by the Newspapers that we are all alive here again, & are likely to have even a more troublesome Winter than the last. Unions have been formed all along the Frontier Towns of the States of Citizens who are determined, as they say, to free the Canadians from the British Yoke. At least 200,000 Persons are sworn Members of these Unions, & 40,000 have pledged themselves to join in the invasion—they expect to be largely co-operated with by the Canadians. I fear there are too many disposed to join them!

Nothing will do, but fortifying the Province upon an extensive scale, if Great Britain determines to retain it.

[Enclosures lacking.]

[412] CHA[RLE]S BULLER TO ARTHUR: A.L.S. 4p.

Oct. 31 *Quebec.*

The bearer of this is my friend Mr. Atcheson[?] a very intelligent gentleman from England who is now in Upper Canada on some private business. He is also well known to Ld. Durham; & I am sure you will find him an intelligent & estimable man.

He is very desirous of making statistical inquiries respecting Upper Canada: and you will not only oblige but greatly serve Ld. Durham by aiding him in these as far as supplying any official information,—which he may want.

I am sorry that I shall not see you again before quitting America. I fear you will have a sad winter of it.

[Endorsed in pencil "recd—12th April".]

[413] [GEORGE, BARON] DE ROTTENBURG TO DEP[UT]Y COM[MISSAR]Y GEN[ERA]L [F. E.] KNOWLES: LB.4, p. 9.

Oct. 31 *Government House, Toronto.*

I have the honor to acknowledge the receipt of your letter of the 30th Inst which I have submitted to His Excellency the Major Genl Commanding, and am directed to inform you that His Excellency approves of your making application to the Commissary General for the further assistance of one Assistant & one Deputy Asst Commissary General[.]

[414] R. B. BLAKISTON TO ARTHUR: A.L.S. 2p.

[1838] *[Place not stated.]*
[c. Nov. ?] Captain Haliday the Son of one of our nearest neighbours, and a personal friend of my own, is just gone to Canada to join his Regiment the 93rd.—and I beg to introduce him to your acquaintance[.] You will find him a very pleasant intelligent and Gentlemanly Young man and very deserving of any attention you may be disposed to show him[.]

I hope that Lady Arthur and your family are well and that the climate agrees with you all. I beg my kind regards to Lady Arthur[.]

[415] ARTHUR TO COLBORNE: LB.1, p. 113-116.

Nov. 1 *Government House, Toronto.*

Your messenger arrived yesterday, and brought me your demi-official and Letters.—

All the information I receive from all quarters conveys a confirmation of the coming storm. The Unions in the States have gradually augmented their numbers, and the scheme has been conducted with extraordinary secrecy. The statement which Colonel Foster received during my absence in July, of 14 000 persons being then members of the Unions, turns out to be quite correct, and his Informant stated, I believe, what was quite the truth—however improbable it seemed at the moment.— The proceedings from that time appear to have been conducted with great secrecy, and, certainly they must have been forwarded by some abler men.— Papineau and Rolph, in my opinion, have cheifly [*sic*] directed this conspiracy, and Governors Marcy and Mason have been deep in their secrets.— But, no matter by whom these projects have been concocted, we must endeavour to destroy their effect.

The men will not turn out as volunteers. Colonel Turner writes from Cornwall, that the proposition left by Colonel Phillpotts, has not given satisfaction.— He has, I understand, communicated with you, and therefore, I need not forward his Letters.— But, I have now required them to turn out as Militia Men, under the Provincial Law.— I enclose the Militia General Order; but, as I do not wish it to be in possession of the Enemy, it will not be published—but instructions sent to each Militia Colonel, directing him to furnish his quota of Men forthwith.—

I hope, above all things, you have it in your power to send us a large supply of Arms.— Months ago I sent a requisition to Quebec to be forwarded to England, for 20,000 stand for this Province, for arming the Militia, and I begged the Secretary of State to stir in it—also, 2,000 sets of Cavalry appointments were applied for, but I have heard nothing of them.— The best People in this country are the Cavalry Yeomen!— They are well horsed, but have no arms.— We shall have, I suppose, a deeper note of complaint from the Militia, than was even uttered last Winter, about clothing, Blankets, Great Coats—but with all their illwill they will come out, I should hope, at the last—now, however, is the time.

I told your Messenger that his journey was, I thought a useless one, as we had a dozen reports of the same kind from the same place. I need not trouble you with all I have received, but they all confirm Mr Kent's statement which, I doubt not, may be relied on.—

All you have suggested respecting the Regular Regiments shall be forthwith acted upon, and the Detachments relieved by the Militia, with the least possible delay.— Only send me *Arms* and I will manage the rest, by some means or other. I shall be rejoiced to get the 93rd.

I enclose a copy of Mr Fox's last Letter to me just received.—

Major General Macomb is not at all to be relied upon— He is a very weak man, and will be easily duped by the Patriots.

If the American Government will only act with firmness we shall yet avert the storm by preparing for it—but I have not, nor ever have had, the slightest confidence in them.—

They must have known what has been going forward long enough.— I find, from the Captain of the Steamers, that many of the American Patriots have passed down with Canadians to the Lower Province during the last six weeks.

[Enclosures lacking. Enclosure from Fox is apparently item 369.]

[416] [GEORGE, BARON] DE ROTTENBURG TO THE OFFICER COMG R ARTILLERY TORONTO [H. G. JACKSON ?]: LB.4, p. 10.

Nov. 1 *Government House, Toronto.*

I am directed by His Excellency The Major Genl Comg to call your immediate attention to the subject of placing the Artillery here upon the most serviceable footing— His Excellency understands that there are several field pieces which might be rendered available for the Militia if the Gun Carriages were completed & the Major Genl. desires me to say that he expects you will use every exertion to accomplish this.

As the point is one of great importance the expense attending it must be considered as a secondary object.— You will have the goodness to communicate with me as soon as possible upon the subject[.]

[417] H. S. FOX TO AARON VAIL: A.L.S. 31p.

Nov. 3 *Washington.* [Marked "Copy".]

The alarming reports which had reached the United States Government, respecting apprehended hostile movements against Canada from within the American Territory, and which were communicated to me by the friendly orders of the President, have been amply confirmed by intelligence conveyed to Her Majesty's Colonial Authorities through various other channels; and I am sorry to add, that the mischief appears to be far more serious and extensive, and the danger of hostile disturbance more imminent, than had been represented in the information received at Washington.—

It is now ascertained, beyond the possibility of doubt, that a secret combination or conspiracy, of vast extent, and possessed of great resources in money and in military provisions, has been formed, and is at this moment in active progress, within the confines and jurisdiction of the United States, for the purpose of waging war upon Her Majesty's Provinces of Upper and Lower Canada.— The combination extends along the whole line of the Canadian frontier, from Maine and Vermont to the State of Michigan: it extends also far into the interior of the States of New York, Pennsylvania, and Ohio: and likewise into the neighbouring State of Kentucky.— It is affirmed, and believed, that 40,000 American citizens are already enrolled in this criminal association.— The above is the lowest estimate: the depositions of some of the informants carry the numbers to a much greater extent. To these are joined a few vagrant Canadian refugees: the number of the American conspirators is daily and hourly increasing.— The plot is carried on by means of masonic lodges, secretly established in almost every town along the frontier, the members of which communicate with each other by private signs, and are divided into several grades of initiation. A complete system of these secret signs, as well as the cypher or secret alphabet, by means of which the associates correspond in writing, is in the hands of Her Majesty's Authorities.— The regular organization has been completed, of a pretended Provisional Government for Upper Canada, with assumed official rank and commissions, both civil and military.— The names, description, and residences, of the chief individuals composing this pretended Government,—who are American citizens,—are also in the possession of the British Authorities.— A pretended national Bank of Canada has also been organized, to be established and maintained by the seizure and plunder of the public property.— The Superior Lodges of the Association are believed to be situated in the Towns of Rochester, Buffalo, and Detroit: a Grand Central Lodge, or Convention of Delegates, is held at Cleveland: another considerable Lodge is situated at Cincinnati.— Arms, and warlike stores, are secreted at various points; and the conspirators also reckon, that with their present force and number, and complete organization, they will have no difficulty in again forcing and plundering the United States and State Arsenals, whenever the time for showing themselves in arms shall have arrived.— No less than nine Steam Boats, of those that ply regularly upon Lake Erie, the names of which are in the possession of the British Authorities, have been engaged for the service of the conspirators. I am afraid there is no doubt that a number of magistrates, justices of the Peace, and State Officers of the above mentioned States, are involved in the present flagitious enterprize.—

The direct objects of this vast combination are, to invade and conquer Upper and Lower Canada, to subvert and revolutionize the established Government of those Provinces, and to wrest them from the rightful dominion of the British Crown. These are the designs of the chief directors of the plot: but it is probable that a large majority of their followers have enlisted in the scheme, for the sole purpose of rapine and plunder.— The particular mode and time of operation do not appear to have been yet determined upon by the conspirators, but will be made to depend upon circumstances, and the accidental course of events.

The above particulars, a large portion of which is already known to the United States Government, are derived from private information, received through various channels by Her Majesty's Authorities in Canada. The evidence which has been submitted to Her Majesty's Authorities, and also to myself, is of such a nature that we can entertain no doubt whatever of its truth.— There may possibly be error and exaggeration in some of the details,—which must usually happen when secret machinations are to be detected and dealt with,—but the general truth of the information admits of no doubt whatever.

In this critical state of things, the immediate interference of the Supreme Authority of the Republick can alone avert the most terrible and afflicting consequences:—and I do solemnly appeal to the President and Government of the United States, effectually to suppress this lawless association, which is plotting the destruction of Her Majesty's Provinces, and fearfully hazarding the peace of Both Countries.— Vast hordes of banditti and assassins are maturing their plans for the desolation and ruin of a British territory: they are engaged in this work within the jurisdiction of the United States,—where no British Authority can reach them,—but where Her Majesty's Authorities rely confidently upon the friendship and honor of the United States Themselves, to exert the necessary power. It would not be fit for me to suggest modes of proceeding: but surely there must reside somewhere, in every well constituted State, the power to prevent those who live under its laws, from persisting in the perpetration of violent and atrocious wrong against a friendly foreign people.—

I must observe that the present crisis in no way resembles an ordinary case of neutrality between contending foes,—between parties contending in open and legitimate war.— Neither is this a case of neutrality, as between a Government and its rebellious subjects.— No rebellion or civil war is now raging in Canada; nor has been for nearly a twelvemonth past.— The insurrection of last winter, in Lower Canada, was suppressed in a few weeks: the insurrection in Upper Canada, was suppressed in a few days.— Yet from that time to this, Her Majesty's Provinces have been kept in an almost constant state of warlike alarm, by attempts and projects of invasion from abroad; the invaders being the citizens of a friendly Republick, of a Country with whose Government Great Britain is at peace.— Her Majesty's subjects are exposed to the inconvenience and expence, the hazard and suffering of a state of war, while they are precluded from retaliating or making just reprisal upon their enemy.— That enemy is enabled, again and again, to mature his plans of aggression within the confines of a friendly Power, whose laws, from some incomprehensible reason, he still continues to evade or overrule.— I have here presented no exaggerated picture of the extraordinary state of things, which we have witnessed during the last twelvemonth upon the Canadian frontier.— It is true that whenever actual invasion has been attempted, the attempt has been quickly repelled, by the firmness of Her Majesty's Troops, and by the High courage and heroic loyalty of the British Population of Canada.— But it is not just that all these hazards should be encountered; and the burthen again forced upon Her Majesty's subjects, of defending themselves in arms against the hostile citizens of a friendly State.—

If the invasion which is now meditated, be allowed to take place, disastrous consequences will ensue.— If the American invaders, proceeding from within the jurisdiction of the Republick, should obtain a transient success, and overrun a portion of British territory, the United States would necessarily become answerable to Great Britain for the whole amount of the damage sustained, both public and private, for the recovery of the territory, and the reparation of individual loss.— If, on the other hand, which is more probable, the invading armament be repulsed,—is it possible to suppose, that the victorious party, exposed to such unheard of and enormous provocation, will always have the forbearance to respect the American boundary, from within which a lawless and unprincipled enemy will have been enabled to advance?— Is it possible to believe, that a horde of ruffians and brigands shall be permitted, again and again, to issue forth from within the territory of the United States, for the ruin of Her Majesty's subjects, and still, when repulsed, to shelter themselves at pleasure beneath the same extorted and abused protection?— I allude not to these things for the purpose of arguing, prematurely, the question either of the right of self defence, or of national reparation:— I speak only of the probability of events:— and out of either of the cases above supposed, there would arise national discussions and disputes, of which it is painful to contemplate the issue,— painful to those who desire as cordially as I do, to behold a long continuance of peace and friendship between England and America.— It is by timely and instant measures of prevention, under the authority of the Supreme Government, that the mutual calamities, now imminent, may be averted.—

[Superscription reads: "Aaron Vail Esqre: Acting Secretary of State".]

[418] H. S. Fox to Arthur: A.L.S. 20p.

Nov. 5 *Washington.* [Marked "Private".]

I herewith inclose the copy of a Note which I have addressed to the U. S. Government, and I will communicate to you officially their written answer, as soon as I receive it, which will probably be in a very few days.— I do not know exactly what tone they will assume, but I think we are making them bestir themselves.— They have hitherto reckoned upon the complaisance of Great Britain being inexhaustible; and I do not wonder at it, considering the over civil manner in which they have been complimented by all parties at home, and by all our English newspapers, upon their faithful neutrality. I purposely for a few days delayed addressing the Govt:, while the New York Elections were impending; during which time it was vain to hope that they would move hand or foot, in any thing that might endanger the vote of the lowest ruffian or patriot in that State.— The present New York Election is of more than ordinary importance to the administration, and upon its issue depends in a great measure the future political existence of Mr: Van Buren.— The voting, however, over the whole State, will have been concluded the day after tomorrow, and can consequently no longer be influenced from hence.— Mr: Forsyth is absent in Georgia; but I have had much conversation with Mr: Poinsett, Secretary of war, who is more our friend, and has more honorable notions in the present business, respecting the duties of his own Country, than most of his Colleagues.— Together with the inclosed Note, I have delivered to him, in a separate form, an abstract of the evidence, names of persons, and steam boats, cypher and system of secret signs, and other requisite information; withholding only the names and descriptions of our informants; for although I might trust the Heads of Departments here, certainly I could not trust their clerks and subordinates.— Mr: Poinsett declares to me, that the U. S. Government are determined to do all that could by possibility be done, if the plot was one of High Treason against Themselves;— which in fact it partly is.— Certainly this principle, if faithfully acted upon, is the most that we can expect: but after all, their means of controlling their own citizens are almost null.— They neither can, nor will, assume a power beyond the law (which would be done in England in a similar crisis)—nor, I sincerely believe, would Congress indemnify them if they did.— Of regular troops, all that can be brought together are already on the frontier.— If the militia were called out, they would probably join the brigands.— In short, the Institutions of the United States render them unsafe neighbours for other nations: they have before shown themselves so to Mexico: we, unfortunately, are their only other conterminous neighbour, and therefore the rest of the world will never trouble themselves much about the matter.— My Note has been forwarded by the President, to the Governors of all the States involved; with, I understand a strong representation from himself, pointing out how deeply both the interest and the honor of the Country will be compromised, if the threatened acts of violence against Canada be persisted in.— All this may I hope open the eyes of those Authorities, and of influential men, to the danger they are in of a war with England.— No men of power or influence in America, are prepared to risk a war: of this I feel persuaded: but the main difficulty, after all that has been allowed to pass, is to convince them that by the course they are now running they are really incurring the risk of war.— And this conviction I will continue to do all in my power to inculcate.

I shall hope to be able to communicate to you something more precise in a few days.— I shall also probably have some conversation with the President, although I cannot ever rely quite so much upon what he says in private conversation, as upon the official language of his Ministers.—

Upon consideration, and consultation with Captain Roxburgh, I refrained from taking Mr: Kent to any of the American Ministers; not in fact thinking it quite safe to do so: but I was extremely glad to have an opportunity of speaking with him myself.— He has engaged to write to me any future information of value, which he may obtain.— He requested, as Capt: Roxburgh will inform you, to be enabled to go home into Ohio, viâ Pittsburgh, from Philadelphia, not judging it safe to return by the way he came.— I acceded to this, and paid him 150 dollars, which was the remuneration he said he expected for his time and trouble.– I also authorized Capt: Roxburgh, to advance to him at Philadelphia, such small sum further, as may be necessary to pay the journey from thence to his home in Ohio.— There is some degree of mystery, about the conduct of this young man, Kent.— Nor do I comprehend, whether he engaged in the plot, with the design of exposing it, or whether intending to go through with it, and that he afterwards repented.— Probably the latter: as in the other case he would have demanded a larger recompense.— Of the general truth of his information, I cannot entertain any doubt whatever, corroborated as it is, both by the other depositions conveyed to yourself, and by much of the information received here from the U. S. Collectors of Customs.— With respect to the money which I have paid him, I request you to inform me whether you will charge it in your accounts, together with the rest, in which case I will send you his receipt.— Orders have been transmitted, at my request, by the Treasury department, to suspend the sale of the confiscate patriot arms at Niagara.— I hope the orders will have arrived in time.— General Macomb is expected here in a few days, upon leave granted some time ago. He will probably have left the frontier, before the officer whom you despatched, reached his Head Quarters.— But Colonel Worth, who is a very good man, will then have been senior officer at Sackett's Harbour.— I shall be much pleased, if you think right, that you should communicate the inclosed note to your Executive Council; but *not* in such a manner as can lead to its *present* publication.— I was very much obliged to you for your private, as well as public letter, brought by Capt: Roxburgh; and also for the Minute of the Executive Council, which is a very able and interesting paper.— I will not fail to write again in a few days. . .

November 6th: 1838[.]

Copies of the communications which you addressed to General Macomb, have arrived here today; having been transmitted to the Secretary of War by Colonel Bankhead, the U.S. Officer who it appears received them at Buffalo, in the absence of General Macomb.— Mr: Poinsett despatches several confidential agents, this afternoon, to the frontier, furnished with the above documents, and with tho e which I delivered to him— These agents will endeavour to obtain information upon oath, on the spot, upon the strength of which it is hoped that the leading conspirators may be arrested.— The Government doubt, how far without this they can proceed. The reports from their collectors, were only rumours and suspicions, though thoroughly confirmed by our information.— This part of the question, however, is now in the hands of Mr: Grundy, the U. S. Attorney General, the constitutional law adviser of the Govt:, who has not yet delivered his opinion.— I think at any rate, that the stir which is being now made, and much more, the able and extensive preparations of yourself and Sir John Colborne, will show to the conspirators that they are discovered; and will prevent, for the present at least, any open attempt.— And we shall then probably be all rewarded for our pains, by being told that the whole thing has been a delusion!— General Macomb is at New York, and expected here immediately.

[Endorsed in pencil: "Copy transmitted to the Secretary of State in Sir G Arthurs Despatch No 88—14 Nov. 1838—"]

[Enclosure is apparently item 417.]

[419] C. A. HAGERMAN TO THE LIEUTENANT GOVERNOR [ARTHUR]: A.L.S. 3p.

Nov. 5 *Toronto.*

I sincerely assure Your Excellency that I consider any addition to the Proclamation will weaken the good effect it is in its present form, so well calculated to produce, by destroying the *singleness* of purpose for which it has been composed.—

I fear the introduction of opinions, or the explanation of the policy of government on any particular subject, would be productive of Mischief— Some party or other might be displeased with the views promulgated, and it would be dangerous to pledge yourself to any particular course— As it now is, the proclamation is *altogether unexceptionable* and I would strongly advise leaving it so.— A more fit opportunity will present itself for doing away the Misapprehension that prevails on the subject of the Reserves than the present, and it will be better to deal with the question distinct from any other. At the end of the 20th. Paragraph some *general* assurance might be given that all classes of Her Majestys subjects should be protected in those rights to which all are equally entitled, and that to this end, the attention of the Govt. would be at an early period directed to the adoption of some measure which should have the effect of removing all apprehensions that undue preferences would be given or secured to one party over an other.—

It has occurred to me that if the 12th. paragraph ended with the words "*your property*" it would be sufficiently strong, and should your Excellency adopt this suggestion, it will be necessary to strike out the words underscored in the 13th. paragraph. My reason for making this suggestion is to guard against creating unnecessary alarm here, or giving encouragement to the Brigands on the other side, by leading them to suppose we over-rate the strength of their party, or that we are not correctly informed of their proceedings. . .

P.S.—The word "Mystic" or "concealed" may be substituted for "Masonic"—which last is objectionable.— 12th. parah.

[The proclamation referred to is apparently the one dated November 5, 1838. See *Upper Canada Gazette, Extraordinary.* November 6, 1838.]

[420] H. [*i.e.* J. T.] W. JONES TO ARTHUR: L. 17p.

Nov. 5 *Toronto.* [Marked "Copy".]

Having been entrusted with Despatches to General Macomb, I have the honor to report for your Excellency's information, the substance of what he communicated concerning the frontier disturbances; and also what I learned myself from personal observation, and enquiries made in passing along the American frontier to Plattsburgh [*sic*].

At Oswego where I landed from the Steam Boat, I understand that a very strong feeling exists in favor of the Patriot cause; Captain Armstrong who formerly commanded the Sir Robert Peel, informed me that upwards of 600 men had been sworn to the Patriot Cause in this town alone, and that meetings are constantly taking place at which funds are collected for the support of the Patriots. Other persons however who had equally good means of ascertaining asserted that the meetings were chiefly connected with electioneering purposes, and were attended for the most part by fellows who delighted to hear themselves speak, and who would never venture to take an active part in an invasion of the Canadian territory: I am inclined to believe the latter to be the true state of the Case.

At Sacke[t]t's Harbo[u]r, in the absence of General Macomb, I waited upon Coll. Clarke the officer in Command of the Garrison, mentioned the reports which were prevalent in Upper Canada, and requested his opinion upon the state of the Frontier; he said that reports of the same kind had reached him from different sources, and that in connexion with the civil authorities, he had taken great pains to ascertain their correctness; and that he was now convinced there was but little foundation for the alarming reports which had been in circulation; a secret society certainly existed, but their means were very much overrated: he considered the force at his disposal amply sufficient to put down any rising which might take place, any where in his neighbourhood; he had nearly 500 men, with artillery and a Steam boat at his command, and held the garrison in readiness to turn out at any moment:—he mentioned that Oswego, and Watertown, were the strong holds of the rebels at the lower end of the Lake; but that the collectors at each place were on the watch, and reported to him every thing that occurred.

On the remainder of my journey to Plattsburgh where conversation in the boat or stage turned upon the frontier disturbances, it certainly was the general opinion that the Canadas were oppressed by Great Britain and that they ought to be independent; at the same time the most respectable people deprecated all interference on the part of the United States Government, and universally condemned the conduct of the American Citizens who had taken a part, saying at the same time however, that none but worthless fellows, men of ruined characters and desperate fortunes were concerned in the business: and laughed at the idea of an attempt to subvert the British authority, with such men as Johns[t]on and Van Renss[e]laer as leaders: On the whole the coming elections were considered of infinitely more interest than any thing connected with the Canadas.

I found General Macomb at Plattsburgh, he paid the greatest attention to my communications, was himself in previous possession of many of the facts mentioned, but was of opinion that there was little cause for serious alarm: he was determined himself to use every means in his power to preserve the peace of the frontier; the orders to this effect from the Government being most peremptory and his own orders to the commanding officers of posts on the frontier equally strong. Reports of every description were daily reaching him from all quarters, but he was convinced that many *originated*, either with men anxious for employment as spies, or with men in subordinate offices, anxious to shew their zeal and activity, and that all reports were much exaggerated in passing through such hands. He had no power to suppress the meetings which took place, but on hearing of any assemblage of men in arms, he would not fail to take the most prompt measures, for dispersing them, he had not a doubt of the sufficiency of his force for this purpose, and was confident of the cordial support and obedience to his orders, of both officers and men; he mentioned at the same time that the powers of the military officers had recently been enlarged in cases of this kind and they had now the power of acting without any authority of the civil authority in cases of emergency.

He gave me to understand that the hands of Government were in a manner bound until after the coming elections in the state of New York; the result of the elections is very doubtful at present, is of vital interest to the administration party, and would he was sure be influenced if strong measures were used *prematurely* against the sympathisers:—this apparent supineness would however be amply atoned for when the elections were fairly over:—Wednesday November the 7th. is the last day.

The General is inclined to believe that when once the American Government takes a decided part, and uses strong measures to suppress the disturbances, many will at once withdraw from the Society as there are no doubt many at present who believe that the Patriots are secretly encouraged by the administration.

The principal point which I was directed to press upon the General's attention, was the unprotected state of some arsenals along the frontier, he said that he would at once see Governor Marcy on the subject, and offer United States Troops to guard them in case the Governor's means should be insufficient for the purpose; he left the same day for Albany for the purpose of seeing the Governor on the subject.

I furnished General Macomb with the secret signals of the society and he promised to employ some confidential person to attend their lodges, and furnish exact information of what was going on:—he mentioned that he had ample funds at his disposal for expenses of this nature, and that no means shall be left unemployed. He had heard reports of large sums being contributed by wealthy men along the frontier, but gave not the slightest credit to the stories, saying it was very unlikely that intelligent men would embark money in a business which was to be conducted by such fellows as Van Renss[e]laer: he believed that parties might attempt to cross the frontier, and chiefly with the view of inducing the British to commit reprisals, and thus embroil the two Governments: but that so long as a good understanding was maintained between the Governments, and attempts were made by both to preserve quiet, no danger whatever was to be apprehended from the utmost efforts of the Patriots.

With regard to the real intentions of the United States Government, General Macomb shewed me letters and copies of correspondence between himself and many of the authorities which were evidently not meant to be produced publickly, and from the nature and tenor of the letters, it is my firm conviction that there is at present a sincere desire to preserve quiet on the frontiers, and keep good faith with the British Government. He stated to me finally that as many cases might arise of our Government receiving information of consequence, which it would be prudent to transmit by a special messenger, he would furnish me with a letter to all the officers commanding on the frontier, directing them to pay due attention to any communication which might be made by me:—

I enclose a copy of this letter, and also a list of the American posts along the frontier as furnished by the General.

On enquiry concerning the means of transport possessed by the Patriots, it appears to me that little danger is to be apprehended on the Lake shore of Lake Ontario, a collection of boats and sailing vessels in any number would naturally excite suspicion, and require time, and besides in unsettled weather they would scarcely venture across the Lake in sailing vessels, with the knowledge that we have armed steamers on the Lake:— Our own steamers are safe on this side, and of the three American steamers, one is already laid up, a second was to perform her last trip about this time, and the other was expected to be laid up in a short time, and as it is usual to take down the engines and machinery of the steam boats when they are laid up for winter, it is most likely that in the event of either of these boats being seized, the intelligence would reach our Government before they could be prepared to move—

[*Enclosures:*]

[421] *1838*
Oct. 30

H. C. [*i.e.* ALEXANDER] MACOMB TO THE OFFICERS COMMANDING THE TROOPS AND POSTS ON THE CANADIAN FRONTIER: L.

Head Quarters of the Army, Plattsburgh [*sic*]. [Marked "Copy".]

I have the honour of introducing to you Mr. Jones of the British Army, who is the bearer of this letter.— Should Mr. Jones communicate any thing to you on the subject of our frontier affairs, you will be pleased to give it due consideration.

[The signature is given as "H. C. Macomb Major General Comr in Chief" apparently copied in error for Alexander Macomb.]

[422] [*1838*]
[*c. Oct. 30*]

[J. T. W. JONES]: M.

[*Place not stated.*] [Marked "Copy".]

Stations of the American Troops on the Canadian frontier, in the beginning of November.—

Fort Gratiot, at the entrance of the St. Clair River
Detroit—Michigan.
Buffalo
Fort Niagara
Sackett's Harbour
French Mills, on Salmon River
Chazé, near Odeltown, Lower Canada.
Plattsburgh [*sic*]
St. Alban's—Vermont
Troy—Vermont

At Plattsburgh, the Head Quarters of a Regiment, General Eustace commands; Colonel Worth at Sackett's Harbour, the Head Quarters of another Regiment; General Brady at Detroit; and, in case the disturbances on the frontier continue, General Macomb will take up his own Head Quarters at

Buffalo;— I believe that the whole American force along the frontier amounts to 2000 Men.—

[423] [GEORGE, BARON] DE ROTTENBURG TO H[ENRY] DUNDAS: LB.4, p.11-14.

Nov. 5 *Govt. House, Toronto.*

Referring to the confidential letter of the 1st. Novr. 1838 addressed to you by His Excellency the Major Genl Commanding, I am directed by His Excellency, to call your attention to the following subjects, which, from the pressure of business were omitted in it.—

1st. The most active and intelligent of the Magistrates in the District, should be required to communicate frequently with you upon the state of their neighbourhoods, and an immediate report to be made of any attempt at insurrection or disturbance.

2nd. As there is reason to believe that arms have been brought into the Province, and which are now secreted, His Excellency wishes that the Magistrates, (or such of them as you think proper to confer with) would exert themselves to discover the places of deposit, and the Major General authorizes you to offer a suitable reward to any person [who] will give such information as may lead to a discovery, but this reward should be offered privately.—

3rd. It is the more important to establish a thorough understanding with the Magistrates at this moment, as information has lately been ıeceived, that the Brigands, from the other side are passing the Frontier in small parties, with the avowed object of joining the disaffected here, and of establishing themselves in rear of some of our important posts.

His Excellency desires, that you will, without delay, make the requisite communications to the Commanding Officers of Corps, and detachments, upon the foregoing points, so as to supersede the necessity for any further instructions being sent to them, and also send a Copy to Colonels Marshall, Young, Turner, and Carmichael, of the undermentioned distribution of the Volunteer Force and Sedentary Militia, which are to be employed in your District. The detail of these is as follows.

Under Major Warren	Presq[u']isle	100 men	3rd Northumberland
	"	100 "	3rd Prince Edward
	Belleville	100 "	1st Hastings
	Bath	100 "	1st Addington
	Gan[a]noque	200 "	2nd Leeds
	Brockville	200	1st. Leeds
	Prescott	200	2nd Grenville
Col. van Koughnet	Cornwall	400	3rd Provisl. Batt.
Col. McDonald	Charlottenberg	600	4th. Do Do
	Belleville	2nd Hastings Troop of Cavalry	
	Kingston	1st. and 2nd. Frontenac— Troops of 1 Subaltern. 2 Sergts. 1 Trmpet.[?] 2 Corpls and 25 men each.	
	Brockville		1st Leeds—the entire Troop
	Cornwall		1st Stormont—the entire Troop.

A Battalion [*sic*] of Incorporated Militia under Colonel Hill is ordered to be raised at Kingston.

Should these orders not have reached the several Commanding Officers of Militia who are concerned, you will have the goodness to take steps for carrying the same into effect.—

Should the Brigands effect a landing, they must be immediately attacked and destroyed, nor upon any account be permitted to obtain a permanent footing in the Country.

I am further directed by His Excellency to acknowledge the receipt of your letter of 1st. Instant, which has been submitted to the Major General.—

I am commanded by His Excellency to observe that he cannot but think, that many of the reports coming over from the other side, are much exaggerated, and the preparations stated to be going on there, represented as being on a scale of magnitude, far beyond the reality.— At the same time, Sir George Arthur wishes you to continue to use every exertion, and vigilance, in your power, to ensure the safety of the Garrison of Kingston, and the District entrusted to your charge; agre[e]ably to the confidential letter of the 1st. Novbr 1838, addressed to you by His Excellency, and the further detailed instructions conveyed in this; ample powers have been given to you to meet every emergency. His Excellency is of opinion, that the Naval force under Captain Sandom is fully adequate to put down any attempt that Johnston may make, on the St Lawrence or elsewhere, if used energetically.—

With respect to your application to avail yourself of the services of the Indian Warriors, His Excellency does not deem it adviseable to employ them except in cases of the greatest urgency, and where circumstances will not allow time for an application being made to Head Quarters.—

The Major General regrets to find, from intelligence received this day, that great excitement and alarm prevails at Belleville and its vicinity. Instructions will be sent to Captain Swan[,] particular service, to proceed there immediately and assume Command of the Volunteer Corps and Sedentary Militia to be employed for its defence.—

His Excellency is very desirous that you would exert yourself to calm the state of alarm and excitement, which you report prevails at Kingston.— The ample means of defence placed at your disposal, His Excellency had hoped would have quite tranquillized the Inhabitants of that place and its neighbourhood.—

[Superscription reads: "Col The Honble H Dundas Comg the Troops Kingston".]

[424] [GEORGE, BARON] DE ROTTENBURG TO COL [RICHARD] AIREY: LB.4, p. 15-16.

Nov. 6 *Government House, Toronto.*

I have the honor to acknowledge the receipt of your letters of the 27 & 29 Octr 1838 which have been submitted to the Major Genl Commg.

I am directed in reply to state that the Major Genl approves of your detaching a Company from Col Prince's Battalion to Gosfield.

His Excellency is very desirous that ample supplies of Provisions & other Stores should be laid in for the use of the Troops along the whole of the Western Frontier. Instructions to this effect have already been given to the Depy Comy Genl here, but at the same time the Major

Genl authorizes you to give further directions to the Commissariat officers in your District should any deficiency exist upon these points.

His Excellency has directed that the whole of the Regt under Your Command shall be concentrated at Amherstburg as soon as the Volunteer force & Sedentary Militia ordered to be raised for the defence of the district are embodied & you will receive instructions to this effect from the Asst. Quarter Mr General here.

His Excellency authorizes you to embody 1 Subaltern & 25 Privates as an Artillery Company, & you can by means of the Lieut of the Royal Artillery stationed at Fort Malden organize & drill them[.] By this means your Artillery force will be placed on an efficient footing[.]

[Superscription reads: "Col Airey—Comg Amherstburg".]

[425] [GEORGE, BARON] DE ROTTENBURG TO COL [RICHARD] AIREY: LB.4, p. 17.

Nov. 6 *Government House, Toronto.*

I have the honor to acknowledge the receipt of your letter of the 29th. Octr. 1838 addressed to the Asst. Mil Sec detailing the steps you have deemed it requisite to take in consequence of the confidential letter of the 22nd Inst. [*sic*] from Col Halkett & which was delivered to you by Capt Markham D A Q M Genl.—

Your letter has been submitted to His Excellency the Major Genl Commanding & I am directed by His Excellency to say that he approves of the measures you have taken for the security of your Posts & district therein detailed—

With regard to the erection of a Field work at the point you propose viz Bois blanc the Major General desires me to say that Major Barou Comg Royal Engineers in Upper Canada is now upon a tour of Inspection & His Excellency wishes you to confer with that Officer upon the subject. Should Major Barou concur in the necessity you state exists for the building a blockhouse or other work there, Sir George Arthur desires that the same may be forthwith commenced—

[426] [GEORGE, BARON] DE ROTTENBURG TO COLONEL [JOHN] PRINCE: LB.4, p. 15.

Nov. 6 *Government House, Toronto.*

I have the honor to enclose a Copy of a letter addressed to His Excellency the Major Genl Comg by Colonel Macaul[a]y relative to information received of the drilling & organization of men below Fort Gratiot & that these persons intended to invade Canada[.]

His Excellency desires me to say that he wishes you would endeavour to ascertain the truth of this report & communicate the result to Colonel Airey Commanding at Amherstburg.

[Superscription reads: "Colonel Prince Comg Sandwich."]

[427] [GEORGE, BARON] DE ROTTENBURG TO H[ENRY] DUNDAS: LB.4, p. 18.

Nov. 7 *Government House, Toronto.*

I am directed by His Excellency the Major Genl Comg to inform you that 30 Cwt. of Gunpowder is in possession of Messrs. R Barclay & Co at Chisholm's rapids on the river Trent, & 1 Cwt of Gunpowder & 6 Cwt of lead in possession of Messrs. Francis & Hay at the mouth of the Trent—

His Excellency wishes you would take steps, for ensuring the security of this & to prevent its falling into improper hands[.]

[428] ARTHUR TO COLONEL [HENRY] BOOTH: LB.1, p.127-128.

Nov. 8 *Government House, Toronto.* [Marked "Confidential".]

Circumstances, over which Captain Swan has no control, prevented his being over as soon as I wished—and, as the want of a Military Officer at Belleville was *most urgent*, I was obliged to send off Captain De Rottenberg [*sic*] there.— I did think of stationing Captain Swan at Port Hope and Cobourg, where there is no Military Officer—but, finding that the turn out of the Militia on the Niagara Frontier has been a failure, it is better to see what the name of old Colonel Kirby will do—therefore, I have put him in orders for a Regiment, and send back Captain Swan to you, to assist in the formation of the corps.—

We are, at this moment, on a mine which I expect may spring every moment—

I have obtained a great deal of valuable information within the last three days—and, as soon as I get the 10000 stand of arms, which I expect from Quebec every day, I am determined, suddenly to cause several of the principal Traitors to be apprehended.— That measure will, of course quickly bring matters to an issue—and I entreat of you to make the best preparation for it that you can.— I do not think that the Patriots can act with all the effect they fancy upon the Province; at the same time, they have many supporters, of whose proceedings I have a good deal of information[.]

The worst blow is the recall of the 93rd Regiment— It has made a most baneful impression upon the Public mind in this City!!

[Superscription reads: "Colonel Booth Commdg. Niagara."]

[429] ARTHUR TO COLBORNE: LB.1, p. 121-124.

Nov. 8 *Government House, Toronto.*

I informed you that I had sent an Officer to Generals Brady and Macomb—their answers I now enclose for your perusal.—

It appears that they think better of the state of feeling, than the Civil Officers of the States who have reported to their Government,—but in a private letter Mr. Fox says, that he thinks the Military Officers do not know much, and that the truth is kept from them.— Further—General Brady is not far from 70 years of age and is very deaf.—

I have just received your orders for the return of the 93rd Regiment, which landed yesterday, after enduring a most dreadful passage.— It is now blowing most furiously; but they shall reembark tomorrow morning, and, I hope will be, at once, able to proceed downwards.—

This is a most untoward event indeed.— I wish they had not come up—the moral effect will be so bad under the present circumstances of the Province; but we must make the best of it.— The terms which you offered threw a sad damp upon our recruitings for several days. I regret there should have been any difference of opinion upon it, but I reflected upon the subject long and anxiously, and became convinced, that, with reference to the price of labour in this Province, which has much increased [since] emigration was checked, men could not be obtained on any better terms.— And even upon the terms offered, they have come forward most lamentably all over the Province—but, much worse to the

Westward than to the Eastward.— It is a sad affair! We have no supply of Blankets, Bedding or Clothing.— All must be purchased at an enormous expense, and enough is not to be procured *on any terms*. In my mind it seems downright insanity, that the Government have not sent out supplies, and formed large Depots, to meet possible contingencies in the London District, at Toronto, and Kingston. I might almost say, to meet a very probable event.— I regret deeply putting the county to such unnecessary additional expense, but, that consideration is nothing compared with the prejudice it works against the Militia coming forward—and they are very bitter with reference to the past.—

The accounts I have now daily from all quarters, are to the effect that great numbers of these Ruffians are already in this Province ready to burst out upon us.— Mr. Rattan from Cobourgh [*sic*] writes most strongly upon this point today, He is sure they have been coming over in twos and threes for some weeks.—

I hope you will be able to spare Captain De Rottenberg [*sic*], I removed him from Belleville, as I mentioned to you I would, in order that he might undertake the management of all the arrangements respecting the Militia detail.— But the state of Belleville is such, and the neighbourhood also, that I have been obliged to send him back there, as Major Warren is not able to manage the People in that Quarter.- He was ordered down, I understand, under the supposition that his services were not urgently required at Kingston.— Pray do not call him away.—

If the Militia are kept out, we shall be obliged to give their wives and children rations.— I caused the number of Married People to be limited to six on the first order.— But, now we must take such men as we can get.— What do you think of this— Further, if matters get worse, we ought to venture to promise 50 acres to every Militia Man who stands by us during the contest.— This would bring them out—and better will it be to give up a million of acres in this way, than to let the Traitors have them.

I enclose you the proclamation I have just issued.

[Enclosures lacking.]

[430] ARTHUR TO COLONEL [HENRY] DUNDAS: LB.1, p. 125-127.

Nov. 8 *Government House, Toronto.*

The pressure of business that has developed upon me will explain my not having answered before your Private letter.—

Certainly I approve of all you have done, in respect [to] gaining information; and, if you will only take the precaution to confer with the Queen's Council [*sic*] Mr. Cartwright, upon the subject of remuneration, we shall be secure against probable Treasury Queries.—

The recall of the 93rd. is a sad blow upon us; but it cannot be helped I suppose, We must make the best of it, altho I am aware that the *moral effect* will be bad indeed.—

It strikes me that your Sheriff[1] will be a most desirable Person to get out a Regiment *quickly*. I have therefore given him authority, and so I have Mr Gowan, which I hope will have a good effect.—

I find there is much alarm at Belleville, and therefore have sent back Captain De Rottenberg [*sic*]. Let him call out all the Loyal

[1]Allan McDonell.

people in that Quarter, and supply him with 300 stand of arms, and Flints and Ammunition in proportion—and, if he can muster a greater force, by all means supply him.

You will, I hope receive tomorrow 10,000 stand of arms from Quebec, be so good as to send forward 5000 stand to me as soon as possible, and take care to cause the force called out down the River to be well supplied with arms and ammunition.

Dont trust this important point to the Ordnance, without seeing to it with your own eyes— Be sure no arms however are sent by any but a safe conveyance and good escort.— Arms will be required for Colonel Gowan's Regiment.—

Will you desire Captain Sandom to send up the Guns for arming the Traveller, also guns for arming two other Steamers which I have taken up on Lake Erie.—

If he sends the armed vessel to Presqu'Isle I will take care to have an Officer there to take charge of her, with such men as I can muster.—

You are much better off at Kingston than we are here, we have a multitude of disloyal fellows about us.— Presqu'Isle is the place we have most to look to—if all be well there, I have no fear of Kingston.

[431] JOHN PRINCE: A.M.S. 4p.

Nov. 8 *The Park Farm, Sandwich.*

Amherstburgh [*sic*] 15 Miles S W of Sandwich—

The only place of Strength at Sandwich, is the stone Barrack formerly a Seminary—in the Front of the Town on the Beach, is a Wind Mill half Stone—a brick Cottage at the East end of the Town— At Windsor 2 Miles East of Sandwich opposite Detroit is a large Brick *House* 2 Storey and a Brick Cottage— The Ground here is favourable to running up works in many places, and was used for that purpose during the late War with the United States— At Windsor there is also a large 2 Stor[e]y Store of Brick Store [*sic*] with Stone Foundation on the Edge of The Bank—(Dougalls)

The River Canard is Fordable above the *Forks*— There is a good position for a bridge on the 2 Concession line where the road can be opened at small expense[.]

West of Amherstburgh there is [*sic*] also 2 large 2 stor[e]y Brick houses Reynolds & Elliotts, within a mile or mile & a half—of the Town in

At a distance of 3 miles from Sandwich on the Road to Amherstburgh are 2 Stone windmills, within 100 yards of each other and a Tavern near the same place—

4 Miles further on is another Stone Wind Mill and about a Mile further another Stone Wind Mill[;] there are 2 or 3 Taverns along this distance,

The River Canard is a Deep Sluggish River half way between the two places— No Bridge (substantial--) But only a small scow--

Both sides of the Stream is [*sic*] marshy—for many yards[.] On the other side towards Amherstburgh is the Indian Village (Hurons)—and no Wind mills nor Taverns on this side of the River[;] 2 Miles below Amherstburgh is [*sic*] 2 Stone wind mills within 200 yards of each other— and 14 Miles further on the Shore of Lake Erie in Colchester is a Stone Church— Along this route the roads are bad in the fall of the year[.]

On this Road there are 2 or 3 Inns—no mills or places of

sight of the River—

Colborne Furnace or Iron Works— 26 Miles S East of Sandwich

Strength— Tho there is Timber enough at hand [Interpolation here reads: "The Country is flat"] to make block houses or breast works— This road is bad generally speaking and is in a direct line from Sandwich to the Shore of Lake Erie— The Iron works being about 4 miles from the Shore of the Lake— The Irons [*sic*] works is not a place of any strength in itself but the[re] is [*sic*] ample houses &c. for barracks— Point *Pelé* is 8 Miles distant from this point and the Island of that name eight miles distant from the Point— and 15 Miles distant from the Main land—

Chatham is 50 Miles East of Sandwich[.] There are several Mills (wind) along this route or rather along the River & Lake Shore but none of them stone or Brick— After getting ten Miles from Sandwich the Country to the Mouth of the River Thames is impassable from the great rise of the waters— and the Inns are in a great measure deserted— But after the first 10 Miles from Sandwich a road [footnote here reads: "The course of this Road is marked Roughly in the Plan in Red Ink." The Plan is lacking.] can be made back on good ground with the greatest facility to a point on the River Thames, within a few miles of Chatham—fit for heavy Wheel Carriages or Guns—Troops—at a very small expense through Maidstone and Rochester on the Ridge—on the old allowance for road[.] The only communication with Chatham now is by the Middle and Communication Roads 27 Miles further *Round* and in Winter thaws impassable for Guns &c— In the winter to get to Sarnia you must go by Chatham[.]

On the right bank of the R Thames 4 Miles West of Chatham is a Large 2 stor[e]y Brick building on a moderately High Bank Commanding a Reach of the River Thames (McCraes house) —and another middle sized Brick house about a mile East of it— on the River Right Bank [(]Gorse's house)—East of Chatham about a Mile is another Stor[e]y & Half Brick house (left Bank)—on a high Bank—commanding a Reach— At Louisville 5 Miles from Chatham is another Brick house on the River Right Bank—

Sarnia — about 60 Miles from Chatham in a Direct line—and 70 by the bye ways and back roads—

In going to Sarnia you start from Chatham to Baldoon (on the Schnie ecarte a Branch of the which are all very bad—but the Militia can get through any where and bad roads are not considered an insuperable objection to their gaining a point.—

Moore Township— This is opposite Palmer the County Seat of Part of Michigan a good settlement[;] here some Inns no mills—bad roads — high banks to the River, and plenty means of *defence* from its localities[.]

River Thames— The bridge is unfinished at Chatham and there is a small draw bridge to cross the River— The roads through the Country are generally bad in winter during the thaws —for heavy Artillery—but light Artillery can be got along with facility by people who are accustomed to bad roads in the woods and marshes—and heavy loads and the Management of Cattle under adverse circumstances—

From Chatham to the Lake Shore of Erie is about 14 Miles—there is a road or perhaps Two roads but neither of them are good but are still passable[.]

From Chatham East to District boundary — is 25 miles[.] The River Thames has to be crossed Either at Chatham or higher up the River at the Ford on the Flats in Howard (high banks) 12 Miles from Chatham[.] Roads are tolerably good[.] The Inns are few and with little to recommend them, there are no Stone or Brick Mills on this route & no strong points except on the River Banks and the hilly undulations of the soil—which get more frequent as you proceed further East—

River St Clair) by the Town line between Township of Chatham and Camden strike Bear Creek at Taylors Mills & Down Bear Creek to Baldoon a round about of 40 miles, for *waggons* &c—for man & horse there is a more direct road of 18 miles not always good—from thence you proceed to Sombra Township which is settled in Front—neither of Baldoon or Sombra has any Mills (defensible)—which takes you to Moore.

[Most of the second paragraph of the document is written in a reddish ink which has faded almost into illegibility. The transcript of this paragraph rests mainly on item 432.]

[432] JOHN PRINCE: M. 6p.

Nov. 8 *The Park ffarm, Sandwich.* [Marked "Copy".]
[Another copy of item 431.]

[433] ARTHUR TO HENRY DUNDAS: LB.1, p. 128-130.

Nov. 9 *Toronto.*

In addition to the Corps before called out, I yesterday authorized a Corps under Lt. Colonel Allen McDonnel [*i.e.* Allan McDonell] to be raised at Kingston, and one at Brockville under Lt. Coll. Gowan. These Corps will require arms & accoutrements if you can supply them. Also, all the Glengarry Regts are called out.

Be sure to satisfy yourself that you have a good supply of fine grained powder—and if you have not, and there should be any doubt of your being supplied from Quebec, cause all that is to be had to be purchased at Kingston.

I mention this because we have no fine grained powder here, and we are much in want.

After what has occurred below, you had better strengthen your Posts upon the Rideau as these Pirates may now try to cut off our communication in that Quarter.

If possible Colonel McMillan should certainly endeavour at once to raise a Corps at Perth—

The Glengarries must of course be freely used to keep open the communication with the Lower Province, and I shall be delighted to hear that they have made a good turn out.—

Take care to supply Captain De Rottenberg [*sic*] with arms and ammunition, and, then, I think, we shall be guarded at all points to destroy these Ruffians if they venture to Land.

Put up the Militia with all the comfort you can and do not regard expence to this end.

Be sure and ascertain from the officer in charge of the Comt. that you have an ample supply of Flour & Meat. . .

P.S. I expect every moment to hear of an outbreak in the Western District, but am pretty well prepared for it[.]

[434] ARTHUR TO COLONEL [RICHARD] AIREY: LB.1, p. 130-133.

Nov. 10 [*Place not stated.*]

I hasten to let you know that there has been a rise in the Lower Province on Sunday last.

The Rebels were in possession of Beauharnois and had seized the Henry Brougham Steamer which had called at that place. Their object is to cut off the communication between the two Canadas.

They have risen also on the Richelieu, and were expected to make an attack upon Sorel.

By various informations on oath before me I find it is the intention of the "Patriots" to attack the Upper Province as soon as the rebels have commenced their operations below. I have ascertained beyond all doubt that they have a large supply of arms immediately in the neighbourhood of Detroit and all along the St Clair.

I have no report of what success you have had to the Westward in turning out the Militia. It will give me sincere pleasure to find that at Sandwich, Major Reid has been able to muster a considerable force of Militia, so as to permit him to send you back the Dett. of your Corps—and the same at Chatham—from whence I wish your Detachment to be withdrawn as soon as Colonel Chichester can muster 200 men; but I should be glad to hear that he had 700 to support you, if necessary, either at Amherstburg or at Sandwich, or if necessary to move towards the lake if a landing should be effected there.

I shall be glad to hear that you have been able to muster in some strength also at Gosfield.

In fact, I should be glad to find you have as large a force as you can arm, and you need not consider yourself to be limited to the force mentioned in the General Militia Order.

I have sent 1500 stand of arms to London, so that Colonel Chichester can be supplied from thence if you have none to spare.

The Militia must be made comfortable in quarters, therefore whatever expense is *necessary* to this end it must be incurred only report upon it as soon as you can.

Within the last fortnight I should hope you have considerably strengthened your Station. We must not suffer this Banditti to hoist their Colors for a moment in any part of the Province if we can help it.

It will be desirable, indeed necessary that your Commisst. should be amply supplied from Amherstburg to Sarnia with Meat and Flour for the Winter Months—do see to this and consider yourself authorised to direct whatever is necessary. . . .

P.S. I will send you in a few days a Detachment of the Provincial Artillery to work your guns.

[435] ARTHUR TO COLONEL [RICHARD] AIREY: LB.1, p. 135.

Nov. 10 *Toronto.* [Marked "Confidential".]

[There is a space left at the beginning of the letter, and a marginal note which reads: "This letter the same as the preceding down to the cross." *i.e.* see the asterisk in item 436.]

There are I believe a good many colored people in the neighbourhood of Amherstburg— There would be no objection to their services being engaged, and they might act either with you or with Colonel Chichester. I am very anxious to have as strong a force to the Westward as I can arm.—

I have just heard that the 73rd have come up with the Rebels; dispersed, and taken several of them Prisoners.—

[436] ARTHUR TO COLONEL [CHARLES] CHICHESTER: LB.1, p.133-134.

Nov. 10 *Toronto.* [Marked "Confidential".]

You will receive herewith a letter and memorandum respecting the Indians.—

It is my desire to place the Indian warriors out of the way of being tampered with; and, at the same time, to make their services available in the field should these Ruffians cross over to devastate the Province, which seems their fixed determination, from the preparations, which are still in progress, and from the assistance some of the Patriots are already affording in the Lower Province to the Rebels.—

No time should be lost in making the best possible arrangement for assembling the Indians, so that, in their way, they may be comfortably housed, and at the same time, be at hand if their services are required.

An order shall be issued tomorrow for serving out Rations to the Indians thus assembled.—

It will be desirable to carry this measure into effect as quietly as possible, as the Americans, it would seem, are very fastidious, and think the Indians ought not to protect their homes.—

Of course, I need not say to you, that if these people should be called upon to take the field, which I earnestly hope, may not be the case, they should be enjoined to act towards an enemy with all the humanity required by civilized warfare.—*[1]

If any better arrangement for assembling the Indians, and stationing them, than is pointed out in the memorandum occurs to you be so good as to act upon it—only take care to let me know.—

I wish you should have as large a force as you can possibly arm.—

A detachment of the 73rd. have come up with the rebels—dispersed and taken several prisoners.

What number of blacks have you in the neighbourhood of Chatham? I understand they make good soldiers.

[Enclosures lacking.]

[437] ARTHUR TO COLONEL [JOHN] MAITLAND: LB.1, p. 135.

Nov. 10 *Toronto.* [Marked "Confidential".]

[There is a space left at the beginning of the letter, and a marginal note which reads: "The same as that to Colonel Chichester as far as the cross." *i.e.* see the asterisk in item 436.]

I have just heard that the 73rd have come up with the Rebels, dispersed, and taken several of them Prisoners.—

[438] H. S. FOX TO ARTHUR: A.L.S. 21p.

Nov. 10 *Washington.* [Marked "Confidential".]

I have the honor to acknowledge the receipt of Your Excellency's despatch, marked confidential, of the 31st: ultimo, with its several inclosures, brought to me by Lieutenant Bewes.— I have read, with great interest and anxiety, the additional information contained in those inclosures, respecting the meditated invasion of Canada by the combined hordes of American brigands.

Upon the two important questions, which form the principal subject of your despatch, I am afraid that I cannot at present speak as satisfactorily as I could wish.—

With respect to the arming of British Vessels upon the Lakes, to an extent beyond what was stipulated between the Two Governments, the expediency, and the absolute necessity of so doing, are indisputable.— But there seems to be some misapprehension, as to a supposed arrangement made by Lord Durham, with the United States.— No communication whatever, as far as I am acquainted, has passed upon that subject between Lord Durham and this Government. All that has been done in the matter, is this: in the month of June last, immediately after the

[1]For meaning of this asterisk see item 435.

destruction of the Steam Boat "Sir Robert Peel", I addressed a despatch to Lord Palmerston,—in anticipation of what I expected would happen, and which is now happening,—suggesting that Her Majesty's Government should authorize me to enter into an agreement with the Government of the United States, for suspending, in case of emergency, the arrangement formerly concluded:—but to this I have received no answer from Her Majesty's Government.— I sent a copy of my despatch, at the time, to Lord Durham: probably he concluded, that I should in due time receive the necessary authority from home.— I feel certain that Her Majesty's Government have not expected the crisis which has now arrived.—

However,—I do not hesitate in recommending you to disregard the restrictions stipulated in the agreement in question.— The present crisis is one of absolute and overruling necessity; and I do think it is beyond the possibility of things, that the United States Government should be so monstrously unreasonable and perverse, as to raise any complaint or objection; considering that the hostile acts, which render your proceeding necessary, are the acts of their own citizens; lawless and atrocious acts, which the Government avow their desire to prevent or punish, if they could.—

I am not yet certain, whether it will be expedient for me, officially to acquaint the United States Government with the extent to which you find it necessary to exceed the stipulated armament; or whether it will not be better, to leave a case of such evident necessity to be explained afterwards, if any cavil or objection should be raised.— I feel inclined to the latter course: because it may be requisite to vary the amount of the armament, according to circumstances, of which you might not always be able to give me precise or immediate information.— I shall be guided, however, in my decision upon this point, by the course which my pending communications with the Government, upon other matters connected with the present crisis, may take; and I will shortly address you again upon the subject. In the mean time, I repeat that I would recommend the necessary armament to be continued, without scruple, and without reference to the stipulations of the year 1817.

The other principal subject, discussed in your despatch, is of a more important character, and involves very serious and doubtful considerations.— I have always believed, that one of the inevitable consequences of the invasion of Canada, now threatened, by the American brigands, would be, that Her Majesty's Forces, in repelling those invaders, would pursue them into the territory of the United States, and that a risk of hostile collision with the United States Authorities would thus be incurred.— You will have observed, that in the Note which I addressed to the United States Government, I have held out this apprehension, as a strong argument to induce the Supreme Government effectually to interfere, for preventing the meditated invasion.— But with respect to negotiating any specific arrangement, by which the United States Government should agree before hand, to admit of such an infringement,—or violation, as they would call it,—of the Territory of the Republick, I must at once say, that I consider it to be utterly impracticable. Even if the President should be himself willing, which I much doubt, to agree to such a proposal, I am quite certain that he would not dare to encounter the clamour of his citizens.— Any infringement by us of the American Territory, in pursuit of the invaders, must remain to be justified afterwards, by the absolute and paramount necessity of self defence, and the force of uncontrollable and excessive provocation.— I think that it would weaken our argument of justification hereafter, if we are to enter into any regular discussion of the matter with the American Government by anticipation,—beyond the general warning which I have already addressed to them.—

I repeat, that I consider the retaliatory infringement of the neutral rights of the American territory, as almost unavoidable, in the event of the threatened invasion of Canada being actually attempted:—but the consequences would be of such extreme and fearful importance,— involving the instant probability of a national war,—that the act ought certainly not to be sanctioned, so long as any other possible means should remain, of giving adequate protection to Her Majesty's subjects.— These arguments apply, most of all, to the supposed case of a pursuit of the invaders into the American harbours, or of a landing upon the American shore.— In the event of an engagement with the pirates, upon the open waters of the lake, it would evidently be impossible that in the heat of action, the exact line of the American boundary should be respected, or even ascertained.— But these all are extreme cases of necessity; to be defended and justified upon the ground of that necessity, rather than to be provided for before hand, by any specific arrangement or understanding.—

[439] H. S. Fox to Arthur: A.L.S. 2p.

Nov. 10 *Washington.*

I have this evening received the intelligence of the disturbances in Lower Canada,—up to the date of the 5th: instant from Montreal. I had not expected that the mischief would be first renewed in that quarter.— I wait most anxiously, to learn what effect the news from Montreal will have produced in Upper Canada, and within the American border.—

Those here who are ill disposed towards us, will now strive all they can, to make it appear that the whole mischief and danger is *within* the British Provinces, and not from without.

[Endorsed in Arthur's handwriting: "Furnish for the perusal of the Executive Council & to be returned as soon as possible GA".]

[440] J. H. Harris to Arthur: A.L.S. 3p.

Nov. 10 *Park Lodge, Cambridge.*

It having been intimated to me by Dr McCaul, the gentleman selected by the Archbishop of Canterbury for the Principalship of Upper Canada College—that he intends shortly to sail for America—I gladly avail myself of the opportunity to thank Your Excellency for your kind letter of the 9th. August & its enclosure, which His Grace forwarded to me in the first week of Septr.— In compliance with your Excellency's & the Archbishop's joint request I made such enquiry as I was able amongst the few friends whom, from my long absence, & the particular period of the Academic Year, (it being then the Long Vacation, when the University is almost empty) I had the opportunity of applying to—& I wrote particularly to one gentleman whom I had reason to think peculiarly well qualified for the Situation of Principal, offering to bring his name under the Archbishop's consideration, shd. he be willing to become a Candidate—after a little deliberation however this gentleman declined the proposal; and I was finally obliged to inform his Grace that I scarcely saw any prospect, from the circumstances I have alluded to, of *my* speedily hearing of a competent successor for my late office.— About three weeks ago the Archbishop wrote to inform me that he had selected Dr McCaul a Tutor of Trinity College, Dublin, of whom he had received high recommendations as to talent, & character— I have not the pleasure of being at all acquainted with Dr McC. but His Grace seemed to feel the importance of a good selection to the interests of the College, so strongly, that I cannot but anticipate favorable results from his Grace's appointment— I am not sufficiently acquainted with the peculiarities of the Dublin System of Academic instruction to be aware whether there can arise any little difficulties in the first co-operation of a *Dublin* Head with so many *Cambridge Members* of the Corps Instructive: but I am led to suppose that in some quarters at least a *break* in the chain of *Cambridge* succession will not be deemed a subject of regret—& as I believe there is more attention paid at the Irish University to some popular & useful branches than at the English ones, Dr McCaul's appointment will probably be of advantage in carrying out the more *general* features of the Course which has been adopted at U. C. College— I have already written to Dr McC. & purpose doing so again, when I forward this to his care— he cannot I fear reach Toronto before Christmas, so that the College will have been just three quarters of a year without a head, but I hope it will not have suffered materially from this cause— Dr McC. will have the advantage of commencing his superintendence with the beginning of the College Year, after the annual Examination—to which I trust there is no prospect of such an interruption as was occasioned by the insurrection last year— There is much speculation here as to what *will* be the issue of Ld. Durham's annoyance at the parliamentary proceedings relative to his Ordinance— Ld. Normanby is mentioned for his successor, but with little foundation I believe for the surmise—& within the last two days the opinion has been rather entertained that Ld D. after all will not resign—& the arrival of one of His Ldship's A.D.C's., Capt. Conroy, within the last few days seems a little to favor this idea—but of course the public can only *conjecture* on such topics—

I trust most sincerely for your Excellency's sake as well for the peace of the Province, that Upper Canada is in a quieter state, & has quieter prospects, than there seems reason to apprehend for the Lower Province—

About ten days ago I received the handsome testimonial which Your Excellency & the College Council were pleased to adopt with reference to my late official conduct—& for which I beg to offer my respectful thanks— It reached Quebec a few days after we had set sail, & was retained for an opportunity of being forwarded to England by private hand— this opportunity I believe was afforded by the Chief Justice's visit— I have not however yet seen, or heard from, him— Mrs Harris begs to present her Compliments to Your Excellency[.]

[441] ARTHUR TO COLONEL [C. B.] TURNER: LB. 1, p. 136-137.

Nov. 11 *Govt. House, Toronto.*

I am much disappointed at not having heard from you by the last Post. Pray press on, by every means, that are prudent, the raising of men, so that we may be able, effectually to assist the Comr of the Forces in the Lower Province. Do nothing in haste, but having considered well, what can best be done, then act with promptitude and decision. If Lt. Colonel Gowan can rapidly bring forward another Corps, we shall surely be able to spare a thousand men to enter the Lower Province. By all means support Colonel Carmichael in keeping open the communication with the Lower Province. Have an eye also on Hawkesbury in your rear and establish a communication by means of some Cavalry with Mr Hamilton at that Station . . .

P.S. Write to me every day if it be but five lines, whilst affairs continue so anxious, and on the shortest notice, be ready to assist the Comr of the Forces. Pray shew this letter to Colonel Phillpotts from whom I expected to have heard what were Sir John Colborne's further wishes, respecting the Glengarries.

[Superscription reads: "Colonel Turner, Comr at Cornwall."]

[442] ARTHUR TO COLONEL [PLOMER] YOUNG: LB. 1, p. 136.

Nov. 11 *Govt. House, Toronto.*

I am disappointed at not having heard from you by the last post— pray write me almost daily and report progress in turning out the Militia, and furnishing any details, which you consider at all interesting or important at this crisis.

Colonel Turner must be ready to support Colonel Carmichael, and you must support Colonel Turner as far as you possibly can. By all means must the communication with the Lower Province be kept open.

Do not wait for instructions, upon any important point that is urgent, but use your discretion, and act with decision and promptitude at this moment.

[Superscription reads: "Colonel Young Prescott."]

[443] COLBORNE TO ARTHUR: A.L.S. 2p.

Nov. 11 *Odell Town, La Colle.*

I trust that the failure of the Rebels in this Province will have a good effect in Upper Canada. They have been dispersed in every quarter and their arms and ammunition have fallen into our hands.

The Glengarry Regiments of Militia which I took the liberty of directing to cross the Beauharnois have been of much use to us—

I hope I shall be able to send you reinforcements if we succeed in reestablishing order in the Montreal District—

The preparations for this revolt commenced in June last . . .

[P.S.] Nelson, Cote, and Gagnon have escaped to Champlain, but the French General has been made prisoner[.]

[444] D DUNDASS [*i.e.* HENRY DUNDAS] TO MAJOR [J. H.] BLACKER: L.

Nov. 11 *Kingston.* [Marked "Circular".]

The rebels & Sympathisers are now in possession of Prescott[;] it is now important that every Loyal man should be up and doing— Give orders for every disposable man to march to Kingston without a moments delay . . .

a true copy
John S. Cartwright[.]

[Endorsed: "The Adjt Genl of Militia having perused the within, doubts the propriety of the measure— If acted upon it will deprive the whole line of Country along the Bay of Quinté of every disposable man. RB".]

[The letter would appear to be a copy (made by Cartwright, Kingston banker and member of the Legislative Assembly) of a general "Circular" appeal issued by Dundas following the Prescott landing. It is given as being signed: "Yours in haste D Dundass Lt Col 83d Rgt & Col Commanding". It has the superscription: "To Major Blacker 3d Battn Hastings Militia", and when folded is addressed to him at "Shannonville". Refolded, the letter is further addressed: "To Col. De Rottenburg Commanding at Belleville". It might be conjectured that the endorsement by Bullock as adjutant general of militia came between the two addressings.]

[445] A. McNabb to [Arthur]: A.L.S. 2p.

Nov. 12 *Kingston, U. Canada.*

May it please your Excellency

In times of emergency it becomes every loyal Subject to use his utmost efforts to assist the general cause,— I can, may it please your Excellency do so, and under your sanction and authority raise immediately a company of Volunteers from the Bathurst District bordering on the Ottawa River where I am known, to do duty here or elsewhere in the Province, and I deem it my duty to represent this to your Excellency that you may avail yourself of my willingness, and their attachment to serve the Queen and Country . . .

A. Mc.Nabb, Lt.
1st. front[enac], Militia[.]

[446] F. L. Arthur to the Adjutant Gen. of Militia [Richard Bullock]: LB. 4, p. 20.

Nov. 13 *Govt. House, Toronto.*

I am desired by the Lieutenant Governor to inform you that His Excellency has considered it adviseable to increase the Troop of Provincial Cavalry under Major Magrath, and directs therefore that 1 Sergeant 1 Corporal and 23 privates be added to the present strength.

[447] C. C. Domvile to H[enry] Dundas: LB. 4, p. 18-19.

Nov. 13 *Government House, Toronto.*

I am desired by His Excellency the Lieutenant Governor to request you to inform yourself of what quantity of arms—ammunition—accoutrements—flints &c are at Bytown.— (I think a hundred stand have been ordered there)[.]

His Excellency is of opinion that there should be 300 stand at that place, and is anxious, that, if that number are not already there they should be made up to the above complement.

His Excellency is also desirous that 200 stand should be sent to Mr. Hamilton at Hawkesbury, and that his receipt should be taken for the same.

The necessary proportions of ammunition—accoutrements—flints—&c. will of course be sent with the above mentioned arms.—

[448] C. C. Domvile to H[enry] Dundas: LB. 4, p. 19-20.

Nov. 13 *Government House, Toronto.* [Marked "Immediate & Urgent".]

I send you an extract from a letter just received by the Lieutenant Governor from a good authority.—

"I think it right to apprize you, for the information of His Excellency, that I have had positive information, that the Rebels are intent upon getting possession of the Steam Boats, by putting persons on board as Passengers, and otherwise—with arms concealed, so that they may be enabled to seize the Boat unawares."—

In consequence of the above information, His Excellency desires, that no Steam Boat may be allowed to proceed up the Bay of Quinty [*i.e.* Quinte], or in any other direction from Kingston, without an armed party being placed on board—and that all Passengers—sailors—and others, may be searched carefully, before allowed to embark.—

[449] F. A. M. Fraser to Henry Dundas: A.M.S. 3p.

[*1838*] [*Place not stated.*] [Marked "Original".]

[*Nov. 14?*] Instructions conveyed to Colonel The Honorable Henry Dundas—Commanding at Kingston U: C:

Information having reached His Excellency The Major General Commanding, that Prescott has fallen into the hands of Brigands and others, hostile to the Government—I have the honor to convey to you His Excellency's directions as follow.

You will be pleased to occupy the Fort Henry with such a part of your Regiment, the 83rd., as, together with a force of truly loyal men on whom you can depend, will *fully ensure* the maintaining of that post[.]

With the remainder of the 83rd such a Provincial force as you may be able to collect and trust to, with two six pounders, and accompanied by Lieutenant Crawl[e]y R.E, you will proceed down the St. Lawrence and dislodge the enemy from Prescot[t].

His Excellency having previously given you discretionary powers, these orders need not overthrow any arrangements you may have deemed it right to make, as being nearer the scene of action, and possessed of more recent information; but whatever may have been your previous dispositions you will be pleased to consider it, as your paramount duty not to suffer the Brigands and disaffected to occupy a spot in the province, one moment longer, than the most vigorous measures can prevent.

Should the Ruffians have unfortunately succeeded in obtaining possession of the Fort at Prescott—The Major General hopes you will be able to dislodge them with your two Six pounders; and trusts that Captain Sandom R.N. will have proceeded, with the Naval force at his disposal, down the St. Lawrence, with a view to prevent communication between the British and American Shores—

You will direct the officer whom you may leave in Command at Kingston, to put arms into the hands of such gallant and trusty Inhabitants as may be disposed to turn out for the protection of their country[.]
By Command

F. A. MacKenzie Fraser
Colonel—Asst. Qr. Mr. Genl.

P.S. It is His Excellency's wish that if arms have arrived from below, 5000 stand with Ball ammunition in proportion, be sent up by the "Traveller", as speedily as possible; if none have arrived, send up what you can spare—from those in Store.

[450] Nov. 14 ARTHUR TO COLONEL [WILLIAM] COX: LB.1, p. 179-181.
[*Place not stated.*]

Yr. messenger arrived with yr. Letter about 4 O'Clock last evening. I am more and more persuaded that it is necessary to be calm and cautious how we place any great confidence in any statements derived from such sources.

I do not say they are to be disregarded, but that they ought not to be confided in without much abatement for the possible interested motives of the Informant.

When I first saw your messenger, I remember it occurred to me there was a something about him a little mysterious! I have been more struck with it on my second interview with him. His story may be literally true; but, until I knew [*sic*] more of him I am not disposed to give him my entire confidence!

The truth is—although there may be mischief brewing—and although I receive warning after warning that the "Patriots" are going to over-run the Country, yet, I must confess, that I cannot discover from what quarter all this evil is to come—and I do believe that there is a Class of Persons who are making a Market of the times, by originating these Stories.

Under these circumstances, I shall be thankful if you will more particularly enquire of Mr. Law respecting yr. messenger—how long he has known him, or his family—what is his occupation and what his *association* to his *own knowledge.* Although I am anxious for this information, nevertheless, I have told him that whatever remuneration you have promised him he shall have.

In all yr. proceedings—& pray urge the same upon the respectable & loyal People near you—do not forget the extreme importance of not apprehending, or causing any person to be apprehended, for Treason without the most conclusive evidence. Even *One* erroneous arrest brings on very calamitous consequences.

I am much obliged to Mr. Law for his intimation respecting the supposed plot for seizing some of the Government Steamers, and I have given the necessary instructions upon the subject. perhaps he wd. give the Govt. further particulars of this matter wh. may lead to extensively beneficial results.— The rest of the Troop are ordered out as you request.

My opinion is that you will find Captain Macdonald not only a resolute Soldier but very useful in tracing out what is going on in yr. neighbourhood. Rely upon it the schemes of the disaffected are not so deep, but that they may be fathomed. The wicked are too commonly supposed to carry a Charm about them, and this absurdity is prevailing here in all its folly.—

I have been led to make these observations because yr. Messenger came to me intoxicated last night and has wholly disappeared this Morng.

[Superscription reads: "Colonel Cox. . .Comdg. at Whitby."]

[451] C. C. DOMVILE TO THE OFFICER COMMANDING KINGSTON [HENRY DUNDAS]: LB.4, p. 20-21.

Nov. 14 *Government House, Toronto.* [Marked "Immediate & Urgent".]

With reference to the communication sent to you by the Assistant Quarter Master General—I am directed by his Excellency the Major General Commanding to desire that the Posts on the Rideau Canal may be immediately strengthened, and every possible means taken to provide for their security.

[452] ARTHUR TO H. S. FOX: LB.1, p. 141-142.

Nov. 15 *Government House, [Toronto.]*

I did intend to have addressed you, in a private letter, at some length, but I have not a disposable moment.

The outrage committed upon our Territory, immediately in the view of the Military as well as the Civil Authorities of the States removes every doubt from my mind that the Govt must be countenancing these outrages whilst they affect to deprecate them.

I hope you will *threaten* them with your departure, though your last note was as strong as could well be, and move them if any thing would.

Colonel Farquharson, who is the bearer of my Despatch to you, will have the honor to bring me your reply...

[P.S.] Although I have said I hope you will *threaten* to demand your Passport, I ought to say that in the present state of this Province War is to be avoided if it can be.

[453] C. A. HAGERMAN TO THE LIEUTENANT GOVERNOR [ARTHUR]: A.L.S. 2p.

Nov. 15 *Toronto.*

It is a question whether it be desirable to issue a Proclamation at this moment at all or not— the events of a few days, will most probably change the character of any that you would now promulgate.—

In the event of issuing one, it appears to Mr. Draper and myself that it should be confined to a Statement of facts shewing the necessity which may exist for calling out additional force—and not be in itself the order for such measure.—

An allusion to the accountability of the United States to Great Britain we both think most important.—

[454] C. C. DOMVILE TO ASST. QUART. MAST. GENERAL [F. A. M. FRASER]: LB.4, p. 22-23.

Nov. 15 *Government House, Toronto.*

His Excellency the Major General Commanding is desirous that the line of Communication between this and Kingston should be well kept up and secured, by means of Orderly Dragoons, and he begs that you will arrange with Colonel Bullock to call out immediately such bodies of Cavalry as may ensure the complete and expeditious performance of this duty.

By an extract from a letter from Colonel Turner, it appears, that, by the directions of the Commander of the Forces, Colonel Phillpot[t]s "has called out Captain Harvey's Troop for the purpose of extending the line" from Cornwall "to Kingston; and that Captain Jarvis' (Cornwall) Troop, communicates from *Munroe's* (a house I believe below Cornwall) to Coteau du Lac"—

His Excellency would wish you to put yourself in possession of the mode in which the express duty is performed by the above Troops, between Kingston & Coteau du Lac—

[455] C. C. DOMVILE TO DEPUTY COMM[I]SS[AR]Y GENERAL [F. E.] KNOWLES: LB.4, p. 21-22.

Nov. 15 *Government House, Toronto.*

As His Excellency the Major General Commanding is convinced, that, at the present advanced state of the season, and with reference to what is passing in the Lower Province, he cannot expect the necessary supplies of Blankets from Quebec—and, as the Militia and Volunteers have refused to turn out, unless duly supplied with food and Blankets, according to the terms of enlistment—I am directed to suggest to you the necessity of sending some discreet Merchants into the United States—with all due dispatch—for the purpose of purchasing Blankets, at Utica—Albany—New York—and such other town as may appear good to them (consistent with expedition)—and of Shipping them with as little delay as possible from Oswego, for this Place and Kingston, as you can best arrange, with reference to the demands for them.—

[456] JOHN FORSYTH TO H. S. FOX: L. 19p. In Fox's handwriting.

Nov. 15 *Washington.* [Marked "Copy".]

The President, to whom has been submitted the Note addressed by you to the acting Secretary of State of the 3d. instant, conveying information of a secret conspiracy supposed to exist within the confines and jurisdiction of the United States, for the purpose of waging war upon the British Provinces of Upper and Lower Canada,—has instructed me to make the following reply to it.—

The Government of the United States has regarded with the deepest anxiety, the unfortunate disturbances which have recently taken place in Her Majesty's Possessions adjoining the northern frontier of these States, and has spared no exertions whilst enjoining upon their citizens, a proper sense of their obligations to prevent by all legitimate means, any interference on their part in the affairs of their Canadian neighbours.— That measures of this nature were promptly adopted by the President, upon the occasion referred to, you are well aware, as also how far they have proved successful.— Prompted by the same feeling, the reports which have reached this City of apprehended hostile movements against Canada from within the American territory, whether received through official or other channels, have been scanned with lively interest by the Executive; and although the examination has resulted in a conviction that the circumstances detailed in them are of a highly exaggerated character, every precaution that the most watchful prudence can suggest, and perfect good faith towards a friendly nation dictate, has been, and will continue to be taken, to avert the threatened mischief.— If an organized combination against any foreign Government, entertaining the lawless designs attributed to that described in your note of the 3d: instant, exists within the jurisdiction of this Government, it is the duty of the United States, as well to themselves as to that foreign Government, to use their best endeavours to suppress it.— In the determination to fulfil this acknowledged obligation, the Government of the United States cannot with propriety take into consideration the contingent consequences on discussions to which you have alluded; and the President is pleased to find, that you have properly omitted to argue, so prematurely, questions of the rights of self defence, or national reparation, in reference to circumstances that have not happened, and which it is hoped will never occur.—

From the evidence in the possession of this department, highly coloured in its details as much of it unquestionably is, there is certainly room to fear that some attempts may be made during the approaching winter, to excite disturbances in Her Majesty's Canadian Provinces.— No serious uneasiness as to their result can well be entertained.— Such attempts must necessarily prove abortive.— And the President is unwilling to believe it possible, that any difficulties in the friendly relations subsisting between the United States and Great Britain, will be permitted to spring from such a source.— Every thing in the power of this Government to do, will be done, to prevent a result so much to be deprecated; and the President is quite sure, that our efforts to that end will meet with the cordial and efficient cooperation of Her Majesty's Authorities.— It will require the exercise of great discretion, as well as the utmost vigilance of the Officers of both Governments, to counteract the design apparently existing to involve the Two Countries in a war.— Predatory incursions, and acts of violence on each side of the boundary, will probably be the principal means resorted to, to effect this criminal purpose.— The utter impracticability of placing a frontier, extending nearly one thousand miles, in a military attitude sufficiently imposing and effective, to prevent such enterprizes, is evident.— Regular military armaments, and the movement of armed bands to any considerable extent from the American side of the line, will I think be successfully repressed; and all other hostile preparations will also be averted, as far as that object can be accomplished by the active employment of the means at the disposal of this Government.— Whilst thus performing all its duties in this regard, it will expect that under no pretext whatever, will the officers in command of Her Majesty's forces permit a violation of the territory of the United States.— Such a step could not fail to have a most injurious effect on the friendly relations at present so happily subsisting between the Two Countries; and might, to the deep regret of both Parties, lead to their entire disruption.— If any armed bodies of men should take refuge within, or otherwise enter the territory of the United States, they will be immediately disarmed, or expelled by force; and if any American citizen shall have so far forgotten his duty, as to enrol himself among armed bands that shall have crossed our frontier, after being disarmed, he will be arrested, and delivered over to the Civil Authorities for trial and punishment. Orders to this effect have already been given to our Officers, and they will I doubt not be promptly and efficiently executed.— No depredations committed by the insurgents on our citizens, will be regarded by American officers as justifying retaliation upon Her Majesty's peaceable subjects; and with the application of a similar rule on the part of Her Majesty's Authorities, in respect to such unauthorized and lawless incursions from our side of the line, as may be made in despite of the vigilance of our officers civil and military,—and the exercise of great forbearance in all things on both sides, the President allows himself to hope, that the Two Governments will be able to overcome difficulties which he feels to be of the most threatening character.

[The above is apparently one of the enclosures referred to in item 513.]

[457] ARTHUR TO COLBORNE: LB.1, p. 142-143.

Nov. 16 [*Place not stated.*]

I hasten to forward to you the enclosed copy of a report from Captain Sandom detailing the proceedings against the Brigands, who crossed to Prescott on Sunday Last.

I have not received the report of Colonel Dundas of the Sequel of the affair but I should hope the ruffians who escaped to the Mill are before this in our hands. As soon as I receive Colonel Dundas's Report, I will write to you officially.

In the mean time I have again sent off to Mr Fox, and I must say I think it is time for him to leave Washington unless the Govt. of the United States will act with good faith.

My official to him is as strong as I can make it.

I am expecting an attack from these Brigands every hour, as they are full of activity on the other side. . .

P.S. I am impatient beyond measure for the result of your attack upon Beauharnois.

I hope you are pleased at the turnout of the Glengarries. I want arms exceedingly.

[Enclosure lacking.]

[458] [ARTHUR] TO DURHAM: LB.1, p. 139-141. In Arthur's handwriting.

Nov. 16 *Govt. H.* [*Toronto.*]

You will be disappd. not to receive some tidings from Upper Canada by the Great Western, & therefore although I have been writing all day & all night I will not close the Despatch Bag without a very hasty note to Yr Ldp.

You had carcely left the River before appearances grew worse, & four days afterwards the outbreak took place in the Lower Province at Beauharnois the full particulars of wh. you will no doubt receive by the present oppty.

A Body of our Militia immedly crossed the St. Lawrence & one Thousand of them (Glengarry Highlanders under Major Carmichael[)] were ordered to the attack on the Rebels at Beauharnois on the 12th inst.—the result of wh. has not reached me.

No sooner had our Militia proceeded to the Lower Province, followed by the 93 Rgt which was *recalled* from this Province, than the Brigands crossed over in the United States Steamer, and two large Schooners from Ogdensburg having the night before arrived there from Mullins Bay near Sacketts Harbour[.]

They landed about 400, with two Six Pounders. Capt. Sandom followed them down the St Lawrence & the affair then took place wh. is detailed in his report of wh. I enclose Yr L. a copy. Our Soldiers, Marines & Militia behaved admirably & with but little more than half their numbers worsted the Brigands—some escaped across the River—28 were taken Prisoners & about 50 took refuge in a very strong Stone Mill from whence they could not be dislodged without Cannon— before this time I have no doubt they have surrendered. The Frontier is now swarming with these Ruffians & every hour I expect to hear of their having made descents on various parts of our Territory. In Michigan they have some thousands well armed drilled & completely equipped with plenty of cannon.

I have turned out the Militia but we have neither Blankets Clothing Bedding nor arms for them. Such has been the provision made by the Gvt during the summer! I warned the Secy of State of what was to be expected & I anxiously urged Sir John Colborne to concur with me in raising four incorporated Regt & of all things I urged H. M Gvt that we shd have a distinct Comsst Dept to provide for our wants—so that I really am not to blame for our being so unprepared—although no doubt I shall feel the consequences of it throughout the Winter. But I have no doubt I shall retain the Province in spite of the Yankees, whilst Yr Ld is fighting our battles in London[.]

Mr. Whitney[?] a very respectable Merchant residing in Michigan assured me that the news of the Rejection of Yr L Ordinance was received with most enthusiastic joy—the Brigands felt it to be a triumph in the Canadian Cause— Is it therefore to be wondered at that we have to sustain the present shock.

I do not say it has occasioned these Crusades because it is evident that these Lodges have been in progress all the summer but I have no doubt it has hastened these atrocious proceedings.

Such Papers as I think will interest Yr Ldp. are enclosed— Earnestly hoping that you have had a prosperous voyage & that the Countess & all the family are well[.]

[Enclosures lacking.]

[459] ARTHUR TO LORD FITZROY [J. H.] SOMERSET: LB.1, p. 143-146.

Nov. 16 *Govt. House, Toronto.*

Since I addressed you on the 30th. Ultimo events have been brought to something like a crisis. The Right Wing of the 93rd Regt arrived in this Garrison on the 6th Inst— the following day orders arrived for their return to Montreal to assist in putting down the insurrection that had again broken out in the Lower Province.

At the same time a body of the Militia of this Province, which I had caused to be prepared to turn out if necessary, very suddenly in the Eastern District on the application of the Comr of the Forces marched at once into the Lower Province, where they have already rendered good service.

Taking advantage of this movement the Brigands crossed last Sunday to the British side, and took up a position at Prescott on the St. Lawrence. It is by nature a strong position; a stone mill the walls of which are of more than ordinary thickness, with other stone buildings made it still stronger and the Banditti brought Tools with them with two Guns, in order to intrench themselves.

Captain Sandom Comg Royal Navy on the Lakes does not give the minute particulars of the gallant conduct of Major Young (particular service man, all of whom I have found most desirable assistants) but I enclose his report for your Lordsps perusal, together with the Gazette account of that affair, & some other news from the Lower Province.

The Banditti, consisting of about 400 men, and many of them, I regret to say, appear to be young farmers, were routed by about half their force, but not without severe loss on our part— Some got across the river, twenty-eight were taken prisoners and about 40 or 50 got possession of the Mill, from which they can only be dislodged by Cannon or starvation, ere this I expect they are all captured.

Our people, Regulars, Marines, and Militia all behaved admirably well.

Your Lordship will perceive by Captain Sandom's report what part the American Government must be taking— there cannot be a doubt that the whole of the Civil Authorities have been engaged in the conspiracy against Canada for many months.

I am anxiously looking every hour for news from Beauharnois. The Corps to attack it has moved from this Province: Lieutenant Roberts and 24 Sappers and Miners—about two rather weak companies of the 71st Regt. with a thousand of our Militia (Glengarry Highlanders) commanded by Major Carmichael (Particular Service). Whether Sir John Colborne has directed any other Corps to cooperate with this force I do not know.

We have commenced the Campaign, under every disadvantage— We have neither Bedding, Blankets nor Clothing for the Militia—a great deficiency of arms, and those we have are very bad. Under all these disadvantages, we should be more than a match for these Brigands, if we could only depend upon our own people.

I have striven by every means, to touch the honour of the Americans, and to induce the respectable part of the Citizens to discountenance this Crusade;—but, I fear I have been striving to touch what they do not possess.

[Enclosures lacking.]

[460] C. A. Hagerman to The Lieutenant Governor [Arthur]: A.L.S.

[*1838*] [*Place not stated.*]

Nov. 16 Capn. Graham has just mentioned that there are (as he believes) abundance of Ship Cutlasses and Pistols at Kingston,—would they not answer for Cavalry in the absence of a better Weapon?

[461] A. G. Spearman to Arthur: L.S. 5p.

Nov. 16 *Treasury Chambers*, [*London.*]

The Lords Commissioners of Her Majesty's Treasury having had under consideration your Letters dated Toronto 2d. August & 2d. Octr. last in reply to the communication addressed to you by direction of this Board on the 30th May on the subject of the proposition which you had submitted to the Secretary of State for a separation of the Commissariat of the two Provinces of Upper & Lower Canada, I have it in command from their Lordships to acquaint you that my Lords did not, by any of the observations contained in their Letter, intend to interfere in any manner with the most unreserved communication between yourself and the Secretary of State upon any subject whatever to which your attention as Lieutenant Governor of the Province of Upper Canada might be called, or to which you considered it important for the good of Her Majesty's Service to draw the attention of Her Majesty's Government; because they are clearly of opinion that the advantage of the service is always the best consulted by the most unreserved communications, upon all subjects, between the Government at home and the Officers administering the Government of Her Majesty's Colonies abroad; but that they, nevertheless, continue of opinion that in a matter purely of Military Administration, and for which the Officer Commanding the

Forces, (an authority which he exercises directly in both the Provinces,) is responsible, no such change as you suggested could be adopted without the express sanction of that Officer, who must be considered as being, upon the whole, the person the most competent to decide how far it could be made with advantage to the Queen's Service.

I am directed, further, to state that it was by no means their Lordships intention to convey any reproof to you, and that they are quite sensible that you were only moved by a view of what you considered the most advantageous course for the public Service, altho' they did not concur in that opinion, or think it necessary to separate the Commissariat department in the Canadas into two distinct responsibilities, from which so far as my Lords could judge no advantage whatever would arise, on account of inconveniences which, however great, (as they undoubtedly were,) arose out of circumstances which their Lordships trust will not recur, and which could not, indeed, have been avoided, even had the separation recommended previously taken place, unless the strength of the department had been in point of numbers very far beyond what this Board could, prior to the insurrection, have considered in any degree justifiable.

I am desired further to state, also, that my Lords are confirmed in the opinion thus entertained by them, by that which has been expressed by the Commander of the Forces and by the Commissary General to whom the proposition made by you was referred, and they trust the directions already given and the steps taken will prevent the recurrence of any such difficulties, as those complained of, on any future occasion.

[462] C. C. Domvile to Colonel [C. B.] Turner: LB.4, p. 23.

Nov. 16 *Government House, Toronto.*

With reference to a communication from you, in which you state that you are very hard pressed in consequence of having no one to assist you.— I am directed by His Excellency the Major General Commanding to inform you, that, should you still experience the same difficulty, he authorizes you to select some active and intelligent Militia or Volunteer Officer as your Assistant, until such time as you may cease to require his aid.—

The Major General also authorizes you to afford to such officer as you may select, whatever allowances you may consider necessary, according to the nature of the services he is to be employed on.

[463] Arthur to Colonel [W.] Thompson: LB.1, p. 146-147.

Nov. 17 [*Place not stated.*]

I directed the Adjutant General yesterday to instruct you, that I wished about 300 Men of the Regiment under your command to be mustered for the purpose of proceeding to Toronto.

It does not appear to me to be necessary, that this measure should just now be carried into effect; but, I shall be glad to hear that your gallant fellows have mustered well, and I shall always depend upon them for any service that may be required—and such as left their Homes on this occasion to repair to Toronto, both officers and men will be entitled to draw two days pay—

I beg you will let me know how the proposition of turning out one day in the week for muster and drill has been received the men being for that day paid at the rate of 2/6.—

[Superscription reads: "Colonel Thompson 2nd. West York."]

[464] [LORD] FITZROY [J. H.] SOMERSET TO ARTHUR: A.L.S. 2p.

Nov. 17 *Horse Guards, [London.]*

Although I have nothing to impart to you in return for your very interesting letter of the 12th October, containing the copy of Lord Durham's proclamation I trouble you with this note to express to you my acknowledgements for it, and to assure you it will afford me great pleasure to hear from you, whenever you may have any thing to communicate which you think Lord Hill may like to hear.

[465] JOHN EDEN:

Nov. 17 *Head Quarters, Montreal.* [Marked "(Extract)".]

General Orders.

No. 9.— His Excellency, The Commander of the Forces, is pleased to approve of the issue of Field Allowance to the Staff, Troops, and Departments serving in the Canadas.

Returns for the present Quarter, ending the 31st. December next, will be sent to the Deputy Quarter Master General, in Quadruplicate; these Returns to be made according to the Royal Warrant, dated 22d. July 1830, and signed by the Respective Heads of Departments, and Commanding Officers of Regiments.

(Signed)
John Eden
D.A.G.

[466] ARTHUR TO COLONEL [CHARLES] CHICHESTER: LB.1, p. 151-154.

Nov. 18 *Govt. House, Toronto.*

I have just received your Letter dated the 16th. instt., and am glad to find that the Roads still enable us to keep up pretty rapid Communication.—

The information I have received all the way from Ogdensburg to Detroit is so complete as to leave me nothing to desire in that way except the exact points to be attacked, and the time of attack, which has hitherto been kept a profound secret amongst the Leaders. If Van Allan can give any information upon this point it will be very valuable, and you have done quite right to employ him. And, certainly, if he does give information that is really important, he shall be well rewarded.—

Some of these Brigands I have positive information have been training near Fort Gratiat [*sic*].—that is, between Fort Gratiat and Fort St. Clair about four or five miles in the Interior.

It would be desirable to know the exact amount of this force. Van Allan might also be induced to let us know who are the disaffected in the Country—and whenever the information *is strong*, and can be quite depended upon, the parties should be apprehended, and, at all events, dispossessed of their Arms.

The foregoing is an answer to your letter marked "private" of the 16th. — Another letter accompanied it, not dated, most probably written at the same time—upon which I will offer one or two remarks.—

You observe that as soon as the Commissary returns you shall order those who have given in their names to march to his Office to receive their bounty.—

My apprehension is—that, as soon as they receive it, they will march off, & it was on this account that it was directed that the bounty should be expended in procuring Necessaries, and the balance only given.—

With regard to your having put the Law in force against two men, you must take care to proceed legally—only the Colonel of the Regiment, I think, has the power— I have not time to refer to the Act, but I will desire a Copy of it to be put up with this.—

Undoubtedly, it is a dreadful tax upon the people of the country to come forward in this way, and we must try every expedient to induce them to do so con amore—

How would it answer to let them form in Companies in the neighbourhood of their own homes, so as to drill once a day and be ready to turn out the moment an enemy is known to be actually about to embark for the purpose of invading us?—

I mention this because it was a proposition of Sir John Colborne's—only he said once a week for drill paying the men 2/6. for that day. In fact, I would approve of any thing so as to be as far as possible prepared, and to keep the men in as good humour as we can.—

It is so impossible to find arms for the force I wish to be prepared, that I have issued an order today giving a bounty of 10/– to such men as bring their own arms, but the order is so worded as not to make it appear that this proceeds from a want of arms.

So also with regard to blankets, I have authorised 10/– as a bounty to Men who bring their own.

As to Bedding, there is plenty of straw, & under the General authority I have issued to Officers Commandg., you must do your best to make Pailliasses— I rely upon all endeavouring to incur no expense that can be avoided, and yet keeping the Men in good humour—by wh., I mean, of course, that such expense must be incurred as cannot be avoided; but what cannot be avoided must be incurred.—

The plan I have suggested of drilling the Men at their Homes would answer for the Blacks to whom you allude, & with a good Officer or noncommissioned Officer to train them they would be ready for the hour of need.— With regard to the communication between Bear Creek & Chatham, I have no objection to your improving the piece of road to which you allude only take care not to make a way for the enemy.—

As regards the Indians, as affairs are now looking so serious, & as it seems scarcely probable that we shall be able to avert through our Minister at Washington, the invasion of these Ruffians, I leave to the control of the Officers Commandg. at the several stations the future movement of the Indian Warriors.—

You may call out any additional Cavalry, if you can use them with effect. We have no Cavalry appointments, and I am now trying to make use of some Sea Cutlasses of which there are about 1200 in Store; this is so expensive an army that I wish not to encrease it beyond what is necessary.

There should be a perfect understanding between Colonel Air[e]y—Colonel Elliot Commanding at Sarnia—& yourself.— So that you may promptly be able to support each other— I will mention this to Colonel Air[e]y.

All I can further add, is—that, altho' these Vagabonds may not attack us for a month or six weeks to come, yet, in my opinion, not a day should be lost in our being as prepared as under all our difficulties we can be.—

[Superscription reads: "Colonel Chichester Comg at Chatham".]

[467] J. SISSON: D.S.

Nov. 18 *Office of Ordnance, Montreal.*

Return of Arms & Accoutres. &cc issued to Upper Canada since the first May 1838.

Date, when sent from Montreal.	Musquets Complete.	Accoutrements sets.	Musquet Cartridge.	Pistol Cartridge.	For what Service,
July 2nd. 1838.	1370	.	.	.	For. Kingston
Do. 4th. "	720	1425	.	.	" Do.
Do. 5th. "	742	720	.	.	" Do.
Do. 11th. "	400	.	.	.	" Do.
Do. 12th. "	5000	.	100,000	.	" Do.
Do. 14th. "	.	1813	.	.	" Do.
Do. 20th. "	1116	.	.	50,000	" Do.
Octr. 24th. "	400	400	1,000,000	.	" Do.
Do. 27th. "	1000	1000	.	.	" Do.
Do. 30th. "	200	200	30,000	.	" Cornwall.
Do. 31st. "	400	400	.	25,000	" Kingston.
Novr. 6th. "	500	500	10,000	.	" Coteau du Lac.
Do. " "	1200	1200	20,000	.	" Carillon.
Do. 10th. "	8964	10,000	223,000	25,000	" Kingston.
Do. " "	.	.	100,000	.	" Brockville & Prescott.
Do. 14th. "	.	.	20,000	.	" Carillon
Do. 16th. "	.	.	40,000	.	" Coteau du Lac
Total......	22,012	17,658	1,543,000	100,000	

[The above is probably the first enclosure referred to in item 470.]

[468] ARTHUR TO COLONEL [HENRY] BOOTH: LB.1, p. 158-160.

Nov. 19 *Govt. House, Toronto.*

Sir Allan Macnab has forwarded to me your letter to Him of yesterday in which you communicate that you had received information of a meditated attack near Niagara and that you expect the same between Fort Erie and Chippewa—and request Sir Allan's cooperation.

If the armament consists of only 800 men as you mention, I think you will have no difficulty in overwhelming them before Sir Allan can come to your assistance, but it seems to me far more probable that their destination is Hamilton if they have Guns, and I would far rather Sir Allan should take care of that post, or certainly he should not leave it without a sufficient force.

I have directed him therefore to call out the Sedentary Militia and if I can only supply them well with arms he may both assist you, and take care of himself.

I ordered two hundred Stand of Arms to be sent to St. Katherines [*sic*] and directed 200 men to be called out there— this morning I directed another hundred to be called out there, and the whole to be under Colonel Clarke.

Unfortunately, Colonel Clarke though a loyal man, and an old Militia officer is not a good officer—it would be very desirable therefore, if you could associate some person with him who does know something if [*sic*] the matter—either as an Adjt or otherwise. I enclose you the names of some applicants, but I do not know them.

It occurs to me that Mr Robinson of St. Catherines [*sic*] is an intelligent Person, who would be of great service to you. He may have a Company of Volunteers if he can raise them, or you may employ him in any way in wh his services can be useful.

I wish to give you the utmost Latitude in calling out Infantry or Cavalry in the confident hope that you will not suffer an enemy to remain, in any part of your District,—or,—indeed, out of it if it be within your reach—any longer than is necessary to get at him.

I have already mentioned that I sent orders for calling out a hundred men at Grimsby from Lt. Coll. Henry Nellis [*i.e.* Nelles] Regt.— The Troop attached to that Regt. had also better be called out which the Adjt. Genl of Militia orders by this opportunity.

Employ any officers of your Corps you think proper to assist you in any way essential to the Service at this Crisis—either in forming the Militia or otherwise, and whatever allowance you think it proper to give, either forage or Pay I will confirm myself so far as I can, and will recommend to Sir John Colborne, if it rests with the Comr of the Forces.

I am most anxious that Commodore Drew should be on the Lake, and have written to him by this opportunity urging him to equip without delay.

In a former letter I mentioned to you that I would approve of your calling out either Captain Rykerts, Capt Macdonalds or Capt Macleods Troop of Cavalry; the preference should of course be given to the two first offering themselves[.]

[Enclosure lacking.]

[Date appears to have been changed from Nov. 22.]

[469] ARTHUR TO HENRY DUNDAS: LB.1, p. 147.

Nov. 19 *Government House, Toronto.*

I have the honor to acknowledge your letter giving me the account of your proceedings at Prescott— whatever the expence may be, I certainly approve of the Windmill at Prescott and at Maitland being armed and occupied.—

The result of your proceedings at Prescot[t] I await with the greatest anxiety.

[470] COLBORNE TO ARTHUR: L.S. 6p.

Nov. 19 *Government House, Montreal.*

I beg to thank you for your letter of the 10th. You will be delighted to hear of the Conduct of the Glengarry Militia, and the whole of the Militia of the Counties of the St Lawrence[.] The Glengarry Regts turned out at a few days notice more than 1500 men, and I understand about 5000 men speedily assembled at Prescott to repel the invaders— I hope therefore that you will find that the spirit which existed last year has not evaporated and that when the Militia are persuaded their services are required they will not be less backward [*i.e.* forward?] than their Comrades of Leeds, Stormont, Dundas and Glengarry—

The enlistment of men for eighteen months appears to me a proceeding which few Agriculturists will approve of. Some of the best men of the Province would have no objection to serve till May and then return to their homes. Neither Clergy Reserves, the supposed debts of the Government, nor dissatisfaction of any kind, are connected with the dislike to turn out at present— The emergency of last winter roused every man that was not disaffected; but when Militia are liable to be exposed to frequent Calls, and to the privations of winter duty on the frontier, they will think twice before they quit their homes in expectation only of a fight— The enclosure will explain to you the arms that have been forwarded as soon as Conveyance and escort could be procured for them— They must have been at Kingston some time—

By the accompanying return of Blankets and Articles of Clothing you will see the assistance you can expect from this Province— I hope you will find no difficulty in obtaining blankets and bedding from the United States— The large bodies of Rebels have been dispersed in this District, we must however be on our Guard as in every District they are prepared to rise— The Prescott affair will I think make the Brigands more cautious in their expeditions— The 93rd. Regt will be ordered to Kingston at your disposal in a few days—

As soon as I heard of the landing of the Brigands near Prescott I directed Colonel Wetherall to proceed to that place with a Detachment of the Royals and 71st. Regt, the 93rd. Regt and the Glengarry Militia[.]

[First enclosure is probably item 467. Second enclosure lacking.]

[471] C. C. DOMVILE TO DEPUTY ORDNANCE STOREKEEPER: LB.4, p. 25.

Nov. 19 *Government House, Toronto.*

I am directed by His Excellency the Major General Commanding to desire that 50 Indian Guns, with Ammunition (half ounce balls) and Flints in proportion may be issued by you, and sent to Cobourg tomorrow morning in the Steam Boat that takes the Blankets.—

They are to be forwarded from thence to Major Anderson[,] Rice Lake accompanied by an escort.—

[472] C. C. DOMVILE TO MAJOR [S. P.?] HURD: LB.4, p. 24.

Nov. 19 *Government House, Toronto.*

I am directed by His Excellency the Lieutenant Governor to acknowledge your communication of the 16th Instant.— And to express his satisfaction at having it in his power to avail himself of your valuable services and assistance in the Quarter Master Generals Department.—

[Superscription reads: "Major Hurd Dept. Asst. Qur. M: General of Militia."]

[473] C. C. Domvile to Colonel [A. W.] Light: LB.4, p. 24-25.

Nov. 19 *Government House, Toronto.*

I am directed by His Excellency the Lieutenant Governor to acknowledge the receipt of your Communication of the 30th. of October.

Of the gentlemen you mention, Captain Muttlebury has the command of a Colored Company on the St Clair Frontier—and Mr Stuart will be, if possible, employed in the way he wishes.—

His Excellency coincides in your opinion of the danger of a descent upon Natawasaga Bay or Penetanguishine, and will take measures for rendering such plans abortive.—

[474] Arthur to Colborne: LB.1, p. 148-149.

Nov. 20 *Toronto, Govt. House.* [Marked "Private".]

I heartily congratulate you on your entire success, and most anxiously hope it may be the means of putting an end to any further insurrection in the Lower Province—but, I cannot believe that you will be let alone quite so easily. Papineau has surely concerted his Plans better than to be discouraged by the first defeat, and his American friends will perhaps desire to try their luck once more.

You have, of course, long since heard of the affair at Prescott—there was a little more time taken up than I expected, but it has been well done at last.

I have ordered a Court Martial to assemble at Kingston on Monday next, and there will commence the difficulty of the Government. My Lord Glenelg cannot wish these Brigands to be encouraged to cross over again, and, yet, if they be not severely punished, the Inhabitants of Upper Canada will be continually harrassed [*sic*] by their wicked and atrocious conduct.

I am now every day expecting to hear of an attack upon the Western Coast and also Southern Coast of Lake Erie, as I have very certain information of the Brigands collecting in considerable numbers from Buffalo upwards. The Militia continue to turn out very very slowly, and with every effort I can make I have not yet been able to collect more than 300 men at Brandford [*i.e.* Brantford.]

If I had a Regiment of the Line there, and some *more arms* I should feel quite confident of *directly* putting down any attempt from whatever quarter it might come—and it is a great object, in the present state of this country, to give the Invaders no breathing time.

It is hardly to be believed the extent to which these Hunters Lodges have been carried in this Province in connexion with the Patriots[.]

I have had the greatest trouble in procuring any Steamers in Lake Erie[;] at length two have been delivered over, and Captain Drew is preparing to go up the Lake—but, to my great annoyance, I do not think He can be ready for 5 or 6 days. We must make the best of it!

I hope you will recommend that Major Young should get a Lieutenant Colonelcy—it will have the best effect, and I am sure the Glengar[r]ies wd. be highly delighted if Major Carmichael were promoted.

Under existing circumstances I am sure you will give me much latitude and I have therefore directed that the Mill at Prescott and the Mill of Maitland shd. be armed and occupied.

The expense will not be considerable.

I want a further supply of Arms very much for an extended frontier . . .

[P.S.] I have been obliged to make many captures of the disaffected.

[475] ARTHUR TO HENRY DUNDAS: LB.1, p. 150-151.

Nov. 20 *Toronto.*

I most sincerely congratulate you on the success of your Expedition and the determination you manifested not to let those vagabonds escape[.]

Nothing cd. have terminated better except that now comes the awful ordeal of punishing the Brigands, and from this I should most earnest desire to be releived [*sic*].

Accept my best thanks for the successful service you have rendered to this Province. All engaged deserve the highest commendation; and, I hope, you will concur with me that Major Young ought to gain a step for having so promptly met these Robbers & Murderers. I shall urge it strongly. I have directed that a Civil Court Martial shall assemble at Kingston on Monday next for the trial of the Prisoners, and until the trials are over you had better keep a good body of Militia at Kingston. The Leaders had better be the first brought to trial, & I shall thank you to order the Sheriff or deputy Sheriff, or some other competent Person, to prepare a Memorial return of them with such information or particulars of His History as can be extracted from each, forwarding a copy to me with as little delay as possible for transmission to our Minister at Washington.

I hope Major Bonnycastle is better[;] be so good as to desire Him to arm and occupy both the Mills at Prescott & at Maitland[.]

I am very anxious, if they can possibly be spared, to have there a four thousand[1] stand of arms sent *as soon as possible to me* to be forwarded chiefly to the London District, where I am almost daily expecting a far more serious descent in point of numbers than you have had to the Westward [*i.e.* Eastward.]

I could very badly spare them but I ordered a supply of Arms to be sent from hence to Presq Isle.

[476] JOHN GRIFFIN TO ARTHUR: A.L.S.

Nov. 20 *Philadelphia.*

I send you a present herein knowing what effect it will have on your blood-stained hand—the blood of Lount and Matthews [*sic*] cries aloud to Heaven for vengeance. Thou foul villain of the damned the very convicts at Hobart Town had your demon person removed for your murders on their persons. You promised, in your proclamation of the 5th. inst. concessions in Church reform; could you not do it at first instead of committing murder on the Citizens of America . . . this is not classic language for a man of your office: but you incarnate devil of hell, Robespierre was an angel to you. I am an Irishman and the blood of Emmet and of .98 is in soak for every English damned murderer. My ignorance of the English language prevents me of not applying harsher names to your murderous person. I have a knowledge of all the movements on the frontiers and would rather see your damned head speared than even the freedom of the Canadas and I would be executioner.

Farewell wishing, thou Devil, your habitation will be that of Dives in hell.

John Griffin

Recruiting Sergeant for the Patriots

No. 89. South Wharves[.]

---

[1]Possibly a copyist's error for "three or four thousand".

[477] C C DOMVILE TO LT. COLONEL [GEORGE] THE BARON DE ROTTENBURG: LB.4, p. 25-29.

Nov. 20 *Government House, Toronto.*

I am directed to acknowledge your letter of the 17th. Instant.—

The Lieutenant Governor has heard with the greatest regret, that the Townships of Rawdon and Sydney are in such a state, as you represent, upon the information of Captain Fiddler—and which must of course be put a stop to.—

It gives the Lieutenant Governor the deepest concern to find, that the inhabitants have been placed in circumstances of so much alarm at Belleville.— and it does appear to His Excellency to be extraordinary, as he certainly has information from good authority, that, a great portion of the Inhabitants both of Sydney and Rawdon, are loyal People.— But you have of course, done quite right in making every preparation either for offensive or defensive operations.

Should any number of men actually have risen in arms, either in Camden or Rawdon, the only way is to march a force upon them immediately, without waiting for them to come to Belleville.—

It is the Lieutenant Governor's impression however, that those people cannot be so mad, as to think of moving, unless there is an attack of foreigners from the American Shore upon Presqu-Ile.—

The Lieutenant Governor has a report from Kingston, informing him that the Len[n]ox and Addington Cavalry had been sent down to scour the Country of Richmond and Camden.—

With regard to arresting individuals, if there be information information [*sic*] on oath, of their disloyal intentions, it would be of course proper to cause the principals to be apprehended.

With regard to drafting from the Militia, it certainly seems but just and proper, that the disaffected should be punished for non attendance.— At the same time, it is almost questionable policy whether it is prudent to put arms in the hands of such people.—

With respect to the men serving for six months, the Lieutenant Governor wishes it to be understood, that he does not desire to call out the Militia for any longer period, than is absolutely necessary to put down this wicked conspiracy, so that you may take men for shorter periods.—

The Lieutenant Governor quite approves of Captain Bunters and Captain Murray's companies being increased (as you recommend) to 100 rank and file.

The Lieutenant Governor is highly gratified at Colonel Lander's [*i.e.* Landon's] having sent a company of the 3rd Hastings to your relief, and it may be increased also to 100 rank and file, if so many men will volunteer.

His Excellency is very sorry to find, that the armed boat has arrived so unprovided as you represent.— But if volunteers have come forward well at Bell[e]ville probably you will be able to detach a few men for that service.— And with regard to necessaries, you are authorized to purchase whatever is required.— 250 Blankets however are being forwarded by this opportunity for Presq'Ile and 250 for Belleville, a general Militia order also has been published, authorizing a gratuity of ten shillings currency to such men as bring their own Blankets for their own use.—

Mr Petrie's service may be accepted for the Provincial Marine, and you will no doubt find him very useful in the Bay of Quinty [*sic*], or even at Presq'Ile, without superseding Lieutenant Hayter.—

With regard to the attempt which has been made to plunder another individual at the carrying place, His Excellency is satisfied that the Loyal men have only to act with a little determination and they will soon put down these nefarious proceedings—

[478] ARTHUR TO COLONEL [RICHARD] AIREY: LB.1, p. 229-230.

[*1838*] *Govt. House, Toronto.*

[*c. Nov. 21*] Coll. Maitland continues so very unwell that I feel it to be prudent to direct that Major Reid should *forthwith* join his Regt.— I request you will direct accordingly.

I feel the greatest regret at removing Major Reid from a Station with wh. he is so well acquainted, & where he is so much respected; but, it is unavoidable.

You can replace him by Major Deedes if you consider it necessary— I hope the Militia are accumulating in force at Sandwich, so as to leave you at liberty to act upon your flank should a descent be made at Gosfield wh. I much expect.

By all means draft from Colonel Prince's Regt., so as to put him in force, and relieve yr. people from Sandwich— Otherwise, yr. corps cannot be efficient.— It will be a great object for you to have such a force as will allow you to guard the Fort with a sufficient force and freely to march off with the 34th Regt. To effect this, get hold of any loyal men you can, no matter from what Militia Regiment or of what colour.

Colonel Chichester should do the same.

I did not before know the localities of Isle Bois Blanc— there can be no doubt the Enemy will endeavour to get possession of it if such possession will render Fort Malden untenable. I am surprised the Commander of the Forces did not issue some order upon it—or that Capt. Barou has not reported.

Under the general authority you have already recd. from me you are fully authorised to take every measure for the defence of yr. Position—&, consequently, in that Instruction Isle Bois Blanc is included.

I have issued an order giving a Bounty of 10s/- to every Militia Man who brings his own arms & the same sum to any Man who brings his own Blankets— This, I hope, will be of some service to you at this moment when Arms & Blankets are so difficult to be procured. You should take great care to have a distinct understanding with Colonel Chichester & Colonel Maitland, & to keep up the most rapid communication with them.

[479] ARTHUR TO P. B. DE BLAQUIERE: LB.1, p. 230-231.

[*1838*] *Govt. House, Toronto.*

[*c. Nov. 21*] I thank you for yr. very kind and considerate letter, & am most thankful to yrself. or any other reputable & influential Inhabitant of this Province who will take the trouble to give me information.

I do not know in what manner I could at this moment avail myself of your services in a Military Capacity. Would that I had Arms & Accoutrements to send in greater abundance, but this is only one of the very many difficulties agt. wh. I have to contend at this critical moment.

To provide, as far as I can for this want, I have offered a gratuity of 10s/. Bounty to every man who brings his own arms and the same sum for those who bring their Blankets.

A Meeting of the Magistrates and Inhabitants wd. be of great service to concert measures for reasoning with the People, & of ascertaining whether any of the disloyal are armed & if so they shd. be deprived of their arms.

I quite agree with you that Duncombe's Country should be narrowly watched & I hope the Magistrates are doing so.

[480] ARTHUR TO BRIGR GENL [HUGH] BRADY: Df.L. 3p.

Nov. 21 *Government House, Toronto.* [Marked "draft".]

I have the honor to express my thanks to you for your obliging attention to my communication presented to you by Captain Herbert Taylor, and I should forbear from troubling you again, had I not received from several very highly respectable citizens of the United States, communications of the progress of those infatuated People who are threatening to invade this Province from the Westward, along the St. Clair from Amherstberg [*sic*] to Sarnia, on the plea of assisting the Canadian People on no better grounds than because they have been misled by a small faction of the Community to believe that Her Majesty's Subjects are desirous of their interference.

Under the like misrepresentation a body of these Brigands made a descent upon Prescott, on the St. Lawrence, where they had been given to understand that they would be joined by a considerable number of the British. But, to their utter disappointment, not a Man joined them—on the contrary, their landing was most fiercely and successfully opposed by the People, before any of Her Majesty's Troops arrived, and finally, after fifty of their party had been Killed, nearly Two Hundred were taken Prisoners— [The following passage is here deleted: "and are now on the point of being tried for the Felony they have committed."]

It is under feelings of the most earnest desire that these infatuated People should be checked in their wicked project, in which so many of them must inevitably fall, that I once more address you on the subject, earnestly trusting that their mad design may be prevented by your firmness and decision in the important duty entrusted to your charge.

It has afforded me great gratification to find that the Civil Authorities at Rochester have at length earnestly [the word "warmly" is here deleted] interfered, and are causing, as I am informed, these People to be apprehended, which I am sure is an act of just mercy towards them.

[481] ARTHUR TO COLBORNE: LB.1, p.221-224.

Nov. 21 *Govt. House, Toronto.*

Since I wrote to you, I have received such further information as does not leave a doubt, that we shall be *very shortly* simultaneously assailed in several quarters especially to the Westward.

I am anxiously looking for the 93rd Regt. back, and earnestly wish that I had a Corps of the Line at Brantford, where, hitherto, I have ineffectually endeavoured to induce the Militia to volunteer or turn out even for a Short time.

Not a day should be lost in sending to this Province as many arms as can possibly be spared. Colonel Phillpotts assured me that I might depend on 10,000 Stand.

There should certainly be if possible 5,000 Stand more in the Western

District, so as to enable us to meet an invading Foe the moment he lands at any point, for I am certain that if he can hold out for a short time, he will be numerously supported; such, most unhappily being the feeling of the Country all the way up from Kingston to Detroit.

The whole Western Country is full of Traitors, and there is a goodly nest of them in Toronto they having formed "Hunter's Lodges["] ever since the Month of June last. But, only send me arms, and we shall yet do well.

We ought to have had at least 2000 men more in this Province, in order not to coax these rebels, but to punish them well, and not to suffer the Loyalists to be thus harrassed [*sic.*]. I assure you I do not think the Militia would turn out again; they are seemingly even now indifferent to the result.

Do not consider me utterly unreasonable when I ask, whether you think you could spare Colonel Cathcart for this command. I have now called out a very considerable Cavalry force and as he has two troops in the Upper Province you might possibly not object to making it his Head Quarters. In that case, I would place him—without moving his Squadron from Niagara in command of the whole Western District, which I could well do as poor Colonel Maitland is, and has long been exceedingly ill, and writes me that he cannot move with his Regiment.— I have consequently desired Major Reid to proceed from Sandwich to London.

Colonel Booth has also been confined for many weeks with little prospect of being soon able to move. He is an excellent officer, but it would appear too excitable though this is probably induced by indisposition.

I enclose for your perusal copy of a Letter which Mr Allan gave me this morning from a very respectable person at Pittsburg[h]. It is important as he is a person of known integrity and attachment to Great Britain, and I send off an officer in the evening to obtain the information which He professes to be able to give.

To my mind the Govern̉t of America has long been at the bottom of all these proceedings, and it will occasion me some surprize if War be not proclaimed against Great Britain as soon as Congress meet and Mr Duncan McIntyres secret in my opinion is this.—that the American Government have been for some time preparing for it.

[Enclosure lacking.]

[482] ARTHUR TO CAPTAIN [ANDREW] DREW: Df.A.L.S. 3p.

Nov. 21 *Govt. House, Toronto.*

I lose no time in informing you that from the information now before the Government, no doubt can exist of the determination of the Brigands to cross in considerable numbers at the Westward perhaps along the St. Clair but some accounts state to the westward of Amherstburg.

Also, there is great reason to believe, that they will cross from Cleveland & attempt a descent at Port Stanley—or, possibly Port Dover.

Under these circumstances, not one hour should be lost in your pushing up the Lake, and watching the Enemy at every probable point.

I have not heard any thing for some weeks past of the Toronto. I know not whether she is or is not at Amherstburg where I desired she might be stationed, & where, if any *where*, she might be of greater use—

I do not know what arrangements you made for having men assembled; but I have desired Captn. Elmsley to send you any He can collect,

& I have also desired an officer of the Navy who called upon me from Hamilton to do the same & said that He had already supplied you with about 25 Sailors.

Colonel Thorn sends you a detachment of Marines— they are, as he informs me, *all Volunteers* & men well adapted for the Service.

I do not know whether there is a supply of Coal at the Grand River but, I trust, care has been taken to provide a large supply of Fuel. If not, it shd. be had immedly on any terms, for, if the Steamers are to be of any service to us now is the moment.

I would have complied with your request of giving you a party from the 43rd Regt—but, the Comdr of the Forces has expressed a particular wish that Detachments shd. not be taken away from any Corps of the Line as it tends so much to weaken them.

[483] ARTHUR TO SIR A. [N.] MACNAB: LB.1, p. 156-157.

Nov. 21 *Govt. House, Toronto.*

I hasten to acknowledge yr. letter wh. I have this moment recd.—

It strikes me that an attack, such as Colonel Booth apprehends, cannot require a larger force than he has at his command and considering also that he has a supply of arms of at least six or seven hundred stand which you have not.— However, if these Brigands do venture to cross over we must be at them from every quarter, and give them no time to accumulate. You will, however, take the greatest precaution not to leave Hamilton unprotected.—

There is, at present, no steamer in the Port—but, tomorrow, I will endeavour to send you three hundred stand of arms more. We are very badly supplied, and I know not what to do for arms.

Certainly call out any of your Sedentary Militia, and, under the order I have issued, I should hope you will be able to get a good body of men together who will come with Arms and Blankets.—

I directed the Adjutant General to call out a Company of 100 men at Grimsby and 200 men at St. Catherines[*sic*]— in case of any accident having happened to the first order I send another from Coll. Bullock,— will you be so good as to forward it.—

I am expecting the 93rd. Regiment from the Lower Province— if they come I shall, if I can possibly manage it send a Regiment of the Line to Brantford wh. must give great confidence.—

I shall thank you to send on the accompanying Despatch to Commodore Drew and Colonel Booth.—

It is most important that you should at once apprise the Adjt. General of Militia of any force you call out wh. has not been ordered by me through his office.

[The despatches referred to are probably items 468 and 482.]

[First enclosure lacking.]

[484] ARTHUR TO COLONEL [JOHN] PRINCE: LB.1, p. 155-156.

Nov. 21 *Government House, Toronto.*

I have not the opportunity of sending an answer to your letter of the 8th. instant through the Adjutant General of Militia, but I lose no time to hastily replying to it myself.

Without further explanation, I cannot very well understand why Major Girty has not been called out with your Regiment; but, as there is no time for discussing the matter, I beg at once to place his services at your disposal, and request you will notify the same to him.

Pray exert yourself to the utmost to get out men. As it is not possible to arm and equip suddenly so large a force, I have caused an order to be issued offering a Bounty of 10/– to every Man who brings his own Blanket and the same to every Man who brings his own Arms.— This, I hope, will do some good.

Gosfield, or some Indian Village near it, is a part of the Country which I have always fancied might be thought of by persons intending a serious invasion in order that they might at once from thence march upon London. Certainly, in some way or other, I heard many months ago that this was contemplated, but we have had so many reports that it is impossible to rely upon any.—

You will hear that the whole batch of Brigands who attacked Prescott have fallen into our hands, except about 50 who were shot, and, probably, about 10 or 12, who made their way back to the American Shore.

May I take this opportunity of requesting that you will be so good as to report to Colonel Airey any expense incurred that is not strictly according to the Regulations of the Service—and I am aware in times like the present this must happen—so that it may be *at once* approved and that dissatisfaction avoided which most unhappily resulted from the last turn out.— All the onus of which fell upon me although I had in fact nothing to do with it, and have been drawn into the most unpleasant Commissariat misunderstanding.—

My earnest desire now is that every just expense that is incurred should be directly discharged. I trust to the prudence and good feeling of every officer in command not to incur any unnecessary expense but what is necessary must in such an emergency be incurred.—

[Superscription reads: "Colonel Prince 3rd. Essex Militia."]

[485] R. B. Sullivan to The Lieut Governor [Arthur]: A.L.S. 4p.

Nov. 21 *C[rown] Lands Office, [Toronto.]*

I hope Y. E. will excuse me for suggesting a suspicion which Mr Allan & I entertain from a consideration of the communicatn submitted by Mr Allan this morning and a comparison of its contents with past and passing events.

We think that the American Government is secretly preparing for a declaration of war, which cannot however take place without a meeting of Congress or without the assent of the senate, the object of the Americans would no doubt be to pour an overwhelming force into Canada. The Am. Government cannot as is done in other nations make regular preparations, but they can effectually make ready for a war by a gradual exasperation of the public mind. which would perhaps produce a unanimous and cordial assent to the war, into which the Govt would appear to be dragged unwillingly though in fact the promoters of hostility from the beginning.

We know nothing in this country of the negociations respecting the Caroline, that affair may at any moment be made the pretext for war, and yet for aught we know Mr Fox is as ignorant of the progress of negociation as Your Excellency. he may be taken by surprise as easily as the Govt here—

If in reality Officers of the United States are in league with the enemy, and offer to lead them to the conquest of Canada it would be infatuation to believe they would adopt such a course without they expect to be redeemed from the dishonor of heading a band of pirates by the open sanction of their Government, or that they would have the folly to organize a large army without expecting the whole rescources [*sic*] of the Union to support them.

We therefore would suggest to Your Excellency that an early opportunity should be taken (in addition to the general warning that war was approaching) of representing to Mr Fox the danger of the Americans anticipating the movements of our Government by a declaration of war on their part. this was their course last war, and it is obviously their most politic measure, if the conquest of Canada is their object.

[486] C C Domvile to Major [R. J.] Barou: LB.4, p. 29.

Nov. 21 *Government House, Toronto.*

I am directed by His Excellency the Major General Commanding to acknowledge your letter of today's date, and to inform you that he approves of your estimate for the BlockHouses, and authorizes you to take such immediate steps as may cause the expeditious completion of the works referred to (viz the Blockhouses)—

His Excellency is desirous that you should put yourself in communication with the owners of the land on which the Block Houses are to be built, and cause the best possible agreement to be made with them.—

[Superscription reads: "Major Barou Commanding Engineer Toronto".]

[487] Jno. Macaulay to Commodore [Andrew] Drew: L. 2p.

Nov. 21 *Government House,* [*Toronto.*] [Marked "Copy Confidential".]

It has been stated to His Excellency, upon authority which cannot be questioned, that Lieutenant Clarke of the Royal Navy is a person of eccentric and irregular habits, and I am therefore directed to give you intimation of this circumstance and to express His Excellency's desire that you will be very cautious in assigning the command of any of the Steamers on Lake Erie to an officer, in whose steadiness and discretion you cannot place the fullest reliance.

His Excellency, in directing this communication to be made to you, does not intend to disapprove of your employing Lieut: Clarke in a subordinate Post, if you should be disposed to make such a use of his services,—but, as His Excellency is most anxious to avoid the remotest possibility of such collision with the people or officers of the United States as may lead to a national War, he desires that you should be very particular and careful in the selection of your officers.

[488] C. C. Domvile to Capt. [James ?] Leckie: LB.4, p. 30.

Nov. 22 *Government House, Toronto.*

I am directed by His Excellency the Lieutenant Governor to request you to inform him of your reasons for not having taken means to discipline and drill the company under your command, and, at the same time to suggest to you, that no time should be lost in so doing, and that, as much attention should be paid to training the men to the Great Guns, as their other occupations will possibly allow.

[Superscription reads: "Capt. Leckie 1st. Provincial Artly."]

[489] ARTHUR TO COLONEL [RICHARD] AIREY: LB.1, p. 166-167.

Nov. 23 *Government House, Toronto.*

Your letter with its enclosure arrived this morning.

From General Brady's account it would appear that these vagabonds have determined to try their fortune[.] I feel persuaded you will give a good account of them—

The Right Wing of the 93d Regt. returned this day from the Lower Province—thereupon, I lost not a moment in ordering you to be supported & the 85th Regt will embark in the Course of this night and will proceed on in Waggons to support the 32d. which will enable the 32d to support you if necessary[.]

As I have given you many warnings since I despatched Captn. Markham this day month I am satisfied you have done all that circumstances permitted to prepare to give these vagabonds a warm reception[.]

Should their attack be still deferred allow me to suggest your engaging as many pentioners [*sic*] as you can to man and defend the Fort so that you may be able freely to take the field with the 34th Regiment[.]

My idea is that they will not venture to face the fort, but will rather land on the lake between Gosfield and Port Stanley—but, come as they may I feel confident that you will give a good account of them[.]

After enduring much delay and disappointment I have at length succeeded in getting two fine steamers well armed the "Milwa[u]kie" & "Webster" & Commodore Drew proceeds upon the lake tonight as I hope & trust— He left Toronto yesterday morning assuring me, that He was quite ready for sea, and I pressed him not to lose a moment. . .

P.S. The Sedentary Militia should of course now be called out—

[490] ARTHUR TO COLONEL [HENRY] BOOTH: LB.1, p. 173-174.

Nov. 23 *Govt. House, Toronto.*

I have just recd. information from Colonel Airey that a most formidable descent is *on the eve* of taking place to the Westward—formidable, I mean, as to numbers—&, I believe, in equipmt. also.

Yesterday, I desired that Commodore Drew would hasten his departure up the Lake & I gave him a good party of Volunteers from the Militia. His intention was to go up in one of his Steamers, and to leave the other off Point Abino.

I have now sent him word that he had better proceed at once himself & send the other Steamer to Fort Erie where I wish you would *at once* embark a party of 150 men. You may select whatever men you deem best to part with for such a service. Either the 43rd.—or Colonel Kingsmill—or Colonel Kerby's—or, Sedentary.

The great point is—despatch!—and as well equipped as circumstances admit— purchase Blankets or Great Coats if they are to be had for money and you have none in Store.

A force in rear of these Vagabonds will be the most effective.

The rumour of an Attack upon Niagara was a mere deception to hide the intended attack upon the West. If there be occasion for it, I shall not hesitate to leave the Niagara Frontier to the Militia and move off the 43rd.— Be so good, therefore, as to have the Corps ready to move at a moment's notice.

I have just sent off (—that is, they embark in the Morning—) the 85th. for London—which will enable Colonel Maitland to advance with the 32nd. Regiment to support Colonel Airey.—

The right wing of the 93rd. regimt. returned here this evening.— I hope Sir John will be able to send me another Corps.—

[491] ARTHUR TO COLONEL [CHARLES] CHICHESTER: LB.1, p. 164-166.

Nov. 23 *Government House, Toronto.*

I conclude from Colonel Airey's letter that the Brigands have been induced to try their fortune in the West and although they have hitherto been reluctant I will not doubt, that when these vagabonds are known to have landed, that the Militia will come forward as they have hitherto always done with good spirit—

The difficulty I have had in getting a couple of Steamers is not to be described—but, at length it has been accomplished, and Commodore Drew sails with two steamers well armed in the morning, [marginal note here reads: "The Milwaukie The Webster"] and I hope will be ready to play his part in the West. The Naval people here tell me, that the Brigands will not venture across the Lake at this season, but it seems to me that they are made [*sic*] enough for any exploit[;] it will be well therefore to look to your flank as well as to your front, as it is evidently a most important matter with them to get to London[.]

I am of opinion that they will not attempt to penetrate by way of Sarnia, in that case Colonel Radcliff had better move to support you with all the force he can muster—

I have no idea what the state of the road is between Chatham & Amherstburg but you had better take up the Steamer that is on the Thames for the service of the Governmt[;] great care however must be taken to prevent her falling into the hands of the Brigands.

The Right Wing of the 93rd Regt. arrived this day from the Lower Province, & I have not lost a moment in sending forward the 85th Regt. the 32nd. will therefore support you, and the 85th will come up to support the 32d..

I shall also move forward the Gore Militia if I find by tomorrow's post that matters are such as to require it— I am sure when an enemy is known to have landed that our Militia will do their duty...

P.S. The Sedentary Militia should of course now be called out—

[492] ARTHUR TO COLBORNE: LB.1, p. 161-164.

Nov. 23 *Toronto.*

I enclose copies of two letters from Colonel Airey with their enclosures & one from Mr. Whiting from Detroit.

Also one from Sir Allan Macnab with its enclosure from Colonel Booth.

You will perceive that the Brigands threaten in considerable force to make a descent upon the Western Coasts, and in considerable force upon the Niagara Frontier.

From the nature of General Bradys information, which is corroborated by Countless reports from other Quarters, I think it is beyond all doubt that we shall be assailed in many Quarters at once.

As to the attack threatened upon Toronto, I scarcely know what to make of it. The particular scheme of the Patriots has been conducted with so much secrecy that their movements are not easily discovered.

The turn out of our Militia as I have before informed you has been most discouraging.

Colonel Airey, you will observe, accounts for it, just as others have done throughout the Province; but I can with difficulty bring myself to believe that all this bad feeling has originated or rather been kept up from the non-adjustment of accounts.

The right wing of the 93d. Regiment has just landed, and I have therefore instantly ordered the 85th. to proceed viâ Hamilton to London with all Despatch and the 32nd to advance to the support of Colonel Airey provided there be not a descent at the same time at Port Stanley.

There has been the most extreme difficulty in getting any Steamers in Lake Erie— they were however, ready yesterday, and Captain Drew has I conclude pushed on up the Lake this evening according to the orders which I gave him.

I ran the risk of leaving Toronto without any spare arms and sent off 2,000 Stand to London about 3 weeks ago; but Colonel Maitland and Colonel Airey still write in the most urgent terms for more arms and of accoutrements we have none.

We have such an extended frontier that our demands are necessarily much greater than they would be otherwise.

We are still without Clothing or Great Coats or Blankets and without them, the reluctance of the militia to turn out is increased ten fold.

In this extremity a Board has recommended that an allowance should be given to each Militia Man to provide his own Clothing—Great coats excepted—and, whilst the Deputy Commissary General thinks this will be a saving, the Commanding Officers of Regiments are of opinion that the men will supply themselves.

I have also offered a Reward of ten Shillings to every man who supplies his own Arms and the like sum to every man who furnishes his own Blankets.

Just at this juncture, rather strangely, a supply of 10,000 Stand of Arms has been sent to the States Dêpot [*sic*] near Detroit, which the Regular Force cannot take care of; and the General Govt. has liberally made a present of ten pieces of Ordnance to the City of Buffalo. The whole of these arms and Cannon are in possession of the Brigands in an hour if they are pleased to take them! ! !

What took place last Winter, in this way, ought to have convinced our Government of what the true design of the United States is, and five thousand Troops ought to have been sent out, with Clothing Blankets and Great Coats for the Militia. . .

P.S. 9 oClock P.M. I send orders for the Left Wing of the 93d Regt. to proceed on to Toronto immediately; and, if your position admits of it, a reinforcement ought to be sent into this District *without delay.*

[Enclosures lacking.]

[493] [ARTHUR] TO HENRY DUNDAS: LB.1, p. 171-172.

Nov. 23 *Govt. House, Toronto.*

I regret that I am obliged to take from you the left wing of the 93rd. Regiment—but, affairs are so pressing in the West, that there is no help for it.—

A descent, formidable as to numbers, is on the eve of taking place to the Westward.— I have, therefore, lost not a moment in sending on the 85th. Regt. to London—&, as soon as the left wing of the 93rd. Regt. arrives at Toronto I shall send forward to London the Right Wing if the Service continue urgent. The 85th. proceed in the Morng.

Call out whatever Militia you require, & be sure that whatever can be done, is done for their comfort. We have the Province to secure, & expense, in all that is essential, must be no consideration.

I write to Sir John for more Troops, & I trust he will be able to send me two Regiments.—

No report of it has reached me, but I am told the 73rd. are at Cornwall, if so, they will be the sooner up.—

I have urged Sir John Colborne to send more arms *immediately*—pray send up as many stand as can possibly be spared with accoutrements.—

Mr. Routh has promised to send Blankets & Clothing. do not let a moment be lost in forwarding the same, retaining, of course a proportion for Kingston.

I do not know at what points the Brigands can cross in the St. Lawrence when the Ice sets in—but you had better look to this and fortify accordingly.

General Brady has informed Colonel Airey that he cannot prevent the Brigands from crossing over their numbers are so great—&, yet, at this very time, 10,000 Stand of Arms are sent to Detroit for the *public service* & 10 pieces of cannon to Buffalo all, of course, at the Command of the Brigands.

[494] ARTHUR TO JOHN MAITLAND: LB.1, p. 167-168.

Nov. 23 *Government House, Toronto.*

In consequence of Colonel Airey's communication this morning that the Brigands had determined to proceed with their attack I ordered the 85th Regt. to embark immediately to move to your support which will enable you to support Colonel Airey or Colonel Chichester, as circumstances may require[;] the great object will be to crush these vagabonds effectually at every point. Should your health prevent your taking the field it will be necessary for you to inform Colonel Chichester who will in that case the the [*sic*] senior Officer—and will act accordingly.

I have at length succeeded in getting two good steamers the Milwa[u]kie and the Webster and Commodore Drew starts tonight I hope, for the Westward, and if he gets in rear of the Brigands, I trust he will put an end to these exploits. . .

[P.S.] The Sedentary Militia should of course now be called out.

[495] J. B. ROBINSON TO ARTHUR: A.L.S. 4p.

Nov. 23 *Cheltenham, 7 Lansdown Place.*

The day before I left this for London, I received Your Excellency's letter written at Sorel, and the papers which accompanied it—and about the same time I read in the Newspapers Lord Durham's *Proclamation*, which I confess I was sorry to see— It has put Ld Brougham & all others who are disposed to treat him with ill nature, in full possession of his case, & the issuing such a proclamation must be admitted to be a highly exceptionable act— The press has hit hard upon some palpably weak points which it contained—while others escaped their detection, from their want of knowledge of facts— I shall of course not let the papers sent to me be seen—& if upon the arrival of Ld. Durham who is daily expected, he desires any help that I can give him, he shall certainly receive it to the utmost of my power, provided the course he recommends is such as I shall think judicious & just— But I confess I never was, & am not now sanguine in my hope that Ld. Durham's mission will have a satisfactory result— He is unsound in important points—does not look temperately at difficulties—is rash in action—& is so deeply committed to a destructive party & a destructive policy that it would be almost a miracle if he should arrive at a result that ought to be satisfactory— However I am most happy that he resolved to persevere in maturing his plan whatever it may be, for it is just possible that he may bring himself to recommend a sound measure, without defacing it by absurd notions taken from the United States; & at any rate it would have been ruinous to his character if he had ended his mission without submitting a scheme of some kind— In regard to the past, his case seems now to stand very fairly before the public— that he must have meant & desired to do what was right in respect to the Ordinances is not doubted, I think by any considerable, or respectable portion of the public—& any merit beyond that of meaning well can not I think be claimed for him by any who values his own reputation— He set out ill—and has done many things in a bad spirit—erring in feeling no less than in judgment— Whatever could be honestly said in vindication of his absurd ordinances, has been said by himself in his proclamation & dispatches, & said well,—and these contain moreover some reasonings & assertions which I could not with due regard to the necessity of preserving a good conscience have advanced in his behalf— It is comforting at any rate to reflect that he is well able to take his own part, & is therefore very likely to obtain at the hands of the public all the justice he is entitled to— If by saying what I knew & what I really felt, I could have been of service to His Lordship, I might on so particular an occasion have occupied for the first time in my life the columns of a newspaper with my lucubrations in the hope of helping to withstand prejudice, but I fear my whole testimony would not make out a flattering case—

Being told that Lord Glenelg would return from Leamington last Saturday week, I went to London the following tuesday, allowing his Lordship three days grace, but on my arrival I found he had given himself another week at the Spa & I returned to Cheltenham— I had a long chat with Mr. Stephen & a short talk with Sir George Grey—

The latter I should judge when he began his official career, must have had many pernicious notions to unlearn, at the expense of the Colonies—& I think he gathered from our half hours conversation that I was probably as open to imputations of prejudices of another kind— I found him very civil & pleasant to talk with— Mr. Stephen was beyond measure condescending & explanatory & from what he said, I suppose I shall before it is long have some communication with Ld. Glenelg either verbally or in writing— Mr. Spring Rice, I was told has been requested to receive me, if I came in Ld. Glenelg's absence, but the illness of Lady Theodosia had taken him to Brighton, the day before I got to town—& I could not conveniently delay my return[.]

Unless my presence is desired I shall probably not go to town till Parliament meets, but from what was said by Mr. Stephen I do not expect to be allowed to remain in quiet so long—

I inquired of both the Under Secretaries respecting the proposed additions to the Leg Cl. but they seemed to know nothing of it— as soon as I see Ld. Glenelg, I shall speak of it, & I did indeed urge the matter as strongly as I could in the office— I was pleased to find that Mr. Stephen really seemed to sympathise with Mr. Boulton late C. J. of Newfoundland as a person who had been most hardly dealt by— It is not my intention to intrude my opinion or advice unless I see something about to be done which I think wd. be unfortunate & therefore so far as I am concerned I may be no wiser than I am now in Canadian Matters till Parliament meets— Sir Wilmot Horton pressed me much to spend some days with him at Twickenham & I did manage to stay one day with him— He has been ill—but is now recovering—& very anxious to succeed to the Government of Bombay, if Ministers will let him—but I see, John Bull says Sir George Grey is to be the man— I think this rather unlikely—

We hear rather alarming reports here about projected movements agt. L. Canada by the Americans—& I believe there is no subject on which more anxiety is felt— I am prepared to say what I think shd. be done for putting an end to these annoyances—but I doubt a little the firmness of the present rulers— What an atrocious part that fellow OConnel[l] is acting in Ireland!—

We are all well—not making an exception of myself though I am not just now quite what I have been. . .

[P.S.] I asked particularly whether information was desired respecting the disposal of any of the prisoners, but there seemed to be noth[in]g pending.

[496] C. C. Domvile to Colonels [Henry] Dundas and [Plomer] Young: LB.4, p. 32.

Nov. 23 *Government House, Toronto.*

I am directed by His Excellency the Major General Commanding, to request you to forward, for his information, a correct return of the numbers killed and wounded on the side of the Rebels and their allies from the other side, at the affairs at Prescott.—

His Excellency is also desirous, if possible, to be informed of the original numbers of these marauders.

[497] C. C. Domvile to Captain [Williams] Sandom: LB.4, p. 30-31.

Nov. 23 *Government House, Toronto.*

I am directed by His Excellency the Lieutenant Governor, to request, that you will be good enough to forward to him with as little delay as possible, an attested copy, of that part of the Log of the Experiment, in which the late affairs at Prescott are recorded—for the purpose of its being transmitted to the Secretary of State.—

His Excellency is desirous, by this means, to put the Secretary of State in possession of an account that can be depended upon, of the whole proceedings of the "United States" Steamer, and of the Schooners—together with the circumstances under which she was fired into.—

I am also directed to acknowledge your letter of the 18th. instant, and to convey to you His Excellency's thanks, for the able and judicious cooperation you afforded to Colonels Dundas and Young, in defeating and capturing the Band of Marauders at Prescott.— At the same time, His Excellency regrets, that there should have been any opinions expressed in your letter of the 14th. Instant, which you are now desirous to withdraw, as copies of that communication have been forwarded to the Secretary of State, and to our Minister at Washington.—

A copy of your letter of the 18th. instant will be forwarded as soon as possible to Mr Fox.

[498] ARTHUR TO COLBORNE: LB.1, p. 168-170.

Nov. 24 *Toronto.*

You will of course be anxious for further information from Niagara and the Westward; I write therefore, simply to say, that the Brigands who were at Lockport have moved to Buffalo where these Vagabonds are in considerable force as stated in several reports.

My latest letter from Colonel Airey is dated 21st. Novr. 12 o Clock P.M. No attack had been made up to that time, but he seemed to expect it hourly.

I have also every [*sic*] accurate information from Cleveland, the Brigands are in great force there[.]

What an incomprehensible state of things this is.

The whole border of a *friendly* power turning out with an armed force and that power using no effort, that is, no effectual effort to suppress the outrages for which the force is assembled.

It is a happiness to consider that this state of things cannot last.

The 85th. proceeded early this morning. I shall be more at my ease, when I find they have advanced to London.

Putting together all the accounts I have received, the conclusion I draw is, that there will be an attack upon the Western Frontiers from the St. Clair;

Upon the Southern [*sic*] Shore of Lake Erie—Port Stanley, I suppose, from Cleveland—and upon Port Colborne from Buffalo and upon Presqu'ile from Oswego or Sacketts Harbour.

If Commodore Drew is in time to the Westward & Captain Sandom keeps a good look out below—these vagabonds ought never to reach our Shore, and as they have very accurate information of all that we do, our extensive preparations will I trust deter them—for I have already more prisoners on my hands than I know what to do with. But if they do come, I have little doubt we shall give a good account of them[.]

All our endeavours to get Blankets and Clothing from the States have failed.

[499] ARTHUR TO H. S. FOX: LB.1, p. 181-182.

Nov. 24 *Govt. House, Toronto.* [Marked "Private".]

I avail myself of the return of the messenger from New York, who brought up my Despatches by the "Great Western" to communicate to you the conclusion of the Drama at Prescott; and although exceedingly pressed for time I have endeavoured to give you the fullest information.—

In putting many circumstances together I am strongly impressed with the notion that being defeated in over-run-ning this Country in the way they intended they will declare War *suddenly* if they can find a good pretext for it—and the Caroline affair is still open to them.

A few days ago I received a letter from a Gentleman, who has a relative—a native of Scotland—residing at Pittesburg, [*i.e.* Pittsburgh] in which his relative hints in strong terms at certain preparations, & offers to give full information, if I will send a confidential person to whom he can make disclosures of great importance.

He asks for no remuneration and says that he is wholly influenced by a love of his Country and as I have ascertained that he is a person of excellent reputation, I have sent an Officer to confer with him. You shall know the result as soon as I am in possession of the secret.

I am quite satisfied that you have taken a [blank in M.S.] in not applying to the American Govt. respecting our possible violation of their Territory in the pursuit of an enemy. I shall continue to use every means to avoid misunderstanding, & I shall rejoice to find that you can steer us out of our present danger;—for, I must admit that War should if possible be avoided.—

[500] ARTHUR TO LORD FITZROY [J. H.] SOMERSET: LB.1, p. 174-179.

Nov. 24 *Government House, Toronto.* [Marked "Private".]

The affair at Prescott terminated by the surrender of the party of Brigands who took refuge in the Mill on the 17th. instant.—

The Accompanying Documents will give Yr. Lordship a full idea of all that has transpired. You will imagine me sufficiently profuse in my Orders, Proclamations, &c;—but, the plain truth is—that, the people of this Province require to be roused into action and driven from poring over their grievances whether real or imaginary.—

This Invasion was in every sense an American one.— Only four of the Canadian refugees were concerned in it.

The American Government I believe, to have been at the bottom of the whole conspiracy— they had a Political end to gain, but the worthy citizens have entered into the Crusade as a matter of speculation— it was a cheap way, they had been induced to believe, to get land and that was a high temptation for them.— I am inclined to hope, however, as soon as it is well known that Possessions are not to be had in Canada without fighting hard for them that the feeling of sympathy will greatly abate.

The speculation is attended with greater risk than Jonathan *guessed*.—

The Citizens of Oswego you will observe by one of the enclosures say that Men's minds begin to be opened and they are sure there is a strong reaction and therefore beg to intercede for the "deluded" persons who have been guilty of this act of atrocity.—

Their admissions whether sincere or not & Colonel Worth's language are likely to have a good effect in the states and I therefore directed the correspondence to be published.—

I have not received any official account of the loss of the Brigands, but, I believe, the account given in the Papers is correct—160 Prisoners—18 wounded and 102 killed— Our loss considering that the number engaged in the affair was so small, was very severe—killed 13—wounded 67— The Militia, I really believe, would have put every one of the Brigands to instant death upon the spot had not Colonel Dundas resolutely interefered with the Regular Troops to prevent it.

I do hope Her Majesty's Govt. will mark their sens[e] of Colonel Dunda's [*sic*] conduct— He has been highly zealous and useful as well with the Militia as with the regular Troops and also in some civil affairs within his Military Command wh. has induced me to notice him particularly to the Secy. of State.—

I have also strongly noticed the conduct of Major Young who deserves great credit for his promptitude and decision in attacking these Vagabonds with an unorganized Militia Force.

I am also sure Lord Hill will be well pleased with the conduct of Major Carmichael who mustered a thousand of our Glengar[r]y Militia from their farms and marched with them into the Lower Province almost as quickly as Out posts could have been brought in[.]

These Highlanders were very orderly whilst there was any thing to do; but, afterwards, they ravaged the Country most awfully!—

I enclose Copies of the last reports of Colonel Airey and Colonel Booth by which Your Lordship will perceive both were then expecting immediate attacks on the Western and Niagara Frontiers.—

Your Lordship will observe that General Brady states that he cannot prevent the descent of the Brigands in the West who are very formidable *in numbers*— I have sent off therefore the 85th. Regt. to replace or to support the 32nd.— I have ordered the latter Corps, if necessary, to advance from London to Amherstburg to support the 34th.— I shall expect, however, that the Militia will now come forward in the West and then I shall have no further anxiety respecting the result of any attack.—

Very lately 10 pieces of Cannon were made a present to the Citizens of Buffalo & 10,000 Stand of Arms were sent to the Arsenal at Denburn [*i.e.* Dearborn], near Detroit.—

These are not *Peace* offerings and must be intended either to enable the Brigands to continue to help themselves as they have hitherto done from the Public Arsenals or the American Govt. have an eye to the probability of immediate War. Many circumstances lead me to come to the latter conclusion & I have lately dispatched an Officer to the States to confer with an English Gentleman who has undertaken to give me some important information on this point.

The Americans still harp upon the affair of the Caroline as a national injury for wh. they demand satisfaction. Could any people on the earth, but the Americans advance such a claim in the face of all the injuries & outrages their Citizens have been inflicting upon the people of Upper Canada.

Do let me entreat of you, My Lord, to use your influence in strengthening these Provinces *as soon as* the navigation opens. We ought to have the fortifications constructed which, I believe, the Duke of Wellington approved years ago.—

There should be large depôts of Great Coats—blankets & Clothing for the Militia with an adequate supply of arms and ammunition—

Equipments complete for 2000 or 3000 Cavalry for which force the Yeomen of this Country are admirably qualified and dash through the Bush in fine style and above all things promote the emigration of good loyal Men.—

I have embodied 4 Regts. of Militia for 18 months in order to give confidence and I wd. urge upon every consideration that the Frontier duty should always be undertaken by the Militia— it is unjust to place our regular Troops under the violent temptation of taking the Frontier duty. They have all relations or friends settled in the States and what will bind an Irish Soldier if he has the opportunity of seeing his *cousin*.

If War be averted now which I trust in God it may[,] come it must at any [*sic*] early period from the Sovereign People whose arrogance is unsufferable and we ought to be always prepared.

I have no doubt the American Govt. intended on this occasion to make another Texas affair of it but they have been disappointed in this—

our preparations for defence were indeed too long deferred; but they have, since determined upon, been carried on so extensively & vigorously that all apprehension of surprise is removed—but the expense is frightful.— The only comfort is the reflection that it would have cost twenty times more to have recovered the Province if the Conspiracy had succeeded.

I wish Your Lordship could find time to look into the confession of Charles Hindenlang the French Officer who was captured at Odeltown.— You will find it in the Montreal Herald of the 17th instant.—

The statement,—I have no doubt, of the miserable delusion under wh. the poor Canadians have taken up arms—is quite true,— Hindenlang himself & many others of his standing were duped by the wicked Traitors who in connexion with the Americans have hatched this conspiracy, but all these People knew the wickedness they were about and are undeserving of any compassion beyond that which every Christian must feel even towards the most depraved.—

[Enclosures lacking.]

[501] ARTHUR TO COLONEL [RICHARD] AIREY: LB.1, p. 183-184.

Nov. 25 *Governmt. House, Toronto.*

There is but one point in Your Letter of the 21st. inst. to wh. it is necessary for me to refer— I allude to the Steamer in the Thames! In my letter to you of last Eveng. I mentioned that I had procured two fine steamers the "Webster" and the "Milwaukie"—these are chartered at an enormous expense, and, I trust, will fully answer all yr. purposes.

I am very anxious to press upon you the necessity of keeping open a rapid Communication with Sandwich, & Chatham, so that if the Brigands attempt to *establish* themselves you may be promptly supported in assailing them.

This, I conclude, will be their object, tho' from not knowing the ground I cannot guess where their projected Fortress will be attempted to be established—most probably, somewhere near the St. Clair, so that the means of escape may be open but with the two Steamers you will effectually cut off their communication with the opposite shore. Commodore Drew, I venture to hope, will be at Amherstburg this day or tomorrow.

I enclose an extra Gazette which I am desirous should be circulated on the American side as far as possible. Also a General Militia Order which I hope may do some good amongst the Militia.

As there is no letter from you to day I am in hopes the Brigands will yet abstain from their mad design.—

[Enclosures lacking.]

[502] ARTHUR TO HENRY DUNDAS: LB.1, p. 183.

Nov. 25 *Govt. House, Toronto.*

I am anxious that the Correspondence wh. you sent to me sd. be circulated on the American side. I think it will do great Service. May I beg your assistance in this matter.

The General Militia [Order] will, I hope, do some good also amongst our own People.

I have requested the Commander of the Forces to send us up another Regt. You will, of course, retain one wing with You if my request be complied with.

I have nothing new to day from the Westward.

The service you have rendered in bringing the affair at Prescott so speedily to a close was rendering a great service to this Province, & I have endeavoured, in a Despatch to the Secretary of State, to do justice to the great zeal & unremitting attention You have given to the public Service ever since my arrival whether the Service has been Civil or Military.

[503] ARTHUR TO COLONEL [JOHN] PRINCE: LB.1, p. 170-171.

Nov. 25 *Govt. House, Toronto.*

I have before me yr. letters of the 16th. & 17th. November addressed to the Adjutant General of Militia.—

The Adjutt. General will notify that all yr. recommendations are approved; but the emergency being now so great and pressing, you had better at once call out your whole Regt. under the Militia Laws.

Capt. Leslie's resignation shall not be accepted.—

By all means let Mr. Chewett raise a Corps of Artillerymen— I never heard of such a company being proposed by Colonel Elliot— pray take care the 9 Pounder does not fall into the hands of the Brigands or at all events take care to make it useless to them.—

It is impossible to conceive that, for any complaints against the Commissariat, there should be such a reluctance on the part of the Militia to turn out. I cannot conceive to what you allude by the 14 days pay due to the Men who turned out in July. The Military Secretary assures me that he is unconscious of any such pay List having been rejected. He says, on the contrary, that he is convinced there must be some misapprehension or mistake about it for none has been rejected—but he will look into it Tomorrow.—

With the Enemy now before them, however, I cannot doubt the Loyal Militia will come forward to a man—and hope to hear from you more cheering accounts. . .

[P.S.] I have ordered Commodore Drew to proceed with his two Steamers immediately to the West.—

Nov. 25 H. S. FOX TO JOHN FORSYTH:
[See item 510.]

[504] C. C. DOMVILE TO COMMODORE [ANDREW] DREW: LB.4, p. 32-33.

Nov. 26 *Government House, Toronto.*

I am directed by His Excellency the Lieutenant Governor, to state to you that he is very anxious to have some stores, consisting of Gun Sleighs &c. conveyed from Chippewa (to which place he orders them to be sent, hearing that the Welland Canal is closed) to Amherstburg.—

From a letter dated the 23rd instant which His Excellency has received from Colonel Airey, it would appear, that all is quiet at present on the Western Frontier.— You will however, by this time, have arrived at Amherstburg, and will be the best judge of the possibility of sending a Steamer for these stores at present, without endangering the safety of the Frontier.—

In case you should think it dangerous to send a Steamboat so far down the river as Chippewa, His Excellency will direct these gun sleighs to be sent on to Fort Erie,—and he is anxious to hear from you upon this subject as soon as possible, by express over land.—

The moving such heavy articles from Chippewa to Fort Erie, would, of course, be attended by a very heavy expense.

[505] COLBORNE TO [ARTHUR]: A.L.S. 4p.

Nov. 27 *Montreal.*

I have received your letters of the 20th and 23d inst; and the inclosures which accompanied them.

The 93d Regt must have arrived at Toronto before the 25th inst; and the 73d Regt. will leave Montreal this day for Upper Canada. Colonel Love, who commands this Corps, is an excellent Officer and fit for any service; and may be employed in the London District with great advantage. A demi-battery will also proceed to Upper Canada; tomorrow or the following day; to replace the d. Battery which I have directed to be embarked at Kingston for Toronto with a view of your ordering this reinforcement to the London District. You will I hope be enabled to have four Regiments of the Line in the London and Western Districts; and a Battery; besides the Guns at Amherstburg.

I beg that you will make arrangements for concentrating the regular force the moment the principal point of attack may be declared, or the one against which you think it best to move; and not to endeavour to guard any points however important they may appear, if they cannot be defended without dividing our force— By attacking in one quarter we are certain of success; provided we can unite speedily.

I find that the arms forwarded from Montreal on the 6th[?] inst arrived at Kingston on the 23d. Thus 10,800 have been sent to Kingston since October 27th. and 1700 to Cornwall.—

The Rebels to the Southward of the St Lawrence were so completely dispersed, that they have had no time to recover from their panic; the Brigands intended for their support are consequently without work for the present. The conspiracy however has been extensively organized in most parts of the Province. 3000 persons have taken the secret oath in the suburbs of Quebec; and to the Northward of Montreal certain leaders which were destined to collect their Rebel Corps if a stand had been made on the Richelieu, are still waiting for an opportunity to disturb the Province.

It is my intention to send two or three Battalions to visit that section of the District. A large quantity of Arms and Ammunition are in the villages. We have succeeded in taking many of their depots— The greater part of our force is between the Richelieu and the Yamaska. After the search for arms we shall draw in, towards Montreal. For we must not only be strong here, but shew that we have a disposable force to march to any part of the District.

[506] [SIR] R. [W.] GARDINER TO ARTHUR: A.L.S. 5p.

Nov. 27 *Melbourne Lodge, Claremont, [England.]*

I dont think you would forgive me if I was to suppress a wish I have to make known to you a Boy of mine, who has recently joined at Kingston —in the Artillery— In the chances of Service, he may fall under your notice—and if so—I am sure he will receive every kindness at your hands—

We are all looking with anxious eyes upon you all— Every thing that comes home in private letters, seems to foretell a stormy Winter along the Frontier. . . [Sends wishes.]

[507] C. A. HAGERMAN TO ARTHUR: A.L.S.

Nov. 28 *Toronto.*

I have just received the enclosed from Mr Draper which I send for Your Excellency's perusal.

[Enclosure lacking.]

[508] C. C. DOMVILE TO LT. COL: [GEORGE] THE BARON DE ROTTENBERG [*i.e* ROTTENBURG]: LB.4, p. 33-36.

Nov. 28 *Government House, Toronto.*

I am directed by His Excellency the Major General Commanding, to acknowledge your communication of the 27th. instant—and to express his great regret, that an outrage, such as that which you describe, should have been perpetrated at Belleville, particularly at this moment, when it is so desirable to avoid exciting the feelings of people of doubtful loyalty.— This rash act (committed, no doubt, through mistaken ideas of zeal) will, perhaps be the means of restoring to the "Plain Speaker" its former popularity.—

His Excellency perfectly approves of the steps you have taken in this matter, and has heard with great satisfaction of the course the Magistrates have pursued.—

With respect to your suspicions of the views of some of the Militia soldiers and the sergeant you mention—His Excellency is confident, that you will take all the necessary precautions against the probable danger from their disaffection, and is desirous that you should make what arrangements may appear best to you under the circumstances.— Should your suspicions be confirmed, prompt measures will of course be the most effectual.—

With regard to your opinion of the state of the neighbouring Townships—His Excellency cannot but hope, that the reports you have received of their readiness to rise may be greatly exaggerated.—

In a conversation which His Excellency had with Colonel Campbell, who resides in Seymour—that Gentleman stated positively, that the inhabitants of his Township are loyal, and that in Percy and the neighbouring country, half the bad feeling represented does not exist,—at Rawdon it certainly is bad.— Some discreet person should be sent to the latter place and its vicinity, to ascertain as accurately as possible the real state of that country.—

His Excellency is desirous, that, while all due precaution is taken, and the utmost vigilance exercised, the greatest forbearance both in word and deed should be observed, for much bad blood and irritation is always created by taunting and insulting expressions; and open suspicion often drives people to acts which otherwise they would not venture upon.—

With regard to the general rising you expect, His Excellency agrees with you in thinking, that if it should ever take place in the District under your command, it will be regulated by assistance from the other side.— And that any movement in Major Warren's neighbourhood will also depend upon support from the Americans.— He is at the same time confident, that by the exercise of an active vigilance, and by a judicious disposition of the force under your command, all such disturbances and inroads as can be apprehended in your neighbourhood will at once be crushed.—

Should any such movement take place at Presqu'ile, the Inhabitants of Prince Edwards must be called upon to lend their aid.—

His Excellency is much gratified by the effect that his measures for the defence of the country have produced upon the Loyal Inhabitants of Belleville—and is glad to hear that confidence, so necessary at present has been restored.—

With respect to the still unsettled claims of the Militia and Inhabitants—the Asst Military Secretary has been directed to write again to Mr Clarke upon the subject—and to forward a copy of his answers to the Commander of the Forces.—

His Excellency is perfectly confident, that every means in your power will be used, and all your attention will be directed, not only to defend your District against our enemies, and to quiet the apprehensions of the people, but, to avoid any unnecessary collision with such individuals as may be only under suspicion.—

[509] H. S. FOX TO ARTHUR: A.L.S. 4p.

Nov. 29 *Washington.* [Marked "Confidential".]

Finding by conversation with the Secretary of State, that it was probable the United States Government might think it necessary to ask from me some explanation, respecting the British naval armament equipped upon the Lakes and Rivers of the Canadian Frontier,—I judged it best to anticipate the enquiry; and I have accordingly addressed an official letter upon the subject to Mr: Forsyth, of which I herewith inclose you a copy.—

Considering that the necessity for the equipment of this force is occasioned by the piratical war levied against Her Majesty's Provinces by lawless citizens of the United States,—I have not thought it becoming to shape my communication to Mr: Forsyth in the form of requesting the consent of the United States Government; but have confined myself to stating the fact of the increased armament, and declaring the motives.

[*Enclosure:*]

[510] *1838*
Nov. 25

H. S. FOX TO JOHN FORSYTH: A.L.S. 4p.

Washington. [Marked "Copy".]

I am informed by H. M. Authorities in Upper and Lower Canada, that in consequence of the unlawful and piratical acts of hostility to which those Provinces are at present exposed, it has been found necessary to equip, under the British Flag, a more extensive naval armament, upon the Lakes and Rivers which include the boundary line between the British and American Possessions, than either Government would be authorized to maintain, according to the stipulations of the Convention of 1817.—

I certainly do not apprehend, that any objection against this proceeding is likely to be raised, on the part of the Government of the United States.— But in order to prevent the possibility of misapprehension in any quarter, I think it expedient distinctly to assure you, that the armament is equipped for the sole purpose, as above expressed, of guarding H. M. Provinces against a manifest and acknowledged danger; and that it will be discontinued at the earliest possible period, after the causes which now create that danger shall have ceased to exist.—

[511] F. L. ARTHUR TO LIEUTENANT ROCHE: LB.4, p. 37.

Nov. 29 *Government House, Toronto.*

I am directed by the Lieutenant Governor to request you will proceed on board the Government Steamer "Cheif [*sic*] Justice Robinson" and take upon you the command and charge of that vessel until further orders.

[512] ARTHUR TO COLBORNE: LB.1, p. 185-188.

Nov. 30 *Government House, Toronto.*

There has been no attack yet reported either to the Westward, or at Niagara.

About 2000 of these vagabonds were collected at Buffalo last week; but, from information which I received yesterday, it would appear that they have moved from thence up the Lake with the exception of 600 or 700.

About a thousand or fifteen Hundred are at Huron on Lake Erie 40 miles above Cleveland, and a considerable number have assembled at "Put in Island".

In the neighbourhood of Detroit there are about a thousand Brigands. What number there are at Cleveland and in Ohio State generally, which is the Hot-bed for these Vagabonds to the Westward, I cannot exactly learn. There appears to be no stability in their Plans; and I infer that their Leaders have no great power over them.

Sir Allan Macnab sent me by express the letter which I enclose, and from which you will find that a serious descent is meditated at Wilberforce about twelve miles below Amherstburg.

The information comes through a very respectable Quarter; but, although I have provided for it, I doubt very much the execution of the plan. In the first place, several Steamers have been lost, and others seriously damaged in Lake Erie, which were in the service of the Patriots —by this their movements have been seriously crippled.

In the next place, your energetic and successful measures in the Lower Province; and the result of the affair at Presscott [*sic*] have abated the ardor of the Brigands, and the extensive preparations, which have been made in this Province, both to *prevent* insurrection, and to defeat invasion, must convince the Conspirators, who thoroughly well know all that has transpired Here or is now going on that the execution of their design is hopeless.

Nevertheless, I have moved the 32d Regt. to St. Thomas, and the 85th. Regt to London, where they can act together, and will be in the way for any thing that can possibly happen, and, at the same time check the disloyal in that section of the Country who would up to the present time, have undoubtedly joined in considerable numbers in the event of any invasion.

We have ascertained beyond all doubt that Lodges have been formed throughout this Province, in connexion with the infamous Vagabonds in the States; and had matters taken a different turn in the Lower Province, we should have been in a blaze long before this.

In the neighbourhood of Belleville, there is a very bad feeling, and one company of the Militia formed there have acted so ill that Captain De Rottenburg has reported to me the necessity of forthwith disarming them.

Another company from Prince Edward have also behaved ill which has much surprised me. I enclose copy of Captain de Rottenburg['s] letter [footnote here reads: "His Second letter which is the most important I have forwarded directly to Mr Ruttan & I have retained no Copy of it."] —the better course, I thought, was to send down the Sheriff Ruttan to enquire into the Matter and to reason with the men. I have found him a very influential person amongst the people in that Quarter.

An extensive well organized insurrection in this Province will be a very different affair from one in the Lower Province; and, I believe, no Country ever had a nearer escape from such an awful calamity than we have had.

The public mind, I trust in God, is undergoing a most desirable change, and it may be hoped that we shall be in a far better position in a few weeks—but I by no means feel confident in this matter—and a recurrence of mischief with you would produce a great convulsion Here.

A feeling of discontent, or dissatisfaction or disaffection or disloyalty —or, by whatever name it may be termed, has extended far and wide— broad and deep. The concessions and surrenders which were made by the Home Government to the Mackenzies and Bidwells of former days have had the most baneful influence, and if this Province be eventually saved from going into a Democratic State, it must be by the Special interposition of Divine Providence.

[Enclosures lacking.]

[513] H. S. Fox to Arthur: A.L.S. 9p.

Nov. 30 *Washington.* [Marked "Official".]

I herewith inclose to Your Excellency the copy of an Official Note, which I addressed to the United States Government on the 3d: instant, [marginal note reads: "forwarded in a former letter.—"] upon the subject of the extensive conspiracy, which it has been ascertained exists within the territory and jurisdiction of the United States, for the prosecution of lawless and piratical hostility against Her Majesty's North American Provinces.— I also inclose a copy of the official reply, dated the 15th: instant, which I have received from the United States Secretary of State.—

I further transmit to you a proclamation by the President of the United States, which was issued on the 21st: instant, after the intelligence had been received at Washington of the actual invasion of Her Majesty's Province of Upper Canada, in the direction of Prescott, by an armed body of Americans proceeding from Oswego and Ogdensburg in the State of New York.—

It will be well if this earnest exhortation, addressed to his fellow citizens by the Supreme Magistrate of the Republick, shall succeed, before it be too late for the peace of Both Countries, in arresting the present atrocious course of violence and crime.—

I continue to receive from the President, and from his Government, distinct assurances of their resolution to employ all means which the law permits, for the prevention or punishment of those acts of hostility, which are now being perpetrated against the peace of Her Majesty's Possessions.

It is my duty however to add, that it becomes each day more manifest and certain, that the authority which the laws and institutions of the United States place in the hands of the Executive Government, is not sufficient to enable that Government, in the crisis which we are now witnessing, to fulfil Its national duties towards the Crown of Great Britain.

We must still mainly rely, for the defence of Her Majesty's Provinces, upon the firmness and valour of Her Majesty's Troops, and upon the well tried honor, courage, and loyalty, of the inhabitants of British race in Canada.— And we may all rest secure in the heartfelt and proud conviction, that the whole strength of the British Empire will be exerted, when necessary, to guard or to avenge the attached and faithful subjects of Her Majesty in North America.

[Filed with the above is a newspaper clipping giving a copy of the proclamation by President Van Buren dated November 21, 1838. The other enclosures referred to are obviously items 417 and 456.]

[514] HOWICK TO [ARTHUR]: A.L.S. 3p.

Nov. 30 *War Office*, [*London*.] [Marked "Private".]

I had the pleasure some time back of receiving your letter of Octr 11th & the accompanying packet for Mr Robinson was forwarded according to your directions.—

I have heard with very great regret of the present threatening aspect of affairs in the Canadas, & I shd be exceedingly glad if effectual measures could be taken to encourage emigration to those provinces.— I do not entirely agree with you as to the preference to be given to English settlers, I believe that settlers from any of the three kingdoms would answer equally well provided no narrow & exclusive policy is pursued upon Church matters.— This too upon other grounds is most important, it is impossible not to perceive that an exclusive church is opposed to the feelings of the great body of the present inhabitants of Canada, & if we run counter to those feelings upon this subject we shall undoubtedly alienate their affections & undermine the only foundation of our power.— I think every possible encouragement shd be given to the diffusion of religious instructn by all denominations of Christians.—

The prevention of desertion is a subject which occupies much of my attention & I am still of opinion that the formatn of military colonies would be an advisable measure, nor do I think it impossible that something of the sort may be attempted.— Upon the subject of desertion I have seen with much alarm a suggestion contained in a letter from yourself to the Govr of Lower Canada which I read today at the Colonial Office, I mean the suggestn that the troops shd be relieved from the stoppage for their rations to put them on a footing with the militia.— You must be sensible that this wd. be equivalent to an augmentatn of their pay of 5d a day a boon which could not possibly be given to the troops in Canada without being extended to the Army generally, & the expense of doing this wd be enormous, I trust the idea has been abandoned.—

Having only learnt this afternoon that there was an opportunity of wrịting to Canada I have written this letter in great haste & have no time for more.—

[515] [Lord] Fitzroy [J. H.] Somerset to Sir John Gardiner: L.S.

Nov. 30 *Horse Guards, [London.]*

I have not failed to lay before The General Commanding in Chief your Letter of the 27th. Instant, and am directed to acquaint you, that the name of Captain Arthur of the 4th. has been noted for removal to a Regiment serving in Canada, and His Lordship will be glad when He shall be enabled to meet your wishes on the subject.

[The above was apparently an enclosure in item 548.]

[516] Arthur to Colborne: LB.1, p. 188-191.

Dec. 1 *Government House, Toronto.*

I had the pleasure to receive last night your letter of the 27th. November informing me of your having ordered up the 73rd. Regiment, & a demi-battery from Kingston.

From my letter of yesterday you will find that no attack had taken place either at Niagara, or to the Westward; and my reasons for thinking that the Brigands are not quite so eager for the work as they were.

Mr. Kent, who you will remember brought us the first intimation of the intended attempt to seize upon Fort Malden, & who[m] I sent off to Washington, has just arrived from Detroit which he left on Saturday night.

His statement is that the Brigands have collected in considerable force at and near Detroit, & that their settled plan was, to attack Sandwich last Monday, & from thence to proceed to Amherstburg. He gave Colonel Prince notice of this movemt. & also communicated it to General Brady. Their number he computes to be about 1200! and, he adds, that if he [*sic*] can get a footing their force would soon be largely augmented.—

I still feel strongly impressed with the conviction that they are much discouraged; and, although they had collected for it, they could not have made the attack upon Sandwich on Monday—or, I should have heard of it last night.

Under these circumstances, until I hear from you again, I have ordered, the left wing of the 73rd. Regt. to halt at Kingston and will retain the right wing at Toronto.

If the state of the Lower Province induces you to conclude that you will require the 73rd. Regt., or some other Corps back, I think it will be better not to send this Regt. to the Westward, as withdrawing them will have a bad effect. Of course, if, contrary to my expectation, these Ruffians continue to threaten us in the West I shall not hesitate to forward the 73rd.—but, I am most anxious not to take any force from you that you may require; for, on yr. success or otherwise our situation must be mainly influenced.

In a private Letter Mr. Fox informs me that the Upper Province is the grand object; but, unless there be a serious insurrection in the Lower Province, I cannot think that we shall be seriously endangered.

I feel satisfied that the public mind is undergoing a beneficial change, and my apprehensions all along have been raised far more by the movements of the disloyal than by the threatenings of the Brigands.

The objection wh. was first made to turning out obliged me to draft from the Militia; but I have this Morng. issued an order to check the augmentation of our force, until I see further what is likely to happen; and I shall thank you to afford me the best information you can of what is in yr. view likely to be the result, for my guidance.

When you requested me to take up all the Vessels in Lake Erie you cd. not have been aware that the Americans have above Fifty Steamers in that Lake. I took up two on the best terms that were to be made; and, most unfortunately, they have both been seriously damaged, & are still at the Mouth of the Grand River.—

The Toronto has been totally useless.—

I observe in the President's Proclamation of the 21st. November that he asserts that "disturbances have actually broken out anew in different parts of the 2 Canadas["]. This is untrue. The great expense I have incurred in calling out the Militia, originated in the Rebellion in the Lower Province, & in the preparations for the invasion of Upper Canada wh. were carried forward upon so extensive a scale as to cause the Communication wh. was made by the American Government to Mr. Fox—and, certainly, I carried out the embodying of the Militia much further than I had first proposed, or thought necessary in order to *prevent* internal disturbances in wh. we have fully succeeded. Mr. Van Buren, therefore, is not justified in stating that they had broken out in Upper Canada.

Preparations for the most extensive disturbances in concert with the conspirators in the States, I admit had gone to a most alarming length; & I have been obliged tempor[ar]ily to put forth the whole energy & means of the Government to defeat the Plot; but there has been no insurrection in wh. the slightest excuse could be raised for foreign interference.—

It is of great importance to keep this in mind.—

I have received a whole mass of Papers from Downing Street respectg. the affair of the Caroline in wh. the American Government demand *satisfaction* in a very high tone. How this will terminate there is no saying. The subject is referred to me for further evidence upon some points wh. are deemed essential.

[517] ARTHUR TO COLONEL [RICHARD] AIREY: LB.1, p. 196-197.

Dec. 2 *Govt. House, Toronto.*

Yr. letter dated 29th. Ultimo ½ past 12 O'Clock P.M. I have only this moment received.

Such contradictory accounts have reached me that I have scarcely known what to believe.—

From statemts. lately received I had begun to hope, that, from what had occurred at Prescott, and from the failure in the Lower Province there would have been an end to this wicked warfare. But, the statemt. contained in yr. letter is corroborated by the information wh. I have this day recd. from Coll. Macnab that Doctor Duncombe with 500 of these Vagabonds has proceeded from Buffalo to the West.

The Officers, generally, have sent in no returns of the Force they have assembled, & I was therefore obliged to issue an order suspending the calling out further re-enforcemts. until Returns were sent in— I enclose Copy of that order, but I have further modified it by a subsequent order today.

Of course, neither of these Orders set[s] aside the provision made by Law, & you have done quite right in calling out the whole of the 3rd. Essex— do not hesitate to employ the most popular Officers you can lay your hands upon— I know nothing of Major Girty— he was so strongly recommended by Colonel Prince who I have understood is himself a popular Man that I concluded Major Girty was Popular also.—

It is necessary also to have a strong efficient Militia force at Gosfield— Whatever you do at the spur of the moment I shall approve.

I cannot find in any of yr. letters what force, exclusive of yr. Regt., you can turn out at Amherstburg, but I have been calculating upon 400. or 500. at least, &, if so, you will be more than a match for any force these People can bring over. But, it is most desirable, that you should have a rapid communication open with Chatham & London, so as to be timely supported...

P.S. You cannot imagine how grieved I have been at finding the "Milwaukie" and "Webster" Steamers have not been able to leave the Grand River, but I have every reason to hope they will be off tomorrow.

[Enclosure lacking.]

[518] ARTHUR TO COLONEL [CHARLES] CHICHESTER: LB.1, p. 194-195.

Dec. 2 *Govt. House, Toronto.*

The Officers generally in command of Corps & Stations, with some exceptions, have been so remiss in sending in Returns of the Force that has actually joined, either under orders from myself—or, tempor[ar]ily, upon their own Authority, that I cannot form an opinion what Number of Men we have out—except from a return wh. the Adjt. Genl. of Militia has laid before me by wh. it wd. appear that above 20,000 men have been called out.

To correct this, & arrive at the truth, I have by the accompanying order checked the further augmentation, until Returns are sent in; but I am anxious you should understand that this order is not to prevent the assembly of any number of the Sedentary Militia that may be required in any part of the Province that may be seriously threatened or invaded.

I have, also, particularly excepted Colonel Prince's Corps which I much wish should be completed. Sandwich is a point to which I think, it likely the Enemy will direct themselves, if they attack any where; & we ought to be in good force there, and every possible arrangement made for re-enforcing it in the event of invasion at that point.—

If Colonel Prince's People are not to be got out in force, had you not better order the few men raised by Colonel Cameron—I mean the Skeleton Regt. to march to Sandwich; or to send them any other disposable force.

At London I conclude you will always be able to assemble, on an emergency, as many men as he can require, but I am not sure this can be done at Sandwich—from the neighbourhood of Maidstone, Rochester, Tilbury—

Be so good as to look to this & let me know. I beg that you will make arrangemts. for concentrating the regular force the moment the principal point of attack may be declared, or the one agt. wh. you think it best to move & not to separate the Regular Regts.— two regular corps concentrated will destroy any thing these Vagabonds can collect.—

I shall send another half Battery to London. At present, I shd. be of opinion that London & St. Thomas' is a good central position for the regular force.

Has the order offering a Gratuity been the means of inducing any men to bring their own arms & Blankets.—

How does it happen that Colonel Radcliffe [*i.e.* Radcliff] is so little likely to be of use. I thought there had been at least 250 Stand of Arms amongst his people, & that they would be ready at any moment.

Pray do not let the Ammunition be issued to the Indians until *it is required*. . .

[P.S.] Will you be so good as to communicate the contents of the first part of this letter to Colonel Airey and Colonel Prince as there is not time to write to them from hence?—

[Enclosure lacking.]

[519] ARTHUR TO COLONEL [CHARLES] CHICHESTER: LB.1, p. 198-199.

Dec. 2 [*Place not stated.*]

Since I wrote to you this morning, I have recd. a letter from Coll. Airey in wh. he states that the Brigands are collecting in some force opposite Amherstburg. Whether they will venture to land or not it is impossible to say—

I enclose you a memorandum of which I have enclosed Copies to Colonel Airey & Coll. Maitland not knowing exactly where this Letter may find you.

By all means get if possible a good force at Gosfield that it may be at hand to support Coll. Airey.—

You cannot be too particular in ensuring rapid and certain communication between Amherstburg and London, and Waggons should be ready for the rapid advance of the regular force should it be necessary.

Commodore Drew has repaired Damages & I hope is on the point of proceeding up the Lake— He has 200. men on board his Steamers.

The Asst. Quarter Master Genl. is on the point of starting for the West.

[Enclosure lacking.]

[520] ARTHUR TO SIR ALLAN MACNAB: LB.1, p. 192-193.

Dec. 2 *Governmt. House, Toronto.*

The Officers Generally in Command of Corps & Stations—with some exceptions—have been so remiss in sending in Returns of the Force that has actually joined them either under the orders from myself, or, tempor[ar]ily, upon their own Authority that I cannot form an opinion what Number of Men we have out—except by a return which the Adjutant General of Militia has laid before me from wh. it wd. appear that above 20,000 Men have been *Called out.*

To correct this, I have by the accompaning Order checked the further augmentation until Returns are sent in but I am anxious you shd. understand that this order is not to prevent the assembly of any number of the Sedentary Militia that may be required in any part of the Province that may be seriously threatened or invaded.

I am much obliged to you for sending me the information Contained in your Letter of yesterday's date—it seems difficult to know what to believe.—

On Wednesday just after I had received your Letter, in which you informed me of the formidable force destined to attack us at Wilberforce, a Person arrived from the Westward who has for some time been employed by Government, & whose statements have hitherto entitled him to much confidence.

He left Detroit on Saturday afternoon at about 4 O'Clock. There were about 800. Patriots there, and in the neighbourhood who *meditated* an attack upon Sandwich and Fort Malden of wh. he had informed both General Brady & Colonel Prince & thought they would not carry it into effect. At Cleveland he was confident there were no more hunters than a party of about 250 who had come down to Buffalo at the same time he did with the determination of attacking Commodore Drew at the Mouth of the Grand River.

He spoke of the Patriots being much discouraged.—

Yesterday, a Person in the Royal Navy arrived from Detroit. He left it on Sunday. He corroborates the statement of the Person who had preceded him, & having touched at "Put in Island" he assured me there was no force there— But he thought a Force would be collected there during the Winter.

Another Person employed by Govt. was at Buffalo on Wednesday last— He is the Individual who gave to Colonel Dundas notice of the movements of the Patriots to Prescott & is now employed to the Westward. He has been in all the Lodges. His statement is that the Patriots were much dispirited—that many had left the Concern as a bad speculation. There was nothing he was persuaded to be apprehended from Buffalo. He is now, I should suppose at Detroit.

Under all these various conflicting Statemts. it is difficult you will perceive to know what is to be provided for, but my idea is—that if any thing is attempted it will be—not at Wilberforce, but to the West from whence they can more easily retreat— However, we must be watchful every where.—

[Enclosure lacking.]

[521] ARTHUR TO JOHN MAITLAND: LB.1, p. 197-198

Dec. 2 *Government House, Toronto.*

I have intended for a week past every day to address a few lines to you but I have literally not had one moment.—

As you mentioned in two letters that yr. health wd. not enable you to move with your Regt., I thought it better not to leave the notification until the last moment as it might inconvenience the public Service.

I feel satisfied you will have rightly appreciated my motives and be convinced that I have most sincerely regretted the cause.

I am sure you will still render what assistance you can in furthering a service that has called you its own for so many years.

It is most distressing that the Militia have so reluctantly turned out in yr. district— pray, if you can, suggest any other measure[;] do intimate it to Colonel Chichester— perhaps Colonel Askin would be a likely man to head some Volunteers—

[522] C. A. HAGERMAN TO ARTHUR: A.L.S.

[*1838*] [*Place not stated.*]

Dec. 2 I send your Excellency the enclosed from Mr Draper.— I have not received the papers to which he refers, but I suppose he has sent them to Mr. McAulay[*sic*].—

[Enclosure lacking.]

[523] W. H. DRAPER TO COLONEL [RICHARD] BULLOCK: A.L.S.

Dec. 3 *Kingston.*

You will receive herewith an official &c &c &c—

One of the minutes that of Abbey got a roll in the Snow & it has rather spoiled its appearance but I did not like to delay getting it off—so send it with its faults instead of stopping to draw up another[.] Pray explain this to H Excy as my apology for sending such a rough looking concern[.]

[524] ARTHUR TO COLONEL [J. B. B.] ESTCOURT: LB.1, p. 200-205.

Dec. 4 *Govt. House, Toronto.*

My extreme occupation will, I trust plead my excuse for not having earlier acknowledged & replied to yr. letters, but, I have really been so overwhelmed that it has not been in my power.

I have felt deeply concerned that the Militia did not more readily volunteer—it has occasioned me the greatest perplexity, and when drafting was at length resorted to, so many cases of extreme hardship were daily presented that I was under the necessity of checking it until Returns were made—

Scarcely any of the Militia Officers sent in returns, & many Corps were called out without my knowledge, so that it was impossible for me to judge what force was on Service.

This will account to you for the temporary suspension which was ordered of drafting, &c.— I was anxious to explain what must have appeared to you extraordinary whilst you needed men so much and I will now proceed to make some remarks upon the points you have adverted to in the order in wh. they occur in yr. letters.— With regard to arms—alluded to in yr. letter of the 24th. I ordered 1500 to be deposited at Fort Erie during the summer, considering that, independent of the 43rd., it was not probable you wd. require to arm a larger force— 200 of these, I desired to have sent to St. Catherines [*sic*], but I am not aware of any other deduction— 1300 therefore must have been distributed on the Frontier which I should certainly consider an adequate force.— Will you be so good as to let me know, thro' the Asst. Adjt. General, how these Arms have been distributed. I have, however, directed 300 more to be forwarded to Fort Erie.

In the emergency of the moment, I thought it better to order 150 men to be sent to the Westward where a considerable force of the Brigands has been assembled.

It was my expectation that Commodore Drew wd. have sailed a week ago; but, as it is possible he may not even yet have taken his departure I have sent off an Express desiring him to take no more than 50 men—& to leave the rest at Gravelly Bay. If the Despatch be not in time to prevent the embarkation of the Party I will endeavour to send you the like re-enforcement.

With respect to the information conveyed to you by Maxwell noticed in your second letter of the 24th. I attached very little importance to it, as I had the same day received very full information and the reports are so contradictory that it appears impossible to rely upon them.— The Movemts. of the Brigands are, in fact, as unsettled & changeable as their designs are wicked.

It is highly probable that some of these Fellows have crossed over & are prowling about, but it is not likely that they are numerous— If you will be so good as to stir up yr. Sheriff,—& more especially your under Sheriff who is a very active person from time to time,—as well as the Magistrates—to keep a sharp look out it is not likely that any Considerable number of these Vagabonds can remain in your District.

For work of this kind I shd. think yr. under Sheriff a very competent Person and any reasonable expense that you authorise will be readily approved— The Under Sheriff assured me that he was convinced the People in the Niagara District, generally, were not by any means disaffected and that there wd. on any emergency be a good turn out of the Militia.

He spoke of a great many respectable Men who wd. upon emergency turn out Mounted and I told him that I wd. gladly supply 200 or 300 cutlasses for them which, when Sabres are not to be had, are good weapons.—

A Sedentary Corps of this kind—proper places being fixed for their assembling—wd. be a most desirable force & the probability is that many of them have Rifles or Guns or Pistols.—

I shd. recommend you very much to confer with Mr. Mc.Leod upon this matter, & whilst employed in organising the force I shd. be most willing to admit his claim to Compensation— proper & convenient places for the assembling of this independent Cavalry & signals of alarm being settled wd. give you strength at no great cost.— Mr. Robinson of St. Catherines I am also sure you wd. find a most intelligent & useful auxiliary—he wd. perhaps himself suggest some useful hints.—

A good many of the Sedentary Militia of yr. district must I presume have Arms & if these were coaxed with a little kindness they wd. perhaps shew a good disposition to be useful.—

In addition to the 300 Stand of Arms & 200 Cutlasses I will send you 50 Muskets that have been cut down for the use of the Cavalry & it makes an excellent weapon—

These would answer for Captain Mc.Meachin's Troop.—

I shd. have real pleasure in acceding to yr. proposition respectg. Mounted Musketeers but the expense of 250 more Cavalry is quite startling. We already have nearly 900. out & the Govt. will never forgive me the expense— this, & this only deters me from encouraging yr. proposal, the benefits of wh. I see clearly.

With respect to the information brought by Maxwell, who arrived last night, I have no doubt he has stated what be believes to be true; but his story is not quite consistent, & I was sorry to observe that he labored under much excitemt. when I first saw him.—

This class of Persons being obliged to frequent Taverns in order to pick up information are led into bad habits wh. considerably detract from the value of their Communications.

I incline, however, to think that he believes all he states— The wise course, I apprehend, for us to pursue is—to be as well prepared to resist mischief as we can,—come when, & from what quarter it may.—

That these Vagabonds will attack us if they can get any opening I have no doubt; and I entirely believe that there is a considerable force being raised in Kentucky wh. may soon be on the Frontier; but I expect these people will demonstrate themselves in the West & not at Niagara.—

Allow me to suggest—that, from several reports wh. I have received, I am inclined to doubt whether matters are going on well at Waterloo Ferry. I should recommend yr. placing one of the most prudent & intelligent Militia Officers you have under yr. command in charge at Fort Erie, & subjecting the Ferry to very strict regulations, or, if you please, place an Officer of the 43rd. there.

There are now about 600 Indian Warriors in a state of preparation at the Grand River & who could at any time be collected in a few hours.

Sir Allan Macnab will always we [*sic*] ready to advance with *at least* an equal force—so that if you keep yr. communication open with Sir Allan Macnab at Hamilton, & with the Officer Comdg. at Brantford you will always be rapidly supported— I have not finally determined upon it, but I think the 73rd. Regt. will occupy Brantford with a demi-brigade of Artillery. I wd., however, on no account allow these supports to interfere with the aid you may more readily expect by looking to yr. Sedentary Militia and to the Companies formed at St. Catherines & elsewhere—these I trust are being well drilled—and will shortly be,—if not at present,—in every respect Serviceable.

I think you wd. be quite right in being at the expense of occasionally despatching an Officer to Buffalo and Lockport or up so high as Cleveland to give intelligence of the force & intended movemts. of the Brigands.— I am expecting Mr. Jones daily from an important Mission—

I shall always be glad to hear from you and most happy to afford you every possible support— There never was a time when the temperate— judicious & zealous exertions of all Officers in Command was [*sic*] of greater importance.—

[Superscription reads: "Colonel Estcourt Comdg. Niagara Frontier."]

[525] H. S. FOX TO PALMERSTON: A.L.S. 5p.

Dec. 4 *Washington.* [Marked "Confidential Extract".]

"The Three important Paragraphs in the President's Message of this day to Congress, which relate to the hostile movements against Canada, will no doubt more deeply engage the attention of H. M. Govt:, than any other part of that document.—

The Two First of these Paragraphs do certainly recognize and declare the extent of the mischief, and the existence of lawless designs of hostility on the part of American citizens, as broadly and explicitly, as could be expected from the Executive Administration of a popular Government.—

In the Third Paragraph, the Constitutional feebleness of the Executive Govt: of the United States, and the inadequacy of its authority to meet the present crisis, are most apparent.— In this part of his Message, the President does in fact little more than implore and beseech his fellow citizens, to desist from a career of acknowledged and infamous publick crime.—

If H. M. Government shall judge it expedient to recommend the insertion of a clause in H. M. Speech to Parliament, declaring H. M. resolution to defend the North American Provinces against all dangers from within and from without,—in a tone which shall make it clearly intelligible to the American People, that by persisting in their present course of aggression, they will draw down upon themselves the vengeance of England. and the ruinous penalty of a national war,—I feel convinced that such a declaration would exercise a more immediate influence over the conduct of the American nation at large, and be of more avail in staying the progress of hostile aggression, than all the deprecating language which has been hitherto used in the Proclamations and Messages of the President:—"

(Signed) H. S. Fox[.]

[The above was apparently an enclosure in item 533.]

[526] ARTHUR TO H. S. FOX: LB.1, p. 199-200.

Dec. 5 *Govt. House, Toronto.*

From the information I have received, from various quarters, & thro' highly respectable sources, I do not doubt that a large force is being collected in the State of Kentucky—for the purpose of joining in the invasion of this Province.—

Will you allow me to suggest,—as the President's Proclamation may mislead many Persons, and induce them to believe that disturbances have broken out in Upper Canada, as he has erroneously stated, & that, therefore, their interference is the more justifiable,—that the Government of the United States should without delay endeavour to remove the mischief which they have unintentionally done.—

I pledge myself that there has been no political disturbance whatever in this Province beyond great excitement occasioned by the audacious proceedings & preparations on the American Frontier.—

I am obliged to write in great haste to save the Steam Boat.—

[527] C. C. HAGERMAN TO ARTHUR: A.L.S. 3p.

Dec. 5 *Toronto.* [Marked "Private".]

I send your Excellency a private letter from Mr Draper received last evening, which you may find interesting.— I also enclose the statement made by a principal Brigand and of the name of Bulkley which contains a good deal of information.—

I have several times thought of mentioning to your Excellency that it strikes me it would be an Act of *Justice* as well as good policy to request Mr McLean (Judge) to resign the command of the Regiment of Militia of which he is Colonel, and confer it upon D. E. McDonell [*i.e.* D. Æ. Macdonell] who headed them and conducted himself so creditably at Beauharnois.— I do not know whether you have read Major Phillpotts report of the expedition from the Eastern District to Lower Canada; if so you will have observed some remarks on Colonel McDonells *political* principles quite out of place and calculated to give offence, and this renders some notice of the latter (as it appears to me) the more necessary.—

[Enclosures lacking.]

[528] J. B. ROBINSON TO ARTHUR: A.L.S. 9p.

Dec. 5 *Cheltenham.*

The mail bag must not go without a letter from me, though one has little satisfaction in writing by so tardy a conveyance— Before this letter reaches you, I trust you will have received one of a later date in which I may have something of more interest to communicate than I have at present— It was most kind of Your Excellency to take so much trouble in the midst of your perplexing difficulties to furnish me with the means of judging of your prospects in the coming winter— Having read carefully as well *as with* avidity all the papers transmitted to me (which were forwarded without delay from the Colonial Office,) I am beyond measure gratified by the attitude of preparation which has been assumed in both Provinces— I quite agree in the sentiments expressed in your letter to Ld. Glenelg that what is wanting is the adoption of such measures for permanent security & tranquillity as are most likely to drive (if any thing will) the disaffected within, and the lawless ruffians without the Province to abandon their infamous projects— By this time, I dare say you are much better able to judge whether any formidable attempt upon Upper Canada will be made this winter— I have no doubt that the kind of organization which Sparks & others describes has been going on, & that the signs & pass words &c have been in general truly stated by your informants, but at the same time I think it likely that the conspirators have no desire that their proceedings or at least the main scope & object of them should be concealed; but on the contrary they would rather I dare say that very exaggerated accounts of them should be reported to you— And indeed I should not wonder if some of the informants were not sent upon their errand by the persons whose infamous doings they have been detailing[.]

At the same time, it is very certain that if these rumors were disregarded, & the Country left exposed, then serious attempts would be made, & with some prospect of success.

It naturally occurs to me that if a hope was entertained by any number of rational & influential persons of revolutionizing the Canadas & if these persons could control the movements of their associates, they would have thought it prudent to let at least this winter pass over quietly, in the expectation that our Government would be encouraged by the calm to withdraw—a large portion of the troops next year—

The proceedings of the rebels in Lower Canada seem rather unaccountable— It can not be that they place any reliance upon the probable unfaithfulness of the army— Their insane leaders may have led them to entertain such a hope— When one considers the body of troops in L C. it can only be supposed that the outbreak was the mere wicked ebullition of bad passions uncontrolled by any calculations of prudence—or that it is really known & understood by the rebels that there is a large (& it ought to be an overwhelming) number of Americans ready, to pour in, if *they* can only first make a lodgement somewhere, & exhibit some semblance of an achievement in the sacred cause of liberty— I am delighted that Sir John moved upon them so promptly & in such force, & I confess I am charmed to see the former Special Council restored, & some good ordinances passed for the protection of the Country— I trust it will be followed up by the instant trial by Court Martial of some of the most notorious offenders—

I can not understand how Theller could have escaped from the Citadel—or how it happened that he had not been sent to England on his way to Australia— By the way a fellow passenger with me in the Great Western, knew Theller well in Ireland— He told me he had been his fellow student when Theller was past the age of 20—& that after that Theller procured the appointment of assistant Surgeon in the Navy & to his knowledge he was some time in that capacity in an English Ship—

I am glad to find several Corps of Militia are to be embodied— Without such a preparation, I am convinced the Province of U.C. wd. have been attacked at several points, & I am not without my fears that it will be at all events when the ice takes on the Sinclair— our most formidable enemies are in the West—

I read with much pleasure the report of the Council upon the state & prospects of the Province— It is an able & excellent paper in all respects & I wish it may obtain publicity—but I doubt whether the Ministry will do it that justice— We Canadians I confess have a sorry prospect before us— The efforts already made for our protection are most costly to Great Britain— Are they to be,—*will* they be continued for a series of years?— If not who can safely foretel[l] when any portion of them can be prudently withdrawn?— The truth is the decision must now be taken by G. Britain in justice to her Colonial subjects, & to the Empire—she must look the difficulty in the face fairly—& make suitable provision for meeting it—or she would consult every interest better, including the interests of humanity, by honestly telling us at once that she feels herself unequal to the struggle that will be necessary for preserving us— We could easily I think, suggest such measures as would protect us against any thing but the contingency of a public war— When that comes the struggle will doubtless be severe, but I think we can not doubt the power of England to retain her American dominions so long as she retains her naval ascendancy—

I quite agree with all that has been said by Your Excellency to the Secretary of State upon the present state of things—& I hope the Government will act in future a little more worthily than they have done— The moment I saw, in U. Canada that a question had been asked in the House of Commons as to the employment of the Indians, I was satisfied it would be followed by a dispatch almost insisting upon your abandoning that important aid in your struggle for self preservation— This is quite in character with the mawkish feeling that has disgusted the loyal people of both Provinces— I wish Mr. Sullivan had been reading (as I have lately) the life of Joseph Brant written by Mr. Stone of New York, the perusal of it would have suggested to him some rather striking arguments agt. the scruples of the Ministers—

I trust there is no idea of throwing the slightest discouragement upon the zeal of the brave Indian Warriors to defend their Country & support the cause of their Queen— I wish we had ten thousand of them— The Comparison of these fine fellows with the ruffians who threaten to invade you is very well put by the Council in their report— I wish I could venture to make it as public as it ought to be—

I can not express how much I am astonished at the last opinion of the Crown Officers in respect to foreigners being tried as traitors— I did not think it possible as one of my brother Judges did, that they would be so reckless of their reputation as to venture to rest in the conclusion they had too hastily formed, & to support it by such references, in opposition to such authorities as they have done— They knew & felt while they were writing this discreditable paper (for it is really discreditable) that if they were Judges they could not & dare not act in conformity to what they profess to be their opinion— I think I must for my own satisfaction place the whole discussion before some eminent & experienced Criminal lawyer and obtain his opinion upon it— The weak points in their paper & the style of the whole are really such as amaze me—

Lord Durham is yet in or about Plymouth—& the London Editors seem wearied with watching his movements— He was most unlucky in being detained for days on board the frigate in the harbour, by the tempestuous weather which prevented all intercourse with the shore—and when at last he did land, he seems not to have posted up to town as all the world expected—but to have kept himself quiet at Plymouth, for all I know to this time— It is probable he is now in town— I shall probably see him when I next go to town—which I do not intend doing till I have returned from a visit to Sir Francis Head—who is living in Warwickshire about 60 miles from hence— I am sorry I did not meet Ld. Glenelg in town when I went for that purpose—but I could not wait his return & I had no desire particularly to see him until Ld. Durham had presented his scheme, when the Govt. would better know their position—

I am feeling, & looking I believe, a good deal the better for a month's peace & rest in England, though I am not without my grievances which I trust my naturally good constitution will surmount— Mrs. Robinson & our children are quite well— I trust Lady Arthur & your family will suffer nothing from the cold of a Canadian winter—

[529] ARTHUR TO COLBORNE: LB.1, p. 214-216.

Dec. 6 *Toronto.*

I take the opportunity of the "Traveller's" proceeding to Kingston to inform you that we have recd. nothing new from the West. It is nothing new to say that Colonel Airey, in a letter dated the 3rd. inst., writes that an attack is expected every hour at Sandwich, the Brigands having assembled to the extent of about 600 men immediately opposite that Town.

Colonel Prince is quite alive to the intention, & is in force enough to resist, if not to destroy the assailants. Col. Airey says he is ready to support Col. Prince with a hundred men, & a nine pounder if necessary; but I have thought it better to order him to be re-enforced from Chatham wh. I did on the 2nd. inst.

That Supreme Vagabond "Theller" is with the Brigands at Detroit—If they do venture across, I hope he will be of the party; for I am sure that not one of them ought to be suffered to return.

Lt. Jones of the 43rd. Regt. has just returned from Pittsburg[h] where I dispatched him for information from a Mr. Mc.Intyre a Scotch Gentleman who wrote to me to say that he cd. give important information if I wd. send a Confidential Officer to receive it. I enclose a copy of the information wh. he gave to Mr. Jones. It is just a corroboration of all we have had before; but his confirmation is important, & he is, no doubt, well informed as to all that is going forward.

The plan of the Brigands seems to be to make an attack on the Western & Niagara Frontier when the Ice will bear them.

Mr. Jones describes the feeling all along the frontier to be quite enthousiastic [*sic*] in favor of the Brigands, and the support and encouragemt. they have received in money and means is quite extraordinary.—

In the Interior, he says, a very different feeling exists and that the conduct of the Brigands is severely condemned.

I have considered the cases of the first 3 prisoners who have been tried.— Sch[o]ultz—Abbey—& George, and have ordered them all to be executed. Schultz on Saturday & the other delinquents on Wednesday[.]

It is awful work but I believe it to be absolutely necessary.

Five more have been convicted, & are sentenced to be hanged, but I have only this eveng. recd. the proceedings & have not decided upon them.

[Enclosure lacking.]

[530] [ARTHUR] TO COLBORNE: LB.1, p. 208-209. In Arthur's handwriting.

Dec. 6 *Toronto.*

[Another copy of item 529 with slight variations. It is cancelled by being scored through. The final two paragraphs read:

"If there sd. be any serious attack upon our Western frontier I shall of course be off for it immedly(.)

"But Genl Thellers division I do not imagine will be a very formidable affair—"]

[531] ARTHUR TO HENRY DUNDAS: LB.1, p. 205-206. In Arthur's handwriting.

Dec. 6 *Govt. House.*

I send down the Traveller with Warrants for the execution of Abbey & George.

What an awful concern it is & where is it to end?

Be so good as to send me a state of yr garrison at Kingston, & what duties they take. Is the conduct of the Militia in quarters good, & are the men comfortably lodged, clothed, & Blanketted!

Do be so good as to advise the officers commanding to persuade their men agt. drinking to the excess they did in the Spring when last embodied[.]

From several reports wh. I have received it certainly appears that a considerable body of Kentucky Men not less than 2000 are on the move to Detroit.

You must keep, therefore, an adequate force of Militia to take all the duties for if the plot thickens in the West, I shall be obliged to send there the whole of the 73 Rgt, but from the reenforcts expected from Engd Sir John will be able to send up another Corps if we require one, if all goes on well in the Lower Province[.]

As I have no Staff officer at hand at this minute will you be so good as to desire the Ordnance Storekeeper to send up a return of Arms & accoutremts in Store at Kingston & what number of Cutlasses— These make a good substitute for Swords for the Cavalry[.]

One of our Troopers cut a fellow down in fine style with a cutlass about a fortnight ago & proved beyond all doubt that it is a deadly weapon[.]

The Fellow endeavoured to stop Him on the road. . . .

[P.S.] Col: Airey writes me on the 3d Ins that He was expecting an Attack every hour— Theller is at Detroit with a pretty considerable body of Patriots[.]

[532] ARTHUR TO THE BISHOP REGIOPOLIS, [ALEXANDER MACDONELL]: LB.1, p. 206-208.

Dec. 6 *Govt. House, Toronto*

Pray be so good as to excuse my not having earlier acknowledged your letter of the 24th Inst.[*sic*], forwarding the petition of Thomas Raill[?], but I really have not had it in my power.

I have referred the Petition for explanation, so that I am not at this moment able to speak upon the merits of the case; but I cannot believe it possible that any officer serving under me will object to any just Claimant for promotion on the ground of his being an Irish Catholic. There is nothing I should more strongly animadvert upon, and I must say, that I have never yet known such an objection raised since I have been in the Province.

I thank your Lordp for sending me a copy of your admirable address to the Inhabitants of Glengarry, and I am much gratified to find, that it is your intention to publish one of the same kind to the Irish Roman Catholics.

Your recommendation of your friend Colonel McDonnel [*i.e.* Macdonell of Peterborough, I attended to as soon as I received it, and if he can only meet with a body of Brigands the field of Glory will be open to him!

Your friend Captain Wilson, (London District) has applied for the office of Clerk of the Peace to which I have this day appointed him.

His application was accompanied by a Letter which Your Lordship had addressed to him eighteen months ago—but you will see it had not lost its "value"—

[533] H. S. Fox to Arthur: A.L.S. 31p.

Dec. 6 *Washington.* [Marked "Confidential".]

I have delayed sending off my despatches to you, till after the appearance of the President's annual Message. I am glad that I did so, as I have in the mean time, this day, received your public and private letter of the 24th: ult:, with the several interesting and important papers inclosed.—

You will perceive that in the President's Message, as well as in his previous proclamation of the 21st: ult:, he sets forth the existence and extent of the mischief, denounces the lawless and infamous designs and acts of American citizens, and recognises the duty of his Government to frustrate and punish those acts and designs, as broadly and explicitly as can well be.— It seems hardly possible, that any Government could have the effrontery to use such language, if intentionally conniving at the crimes which it denounces.— At the same time, you will observe that these proclamations amount, in fact, to little more than exhortations, addressed to the citizens of the United States, imploring them to desist from their present career of violence. The President can of course only threaten the enforcement of such laws as exist; and the existing laws and institutions of this Country do not enable the Executive Government, in the present crisis, to fulfil its national duties towards Great Britain. There is the real mischief: and it will not be remedied, until the British Government shall resolve to speak out, to the American people at large, in a very different tone from what has hitherto been used.—

I really believe,—and I have anxiously watched, and reflected upon, all that passed,—that the President's Government is sincerely striving, as far as so weak and feeble a Government can be said to strive at any thing,—to fulfil its national duties: but most assuredly, the American nation and people are obstinately and scandalously betraying those duties.— They neither desire, nor dare, to go to war with us.— But they hope, by continuing their present conduct,—the multitude making war while the Government professes peace,—to obtain Canada without the risk of a national war.— They expect, to use an expression I believe of your predecessor Sir F. Head, to "hustle us out of Canada."— And it is partly by the fault of our own countrymen at home, that this hope and delusion is indulged in.— It must, by some unequivocal act or declaration, on the part of Great Britain, be made intelligible to the American people at large, that they *shall not* continue this course of aggression, with impunity.— Such act or declaration would have more effect, than all that either can or will, be done or said, by the President.— The great bulk and majority of the nation, who I am persuaded are not for war, would then interfere to put down the invaders; and would interfere with more effect, than any Government, acting as a Government, can be expected to do in this Country.— But unless something of this kind is done soon, I see little chance of a favorable termination of our difficulties.— I inclose to you a short extract of what I wrote home upon this subject, yesterday, upon transmitting the President's Message.— I have before written in the same sense, and shall continue to do so.—

You will perceive, that with regard to the real intentions of the President and his Government, I think better of their sincerity than you do.— But the difference between us is a mere point of criticism, and is of no practical consequence: for as long as a Government is so entirely helpless to prevent its laws from being broken, the greater or less sincerity of its real wishes little signifies.— And I am well aware, that the least relaxation of defensive effort and preparation on our side, or a transient success on the part of the invaders of Canada, would drive such a Government, whether willing or unwilling, into a tacit acquiescence in the crime.—

I consider a continuance of the present full state of warlike preparation in the Provinces, to be absolutely necessary for their preservation.— But it will be intolerable, if the hazard and vexation of such a state of war are to be entailed, season after season, upon the loyal inhabitants of Canada,—and the expence ultimately upon the people of England,—in order to repel open invasion from a nation, which is in the mean time, in other quarters, reaping all the profit of peaceful intercourse with us!—

I have addressed to you, under an accompanying cover, a letter marked official, dated the 30th: ult:, inclosing to you, officially, my Note of the 3rd: ult: (which you already have) to the United States Government, and Mr: Forsyth's answer to that Note.— I think it will be of advantage to our interests, both here and in Canada, that these documents should be published.— I do not expect that the United States Government will lay them before Congress, or print them here: and it would be contrary to diplomatic regulations, for me to give publicity to official corrrespondence, in the country to which I am accredited. Under these circumstances, I would suggest to you, if you see no objection, to publish these documents in Upper Canada, either by laying them before the Provincial Parliament, or in any other way that you think proper.— The papers to be so published, would be, your first despatch to me, dated the 22d: of October: my present official letter to you dated the 30th: ult: (which I have carefully worded with that view,): and its two inclosures, namely my Note of the 3d: ult: to the United States Government; and Mr: Forsyth's answer to that Note, dated the 15th: ult:— The public cause will I think be benefitted [*sic*] by the circulation of these papers; and I feel a personal wish, that the loyal people of Canada should know that I am not remiss, as far as my means go, in serving them.—

I send to you here inclosed, two singular papers which have been given to me, unofficially, by the President.— Mr: Warren Green, the writer of the letter to Abraham Van Buren, the President's son, is, I understand, unknown to them personally.— The letter to this Warren Green, from Von Schoultz, the Polish brigand taken at Prescott, will speak for itself.— The President daily receives innumerable demands and supplications, to interpose in behalf of the prisoners at Kingston. He has positively refused to undertake any interference.— But he has at the same time expressed to me, privately, his opinion,—upon giving me these letters,—(and also upon communicating to me the proceedings of the Oswego Committee, which you have received through Colonel Worth, and published:) that the exercise of clemency, on the part of the British Authorities, will essentially tend to subdue the spirit of violence and aggression within the American border. I have replied, that I have no objection to convey to your knowledge, confidentially, that such is the President's opinion: but I have distinctly acquainted him, that I will not support that opinion by any expression of my own: my conviction, upon this painful part of the subject, being entirely the reverse.—

I do not know what the fate of this Von Schoultz may be: but it strikes me, in reading his letter, that he might probably be able and willing to make important disclosures.— I request you to be so good as to return these letters to me, after you have read, and if worth while, had them copied.—

I am afraid that the worst of the delinquents will never fall into our hands.— The real movers of the invasion of Canada are the wealthy citizens of the great towns within the American border.— These villains have a deep and permanent land-speculating interest, in maintaining the movement: they will continue, again and again, to hire and delude fresh bands of adventurers to serve in this infernal crusade: and I am afraid it is not by repeating former acts of clemency, or by indulging those adventurers in the hope, that when taken their lives will still be begged off upon the plea of delusion,—that we shall succeed in subduing the present organized system of crime and violence.—

You will have been glad to see that Governor Marcy has lost his election. Of his successor, Seward, I know nothing: but he cannot be so bad as the other.—

General Scott has been again ordered to the command on the frontier. But after a short stay there, I believe he will come to Washington.— I did not hesitate to say to the Secretary of war Mr: Poinsett, and to the President, that I regretted the appointment of Scott; for that, whether right or wrong, he had not so conducted himself, last year, as to engage the confidence of our Authorities.— Mr: Poinsett tells me that he shall himself candidly state this to General Scott; and that he feels quite sure, that if confidence is shown to General Scott, you will not find him undeserving of it.— General Scott is punctilious, and incredibly vain; but the impression upon my own mind is, that he is honest, and that what appeared abnoxious in his conduct last year, arose from mutual misconception.— General Macomb has proved himself quite unfit for the occasion.— He is now here, and even yet scarcely believes in the existence of the conspiracy against Canada.— He is a well meaning man, but has been thoroughly imposed upon.—

I shall be most anxious to hear the result of your enquiries at Pittsburg[h]. My present belief is, that the United States Government has no thought, or intention of war.— All the information which I have, respecting the American army and navy, confirms me in the belief.— I feel as certain of this, as I can be of any thing that regards the secret intentions of others.— But it is not a bit the less necessary to keep a vigilant eye upon all that passes; for the present crisis is one, which, if much further prolonged, must inevitably end in war, whether the Government desire it or not.—

I have heard nothing for a long while respecting the claim for the "Caroline".— I suspect that the United States Government regret, and are ashamed of, having spoken so loudly upon the subject; and that they will willingly let it sleep, if not pressed by violent demands in Congress.—

I forward my present letters by Colonel Farquharson, who is waiting at New York.— I shall continue to write to you by the post, which, though slow at this season, is I believe tolerably safe.— I find Mr: Moore, the agent at New York, always exact and careful in transmitting my correspondence.

[First enclosure referred to is apparently item 525. Other enclosures lacking.]

[534] ARTHUR TO COLONEL [CHARLES] CHICHESTER: LB.1, p. 210-211.

Dec. 7 *Govt. House, Toronto.*

I have received your Letter of the 5th. Inst., as well as Colonel Aireys of the preceding day[.]

Nothing could possibly be better than your having decided upon moving with 200 men at once to Sandwich— it must bring you upon these vagabonds, who it appears took to the Woods, and by sending the Indians in to drive them out, I should hope that they have been all secured long ere this.

You have done well in moving Colonel Cameron to Chatham, and at once collecting a good force there. I do not leave myself to doubt for one moment that the Militia will now turn out well and do their best to destroy or capture the Brigands.

Not one of these audacious Pirates will I trust be able to return to the American Shore.

The Asst Quarter Master General writes me that the 32nd had advanced to support the 34th. This does not strike me to be necessary; as it would appear that 300 Militia have already proceeded to Gosfield from London; which force, in addition to the Militia already stationed there, would seem more than enough to crush the Brigands whom Colonel Airey does not estimate beyond 300 men.

The 85th. should be held fast for the defence of London and its vicinity— I have ordered the 73d to proceed to Brantford with a demi Battery of the Royal Artillery, which will make all safe in that Quarter.

I shall look with impatience for further tidings from you.

[Superscription reads: "Colonel Chichester Comg Western Dist."]

[535] ARTHUR TO COLBORNE: LB. 1, p. 216-218.

Dec. 7 *Toronto.*

It has blown a violent tempest during the last 24 hours, and in consequence the "Traveller" is still detained.

An hour ago I recd. from Colonel Airey by Express, the letter of wh. I enclose you a Copy with its enclosure.

Three hundred & fifty of these Vagabonds crossed over on the Morng. of the 4th. & landed at Windsor about day light.—

The Militia under Colonel Prince immediately turned out to attack them, and Col. Airey says after a few exchanges of shot dispersed them—that they took to the woods, where "Col. Prince did not consider it prudent to pursue them".

This I do not quite understand, because in a subsequent part of his letter he states—"the pursuit of parties of the Militia is still going on, but, up to 3 hours ago, only 9. prisoners had been taken".—

By Col. Prince's verbal statemt. it wd. appear that 25 of the Brigands were killed—this was letting them off too easily.— But, I should hope, that all of them must have since fallen into our hands—for, I wrote to Colonel Chichester to increase the force at Sandwich, and early on the Morng. of *the 5th.*, he moved with 200 men by the St. Clair shore road, so that he must have been in the way of the Brigands the day after their defeat.—

Coll. Cameron moved on from London to take the Command at Chatham with 120 Men & a force of the Sedentary Militia was also called out—so that Coll. Chichester says he feels all will be safe at Chatham.—

3 weeks ago I ordered all the Indians to be collected at their several Villages to prevent their being tampered with; and those to the Westward will, therefore, now be ready to scour the woods, if their Services are required.—

Not a man of the 350 I shd. therefore hope will escape.— Colonel Airey mentions that General Brady had informed him that an Attack in force wd. be made on Fort Malden on the night of the 4th—but the Express did not leave Amherstburg until ½ past 3 OClock on the Morng. of the 5th.—and up to that time no attack had been made.

I ordered some days ago, as the turn out of the Militia had been so slack at Gosfield, that Col Ball's Regt. shd. move forward to Gosfield from London— they are 300 strong & will be an efficient support to Col. Airey, if He requires them.—

Col. Airey has not sent a return of the Militia force he has at Amherstburg—indeed in this respect all the Officers have been exceedingly remiss—but, I apprehend he has about 300 men—so that supposing his information to be tolerably accurate—that the Brigands had, on the whole, about 600 men—He must outnumber them exceedingly.— If they do venture, it must be an act of desparation [*sic*]. We shall be next attacked, I conclude on the Niagara Frontier, as the Brigands still continue numerous about Lockport & Buffalo.

It is prudent, therefore, certainly to send forward the 73rd. to Brantford, & I must bring up the left wing from Kingston, wh. I regret very much, whilst the trials are going forward; but, at present I do not think there can be any danger in that quarter.—

The demi-Battery has not arrived from Kingston, but I shall not wait for it, but forward the demi-battery from hence with Col. Love.—

The Scotch part of the Community have come round very much lately—so that I have less apprehension than I had of our own people, & consequently care less for the movements of the Brigands. Not but what enough remains to make me anxious & quite alive to the danger of the extensive conspiracy that has been formed between the Worthies here & in the States for some months.

The enclosures in the letter from Col. Airey from Messrs. Murphy and Latimer shew, what class of persons have been engaged in this Patriot enterprize—

[Enclosures lacking.]

[536] ARTHUR TO COLBORNE: L. 10p.

Dec. 7 *Toronto.* [Marked "Copy".]

[Another copy of item 535 with slight variations.]

[537] ARTHUR TO HENRY DUNDAS: A.L.S. 4p.

Dec. 7 *Toronto.*

I am sorry to be under the necessity of taking from you the left wing also of the 73rd—but the whole Regt. must go at once to the Westward.

On the morning of the 4th the Brigands landed about 350 Men at Sandwich— they were met by Colonel Prince's Militia—made a bad fight of it, & dispersed into the Woods—after losing about 25 Killed & 9 Prisoners.

It is supposed, by General Brady's Statement, that this was not the main attack, but that a more formidable attempt would be made upon Amherstburg.

I am also in the full expectation of an attack upon the Niagara Frontier.

Be so good as to send forward therefore the Left Wing of the 73rd with the least possible delay—with a Demi-Battery.

I have written to the Commander of the Forces & He will most probably send up another Regiment forthwith.

It gives me great concern to find that there has been a doubt about the place of Execution.

Although the Attorney General worded the warrant at or near Fort Henry I understood Him to mean the Jail at Kingston.

But we are to blame, & nothing should have been left open for doubt.

The Steamer would have gone off to you with this early this morning, but it has blown furiously all day.

[538] ARTHUR TO COLONEL [F. A.] M. FRASER: LB.1, p. 211-214.

Dec. 7 *Government House, Toronto.*

I have received both your letters from Brantford, and have attended to your suggestions.

Not being certain that I could retain the 73d Regiment in this command, I thought it better not to advance them to Brantford until I should hear from the Commander of the Forces—as the moral effect of recalling a Corps does much mischief.

Having however, this morning received information from Colonel Airey of the descent made at Sandwich as well as your letter from London upon the same subject dated the 6th. Inst.

I have now ordered the 73d to proceed to Brantford as soon as the weather will admit of it, but it has been blowing a tempest during the last 24 hours.

I wrote to Coll Chichester on the 2nd Inst to reinforce Sandwich and to move in Coll Cameron[;] this he writes me he carried into effect on the morning of the 5th. Inst. which I think must have brought him in contact with the Brigands, who were dispersed on the 4th. I am glad to perceive also, my wishes were promptly carried into effect by Colonel Ball's to Gosfield.

If Colonel Airey's information was tolerably correct, and the Brigands remaining to be crossed over did not exceed 300 men I do not see the necessity for advancing the 32nd, but as the Papers to which you allude as being found in one of the Ruffian's pockets you have omitted to forward I cannot form an opinion on the subject.

I would not however, under any conce[i]veable circumstances concur in separating the 85th Regt[;] rather far would I leave London to be occupied by the Militia until the 73d move up to London, which of course they will do, if the service requires it, which I think will not be the case.

As the demi Battery has not yet arrived from Kingston, I have forwarded the one from Toronto with the 73d Regt.

If the Sedentary Militia did not turn out at London as they ought to have done, there was of course nothing for it but to bring up the men you have ordered from Brantford, and it was quite proper to replace them from Hamilton.

I will cause Hamilton to be reinforced by some of Colonel Thomsons [*i.e.* Thompson's ?] Sedentary Militia if the next information from the West does not bring tidings of the destruction of the Brigands or that at least their power to do mischief has been removed.—

The 7th 10th and 42d. are under orders for Canada with more of the Guards—Artillery &c &c so that it would appear we are not forgotten at home. . .

P.S. Pray forward to me the papers found in one of the Ruffians pockets to which you advert in your letter. They may be of importance.

[539] C. C. DOMVILE TO THE VARIOUS COMMANDING OFFICERS: LB.4, p. 39.

[*Dec.*] 7 *Government House, Toronto.*

I have the honor to enclose, by the command of His Excellency the Major General Commanding, an extract of a letter from Mr Draper (dated Kingston 3rd. December) Depy. Judge Advocate at Kingston, for your information and guidance— [Marginal note reads: "Relative to identifying Prisoners."]

[Enclosure lacking.]

[540] H. S. FOX TO LT: COL: FARQUHARSON: A.L.S. 5p.

Dec. 7 *Washington.* [Marked "Private".]

I send by this night's post, *3* despatches for Sir George Arthur, under cover to Mr: Moore the agent at New York, who will deliver them to you.— I shall feel much obliged, if when you reach Canada, you will write me word any thing remarkable, respecting the designs against Canada, which you may learn or observe on the frontier, or in the course of your journey.— If in passing through Buffalo, or elsewhere, you should hear of the presence of General Scott, who is about to take the command on the frontier, I think it would be adviseable that you should call upon him, saying you do so at my request, and offer to be the bearer of any confidential communication which he may have to send to the Lieutenant Governor.— There is, I am afraid, some mistrust of General Scott, on the part of our Authorities, arising I think from mutual misconception.— General Scott is punctilious, and incredibly vain; but I believe that his intentions in the present crisis are honorable, and that if confidence is shown to him, he will not be found undeserving of it.— He has more influence with the officers and men of the U. S. regular army, than any other man in their service; and it is of the most extreme importance that no needless distrust or misunderstanding should take place.—

[541] [J. B. ROBINSON] TO SIR GEORGE GREY: L. 6p.

Dec. 7 *Cheltenham.*

It is necessary that I should incur no delay in answering your letter of the 5th. Inst. enclosing a despatch from Sir George Arthur of the 23rd. of July last, respecting proposed additions to the Legislative Council of Upper Canada, otherwise it might have been desirable that Lord Glenelg should have had the opportunity of discussing in conversation two or three points to which it would probably occur to him that consideration should be given—

The increase which the Lieut Governor proposes is large certainly—much larger I imagine than has been made on any former occasion in U.C. or in any other Colony—but I am inclined to think this not objectionable—considering the great extent of U.C., its various classes of population,—and the importance of having this branch of the Legislature so composed as to entitle it to confidence and respect[.]

I think there are at present 26 members of whom there are 9—who from age or other circumstances do not attend— Sir George Arthur proposes to add 27 members which would make the actual number in all 53 and of effective members 44—

It is not probable that more than 30 members would be generally in attendance and that number I think would not be excessive either in public estimation or with regard to any inconvenience likely to arise from it— His Lordship will consider whether so wide a departure from what has been usual may form an embarrassing precedent with respect to other Colonies, and lead to expectations with which it may not be easy to comply—

If the extent of the proposed increase be not objected to, then in regard to the individuals named His Lordship I think may securely rely upon their being all Gentlemen firmly attached to the British Govt. and whose principles and character entitle them to general respect—

As Sir George Arthur has deliberately considered in what order he would wish them to stand, which is important in case any curtailment of the list should be thought adviseable, I will make no observation on that point— If the whole list be adopted then of the 27

2 will be from the Eastern District—
1 from the Bathurst Dist—
2 from Johnstown
3 from the Midland Dist.
2 from Prince Edwards Dist.
7 from the Home Dist—
5 from the District of Gore
2 from Niagara Dist.
3 from London Dist—

As to Country I believe that they stand thus

English 4
Irish— 6
Scotch 5
Native Canadians or
Americans 10
From other Colonies 2 — 27 —

Eight I think have been Officers in the Army or Navy and the rest excepting the Vice Chancellor and Mr Sullivan are chiefly Gentlemen living in the Country on their Farms, or engaged in Commerce[.]

I apprehend however that neither the Country nor religious denomination of the individual have been considered by the Lieut Governor, with any view of attempting to keep an even balance in these respects[.]

I take it for granted His Excelly. has thought it a more satisfactory course to be guided solely by the character and fitness of the individual, not allowing it to be either a qualification or disqualification that he happens to have come from any particular part of the British Dominions, or to belong to any particular Church—

I believe tho' I may be in error in two or three instances, that in point of fact of the 27—

20 are of the Church of England
5 of the Church of Scotland
1 Roman Catholic
1 Methodist—

With respect to the Districts from which none are proposed to be taken—

the Western District contains now one Legislative Councillor
the Dist. of Newcastle 3
and the Dist of Ottawa—1— Mr Hamilton of the last mentioned Dist. for whom a mandamus was sent out I believe some years ago has declined to act[.]

His Lordship I daresay has been made aware that the Assembly contains several gentlemen who have every claim to the distinction of a seat in the Legislative Council & who would be most useful members of that Body but it seems to be thought by His Excelly most advisable not to deprive the Assembly at present of their services— I do not suggest any additions or substitutions because that is not desired— It may not be thought improper in me however to mention that there are some gentlemen whose names I have reason to know Sir George Arthur had under consideration but he doubtless felt it to be impossible to include all who might be thought eligible— I recollect the following names, and I mention them in order that if Lord Glenelg should desire it, and should have the opportunity he may converse with some one having knowledge of U. C. respecting them—

George Catchmeyde Salmon
David Jones
James Ingersoll
George Langley
Charles Baby
Charles Elliott
Guy Carleton Wood
William Johnston Kerr
William Thompson
Robert Land
James Cumming
John Arnold
Hammett [*i.e.* Hamnet ?] Pinhey

Some of these for various reasons I should have liked to have seen included. Mr Tucker who has lately been made Provincial Secretary would probably be a good addition, and his Office makes it proper he should be appointed, if there be no particular objection— I am aware of none—

If His Lordship should think it inexpedient to adopt the whole list, I venture to suggest that either the measure might be at present limited to the Confirmation of the 9 or 10 recommendations made by Sir Francis Head—adding Mr Tucker—

Mr Robert Neilson
Mr James Sampson
Mr Alexr. Fraser
Mr John McGillivray

or, if it were thought well to appoint 20, *the first 19* on his Excellys list, with Mr Tucker

or, if there were to be any appointments made out of His Excellys list, which I should not think it right however to press, they might stand thus—

Vice Chancellor
Mr Sullivan
Mr Tucker
Wilson [*i.e.* Willson ?]
I. Fraser
Wilkins
Fergusson
Radcliffe [*i.e.* Radcliff]
Street
Alexr Fraser
Dickson
Neilson
Macaulay
Hatt—
Sampson
McGillivray
Vansittart
Charles Elliott
Hammett [*i.e.* Hamnet ?] Pinhey
Henry Graham

Mr Jones who stands on Sir George Arthurs list is most probably known to Lord Glenelg— he would make I think a useful member—

There are many considerations which make it exceedingly difficult for a person intimately acquainted with the Province to settle a list of names—numerous enough and not too numerous, but on the whole tho' I should have made a selection somewhat different I am inclined to recommend the precise adoption of Sir George Arthurs list, adding Mr Tucker, unless in any despatch subsequent to that sent to me His Excelly seems himself to be undecided in respect to it—

[The above is apparently the letter referred to in item 555.]

[542] ARTHUR TO COLBORNE: LB.1, p. 219-221.

Dec. 8 *Govermt. House, Toronto.*

Since I addressed you yesterday, I have received several letters from Colonel Airey.

Also one from Colonel Chichester, and from Mr Whitting of which I enclose you copies.

It would certainly appear that Colonel Prince did not manage matters well, and the Brigands in consequence escaped much better than they ought to have done.

This has given me a good deal of concern.

There had been a Detachment of the 34th. Regt. at Sandwich for some time, but they were withdrawn only a few days before the attack agreeably to your wish that the Corps should be concentrated.

By Mr. Whitting['s] letter to Mr Macaulay, you will observe that he considers the mischief was extending very widely.

Matters have gone too far to render the interference of the Government of the United States effectual, however sincerely they may desire it; and I must say that General Brady does appear to have acted zealously and faithfully.

It seems to me not to be safe to leave the 34th. any longer so far from effective aid from the Regular Troops:—at present they are, as it were cooped up and would appear to be employed in taking care of a particular Fort in place of protecting the Country.

I have therefore determined to order the 32nd. to advance so as to be near enough to act in concert with the 34th. and I must manage to make the 73d and 85th. cooperate.

The only objection to this is leaving Brantford.

I am anxious before the Ice is strong enough for the enemy to get a strong force of Militia at Chatham and at Brantford, but I have not yet been able to manage it. They turn out very reluctantly in the Western and London Districts.

The number of persons, who have left the Province and gone to the States is astonishing. I do not believe that all are disloyal, but many have emigrated from fear.

This gives a fair opening for Military Settlements and I should rejoice to see the Government resorting to such a scheme.

It is in vain for me to trouble you with all the statements and affidavits, which are before this Governt.; but the upshot is, that the Brigands are largely augmenting their force, and will give us warm work of it during the winter.

The means they have at their disposal is quite extraordinary and beyond all question, shews how generally the cause must be supported in the States.

Do you think Gosfield would be a good station for the 32 during the winter? Would the Corps be near enough to work together?

I suggest this thinking it will be the most open point to the Brigands during the winter.

[Enclosures lacking.]

[543] F. L. Arthur to Colonel [Charles] Chichester: LB.4, p. 37-39.

Dec. 8 *Govt. House, Toronto.*

The Major General Commanding has directed me to answer your letter dated from Tilbury 6th. instant which His Excellency received this morning.

Nothing can exceed the Major General's disappointment that the Brigands who landed at Windsor dispersed with so little loss, and were not at least briskly followed up so as to prevent their escape across the Detroit— no official account of this affair has as yet reached Head Quarters.—

It would seem you have not any line of Troopers opened out between Chatham and Sandwich, or the information would earlier have reached you of what transpired at Sandwich.— Could not this be managed during the Winter— The Major General considers it of the utmost importance that the communication should be kept open from Post to Post.

If the Brigands did not get away by canoes or boats across the Detroit, it would seem that the Post you have occupied at Tilbury must bring them up, for there appears no other escape for them but by the St. Clair—and that is a long round.

Perhaps Gosfield would be a good position for the 32nd Regiment during the Winter? will you be so good as to state your opinion upon this point for the Major General's information.—

The Troops suffered much during the Summer at Chatham— The Major General would be glad to know to what probable cause the sickness is to be referred.

The bad quality of the Water has been mentioned, might not that be remedied by bringing the water into the Town from a higher source, or is it from any other cause that can be remedied.—

I am instructed to make this enquiry because the Major General thinks, whilst the Militia are out, it would be a good opportunity to get some useful labour at a moderate cost.

[544] C. C. DOMVILE TO COLONEL [C. J.] BALDWIN: LB.4, p. 41.

Dec. 8 *Government House, Toronto.*

I am directed by His Excellency the Major General Commanding to inform you that in consequence of the late disturbances in the West, further reinforcements will be necessary in that quarter.

He is accordingly desirous to know if a company of 100 men of your Regiment can be immediately held in readiness to march if required.

[545] ARTHUR TO COLONEL [RICHARD] AIREY: LB.1, p. 224-227.

Dec. 10 *Toronto.* [Marked "Private".]

The Asst Adjt. General laid before me this morning your letter of the 6th Instant, with an enclosure from Colonel Prince. Colonel Foster will reply to it tomorrow— in the mean time, I lose not a moment in saying that you have acted rightly, in sending a Company to Sandwich, and placing Major Deedes in command as Colonel.

I had proposed, not knowing what you wished yourself—some days ago, to Colonel Chichester, whether it would not be desirable to move the 32nd. to Gosfield during the Winter Months—as *there* they would be ready to support you in a few hours if necessary—whilst they would be in a good position for Winter Work.— Consequently—I am now quite concerned to find that the Asst. Qur Mr General is sending that Corps back to London. I send off express to direct their advance—and enclose a copy of my letter for your information.—

To describe to you my feelings at Colonel Prince having caused four men to be shot after they were taken, or had surrendered, is not in my power.—

Knowing that I had again and again urged upon every one to forbear, & to leave the punishment of these delinquents to the Laws, it is, even if it were legal, which I believe it is not—most unjustifiable to have taken such a step—

Her Majesty's Government evidently desire to maintain Peace with the United States— As a Servant of the Queen, subordinate to Her responsible advisers, I wish to pursue their policy to the best of my ability; and such an act as Colonel Prince has committed, may so influence the American People, that it is not improbable that they will make a handle of it to force their Government into a war.—

Pray let me entreat you, to cultivate, so far as you can, a good understanding with General Brady— I hope Colonel Prince's act may be understood to have been dictated by a sudden impulse in the Field, and that the American Government may regard it in that light.—

Do you think that General Brady has been acting in good faith towards us— from the President's last Proclamation the Government is now desirous, as I infer, to take a decided part to maintain peace.

I have been obliged to address you in much haste. . .

P.S. You may cause all the Prisoners to be removed as soon as you think proper to London, where I propose they shall be tried— Have the kindness to cause every possible information to be drawn from them, and the necessary witnesses to identify them &c &c. to be sent to London. Employ any professional person to do all that is needful in this, & if there be no professional person, then the most intelligent Officer you can find—

The information should be addressed to Mr. Sherwood (Queen's Council [*sic*]) London, as he will be appointed to act as Judge Advocate and will proceed there forthwith.

[Enclosure is possibly item 547.]

[546] ARTHUR TO COLONEL [CHARLES] CHICHESTER: LB.1, p. 227-229.

Dec. 10 *Govermt. House, Toronto.*

Your letter of the 7th. Inst. from Tilbury addressed to Colonel Foster, he received this morning, and will answer tomorrow; in the mean time I wish to make one or two observations to you.

You have no doubt done quite right in proceeding to Windsor, but you will have found on your arrival that a company of the 34th. had been sent there by Colonel Airey, and Major Deedes, as Colonel placed in Command.

Colonel Fraser Asst. Qr Mr General had moved on according to a wish I had expressed under certain contingencies—the 32d Regt so far as Adairs Tavern; but on the 9th. he writes me that he proposes they should again return to London.

I have written to him, and enclose copy of my letter to advance the Regiment to Gosfield, where there are as I am assured good Quarters to be found, and it is a good position either to support Colonel Airey or to support the force at Sandwich or to face the Brigands should they cross from "Put In Island"—(where they have a supply of Provisions Ammunition &c) when the Ice will enable them to cross by Point Pelé.

Do all you can to make the Troops comfortable, both Regular and Militia— Let the latter feel that they are as much an object of the regard of the Govt. as the Regular Troops, and let them be well trained, especially, in loading and firing and charging and one or two simple movements.

I have ordered two Guns also to move with the 32nd Regt. It gives me pleasure to find that you have taken seven of the Brigands, and, especially George Putnam.

You had better send them, under a safe escort to London where I have ordered a General Court Martial to assemble. I trust the Indians will bring out the rest of these Murderers from the woods; there must yet remain many who cannot have crossed into the States.

Never was I more shocked to find that Colonel Prince had ordered four of those, who had surrendered to be shot.

You will hear from the Assistant Adjt Generall [*sic*] upon this subject; I am obliged to write in much haste.

[Superscription reads: "Colonel Chichester Comg London & Western Districts".]

[Enclosure is possibly item 547.]

[547] ARTHUR TO [F. A.] M. FRASER: LB.1, p.231-233.

Dec. 10 *Government House, Toronto.*

I have this moment received your Letter commenced on the 8th. and concluded on the 9th. instant.—

As the object of yr. advancing the 32nd. Regiment was to support Colonel Airey, if he should require support, I am rather surprised that—at the moment when I think he has very properly sent one company to Sandwich, and requested to be re-enforced—you should have determined on sending back the 32nd. Regt. to London.

I regret exceedingly that this course has been taken, and hope that Colonel Chichester may have arrived in time to put a stop to it; wh. I think it probable he may do as I proposed for his consideration whether the arrangement of occupying Gosfield with the 32nd. Regiment might not be desirable, without knowing that Colonel Airey had detached a company of the 34th.—

If the 32nd. be stationed at Gosfield, they will be able to act with the 34th. just as the Commander of the Forces desired; and, it will be a most convenient quarter during the Winter Months to watch the Brigands if they muster strong at "put-in-Island".

Be so good as to make the best arrangemt. you can for quartering the 32nd. comfortably during the Winter. I would still keep a Militia force at Gosfield to act with the 32nd.

The whole of the 85th. Regiment may be stationed at London, & the Militia may occupy St. Thomas; but now, and during the rest of the Winter, there is nothing to apprehend from *Point Abino to Gosfield.*

The Guns may remain with the Head Quarters of the 32nd at Gosfield, & I hope the Officer Commandg. the 32nd. will make the best arrangement he can, as soon as the Ice is formed,—and, indeed before if possible for ascertaing. what is going on at "Put in Island". By keeping himself quiet, & watching the Brigands from Gosfield we may take them by surprise where they may little expect to find a body of Troops.—

It was only by the express this day that I found Colonel Airey had detached a Company to Sandwich.

So far as I can form an idea by my map, I apprehend that Gosfield is about 30 miles from Amherstburg and a little more by the cross road to Sandwich.— A communication should be established by Sedentary Cavalry between these Stations and also between Gosfield to Chatham which, I presume, must be about 42 miles.—

[548] SIR J[OHN] GARDINER TO ARTHUR: A.L.S. 7p.

Dec. 10 *H[orse] Guards, [London.]*

I was truly gratified by the assurances conveyed to me, in your letter from Montreal— I think, however, you will agree with me, that, I have very little to thank *them* for; I do not mean that, I do not attach importance to the thing itself, but that my claims entitled me to earlier consideration.

I find, that, my nephew a Lt. in the Royl. Artillery is in your neighbourhood that is, in your Comd—Lynedoch Gardiner[.] He is, I think, a very promising Lad and if He comes across you, I know I may calculate upon your countenance and protection— Our Assistant here Col Cochrane has just put the enclosed, into my hand, begging me to interest you in favour of a nephew of his in the 32nd.

I lost no time in making known your wishes for the removal of the *Captn.* from the 4th to Some Corps in Canada. You will perceive from the enclosed note to me, from Lord Fitzroy Somerset that, Lord Hill has approved of his being listed, and I am persuaded there is a readiness to do it, whenever the Oppty. may offer— If you can Suggest any thing, or that, there Should be any opening which you may at any time point out, you had better write to me immediately[.]

From the tenor of your letter, I conclude you fully expected, all that, has occurred in your part of the world, it has had one good effect, which is, that, the Govt has at last been induced to Sanction an encrease to the Army of about 5,000—by allowing Regts. to Recruit to 740— I cannot help thinking that the return of your Governor Genl is deprecated in most Quarters, tho' many people Seem to think, He had great grounds of Complaint against Ministers— Lady Durham, I see, has decided on extinguishing her appointment about the Queen, and many infer from it, that, there is no chance of any arranget. between him and the Govt— it is Said, that, He will have the Support of his father in Law, Earl Grey— I have not read your proclamation yet, tho' I am told it is worth reading, and if you had only omitted one part, that, relating to religion, it would be a capital document— By the bye what do you say to the Speeches made at the Military dinner given to Lord Durham before his Embarkation from Quebec— Entre Nous, I must say, I am inclined to impute a little want of consideration, in the frequent allusions made on the above occasion to matters of a political tendency, and in which we Soldiers have really no business to interfere—

I am afraid, as you Seem indeed to apprehend, that, you will have no idle time of it, during the Winter—but I have no fears for your not getting through it— God bless you—

[First enclosure lacking; second enclosure is apparently item 515.]

[549] C. A. HAGERMAN TO [ARTHUR]: A.L.S. 2p.

[*1838*] [*Place not stated.*]

Dec. 10 I send you Hough on Courts Martial and refer you to page 254 for distinction between *Finding* and *Sentence* of Court Martial.—

I do not mean that the doctrine laid down is *conclusive* as respects the Kingston case— I should require to look more closely into it, (which I shall do when the proceedings are referred back) but it favours the opinion of Mr Draper, in which I am *disposed* to concur, although it may turn out not to be the correct one,—

I send your Excellency Dr. Sampson's letter:—the events in the West should I think be considered in connection with the question— What is the proper limit of Capital punishment in the case of the Brigands taken at Prescot[t]?—

[Enclosure lacking.]

[550] W. H. HAMILTON TO ARTHUR: A.L.S. 5p.

Dec. 10 *67, Oxford Terrace, Hyde Park, London.* [Marked "Private."]

We have indeed been very desirous for some time past to hear from you or Lady Arthur and to know your feeling on the state of the Province at the last outbreak, for we could not but be very anxious concerning you all. Your letter of the *31. October*, and Lady Arthurs to Mrs. Hamilton have relieved us greatly as to any apprehension of immediate annoyance to you from the Rebels—and the defeat of the Party that landed at Prescot[t] has given a new tone to public feeling—but there is a long Winter to be got over—and your mind, at the least, will be much harrassed [*sic*] by the vigilance it will be necessary to exercise against an Enemy so active and powerful. A rightful cause and the protection of an all wise Providence will, I firmly hope, enable you to maintain the British authority effectively so long as it may be deemed expedient for the Mother Country to retain these Colonies. That we must part with them in the course of a very few years seems to be the general impression here.— Every arrival from New York is now looked for with the most intense interest—and the political conflict pending between Lord Durham and Ministers, yields place in public attention to the more important and actual one in which the Canadas are now engaged.

I have more than once regretted I did not accompany you this time last year: but as events have occurred, my services, which are of a peaceful and ordinary caste, would have availed you little, and it seems as if much time must elapse before the business of your Civil Government can fall into its usual routine. Moreover, as you say you would, on no account, recommend my joining you, I give up all idea of it—unless indeed quiet is restored by the Spring, and I can run over and back again as a mere visitor among the many who now avail themselves of the communication by Steam.—

I will now reply to that portion of your letter which relates to business.— Montagu acted, no doubt, under a persuasion that the Sheep speculation to [*sic*] Port Phillip would be very advantageous to those concerned,—and having kindly offered me a share in it, which I have declined. I shall be glad to learn that his expectations are realized.— With regard to my drafts on him for your account previous to Lady Arthur leaving England, you are mistaken as to my having authority to make another for £300.— Your letter gave me warrant to negotiate for £2500—which I did—in two Bills (£2000 & £500) *at 5 per Cent discount;* the first Bill through the *Australasian* Bank (the Chartered) with Mr. Arthur Willis's indorsement—which was required—and the second through Mr. Fredk. Bell—who took it without any indorsement.— I have already hinted to you that Mr. Willis's act was a voluntary one—but it is nevertheless *a favor*, which I sought to avoid a repetition of, lest it should place you under obligation, and I still would avoid, it, if I can. As Mr. Hyde's Son will not go out until the Spring (if at all, for his wife is averse to it) I have no resource but the Banks. I yesterday called on Mr. Angas, who, you are aware, is in the Direction of the *Union*, and asked him to ascertain whether my draft on Montagu for *your account* would be taken without a third name—and he will do so on Thursday next.— If it will not, I must, of necessity, have recourse to Mr. Willis.— I drew lately on Montagu, on my *own* account, £500 at 5 per Cent discount—but was obliged to get Mr. Lyttleton to indorse my Bill—such being the rule of the Banks—and I must shortly do so again, as Montagu has not sent me Money so soon as I counted on. The loss by drawing is not so great as it appears, as we have the use of the money Six months earlier than we should have it by remittance from the Colony—and that might be made at some loss if Bills in England were at a premium.— You will find in the Pass Book of Coutts & Co. which Lady Arthur took out, credit given for the *proceeds* of my two Drafts vizt. £1900—& £475. I must now negotiate on the authority of *your last letter*, and I propose to do so for £500 only, in the first instance, to pay Mr. Hyde's account (£170) and Mr. Walton. I have written to the latter for his Bills. When they are discharged I will pay the remainder to Coutts & Co.— I saw Mr. Marjoribanks and obtained from him a statement of your Account, which I will copy for your information. Should your drafts on them appear beyond the balance at your credit, they will let me know immediately, and I will draw on Montagu. This will prevent any over accumulation with them, as they pay no interest.— I hope I have made myself clearly understood by you as to Money Matters: if not pray require further explanation.

There is every reason to believe that the Derwent Bank will fall into the *Union*, as the *Tamar* Bank has done. I have therefore willingly met Mr. Angas's obliging suggestion that I should take a place in the London Direction. The emolument will be trifling (not beyond £50 a year at present) but it will give me employment, which I much want, and it will keep me well informed of the pecuniary condition of V. D. Land and New South Wales.— I have seen a Hobart Town Paper of the 12. July, received by way of Sydney. I am sorry to find there are still some Bushrangers out. The Legislative Council was sitting. The vote of £1700 to Lewis for compensation, was unanimous, with the exception of Swanston—who again protested against it, spite of Lord Glenelg's Despatch. The appointments of Collector of Internal Revenue, Assistant Treasurer, and Civil Engineer are abolished. O.Connor and Mr. Moore are carrying on a Paper War in no very measured terms, regarding the differences between the former and Mr. Barnett.— O'Connor has at great length *refuted* Mr. B's "refutations"—and the latter is now employed in writing a further refutation. There appears to be no end of this course of attack and defence.— Mr. B. is till at Dunkeld with the Duchess of Atholl.— I shall have the pleasure of writing to you again soon. Mrs. Hamilton will then also write to Lady Arthur. Pray accept our kindest & best wishes[.]

Copy of Coutts & Cos Account.

1838	Cr.		
June 11.	By balances at the time the book was made up —		30 . 8 . 3
Aug. 26	" Treasury Warrant – (less Stamp 7/6).		499 . 12 . 6
Oct. 13	" Divd. on £233.3.7 Red 3·PCents		3 . 9 . 11
" 23	" Proceeds of Sale £233.3.7 Red. @93–	216 . 12 . 2	
	less Brokerage –	5 . 10	216 . 11 . 4
			750 . 2 . –
1838	Dr.		
June 20.	To paid Mr. Holberton——	43 . 15 . 0	
27.	— " —— Marsh ——	14 . 7 . 0	
Aug. 30	— " —— Lady Arthur's Bill to Parker & Co.	100 . – . –	
Dec. 6	— " —— Major B. Willis —	50 . – . –	
		208 . 2 . 0	
	– Bill under acceptance due 2. February ——	270 . 8 . 7	
			478 . 10 . 7
	balance at Sir Geo Arthur's Credit 10. Decr.		271 . 11 . 5

P.S. I was requested by Miss Consett to trouble you with her recommendation of a Gentleman resident in Upper Canada, and she has sent me a duplicate of her note, in case the former should not reach you. I therefore do so, though I hope the troubles on the frontier do not extend to the interception of letters.— Mrs. Hamilton wrote to Lady Arthur last month.

[Enclosure lacking.]

[551] C. C. DOMVILE TO COLONEL [F. A. M.] FRAZER [*i.e.* FRASER]: LB.4, p. 39-40.

Dec. 10 *Government House, Toronto.*

As it appears by your letter of the 9th. Instant to the Major General Commanding, that Colonel Airey has requested a further reinforcement of Troops, I am directed to desire that the 32nd. Regiment may be moved on to his support.— four Companies of the Regiment may be stationed at Gosfield, where the Major General is informed that good accomodation for them may be procured, where they will be ready to support and act with the 34th. Regt. and where they will be available when the Ice enables the Brigands to cross at Point Pelée.— And two Companies may at once move to Amherstburg.

If the State of the Western Frontier requires it, of Course, the whole of the 32nd. Regt may proceed to Amherstburg—

The Major General has directed this instruction to be forwarded direct to you, not knowing exactly where Colonel Chichester may be found—

The whole of the 85th Regt may be stationed at London & the Militia may occupy St. Thomas, but now, and during the rest of the Winter there is nothing to be apprehended from Point Abino to Gosfield.

[Superscription reads: "Colonel Frazer Ass Q M General & Copies to Colonel Chichester Col Airey & Officer Commd at London".]

[552] C. C. DOMVILE TO OFFICER COMMANDING AT LONDON: LB.4, p. 41.

Dec. 10 *Government House, Toronto.*

As the Major General is not certain where Chichester may be found, I have the honor to enclose you a copy of His Excellency's instruction to Colonel Frazer [*i.e.* Fraser], and to request you to act upon it, in the absence of both these Officers[.]

[Enclosure is apparently a copy of item 551.]

[553] ARTHUR TO COLBORNE: LB.1, p. 235-237.

Dec. 11 *Govt. House, Toronto.* [Marked "Private".]

I have just addressed you upon the affair at Detroit, and forwarded to you the correspondence, or rather reports, from Colonel Airey and Colonel Prince.

The Militia acted with their usual gallantry and spirit, but as far as I can make out Colonel Prince's report never was there more confusion and unnecessary excitement.

It seems the Brigands were frightened to death as soon as our people faced them, and never was less advantage taken of the panic of an enemy.

To make amends for what was wanting in the field, Colonel Prince determined upon severity after the affair was over. In his own language, "Of the Brigands and Pirates 21 were killed, besides 4 who were brought in just at the close and immediately after the engagement, all of whom I ordered to be shot upon the spot, and which was done accordingly."

Notwithstanding the extreme provocation of this band of ruffians, and notwithstanding some strong language used by Lord Durham, upon the subject, and still stronger by our Attorney General, I cannot think that it was lawful, much less justifiable for Colonel Prince to have taken the Law into his own hands, and put these men to death, after the action was over, and after they were disarmed and Prisoners.

At all events, I am sure, it will be made a handle of by the Americans, as grounds for making more proselytes to the Patriot cause, and, therefore, was most impolitic.

On this account I have determined not to give publicity to Coll. Princes report *officially*: (Prince in independent Militia style published his report before it was forwarded to me) but rather to publish a District Order, recapitulating the particulars of this audacious invasion, without noticing this very tragical event.

If we fall into work of this kind, we shall find the Brigands quite our equals in such deeds.

I have nothing new from the Westward this morning.

[554] [ANONYMOUS]: to ARTHUR: A.L. 2p.

Dec. 11 *Buffalo.*

I am about to propose that which will be of service to the Gover[n]ment (provided it is to my interest) I am offored [*sic*] the *corresponding secataryship* of the *secret society* of *Patriots* of this place. in the place *of Marcellus Mills* who leaves here for Detroit[.]

I am willing to take this office and betray the confidence of the society and give all information to the *Brittish* [*sic*] Government that lays in my power, if I can get sufficient recompense to cover any loss that may accrue in the event of detection[.]

I am proprietor of a public house here that is the *rendezvous* of the leaders of the Patriots and this place is the very focus of the rebellions[;] consequently in holding the above office I shall be apprised of every movement along the frontier. I do not wish to accept the office or to interfere in any way as I am doing an excellent business except for the above stated reasons[.] As *money* is my only object and very little Patriotism except as far as interest is concerned I am willing to render any service to the Gover[n]ment £500 down and £50 pr month will buy me.

If you think well of this direct to ("Miss Lucetta Thornton Buffalo") and I will disclose my name or if you can make arrangements appoint some one to meet me here and name time and place[.] Send *Capt Mathias* and write me when and where to meet him[.] I will attend to it as I know him[.]

For fear of incur[r]ing suspicion I direct this under cover to the Post Master at Toronto[.]

If the Government wishes I can abstract a *Patriot Dictionary* from the society.

[555] J. B. ROBINSON TO ARTHUR: A.L.S. 4p.

Dec. 11 *London, Spring Gardens' Hotel.*

A long letter from Mr. Morris of 17 Novr. has just put me in possession of the whole affair near Prescott, the most impudent attempt certainly that has yet been made— From this demonstration, I look for accounts of further outrages—nothing below Lake Erie is to be apprehended, I think, but on the Western frontier an advantage may possibly be gained—& there is no point on which a temporary success would be more disastrous— Whatever force we have there can not be very quickly reinforced, & the adjoining States are full of our worst enemies.— Sir John might safely, after the complete frustration of the attack below, send another regiment to that frontier or to London & I hope he has done so— The London Press, I am happy to see is giving your Excellency great credit for your action & thorough preparation to meet the looked for storm— I shall continue to be anxious till I hear from, or of, the West—

Some days ago I got a letter from Ld. Glenelg on the subject of the Leg Council, to which I believe I should have called attention in vain but for your recent letter of 29th. October— I answered it promptly & regret I have not the draft of my answer with me that I might send it to you, but I shall send it on my return to Cheltenham— I recommended your list being taken as it was—adding (if Ld. Glenelg thought fit) Mr. Tucker, who should be in, I think. My letter produced a request that I shd. if possible come to town to see Ld. Glenelg on that & other matters[.]

It was not quite convenient—but of course I came & I commenced my acquaintance with Ld. Glenelg to-day— He seemed to have made up his mind to take only part of your list— Sir George Grey was with him, & between ourselves, I think his Lordship would do in some respects better without him— I fought hard for the admission of the Vice Chancellor & Mr. Sullivan but am not sure that I succeeded—the objection being that the latter is an officer of the Govt's. and the former a *Judge*, & that the House of Commons were against any Judges being appointed &c. I assured them that recommendation did not extend to Equity Judges, for evident reasons but whether the objections will be finally withdrawn in regard to both or either I cant say— However there will be small time for reflection, for His Lordship I believe expects to get the Mandamuses signed tomorrow—

Sir John Colborne is made Governor in Chief—the Commission will be signed tomorrow— It will be very flattering to the General; & is a better step than the sending out Lord Spencer or any of that class of politicians, & better I think than the vesting the Govt. in any Civilian just now, unless indeed some person could be found of very superior qualifications— I doubt whether Sir John will altogether like it— He hoped & wished to escape from the turmoil of a Colonial government, & I am inclined to think his health requires it— His reign I dare say, will not (with his own consent) be long—

Lord Glenelg discussed many matters with me very agreeably & apparently with much cordiality & confidence— He is obliged to attend a Cabinet Council tomorrow at Windsor—& on thursday I shall leave this to join Mrs. Robinson who is on a visit to Lady Head— Soon after we return to Cheltenham I shall again visit London—& should have staid a day or two longer now, if Ld. Glenelg had wished it, but he did not press it, & it is more convenient to me at present that he did not—

Lord Durham is in town, & I shall see him tomorrow— I am told his papers have not yet arrived, or at least that they had not very lately, & that he has not yet submitted his scheme— I doubt whether he is prepared to lay before the Govt. any measure complete in it's [*sic*] details—but I shall learn tomorrow I dare say, & I think I shall keep my letter open, & let you know— I should like to hear what others suggest, & what the Government are inclined to, before I propose my own course, which however (be it right or wrong), I think I have fully made up my mind to.— You will easily understand that I am placed in a situation of some difficulty, for more reliance seems to be placed in my judgment I fear, than it deserves & moreover let whatever course be adop[ted] so much depends on the policy of the executive afterwards, that we can feel no confidence that any experiment will have a fair chance— The Montreal Merchants, the Military, the Govemt.—Lord Durham, all have their notions of what *alone* will save the Country—& no doubt they are right in some things—& wrong in others, & will agree only in crying out agt. any plan that does not exactly tally with their opinions— For my own part I have no ambition to be the originator of a scheme—though I would not shrink from it— I am at any body's service, to help in a good measure, & at nobody's service in a bad one— I feel no other embarrassment than a serious difficulty in assuring myself that I can discern the true road among so many that lie open to our choice—Something must now be done, it ought to be final and decisive—whatever it may be, & from whatever quarter it comes, I shall leave nothing undone to guard the interests of Upper Canada, as I understand them—I may in my zeal miss my road as many a much wiser person has done before me—

I suppose the Govt. must wait for Ld. Durham's communication but this is the time for consideration, & I much fear the multitude of other pressing business may drive it off, till the Parlt. meets, or nearly so, & then all will be hurry— I shall probably however hear more in a very few days— In the course of tomorrow I shall be able I hope to drive down to Sir W. Horton, who is not yet quite recovered— He had a narrow escape. . .

[P.S.] Lord Glenelg told me today a Principal for U C. College had gone out a Dr. Mc.Call [*i.e.* McCaul] (*Irish*)—

[The letter referred to is apparently item 541.]

[556] C. C. DOMVILE TO COLONEL [FREDERICK] MAUNSELL: LB.4, p. 42.

Dec. 11 *Government House, Toronto.*

I am directed by His Excellency the Major General Commanding to enclose you a Copy of an intercepted letter from a deserter of the 85th. Regt (named Henry Rose) dated Buffalo N.Y. 5th December—to Richard Cluff a private in the above Corps.

His Excellency is desirous that you should direct the Private Richard Cluff to answer the enclosed, and to upbraid the Writer with his dishonorable and criminal conduct, with such other matter as you may think proper to insert.

It will be desirable to avoid letting Rose know that his letter has been intercepted.

[Superscription reads: Colonel Maunsell 85th Regt London."]
[Enclosure lacking.]

[557] C. C. DOMVILE TO [RICHARD LOVE ?]:[1] LB.4, p. 42-43.

Dec. 11 *Government House, Toronto.*

I am directed by His Excellency the Major General to inform you that the left wing of your regiment will be with you immediately.—

His Excellency has just heard that in consequence of stress of weather the Traveller in which they were was obliged to put into Presqu'isle.

The Major General hopes that you will be able to procure good quarters for the left wing at Brantford[.]

[558] COLBORNE TO ARTHUR : L.S. with emendations in Colborne's handwriting. 10p.

Dec. 12 *Montreal.*

I intended to thank you for your letter of the 1st inst, soon after I received it, and I can scarcely offer any excuse for the delay which has taken place in my reply, except that for the last week I have been much perplexed and embarrassed by the provoking conduct of Judges and the conflicting opinions of Crown Officers— I am persuaded that the Brigands, trusting to their reported numbers, will not disperse unless we can shew a respectable regular force to receive them on our side—

It appears from the several accounts that the point at which the Brigands are to assemble is to the Southward of Detroit, and that they think themselves sufficiently strong to disembark below Amherstburg— The Fort at Amherstburg was repaired that the Militia might occupy it on an emergency and maintain themselves till the Brigands could be attacked in force.—

We must use every effort to keep our ground at Sandwich, and Amhers[t]burg; and prevent the Marauders from pouring in by the Detroit; But to lock up the 34th. merely in defending the Fort would, I think, be a great error.

Gosfield is a very good point to occupy if you can find cover for a Regt.; I should however wish to post another Regt. of the Line at Amherstburg—

The easy passage to deserters is the only consideration against this move. I should recommend provisions to be kept in the Fort for 300 men, for fourteen days, and a Garrison of Militia appointed to cccupy it on an emergency, for we must not suppose that the Brigands will be able to break ground or make any impression on it— In this case, if two Regts. of the Line, with about 500 Militia attached to them, are ready to move against any force landing above Sandwich, or in the Townships of Malden Colchester or Gosfield,—this column wd. probably disperse any force the Brigands might land; and return to Amherstburg— It must however much depend on the judgment and intelligence of the Officer in Command what force should be left to guard Amherstburg and Sandwich—as it will of course be a great object with the Brigands to draw off the Troops from the Detroit and open thus a passage, and establish themselves—

I have no doubt that two Battalions of the Line should be well closed up at Amherstburg or near it— They will find their way through any

[1]Love was lieut.-colonel commanding the 73rd Regiment which, after being in action in Lower Canada (items 435, 436, 437), was moved to Upper Canada (item 505), evidently to Kingston (item 537), and thence to Brantford (item 538). The letter was probably written to Love concerning his regiment.

force landing in their rear— With these moveable Columns the Brigands cannot succeed— Colonel Maitland being ill will I imagine remain at St. Thomas or London. Major Lloyd of the 73rd., if Colonel Love can spare him, might be sent to Sandwich.—

We may safely calculate on the difficulty the Brigands will find in making their movements simultaneously and preventing our attacking them in detail— I cannot imagine you have much to fear from any internal movement in the London District except the Brigands maintain their ground for any time— I should prefer two Regiments of the Line being placed at London with 500 Militia attached to them—

This Column would be prepared to move either on Amherstburg or on any Brigand force which might have effected a landing on Lake Erie Shore or the St. Clair— The Niagara frontier and the coast from Fort Erie to the Mouth of the Grand River we must always be anxious to protect[.]

The 43d. Regt. might be supported from Toronto by a wing of the 65th. or the 93d., if the Brigands collect at Buffalo, with 500 Militia.

This Column would be able to make head against any force that could be suddenly brought against it— Major Es[t]court should Col: Booth continue on the sick list you may rely on; he will perform his part well—

Three Comps. of the 65th. Regt. move on Thursday Morning— They had better proceed to Toronto if things go on well at Kingston— The remainder of the 65th. are at Quebec but will be prepared to Move the moment I can ascertain that the 11th. Regt. can be spared from New Brunswick— A Battery of Artillery shall be sent to Kingston before the end of this month or the beginning of Janry.

I cannot send the demi-Battery which I promised you immediately— Col: Cubitt must remain for a time with a reduced force—

At Boston, they are recruiting for the Detroit frontier from the unemployed Irish—150 started a few days since for Burlington, in Vermont, with arms packed— Gagnon is on our frontier with about 400 Canadians—

We have in the Montreal Goal about 650 Prisoners— The Court Martial has tried 12[.] I have ordered the Court to adjourn till the Law Officers can determine whether the Offenders can be tried, under the Ord[i]nance of the Special Council for Treason— The word Treason not being mentioned in it "eo nomine"[.]

If Col: Maitland cannot proceed with his Regt. the 34th. and 32d. will be under the immediate Command of Lt. Col. Airey and the 73d. & 85th. under Col: Love— I should think you need not be uneasy about Brantford— The Troops from London would menace the disaffected near the Grand River and keep them in order; as they would reach them in two marches waggons being prepared for their conveyance[.]

I hope to be able to send another Regt. for the Niagara Frontier before the Navigation closes[.]

If the Brigands were in great force, they surely would not come across in small gangs as they have lately done— I agree with Mr. Fox that a fearful example must be made of the Ruffians who are taken—

[559] [ARTHUR] TO [RAYMOND BABY AND PAUL L'EVEQUE]: Df.L. 6p.

[1838] [*Toronto.*]

[*c. Dec. 13*] Messieurs,

J'ai reçu avec beaucoup de plaisir l'Addresse que vous m'avez presentée de la part des Canadiens d'origine française residant dans cette ville et ses environs, en assurance de leur attachment inviolable a l'Empire Britannique et de leur détermination à en maintenir la Suprematie dans le Haut Canada par tous les moyens en leur pouvoir.

Cette declaration de leurs Sentimens est d'autant plus appréciable qu'elle forme un contraste agréable à la conduite d'une partie des Canadiens d'origine française dans la Province inférieure; conduite dont les suites se sont retombées, dans deux occasions récentes, sur eux-mêmes et sur les instigateurs de leur crime d'une manière, quoique juste, bien effroyable.—

Il serait bien surprenant à la verité, qu'aucun individu parmi nous, de quel-que soit son origine fut il vraiement pénétré des sentimens qu'ont exprimés ceux que vous répresentez, pût considérer sans éprouver la plus parfaite indignation son pays natal, ou le pays qu'il a adopté, envahi,— ses frères et ses co-sujets massacrés et ses proprietés ruinées par une horde d'étrangers barbares et déréglés, venus d'un état apparemment amicable et au milieu d'une paix la plus profonde.

Je remercie les Signataires de cette Addresse [*sic*] de l'offre spontane qu'ils me font de leur services pour aider à venger les droits outragés de notre Souveraine très gracieuse et j'en userai bien volontiers dans l'occasion.

J'aime à croire cependent et je le desire bien sincèrement qu'à l'avenir aucune circonstance ne m'obligera de les mettre en operation.—

J'apprecie grandement aussi l'aveu que contient cette addresse où les Signataires reconnoissent qu'ils ont jouis sous la Couronne Britannique de la liberté la plus entière, et que la gratitude et l'intérêt doivent également les porter à prendre les armes pour sa défense, car indépendamment de l'hommage que la Justice rend à la Verité, elle renferme un fait, lequel dans ses circonstances principaux est rigoureusement applicable à tous les Canadiens d'origine française dans les deux Provinces—

L'expression de l'entière confiance avec laquelle il se reposent sur mon administration ne peut que m'être tres flatteuse, mais son succès dépend beaucoup de l'union qui regenera parmi nous. Je vous assure que je continuerai à faire tous mes efforts pour m'assurer cette coopération que je desire si ardemment, en adoptant les mésures les plus propres à avancer les intêrets du publique.

[The above is apparently a draft of a reply to an address from the Canadians of French origin residing in the City of Toronto, presented to Arthur on their behalf by Baby and L'Eveque. It appears in English, along with the address, in the *Upper Canada Gazette, Extraordinary*, Dec. 13, 1838.]

[560] ARTHUR TO COLONEL [CHARLES] CHICHESTER: LB.1, p. 233-235.

Dec. 13 *Government House, Toronto.* [Marked "Private."]

I transmit to you a letter from the Military Secretary, marked Confidential— The subject speaks for itself, and has given me extreme vexation.— My wish is, that you would use the best means of getting the information required, in a manner, the least calculated to wound Colonel Prince's feelings, which I wish to avoid, forward a copy of the confidential to him, with a very few lines simply requesting the information I have desired.—

Last night I received your letter of the 10th. Instant on your return from the West.—

I quite agree with you about not separating the Regular force—it has been *my earnest wish*, that not less than two Regiments should be able to act together; and by sending on the 32nd. to Gosfield, I thought this end would be best attained, so far as the Western District is concerned.

The 73rd. & the 85th. might then be brought so near that they might also act together to meet any force that should penetrate towards the London District, from Sarnia or elsewhere on the St Clair Frontier.

If a good look out be kept on the St. Clair we can always be before hand with any movement from that quarter—if the Officer Commanding sends off information to the London District, as well as to Chatham.—

I thought Colonel Radcliffe [*i.e.* Radcliff] had been so popular a person that he would readily have completed his Battalion; and, if so, I was satisfied from the nature of the Country, that he might have kept almost any hostile force in check, even if he was not able to destroy them.

Whatever Militia we have out should be well trained in essentials, for they would then soon become efficient— I allude to this because I observe all the Militia Officers are too much disposed to overlook the advantage of Military Movement—pray enjoin it everywhere, it strikes me they must have been surprised[.]

I am glad so many stragglers have been picked up since the affair at Windsor, as you mention; but, still, I cannot comprehend, with the Force at Sandwich, how they got off so well—it is not easy, from Colonel Prince's report, to know how many Troops he brought against them.

I purpose crossing to the Westward in a few days— will you previously consider, what force horse and foot, you think you will require for the London and Western Districts during the Winter—and where you would recommend that they should be stationed— Not only for the sake of economy; but for the comfort and well being of the Yeomanry I should wish not to keep any Militia out—except Volunteers—beyond what are absolutely necessary.

[Enclosure lacking.]

[561] [ANONYMOUS]: TO ARTHUR: L.

Dec. 13 [*Postmark: Waterford* (?), *N.Y., and Kingston.*]

To His Exellency Sir George Arthur k c n &c &c &c

I was greatly astonished to hear of the execution of the brave and jeneros Von Scholtz and the intended execution on wensday of George & Abbey. as to the testimony given by Chipman it is utterley and totally false but your officers have hired him to lie. but if you go on with the exicution of the unfortunate but inocent men your tyrany and inhuman butchery will meet from heaven the dreaded vengance which you deserve and i hope it will come soon. if you do inhumanly butcher all those men you will arouse the indignation of every good citizen of the United States. (and mind ye that our next President does not row in the same boat with those Hellish British governers in the Canadas as Van Buren has done) who will do as did the jeneros Lafyette but with a more just right, The reports by the Loyal papers concerning the treatment of Lieu Johnson are a pack of confounded Lies as base as your hirelings could invent. but Lieing is a prominent charactaristick of your prentended Loyal subjects. Your treatment to Miss Lount is enough to call down vengence upon your infamous head. but the time is fast coming when if you remain in this continent you will be placed in worse condition than Lount who died in the glorious cause of liberty when you are beging for life then will you think of those martyrs whom you unjustly condemned to death[.]

if you wish to know who i am

i have got a plenty of cast iron steel & brass and pills nade of lead also some charcoal sal nitre &c[.] i am thinking that you want to take a dose of those pills[.]

I am from Van Deimans land and know you well[.]

[562] [ANONYMOUS]: TO ARTHUR: L.

Dec. 13 *Syracuse.*

Vile and Misserable wretch

I improve this opertunity of sending you those few lines merely to hint in the most delicate manner in the world that you are a damd murderer and Cut throat the Cries of those poor victims that you butcherd has assended to the almity and he has Chosen us to be thair evengers thare in know at this vary moment 9:000 Brave fellows ready to march in to Canada and send evary john bull that there is in it to perdition and you you infemous wretch [tear in MS.] head and that in not all are another mount pases away you will see the Stripes and Stars on eavary wall in Canada and then john bull will Curse the day that eavery hung Von Shoult and his Companions was it in my power which i hope it will be are long i would erect a gallows high as hamon to Hang your Cursed Carces. on

The star spangled banner in trioumph shall wave
ore the land of the free and the home of the brave—

A friend to liberty.

[563] C. C. DOMVILE TO COLONEL [HENRY] DUNDAS: LB.4, p. 43.

Dec. 13 *Government House, Toronto.*

I am directed by the Major General Commanding to call your attention to the defence of Wolf's [*i.e.* Wolfe] Island, and to suggest to you Whether, from the temptation its position holds out to the Brigands from the other side to endeavour to cut off the small force at present stationed there, it should not either be occupied by a large force, and one competent to defend it or left without any—and whether it is a position of sufficient importance to be garrisoned at all.—

In case you should think it desirable to occupy the Island, His Excellency would suggest the propriety of sending an Engineer Officer to examine its capabilities of defence, and to report upon the number of men that would be required to hold it.—

[564] ARTHUR TO COLONEL [F. A. M.] FRAZER [*i.e.* FRASER]: LB. 1, p. 240-243.

Dec. 14 *Government House, Toronto.*

I have this moment received your letter of the 11th. Instant, and, as I understand there is a return orderly I lose no time in acknowledging it.—

The information you afford me in so clear and concise a form is very acceptable.—

At the same time that I received your former letter Letter [*sic*] informing me, that you were going on to Amherstburg and that Colonel Airey had applied for two Companies and the Guns, I received a letter from him, intimating that he had been assured from General Brady, that the attack on Sandwich was a feint, and that the main attack would be made upon Amherstburg.

On the same day a deposition was laid before me, to the effect that a very considerable force of the Ruffians, calling themselves Patriots, were on their way from the interior of Michigan and Ohio, to join in the attack on the Western Frontier—and also, that a depot of Provisions and Ammunition had been formed at "Put in" Island.

Under these circumstances I thought the advance of the 32nd Regt to support the 34th. was a prudent measure, and would rather be in in [*sic*] unison with, than in opposition to the view I have taken of not separating the Corps of the line. I wrote off therefore instantly to direct the advance to Gosfield of the 32nd. Regt, which had already advanced sixty miles on the road.— It struck me, as Colonel Airey had requested to be reinforced, that, on reflection, you would have paused in sending back the 32nd. Regt. until you had communicated with Colonel Chichester & therefore hoped the Corps would not have returned to London.—

I should wish of all things that the whole Frontier duty should be taken by the Militia, and that neither Amherstburg nor Gosfield were occupied by Troops of the Line, but that they were held in reserve at Chatham or some still more convenient station.—

Just now however, this could not be done, and, as I shall have the 73rd & 85th. to act together, & as I do hope desertion is not now to be apprehended, it will be as well for the 32nd. Regiment to be stationed at Gosfield, where I expect, good accommodation will be found for them, as well as for the Militia.—

My former letter was written in the hope that the 32nd had not returned, if under any circumstances the Corps should still be at London, there let them remain until further orders.

I am much gratified to find that the conduct of the Troops was so good during the March.—

With respect to Isle Bois Blanc, I was not aware that more than one blockhouse had been ordered— Colonel Barou is ordered to visit the West immediately.—

If the clearing of the Island were absolutely necessary to the defence of Amherstburg, I conceive the authority I gave to Colonel Airey was quite sufficient.—

With regard to the St Clare [*sic*] I am of opinion that 200 men are not enough for its defence, because I think it is a point from whence we are most vulnerable, and I have lately written to Colonel Chichester upon the subject.—

Colonel Radcliff's Corps in Adelaide however should be quite enough, if he can raise one so promptly as was expected, if not we must have other Troops there.—

I am glad to find that the Coloured People are turning out better, but I do not wish that any men who have been drafted should be kept out a day longer than is necessary.

We have too many cavalry out, and they are not so conveniently stationed as might be desired.—

I do not think there is any reason to regret your tour, as Personal Knowledge of the country is so essential, especially in your Department, provided all has been well done in your office, and no unnecessary expense incurred.

I propose at length prosecuting my long intended journey to the West, and shall leave Toronto on Monday, reach Brantford that evening—Woodstock the following day & from thence on to London—this may perhaps enable me to inspect the 34th Regt. on Saturday.

[565] H. S. Fox to Arthur: A.L.S. 2p.

Dec. 14 *Washington.* [Marked "Private".]

The inclosed is the copy of a letter which I have written this day to Sir John Colborne.— The matter refers to Lower, rather than Upper Canada; but I shall equally apprize you of any thing further that occurs in it.— And perhaps you will be able to furnish me with information similar to what I ask from Sir John Colborne.— We must be excessively cautious with regard to names.—

[Enclosure is apparently item 570.]

[566] C. A. Hagerman to Arthur: A.L.S.

[*1838*] *Toronto.*

Dec. 14 I send your Excellency a letter I received to-day from Mr. Draper—I will call in the course of tomorrow morning and take your Excellencys Instructions upon it.— Difficulties appear to have arisen which ought to have been guarded against, but for which he is in no way blameable.—

[Enclosure lacking.]

[567] C. A. Hagerman to Arthur: A.L.S.

Dec. 14 *Toronto.*

I must beg your Excellency to receive as my excuse for the imperfect and slovenly appearance of the accompanying paper, the constant interruptions to which I have been subject while writing it.— It may serve as a suggestion of some arguments in favour of an application to the American Authorities,—others, and of greater weight, will I doubt not occur to your Excellency.—

[Enclosure referred to is probably item 568.]

[568] C. A. H[agerman]: A.M.initialled. 4p.

[*1838*] [*Place not stated.*]

[*Dec. 14?*] Should the Lieutenant Governor think it expedient to make any requisition upon the Government of the United States, to deliver up the leading rebels and Brigands now in that Country it appears to me that arguments founded on the following views of the question may be with propriety adopted.—

It is impossible for any intelligent and dispassionate person not to see, that the two Countries are placed in circumstances of the greatest danger of coming into hostile collision, from the extensive organization among the Citizens of the United States having for its object the subjugation of these Provinces, and their separation from Great Britain;— in furtherance of the designs of this party, this Province has been invaded, while in a State of internal peace, not less than six times [marginal entry here reads: "Navy Island Schooner Ann Point Pelé Short Hills Prescot(t) Sandwich Fighting Island"] by several hundreds of the

Citizens of the United States within the last 12 months;—and in the course of the Contests which ensued, many of Her Majesty's Subjects were murdered, their houses burnt and their property destroyed.— Retaliation for these great injuries, would be regarded by most men at least excusable, but the Inhabitants of the Country have hitherto forborne to seek it at their own hands, although it is not to be disguised that there are indications of growing impatience, and a desire for summary retributive justice, that may lead to a vindictive border Warfare that no humane mind can contemplate without a feeling of horror.— In the mean time the British Nation, is compelled to incur an expense in protecting these Provinces from invasion from the United States—a Country with which it is (nominally) at peace,—little less in amount than if a War between the two Nations actually existed.— Giving credit to the American Government for a Sincere desire to put an end to outrages committed by its Citizens, so disgraceful to their national character—and so destructive of the peace and happiness of the Canadas,—it nevertheless ought not to be over looked that Great Britain may not long submit to receive as an excuse for the non-fulfilment of the treaties that bind the two nations to the maintenance of Peace with each other, that it has not the power of compelling its Citizens to observe and pay respect either to their own Laws, or the Laws of any civilized community—and should this attitude be assumed by the British Government, there is little doubt but a National War would be the result.—

Hitherto the Troops of the line and the Militia of the Province, have successfully repelled all attempts to keep possession of any part of the Country by the Invaders, and in the course of their opperations [*sic*] they have captured some hundreds of the Brigands opposed to them, who are now in prison at the Mercy of their Captors, and liable to be executed for their Crimes.— To inflict extreme punishment on all those guilty persons (however right in the abstract) is repugnant to the feelings and disposition of the Government; and it would gladly avail itself of any reasonable ground of excuse to the injured people of the Country, for setting at liberty a large number of these Criminal[s] in the hope that such clemency might have a favourable effect on the conduct of others, and prevent their falling into similar acts of wickedness.—

With the double object of punishing the first instigators and principal leaders of the invading party, and supplying a motive for indulgently treating the least guilty of the Brigands it might be proposed to the United States Government to deliver to the British Authorities the persons of William Lyon McKenzie, Duncombe—Johns[t]on—Birge and any others that may be selected.—

Against each of these persons charges may be established not in their nature political:—such as Murder and Robbery against McKenzie and Duncombe; and of felony in appearing in Arms against Her Majesty in this Province from a foreign Country—against Johns[t]on and Birge—an offence which should not be regarded as a political offence any more than a Riot or other unlawful assembly.—

If these persons were delivered up and punished, there is little doubt but that an effectual check will be put to further aggressions— if not— they will be continued—and for the consequences the American Government will be alone responsible.—

If His Excellency should make any communication to Mr. Fox—I would recommend [its] being Confidential.—

[569] [LORD] FITZROY [J. H.] SOMERSET TO ARTHUR: A.L.S. 2p.

Dec. 14 *Horse Guards, [London.]*

I have received your private letters to the 14th Novr. and beg to offer you my best acknowledgements for them and the interesting papers you inclosed with them[.] The same Mail brought us letters of a later date from Montreal with the Official report of the capture of the Sympathizers at Prescott; and I avail myself of the present opportunity to congratulate you on this first result of the Invasion which will probably serve[?] as a Wholesome Check on such Enterprizes in future.

Pray continue to let me hear from you—

[570] H. S. FOX TO COLBORNE: A.L.S. 7p.

Dec. 14 *Washington.* [Marked "Copy Private and Confidential."]

The name of the Polish brigand officer, now at New York, alluded to in my letter to you of the 7th. instant, who has offered to make disclosures to me upon being paid for it, is Oklamski.— Mr: Featherstonhaugh, an English Gentleman in whom I have entire confidence, is the medium of my communications to him.— This Pole has been formerly in the Russian, and in the French service; and is apparently an active and intelligent man.— He states that he was engaged in the affair at Odell Town, and after the failure there escaped into the United States.— He declares that he is in the full confidence of Papineau, and the other leaders. He says that they are now engaged in organizing a plan for another outbreak in *Lower* Canada; and that he expects, in about a week later, to get possession of, and show to Mr: Featherston[haugh], the original sketch of this plan, drawn up by Papineau and Nelson— Mr: F. has the means of verifying Papineau's handwriting, but not Nelson's. The contents of such a paper would be well worth my obtaining for you.— But of course there is a risk of the man being either an impostor, or a double traitor.— The evidence taken in the trials now going on at Montreal and at Kingston, and the disclosures made by those amongst the prisoners, if any, who are turning Queen's evidence, may perhaps enable you to assist me in judging of the probable usefulness of the Pole's information.— If he was of the party at Odell Town, he must be known to the Frenchman, Hindenlang, who was taken there.— It wd. be very desirable to know, whether he is likely to be speaking the truth, when he says that he is in the confidence of Papineau and the leaders.— The value of his disclosures will depend of course chiefly upon that point.— He may probably be known to Von Schoultz, the other Pole, who was taken at Prescott, who I suspect is willing to make disclosures also.— I shall send a copy of this letter to Sir George Arthur: but in the mean time, you will be able to communicate upon the subject, if you think it right, with those who conduct the trials at Kingston, more quickly than the same can be done viâ Toronto.— I will write you word, as soon as I obtain any further intelligence: you will naturally perceive the necessity of great caution and secrecy with respect to names.—

[The above was apparently an enclosure in item 565.]

[571] J. S. MACAULAY TO ARTHUR: A.L.S. 8p.

Dec. 15 *Toronto.*

In a recent conversation I had the honor of holding with Your Excellency, you seemed, as I thought, to indulge the expectation, that, because certain very respectable American Citizens, discountenance the proceedings of the Societies organized for the attack of this Province, and because the public authorities are in some instances acting with good faith, we may relax in our military preparations, and thus save further expence: the more so since the results of the late piratical attacks, and the explanations which have been consequently promulgated by the Government, have done much to dissipate the delusions of the American people.

Your Excellency cannot have forgotten that when the piratical attacks of last winter had been repulsed, and our Jails were tenanted by many American Citizens, similar assurances were given by the respectable portion of the American people, who, as now, desired to divert Your Excellency from the painful duty of punishing the Americans who had fallen into our hands.

Waite assured Your Excellency, that the fact of his not having been joined by any of the Canadians at the short hills, would of a certainty dissipate the delusions of the Frontier people,—yet they have not been dispelled, simply, because the American people are not under any delusion; unless it be a delusion, to imagine that they can worry the British Government into the abandonment of the North American Possessions.

The Americans generally, and our frontier neighbours particularly, know that when an attempt at insurrection was made last year, the people of this Country put it down, without the aid of a single British soldier: and they do not believe, that a people who would not accept republican institutions, when no impediment to such acceptance existed, would declare themselves favourable to those republican institutions, when the Country is filled with armed men, and soldiery, resolved to perish, rather than submit to their introduction.

Von Sch[o]ultz may possibly have been led to believe that trial by Jury was unknown in Canada, and that those who came to introduce it, would be hailed as deliverers; but Theller can plead no such ignorance, yet this man after the merciful treatment received from the British Government, shews, not that acknowledgement of error, which might have been reasonably expected, but on the contrary is now taking an active part among the enemies of the British name; and will, I feel assured, be one of a party to assail this province again, next winter, if not during the present season.

If it be true that the respectable Citizens of the United States repudiate the conduct of our frontier foes, is it not strange, that throughout the extended domain of the Union, no public meeting of that respectable class has yet been held to give expression to their opinions? Does it not necessarily lead to the conclusion that the respectable portion of the American Citizens, are either insincere in their professions, or are so numerically contemptible, that they dare not give public utterance to their sentiments.

Johnston and Birge have both escaped from the custody of the American Authorities— Had they been two run-away slaves, seeking this land of true liberty, would such escape have been permitted?

Be assured Sir, that the game now playing by the American people will be persevered in, until they drive the British out of Canada, or until a war with Great Britain, shall have taught them the impossibility of subjugating the Canadas, and shall have dismembered their Union.

Foiled this year in their piratical attacks they will renew them next winter, if not sooner, and though they have no expectation of gaining a footing in the Country, yet they *calculate* that by compelling the British Government to incur an enormous annual expenditure in defence of Her North American Provinces, that Government will soon arrive at the conclusion, that the possessions so maintained are not worth the cost.

In this expectation the Americans shew their usual sagacity, for if the British Government permit this system of border warfare to be continued from year to year, and the same cost of defence to be annually incurred, the British people will soon compel the Government to give up the Colonies, or to draw the sword. They confidently look to the former alternative being chosen, we, the latter: and if our judgment be correct, the sooner the conclusion is arrived at, the better.

The Americans unprepared for war would not long be able to withstand the force, moral and physical, with which they would be assailed; assuming always that the British Government embarked in this war, with the intention, (and consequent exhibition of strength), of bringing it to a termination, before other Powers could have time to make the necessary preparations for engaging therein.

If the British Government desire the peaceful occupation of these Provinces, they must compel the Americans to respect our soil, which they never will unless they are made to pay well for their late most unjustifiable and barbarous attacks.

Judging from the conduct of the Americans generally, it appears not unreasonable to assert, that the assurances of a class which does not embrace the majority of the people, is of no value whatever.

While certain respectable persons at a distance are assuring Your Excellency, that there is an end to the sympathy (as they are pleased to term it) of the American Citizens, and that no further attacks will be made upon us, a meeting at Buffalo, in our immediate neighbourhood is attended by thousands, where it is asserted (as I am informed) that the people have a right to wage war without the consent of the Government, and that any attempt of the Executive to restrain them is unconstitutional. These circumstances lead to the conclusion that we should wait to see the action of the multitude; putting no faith in the assurances of the few, however respectable, and persevering quietly in making preparations for that war, which however amiably disposed the American Government may be, they apparently lack the power to avert.

I have preferred addressing Your Excellency in writing, rather than expressing verbally my opinions on the subject matter herein contained, because should you deem those opinions of any value they are in this form more available for the consideration of others, who from their longer residence in America, and their more intimate acquaintance with its inhabitants, may fairly be deemed more competent to give an opinion as to the probable action of the people under existing circumstances.

[572] J. S. MACAULAY: A.M.S. 2p.

[*1838* ?] [*Place not stated.*]

[*Dec. 15* ?] Memoranda for the Attack of Fort Niagara[.]

Let all the Boats that can be procured be assembled under a Guard, in a position favourable for embarkation, the pretence being that they are collected least [*sic*] they should fall into other hands.

Let the Sappers and Miners make a few, (8 or 10) light ladders, and a good supply of gabions, and chevaux de Frise[.]

Let three leather bags be prepared capable of holding about 60 Pounds of Powder each, with a short port fire attached ready for ignition.

A Battalion of Infantry being at no great distance will take, a rather unfrequented route (known), to arrive near the point of embarkation towards evening, care being taken that the inhabitants are not made acquainted with the intended attack.

Two divisions will proceed to the attack, the one landing between the village and the fort, the other attacking on the river side.

There is a door on the north side of the main building which probably might be easily reached by a Sapper with a bag of powder, who will attach and light it; twelve men will be ready to rush forward, on its explosion.

The Sappers will carry the ladders and axes, each of the attacking parties having a bag of Powder and a proportion of scaling ladders with them.

The two first divisions landed, the boats return to take over the remainder of the infantry, who if the place is carried, proceed immediately to attack the village and entrench themselves there[;] for this purpose the gabions and chevaux de Frise will be passed over with as little delay as possible.

If the place should not be carried the troops entrench themselves in the most favourable positions, and form a cordon round the Fort. A Rocket Brigade will then be passed over and an attempt made to fire the buildings which as they are all covered with and some are entirely composed of wood, will not be a very difficult operation.

In the mean while the heavy ordnance are to keep a constant fire of round shot upon the reverse of the land fronts which may be carried by day should the night attack fail of which there is however little probability if the details be well managed and perfect secrecy as to the intended attack be preserved.

[The above is filed with item 571 and is written on similar paper, with corresponding folds. Item 571 is endorsed: "Mr Macaulay 15 Decr 1838 Fort Niagara." It is therefore probable that the two items approximate in date.]

[573] [JOHN] TUCKER & [GEORGE] LAURIES TO ARTHUR: A.L.S. 3p.

Dec. 15 [*33, Broad street,*] *New York.*

We have received a letter from Messrs. Hyde, Hodge & Co of London per. Ship 'Westminster' dated 8th. Octr., requesting that we would aid Ketunah Hammond (whom they had sent by that Vessel as a servant for Lady Arthur), and put her in the way of proceeding to Toronto:—also to enter at the Custom House & pay the Duty, on two cases containing wearing apparel, which were sent by the same Vessel.—

On going to the Custom House, the Collector promptly & courtiously [*sic*] gave us a free permit for the two cases, to be landed without duty & without examination, on the ground that they contained the baggage of Your Excellency— and as the journey is long, & the Rivers & Canals closed by ice, we have had the cases covered with tarred canvass—to protect them as much as possible, from the weather while in the Boot or on the top of Stage Coaches.— We have had them marked as the baggage of Kitunah [*sic*] Hammond, in order that they may go more easily forward.

As the extra expense of transporting these cases will probably be considerable; and as Mr. Hyde expected that the Young Woman, as well as the cases, would have been here in time to go by the Rivers & Canals, he did no[t] furnish her with sufficient funds for her journey by Stage Coach—& we have therefore given her Fifty Dollars here—which Messrs Hyde Hodge & Co will repay us.

This sum, no doubt, will be fully more than what she will require—& we have requested her to pay the extra charges for transporting the cases, & to account for the same on her arrival at Toronto.— A passenger in the Westminster, (a Mr. Evans—) who is on his way to Toronto, has kindly promised to give his protection to the Young Woman on the journey.—

Mr. Evans has promised to deliver this to Your Excellency—& in the hope that the cases may reach Canada in safety, We remain—

[574] [G. Evans ?]:[1] M. 2p.

[*1838*] [*Place not stated.*]

[*c. Dec. 15*]

Pd. extra for luggage from New York

	$ c
Freight by steamer from N. York to Newbury	2. . 0
Do by stage from Newbury to Albany the fares of 2 persons	13. . 0
Porterage from boat	0..50
Sleigh from stage across the Hudson	2..00
Porterage to railroad by sleigh	0..75
Freight by railroad to Utica the fare of one person	3.,75
Porter at Utica	0..25
Freight by stage from Utica to Rochester the fares of 2 persons	16. . 0
Porterage at Rochester	0:.50
Freight by stage to Lockport the fares of 2 persons	4. . 0
Freight by stage to Lewiston the fares of 2 persons	2. . 0
Porterage at Lockport	0..50
Sleigh at Lewiston to Ferry House	0..25
Ferry Waggon & taking charge of luggage	0..75

Paid for travelling expenses &c for K. Hammond

	$ c
Tea on board steamer for Albany	0..50
Fare of steamer	2. . 0
Stage from Newbury to Albany	6..50
Breakfast on road to Albany	0..50
Dinner on road to Albany at Hudson	0..50
1¾ days board fuel etc at American Hotel Albany	3..50
Dinner & tea at Utica	0..50
Railroad fare from Albany to Utica	3..75
Stage from Utica to Rochester	8. . 0
Bed & breakfast at Rochester	0..75
Stage from Rochester to Lockport	3. . 0
Dinner on road from Rochester	0..50
Hotel at Lockport	2. . 0
Stage from Lockport to Lewiston	1. . 0
Bed & breakfast at Lewiston	0..75
Hotel at Lewiston 2 days	3. . 0

[1]This undated document is doubtless some days later than the date here given to it. It is placed here because of its association with item 573.

	46 25	Ferry fare & luggage	0..37
Deduct Mr. Evans's share of porterage say	0..50	Tea bed & breakfast at Queenston	1..25
	2)45..75	Dinner on road to Hamilton	0..44
K. Hammond's share of freight say one half	$22.87	Tea on road to Hamilton	0..50
		Bed & breakfast at Hamilton	0..75
		Stage from Queenston to Hamilton	3..0
		Stage from Hamilton to Toronto	3..0
		Sleigh to Ferry House	0..12
			$46..18

Dr. Mr. Evans in Account with K. Hammond Cr

	$ c		$ c
Recd. of K. Hammond	10..0	Amount paid for travelling expenses board &c	46..18
Do	33..0	Amount of freight for luggage	22..87
Do	10..0		
Do	2..0		
	$55..0	Total paid for K. Hammond	69..5
		Total recd. by G. Evans of K. Hammond	55..0
		Balance due to G. Evans	$14..5

[575] ARTHUR TO GLENELG: LB.5, p. 304-314.

Dec. 17 *Government House, Toronto.* [Marked "Confidential".]

At so early a period as the 3rd. April last, I communicated to the Executive Council my desire for an investigation of the circumstances connected with the destruction of the Steamboat Caroline, with the intention of subsequently transmitting to your Lordship without delay such information as should be procured on that subject.

The mission of the Earl of Durham, combined with other events of pressing and immediate importance, caused the matter to be in a manner lost sight of, and the interest at first taken in it to subside, until at length demonstrations of hostility on the American Frontier and doubts of the sincerity of the United States Government seemed to promise an elucidation of the Caroline affair and the relations which were to subsist between the two Nations, if not more satisfactory, yet much more conclusive than would arise from a development of the facts attending the destruction of that vessel.

If the delay has occasioned no particular inconvenience to Her Majesty's Government (and I must observe I was not called upon for any Report) I cannot altogether regret that it has taken place, because so far as I understand the subject in dispute, events which have occurred in the interim have materially strengthened the ground to be taken by the British Government, and weakened in proportion that assumed by the United States; moreover, the communication by your Lordship of the correspondence of the American Minister and the affidavits and other Documents on which he so confidently asserts his right to demand reparation, have enabled me to direct the enquiries instituted in this country to the refutation of the Stigma of ferocious conduct and wanton cruelty attempted to be cast upon the Force engaged in the transaction, founded on Statements which, however worthy of the "Patriot" Newspapers of the American Frontier, I could never have expected would be seriously brought forward in an important negociation.

I have the honor to transmit herewith to your Lordship the several Depositions of persons engaged in the destruction of the "Caroline," all of whom are men of undoubted veracity, and I am satisfied that your Lordship would not easily believe them capable of the savage conduct that has been ascribed to them.

Your Lordship will perceive from the Documents

1st. That the destruction of the Steamboat in question was resolved on by Colonel Macnab, at the exigency of the moment without Orders from the Lieutenant Governor.

2ndly. That this Resolution was adopted in actual view of the Steamboat whilst she was engaged in carrying Troops and Munitions of War for the invasion of Upper Canada from the American Territory.

3rdly. That the Orders given by Captn Drew to his men and the arms with which they were furnished, namely sabres and pikes, alike shew that wanton injury, vindictive or just punishment, or even retaliatory measures of aggression against American Citizens, then in the actual commission of hostility, were not sought for.

4thly. That as it was decided to attack Navy Island, situate cloes above the Rapids leading immediately to the pitch of the Niagara Falls, in the midst of a strong current, and in a position, therefore, as easy of defence as it was difficult of approach, it became of the greatest and most urgent consequence to cut off the means of transporting artillery and ammunition from the American shore, as the acquisition of them might render the island, if not actually impregnable, at least difficult of capture without considerable sacrifice of life during a severe conflict.

5thly. That the Steamboat, having been laid up for the winter in Buffalo Harbour, was cut out of the ice under pretence of being employed to carry freight and passengers from the City of Schlosser, a place of no trade or resort, and to which, at that inclement season, a passage by water was most inconvenient, not to say dangerous, while, on the precise route along the shore, a railroad was in active operation.

6thly. That the Steamboat was cut out from the ice by a large assemblage of men at Buffalo, who individually could have no legitimate interest in her, or any lawful or merely contraband trade in which she could have been possibly expected to engage.

7thly. That the Caroline, instead of being employed in the route pretended, was actually engaged during the day and part of the night of the 29th December between Schlosser and Navy Island, the latter place being almost uninhabited except by the Brigands who had invaded it.

8thly. That, in the night of the 29th December, and when attacked, she had armed men on board, though probably not in great numbers, and also that there were armed men in the House at Schlosser who could have been no other than a part of the soi-disant Patriot Force.

9thly. That there was not for many days any civil or Military force of the United States at Schlosser, and that, at Buffalo, the authorities were either unwilling or unable to prevent aggression against Canada.

10thly. It appears from the letters of General Arcularius that the Patriots had committed acts of hostility against the Sovereignty of the United States in taking possession of the Ordnance and Arms of the Republic; and that there was no force at hand and no authority which could prevent these Ordnances and arms from being directly used as a part of the *Materiel* of the Patriot Army.

Lastly. It appears from the affidavits that there was no intention on the part of Captain Drew's Force of taking life: and that, in fact, only one or at most two lives were lost on the part of the "Patriots"; that these lives were taken in the Prosecution of an enterprize, undertaken and effected simply for selfpreservation; that the utmost humanity and forbearance and even protection were shewn by the attacking party, and that no one either dead or living was on board the Caroline when she was abandoned by the British Force.

Although, My Lord, I cannot be considered as having any personal interest in upholding or applauding the acts or conduct sanctioned by my Predecessor upon his own responsibility, I yet feel that I should be scarcely doing him justice were I not to offer for the consideration of Her Majesty's Government the arguments which occur to me in justification of the destruction of the Caroline.

My opinion is that not only that act was justifiable, but that a much more decided course of reprisal and occupation of American Territory might have been adopted without giving ground of offence to the United States Government, whereon it could justly demand reparation in accordance with the Law of Nations.

While expressing this opinion, I feel strongly that, viewing the question as one of expediency, Upper Canada is not the place for making reprisals, or provoking the U. States to retaliation, or even for the adoption of preservative measures which would involve the occupation of American Territory. England has so many available means of vindicating the honor of the Nation in other Quarters that I should prefer even the suffering of injury here, with the expectation that our National Rights would be asserted by the Government at Home, to any attempts which, with the means at my disposal, I could make in Canada to vindicate them.

I do not now consider what I should have done had I been placed in the same circumstances with my Predecessor; but I confidently maintain that the act sanctioned by him, namely the destruction of the Caroline, was fully justified both by circumstances and the Law of Nations, and that the United States have no reasonable ground for offence, or demand for reparation.

Considering the question in the view warranted by the facts, I should reject, as totally inapplicable, the term "Neutrality of the United States" made use of in the correspondence of the American Minister because, in fact, at the time of the occupation of Navy Island, there was no Civil War, nor any other War in Canada.

When the United States chose to receive within their Boundaries certain fugitives from justice in Canada—these persons would seem to have become, by the protection afforded them, United States Citizens, entitled to the protection of and bound to obey the laws of the country wherein the[y] sought refuge— The United States, on the other hand, being accountable for their conduct to a friendly power while under the flag of the Union and within it's [*sic*] jurisdiction, precisely as in the case of it's native Citizens.

Supposing, therefore, that the whole of the invaders at Návy Island had been previously fugitives from Canada, their invasion of the Province in hostile array could only have been considered as an invasion from the United States by American Citizens.

If American Citizens choose to make use of American Territory for the collection of an invading force, and use American vessels to transport the invading army with its arms and Munitions of War, the vessels which are thus used, and the Territory which is so occupied must, in my opinion, at least be considered as hostile.

The Profession of peace or of inability to restrain its citizens on the part of the Government does not relieve it from the imperative duty of preserving peace with an ally; nor can it prevent the territory openly used, or the vessels openly employed in hostility from being considered hostile, though it may be a sufficient ground for the preservation of peace between the two Nations.

In other words I do not consider it any insult to the flag of the United States to enter a portion of the American Territory if that portion be actually occupied by a number of it's citizens levying War against Great Britain in opposition to the will of the United States Government and beyond it's actual control for any purpose friendly or beneficial to England.

I consider it, My Lord, the duty of the United States Government not only to restrain it's citizens; but also, should these Citizens violate the bounds of Treaty and International Law, to bear all the expense, and repair all the injury of the conflict, consequent upon the nonperformance of this duty. When, too, the power of the United States Government ceased to exist during a given time, within any portion of the Union, I consider that the U. States Flag could then receive no insult from a foreign power acting in its own defence, and that where American Citizens were committing a flagrant breach of Treaty and International Law, they could not justly claim the protection of a National Flag.

But, My Lord, to make the case on the part of Great Britain still stronger, the invaders of Navy Island were, with the exception of perhaps one fiftieth of their number, American Citizens, and not fugitives from Canada; and they fought with American Arms that were the Property of the Government. If the Government assented it was an act of War. If it did not assent, it was still an act of War on the part of those who committed acts of hostility, while the vessels they employed, the ground they occupied, and the arms they wielded, were hostile vessels, ground, and arms to all intents and purposes.

The facts afford an illustration of the position to which I cannot forbear alluding. Acts of hostility were committed by the Navy Islanders upon the United States. When these men came within the British Boundaries, let us suppose that the United States made a demand for the twenty two pieces of cannon, the muskets, rifles, and ammunition plundered from American Arsenals—and suppose further that the British Government were to answer "Navy Island is not at present within our control; it is occupied by a hostile force."— Would, in such a case, an attack on Navy Island by American Troops be considered an invasion of British Territory, or an insult to the British Flag?— On the contrary, it would seem to be an act in aid of British Power, and it was one which a truly friendly Nation not only might, but assuredly would have done.

The case which I have thus endeavoured to make clear upon the actual facts is not weakened by adopting the American notion of Neutrality, which, however, is not founded in fact, insomuch as there was no War in Canada;— but let us suppose that there was a War,—England then would be one power, the United States of America the second, and the Navy Islanders the third. Why are the Navy Islanders considered a belligerent power?

Because they, in a small desert island belonging to Great Britain hold her power at defiance and openly disobey her laws, therefore say the Americans the invaders of Navy Island must be considered a belligerent power!

But at the same time that Navy Island is occupied by this power, so also is Fort Schlosser in the American Territory—the same power having besides extended it's influence in defiance of the United States to the City of Buffalo, and along the entire frontier.

The Americans say that, so far as regarded them, Navy Island, in which place England had no actual authority to enforce Treaties, was for the time being independent. On the other hand, we say that Schlosser, and even Buffalo, in which the United States had no power to enforce Treaties, or to carry into effect her own Laws were for the same time independent— If the Americans deny this, they must acknowledge connivance with the Patriots and assistance to them. This, however, they refuse to acknowledge, and their officers profess not to be able to enforce the Law within certain bounds.— In these the Patriots, so far as we are concerned, were supreme. They plundered no arsenals, they took no cannon, they seized no munitions of War, and they had no British Steamboats in their employ, in Canada; they only possessed a small desert island in which they held for a time English Law at defiance. They did plunder arsenals, they did take cannon, they seized Munitions of War, they had an American Steamboat in their employ within the United States, and they held the City of Buffalo partially, and the ground at Schlosser wholly in their power and occupation during many days. This is not proved by our assertions, but by the earnest allegations of U. States Officers from which they cannot retreat without admitting their connivance and assistance to the Patriots, in acts contrary to the letter of their Laws, and to the professions of their Government.

In short either the United States invaded Navy Island; or, according to their version, a belligerent power occupied their territory, committed hostilities against them, against their Will and contrary to their Laws, and from the ground belonging to the U. States *de jure*, but in the occupation of the Patriots *de facto*, invaded British Territory; the first occupation being of U. States Territory, and the occupation of both American and British ground by the Patriots being, for many days, simultaneous.

But the claim for reparation on the part of the United States for the Steamboat "Caroline", as American Property, and for the injury inflicted on those on board, as American Citizens, is quite repugnant to the assertion that the United States Government is neutral between the belligerents. The new power which the Americans recognize arose within their own Territory.— War commenced within the United States by the formation of an invading force with arms and warlike stores;— The invasion was begun when that force embarked in the American Waters; and, if the individuals composing it were acting as the American Government asserts, independently of and contrary to, the will of its Authorities, the recognition of the existence of the Patriot

Power must commence in the United States Territory. Who, then, were on board the "Caroline"? Patriots! In whose service was the Steamboat engaged? That of the Patriots! In whose possession and control was the ground at Schlosser? In that of the Patriot Army! Otherwise why was the that [*sic*] Patriot Army allowed to work its will, in spite of American Authority, even to the open plunder and carrying away of the arms and Munitions of War of the U. S. Government.? The Force thus acting in defiance of American power within the American Territory cannot be considered, while there, at one moment American Citizens, and, the instant the Steamboat crosses the boundary line, a belligerent power. If they formed a belligerent power, the U. States would be but performing their own Professions of Neutrality by leaving it to the Patriots to seek redress for the loss of their own Steamboat and the lives of their companions.

If, on the contrary, this ground of Neutrality is forsaken, and the Caroline claimed as American Property, the armed force assembling at Schlosser as American Citizens, and the place as *de facto* under the control of American Authority, the non exercise of that control throws the guilt of a most flagitious invasion of British Territory upon America as a Nation

Hence she becomes accountable for all the expense of defensive Preparations on the British side, and for the loss of life and injury to Property caused by the invading army[.]

The simple fact cannot be disguised by the misuse of terms. There was in fact no civil War in Canada— She was invaded from the United States either with or without the connivance of the Government. If the Government were, as the United States authorities assert, unable to control the aggressors, it was no act of hostility in us to do so, nor was it any interference with American power for us to act for our preservation in a place where American Power for the time did not exist. If the American Government could, but did not control them, the inviolability of the United States Territory ceased, and we were committing an aggression on an enemy in the act of invading us.

As to the proof that every individual on board the Caroline, or who crowded the House at Schlosser was part of the Pirate force *in transitu*, as it were, for Navy Island; the question is to be asked—What brought the "Caroline" to Schlosser? It could not have been trade, for there is no trade at the place. It could not be the transport of peaceable passengers because a railroad in full operation ran parallel with the river, and the season for navigation had closed! What business had the Caroline at Navy Island, an almost uninhabited spot of ground in the middle of the Niagara River? The transport of Passengers and freight! The passengers were and could be no other than a portion of the invading force; and the freight no other than the arms and stores of the Hostile Army. It may be a question in the Court of requests before a Justice of the Peace whether each man was bound to pay his own passage, and whether his baggage was to go free, or whether there was a Charter Party executed which contracted for the payment out of a common fund. But this question is to us wholly unimportant and the assertion that the Steamboat was employed in the Prosecution of lawful, or even peaceful contraband trade, is so strongly contrary to fact, that it can be only considered in the light of a crafty and unworthy equivocation. Who were the respectable citizens that crowded the beds, and promiscuously covered the floors of the Tavern at Schlosser, so that it was necessary to afford them accommodation on the floor or decks of the Caroline in the midst of a Canadian Winter? Patriot soldiers, taking up their quarters for the night, their names so perfectly unknown that they are told off by numbers— Whether any were lost or not cannot be ascertained by the strictest scrutiny in the neighbourhood unless by recollection of the numbers told off. What prevented the American Authorities from interfering?— Surely some visible force! Where was it? At the Tavern at Schlosser and on board the Steamboat!

The only difficulty to the negociation seems to me to be the wound to American pride in acknowledging that any portion of the American Territory was at any time beyond the authority of its Government, and, consequently beyond the protection of its flag. But this part of the case is too strongly founded upon American Documents to be shaken and the denial of it involves the adoption of the acts of hostility by the American Government.

I shall conclude my argument, My Lord, by referring to many documents in which the American Authorities, at the time of the occupation of Navy Island, and since, have confessed, directly or indirectly, their inability to control the Frontier Population; or which tend to prove the fact. Some of these, I perceive, have been considered in the Memorandum transmitted by your Lordship. When the complete impunity attending breaches of the *Neutrality* Laws, and the contempt in which the authority of the General Government, as well as the Laws of the Union are held by sectional portions of the Population, are recalled to recollection; when it is considered that even the atrocious outrage on the Steamboat "Sir Robert Peel" has passed without the punishment of a single individual among the Perpetrators, and that the notorious William Lyon McKenzie, the robber of the United States Arsenals and the instigator, and *primum mobile* of all the insubordination that has taken place upon the frontier, is found to be even now lecturing on "Patriotism" in New York, unmolested; when, My Lord, all these things are passed in review, it will, I think, be manifest that the necessity which existed to cross the American Frontier line for the purpose of depriving the enemy of a means which he was then using of making war upon and invading the Province, arose from default in the Laws, or failure in their execution, in the United States.

It will, too, I conceive, be further manifest that it was not until such failure was demonstrated by repeated and uninterrupted aggression that the preventive and strictly defensive measure of the destruction of the Caroline was resorted to.

It is likewise evident from a continuance and recurrence of like events that the want of efficient energy on the part of the United States Authorities was not casual or momentary; and that it is the same continuous default, whether involuntary or otherwise that keeps so large a number of Her Majesty's Subjects in Arms in Upper Canada, for its defence against a force which it is the bounden duty of the United States to restrain while under their flag within their Nominal jurisdiction.

[Enclosures lacking.]

[576] ARTHUR TO COLONEL [PLOMER] YOUNG: LB. 1, p. 243-245.

Dec. 17 *Government House, Toronto.*

From statements which I have received to-day, I am led to believe that the Brigands intend to try their fortune again at Prescott. I have therefore desired Sir John Colborne to allow the Left Wing of the 65th.

Regt. to remain with you during the Winter, and I should hope you would be able to accommodate the men comfortably.

Keep them off duty as much as you can, so that they may always be prepared to move.

I should be glad to know your exact strength at present. I make it out to be 577 Rank & file.

What kind of men are they? How are they officered? Would not two or three good drill Sergeants or Corporals be of great service to you. if so, Colonel Dundas will either from his own Corps or from the Right Wing of the 65 Rgt (which I conclude is now at Kingston) afford you this assistance.

I have ordered a very good Sergeant and fifteen men of the Toronto Provincial Artillery to proceed to Prescott.

Is the Fort yet completed? if not, what occasions the delay? the officer in charge of the works must make every exertion to complete it.

What force can you look to to reinforce you upon any emergency? Have you any spare arms? are you well off for ammunition? To what use have you converted the Mill?

Have you Clothing and blankets for the Militia and are they upon the whole well taken care of and satisfied?

My wish is that they should be in all respects as well taken care of as the Regular Troops. Would Captain Sandom's Marine Force be of any Service to you during the Winter months? if so, you had better write to Colonel Dundas to that effect.

Of all things get the Militia into the best and most orderly state you can—and teach them never to hurry or throw away their fire and always to rush on with the Bayonet.

[Superscription reads: "Colonel Young Comg at Prescott."]

[577] C. A. Hagerman to Arthur: A.L.S. 3p.

Dec. 17 *Toronto.*

With reference to Mr. Drapers private letter to your Excellency in which he suggests for consideration the pardoning a certain number of the prisoners taken at Prescot[t], I take the liberty of mentioning that should the suggestion be adopted, it is desirable that he should be immediately requested, to examine into the cases of such of the prisoners as have not been tried, and who[m] he considers best entitled to indulgent consideration,—and that he make a *confidential* report to your Excellency upon them.—

I am happy to find from Mr Drapers last letter to me, that he appears in better health and Spirits than when he wrote a few days since— he appears to feel it necessary for him to complete the duty assigned to him, and is prepared and willing to go through with it.—

As respects the notification of the approval of the proceedings of the Court Martial, to which Mr Draper alludes—I beg to recommend that Copies of the several orders of your Excellency in Council, in relation to these proceedings, and the Judgment of the Court, be transmitted officially to Mr. Draper by Mr. MacAulay, with some expression of approbation of the manner in which the Court has hitherto performed the important duties in which they have been engaged.—

If Your Excellency has no objection to my seeing Hunter C. Vaughans letter to Mr. Draper I should be glad to peruse it.— I think I know something of the young mans Father, and I am also desirous of making some enquiries respecting the William Fletcher to whom he refers— One of this family (a Son of John Fletcher and a cousin of Williams) was permitted to return home some weeks since, and he exhibited great gratitude and contrition— I thought him sincere, and I believe he would give me true information on any point I might think it right to question him upon.—

[578] [ARTHUR AND COLBORNE]: M 12p.

[*1838*]
[*c. Dec. 18*] [A digest of the correspondence between Arthur and Colborne from May 5, 1838, to Dec. 18, 1838, concerning the maintenance or reduction of militia and other forces in Upper Canada. In effect Arthur wants regiments; Colborne wants companies; Colborne thinks Arthur's terms too high; Arthur finds great difficulty in getting men on Colborne's terms; Colborne, eventually realising the situation, swings over to "recommend your calling out 10,000 men, if you can, by your exertions and rousing the spirit of the Loyal Districts, obtain their services." "Employ 3 or 4,000 labourers *at any wages* to make the Coast Roads practicable for Troops— Engage as many Steamers as you like on Lake Erie." "Raise as many Corps of Cavalry as you may think can be brought forward to act." Where the original letters represented in this digest are preserved, they are transcribed in their ordinary chronological sequence. Several of the actual letters are lacking. In these cases the entries in this digest have been transcribed and placed in their chronological sequence to represent the original letters. A letter from Colborne, dated July 19, is noted in the digest as "lost"; it now appears in its proper place.]

[579] ARTHUR TO COLBORNE: LB. 1, p. 245-249.

Dec. 18 *Govt. House, Toronto.*

Thank you for your letter of the 12th. Inst.

The detail into which you have entered is most useful, and, I think I understand your views perfectly. Circumstances however, have rendered some deviation necessary and I will endeavour to explain them.

Most providentially the affair at Sandwich terminated upon the whole well as a deterring example, although never was anything equal to the mismanagement of Colonel Prince. The ruffians took no advantage of all his errors and were routed as you have heard before the reinforcement arrived from Detroit, which was really owing to the firm and decided conduct of Genl Brady.

Whilst matters looked so threatening Colonel Airey sent off a Company of the 34th. Regt to Sandwich giving Major Deedes the command as I had indeed proposed some time before and at the same time an express to be reinforced by two companies of the 32d and the two six pounders. As you had with your accustomed rapidity of action sent me up the 73d Regt which I determined to employ in the Westward, I thought it most desirable not to separate the 32nd Regt and therefore ordered the whole corps to advance to Gosfield, to act and form a junction, if necessary with the 34th Regt.

Colonel Airey, you will observe by his letter, wishes now to withdraw his Company from Sandwich and send them two companies of the 32d. This will leave four companies of the 32d with about 300 Militia and the two six pounders at Gosfield, which is a most desirable Station for supporting either Sandwich or Amherstburg, or for being supported if necessary from those stations.

It would certainly be better to have the whole of the 32d Regt collected at Gosfield, but, really, the Militia are not to be trusted at Sandwich and Windsor where the greatest excitement exists, and I am not surprised at it.

It is very well to talk of our Gallant Militia, but they are just what may be expected of officers and men *totally untrained*. If they ever meet with a reverse, before they are got into better order, it will be most injurious, and therefore spite of all its disadvantages, some arrangement appears to be essential to give them some Detachment of regular Troops to form upon and be instructed by.

The American Govt. seem well disposed to avoid a war, but I do not think it will be possible with such a feeling as exists in the States apparently amongst all classes and increasing so far as I can hear every day. To prepare for far more serious encounters than any we have yet had, there cannot be too soon some system for training the Militia and this can only be done by mixing them with our Regular Troops and affording them the benefit of being drilled by some experienced officers and non Comd Officers.

Whatever may be the result of the present commotions, we ought certainly, to turn to the best advantage the present opportunity of training—the expence, compared to the benefit would be inconsiderable.

There is a considerable force of the Brigands again collected at Buffalo and Lockport and the numbers are increasing. The enclosed letters from the Under Sheriff at Niagara who has good information generally contains [*sic*] the latest intelligence I have received that is to be depended upon. There are many exaggerated reports but I do not believe them.

There is enough, however, to put us upon our guard, and it strikes me—that, as there is nothing now to be apprehended from Point Abino to Gosfield, along Lake Erie that it will be desirable for the 73d to remain at present at Brantford, which in Waggons would enable them on an emergency to support the 43d. in the mean time Colonel Love's experience will be of the greatest service in putting the Gore and Talbot Districts into some good order, which is very necessary, and Sir Allan Macnab I am glad to find although at first a little doubtful has at length recognised Colonel Love as an officer of rather more experience than Himself.

I heard some days ago that the Brigands were again collecting in some force on the St. Lawrence. Last night I received a letter from Captain Sandom of which I enclose you a copy, from which it would appear that another attempt is to be made upon Prescott.

We have there at present, 500 Militia, at least had by the last returns. It is a very important point and I should think it would be very desirable to retain there two companies of the left Wing of the 65th. and one company at Brockville with a field officer. By this means we should be training the Militia and have a force to be depended upon.

I can scarcely doubt that the Brigands will be urged to make reprisals for the serious loss they have sustained; but, if we make a good display of force it is not so certain that they will be able to muster men who will take the field.

The expence of all our arrangements is very distressing, but if war be averted I am sure that both Grt Britain & the Canadas and I may add America also will have reason to acknowledge their gratitude to you.

[Enclosures lacking.]

[580] ARTHUR TO THE BISHOP OF MONTREAL [*i.e.* G. J. MOUNTAIN, BISHOP OF QUEBEC]: L.S. 15p.

Dec. 18 *Government House, Toronto.*

I have the honour to acknowledge Your Lordship's Letter of the 20th ultimo.

It has been to me, I do assure Your Lordship, a subject of the deepest concern,—on the highest of all grounds, the well-being of the Church,—that I was deprived of the gratification, and advantage of a personal interview with you whilst you were in the Upper Province.

I should not have regarded any distance or personal inconvenience to have derived the benefit which I think might have resulted from a mutual interchange of our thoughts and views upon the state of Religion and Education in this distracted Province;—but, it untowardly happened, there were such pressing public matters at the time, admitting of no delay, that I was obliged to proceed to Quebec at the very period of your Visitation.

I did, indeed, push on for London with the utmost Expedition I could use in order to meet your Lordship there, and was sadly disappointed that I did not see you.

There are many points which, in mutual confidence, we might personally have discussed, that I should scarcely feel at liberty to touch upon in any less unreserved manner of communication.

Upon the first point which Your Lordship has adverted to, I hesitate not to record my conviction,—that, to the extreme neglect in supplying pious and well-qualified Clergymen, and good and well-intentioned Schoolmasters from Home, much of the frightful Evil that has all but plunged this Province into a Civil War and severed it from the Mother Country, is to be ascribed. Never did I see Cause and Effect more strongly marked.

I could, during a personal conference, whilst requesting you to make every allowance for my limited Experience, have ventured to have set all my reflections and views freely before you in this matter,—but I must now content myself with remarking that I do not impute all the blame to the Home Government.

Sad, indeed have been the consequences resulting from the Mother Country's having so utterly neglected to nourish The Church when it was first planted in this Province; and no less so from Her having delayed to appropriate the Clergy Reserves until such strife and contention were raised respecting them, as led the way to all the dissensions and bitter feelings that have resulted therefrom.

It is impossible, humanly speaking, at this time to adjust that question in this Province: that which other denominations would have taken thankfully some years ago, they would spurn at, if offered now, as a surrender by The Church of England. Nothing remains, so far as I can discover, but re-investing the Lands in the Crown, and placing them at Her Majesty's disposal with the advice of Parliament,—and that measure it is my present intention to endeavour to carry through, but I believe it will be strongly opposed by the Presbyterians and Methodists, who insist upon having the question settled by the Provincial Legislature, but not, they say, by the present Legislature. Any observations which Your Lordship will favour me with upon this point I shall thankfully receive.

Upon the Second point I concur most entirely with Your Lordship, and do think a division of the Diocese, and the appointment of a Bishop, for the Upper Province ought not to be delayed,—and that the delay of this measure has already occasioned incalculable injury to the interests of The Church of England.

Had a wise and spiritually minded prelate presided exclusively, from the very first, over the interests of the Church of England in this Province,—devoting himself largely to her Spiritual interests,—I have not a doubt that she would have been a *pre*dominant Church,—which is what should most have been desired. In transmitting a copy of Your Lordship's Letter, I shall urge upon Her Majesty's Government in the strongest terms I can use the mischief of delay.

Your Lordship most justly remarks upon the lamentably defective condition of the Common Schools. The mischiefs which have resulted from this cause are not to be told, and the madness of allowing Americans to be the instructors of the Youth of the Country, as is so commonly the case, is an evil which, even if the Province be now saved, must be felt beyond the present generation. I hold it to be impossible that the Province can be retained by Great Britain, if this evil be not got rid of, root and branch, and that too *at once!*

The state of the Indians is a question interesting in the highest degree: they have been intruded upon in every way, and it is remarkable that no Law has ever been passed for the summary removal of intruders upon their lands.

In the mean time I will, as far as I possibly can, endeavour to meet Your Lordship's recommendation with reference to the Mission at Sault St[e] Marie and Delaware. I have all the inclination to do so that you can desire, but the difficulty is to command the means.

When I proceed to the Westward I will make it a point to see Mr. Flood, and will cheerfully strengthen his hands. At present, I would rather not extend my remarks upon this point. I have caused the whole subject to be most fully gone into by the Provincial Secretary, and Mr. Tucker is a gentleman, who will feel it to be a conscientious duty to befriend the Indians, and to exert himself to bring their case forward, so as to remedy the past, as far as it admits of a remedy, and to provide for the future.

The whole of the Missions to these interesting and much ill-used People I will willingly attend to, if it should please God to remove the difficulties which have pressed so heavily upon the Province since Sir Francis Head resigned the administration of the Government into my hands.

The claims to consideration of the Reverend A. Palmer,—Atkinson,—Green,—Strong,—& Archbold, I am not altogether ignorant of. I believe them all to be Exemplary Clergymen, and nothing could give me more pleasure than to assist them—but until the Clergy Reserve Question is settled, nothing can be done, as there literally are no unappropriated funds to which the Government can have recourse.

I had not before heard of the case of the Rev. V. P. Mayerhoffer, but I will inquire into it with a desire to be of service to him.

The subjects brought under my consideration in Your Lordship's Letter, I am conscious are of the deepest importance.

I will give what attention to them I can bestow at present, and do assure you I shall have pleasure in doing so; but I lament there should be occasion to undertake, in the midst of commotions from within and troubles from without, measures which should have been adjusted in the day of tranquillity and of peace.

[The above does not form part of the *Arthur Papers* but is found in vol. 3 of the *Henry Scadding Scrap-books* in the Toronto Public Libraries.]

[581] W[ILLIA]M ROWAN TO ARTHUR: L.S.

Dec. 18 *Head Quarters, Montreal.*

Having had the honor to submit to the Commander of the Forces your Excellency's letter of the 12th. Instant, I am directed to acquaint you, that, as a Copy of your Communication of the 15th. of September has been transmitted for the Consideration of the General Commanding in Chief, His Excellency approves of the Continuance of Captain Halkett as Assistant Military Secretary at Toronto until further Orders.

[582] ARTHUR TO COLONEL [RICHARD] AIREY: LB.1, p. 258-260.

Dec. 19 *Government House, Toronto.*

I have received your [letter] of the 15th. Instant, and am glad you have given me the useful information it contains.

When Colonel Frazer [*i.e.* Fraser] moved on the 32nd. Regt towards Amherstburg, I wrote to Sir J Colborne informing him of the movement, and expressing my opinion, that it was proper that two Regiments should be brought near enough to act together.—

When therefore I found the Asst Qrtr. Mtr. General had hesitated about proceeding with that Corps, I wrote to him on the 14th. Instant to advance—or, if the 32nd had actually returned to London, to keep them there until further orders.—

This precaution I took, expecting every day to hear from Sir J. Colborne.—

I have now received a letter from the Commander of the Forces, dated the 12th Instant, & as he concurs with me that two Regiments should be at the Westward, mutually to support each other, I have ordered the 85th Regt to proceed to Gosfield with the two six pounders.

According to full information of all local circumstances, I leave it to Colonel Chichester to detach one or two Companies of the 85th. or from your Corps to Sandwich—taking care, at all events, that an Officer of the Regular Service is in Command.—

I have written to the Asst. Qutr. Mtr General, to make every possible arrangement for quartering the Regt. at Gosfield as much together as possible, and that any attention should be paid to making them comfortable.—

Colonel Frazer will be on his way to Toronto most probably, & therefore I shall thank you to give orders in this matter, should Colonel Chichester be out of the Way.—

I should still wish to retain a Militia Force of 200 or 300 men at Gosfield.—

By keeping open the communication with cavalry, a junction may rapidly be formed of any of the Troops stationed in the West.

The Commander of the Forces is of opinion that a Militia Force should be appointed to garrison Fort Malden, so that your Regiment may not be locked up to defend it, and that provisions for 300 men for 14 days should be kept in the Fort.

It is of great consequence that, whilst we have the Militia are out [*sic*] that they should be as well trained and drilled as possible—to this end, I would approve of your incurring any reasonable expense, either, in remunerating Officers or Non Commissioned Officers, employed in this most useful service.

It is quite remarkable, how quickly some of the Militia have been brought forward.

General Brady seems to have acted exceedingly well, and, whenever you have an opportunity, I shall thank you to say how much I am gratified by his hearty cooperation— it is some relief to me to find, that He and General Scott have taken the view you mention of Colonel Prince's unfortunate conduct, which has given me the most painful distress.—

I have accounts today from Buffalo and Lockport— There is to be a feint made upon the Niagara frontier, but a more formidable attempt to the Westward— these accounts, which differ as to the numbers, give the Brigands about 6,000 men altogether, collected, & collecting for the West.

[583] ARTHUR TO COLONEL [RICHARD] AIREY: LB.1, p. 257.

Dec. 19 *Govt. House, Toronto.* [Marked "Private".]

I enclose you *confidentially* an extract of a letter received by a Gentleman in Toronto and as this Statmnt differs so materially from Colonel Princes report, I am induced[?] to enclose [it] to you thinking you might be able to let me know whether it is to be credited. I am sorry you cannot make use of it officially, but the Gentleman who handed it to me is particularly anxious it should be considered *strictly private.*

[Enclosure lacking.]

[584] ARTHUR TO COLONEL [CHARLES] CHICHESTER: LB.1, p. 254-257.

Dec. 19 *Toronto.*

I have received your letter of the 12th. Inst. Bowerman's[?] escape is much to be regretted, but I am glad you have picked up with so many of these vagabonds as have fallen into your hands.

I felt satisfied that you would do all you could to cut off their retreat. The business appears to have been most miserably managed at Sandwich.

I sent off Mr. Sherwood the Queen's Counsell [*sic*] to investigate all the cases of those Prisoners, and to prepare them for trial. I am quite satisfied that you have done right in the investigation which you have ordered. The greatest inconvenience always results from delay.

The Queen's Counsel will admit any to become Queens Evidence whose testimony is essential in that way.

It is not safe, I believe, to hold out a promise of mercy to those whose evidence you take in this way, but, I conclude, it is always so understood.

We must, I fear, make every [*sic*] examples of these wicked People.

I am very glad that you reinforced the Sarnia Frontier—their next descent will be from that Quarter if the accounts I have received are to be depended upon.

No doubt can exist that they have still a considerable force upon the Western Frontier.

Colonel Fraser unfortunately sent back the 32nd Regt—in the mean time I had written to Sir John Colborne who entirely approved and thought there should be two Rgts to the Westward.

I have therefore directed that the 85th shall proceed to Gosfield, where, I still think that 2 or 300 militia should be stationed with 2 six pounders.

From the 34 or 85th one or two companies might be detached to Sandwich, as information on the spot may seem to render necessary. Gosfield appears to be a very desirable Petition [*sic*] as it seems to offer the means of rapidly supporting or being supported from Amherstburg and Sandwich & is also within reach of Chatham.

Pray make all the Troops as comfortable as circumstances will admit. I have written to this effect to Colonel Airey in case of your absence so that the 85th. may be in good Quarters—at least as good as can be had.

As to pouches upon which you have written to Colonel Foster.

I find that you have agreed for some—of course I shall approve, and I beg to say, once for all, that under such circumstances, when an officer is doing his best for the good of the Service He will always be sure of my support. It seems there are some accoutrements at Kingston, but when he may get them it is impossible to say—in the mean time if you wait for them, the loss of ammunition will be greater perhaps than the charge for the pouches.

I approve of the Petition for the two men, if you should not have received the notification act upon it on the receipt of this letter, and cause them with an admonition to be discharged!

I am every moment expecting to hear of another attack in the St. Lawrence where these ruffians have again collected in some force. . .

P.S. The two Six Pounders should remain with the 85th.— if you have not sleighs order them to be made at Amherstburg as they ought to be ready for moving the Guns at any moment.

[585] ARTHUR TO COLONEL [HENRY] DUNDAS: LB.1, p. 237-240.

Dec. 19 *Government House, Toronto.*

By a letter which I have just received from Captain Sandom, I learn, that from a person who has hitherto given him very authentic information, he has been apprized, that a considerable force of Ruffians is again collecting, to make a descent upon Prescott.—

I have heard of this intention from other quarters, and we must therefore endeavour to place Prescott and other Places on the St Lawrence, which may be open to attack, in the best state we can for defence.—

The returns sent in are so confused, that I find it difficult to estimate exactly what force I have to depend on any where; but, I apprehend, at Prescott there are

1	The Glengarry Highlanders————	64
2	Independent Company————	40
3	1st Grenville Regt.————	357
4	2nd. Do Do ————	116
		——

making a total of 577 Rank and File.

This is of course a tolerably good force, ***provided,*** it were well commanded, and the men well drilled; but, of this, I am quite ignorant.— Would it not be desirable to send two or three good drill Sergeants or Corporals either from your Corps or from the 65th to Drill the Militia at Prescott.—

I think, at all events, that there should be no time lost in adding at least 100 men to the Force at Prescott—and if the Commander of the

Forces can spare the other wing of the 65th. Regiment, I think Prescott and Brockville would be good stations for them, and so, I have Communicated to Sir John Colborne, and should be glad if he could at once send them up there.—

I have ordered a party of the Toronto Company of Provincial Artillery, consisting of a Sergeant and 15 Gunners, all well drilled, to proceed to Prescott.—

Is the Fort yet completed at Prescott?—if not, do give the most positive orders to have it made defensible, as soon as possible.—

How would you propose disposing of the Marine force during the Winter?— Captain Sandom will have a considerable body of men to Winter somewhere, and they might be made available for Brockville or Prescott and Gananoque— will you confer with him upon the subject, and act as you may think best, only take care to let me know what you decide upon.—

It strikes me, that, as during the Winter Months, there can no longer be apprehension respecting Presqu'Isle, so it cannot be necessary to keep so large a force there, or at Belleville as Colonel De Rottenberg has under his command.— If you think proper therefore, you may withdraw any portion of that force and place it where you deem it more essential.—

I enclose you a statement of the Force in the Newcastle and Midland Districts, as I understand it to be.—

Major Mc.Bean will be more useful to you than to me, and I have therefore approved of his returning to Kingston.—

Sir John Colborne has assured me that he will send you another Battery, and, had I not depended upon his doing so, I would not have brought away the demi-battery, as I am more anxious about Kingston than Toronto.

[Enclosure lacking.]

[586] ARTHUR TO COLONEL [F. A. M] FRAZER [*i.e.* FRASER]: LB.1, p. 249-250.

Dec. 19 *Government House, [Toronto.]*

I received your letter commenced at Sandwich and concluded at Amherstburg.—

As soon as you had moved on the 32nd Regt towards Amherstburg, I wrote to Sir John Colborne informing him of the movement, & expressing my opinion that it was proper that two Regts. should be stationed to the Westward.— I therefore wrote to you on the 14th still to advance— but if the Regt. had already returned to London, then, I desired they might remain until further orders—as I was in daily expectation of being made acquainted with the wishes of the Commander of the Forces.—

Sir John Colborne, in a letter dated the 12th. Inst. much approves of two Corps being stationed in the West, and does not apprehend that desertion is much to be dreaded during the expectation of attack.—

I therefore now send orders for the 85th Regt to proceed to Gosfield, which strikes me [as] being a most desirable station, as, from thence, Amherstburg or Sandwich may easily be supported or vice versâ.—

Supposing there are 300 Militia at Gosfield, it may be made a strong post, and at the same time, allow Colonel Chichester to detach one or two Companies of the 85th from Gosfield, or two Companies of the 34th. from Amherstburg, to Sandwich, as, under full information of all the local circumstances he may deem best.

The two six pounders will move from London, and be attached to the 85th Regt.—

I should wish every possible arrangement to be made for quartering the Regt. at Gosfield, as much together as possible, & that every attention should be paid to make them comfortable.—

By keeping open the Communication with Cavalry, a junction may rapidly be formed, of any of our Troops to the West, Gosfield being 50 miles from Chatham, 32 from Sandwich & 24 from Amherstburg.—

I do not add more as I conclude this letter will not reach you until you have left the West.

[587] ARTHUR TO GLENELG: LB.5, p. 253-255.

Dec. 19 *Government House, Toronto.* [Marked "No 115."]

At a period when I have so many pressing public cares upon my mind, I would not willingly devote any portion of my time to personal considerations. But I feel it to be a duty respectfully to offer a few observations upon Your Lordship's Despatch No 156 of the 24th. October in reply to the Despatch which I did myself the honor to address to your Lordship on the 29th. September, marked "Separate," respecting my allowances as a Major General on the Staff.

It is certainly the case that, in Despatch No 7 Your Lordship has stated that "Where, as in your own case, and that of Sir Francis Head, the only remuneration received from the Public is the Civil Salary attached to the Office, Her Majesty's Government are of opinion that that Salary should be not less than £3500."

Your Lordship's Despatch to which I have referred is dated the 28th. December last, and I received it when on the point of proceeding to Portsmouth for Embarkation, and when it was wholly out of my power to offer any observations upon the subject.

I request you will permit me to remark that, when your Lordship was pleased to honor me with the appointment to this Government, I very naturally enquired what the Salary and allowances of the appointment were; and, through Sir George Grey's kindness, I was permitted to take the Blue Book of 1835 to my House: therein I found that Sir John Colborne drew £3500 as salary, and £500 in lieu Staff Pay and allowances.

Unconscious that there had been any alteration in the Salary, I should have laboured under the misapprehension of supposing that I should have been allowed the same salary as Sir John Colborne had enjoyed, when holding the same offices, had not the Secretary at War, in the course of an interview, recommended me to ascertain distinctly what was the intention with respect to my Staff Appointment.

I did accordingly enquire, and Your Lordship's Under Secretary informed me that Military Pay had been discontinued on Sir Francis Head's appointment; that the salary had not been finally determined but he believed it would be fixed at £4000.

On reading Sir Francis Head's Correspondence, I observed that he had stated over and over that the Salary granted to him was quite inadequate to support his station as Civil Governor; and your Lordship, I presume, must have been quite satisfied of the accuracy of his Representations since you have been pleased to sanction his receiving the difference between £3000 and £3500 during the period of his Administration.

I am convinced your Lordship has not a just idea of the expence of supporting a public Establishment in Upper Canada, or my Communication would have been deemed most reasonable; but, independently of the burden which must ordinarily fall upon the officer administering this Government, the circumstances of the Country since my arrival and the consequent encreased Military Force employed it may be well supposed have in various ways thrown additional expense upon me as well as upon the rest of the officers of the Army, to all of whom, myself excepted, Field Allowances have been granted.

Had I not considered that I might with strict propriety have expected to receive my Military allowances whilst in command here, as I did in Van Diemen's Land under the same circumstances, I would not on any account have made the Representation; and I beg your Lordship will have the goodness to consider that I have troubled you with this Despatch only in Explanation, and not from the slightest intention of be ng further importunate upon such a subject.

[588] ARTHUR TO COLONEL [J. F.] LOVE: LB.1, p. 251-254.

Dec. 19 *Government House, Toronto.*

During the last eight days I have had no less than 36 capital cases to consider in Council which has been such an addition to my labour, whilst preparing dispatches for England & for Washington, that, I have not had one moment to acknowledge your letters.

Your representations respecting the Barrack Master, I have referred for enquiry— He is an old Servant, & I fear, not equal to the active duties of the present day. But it is not just that the Troops should suffer & I will propose to the Commander of the Forces whether he cannot contrive to give him some retirement.—

It has given me much satisfaction to find, that you have got on so well with Sir Allan M[a]cNab, and I shall be much obliged for any assistance you will afford in bringing forward the Militia.

I am most desirous to keep out none but volunteers & those who remain cheerfully, unless there be an unavoidable necessity for it—, but, whilst they are out, it is most desirable that we should do the utmost to drill them— Any expence in affording the aid of Officers or Non Commissioned Officers in training the Militia that you recommend, shall be immediately approved.— In this way much may be done in a very short time— The misfortune is that the Militia Officers are so totally ignorant of drill, that they can render but little assistance to the men.— Does your plan, to which you alluded, provide for the instruction of Militia Officers—and if so, can we put it into practice here.—

With respect to Captain Welby's troop, I scarcely know what to say.— There are not less than 900 cavalry now out & the expence is enormous.— I wish very much to see the nature of the first application and my approval of this Troop—perhaps It might be limited to fifty.—

There is a great complaint[?] springing up about the Cavalry. Men Volunteer fast enough for this force, as it saves them from the Militia duty. In such a state of things there are difficulties on all sides, but the extent of these I have not time to explain to you.

You will however confer a great favor if you will make your observations, and let me know how we can best use the Militia with the least possible hardship upon the people of the Country.— It is in vain to suppose that they will submit to this tax upon their time, & their comfort, year after year.

I expect the first wing of the 65th will be at Kingston to-day— Sir John Colborne says he will send another Regt for the Niagara Frontier if possible, before the navigation finally closes.— He writes me that those Vagabond Patriots have now engaged a number of Irish from Boston and Plattsburg to join their cause, and that these deluded beings are moving up to join the Brigands in their attacks upon this Province— A considerable number have again formed near Ogdensburg, and threaten to try their fortune once more upon Prescott.—

There is no doubt, I think, that they are in considerable force in that quarter, & I am endeavouring to strengthen our force from Kingston downwards to Prescott. If Sir John can spare the other half of the 65th Regt I shall station them on the St Lawrence.

There is also a large assembly of these Ruffians again at the Westward, I expect they now attempt to penetrate by the St Clair.

Your Force is well situated to oppose any descent from that quarter, & by moving on to London you will be able, with the 32nd, to form such a corps, as nothing these people can bring can stand before for an instant.

So, also, if they endeavour to penetrate by the Niagara, you will be upon them, before they can, with the greatest force they can bring, do any serious mischief—

Have you sleighs for your Guns—if not by all means order them.— Are your men and horses well taken care of? If not, all I can say is that I approve of any reasonable expence, because I know it is the particular desire of the Commander of the Forces to render the Troops as comfortable as the nature of the service will admit.

It will be of importance to ascertain where Waggons can be had at any moment when required. Wherever these Ruffians appear, it is of great moment, with *reference to many considerations* to give them no breathing time.

[589] ARTHUR TO JOHN MAITLAND: LB.1, p. 258.

Dec. 19 *Government House, Toronto*

I have received your letter of the 12th instant.

Had the 32nd Regt not returned to London, it was my wish that they should have proceeded on to Gosfield—but, as I had written to Sir J Colborne upon the subject, I was desirous to know his wishes, before they were again advanced, supposing the Corps had actually returned to London— This was the cause of my instruction to Colonel Frazer [*i.e.* Fraser] of the 14th Instant.—

I have now heard from the Commander of the Forces, and he entirely concurs in the opinion, that two Regts. had better be stationed to the Westward.—

I have therefore directed that the 85th. Regt. shall proceed to Gosfield with the two 6 pounders, and I should wish them to advance at once.—

I am glad to hear that your health is improving, and hope, with care, it may soon be entirely restored.

[590] C. C. DOMVILE TO COLONEL [RICHARD] AIREY: LB.4, p. 44-46.

Dec. [c. 20] *Governt. House, [Toronto.]*

I am commanded by the Major Genl. Comg. to acknowledge your Letter of the 17th Inst. covering the Copy of a Letter from Col: Prince; in which he declines rendering any assistance in the previous examination of the Prisoners, & preparing their Cases for trial, considering it inconsistent with his standing at the Bar, in consequence of Mr. Sherwoods having been directed to conduct those Trials as Judge Advocate.

The Major Genl. also observes with regret that Mr. Prince appears to consider the course taken by the Governt., in directing the Prisoners to be tried at London, as likely to interfere with the due administration of Justice.

You will recollect, that, in your Letter, written during the night of the 4th., & despatched from Amherstburg at three o'Clock on the morng. of the 5th Inst. you stated, that you had been apprized by Genl. Brady, that it was the positive intention of the Brigands to make an immediate attack on Amherstburg; and on the following day, at 12 o'Clock at Night, in your Letter to the Asst. Adjt. Genl. you urgently request to be furnished with early instructions as to the disposal of the Prisoners, having no other place of custody than a Barrack-room fitted up as a Cage.

The Major Genl. had also the opportunity of seeing two Letters from Sandwich & Windsor, dated the 5th & 6th Inst., in which the excitement was described to be extreme; & that a further descent of those atrocious Villains was hourly expected; as still greater numbers of them were known to be congregating, & wou'd undoubtedly attack in force when the Ice shou'd be strong enough to bear them.

On the receipt of your Letter of the 4th, & of Col: Chichester's of the 5th, in which he stated that 6 Prisoners had been taken by the Party under his Orders, His Excellency, in Council, determined on ordering One Court Martial to assemble at London, & another at Amherstburgh[*sic*]. But when your Letter of the 6th. announced the difficulty you felt in the disposal of the Prisoners; & when the existing excitement, as well as the strong expectation of further Attacks were made known, it appear'd to the Major Genl. to be an act of common prudence to withdraw the Prisoners as soon as possible from Amherstburgh, & to place them where they might be tried without any probable interruption, & without taking the Officers on the Frontier from their Military duties to act as Members of a Court Martial.

Another circumstance which weighed strongly with the Major Genl. was, that the removal of the Prisoners was, in fact, the removal of a Cause that wou'd naturally increase the existing excitement: and moreover His Excellency thought, that, as the enormity of the Crime render'd it almost certain, that the severest examples of punishment must be made, on an extended scale, it was most desirable that the Members of the Court Martial shou'd not be taken from Gentlemen residing immediately upon the Frontier.

It is a point on which a difference of opinion may exist whether it will have a more salutary effect to try & execute the Prisoners on the spot, & in sight of the American People; or to march them off to the Interior, & there administer Justice upon them free from those exciting circumstances which frequently support the Culprit in his last hours. The Major Genl. strongly inclines to the latter opinion; &, if it were in His Excelly's. power to depart so far from prevailing usage, he wou'd cause every Criminal to be executed in the dead of night, & in the presence only of a few persons appointed to attend the execution.

I am glad to add, that if a doubt had existed in the mind of the Major Genl. as to the propriety & justice of sending the Prisoners to London for trial, the strong observations in your Letter wou'd have entirely removed them.

The course of trying at Kingston, & not on the spot which had been the scene of their atrocities, the Prisoners who committed the outrage at Prescott, has, there is good reason to believe, been well rece'd by the

Inhabitants of that part of the Province who appear to have duly estimated the motives of the Govemt. in endeavouring to lessen the excitement in the immediate vicinity of those atrocities by removing to some distance the perpetrators of them.

The Major Genl., therefore, sees no reason to alter the decision at which he has arrived of trying these Prisoners at London: but, if there are any cases in which there is sufficient cause to apprehend that a Conviction at such a distance as London cannot be obtained, a general Court Martial may, in that event, be hereafter assembled at Amherstburgh.

The Major Genl. has every reason to believe that Mr. Sherwood has visited both Sandwich & Amherstburgh, & investigated carefully all the Cases. It will accordingly be left to his judgment to determine whether it will be eventually necessary for the Genl. Court Martial to adjourn to Amherstburgh.

With the exception of such Cases as Mr. Sherwood may recommend to be tried at Amherstburgh, the whole of the Prisoners will be forthwith removed to London.

[591] ARTHUR TO COLONEL [RICHARD] AIREY: LB.1, p. 261-262.

Dec. 20 *Govt. House, Toronto.*

I have just directed an answer to your letter of the 17th. Inst.; I have fully explained therein my reasons for trying the prisoners at London, where, with the exception of any cases which Mr Sherwood should think it necessary to try at Amherstburg, I wish to have all the prisoners removed forthwith.

For all the reasons stated by the Mly Secretary I am quite convinced that this is the proper course—otherwise, I never would subject the Government to the additional expence occasioned by trying the Prisoners at London.

It gives me a good deal of concern to find by a letter which I have this day received from Colonel Fraser that the 85th. Rgt will be very indifferently accommodated at Gosfield and far too much scattered.

Cannot this be avoided, is there not a Foundry at Gosfield that might be converted into a good barracks?—if not, rather than have the Regt scattered to an extent that would interfere with discipline and expose a Detachment to be cut off, I would much rather move on the whole corps to Amherstburg. But actually I cannot ascertain whether Amherstburg affords accommodation for two Regts, so void are the Departments of information.

I should not regard any reasonable expence in putting up the Regt. comfortably at Gosfield, and from its local position it is a most desirable station and the one I should wish to occupy.

The Asst. Qr Master General recommends three or four Large Log Musket Proof Barracks—to this, I should have no objection, and by employing the Country People and the men themselves such Barracks might be rapidly erected. I suggest this in order that enquiry and consideration may be given before the 85th come up.

I cannot avoid expressing how very highly I am pleased with all your proceedings whilst you have commanded on the Frontier so far as I am acquainted with them. I know of nothing to regret, except your not having sent Major Deedes to Sandwich when Colonel Reid was withdrawn from it, and I am aware as there were no Troops of the Line at Sandwich, that you might have felt a delicacy about it.

[592] ARTHUR TO LORD FITZROY [J. H.] SOMERSET: LB.2, p. 3-7.

Dec. 20 [*Place not stated.*]

I did myself the pleasure to communicate to you in my Letter of the 24th. Ulto. the result of the affair at Prescott.

Fifty nine of the Prisoners captured in that affair have been tried at Kingston—eight of them have been ordered for execution the remaining cases have not been decided upon and one hundred more are for trial. The trials have proved beyond all question that Multitudes of American Subjects & many of them persons of opulence have been parties to the conspiracy against this Province as Members of the Unions named "Hunters Lodges."

These Lodges were first fostered in the States—not less than a 150,000 persons are said, & I believe truly to have been sworn in as Members. Corresponding Lodges have been formed in this Province—the exact number of Members has not been ascertained but they are very numerous. I think I enclosed in a former letter to Yr Ldship a Paper containing the oaths & signs of this wicked fraternity; but not being quite certain I now forward a Copy. The Funds & Means these People have had at their Command are scarcely to be credited, & their scheme was that Invasion and Insurrection were to have burst upon us simultaneously. But, by the Providence of God, we recd. warning of the storm just in time; & by at once calling out the Militia the connection was cut off—no invasion has been successful nor has one Inhabitant had the opportunity of taking up arms in hostility to the Govt. This has led the Conspirators to mistrust each other, & their Measures hitherto have proved abortive.

It seems almost incredible in these "Enlightened Times," that such a body of Persons cd. have been found in any Country to bind themselves together by oaths to commit murder and Robbery upon such a wholesale scheme. I do not think such a multitude of Villains could have been found in any Nation on earth called civilized but in the United States of America!

A large body of these Ruffians calling themselves Patriots rather suddenly collected at Detroit—Brest—and other Places on the Detroit River, and at day light on the 4th. Instt. about 350 of them made a descent upon Windsor (Lake St Clair) about three miles west of Sandwich— It was intended as a feint, and, expecting that the 34th. Regt. stationed at Amherstburg, distant eighteen miles, wd. have hastened to the support of the Militia at Sandwich, it was determined to make the main assault upon Fort Malden—Amherstburg!

I cannot say that the affair at Windsor was managed very well. Coll. Prince who commanded the Militia at that Station was not cool at the work; and the consequence was that proper advantage was not taken of the miserable conduct of the Brigands. However, they were soon routed and dispersed—twenty five were killed and twenty five were taken Prisoners the first day. As many more were taken on the following day, and numbers of them have since been discovered to have perished in the woods. About 50 are supposed to have made their escape back into the States by crossing the St Clair nearly as high up as Sarnia[.]

After the action was over, four of the Prisoners were brought forward by order of Col. Prince & shot upon the spot. That they well deserved such a punishment is true enough, but it was a most unwise proceeding & is likely to occasion me no small trouble. Coll. Prince's Report in wh. he gives an account of this Instruction I determined not to publish; but, to my extreme annoyance, I found the following day that he had published it Himself & sent it through the States—and the great mass of People in this Province applaud his conduct not looking to the consequences!

A General Militia Court Martial is ordered to assemble at London for the trial of the Prisoners and we shall have to make some severe examples.

The feeling on both sides becomes more & more bitter every day and unless these atrocities are put down *speedily* neither Mr. Van Buren's Proclamations nor mine will much longer prevent far more extensive hostilities.—

I am now expecting every hour another descent on the Western frontier, & a more serious one, in point of numbers, than any we have yet had on the St Lawrence between Prescott and Kingston.

Your Lordship will have observed that the President in his Proclamation of the [blank in MS.] and since, in his message to Congress, has asserted that Disturbances have broken out anew in both the Canadas. This is incorrect & a very serious error, for if there were disturbances in this Province, the Banditti would use it as an excuse for their interference—but, whatever may be wished and was intended no disturbance has taken place & of course I am not bound to let Mr. Van Buren know that we have narrowly escaped insurrection.

The municipal authorities of Toronto presented an address to me upon this subject wh. Yr. Lordship will find in the accompanying Gazette, wh. I have cause[d] to be circulated in the States that it might be known that there was & had been no disturbance in Upper Canada.

The 34th Regt. is at Amherstburg where I do not like to leave them any longer unsupported by Regular Troops, & the 85th. is therefore now under orders to proceed to Gosfield on the Lake Shore 25 Miles from Amherstburg that they may act together as soon as the ice affords the Brigands a bridge to cross over the Detroit.— The 32nd. Regt. is stationed at London just in the centre of the Western Country—the 73rd. at Brantford from whence in 24 hours they can form a junction with the 32nd. or, within the same time, with the 43rd. and Dragoon Guards on the Niagara Frontier.— The 93rd. is at Toronto—the 83rd at Kingston, with one wing of the 65th. We have 12,000 Militia embodied & these are ready enough for work, but rough indeed!

It is impossible to express any opinion that can be depended upon as to the future— I hope to draw a strong expression of condemnation from the Southern States upon the lawless outrages wh. have been committed by the Inhabitants of the States adjacent to Canada & to this end I propose publishing part of my correspondence with our Minister at Washington & if the Southern Members in Congress are not decided against those outrages I shd. suppose War must be inevitable—& a heavy calamity it will be upon Upper Canada, although, if we be well supported from England there can be no doubt of the issue.— I have pressed H. M. Govt. ever since I came to Canada to undertake the Fortifications wh. the Duke of Wellington *as I have understood* had approved. It is infatuation of the most unreasonable kind to trust to the honor of the Americans—there is scarcely such a thing in the States—it is the *interest* of that country that shd. always be calculated upon for that they will follow where ever there is any chance of success.

Upper Canada is of incalculable importance to the Union, & it is what such a power will gain rather than what Great Britain will lose by wh. the value of these Provinces must be estimated. To my mind the loss of the Canadas wd. be a blow from wh. Great Britain never wd. recover—but I am a very superficial Politician. I enclose for your Lordship's perusal copy of a letter wh. has just fallen into my hands from a Deserter from the 85th. Regt. who has enlisted into the United States Regular Forces. This man deserted only a few months ago & an officer of the 85th on visiting Buffalo lately found him acting as Orderly to the Officer Commanding the Troops at that Station. You will perceive he holds out pretty good encouragement to his *Comrades* to follow him.

[Enclosures lacking.]

[593] ARTHUR TO GLENELG: LB.3, p. 1-2.
Dec. 22 *Govt. House, Toronto.* [Marked "Separate".]

[Requests confirmation of an appointment of Charles Arthur, now a police magistrate, formerly a barrack master, in Van Diemen's Land, and explains the circumstances.]

[594] ARTHUR TO JAMES STEPHEN: LB.3, p. 2-3.
Dec. 23 *Toronto.*

I shall feel much obliged if you will give an Office cover to the accompanying Letter to my Brother.

You have in my Officials all the information I can impart—it is useless to hazard opinions, for it seems impossible to predict with confidence today what may happen tomorrow. Every effort has been made by a most powerful party to excite rebellion here, & to bring on a National War. The first object has I trust been effectually defeated; and I hope Lord Glenelg will be satisfied that I have so shaped my course as not to leave the American Governmt. ground to complain of one single act of retaliation on our part which has been no small display of magnanimity for I had it in my power to punish them severely— all the injury to be complained of is on our side—& although so far as Upper Canada is concerned War should be by all means avoided—yet Great Britain must resolve to speak out to the American People in a very different tone from what has hitherto been used.

The President's Proclamations are nothing more than mere exhortations; &, in spite of them, it would not in the least surprise me if the People in Ohio, Michegan [*sic*], and New York & some other States were to carry on this predatory Warfare— But, it is my opinion, that the Sympathisers regard the rough reception they have met with in Upper Canada much more than they do Mr. Van Buren; and, notwithstandg. all I hear to the contrary & however necessary it may be to be prepared for the worst my impression is that the Speculation of taking Land in this Province is rather abating.—

The fearful duty remains of punishing the Ruffians who made war upon us—and what a responsible duty it is!—

If Tragedies of this kind are to be performed every Winter the People of Canada will be driven to desperation.— I hope, however, to get through this season with success but I do assure you from any thing I ever heard at the Colonial Office, H. M. Government have no just idea of the State of the People in this Province.

When you have an opportunity will you do me the favor to mention to Lord Glenelg that I sincerely regret his late sad bereavement— Every person who knew his late excellent brother both esteemed & regarded him.

[595] ARTHUR TO COLONEL [HENRY] BOOTH: LB.2, p. 1-2.

Dec. 24 *Toronto.*

It has given me sincere pleasure to find that you are so far recovered as to be able to resume your command, and from the same cause, I trust you may never again have occasion to resign[.]

Colonel Estcourt has given me a very able outline of his views respecting the Niagara Militia in the Niagara District and I am glad to find that you concur with him. It is my intention to amend the Militia Laws at the next session, and previously I propose referring the subject generally for the consideration and report of the Committee. Any remarks therefore with which you will favor me I shall be very thankful for. There are two points to be kept in view and they rather clash with each other—the efficiency of the Militia and expense.

At present, I am most anxious to get all the Militia who have not been attested to their homes; and to make the force we keep out as efficient as possible. It is impossible not to feel for those who are kept unwillingly from their Families & farms. Pray do what you can consistently to the public safety to forward my views in this matter. The Militia will turn out with more alacrity when we require them.

Just at present no serious attack is meditated; but I expect you will be harrassed [*sic*] with small parties of these Ruffians crossing over to do mischief and, you will not understand me that I intend so to reduce our strength as to suffer them to do this with impunity—

Coll. Baldwin's corps are to proceed to Niagara as soon as the Traveller can take them across, wh. I expect will be in three or four days at the utmost. There has been some difficulty about their clothing— they muster about 300 R and file.

I have another such a Corps disposable; & if they are not required more pressingly elsewhere I will likewise send them to you.

This will render it unnecessary to raise any of the Provincial Marines under Captn. Drew as I intended.

Do not think of over exerting yourself until you are quite reestablished in Health & strength...

P.S. I cannot avoid adding, with reference to yr. recent communication with the Adjt. General, that it never entered my mind for a moment that you or Coll. Estcourt shd. be interfered with in the immediate command of Niagara—but, with reference to the Militia I thought it better to determine what shd. be done if the whole of the Troops were to act together in that part of the Territory[.]

[596] ARTHUR TO COLBORNE: LB.2, p. 11-15.

Dec. 24 *Toronto.*

Nothing new has transpired since I last wrote to you; and in these times, that is satisfactory.

At the affair of Sandwich all the officers of the Brigand Forces who had collected in the Western District, took a part—and with one exception, all were either killed, wounded or taken Prisoners.

So that, although the affair was not well managed, the result has been good.

More Canadians were concerned in that affair, than in the attack at Prescott, and the object was to reach London. A man named "Putnam" was the leading Canadian; and a Citizen named "Bierce" who has been throughout a leading character amongst the Patriots officiated as General in Chief.

This vagabond got away— I had rather he had been taken than ½ a dozen of his followers—but the second, a bold Kentucky man of most extraordinary stature was secured,—and is likely to pay dearly for the expedition. His name is Colonel Arsill— He is in good circumstances, and the greatest interest has been expressed for his safety amongst the Americans.

There never were such Idiots, as these Ruffians have proved themselves. At the time they made the attack they had about 1500 collected at or close to Detroit: their only chance of success was to cross over in a body, or as quickly as possible by Detachments; in place of which they suffered their first Division to be destroyed or dispersed, before the next division attempted to push off, and then old General Brady intercepted them and drove them back—which I believe they very willingly allowed.

The two Companies of Militia that were first on the Ground to meet the Brigands were dressed in Red, and it was mistaking them for regular Troops, I am persuaded quenched the ardour of the Invadres [*sic*] and rendered them so passive to the bidding of Genl Brady.

I enclose a Deposition which was made a few days ago by an American, the only one I have yet met with, who does not ask for or expect some gratuity. He has been giving Colonel Dundas and Captain Sandom information for the last two months, and they say it has proved very accurate.

It is his opinion that in a few weeks the Sovereign People in the State of New York will declare for the Patriots in defiance of their Government, and that we shall have invasion upon a much more extended scale, and Mr Kent from Ohio is decidedly of the same opinion as regards that State and the State of Michigan unless they have a serious convulsion nearer Home. Mr. Fox also writes me, that we have no prospect of security but by keeping up a very strong force— The Government is so weak it can do nothing. But, notwithstanding these predictions, I feel far more at my ease because I am convinced there is a great change in the feelings of the People of this Country. Numbers who desired another form of Government, have no wish to run the risk of having their throats cut, or of losing their own property, and they might now be trusted to defend the Province against the Ruffians who have been employed in this border Warfare. In this respect I think the hand of God is very visible, and the greatest good has thus been brought about entirely by the overruling of Providence.

We cannot feel too grateful for this—early in November, and indeed towards the end of the Month, I was under very serious apprehension of an extensive insurrection— "Hunters Lodges" kept up an extensive correspondence and numbers who were not disloyal were exceedingly out of humour—but the two descents that have been made have done great good in clearing up our political atmosphere.

Enough, however remains to make us watchful and I should say that whilst I form the favorable opinion of the change that has taken place, others, whose judgment is to be respected, think that the disaffected have only been quiet, because they have been overawed by the exhibition of Force which has been every where exhibited.

On examination I found that the accomodation at Gosfield was very bad indeed. Three hundred Militia are stationed there, and they are very much scattered. Scattered in a way that would never do for a

Regular Regiment. In place of sending the 32nd Regt therefore to Gosfield, I have sent the left wing of the 85th to Sandwich, which enables Colonel Airey to keep the whole of his Regt together at Amherstburg.

Colonel Airey thinks it is not safe to leave Sandwich without some Troops of the Line, but with this force and the Militia on the Frontier He feels quite secure.

If you wish it, I will send on the Right Wing of the 85th Regt; but, I do not at present consider it necessary; all they want is to recover their confidence in that part of the Country, and my information from Detroit is so much to be depended upon, that I am satisfied I can always reinforce that Frontier in time.

By this arrangement, some of the Sedentary Militia, who are at Sandwich much against their will, may return to their Homes.

I will not now enlarge upon the Subject, but, certainly other means must be resorted to for defending the Country on future occasions.

Colonel Young has applied to have the assistance of some officer as Town Major at Prescott; if you approve of it I could spare an officer of the 93d Regt who would assist in drilling the Militia both at Prescott and Brockville. At the latter place we want an officer of the Line very much.

The arrival of the 65th. Regt has made all secure there, whilst the trials are going on. Colonel Dundas has put a Corps of Militia into the Fort, so as to have the Regular Force ready to move. It is the Sheriffs Regiment and they are men of good character and loyal to a man. I have no fear to trust them, but I do not like to continue the arrangement, without your approval, because I think your arrangement was that the half Regiment should take the Fort Duty.

If you think it will not be convenient to you to spare the other Wing of the 65th. Regt, we should send an officer or two and two or three N. Comd Officers to drill the Militia at Prescott and Brockville: and if the same course were pursued at Cornwall great benefit would result from it. All the Militia require is the most simple movements and to handle their arms a little better, and to acquire the habit of order.

If we could give them this they would do well.

I intend to go to the Westward as soon as I can manage it; but my horse fell with me three weeks ago, and although I have been able to get through, or, rather I should say, on with my office work, I have not been able to ride.

The trouble and perplexity exceeds all I can describe, respecting the Militia. It is my intention to amend the Law when the Legislature meets, which I suppose must be soon.

[Enclosure lacking.]

[597] ARTHUR TO COLONEL [J. B. B.] ESTCOURT: LB.1, p. 262-263.

Dec. 24 *Toronto.*

I have read your letter of the 17th. inst. with much interest, and have to thank you for the trouble you must have taken to master the subject so thoroughly[.]

There are none of your propositions in which I shd. not be disposed to concur in case of a War— At present, I am so much inclined to hope that the Brigands have had enough of it, that I am very desirous that all the sedentary Militia—i.e. the men who have not been attested for six months service—should be allowed to return to their Homes, unless, in any particular instance their services cannot well be dispensed with.

Your idea of calling out a certain number of this Militia by rotation is very good, and quite accords with my view. In a few days I hope to have it [in] my power to go more fully into the subject.

The men called out at St Catherine's [*sic*] and Grimsbay [*sic*] may, I shd. hope, at once be sent to their Homes—but I leave the matter entirely in Coll. Booth's hands, whose restoration to health has given me sincere pleasure.

Allow me to assure you that whilst the Frontier duty at Niagara was in yr. hands I felt the most perfect confidence that the character of the service, and the security of the country wd. be most ably sustained[.]

[598] ARTHUR TO COLONEL [W. H.] DRAPER: LB.2, p. 15-17.

Dec. 26 *Govt. House, Toronto.* [Marked "Private and Confidential".]

I received at a late hour last night your letter of the 24th. Inst. with the Courts Martial which accompanied it.

All the cases that had previously arrived have been fully considered; and Lawton, Delino, Anderson, Buckley [*i.e.* Bulkley ?] Phelps and Leeper have been ordered for execution. We have been, I trust, providentially guided in the selection and no pains have been spared to come to a right conclusion.

Of the List two other Prisoners were selected, but the cases are still reserved to be considered in connexion with the cases of other delinquents.

Never was anything more difficult than to make the selection.

With regard to John Thomas, I hope you will be able to ascertain the fact whether he was brought forward on the charge of attempting to destroy the Locks of the Rideau Canal; because if he were only brought forward for that offence, a distinction might be made in his case.

It has occurred to me that if you employed some very intelligent person to be with the poor Criminals after they are made aware of their fate, and they were entirely separated from the other Criminals, that important information might be drawn from them with reference to the cases yet untried; and also, as respects the parties generally, who have been concerned in this infamous conspiracy.

Independent of the present utility of such information, which is of the utmost importance, a short history of the transactions would most properly accompany the last of the proceedings of the Court Martial to England to be laid before Parliament.

You will understand that all your official letters which accompany the Proceedings will be sent to England.

I should strongly recommend, if *it be possible*, that all the cases should be disposed of—and not one left.

You may take *any* or as many of the young men, who can be useful as "Queen's Evidence,["] and the two who are acquitted may be useful to give information. But, although I had rather have every case disposed of, yet I shall be quite satisfied with whatever you think most proper to be done.

I now wish to say to you, in the most perfect confidence, that I should be glad to limit Capital executions to Fifteen! that is one for every life lost in the Prescott affair; if this can *with Justice* be done, only three more remain for the extreme sentence of the Law; and it is of so much consequence to select the worst that I propose not finally deciding upon any other case until the Trials are concluded! Will you favor me with your opinion upon this?

Warners case was decided—on what grounds I cannot recollect,—but he was to be sent to the Penitentiary for 14 years. His name was on the List which I showed you on my way to Quebec.

I propose that all the Point Pelée Prisoners should be sent to London to take their trial—do you recommend this course. . .

[P.S.] I enclose for your perusal a private and confidential letter from Mr Fox—can you obtain any information upon the point to which he alludes. Be so good as to return the Papers[.]

[Superscription reads: "The Honble. Colonel Draper Judge Advocate at Kingston."]

[Enclosure is possibly item 570.]

[599] ARTHUR TO SIR JAMES MACDONELL: LB.2, p. 19.

Dec. 26 *Toronto.*

You must have the kindness to excuse my not having replied to your note some days ago, but it has been quite out of my power.

I have not failed, however, to pay every attention to your wishes.

Captain Macdonnell, I find, has two objects in view. One, to be exchanged from the 2nd. Len[n]ox to the 2nd. Frontenac—the other, to have the command of the Troop of the 2nd. Frontenac.

With regard to the last of these objects, it appears, there is the serious impedimt. of there being no vacancy, &, that if a vacancy were to occur the Senior Lieutenant has so strong a claim that it could not in common justice be passed over— With respect to the first object I find that an objection has hitherto existed to the exchange on account of the number of old officers who would have felt disappointment.— but, I have spoken to the Colonel of the Regiment & it has been arranged this day that Capt. Macdonnell's wishes should be complied with, so that, having done the best I can, I am sure you will be satisfied.—

I shall always feel the greatest pleasure in attending to any wish you may express, for I know no greater Satisfaction than being of any use to a Soldier who has served his Country so long & with so much honor as you have done.

[600] ARTHUR TO COLBORNE: LB.2, p. 17-18.

Dec. 27 *Toronto.* [Marked "Private".]

Last Friday I made time to attend for two hours at the Examination of the Boys of the College previous to the distribution of the prizes, and was as much surprised as gratified. Doctor Harris must have been admirably qualified. The appointment of his successor I expect to hear of every day.

So much pleased was I with the establishment that I have determined to send one of my little Boys there, who is just Eight Years of age, as a day scholar—and, as I recollect Lady Colborne told me you had a wish of the same kind with regard to Your Youngest son, if you will trust him with us we will take good care of him, and send him daily with our Youngster.—

The College re-opens in the course of a fortnight so that there is no time to be lost.

It has given me sincere concern to hear of your indisposition—for, I Say it with sincerity and truth, I do not know what we should now do without you. I fully expect the Queen will offer you the Government & your health I trust will enable you to accept it.

Your name is worth something amongst the Yankees—but, General Scott, I am told, looks high, and says he wishes a fair field & the Duke of Wellington. . .

[P.S.] I have now issued Warrants for the execution of twelve of the Criminals at Kingston— I hope to limit this shocking work to 15—which will be Life for Life.

The new scene of Trials opens at London this day.

[601] C. A. HAGERMAN TO JOHN MACAULAY: L.S. 2p.

Dec. 28 *Attorney Generals Office, Toronto.*

In reply to your note of this day's date in which you request me to inform you whether the prisoners taken at Amherstburgh [*sic*] on board the schooner Ann[e], & who are now in custody at Cape Diamond, can be tried before the Court Martial now sitting at London, or any other Court,—I have the honor to state, that the Statute authorizing the trial of foreigners taken in arms against her Majesty in this Province, by Court Martial, having been passed subsequent to the offence committed by the Prisoners alluded to, they cannot be prosecuted under its provisions;—and a reference to the correspondence with the Secretary of State, and the opinions of the Crown Officers in England, and of the legal authorities in this Country, in His Excellency's possession, will explain the causes that prevent their being brought to trial before the Municipal Courts of the Province.

[602] ARTHUR TO COLONEL [RICHARD] AIREY: LB.2, p. 25-26.

Dec. 29 [*Place not stated.*]

I simply write one line to acknowledge your letter of the 26 Inst and to say that I am quite satisfied your proposition of trying the Prisoners at Amherstburg, and of leaving Colonel Prince in Command at Sandwich was all well intended.

And although under the several reports made to me I am satisfied it was proper the Court Martial should assemble at London; yet I beg you to understand that if there are cases in which Convictions are not likely to be obtained at London from the want of evidence—in that case I would readily order a Court Martial at Amherstburg, as I do not wish any of the Prisoners should escape from Public justice.

Nothing will, I trust prevent my setting out for the West on Thursday next, as I have pretty well recovered from the accident which has confined me to my office.

[603] ARTHUR TO W. H. DRAPER: LB.2, p. 24-25.

Dec. 29 *Govt. House,* [*Toronto.*]

I have this mng received your letter 27th [?] Inst with the Courts Martial wh accompanied it.

Your want of success in not getting the evidence you wish from Prescott I regret very much; but, I hope by other means you will succeed. In addition to the observations made in my former letter, I would suggest that some of the Wounded men might be made useful as evidence. To identify the man who was engaged in burning the Sir R. Pele [*i.e.* Peel] is of great consequence certainly; but still we must be satisfied with what has been done.

When you first wrote upon the subject, I apprehended that the difficulty in apprehending the Prisoners might have proved far more fatal to justice than has been demonstrated by the result.

I have received a communication from Mr Dix with a Memorial signed by apparently many highly respectable People in Albany in behalf of a Prisoner named "Sweetman", whom they represent for some time to have been under insanity.

All the Persons engaged in the affair at Prescott one might believe readily must have been mad—but, it will be a relief to find there is anything to excuse any one of these Ruffians from the heavy guilt of such atrocious conduct.

I am glad indeed to find, that the Community begin to think there has been enough of the severest punishment—Death! and, I look with some anxiety to the expression of your opinion in answer to my last letter. Never did I feel deeper anxiety and now there must be the same work at London.

It is, I am sorry to say, absolutely necessary, that I should proceed to Amherstburg on Thursday next.

As soon as I receive your reply to this letter, I will determine what shall be done with reference to closing or adjourning the Court Martial—and will take care to leave the necessary authority with Colonel Foster to act during my absence.

[604] ARTHUR TO COLONEL [J. F.] LOVE: LB.2, p. 20-23.

Dec. 29 *Govt. House, Toronto.*

I am very much obliged to you for your letter of the 26 Inst. and for the information it contains.

Your assistance, in the way you purpose in forming the Militia, will be most valuable. Colonel Burrowes, with such aid, will soon have an efficient Battalion, and Sir Allan Macnab will, I trust, avail himself of your valuable offer.

I am very glad to find that the Sedentary Militia have been permitted to return to their Homes. Why the embodied Militia are not punctually paid, I cannot understand, for I have given the most positive instructions upon the subject. You do not mention the cause of the irregularity.

I concur with you entirely that it is most desirable that the Militia should be better formed, and I should most readily come into your proposition of keeping the Adjutant[,] Quarter Master, Sergeant Major and the non Commissioned Officers embodied if I could possibly do so; but I do not know how this can be ventured upon without authority from England. Possibly the Sergeant Major and some of the most expert of the N. Commissd Officers might be attached as Supernumeraries to Colonel Burrowes Corps; and in that way paid; and if the List of officers be not complete, the adjutant might also be attached to that Corps for some time.

I will approve of whatever you do in this way only be so good, whilst we endeavour to promote the good of the Public Service to regard my responsibility with the Treasury.

I thank you for having adjusted Matters as you have done with Major Welby, who, I have no doubt will make a very superior Troop of it from his experience and intelligence. The establishment shall be notified in orders today.

With regard to Captain Macdonnell his zeal has hurried him beyond the bounds of prudence and led him to misapprehension for which I cannot very well account.

So far from my *directing* him to "form a Troop of Cavalry and to procure arms from whatever source he could", which, of course, I would direct no person to do—I very reluctantly on his saying that he could get arms, went thus far,—that I would approve of his forming a Sedentary Troop, &, if the circumstances of the Country should require it, I would readily call his Troop into active Service— I added if affairs went on, as they were doing, that I thought the time was not distant when I should be glad of his services.

I have seen Mr. Macdonnell, and have explained this to him, in the presence of the Military Secretary, and he accords in the accuracy of my Statement. I have no idea that he has intended the slightest misrepresentation—on the contrary, he has shewn an earnest determination to do his best for the Country and has not stopped long enough for reflection, and has thereby been hurried into an error.

For the time his people have been on Service, as Sir Allan Macnab I find called out some of them—they should be paid. But, unless it can be shewn that their services are now required, I could not consent to keeping them embodied.

The expence of the Cavalry is frightful, and I must keep them down at present as much as I can—but, ere long, I presume we shall stand in need of them for I suppose we are not to expect that Great Britain will quietly acquiesce in the *doings* in the United States without demanding reparation, which they will not grant unless they are forced.

It strikes me that the Cavalry of the Country in the event of a war would be more effective than the Cavalry sent from England—what is your opinion upon this important subject.

We have not arms for all Captain Welby's Troop, and I have not the power to purchase them. But I will see what can be done. The Troops already formed have the first claim. I shall be able, I hope, to send about 30 Carbines.

I have now the most accurate information of what is passing on the Frontier; and, although a small Gang of a hundred or two of these Villains may cross over to Niagara, I am persuaded that for some weeks there will be nothing more serious. I do not see occasion therefore for actually hiring Waggons. It is an expence that may well be spared.

No authority from me has been given for this measure in London, and I have ordered it to be immediately discontinued.

It is my particular wish to have Burlington Heights fortified; but it cannot be done without authority. If the Commander of the Forces would take it upon Himself, I think under the circumstances of the Country, it would not be necessary to refer to England.

So far as I am concerned, I would take the responsibility upon myself, as Governor; but I should retard, rather than promote the Service by any such interference. Indeed in this, and in some other respects, I feel my Military position to be so unpleasant, that if I could do so with credit I would resign the Government immediately and return to England.

I am liable to be involved in consiquences [*sic*] which may be quite ruinous, from causes over which I have no control. This I advert to, that you may understand why things are as *they are* in some respects, which, evidently, require to be otherwise, but, I do so privately!

Upon the subject of Dispatches I have repeatedly called the Asst. Adjt General and the Asst. Quarter [Master] General['s] attention to the matter being quite aware of the evil to which you allude.

In a few days I shall start for Amherstburg and shall be glad to find yr Regt comfortably quartered on my way.

[Superscription reads: Colonel Love 73d Regt. Comg at Brantford."]

[605] COLBORNE TO [ARTHUR]: A.L.S. 9p.

Dec. 31 *Montreal.*

I have to thank you for your interesting letters of the 18th, and 24th inst.

The result of the affair of Sandwich has, I think, had a good effect. I have had several letters from that quarter, and among them a communication from Mr. Francois Baby, who resides at Sandwich, He complains bitterly of the arrangements previously to the Skirmish, and after the flight; he is an old Militia Officer, and adverts to the ingratitude of Government in not recollecting his services on the frontier last war. The deposition, to which you allude in your letter of the 24., was not enclosed. Captain Sandom forwarded me information, which he has received from T. D. on the other side. The accompanying paper is from a Polish Officer in the service of the Brigands—the further reports will be sent to us, provided his communications are kept secret.

I believe part of his information may prove correct. I have no doubt from the reports which are continually sent us from the frontier, that the Brigands are preparing to commence operations on the Rich[e]lieu, and between Hem[m]ingford, and Fort Conington. The lines from Watertown, and Ogdensburg to Platzburg [*sic*], and Champlain are so short, that we may have a Corps of Brigands in our front without much notice. There are about 800 Canadians lingering on the frontier, at Albany, Rouses Point, Perrys Mills, and Champlain.

The sympathisers near the Eastern Townships have also been alarming that frontier. Yesterday morning 12 men, led by a man named Grogan, and West a citizen of the State of Vermont crossed the frontier from Albany in sleighs, and burnt two houses, and four barns about a mile on this side of the line, on Caldwell Manor, and made their escape. I have claimed the felons from the Governor of Vermont. All this may lead to war; but I have no doubt both Governments will endeavour to put off the evil day.

Gagnon, Cote, Malhot, Duvernay, Buchette are at Swanton. Wolfred Nelson and Papineau are expected there in a few days. This activity may be encouraged with a view of keeping us employed, and continuing the excitement. I have considered it necessary to reinforce the frontier. The 15th Regt are in Isle aux Noix, the 66th at St John's, and the 71 at Acadie ready for a turn out. The habitans will not venture to move again, unless they are assured of support from the Americans; but the whole population will act vigorously against us the first opportunity that may be afforded them to shew their hatred of everything British— The Priests have entirely lost their influence.

If I find that it is not probable that we shall be attacked, by any formidable Corps of Brigands I shall send the right wing of the 85th to Upper Canada. The left wing of that Regt, will secure Kingston, and leave a disposable force to act on the St Lawrence. There can be no objection to trust the defence of the Fort to Volunteers or Militia. Capt. Bou[r]ch[i]er of the 93rd, will be of great use to Major Young at Prescott, and I will sanction his appointment. We must avoid exposing companies, or detachments of the Regular force, to be attacked. For, if any advantage should be gained by the Brigands over a Corporals guard even, it would give them courage. In any affair if we can bring two Regiments of the line to oppose four thousand or more of the Brigands, I have no doubt of our success. I therefore beg that no companies may be detached to defend mills &c. but that we may [be] prepared to move, whenever we can venture to leave particular stations, with not less than six or seven companies. I have however directed a subaltern, and 30 men of the 73d Regt to halt at Brockville till further orders, as at present they appear to be in a sad state of alarm.

Although the Brigands may approach us with more security to themselves, when they can pass the ice, our line of defence will be much decreased, when the Lakes and Rivers are partially frozen. Thus, assuming that towards the end of January, we shall have only to defend the Townships on the Detroit and St Clair, the Fort Erie frontier, and Gravelly Bay, and the Johnston, and Eastern Districts, on the St Lawrence, I should wish the whole of the 85th to be moved on to Sandwich; but shall regret any arrangement that will take the Command of that Frontier from Col Airey, who has been so vigilant, and active, and has had really hard work.

If the Brigands shew in force at Sandusky Bay or on the Detroit the 73d Regt should move to London ready to support the Militia you may place at Gosfield. I do not think it probable the Brigands would venture to cross to the Eastward of Malden, with two Regiments of the Line at London, and two in the Western District, at Amherstburg, and Sandwich. Four Battalions of the Line in the London District ought to destroy the Brigands in a few days.

The Niagara District I think must be secure; but I should like to send you another Regiment for that Frontier. You will soon discover that Militia will be discontented, if they are detained on service constantly in expectation of an invasion. At a period of excitement I am persuaded the Militia of the Western District would turn out well for a few weeks; but it is ruinous to them in every respect to be constantly assembled. The Volunteer Corps in the Upper Province will I suspect be chiefly composed of a very idle class; and could you raise a sufficient force will be the lads for permanent duty, but I imagine that the Militia in many Townships would not object to assemble one day in the week by wings, if they were well paid for their day's march,—and prepared to march to any distance for a short campaign—

[606] COLBORNE TO ARTHUR: A.L.S. 4p.

Dec. 31 *Montreal.*

Many thanks for your kind letter of the 27th inst. I am delighted to hear your account of the College; and that you were present at the examination. The young men that will be sent out from that Institution, provided able Masters continue to direct the course of education of the students, will soon prove advantageous to every District; and to those we are most anxious to keep on the right road. I return you my best and sincere thanks for your offer of protection, and shelter under your roof, to my little Gentleman who is now under the tuition of a Tutor at Montreal, Although I am become a convert in respect to an opinion I formerly adhered to, that private education in all cases would be found more advantageous, I cannot venture to send my boy to school, till I can fix him permanently in England. His name is on the Winchester list, but I do not think I shall let him enter at that school—

I was unwell for two or three days, but I am quite stout again, and enjoy a long ride, when I can escape from my office. The Court Martial still continues its labours. I shall be guided chiefly by my own views, and those of the Ex Council, as to the number of offenders, that are to suffer the extreme penalty of the Law. It only remains for me seriously to consider in what manner the safety of the Province can be ensured; and Justice be vindicated with as little sacrifice of human life as possible. I have been compelled to suspend another Judge, Valieres [*i.e.* Vallière] St Real, of 3 Rivers, and to arrest the Editors of the Canadien and the Fantasque, at Quebec.

I hope you feel no bad effects from your fall. You will be required at Toronto, I should say defer your excursion to the Westward.

I wish you a happy a new year, as we are so soon to be out of the old one; but I am afraid we cannot expect a more propitious period than the annus mirabilis that is about to end.

www.ingramcontent.com/pod-product-compliance
Lightning Source LLC
LaVergne TN
LVHW060016210926
848481LV00013B/3719

9781487581381